WRITERS OF
THE AMERICAN
RENAISSANCE

WRITERS OF
THE AMERICAN
RENAISSANCE

An A-to-Z Guide

Edited by Denise D. Knight

Emmanuel S. Nelson, Advisory Editor

GREENWOOD PRESS
Westport, Connecticut • London

Library of Congress Cataloging-in-Publication Data

Writers of the American Renaissance: an A-to-Z guide / edited by Denise D. Knight.
   p. cm.
  Includes bibliographical references and index.
  ISBN 0–313–32140–X (alk. paper)
  1. American literature—19th century—Bio-bibliography—Dictionaries. 2. Authors,
American—19th century—Biography—Dictionaries. 3. American literature—19th
century—Dictionaries. I. Knight, Denise D., 1954–
PS201.W75 2003
810.9′003—dc21
[B]   2003052846

British Library Cataloguing in Publication Data is available.

Library of Congress Catalog Card Number: 2003052846
ISBN: 0–313–32140–X

First published in 2003

Greenwood Press, 88 Post Road West, Westport, CT 06881
An imprint of Greenwood Publishing Group, Inc.
www.greenwood.com

Printed in the United States of America

The paper used in this book complies with the
Permanent Paper Standard issued by the National
Information Standards Organization (Z39.48-1984).

10 9 8 7 6 5 4 3 2 1

CONTENTS

PREFACE

For several decades, the term "American Renaissance" identified an accepted construct in our literary consciousness. Coined in 1941 by F. O. Matthiessen, the phrase referred to a handful of literary giants—Emerson, Thoreau, Hawthorne, Melville, Poe, and Whitman—whose works dominated the literary landscape during the middle part of the nineteenth century. In recent years, however, the very notion of the renaissance that occurred in America before the Civil War has been challenged, expanded, and reconfigured to encompass a much wider selection of literary voices. David S. Reynolds's groundbreaking work, *Beneath the American Renaissance: The Subversive Imagination In the Age of Emerson and Melville* (1988), questioned longstanding assumptions about the writers whose works were privileged to the exclusion of other more marginalized authors, and Paul Lauter's pioneering work in such books as *Reconstructing American Literature* (1983) and *Canons and Contexts* (1991) has forever changed the way we view American literary history. Hence, this volume, with an eye toward presenting a more balanced and democratic representation of writers of the American Renaissance, attempts to be inclusive rather than exclusive, by examining a broad cross section of writers whose works emerged during the period between roughly 1830 and the onset of the Civil War in 1861.

It is fitting that our conception of the American Renaissance—which was for so long considered synonymous with American Romanticism—has been expanded to include lesser-known authors who contributed to the literary and cultural climate of their day. In fact, the term "renaissance," derived from the French word "*renaître*," to be born again, speaks to a broader movement in literary and intellectual activity than that suggested by the more outdated—and homogeneous—meaning, which focuses on the handful of writers canonized by Matthiessen. American Romanticism was undeniably a major component of the American Renaissance, but a recognition of other contemporaneous trends is vitally important in comprehending the complex literary consciousness that emerged in the nineteenth century. America at that time had established political independence, generating a strong sense of nationalism and optimism. Publishing houses had sprung up and stood ready to accommodate an eager readership. At the same time, however, the champions of individualism were being challenged by women and abolitionists who lobbied for equality and an end to slavery. In response, the renaissance produced a rich and diverse body of work, which included not only Romantic literature but also slave narratives, political tracts, frontier adventures, tall tales, social satire, occasional poetry, and moral protests.

This period was, in fact, marked by a wave of best-selling works by female authors, who were dismissed by Hawthorne as a "damn'd mob of scribbling women." The very existence of what Jane Tompkins has called the "other American Renaissance"—a movement characterized in part by massive sales of popular fiction—calls into question long-held cultural assumptions about both literary aesthetics and the inherent value of canonized texts.

Indeed, throughout the first 75 years of the twentieth century, American literature anthologies offered an extremely narrow view of the American Renaissance. As a testament to the ways in which the literature of nineteenth-century America has been reconfigured over the past several decades, I have on my bookshelf a curious relic from an earlier generation—a paperback edition of *The Viking Portable Library American Literature Survey: The American Romantics, 1800–1860,* originally published in 1962. The authors of the volume's general introduction, Milton R. Stern and Seymour L. Gross, note, with no apparent irony, that the American writer of the nineteenth century expresses "a whole-voiced rejection of trammeling orthodoxies, comformities, hypocrisies, and delusions, wherever and whenever they are seen on the national landscape. Keeping that spirit in mind, we offer the following selections," which, the editors declare, "maintain a proper balance of materials and meet the widest demands of common practice, flexibility, and usefulness" (vii–viii). That "proper balance" includes the six Renaissance writers named by Matthiessen as well as Irving, Cooper, Bryant, and the four "Fireside Poets," Longfellow, Whittier, Holmes, and Lowell. No women authors or writers of color are represented.

Today's literature anthologies are much more likely to contain representative samplings from a variety of writers whose works were well known by their contemporaries. The 2002 edition of *The Norton Anthology of American Literature, Volume B (1820–1865),* for example, features writings not only by mainstream American Romantics, but also by such writers as Catharine Maria Sedgwick, Caroline Kirkland, Lydia Maria Child, Abraham Lincoln, Margaret Fuller, Harriet Beecher Stowe, Fanny Fern, Harriet Jacobs, Thomas Bangs Thorpe, Frederick Douglass, Bayard Taylor, Emily Dickinson, and Louisa May Alcott. The fourth edition of *The Heath Anthology of American Literature* (2002) features excerpts from several additional writers in its section on American Literature from 1800 to 1865, including, among others, Lydia Sigourney, Caroline Lee Hentz, William Lloyd Garrison, Sarah Grimké, Sojourner Truth, Angelina Grimké, Fanny Fern, Elizabeth Cady Stanton, Augustus Baldwin Longstreet, George Washington Harris, William Wells Brown, Alice Cary, and Frances Osgood, all of whom are represented in this volume. As the movement to further expand the canon continues, and as more writers are recovered, the offerings included in American literature anthologies are certain to increase even further.

Despite both the resurgent interest in and the increasing availability of recovered literature, however, resources for readers have remained widely scattered. *Writers of the American Renaissance: An A-to-Z Guide,* then, is intended as a primary reference guide to 74 authors who were actively writing during the renaissance in nineteenth-century America. With the recovery process still under way, however, this volume can only be representative of the many men and women who were publishing during the nineteenth century, rather than an all-inclusive edition.

That being said, however, the process of selecting writers for inclusion, by nature, assumes a political dimension. The figures featured in this volume do not necessarily represent the "best" or most "important" writers of the nineteenth century; indeed, while some have been assimilated into the literary canon for a considerable period of time, others, such as Martin Delany, George Lippard, and Henry Timrod, are still relatively unknown. No judgment was made about the aesthetic quality of the literature or of the relative contributions of the authors included; the common denominator is that the writings of each author aid in illuminating the complex social, historical, and cultural climate of the American renaissance. There has, however, been an attempt to include a fair number of women writers and writers of color. Moreover, the emphasis is on those who have left a *written* legacy; thus, while Elizabeth Cady Stanton is included by virtue of her drafting the historical "Declaration of Sentiments" (1848), her friend and collaborator, Susan B. Anthony, who contributed much to the women's movement but left little in the way of written work, is not included.

One further note concerns the names listed for authors included. Because some of the writers published under pseudonyms, I have alphabetized using the name by which the writer is best known today, followed by the alternative name in parentheses. Thus, Sara Willis Parton is located under Fanny Fern; Sarah Jane Clarke Lippincott is listed as Grace Greenwood.

Each of the 74 entries in this volume follows a specific five-part format: a biography containing information about the writer's personal history; a discussion of the author's major works and themes; an overview of the critical studies examining the writer's works, and a two-part bibliography, featuring both works by and studies of the author. The entries are arranged alphabetically and are followed by a comprehensive bibliography listing resources for further study.

To everyone who made suggestions for expanding and refining my tentative list of writers, I owe thanks. I also wish to extend special gratitude to John J. Han at Missouri Baptist College who graciously assumed the task of writing an additional essay—his fifth in this volume—when the original contributor dropped out at the eleventh hour. I am indebted to Lisa A. Long, who allowed me to use her essay from another Greenwood volume as a model for contributors to follow. I also thank George F. Butler, Lisa Rowe, and Lindsay Claire, and my editors at Greenwood, for their support through every phase of this project. Finally, I thank my husband, Michael K. Barylski, for his unwavering support of my various research projects.

AMOS BRONSON ALCOTT (1799–1888)

Gregory Eiselein

BIOGRAPHY

Born November 29, 1799, Amos Bronson Alcott grew up in rural Wolcott, Connecticut. He attended an impoverished and unexciting school from ages 6 to 13, but nourished his intellectual interests by reading religious and literary works outside the school's limited curriculum. As a young man, he became a peddler in the South but gave up this never-quite-successful commercial traveling after spending a life-changing winter with a North Carolinian Quaker community in 1823. Later that year, Alcott returned to Connecticut to become a teacher. Wanting to associate learning with pleasure and imagination rather than dull routine, he made the classroom comfortable and appealing and engaged students' interests and curiosities. In 1828 he took these pioneering pedagogical ideas to Boston where he became the superintendent of an infant school.

On May 23, 1830, Alcott married Abigail May, the youngest child of a prominent Boston family, and they raised four daughters—Anna, Louisa, Elizabeth, and May. The newly married couple relocated to Philadelphia and then Germantown, Pennsylvania, where Bronson spent three and half years attempting to establish schools based on his educational theories. He had also begun to publish articles and short treatises. The family returned to Boston in 1834. With financial support from local philanthropists and teaching assistance from Elizabeth Peabody, Alcott opened a school in the Masonic Temple. Banishing rote memorization and facilitating Socratic discussions, he and Peabody enjoyed genuine educational (though not financial) success. *Record of a School* by Peabody (1835) and *Conversations with Children on the Gospels* (1836–37) documented their pedagogical innovations and generated interest among Boston-area intellectuals at precisely the moment when Transcendentalism was erupting into a full-blown movement. With its unorthodox ideas about miracles and candid discussions of subjects such as childbirth and circumcision, *Conversations* also stirred public outrage, which led to the decline and eventual collapse of the Temple School in 1838. Alcott soon set up a similar school in South Boston. His admission of an African American student (Susan

Robinson) alienated or upset supporters, however, and this school experienced sharply declining enrollments before closing in June 1839.

In 1840, the family moved to Concord. Although he struggled to support the family, Concord allowed Alcott to interact regularly with the like-minded Ralph Waldo Emerson and Henry David Thoreau. After suggesting the *Dial* as the name for what became the most famous Transcendentalist periodical, Alcott contributed a few pieces to the new journal, including the widely mocked "Orphic Sayings" (1840–41). With support from Emerson, Alcott traveled to Great Britain in 1842–43 to meet his British supporters. He returned with plans to establish a utopian community based on high principles and various asceticisms. This communal experiment known as Fruitlands lasted just eight months and became a symbol of the practical failure of Alcott's idealism. Even his daughter Louisa gently parodied the community in "Transcendental Wild Oats" (1874). Although Fruitlands's end was a relief to most of the family, Bronson experienced a period of depression. He gradually recovered, but his wife and two oldest daughters realized that he could not financially support the family. Thus, as he turned to his garden and never-lucrative speaking tours, Abigail, Louisa, and Anna found various ways to provide for the financially strapped family. Relocating several times during the 1840s and 50s, the family finally returned to Concord in 1857 and moved into Orchard House.

Bronson Alcott had been offering various public "conversations" to groups in the Boston area since 1838. In 1853, he began taking these cultural talks to audiences in the Midwest and continued to do so through the early 1880s. From 1859 to 1865, he served as superintendent of Concord schools, a position offering some respect but little pay. Because of this position, the success of his conversations, and his renewed efforts at publication, he gradually recovered his standing as a public intellectual during the 1860s. Roberts Brothers released *Tablets* in 1868, and the book sold well largely because of Louisa's concurrent success with *Little Women* (the sales of which ended the family's years of pecuniary hardship). His post-war writings explored free religion, Hegelianism, and "personal theism," a theology that emphasized the divinity of human beings and the spiritual oneness unifying all souls. During this period, he also composed a number of autobiographical works in various genres.

Despite sad and difficult experiences, such as Abigail's death in 1877 and Emerson's in 1882, Alcott's success continued through the final decade of his active career and culminated in the long-cherished dream of a spiritual-philosophical academy. The Concord School of Philosophy opened in 1879 with Alcott as dean. The School's program of lectures and discussions continued each summer for the next 10 years. In 1882 Alcott suffered a debilitating stroke that left him paralyzed and unable to write. He died on March 4, 1888, two days before Louisa's death.

MAJOR WORKS AND THEMES

Alcott is one of the most important educational theorists of the nineteenth century. At the foundation of his theory is the belief that human beings, especially children, are inherently good. Alcott holds that human beings possess a divinity, and in childhood one sees this divine nature "despoiled of none of its glory" (*Doctrine* 24). Yet his theories also emphasize education's role in the cultivation of morality and conscience. This combination of fundamental beliefs appears to create a contradiction: if children are inherently good, why do they need to be taught to be good? The answer hinges on his understanding of education not as information delivery or social training but as the encouragement of children to realize their divine talents. "Instruction must be an Inspiration" (*Doctrine* 18), he insists. Consequently, he disdains rigid, methodical pedagogies: "systematic instruction is repulsive to the habits and feelings of infancy" (*Observations* 12). Influenced by Swiss educational theorist Johann Pestalozzi among others, Alcott's Romantic beliefs about childhood and education led him to develop several innovative teaching methods. As *Conversations* amply illustrates, he relied on Socratic conversation in an era when rote memorization was the rule. He advocated story-telling, journal writing, art appreciation, and comfortable classrooms full of air, light, books, and art; he disliked corporal punishment and adopted a system of classroom discipline in which students took an active role, a means he says of instilling a "common conscience" (*Observations* 22). His educational works champion active learning—group discussions, physical exercise, games, play, and hands-on lessons. Yet one of the most remarkable aspects of his educational theory is his simple insistence that pedagogical method and child development merit thoughtful study.

Following the negative reviews of *Conversations,* Alcott did not publish a book for over 30 years, though he contributed shorter pieces to periodicals and newspapers. He wrote, for example, several pieces of oracular, Transcendentalist philosophy, including the high-toned, metaphysical aphorisms of "Orphic Sayings." Although much ridiculed, "Orphic Sayings" represents an attempt to condense Transcendentalist debates about the spiritual and natural worlds into compact axioms; it is also an experiment in literary form, an effort to express wide-ranging philosophical ideas without systematic argument. During the 1840s, Alcott also published reform essays on vegetarianism, health, and communal life (notably, "Consociate Family Life" [1843]). The primary themes of his reform writings are purity, self-control, and the transformation of society by adherence to high principles and "primitive instincts" ("Fruitlands" 135).

In his later career, Alcott continued to produce philosophical writing in the unsystematic, testimonial style of "Orphic Sayings." In works such as *Tablets, Table-Talk* (1877), "Personal Theism" (1869), and "Philosophemes" (1873–81), Alcott affirms free will, self-expression, and an openness to ideas, while defending theological idealism against the materialism and determinism gaining ground in post-Darwinian American thought. In addition to philosophy and educational theory, Alcott published memoir and autobiographical poetry. Although not formally or stylistically remarkable, *Sonnets and Canzonets* (1882) is a collection of pleasingly pastoral poems, personal verses on his friends and family, and paeans to Transcendentalist geniuses and antislavery heroes. *New Connecticut* (1881) is an epic about Alcott's early life. Among the most valuable of Alcott's autobiographical works are his remembrances of Concord (*Concord Days* [1872]) and the Transcendentalists ("Transcendental Club" [1863], *Ralph Waldo Emerson* [1865], and "The Forester" [1862] on Thoreau).

On Margaret Fuller, whom he admired greatly, Alcott writes: "She was greatest when she dropped her pen" (*Concord Days* 77). The judgment better fits Alcott himself, however. He struggled as a writer with clarity and style, and his published writings can be inflated and murky. Yet he was an appealing and renowned conversationalist. Some of his best work appears in his voluminous and meticulously kept journals. And, according to a longstanding truism in Alcott studies, Bronson's greatest accomplishments were not his publications but his children. Even Bronson thought so: "Our children are our best works—if indeed we may claim them as ours" (*Journals* 400).

CRITICAL RECEPTION

Critics have not always been kind to Alcott. In his early career, reviewers relentlessly criticized *Conversations;* more than one critic described it as obscene, presumably for its discussion of childbirth, sexuality, marriage, and similar topics. "Orphic Sayings" was one of the most ridiculed and parodied pieces in the Transcendentalist catalog. On the other hand, the Transcendentalists responded to Alcott with high and genuine praise. Journals such as James Freeman Clarke's *Western Messenger* printed decidedly favorable reviews, and Emerson referred to Alcott as the "highest genius of the time" (qtd. in Dahlstrand 181). This support did not, however, always translate into unvarying private admiration. Fuller, for example, valued his educational theory, defended his views, and accepted his writings for publication in the *Dial;* but her journal also records some rather sharp criticism of his thinking and writing, including his propensity to become "lost in abstractions" (qtd. in Capper 198).

Despite notable exceptions (e.g., *The Nation's* ridiculing 1868 review of *Tablets*), the nineteenth-century reception of Alcott's later works is mostly favorable. His critics reveal surprisingly little impatience with his prophetic style or his unwillingness to adhere to logical form. In an essay on *Sonnets and Canzonets,* Franklin B. Sanborn praises Alcott's lack of finish and technical control and urges readers not to expect variety, precision, or "Definiteness" (16). Higher accolades came from Octavius Frothingham's *Transcendentalism in New England* (1876), which ranks Alcott second only to Emerson among the Transcendentalists.

Following his death, Alcott was no longer regarded as a major Transcendentalist writer, and with few exceptions, his reputation has continued to decline. Literary critics such as F. O. Matthiessen have maintained that Alcott had no talent or adeptness as a writer. Social and intellectual historians have disparaged his Fruitlands efforts and the excessive idealism of his educational theories and practices. A review of recent criticism reveals that the discussion of Alcott appears most often now as an ancillary component in the study of writers such as Emerson, Fuller, Thoreau, and Louisa May Alcott. Nevertheless, he is the subject of good biographies, including Frederick Dahlstrand's superb *Amos Bronson Alcott: An Intellectual Biography* (1982). Capturing the energy and diversity of Alcott's thinking and writing, Dahlstrand makes a compelling case for understanding Alcott as a vital representative of nineteenth-century American thought. Moreover, several twentieth-century critics—from Morrow (1929) through McCuskey (1940) to Robinson (1999)—have documented Alcott's efforts as an inspiring pedagogical theorist and the centrality of those educational endeavors to Transcendentalism.

WORKS CITED

Alcott, Amos Bronson. *Concord Days.* Boston: Roberts Brothers, 1872.
———. *The Doctrine and Discipline of Human Culture.* Boston: J. Munroe, 1836.
———. *The Journals of Bronson Alcott.* Ed. Odell Shepard. Boston: Little, Brown, 1938.
———. *Observations on the Principles and Methods of Infant Instruction.* Boston: Carter & Hendee, 1830.
Capper, Charles. *Margaret Fuller: An American Romantic Life.* Vol. 1. New York: Oxford University Press, 1992.
Dahlstrand, Frederick C. *Amos Bronson Alcott: An Intellectual Biography.* Rutherford: Fairleigh Dickinson University Press, 1982.
Sanborn, F. B. "An Essay on the Sonnet and the Canzonet." Alcott, *Sonnets and Canzonets.* Boston: Roberts Brothers, 1882. 13–35.

BIBLIOGRAPHY

Works by Amos Bronson Alcott

Books
Observations on the Principles and Methods of Infant Instruction. Boston: Carter & Hendee, 1830.
On the Nature and Means of Early Intellectual Education as Deduced from Experience. Boston: Carter & Hendee, 1833.
The Doctrine and Discipline of Human Culture. Boston: J. Munroe, 1836.
Record of Conversations on the Gospels, Held in Mr. Alcott's School [*Conversations with Children on the Gospels*]. Ed. Elizabeth P. Peabody. 2 vols. Boston: J. Munroe, 1836–37.
Tablets. Boston: Roberts Brothers, 1868.
Concord Days. Boston: Roberts Brothers, 1872.
Table-Talk. Boston: Roberts Brothers, 1877.
Sonnets and Canzonets. Boston: Roberts Brothers, 1882.
Ralph Waldo Emerson: An Estimate of His Character and Genius in Prose and Verse. 1865. Boston: A. Williams, 1882.
New Connecticut: An Autobiographical Poem. 1881. Boston: Roberts Brothers, 1887.
Essays on Education, 1830–1862. Ed. Walter Harding. Gainesville: Scholars' Facsimiles & Reprints, 1960.

Selected Articles
"Orphic Sayings." *Dial* 1 (1840–41): 85–98, 351–61.
"Days from a Diary." *Dial* 2 (1842): 410–37.
"Fruitlands" [with Charles Lane]. *Dial* 4 (July 1843): 135–36.
"The Consociate Family Life." *Herald of Freedom* 8 Sept. 1843.
"The Forester." *Atlantic Monthly* April 1862: 443–45.
"The Transcendental Club and *The Dial.*" *The Commonwealth* 24 April 1863.
"Personal Theism: A Conversation." *The Radical* 6 (1869): 22–33.
"Philosophemes." *Journal of Speculative Philosophy* 7 (1873): 46–48; 9 (1875): 1–16, 190–209, 245–63; 15 (1881): 84–88.

Letters and Journals
The Journals of Bronson Alcott. Ed. Odell Shepard. Boston: Little, Brown, 1938.
The Letters of A. Bronson Alcott. Ed. Richard L. Herrnstadt. Ames: Iowa State University Press, 1969.

Studies of Amos Bronson Alcott

Bedell, Madelon. *The Alcotts: Biography of a Family.* New York: Clarkson N. Potter, 1980.
Brownson, Orestes. "Alcott on Human Culture." *Boston Quarterly Review* 1 (1838): 417–32.
Buell, Lawrence. *Literary Transcendentalism: Style and Vision in the American Renaissance.* Ithaca, NY: Cornell University Press, 1973.
Carlson, Larry A. " 'Those pure pages of yours': Bronson Alcott's *Conversations with Children on the Gospels.*" *American Literature* 60 (1988): 451–60.
Dahlstrand, Frederick C. *Amos Bronson Alcott: An Intellectual Biography.* Rutherford, NJ: Fairleigh Dickinson University Press, 1982.
Frothingham, O. B. *Transcendentalism in New England.* New York: Putnam's, 1876.
Matthiessen, F. O. American Renaissance: Art and Expression in the Age of Emerson and Whitman. London: Oxford University Press, 1941.
McCuskey, Dorothy. *Bronson Alcott: Teacher.* New York: Macmillan, 1940.
Morrow, Honoré Willsie. *The Father of Little Women.* Boston: Little, Brown, 1929.

"Mr. Bronson Alcott's Essays." *The Nation* 20 Aug. 1868: 151–52.

Myerson, Joel. *The New England Transcendentalists and the* Dial: *A History of the Magazine and Its Contributors.* Rutherford, NJ: Fairleigh Dickinson University Press, 1980.

———. " 'Our Children Are Our Best Works': Bronson and Louisa May Alcott." *Critical Essays on Louisa May Alcott.* Ed. Madeleine B. Stern. Boston: Hall, 1984. 259–64.

———. " 'In the Transcendental Emporium': Bronson Alcott's 'Orphic Sayings' in the *Dial.*" *English Language Notes* 10 (1972): 31–8.

Paul, Sherman. "Alcott's Search for the Child." *Boston Public Library Quarterly* 4 (1952): 88–96.

Peabody, Elizabeth Palmer. *Record of a School, Exemplifying the General Principles of Spiritual Culture.* Boston: J. Munroe, 1835.

Pochmann, Henry A. *New England Transcendentalism and St. Louis Hegelianism.* Philadelphia: Carl Schurz Foundation, 1948.

Robinson, David M. "Transcendentalism and Its Times." *The Cambridge Companion to Ralph Waldo Emerson.* Ed. Joel Porte and Saundra Morris. Cambridge: Cambridge University Press, 1999. 13–29.

Sanborn, F. B. "An Essay on the Sonnet and the Canzonet." Alcott, *Sonnets and Canzonets.* Boston: Roberts Brothers, 1882. 13–35.

Sanborn, F. B., and William T. Harris. *A. Bronson Alcott: His Life and Philosophy.* 2 vols. Boston: Roberts Brothers, 1893.

Shepard, Odell. *Pedlar's Progress: The Life of Bronson Alcott.* Boston: Little, Brown, 1937.

Stoehr, Taylor. *Nay Saying in Concord: Emerson, Alcott, and Thoreau.* Hamden: Archon Books, 1979.

Strickland, Charles. "A Transcendentalist Father: The Child-Rearing Practices of Bronson Alcott." *Perspectives in American History* 3 (1969): 5–73.

Warren, Austin. "Concord School of Philosophy." *New England Quarterly* 2 (1929): 199–233.

LOUISA MAY ALCOTT (1832–1888)

Catherine J. Golden

BIOGRAPHY

Louisa May Alcott, who fictionalized her family as the Marches in her best-known novel *Little Women* (1868, 1869), was born in Germantown, Pennsylvania, on November 29, 1832, on her father's thirty-third birthday. Louisa, nicknamed Louy, was the second of four daughters of Abigail "Abba" May, daughter of a prominent family of social reformers, and the controversial educator and philosopher Amos Bronson Alcott. Abba and Bronson wed on May 23, 1830, in Boston. Bronson's unsuccessful idealistic endeavors gave him notoriety but kept the family in chronic poverty with frequent relocations.

In 1834, Bronson moved his family from Germantown to Boston to found the innovative Temple School (1834–39). After it failed, the Alcotts moved to Concord, Massachusetts, home of three notable literary families—the Emersons, Thoreaus, and Hawthornes—who became their lifelong friends and greatly influenced the developing Louisa. Despite their poverty, Louisa enjoyed living in Concord, taking nature walks with her teacher Henry David Thoreau (whom she greatly admired), and writing and acting in plays with her sisters Anna (b. 1831), Elizabeth (b. 1835, nicknamed Lizzie and Beth), and Abigail May (b. 1840, called May); Louisa immortalized the four sisters as Meg, Jo, Beth, and Amy of *Little Women.*

Louisa read widely and eagerly, finding literature an escape. Her favorite authors included Charles Dickens, the Swedish Frederika Bremer, Charlotte Brontë, Sir Walter Scott, Thomas Carlyle, Goethe, Harriet Beecher Stowe, and her family friends Ralph Waldo Emerson (her intellectual mentor) and Nathaniel Hawthorne. She also demonstrated an early gift for writing, completing her first poem, "To the First Robin," in 1842. She had some formal schooling; for instance, in 1840, Anna and Louisa attended Henry and John Thoreau's liberal Concord Academy. Bronson oversaw the academic and moral education of his "model children" as he waited for Victorian society to accept his progressive ideas.

In 1842, Bronson Alcott traveled to England to meet with reformers interested in his endeavors; with William Lane's aid in 1843, he relocated his family to the town of Harvard, Massachusetts, establishing a vegetarian Utopian community named Fruitlands, where he hoped to foster Transcendentalism. When the community failed after eight months, Bronson had a breakdown, leaving his family to rely on charity and Abba's strong leadership while he embarked on unsuccessful speaking tours.

The Alcotts moved to Boston in 1848 where Abba supported the family by doing social work. Supplementing the family income, Louisa was a companion, seamstress, domestic servant, and teacher. Louisa was exceptionally close to her mother, a relationship that was often a burden given Abba's intense needs and frequent illnesses. To Abba's delight and Bronson's disdain, Louisa was filled with drive, independence, and financial ambition; she aimed to be the son of the family, the breadwinner Bronson never could be. The late 1840s and early 1850s were not without pleasure, however. Louisa organized her sisters into a production company to act out her tragic plays; like Jo March, she played the male roles. At 17, Louisa, aided by her sisters, started family papers—*The Olive Leaf* and *The Pickwick Portfolio*—filled with stories, articles, and poems.

By 1852, Louisa found her vocation in writing. In 1849, she wrote her first novel *The Inheritance,* never published in her lifetime. Her first publication, the poem "Sunlight," appeared in *Peterson's Magazine* in 1851 under the pseudonym Flora Fairfield; soon followed her first story, "Rival Painters," in *Olive Branch* (1852). The year 1854 marked her first published collection, *Flower Fables* (1854), a compilation of fairy tales written for Emerson's daughter Ellen. In the 1850s and 60s, she wrote for prestigious literary magazines, including *The Saturday Evening Gazette* and *The Atlantic Monthly.* Over the next 30 years, Louisa actively published juvenile novels and short stories including fast-paced Gothic tales written anonymously or pseudonymously.

The 1850s brought personal and economic hardship to the Alcotts. Her sister Elizabeth succumbed to scarlet fever, suffering greatly and dying in 1858 in Orchard House at Concord; Louisa fictionally translated Lizzie's death into the most poignant episode of *Little Women.* Soon after, Anna became engaged and married John Bridge Pratt in 1860. Louisa's despair intensified, and she briefly contemplated suicide. Then came the Civil War (1861–65), a pivotal event in Louisa's writing career and health. In December 1862, Louisa enlisted as a nurse to aid the war effort, contracting typhoid in January 1863. As a result of the mercury-based calomel treatment, she lost her hair and her good health. Returning to Concord, she turned life into literature, basing *Hospital Sketches* (1863) on letters written home while serving at the Union Hotel Hospital in Georgetown. While the memoir was a major step professionally, she forever suffered the effects of the treatment for typhoid that gradually poisoned her body.

While living in Boston and Concord, which she found oppressively predictable, Louisa continued her writing career. Unknown to her family and distinguished friends, in 1863 she launched a secret writing career to augment the family income: beginning with "Pauline's Passion and Punishment," she wrote thrillers for "penny dreadfuls" such as *Frank Leslie's Illustrated Newspaper* and *Flag of Our Union.* Her first novel for adults, *Moods* (1865), a tale of thwarted love, received mixed reviews. In 1867, she became editor of *Merry's Museum,* a magazine for children. Moreover, with the publication of *Little Women* (1868–69), an immediate best-seller, Louisa earned international acclaim and financial security for her family. Louisa found the attention unwelcome, expressing disdain for her fans who pressured her to find suitable matches for her "little women" (her readers longed for Jo to marry Laurie, but she did not give in).

Ironically, Louisa won fame for a book that she perceived as an artistic regression (*Little Women*). She despairingly called herself " 'a literary nursery-maid who provides moral pap for the young' " (Saxton 371). She continued writing stories and seven subsequent juvenile novels (some of which appeared serially prior to book publication). *An Old-Fashioned Girl* (1870), *Eight Cousins* (1875), *Rose in Bloom* (1876), and particularly the two sequels to *Little Women*—*Little Men* (1871) and *Jo's Boys* (1886)—enjoyed a wide readership in America and abroad.

In real life, Louisa did not follow the traditional path of her juvenile fictional heroines. She never doted on children as her fans presumed. An ardent abolitionist, she championed reform in dress, diet, child labor, prisons, and gender roles. She reveled in her spinsterhood and grew active in women's suffrage, contributing regularly for the feminist periodical, *Woman's Journal*. Despite her efforts to be dutiful and conquer sin—ideals she presents in her best-loved juvenile books—in her fiction, including *Work: A Story of Experience* (1873), she defended a woman's right to work rather than marry. Moreover, Louisa's success as a juvenile fiction writer made travel possible, and she twice toured Europe (1865; 1870 with May).

From her writing, she supported her family, including Anna and her two sons following Pratt's death in 1870. Louisa's financial savvy and literary success seem all the more remarkable given that from 1863, she was plagued with ill health and addicted to opium for sleep and pain control. She also experienced more significant loss in the late 1870s. Abba died in 1877, and Louisa grew closer to her father, especially when May married the Swiss banker Ernest Nieriker in Paris in 1878. She experienced further grief when May, while launching her art career, died late in 1879, shortly after giving birth to Lulu, named after Louisa.

In the 1880s, Louisa raised Lulu and cared for her aging father, who suffered a paralytic stroke in 1882. Her own health declining, she sought homeopathy and mind-cure treatments while completing *Jo's Boys* and three volumes of stories entitled *Lulu's Library,* dedicated to her niece. From 1887 until her death in 1888, Louisa spent her time living in Dr. Rhoda Lawrence's convalescent home in Roxbury, Massachusetts, and visiting Anna and Bronson. Having transferred her energies to her father following Abba's death and reached a better understanding with Bronson once she achieved the success that eluded him, Louisa—who never lived for herself—seems to have relinquished her will to live while visiting Bronson at his deathbed on March 1, 1888. Louisa died on March 6, 1888, two days after Bronson's death, and a joint funeral was held. Anna Alcott Pratt continued to live in Concord, caring for her sister's estate and Lulu, who returned to Europe in 1893 to live with Nieriker.

MAJOR WORKS AND THEMES

Alcott wrote poetry, short stories, adult novels, thrillers, and girls' books. In her writing across these diverse genres, certain themes dominate: self-sacrifice, duty, domesticity, sentimentality, deception, gender expectations, and feminism. Many of these themes permeate *Little Women*.

Alcott claimed the hearts of her contemporary readers with *Little Women*, published in two parts as *Little Women, or Meg, Jo, Beth and Amy* (1868) and Part Second, *Good Wives* (1869); in 1880, the two parts were reprinted as one volume with illustrations. Alcott insisted the book was "*dull*" (*Journals* 166): "I plod away, though I don't enjoy this sort of thing. Never liked girls or knew many, except my sisters; but our queer plays and experiences may prove interesting, though I doubt it" (*Journals* 165–66). In truth, she wrote her most celebrated work at the urging of her family and Thomas Niles Jr., a literary editor for Roberts Brothers who advised her to capitalize on a growing market for girls' fiction. The work is clearly autobiographical, although she idealized her mother and sisters. Louisa uses John Bunyan's popular *Pilgrim's Progress* (1678; 1684) as a framing device to develop the pilgrimages of Meg, Jo, Beth, and Amy March; in this secular recasting of Bunyan, the four sisters learn duty and goodness from their trials as they make their way toward the "Celestial City" to become model wives, mothers, and homemakers.

Bronson longed for his daughters to be "little women," but he barely features in Alcott's portrayal of New England family life (Father March is a chaplain in the Civil War who remains locked in his study while at home). Louisa transformed Abba into the ideal "mother-woman" of the Victorian era. In Marmee, she glamorizes her mother's nurturing qualities while instilling Abba's commitment to philanthropy and self-denial. For example, at Marmee's request, the girls give away their Christmas breakfast to a poor family, and their self-sacrifice is rewarded when their neighbor, Mr. Lawrence, offers them a Christmas feast. Her eldest sister Anna, whose engagement and marriage were difficult for Louisa to bear, becomes the conventionally feminine Meg, who marries early and has children. Louisa immortalized her sister Elizabeth as the angelic Beth in *Little Women,* revealing the abundance of sentiment common in Alcott's juvenile fiction. Louisa made her baby sister, May, the model for vain, demanding Amy. In Jo March, Louy instilled her spirited nature, drive to write and act, and longing to be a boy, though Louisa also shared Beth's ill health. Nonetheless, Marmee and Jo March are active and influential female role models, revealing Alcott's commitment to feminism, carrying into characters such as Nan from *Little Men* who remain single and develop careers while caring for others. Still, even tomboyish Jo loses her buoyancy, stops writing sensation fiction, and becomes a more sedate, nurturing figure in *Little Men* and *Jo's Boys,* showing how Alcott subscribed to the more conventional gender expectations of her age, at least in her juvenile fiction.

Other works celebrate women's careers and opportunities, another Alcott theme. "Happy Women" (*New York Ledger,* 1868), a counterpoint to *Little Women,* features a community of active and independent single women who have careers in art, literature, acting, medicine, philanthropy, and law. Likewise, Christie Devon, the orphan heroine of *Work,* tries a range of professions—governess, companion, seamstress, nurse, wife, mother, and speaker for women's suffrage—though she hungers for the stage, which she renounces. Here again, in a novel championing a woman's right to pursue meaningful work, we see the kind of renunciation that also characterizes her best-known work. Another Alcott orphan, Rose Campbell of *Eight Cousins* and *Rose in Bloom,* offers a more forceful feminist role model by arguing that women should use their minds and develop talents other than domestic arts. Thus, to varying degrees, feminism infuses Alcott's adult and juvenile fiction.

Alcott had a true passion for sensation fiction, a form of literature brimming with murder, deception, drugs, violence, greed, and other vices that raised the ire of nineteenth-century opponents of women's reading. She admitted to a friend: "'I think my natural ambition is for the lurid style. I indulge in gorgeous fancies and wish that I dared inscribe them upon my pages and set them before the public'" (Davis vi). Women commonly published under a pseudonym in the nineteenth century, so Alcott is not unusual in this respect. But she reveals a markedly different persona in her writings published anonymously and pseudonymously as A. M. Barnard. Alcott flies against the grain of Victorian traditions in her private persona, which seemingly enabled her to unleash her hidden emotions and explore human psychology, sensuality, and evil machinations. In her thrillers, we most forcefully witness the theme of deception. Jean Muir, the quintessential Alcott bad woman, is a consummate actress turned governess in "Behind a Mask, or A Woman's Power" (1866). Before becoming exposed, Muir captures the hand and title of an elderly aristocrat in the English family she serves. In "A Whisper in the Dark" (1863), a Gothic story of madness, excess, and self-control, Sybil's deceivers, who wrongly incarcerate her in an insane asylum, are ultimately punished. In *A Modern Mephistopheles* (1877), influenced by Goethe's *Faust,* Alcott weaves a diabolical story about a desperate deceiver, Felix Canaris, who achieves literary success by selling his soul to his manipulative and diabolical patron, Jasper Helwyze. Octavia Davis surmises that in choosing success over freedom, Canaris is not unlike Alcott: "Canaris's wife and his public audience love him not for who he is, but for the person reflected in his poetry, just as Alcott's audience loved her not for her fierce independence or for her support of women's suffrage, but for her juvenile literature" (xvii–xviii). While Alcott, like Jo, stopped writing sensational stories in the 1860s and turned her attention to children's fiction, her thrillers enlarge our image of Louisa May Alcott as a writer.

CRITICAL RECEPTION

In 1853, the publisher James T. Fields rejected an Alcott story and advised her to " 'stick to your teaching; you can't write' " (*Journals* 109). Happily, she did not heed his advice. Over her career she wrote 28 books, including novels and collections of tales, and published over 300 stories and articles in the periodical press. Moreover, one estimate suggests that between 1868 and 1886, she earned approximately $103,375 just on the sales of her books, excluding overseas royalties. This figure is nearly double that of Henry James's earnings from America and Europe during the same 18-year span (Myerson and Shealy, *Inheritance* vii–viii). Like her literary childhood idol, Dickens, Alcott earned success in her own time and long beyond it.

Alcott's career rose in the 1860s with *Hospital Sketches,* noted for its realism and moral force. The first printing of *Little Women* sold out in its first month, and like her subsequent juvenile fiction, it earned praise for its charm, moral lessons, and liveliness. Although girl readers viewed the March sisters as literary models to emulate, *Little Women* won acclaim from the populace of all ages and both sexes: Jane Addams and Theodore Roosevelt cited it as an adored book that never ceased to entertain (Sicherman 245, 256). By the 1870s, Alcott's work was included in courses on domestic fiction and ranked alongside works by literary stalwart Nathaniel Hawthorne. *Little Women's* longevity as a classic is as noteworthy as its early success. In 1927, it was ranked above the Bible and *Pilgrim's Progress* as the book with the most influence on high school students. By 1947, over two million copies of *Little Women* were sold (Myerson and Shealy, *Inheritance* xli). Over a century and a quarter after its first publication, *Little Women* appears in 263 editions in *Books in Print* (2002, including sound and video recordings).

Nonetheless, Alcott has not gone without critique. Henry James called *Moods* unrealistic and *Eight Cousins* unimaginative and commonplace. Particularly in the 1920s, Alcott's juvenile works including *Little Women* were criticized for their bad grammar and abundance of sentiment. Hailed an American *David Copperfield* in the 1940s, *Little Women* was embraced for its feminist message by the 1960s. Critics still consider *Little Women* a rite of passage for American girlhood and applaud it because, as Nina Auerbach claims, it is "a deathless book, one that contains its author's best self. Its hopes and defeats are those of all women" (470).

Literary critics did not initially give Alcott's work serious attention because she was considered a children's writer. Alcott's first biographer, Ednah Cheney, established a reminiscent tone when she presented the notion of dutiful Louisa in *Louisa May Alcott: The Children's Friend* (1888); this became the "Alcott myth," which influenced the largely biographical interest in Alcott well into the 1950s. However, the complexion of Alcott criticism changed beginning in the 1940s with Leona Rostenberg's discovery of Alcott's pseudonym, A. M. Barnard, and Madeleine Stern's biography in 1950, forever influencing the Alcott reevaluation.

With the rise of the women's movement in the 1960s and the republication of Alcott's sensation fiction in the 1970s, Alcott gained the attention of feminist critics. Collections of Alcott's sensational stories, beginning with Stern's *Behind a Mask: The Unknown Thrillers of Louisa May Alcott* (1975), made public Alcott's double literary life. Alcott emerges as a split personality: a writer of charm and domesticity who assuaged the hearts of Americans weary from the Civil War versus an independent women who reveled in the lurid and overstepped the boundaries of Victorian convention. Martha Saxton's feminist biography *Louisa May,* written after Stern's republication of the "lost" thrillers, uses this material to reinterpret Alcott's life. Like Eugenia Kaledin, Saxton sees Alcott's juvenile fiction as an artistic regression and prefers her adult fiction. The masked sides of Alcott's literary life and the feminist threads in her work also have captured the attention of critics including Auerbach, Ann Douglas, Elaine Showalter, Judith Fetterley, and Elizabeth Keyser. Scholars now value the unresolved tensions in Alcott's works and her ambivalence toward the domestic realm, which she both prescribes and challenges in her wide-ranging works.

Renewed interest in Alcott has also led to the republication of lesser-known works, such as *A Modern Mephistopheles* and *Work,* numerous collections of "lost" stories, and editions of her letters and journals by Joel Myerson, Daniel Shealy, and Madeleine B. Stern. In 1997, Myerson and Shealy brought forth Alcott's first unpublished Gothic novel, *Inheritance.* The larger oeuvre of Alcott's fiction reveals the complexity of a writer who moved through various stages as she consciously shaped her persona and guarded a secret identity, largely unknown but suspected during her lifetime. We see Alcott today as a multifaceted woman who outwardly conformed to convention but inwardly rebelled. Publicly, she projected a wholesome image of American girlhood still passed lovingly from mother to daughter. Privately, she defied taboo, writing sensational works with passion and gusto. The range of her writing continues to engage the twenty-first century critic in ways her domestic fiction never did. Alcott's public persona as a children's writer still assures her "a nearly mythical place in the American imagination" (Davis v).

WORKS CITED

Alcott, Louisa May. *The Inheritance.* Edited and with an introduction and notes by Joel Myerson and Daniel Shealy. New York: Penguin, 1997.

———. *The Journals of Louisa May Alcott.* With an Introduction by Madeleine B. Stern. Edited by Joel Myerson and Daniel Shealy, with Madeleine B. Stern. Boston: Little Brown, 1989.

Auerbach, Nina. "Afterword." Alcott, *Little Women.* New York: Bantam Books, 1983. 461–70.

Davis, Octavia. Introduction. *A Modern Mephistopheles.* By Louisa May Alcott. New York: Bantam Books, 1995.

Saxton, Martha. *Louisa May: A Modern Biography of Louisa May Alcott.* Boston: Houghton Mifflin, 1977.

Sicherman, Barbara. "Reading *Little Women:* The Many Lives of a Text." In *U.S. History as Women's History: New Feminist Essays.* Edited by Linda K. Kerber, Alice Kessler-Harris, & Kathryn Kish Sklar. Chapel Hill: University of North Carolina Press, 1995. 245–66. Notes 414–24.

BIBLIOGRAPHY

Works by Louisa May Alcott

Book-length Narratives
Hospital Sketches. Boston: James Redpath, 1863.
Moods. Boston: A. K. Loring, 1865. Rev. ed. Boston: Roberts Brothers, 1882.
Little Women, or Meg, Jo, Beth and Amy. 2 vols. Boston: Roberts Brothers, 1868–1869.
An Old-Fashioned Girl. Boston: Roberts Brothers, 1870.
Little Men: Life at Plumfield with Jo's Boys. Boston: Roberts Brothers, 1871.
Work: A Story of Experience. Boston: Roberts Brothers, 1873.
Eight Cousins; or, The Aunt-Hill. Boston: Roberts Brothers, 1875.
Rose in Bloom. A Sequel to "Eight Cousins." Boston: Roberts Brothers, 1876.
A Modern Mephistopheles. Boston: Roberts Brothers, 1877.
Under the Lilacs. Boston: Roberts Brothers, 1878.
Jack and Jill: A Village Story. Boston: Roberts Brothers, 1880.
Jo's Boys, and How They Turned Out. A Sequel to "Little Men." Boston: Roberts Brothers, 1886.
Diana and Persis. Edited by Sarah Elbert. New York: Arno, 1978. An unfinished manuscript, first published in 1978 and reprinted in *Alternative Alcott.*
A Long Fatal Love Chase. New York: Random House, 1995. First published in 1995 and a partial source for *A Modern Mephistopheles.*
The Inheritance. Edited with an introduction and notes by Joel Myerson and Daniel Shealy. New York: Penguin, 1997. First published in 1997.

Collections
Flower Fables. Boston: George W. Briggs & Co., 1854.
On Picket Duty, and Other Tales. Boston: James Redpath, 1864.
Louisa M. Alcott's Proverb Stories. Boston: A. K. Loring, 1868.
Hospital Sketches, and Camp and Fireside Stories. Boston: Roberts Brothers, 1869.
Aunt Jo's Scrap Bag. 6 vols. Boston: Roberts Brothers: 1872–82.
Silver Pitchers. Boston: Roberts Brothers, 1876.
Proverb Stories. Boston: Roberts Brothers, 1882.
Spinning Wheel Stories. Boston: Roberts Brothers, 1884.
Lulu's Library. 3 vols. Boston: Roberts Brothers, 1886–89.
A Garland for Girls. Boston: Roberts Brothers, 1889.
Comic Tragedies Written By "Jo" and "Meg" and Acted by the "Little Women." Edited by Anna Alcott Pratt. Boston: Roberts Brothers, 1893.
Behind a Mask: The Unknown Thrillers of Louisa May Alcott. Edited, with an introduction by Madeleine B. Stern. New York: William Morrow, 1975.
Plots and Counterplots: More Unknown Thrillers. Edited, with an introduction by Madeleine B. Stern. New York: William Morrow, 1976.
The Selected Letters of Louisa May Alcott. With an introduction by Madeleine Stern. Edited by Joel Myerson and Daniel Shealy, with Madeleine B. Stern. Boston: Little Brown, 1987.
Alternative Alcott. Edited, with an introduction by Elaine Showalter. New Brunswick: Rutgers UP, 1988.

A Double Life: Newly Discovered Thrillers of Louisa May Alcott. With an introduction by
    Madeleine B. Stern and edited by Madeleine Stern with Joel Myerson and Daniel Shealy.
    Boston: Little Brown, 1988.
The Journals of Louisa May Alcott. With an introduction by Madeleine B. Stern. Edited by Joel
    Myerson and Daniel Shealy, with Madeleine B. Stern. Boston: Little Brown, 1989.
Louisa May Alcott Unmasked: Collected Thrillers. Edited, with an introduction by Madeleine
    Stern. Boston: Northeastern UP, 1995.
Louisa May Alcott on Race, Sex, and Slavery. Edited, with an introduction by Sarah Elbert. Boston:
    Northeastern UP, 1997.

Studies of Louisa May Alcott

Anthony, Katharine. *Louisa May Alcott.* New York: Alfred A. Knopf, 1938.
Bedell, Madelon. *The Alcotts: Biography of a Family.* New York: Clarkson N. Potter, 1980.
Cheney, Ednah D. *Louisa May Alcott: The Children's Friend.* Boston: L. Prang & Company, 1888.
Cheney, Ednah D. *Louisa May Alcott: Life, Letters, and Journals.* Boston: Roberts Brothers, 1889.
    Reprinted, with an introduction by Ann Douglas. New York: Chelsea House, 1980.
Douglas, Ann. "Mysteries of Louisa May Alcott." *Critical Essays of Louisa May Alcott.* Ed.
    Madeleine B. Stern. Boston: G. K. Hall, 1984. 231–40.
Elbert, Sarah. *A Hunger for Home: Louisa May Alcott's Place in American Culture.* Rev. ed. New
    Brunswick: Rutgers University Press, 1987.
Fetterley, Judith. "Little Women: Alcott's Civil War." *Feminist Studies* 5 (1979): 369–83.
Keyser, Elizabeth Lennox. *Whispers in the Dark: The Fiction of Louisa May Alcott.* Knoxville:
    University of Kentucky Press, 1993.
Marsella, Joy A. *The Promise of Destiny: Children and Women in the Short Stories of Louisa May
    Alcott.* Westport: Greenwood, 1983.
Meigs, Cornelia. *Louisa M. Alcott and the American Family Story.* London: Bodley Head, 1970.
Payne, Alma J. *Louisa May Alcott: A Reference Guide.* Boston: G. K. Hall & Co., 1980.
Rostenberg, Leona. "Some Anonymous and Pseudonymous Thrillers of Louisa May Alcott." *Bib-
    liographical Society of America Papers* 37 (2nd Quarter 1943): 131–40.
Saxton, Martha. *Louisa May: A Modern Biography of Louisa May Alcott.* Boston: Houghton Mif-
    flin, 1977.
Stern, Madeleine B. *Critical Essays on Louisa May Alcott.* Boston: G. K. Hall, 1984.
———. *Louisa May Alcott: A Biography.* Norman: University of Oklahoma Press, 1950. Reprinted
    1971. Reprinted by Northeastern University Press, 1996.
Strickland, Charles. *Victorian Domesticity: Families in the Life and Art of Louisa May Alcott.*
    Athens: University of Alabama Press, 1985.

WILLIAM APESS (1798–1839)

Theresa Strouth Gaul

BIOGRAPHY

Little information on William Apess's life exists beyond that which he provides in his autobiography. He was born in Colrain, Massachusetts, in 1798 to parents of mixed Pequot and white ancestry. After moving with his parents to Colchester, Connecticut, Apess lived with his maternal grandparents after his parents' separation and a series of white families to whom he was indentured after being removed from his grandparents' care because of physical abuse. In these years, Apess attended school for six winters—the only formal education he ever received—and became familiar with the tenets of Christianity. He later experienced conversion at the age of 15. Forbidden to practice Methodism by the family whom he served at that time, he ran away to New York in 1813 and enlisted in the militia for the War of 1812, serving in the infantry. After leaving the army in 1815, Apess resided for a period in Canada, where he worked a number of jobs and, by his own admission, drank heavily. He eventually returned to Connecticut, reunited with relatives, and renewed his baptism. He began to preach in 1819, married Mary Wood in 1821 and fathered at least three children, and was ordained a Methodist minister in 1829, the same year he published his first piece of writing. On a preaching tour, Apess visited the Mashpee Indians of Cape Cod and soon became heavily involved in what came to be known as the Mashpee Revolt of 1833–34, an effort to obtain rights to self-governance. Adopted into their tribe to speak for them, Apess wrote petitions and appeals, organized their resistance, served a brief time in jail for his activities on behalf of the Mashpees, and addressed the Massachusetts House. His publications in the years 1835–37 and debt actions brought against him in the years 1836–38 are the only public records of his existence in the years following his involvement with the Mashpee, except for the obituary detailing his death, apparently from the effects of alcoholism, in New York in 1839.

MAJOR WORKS AND THEMES

All of Apess's writings were published in an eight-year period. *A Son of the Forest* (1829) stands as one of the earliest self-authored American Indian autobiographies. Taking the form of a conversion narrative, the autobiography describes the prejudice Apess encountered in his life as well as his understanding of Christianity as a color-blind creed. The sermons *The Increase of the Kingdom of Christ* (1831) and *The Indians: The Ten Lost Tribes* (1831) further articulate Apess's belief in the egalitarianism of Christianity. *The Experiences of Five Christian Indians of the Pequot Tribe* (1833) details the conversion experiences of himself, his wife, and three Pequot women and was published along with *An Indian's Looking-Glass for the White Man,* a scathing indictment of white American racism. Apess uses the rhetoric of the U.S. constitution and the Declaration of Independence to defend his efforts on behalf of the Mashpee in his longest work, *Indian Nullification* (1835). *Eulogy on King Philip* (1836), delivered as a lecture twice to audiences in Boston before being published, presents Metacomet as the greatest of American heroes in a bold revision of the history of Euro-Indian contacts since the seventeenth century.

CRITICAL RECEPTION

An early reviewer in the *North American Review* established a dominant theme for subsequent Apess criticism when he wrote: "We do not consider Mr. Apes and a few other persons of unmixed Indian blood, who have written books, to be Indians. They were indeed born of aboriginal parents, but their tastes, feelings, and train of ideas, were derived from the whites, and they were and are, in all essential particulars, civilized men" (Snelling 68). Indeed, questions of identity have preoccupied critics examining Apess's autobiography. Those looking for traces of an authentic Native voice have been disappointed, while others have pointed out that the desire to ascertain authenticity is a lingering trace of colonialism pervading contemporary literary criticism. Early examinations of American Indian autobiography generally excluded or dismissed Apess as too assimilated for inclusion in a canon of American Indian writers. The publication of Barry O'Connell's edition of Apess's complete works, however, established him as a significant figure and made his writings widely available, as does his increasing anthologization. Recent critics have explored how Apess's familiarity with Euroamerican discourses, most important among them Methodism, enabled and shaped his criticisms of U.S. racism. Apess's autobiographical writings have tended to preoccupy critics, while his other writings generally have received less scrutiny.

WORK CITED

Snelling, Joseph. Rev. of *Life of Black Hawk. North American Review* 40 (Jan. 1835): 68–87.

BIBLIOGRAPHY

Works by William Apess

A Son of the Forest: The Experience of William Apes, a Native of the Forest, Comprising a Notice of the Pequot Tribe of Indians. New York: By the author, 1829. Rpt. as *A Son of the Forest: The Experience of William Apes, a Native of the Forest,* 2nd ed., rev. and corr. New York: By the author; G.F. Bunce, Printer, 1831.
The Increase of the Kingdom of Christ: A Sermon. New York: By the author; G. F. Bunce, Printer, 1831.

The Indians: The Ten Lost Tribes. In *The Increase of the Kingdom of Christ: A Sermon.* New York: By the author; G. F. Bunce, Printer, 1831.

The Experiences of Five Christian Indians of the Pequot Tribe; or, An Indian's Looking-Glass for the White Man. Boston: By the author; James B. Dow, Printer, 1833. Rpt. as *Experience of Five Christian Indians of the Pequot Tribe.* Boston, 1837.

Indian Nullification of the Unconstitutional Laws of Massachusetts Relative to the Mashpee Tribe; or, The Pretended Riot Explained. Boston: Jonathon Howe, 1835.

Eulogy on King Philip, as Pronounced at the Odeon, in Federal Street, Boston. Boston: By the author, 1836; rpt., 1837.

Studies of William Apess

Ashwill, Gary. "Savagism and Its Discontents: James Fenimore Cooper and His Native American Contemporaries." *American Transcendental Quarterly* 8.3 (1994): 211–27.

Dannenberg, Anne Marie. " 'Where, Then, Shall We Place the Hero of the Wilderness?' William Apess' Eulogy on King Philip and Doctrines of Racial Destiny." *Early Native American Writing: New Critical Essays.* Ed. Helen Jaskoski. New York: Cambridge UP, 1996. 66–82.

Donaldson, Laura E. "Son of the Forest, Child of God: William Apess and the Scene of Postcolonial Nativity." *Postcolonial America.* Ed. C. Richard King. Urbana: U of Illinois P, 2000. 201–22.

Gaul, Theresa Strouth. "Dialogue and Public Discourse in William Apess's *Indian Nullification.*" *American Transcendental Quarterly* 15.4 (2001): 275–92.

Gussman, Deborah. "The Politics of Piety in Pequot Women's Conversion Narratives." *Literary Calvinism and Nineteenth-Century American Women Authors.* Ed. Michael Schuldiner. Lewiston, NY: Mellen, 1997. 101–24.

Gustafson, Sandra. "Nations of Israelites: Prophecy and Cultural Autonomy in the Writings of William Apess." *Religion & Literature* 26.1 (1994): 31–53.

Haynes, Carolyn. " 'A Mark for Them All to . . . Hiss at': The Formation of Methodist and Pequot Identity in the Conversion Narrative of William Apess." *Early American Literature* 31.1 (1996): 25–44.

Konkle, Maureen. "Indian Literacy, U.S. Colonialism, and Literary Criticism." *American Literature* 69.3 (1997): 457–86.

Krupat, Arnold. "Native American Autobiography and the Synecdochic Self." *American Autobiography: Retrospect and Prospect* (Madison: U of Wisconsin P, 1991). 171–94. Reprinted in Arnold Krupat, *Ethnocriticism: Ethnography, History, Literature.* Berkeley: U of California P, 1992. 201–31.

———. *The Voice in the Margin: Native American Literature and the Canon.* Berkeley: U of California P, 1989. 132–201.

Moon, Randal. "William Apess and Writing White." *Studies in American Indian Literatures* 5.4 (1993): 45–54.

Murray, David. *Forked Tongues: Speech, Writing, & Representation in North American Indian Texts.* Bloomington: Indiana UP, 1991. 49–64.

O'Connell, Barry, ed. and introd. *On Our Own Ground: The Complete Writings of William Apess, A Pequot.* Amherst: U of Massachusetts P, 1992.

———, ed. and introd. *A Son of the Forest and Other Writings by William Apess, a Pequot.* Amherst: U of Massachusetts P, 1997.

———. "William Apess and the Survival of the Pequot People." *Algonkians of New England: Past and Present.* Ed. Peter Benes. Boston: Boston UP, 1993. 89–100.

Peyer, Bernd C. "William Apess, Pequot-Mashpee Insurrectionist of the Removal Era." In *The Tutor'd Mind: Indian Missionary-Writers in Antebellum America.* Amherst: U of Amherst P, 1997. 117–65.

Ruoff, A. LaVonne Brown. "Three Nineteenth-Century American Indian Autobiographers." *Redefining American Literary History.* Eds. A. LaVonne Brown Ruoff and Jerry W. Ward. New York: Modern Language Association of America, 1990. 251–69.

Sayre, Gordon. "Defying Assimilation, Confounding Authenticity: The Case of William Apess." *A/B: Auto/Biography Studies* 11.1 (1996): 1–18.

Stevens, Scott Manning. "William Apess's Historical Self." *Northwest Review* 35.3 (1997): 67–84.

Tiro, Karim. "Denominated 'SAVAGE': Methodism, Writings, and Identity in the Works of William Apess, A Pequot." *American Quarterly* 48.4 (1996): 653–79.

Vernon, Irene S. "The Claiming of Christ: Native American Postcolonial Discourses." *MELUS* 24.2 (1999): 75–88.

Wyss, Hilary. "Captivity and Conversion: William Apess, Mary Jemison, and Narratives of Racial Identity." *American Indian Quarterly* 23.3/4 (1999): 63–82.

———. "A Son of the Forest and a Preacher of the Gospel: Narratives of Captivity and Conversion." In *Writing Indians: Literacy, Christianity, and Native Community in Early America.* Amherst: U of Massachusetts P, 2000. 154–67.

ROBERT MONTGOMERY BIRD (1806–1854)

Phillip Howerton

BIOGRAPHY

Robert Montgomery Bird, poet, dramatist, and novelist, was born in New Castle, Delaware, to John and Elizabeth Van Leuvenigh Bird on February 5, 1806. Robert's father died unexpectedly in 1810, leaving the family bankrupt, and Robert was sent to live with his uncle, Nicholas Van Dyke, a prominent statesman of Delaware. After graduating from Germantown Academy in 1824, Bird entered medical school at the University of Pennsylvania, earning his M.D. in 1827. He immediately opened a medical practice in Philadelphia, but the profession was not rewarding to Bird because he was too humane to charge for his services and because he became depressed when witnessing incurable suffering (M. Bird 34). Bird quit the medical profession after only one year and turned to literature as a career.

During his years of medical study and practice, Bird wrote a volume of poems, several of which were later published in *Philadelphia Monthly Magazine,* and five plays: *The Cowled Lover, Caridorf, 'Twas All for the Best, The City Looking Glass,* and *News of the Night.* Bird's first important success came in 1830 when he entered another play, *Pelopidas,* into an annual contest sponsored by the popular tragedian, Edwin Forrest. Forrest selected *Pelopidas* to receive the $1,000 prize, and he and Bird quickly became close friends and traveled together throughout the eastern and southern United States.

Bird wrote three more plays for Forrest—*Gladiator* (1831), *Oralloossa* (1832), and *The Broker of Bogota* (1834)—before Forrest's refusal to pay for the use of the plays ended the friendship. The poor treatment Bird received from Forrest and Bird's low opinion of American audiences prompted him to quit writing plays to become a novelist. He then published seven books in five years: *Calavar* (1834), *The Infidel* (1835), *The Hawks of Hawk Hollow* (1835), *Sheppard Lee* (1836), *Nick of the Woods* (1837), *Peter Pilgrim* (1838), and *The Adventures of Robin Day* (1839). During this time he also made a trip to London in a futile attempt to secure British copyright of *Calavar,* and in 1837 he wed Mary Mayer. Their son, Frederick Mayer Bird, was born the following year.

Bird's severe writing schedule during the 1830s wrecked his health, and he moved to a farm in eastern Maryland in March 1840 to recover. Although farm life invigorated him, it did not allow him time to write a history of the United States as he had planned, and after summer storms destroyed his crops, he returned to New Castle.

From 1841 to 1843 Bird taught medicine at Pennsylvania Medical College. He also became involved in Whig politics and, after failing to receive his party's nomination to run for Congress, was eventually awarded a patronage position as director of the New Castle Farmer's National Bank in 1846. A year later he sought appointment as assistant secretary or librarian of the Smithsonian Institute, and when denied those positions he borrowed $30,000 and purchased one-third interest in a newspaper, the Philadelphia *North American.* Most of the editor's duties fell to Bird, and this overwork, combined with incessant worry about debt and about misuse of company funds by business partners, weakened his health, and he died of "cerebral congestion" on January 23, 1854.

MAJOR WORKS AND THEMES

In his major works, Bird adopted and expanded many themes that were currently popular. In *Pelopidas* and *Gladiator,* Bird borrowed from Greece and Roman history to create heroes fighting for freedom from tyranny and oppression, and these themes paralleled Americans' views of their struggles against the British. In *Pelopidas,* Spartans establish a dictatorship in Thebes, and the hero, Pelopidas, an Athenian patriot, returns from exile to free the city and to rescue his wife and child from execution. Such themes are central in *Gladiator* as the slave, Spartacus, leads a rebellion against the Romans. In the end, after his wife and child are slain and his armies defeated, Spartacus fights to his death.

In his last plays Bird followed the American trend of turning away from European subjects and settings. *Oralloossa* narrates the Spanish conquest of Peru and the efforts of Oralloossa, an Indian prince and patriot, to resist the invasion. *The Broker of Bogota,* also set in South America, tells the story of a moneylender, Febro, and his troubled relationships with his children: one son becomes a thief, a daughter elopes, and Febro dies of grief. As biographer Curtis Dahl points out, Bird was ahead of his time with this domestic drama exploring the lives of middle-class people (68).

In Bird's first novels, *Calavar* and *The Infidel,* Cortez' conquest of Mexico is the backdrop for fictional subplots of domestic relationships and struggles for liberty as natives of Mexico resist foreign aggressors. Beginning with *The Hawks of Hawk Hollow,* Bird employed the subjects and settings of his own country. Set in Pennsylvania at the close of the American Revolution, this novel relates the attempts of a Tory family to reclaim a plantation unjustly taken from them during the war. Bird's next novel, *Sheppard Lee,* is an experiment in science fiction and satire as a luckless farmer lapses into a trance and consecutively inhabits the corpses of five people from various classes of American society.

Domestic drama and the American frontier are dominant themes in *Nick of the Woods.* The protagonist, Nathan Slaughter, a peace-loving Quaker in the Kentucky backwoods, is alternately a vicious Indian-killer seeking revenge for the massacre of his family. In this novel, Bird attempted to realistically portray frontier life, and he created some of the earliest authentic frontier dialect, humor, and characterization in American literature, but he was criticized for his portrayal of native Americans as "ignorant, violent, debased, [and] brutal" (R. Bird, 8). *Peter Pilgrim,* a collection of sketches and short stories, also provides accurate representations of frontier life, and *The Adventures of Robin Day* is a picaresque novel that satirizes American life but disappointingly lapses into a series of unbelievable adventures (Dahl 111–12).

CRITICAL RECEPTION

Although generally ignored today, Bird's writings were immensely popular during his lifetime. His poems and short stories appeared in numerous periodicals and many were anthologized. *Gladiator* was the first play written in English to be produced 1,000 times during the lifetime of its author, and Bird's plays were staged regularly until the end of the nineteenth century. His novels were also well received. An early reviewer stated that *Calavar* was "a production of decided talent: valuable and interesting" (Review of *Calavar* 258), and Poe praised *The Infidel* as "a work of great power" (32). Poe also had mixed praise for *The Hawks of Hawk Hollow* and *Sheppard Lee. Nick of the Woods,* in addition to being Bird's most popular novel, was also repeatedly staged as a play. Although Bird never earned a living solely as a writer, his books sold well; the majority of his novels were published in several editions, translated into foreign languages, and pirated by British publishers.

Despite such popularity, Bird's writings often do not appeal to contemporary readers. Much of his poetry was written in a sentimental and moralistic style and seems ornate and didactic today. The weaknesses of Bird's plays were summarized by Curtis Dahl: "the themes of the tragedies are overstated, the characters unreal, and the situations overdramatized" (121). Such weaknesses are illustrated in *Gladiator,* for Spartacus is forced to fight not only for his own freedom but also for the freedom of his wife and child—and is ordered to slay his own brother. Furthermore, in his many speeches, Spartacus displays the ideals and rhetoric more fitting an Athenian statesman or a Jacksonian democrat than a slave.

Complicated plots and weak heroes are also prevalent in Bird's work. His plots are filled with mistaken identities, coincidences, unexplained motivations, and uninspiring lead characters. For example, in *The Hawks of Hawk Hollow* the hero has a secret identity, is wrongly accused of double murder, and is repeatedly rescued and recaptured. There is also a secret wedding and confused familial lineages but, in the end, the legitimate heirs replace the illegitimate heirs, and the hero marries the woman he loves and inherits the plantation. Such melodramatic elements, though representative of Bird's era, mitigate the appeal of his work and have kept this multitalented and prolific writer from being considered a first-rate author.

WORKS CITED

Bird, Mary Mayer. *Life of Robert Montgomery Bird.* Ed. C. Seymour Thompson. Philadelphia: The University of Pennsylvania Library, 1945.

Bird, Robert Montgomery. "Preface to Revision of 1853." *Nick of the Woods or The Jibbenainosay: A Tale of Kentucky.* Ed. Cecil B. Williams. New York: American Book, 1939.

Dahl, Curtis. *Robert Montgomery Bird.* New York: Twayne, 1963.

Poe, Edgar Allan. Review of *The Infidel. Southern Literary Messenger* June 1835. Rpt. in *The Complete Works of Edgar Allan Poe.* Vol. 1. Ed. James A. Harrison. New York: Society of English and French Literature, 1902. 32–37.

Review of *Calavar. The North American Review* 40:86 (January 1835): 232–59.

BIBLIOGRAPHY

Works by Robert Montgomery Bird

Plays

Caridorf; Or, The Avenger. 1827. *The Cowled Lover & Other Plays.* Ed. Edward H. O'Neill. Princeton: Princeton UP, 1941. 69–141.

The Cowled Lover. 1827. *The Cowled Lover & Other Plays.* Ed. Edward H. O'Neill. Princeton: Princeton UP, 1941. 1–67.

'Twas All for the Best; Or, 'Tis All a Notion. 1827. *The Cowled Lover & Other Plays.* Ed. Edward H. O'Neill. Princeton: Princeton UP, 1941. 191–221.

News of the Night; Or, A Trip to Niagara. 1828. *The Cowled Lover & Other Plays.* Ed. Edward H. O'Neill. Princeton: Princeton UP, 1941. 143–89.

The City Looking Glass: A Philadelphia Comedy. 1828. Ed. Arthur Hobson Quinn. New York: Pynson, 1933.

Pelopidas; Or, The Fall of the Polemarchs. 1830. *The Life and Dramatic Works of Robert Montgomery Bird.* Ed. Clement E. Foust. New York: Burt Franklin, 1971. 173–296.

The Gladiator. 1831. *The Life and Dramatic Works of Robert Montgomery Bird.* Ed. Clement E. Foust. New York: Burt Franklin, 1971. 299–440.

Oralloossa, Son of the Incas. 1832. *The Life and Dramatic Works of Robert Montgomery Bird.* Ed. Clement E. Foust. New York: Burt Franklin, 1971. 443–575.

The Broker of Bogota. 1834. *Representative American Plays.* Ed. Arthur Hobson Quinn. New York, 1917. 209–251. Reprint, *The Life and Dramatic Works of Robert Montgomery Bird.* Ed. Clement E. Foust. New York: Burt Franklin, 1971. 579–722.

Novels

Calavar; or, The Knight of Conquest. 2 vols. Philadelphia: Carey, Lea & Blanchard, 1834, 1837, 1847. Reprint, New York: J. S. Redfield, 1854. Reprint, New York: W. J. Widdleton. 1876.

The Infidel; or, The Fall of Mexico. 2 vols. Philadelphia: Carey, Lea & Blanchard, 1835. Reprint, 2nd edition, 1835.

The Hawks of Hawk Hollow. 2 vols. Philadelphia: Carey, Lea & Blanchard, 1835. Reprint, 2nd edition, 1835.

Sheppard Lee. New York: Harpers & Brothers, 1836.

Nick of the Woods; or, The Jibbenainosay. A Tale of Kentucky. 2 vols. Philadelphia: Carey, Lea & Blanchard, 1837.

The Adventures of Robin Day. 2 vols. Philadelphia: Lea & Blanchard, 1839.

Nick of the Woods; or, The Jibbenainosay. Revised edition. New York: J. S. Redford, 1853, 1854. Reprint, New York: W. J. Widdleton, 1864, 1876. Reprint, New York: A. C. Armstrong and Son, 1881, 1890.

Nick of the Woods. Burrows, 1904.

Nick of the Woods: A Story of the Early Settlers in Kentucky. New York: A.L. Burt, 1905.

Nick of the Woods; or, The Jibbenainosay: A Tale of Kentucky. Ed. Cecil B. Williams. New York: American Book, 1939.

Collections

Peter Pilgrim; or, a Rambler's Recollections. 2 vols. Philadelphia: Lea & Blanchard, 1838. Reprint, New York: J. Polhemus, 1877.

Studies of Robert Montgomery Bird

Bird, Mary Mayer. *Life of Robert Montgomery Bird.* Ed. C. Seymour Thompson. Philadelphia: The University of Philadelphia Library, 1945.

Dahl, Curtis. *Robert Montgomery Bird.* New York: Twayne, 1963.

Foust, Clement E. *The Life and Dramatic Works of Robert Montgomery Bird.* New York: Burt Franklin, 1971.

Quinn, Arthur Hobson. *A History of the American Drama from the Beginning to the Civil War.* 2nd ed. New York: Appleton-Century-Crafts, 1951.

Richards, Jeffrey H. "The Gladiator (1831): Robert Montgomery Bird." *Early American Drama.* Ed. Jeffrey H. Richards. New York: Penguin, 1997. 166–70.

Williams, Cecil B. Introduction. *Nick of the Woods; or, The Jibbenainosay: A Tale of Kentucky.* Ed. Cecil B. Williams. New York: American Book, 1939. ix–lxiii.

WILLIAM WELLS BROWN (1814?–1884)

Tim Prchal

BIOGRAPHY

William Wells Brown, a pioneer in African American literature, was the child of a slave named Elizabeth and a prominent white Tennessean named George Higgins. Higgins was a relative of Dr. John Young, the master of Elizabeth and, consequently, of her son. Young moved to Missouri in 1816, and in this region Wells matured amid events that would guide the accomplishments of his adult life. For instance, he heard his mother being whipped by a cruel overseer and felt powerless to protect her. Wells himself suffered repeated whippings for refusing to accept a new name after a nephew also named William arrived in the Young household. He was hired out to James Walker, a slave trader, and compelled to transport fellow slaves to auction. At one point, he witnessed the murder of a slave attempting to swim to safety. The corpse was dumped on shore and left there overnight until finally hauled away in a trash cart. Wells convinced his mother to escape with him, incurring harsh punishment for them both when bounty hunters caught them. These experiences inflamed his lifelong battle against slavery and other forms of racism.

In 1834, Wells managed to escape on his own, forcing him to leave his mother and siblings behind. He adopted the name "Wells Brown" from a Quaker who assisted him during his hard and precarious journey north. In Cleveland, he secured work in the Great Lakes shipping industry, began to teach himself to read and write (antislavery newspapers were among his reading material), married Elizabeth Schooner, and began a family. His employment in navigation let him take action against slavery by smuggling other runaway slaves to Canada. Moving to Buffalo in 1836, he made his home a stop on the Underground Railroad. While also becoming deeply involved in the temperance movement, he started to lecture for the Western New York Anti-Slavery Society. His life story, he learned, could serve the cause of abolition whether told in lecture or written form. Brown's autobiography *Narrative of William W. Brown, A Fugitive Slave* was published in 1847, two years after Frederick Douglass's famous tale of his own escape from slavery appeared.

Brown's book was very successful, and the American Peace Society chose him to speak about slavery at an International Peace Congress in Paris during the summer of 1849. The trip became an extended stay in England and surrounding countries, during which time Brown continued to lecture. He also wrote *Three Years In Europe* (1852) and *Clotel; or the President's Daughter* (1853), respectively, the first published work of travel literature and first published novel by an African American author. (Harriet E. Wilson's *Our Nig* [1859] is considered the first novel by an African American author published in the United States.) Having earlier spurned the offer to purchase his independence, in light of the Fugitive Slave Act of 1850, Brown reluctantly permitted British abolitionists to buy his freedom. Having done so, he could go back to his homeland without the threat of being returned to bondage.

Once back, Brown continued to break ground in publishing. His play *The Escape; or, a Leap for Freedom* (1858) is the first published play written by an African American. An earlier play of his, no longer extant, was titled *Experience; or, How to Give a Northern Man a Backbone* and possibly *The Doughface* in an earlier draft (see Farrison 278.) Brown's *The Negro in the American Revolution: His Heroism and His Fidelity* (1867) is the first work of African American military history ever written. After Emancipation, he continued to work for racial equality through lecturing and writing. Before his death in 1884, he had become an inspiration to writers such as Pauline Elizabeth Hopkins, who in her youth won a literary contest that Brown sponsored.

MAJOR WORKS AND THEMES

As suggested above, race, racism, and slavery are central concerns in most of Brown's writing. Even his European travelogue frequently offers commentary on these topics—as well as on literary celebrities, the World's Fair in London, side trips to the country, and so on. For instance, regarding slavery and racism, he writes, "In America I had been bought and sold as a slave in the Southern States. In the so-called Free States, I had been treated as one born to occupy an inferior position. . . . But no sooner was I on British soil, than I was recognized as a man, and an equal" (*The Travels* 98). The underlying lesson here is that racial oppression is not an inherent characteristic of humanity: it can be eradicated. Brown's primary goal for visiting Europe was to convince his audience there to do what they could to convey this lesson to Americans. Back in New York, his views of abolition were shaped by William Lloyd Garrison, editor of the antislavery newspaper *The Liberator.* According to Garrison, the U.S. Constitution supported slavery. In place of political action, then, the sin of slavery was to be overcome through "moral suasion" (see Jefferson 16). The moral influence that literature was purported to exert was seen as a means to realize social reform, and Brown followed suit.

Significantly, Brown portrays slavery not just as morally corrupt in and of itself but also as having a far-reaching corruptive influence. For instance, in the *Narrative,* he recounts having duped a free black into taking a whipping that Brown's master had meant for Brown himself. This cruel act, he explains, "shows how it is that slavery makes its victims lying and mean. . . . Had I entertained the same views of right and wrong which I now do, I am sure I should never have practiced the deception upon that poor fellow which I did" (*The Travels* 47). In *Clotel,* the hypocrisy of Christians owning slaves is said to encourage religious infidelity (171), and discrimination against African Americans in the North "is attributable solely to the influence of slavery . . . " (218). Brown also refuted the notion of racial inferiority and attempted to fill the void of black history by writing *The Black Man: His Antecedents, His Genius, and His Achievements* (1863) and *The Rising Son; or, The Antecedents and Advancement of the Colored Race* (1873). His final work, *My Southern Home; or, the South and Its People* (1880), returns to descriptions of slave life; however, the forthright didacticism of his earlier books is replaced with the objective feel of realism.

Those new to Brown's writing should be aware that his works frequently came out in new editions, sometimes revised, expanded, and retitled. For example, his *Narrative* was expanded for its second edition, and four American editions were released within its first two years of publications. Four British editions, one illustrated, and an Irish edition followed. While British readers were introduced in 1852 to *Three Years in Europe; or, Places I Have Seen and People I Have Met,* Americans read an expanded version of the work titled *The American Fugitive in Europe: Sketches of Places and People Abroad* three years later. Similarly, *Clotel; or the President's Daughter,* first published in 1853 in England, appeared stateside as *Miralda, or the Beautiful Quadroon: A Romance of American Slavery Founded on Fact* (1860); *Clotelle: A Tale of the Southern States* (1864); and *Clotelle; or the Colored Heroine: A Tale of the Southern States* (1867). Each new title signaled a considerable revision of the novel.

CRITICAL RECEPTION

The many editions that Brown's works went through within his lifetime intimate the original popularity of his writing. William Edward Farrison reports that the *Narrative* "immediately became a best-seller" and the four American editions released in fairly rapid succession totaled 10,000 copies. "It was widely read, no doubt, because it was a good example of what Brown intended it to be, namely, a forceful argument by means of narration," he adds (114). The novel *Clotel* also came out in multiple editions, but it seems not to have been as successful. Farrison says, "Although *Clotel* was potentially sensational, it created no sensation, partly . . . because it was brought out scarcely more than a year after *Uncle Tom's Cabin,* with which it invited comparisons to its disadvantage" (228). In the English edition of Brown's novel, the title character is the child of Thomas Jefferson and a slave. Jefferson is replaced by a fictional senator and a southern gentleman in the American versions, but apparently such sidestepping of controversy was not enough to make the novel as popular as Harriet Beecher Stowe's renowned work.

Brown did dramatic readings of his two plays on the lecture circuit, and local newspapers praised these. The *Vergennes Citizen,* for instance, commented on the first play's "many vivid, graphic and thrilling passages" while, regarding the second play, the *Elyria Independent Democrat* critic felt unable to adequately describe "the beauties of this Drama. It must be heard to be appreciated." The *Seneca Falls Courier* wrote that he had "a dramatic talent possessed by few who have, under the best instruction, made themselves famous on stage" (qtd. in Farrison 281–85). These last comments suggest that Brown's performance was as laudable as the play he read. One senses that Brown had a stage persona that might have bolstered interest in his literary work, something like Mark Twain.

While Brown's literary efforts were generally admired in his own time, academic literary critics seem not to have fully appreciated his contribution to American literature until the late 1960s. In fact, 1969 was a banner year for renewed interest in his work. That year, two book-length biographies were published: Farrison's *William Wells Brown: Author and Reformer* and J. Noel Heermance's *William Wells Brown and Clotelle: A Por-*

trait of the Artist in the First Negro Novel. The latter reprints a version of *Clotel,* competing with editions released by at least three other presses the same year. Along with these, virtually all of Brown's other books were reissued in 1969 by various publishers.

Since Brown's work has become readily available again—both on paper and online—scholars have begun to evaluate his contribution to African American literature. Ann DuCille argues that *Clotel* deserves more attention and greater acceptance from critics: "Despite its seminal position as the first novel by an African American, *Clotel* remains a book in need of both reading and readings, an originary, enabling text in want of analysis and deep theorizing—perhaps in want even of a tradition" (451). While rooted in African American experience, Brown's work also prompts important discussion of nineteenth-century literary genres. Heermance, for instance, looks at *Clotel* in terms of the slave narrative genre while R. J. Ellis examines the novel's intersections with many genres, particularly that of the sentimental novel. A generic study of *My Southern Home* might prove fruitful, if not frustrating, as this work entwines history, autobiography, and fiction.

Poststructural critical perspectives also have gleaned valuable insights from Brown's literature. The character Clotel has facilitated feminist literary study, for instance, leading Angelyn Mitchell to explain "Brown's inability to illuminate and to interrogate the true nature of the enslaved female's plight in slavery . . . " (10). Wilson's *Our Nig,* Mitchell argues, speaks more genuinely of a slave woman's experience. DuCille has since offered something of a defense of Brown's portrait of Clotel, saying that the final version of this novel is his attempt "to write a 'woman's novel,' endowing the title character with new dimensions of heroism" and suggesting a link between "chattel slavery and the bonds of matrimony, a connection many white women of Brown's day had begun to make" (452). Along with examining its gender issues, critics have examined Brown's literature in regard to performance theory. Harry J. Elam Jr. takes this approach, showing that *The Escape* reveals "how blackness is conceived and performed both on stage and in life" (288). While the sheer volume of Brown's body of work is noteworthy, especially given the conditions of his life, the remarkable diversity found within his writing clearly lends itself to a variety of critical approaches.

WORKS CITED

Brown, William Wells. *Clotel.* In *Three Classic African-American Novels.* Ed. William L. Andrews. New York: Mentor, 1990. 71–283.

———. *The Travels of William Wells Brown, Including Narrative of William W. Brown, Fugitive Slave, and The American Fugitive in Europe, Sketches of Places and People Abroad.* Ed. Paul Jefferson. New York: Marcus Weiner, 1991.

DuCille, Ann. "Where in the World is William Wells Brown?: Thomas Jefferson, Sally Hemings, and the DNA of African-American Literary History." *American Literary History* 12, no. 3 (2000): 443–62.

Elam, Harry J., Jr. "The Black Performer and the Performance of Blackness: *The Escape; or, a Leap to Freedom* by William Wells Brown and *No Place to Be Somebody* by Charles Gordone." *African American Performance and Theater History: A Critical Reader.* Ed. Harry J. Elam, Jr., and David Krasner. New York: Oxford University Press, 2001. 288–305.

Farrison, William Edward. *William Wells Brown: Author & Reformer.* Chicago: University of Chicago Press, 1969.

Jefferson, Paul. Introduction. *The Travels of William Wells Brown, Including Narrative of William W. Brown, Fugitive Slave, and The American Fugitive in Europe, Sketches of Places and People Abroad.* Ed. Paul Jefferson. New York: Marcus Weiner, 1991. 1–20.

Mitchell, Angelyn. "Her Side of His Story: A Feminist Analysis of Two Nineteenth-Century Antebellum Novels, William Wells Brown's *Clotel* and Harriet E. Wilson's *Our Nig*." *American
Literary Realism* 24, no. 3 (1992): 7–21.

BIBLIOGRAPHY

Works by William Wells Brown

Novel
Clotel; or the President's Daughter: A Narrative of Slave Life in the United States. London: Par-
tridge & Oakley, 1853. Reprint, New York: Bedford, 2000.

Drama
The Escape; or, A Leap for Freedom. Boston: R. F. Wallcut, 1858. Reprint, Knoxville: University
of Tennessee Press, 2001.

Nonfiction
Narrative of William W. Brown, A Fugitive Slave, Written by Himself. Boston: Anti-Slavery Office,
1847.
*A Description of William Wells Brown's Original Panoramic Views of the Scenes in the Life of an
American Slave, from His Birth in Slavery to His Death or His Escape to His First Home of
Freedom on British Soil*. London: Charles Gilpin, 1849.
Three Years in Europe; or, Places I Have Seen and People I Have Met. Boston: A. G. Brown,
1852.
The Black Man: His Antecedents, His Genius, and His Achievements. New York: T. Hamilton,
1863.
The Negro in the American Revolution: His Heroism and His Fidelity. Boston: Lee & Shepard,
1867.
The Rising Son; or, The Antecedents and Advancement of the Colored Race. Boston: A. G. Brown,
1873.
My Southern Home; or, The South and Its People. Boston: A. G. Brown, 1880.

Studies of William Wells Brown

Adéèkó, Adélékè. "Signatures of Blood in William Wells Brown's *Clotel*." *Nineteenth-Century
Contexts* 21, no. 1 (1999): 115–34.
Berthold, Michael. "Cross-Dressing and Forgetfulness of Self in William Wells Brown's *Clotel*."
College Literature 20, no. 3 (1993): 19–29.
Cassady, Marsh. "William W. Brown." *American History* 30, no. 6 (1996): 16–18.
Dorsey, Peter A. "De-Authorizing Slavery: Realism in Stowe's *Uncle Tom's Cabin* and Brown's
Clotel." *ESQ* 41, no. 4 (1995): 256–88.
DuCille, Ann. "Where in the World is William Wells Brown?: Thomas Jefferson, Sally Hemings,
and the DNA of African-American Literary History." *American Literary History* 12, no. 3
(2000): 443–62.
Elam, Harry J., Jr. "The Black Performer and the Performance of Blackness: *The Escape; or, a
Leap to Freedom* by William Wells Brown and *No Place to Be Somebody* by Charles Gor-
done." *African American Performance and Theater History: A Critical Reader*. Ed. Harry J.
Elam, Jr., and David Krasner. New York: Oxford University Press, 2001. 288–305.
Ellis, R. J. "Body Politics and the Body Politic in William Wells Brown's *Clotel* and Harriet Wil-
son's *Our Nig*." *Soft Canons: American Women Writers and Masculine Tradition*. Ed. Karen
L. Kilcup. Iowa City: University of Iowa Press, 1999. 99–122.

Fabi, Giulia. "The 'Unguarded Expressions of the Feelings of the Negroes': Gender, Slave Resistance, and William Wells Brown's Revisions of *Clotel*." *African American Review* 27, no. 4 (1993): 639–654.

Farrison, William Edward. "Clotel, Thomas Jefferson, and Sally Hemings." *CLA Journal* 17, no. 2 (1973): 147–74.

———. "The Origin of Brown's *Clotel*." *Phylon* 15, no. 4 (1954): 347–54.

———. *William Wells Brown: Author and Reformer*. Chicago: U of Chicago P, 1969.

———. "William Wells Brown in Buffalo." *Journal of Negro History* 39, no. 4 (1954): 298–314.

Gilmore, Paul. " 'De Genewine Artekil': William Wells Brown, Blackface Minstrelsy, and Abolitionism." *American Literature* 69, no. 4 (1997): 743–80.

Heermance, J. Noel. *William Wells Brown and Clotel: A Portrait of the Artist in the First Negro Novel*. Hamden: Archon Books, 1969.

Hopkins, Pauline. "William Wells Brown." *Colored American Magazine* 2 (1901): 232–36.

Jackson, Blyden. "The First Negro Novelist." *A History of Afro-American Literature*. Vol. 1. Baton Rouge: Louisiana State University Press, 1989. 326–32.

Joshi, Madhu. " 'Black Men Don't be Afraid to Show Your Colors and to Own Them': A Case for the Study of William Wells Brown's *Clotel*." *Indian Journal Of American Studies* 19, no. 1–2 (1989): 99–103.

Lewis, Richard O. "Literary Conventions in the Novels of William Wells Brown." *CLA Journal* 29, no. 2 (Dec 1985): 129–56.

Mitchell, Angelyn. "Her Side of His Story: A Feminist Analysis of Two Nineteenth-Century Antebellum Novels, William Wells Brown's *Clotel* and Harriet E. Wilson's *Our Nig*." *American Literary Realism* 24, no. 3 (1992): 7–21.

Mulvey, Christopher. "The Fugitive Self and the New World of the North: William Wells Brown's Discovery of America." *The Black Columbiad: Defining Moments in African American Literature and Culture*. Ed. Werner Sollors and Maria Diedrich. Cambridge: Harvard UP, 1994. 99–111.

Rosselot, Gerald S. "*Clotel*, a Black Romance." *CLA Journal* 23, no. 3 (1980): 296–302.

Schweninger, Lee. "*Clotel* and the Historicity of the Anecdote." *MELUS* 24, no. 1 (1999): 21–36.

Simmons, Ryan. "Naming Names: *Clotel* and *Behind the Scenes*." *CLA Journal* 43, no. 1 (1999): 19–37.

WILLIAM CULLEN BRYANT (1794–1878)

John J. Han

BIOGRAPHY

A poet, literary critic, and journalist, William Cullen Bryant was born to Dr. Peter and Sarah Snell Bryant, at Cummington, western Massachusetts, on November 3, 1794. His father was a physician and surgeon who loved poetry, music, and the classics. A member of the Federalist party, he represented the frontier village of Cummington in the Massachusetts Legislature for several years and then was a member of the State Senate (Godwin, *Biography,* 3). The boy's mother was the daughter of Ebenezer Snell, one of the first settlers in the village and a justice of the peace. While growing up, he was placed under two conflicting religious influences: Calvinism from his maternal grandfather and Unitarianism from his father. Bryant was sent to the district schools until he was 12. He began writing poems at age nine, some of which were, to use his own words, "utter nonsense." In the spring of 1804, when he was 10, he composed a poem describing the school he attended; three years later it was printed in the *Hampshire Gazette,* the county newspaper located at Northampton (Godwin, *Biography,* 22–23). The following year he published *The Embargo; or, Sketches of the Times. A Satire,* a Federalist pamphlet in verse.

In 1810, when he was 15, Bryant entered Williams College but withdrew after a year because of the high expenses. Determining to pursue a legal career, he studied law first with Samuel Howe at Worthington, Massachusetts, and then with Congressman William Baylies at West Bridgewater, Massachusetts. In 1815, at 21, Bryant was finally admitted to the Massachusetts bar and practiced law for nearly 10 years near Cummington in the hamlet of Plainfield and at Great Barrington, Massachusetts. In 1817, the *North American Review* published his "Thanatopsis" and other poems; "Thanatopsis" quickly established Bryant's reputation as the foremost poet in the United States. A year later, "To a Waterfowl," a poem, and "Essay on American Poetry," a critical essay on Solyman Brown's verse, were published in the *North American Review.*

In January 1821, Bryant married Frances Fairchild, to whom he was happily married until her death nearly half a century later. In August of the same year, he was invited to read the Phi Beta Kappa poem "The Ages" at the Harvard commencement. In September, his first collection of verse, *Poems,* was published at Cambridge. This volume contained some of his most famous poems, including "Thanatopsis," "Inscription for the Entrance to a Wood," "Green River," and "To a Waterfowl."

In April 1825 Bryant abandoned his law practice and moved to New York City. There he became co-editor of the *New-York Review and Athenaeum Magazine,* a monthly literary journal. In 1825–26 he delivered four "Lectures on Poetry" before the New York Athenaeum Society. In 1827 he joined the editorial staff of New York *Evening Post,* a daily newspaper. Two years later he became editor-in-chief and part owner of the paper with which he was to remain until his death; newspaper ownership eventually brought Bryant a fortune that was estimated at his death to be about a million dollars (Sillen 11). By the time he joined the *Evening Post,* he had already broken ties with Federalism and embraced the platform of the Democratic party. As one of the preeminent liberal journalists of his time, Bryant advocated free trade, free speech, workmen's right to strike, and abolition, among other sociopolitical causes. His passionate support for the abolitionist cause, however, alienated him from the Democratic party; he then switched his allegiance to the newly formed Republican party.

Bryant's hectic life as a newspaper editor and publisher prevented him from producing serious works of poetry as of the mid-1820s. He managed to publish several volumes of verse, none of which is considered equal to the poems he wrote in his youth. Later volumes of his work include *Poems* (1832), *The Fountain and Other Poems* (1842), *The White-Footed Deer and Other Poems* (1844), *A Forest Hymn* (1860), *The Little People of the Snow* (1863), *Hymns* (1864), *Thirty Poems* (1864), and *Among the Trees* (1874). *The Poetical Works of William Cullen Bryant,* a collection of his poetry edited by Parke Godwin, was published posthumously, in 1883.

Volumes of Bryant's prose published during the final three decades of his life include *Letters of a Traveller; or, Notes of Things Seen in Europe and America* (1850), *Discourse on the Life and Genius of Cooper* (1852), *Letters of a Traveller. Second Series* (1859), *A Discourse on the Life, Character, and Genius of Washington Irving* (1860), *Letters from the East* (1869), *Some Notices on the Life and Writings of Fitz-Greene Halleck* (1869), *A Discourse on the Life, Character, and Writings of Gulian Crommelin Verplanck* (1870), and *Orations and Addresses by William Cullen Bryant* (1873). He also published well-regarded translations of two epic poems: *The Iliad of Homer* (1870) and *The Odyssey of Homer* (1871–72). Bryant died in New York City on June 12, 1878, 12 years after his wife's death.

MAJOR WORKS AND THEMES

Bryant's works comprise mainly two genres: poetry and nonfiction prose. As Albert F. McLean rightly points out in his *William Cullen Bryant* (1989), Bryant's verse can be divided into three groups based on their subjects—poems of nature, poems of death, and poems of progress—although the boundaries are sometimes blurry. The poems dealing with nature reflect the author's pantheistic and Romantic worldview: nature manifests the majesty and beauty of a transcendent Divine Being; nature also is the moral guide for humanity. In the lyric "To a Waterfowl" (1815), for example, the weary poet watches a solitary bird flying across the sky at sundown. The bird's flight teaches him that the creature is providentially guided by "a Power" whose care sustains seemingly lone wanderers (Godwin, *Poetical* 1:26). " 'Oh Fairest of the Rural Maids' " (1820) is a love lyric addressed to the young girl, Frances Fairchild, who was to become Bryant's wife. The poet sees her beauty as nurtured by nature itself (Godwin, *Poetical* 1:39). "Monument Mountain" (1824) is an account of the story of a Native American maiden who loved her cousin. The maiden's incestuous feelings toward the relative drive her to kill herself by jumping off the stiff rock at sunset; the mountain where she died is called the Mountain of the Monument. According to "A Forest Hymn" (1825), God indwells nature, and therefore nature is the right place to worship God (Godwin, *Poetical* 1:134). In "The Prairies" (1833), the poet describes the various sights of the midwestern prairies that he witnesses on a trip: the vast fields, flowers, vines, brooks, insects, birds, and forests. He sees in the prairies a majestic workmanship of the Creator God: "Man hath no power in all this glorious work" (Godwin, *Poetical* 1:229).

Bryant's poems of death reflect his belief in the transience of earthly life, in the stoic acceptance of death, and in the benevolence of God. In "Thanatopsis" (literally "a contemplation of death," 1817), written under the influence of the Graveyard School, the speaker grapples with the mystery of death. A "still voice" from Nature teaches him that he should leave this world with an "unfaltering trust" when his time comes; in the grave, an "eternal resting-place," he will join those who arrived there before him (Godwin, *Poetical* 1:17–20). The "Hymn to Death" (1820) was written after the poet heard of his father's death. The speaker welcomes death because it is a "Deliverer" anointed by God to "free the oppressed / And crush the oppressor" (Godwin, *Poetical* 1:47). "The Indian Girl's Lament" (1823) records a Native American maiden's grief over the death of her lover who has been killed in battle. She sings a "sad and simple lay" in which she expresses her belief in afterlife and her yearning for him. "The Death of the Flowers" (1825) was written on the occasion of the death of Bryant's sister; the speaker associates the death with the perishing of "the fair young flowers" (Godwin, *Poetical* 1:157). The speaker of "To the Fringed Gentian" (1829) observes the flower that outlasts all the other blossoms in the autumn; he hopes that when his summons comes he will have a blossoming in his heart for heaven.

Bryant's poems of progress celebrate the achievements, potential, liberty, and freedom of the human race; they reflect the optimistic view of humanity typical of Romanticism and Unitarianism. In the early poem "The Embargo" (1808), the 13-year-old author satirizes the policies of President Thomas Jefferson, attacks three Democratic newspapers, and urges the audience to rise against the French. A believer in human progress, he foresees a bright future awaiting America. "The Ages" (1821) recounts the past ages—the "golden days of old"—of humanity and the progress it has made. The piece confirms the munificence of God and the poet's confidence in an even better world: "Oh, no! a thousand cheerful omens give / Hope of yet happier days, whose dawn is nigh. . . . / In God's magnificent works his will shall scan— / And love and peace shall make their paradise with man" (Godwin, *Poetical* 1:54, 56). "Song of Marion's Men" (1831), a patriotic ballad, eulogizes the achievements of the frontier troops led by General Francis Marion, whose name makes "the British soldier [tremble]" (Godwin, *Poetical* 1:225). In "To the Apennines" (1835), the speaker celebrates the human aspiration for freedom as symbolized by the peaks of the Apennine Mountains.

The most important of Bryant's essays of literary criticism is the "Lectures on Poetry" (1825–26). It comprises four sections: "On the Nature of Poetry," "The Value and Uses of Poetry," "Relation of Poetry to Time and Place," and "On Originality and Imitation." He points out that poetry is "one of the most ancient of all arts, of the very earliest and most venerable branch of literature" (Godwin, *Prose,* 1:3). According to him, the great fountain of poetry is emotion and the source of poetic inspiration lies in nature. Poetry deals with the most noble ideas and emotions, whereas prose deals with the trivial and the commonplace. The spirit of poetry is "an aspiration after superhuman beauty and majesty, which, if it has no affinity with, has at least some likeness to virtue" (Godwin, *Prose,* 1:15). Bryant contends that the American poet should use native materials for the subjects of poetry; there are numerous interesting traditions in the United States that are awaiting exploitation by the poet. Further, the poet should master the traditional art of versification before he pursues originality: "[The poet] must found himself on the excellence already attained in his art . . . " (Godwin, *Prose,* 1:40). Finally, according to Bryant, poetry is a suggestive art, and therefore poets need to depend upon pure suggestion rather than merely imitating life.

Bryant also wrote countless editorials on important issues, both national and regional. In "The Right of Workmen to Strike" (1836), for instance, he espouses the laborers' right to collective bargaining. Twenty men who had decided not to work were reportedly punished by the court with a fine. Bryant declares that penalizing workers over a wage dispute is morally wrong; he blurts, "If this is not SLAVERY, we have forgotten its definition" (Sillen 77). The essay "Freedom of the Press" (1836) condemns those who attempt to silence the press by force. Bryant accuses those censors of establishing oligarchy of their own and trampling on the people's rights. In "The Murder of Lovejoy" (1837), the author deplores the recent killings of two antislavery journalists in Alton, Illinois. The attack on an abolition press, Bryant contends, is an attack on the liberties of the whole Union itself. Meanwhile, in "A New Public Park" (1844), Bryant advocates building an extensive public garden in New York City. In "The New Federal Constitution" (1857), Bryant stresses that the U. S. Supreme Court's decision on the Dred Scott v. Sanford case will not quiet the discussion on the slavery question. Finally, "The Election of Lincoln" (1860) celebrates the decisive victory Abraham Lincoln of the Republican Party has won in the presidential election.

CRITICAL RECEPTION

William Cullen Bryant is not ranked among the best American authors anymore. However, his poetry enjoyed considerable popularity in the nineteenth century, especially in the early 1830s, and has maintained significance throughout the twentieth century. The enduring merits of Bryant's works are evidenced by the fact that some of his well-known poems are widely anthologized in American literary textbooks today. Willard Phillips, one of the earliest reviewers of Bryant's *Poems* (1821), finds in the volume "a strain of pure and high sentiment that expands and lifts up the soul and brings it nearer to the source of moral beauty" (380). Phillips especially singles out "The Ages," "Thanatopsis," "To a Waterfowl," "Inscription for the Entrance into a Wood," "Green River," and "The Yellow Violet" as commendable pieces. In an 1837 review essay, Edgar Allan Poe identifies "an air of calm and elevated contemplation" as the best feature of Bryant's verse. Regarding Bryant's place among American poets, Poe asserts that, without question, "Few—at least who are fairly before the public, have more than very shallow claims to a rivalry with the author of *Thanatopsis*" (49). In a *New York Times* article in 1878, George W. Curtis points out that Bryant was "the first adequate poetic voice of the solemn New England spirit" although the poet has "no trace" of the English masters; Bryant's genius was "calm, meditative, and pure" (1). According to Henry W. Bellows's "Address at the Funeral of William Cullen Bryant" (1878), Bryant has a "modest, unworldly spirit," and "conscience, humanity, justice, and truth" pervade both his prose and his verse (1). In *William Cullen Bryant* (1890; reprinted 1980), John Bigelow praises Bryant for his moral authority: his career represented a "model which no one can contemplate without being edified, which no one can study closely without an inclination to imitate, and which no one can imitate without strengthening some good impulses and weakening the hold upon him of every bad one" (311). A. Blackwood, in his review "Wordsworth and Bryant" (1899), asserts that Bryant's poems do not simply echo Wordsworth's. Indeed, none of Wordsworth's verse can compare favorably with Bryant's; Bryant is "independent in form" and "intelligent enough so he didn't need to copy" (8).

In his essay, "Our Pioneer American Poet" (1905), Charles Leonard Moore places Bryant alongside William Wordsworth: "Without meaning anything but praise, it may be said of Bryant's poems in general that Wordsworth forgot to write them. A few of them rise to the height of Wordsworth's best, and they never sink to the level of his worst." Bryant's poems recall those of John Milton and Thomas Gray and, in "weight and felicity of single phrase," are superior to those of Edgar Allan Poe (224–25). In *The Posthumous Essays of John Churchton Collins* (1912), the author claims that Bryant's poems "Thanatopsis" and "A Forest Hymn" earn Bryant "the honor of being known as America's Wordsworth" (141). William Lyon Phelps, in 1924, also notes that Bryant's place in American literature is secure for four reasons: "He is the Father of American Poetry: He is pre-eminently our poet of Nature: He is a master of blank verse: He is a teacher of peace and rest." Although Bryant's poems are occasionally "colourless," his nature poetry provides "a pleasure" and "a refreshing shelter" (29–30). In *American Prosody* (1935), Gay Wilson Allen estimates that Bryant is "eminently important in the history of American versification because his technique was finished, effective, and truly artistic" (52). According to Tremaine McDowell, in his preface to *William Cullen Bryant* (1935), Bryant was "a poet of minor rank when judged by absolute standards, but a significant early Romanticist and a distinguished liberal when examined historically" (v). George Warren Arms admits, in *The Fields Were Green* (1953), that Bryant "wrote much that is worthless"; however, the best of his poetry contains "a pleasure and a power" (19). In his widely used book *The Cycle of American Literature* (1955), Robert E. Spiller recognizes the significance of Bryant's role in American literary history: "As [Washington] Irving set the romantic pattern for the American short story and essay, William Cullen Bryant . . . led American poetry out of the stiff restraints of the Augustan mode into a simplicity and delight which accurately reflected the new frontiers of mind and spirit. . . . With Bryant's poetry the first separation of literature and American life took place . . . " (27, 29). Identifying Bryant as "America's first important nature poet" and "the outstanding poet of the first third of the [nineteenth] century," Samuel Sillen notes, in *William Cullen Bryant* (1966), that the poet was "the vital link" between the generation of Revolutionary poets and the poets who were prominent in the mid-1800s ("Introduction" 8–9). In his introduction to John Bigelow's *William Cullen Bryant* (1980), John Hollander praises Bryant as "our first poet of nature"; the poet "[recapitulated] even in the earliest years of his work the movement from the passive speculations of a poetic derived from the later eighteenth-century poets of sensibility, to a meditative mode in which the mind is more actively engaged in intercourse with the natural emblems and figures of itself" (xi–xii).

A significant number of critics have noted deficiencies in ideas, diction, and imagery in Bryant's poetry. In his 1897 essay, "Bryant's Permanent Contribution to Literature," Henry D. Sedgwick Jr. cites the poet's lack of artistic discipline as a major problem: "Bryant's verses, except at their best, show a lack of art. They are a little undisciplined; they betray truancy that he will not submit enough to discipline" (541). Although William Ellery Leonard notes, in *Cambridge History of American Literature* (1946), that "the elemental clarity and simplicity of [the] same few ideas, emotions, modes, [and] methods" make Bryant's work "complete" and "harmonious," Bryant "is not one of the world's master-poets, because he was pre-eminently endowed with intellectual intensity and imaginative concentration. The character of his whole mind was discursive, enumerative, tending, when measured by the masters, to the diffuse" (269, 275–76). John Hollander also points out the limitations of Bryant's later poetry: "Indeed, the inability to build further on his earlier vision, with that power of poetic intellect which interprets the very grounds on which previous intuitions have been received, is what finally limits him as an American poet, when compared with the giants of his century—Emerson, Whitman, Dickinson" (xvi). In *William Cullen Bryant* (1989), Albert F. McLean Jr. finds little originality in Bryant's poetry: Bryant's "aptitude lay not in the creation of startling new effects and prophetic questions but rather in the restatement of old truths and in the resolution of contemporary crises of the heart and mind" (131).

Bryant is generally acknowledged as one of the most influential newspaper editors of his time. Vernon Louis Parrington, in *Main Currents in American Thought* (1930), stresses that Bryant's journalistic career is perhaps quite as important as his poetic career. According to Parrington, some critics have unjustly maligned Bryant's reputation because of the uneven qualities in his poetry, ignoring his major accomplishments in journalism. In Parrington's view, Bryant was "the father of nineteenth-century American journalism as well as the father of nineteenth-century American poetry." Bryant is distinguished from his "shriller contemporaries" in "the lucidity of his comment and the keenness of his humanitarian criticism" (238–39). Meanwhile, in his introduction to *William Cullen Bryant* (1966), Samuel Sillen comments, "One of the great American editors, Bryant had no equal before Horace Greeley. . . . That he should be remembered primarily as a somewhat innocuous nature poet is one of those innumerable scandals of our literary history that make one blush. To read him is to dethrone a legend and discover a man, one of the noblest in our national tradition" ("Introduction" 22, 28).

As a literary critic, Bryant has received mixed reviews. According to Albert F. McLean Jr., the methods of writing poetry as recommended in Bryant's "Lectures on Poetry" are "unstable and too often ineffective," for he "obscured his purpose through the multiplicity of his means" (*William* 108). In contrast, Charles H. Brown, author of *William Cullen Bryant: A Biography* (1971), is more appreciative and understanding: "Bryant's lectures on poetry are not among the great critical statements in American literature perhaps, but they are important. The circumstances of their composition and delivery prevented their being a fully considered expression of his beliefs" (147). Samuel Sillen also contends that the lectures "established him as perhaps the most sensitive and judicious critic of the period before Poe and Emerson" ("Introduction" 11).

WORKS CITED

Allen, Gay Wilson. "William Cullen Bryant." *American Prosody*. New York: American Book Co., 1935. 27–55.

Arms, George Warren. *The Fields Were Green: A New View of Bryant, Holmes, Lowell, and Longfellow; with a Selection of Their Poems*. Stanford: Stanford University Press, 1953.

Bellows, Henry W. "Address at the Funeral of William Cullen Bryant." *New York Evening Post* 14 June 1878: 1.

Bigelow, John. *William Cullen Bryant*. American Men and Women of Letters Series. Boston: Houghton, Mifflin Co., 1890. New York: Chelsea House, 1980.

Blackwood, A. "Wordsworth and Bryant." *New York Times Saturday Review of Books and Art* 7 January 1899: 8.

Brown, Charles H. *William Cullen Bryant: A Biography*. New York: Charles Scribner's Sons, 1971.

Collins, L. C., ed. *The Posthumous Essays of John Churchton Collins*. By John Churchton Collins. London: J. M. Dent and Sons Ltd., 1912.

Curtis, George W. "Bryant, Father of Song—Commemorative Address and De Peyster Reception." *New York Times* 31 December 1878: 1.

Godwin, Parke, ed. *A Biography of William Cullen Bryant, with Extracts from His Private Correspondence*. 2 vols. New York: D. Appleton, 1883.

Godwin, Parke, ed. *The Poetical Works of William Cullen Bryant*. By William Cullen Bryant. 2 vols. New York: D. Appleton and Co., 1883.

————. *Prose Writings of William Cullen Bryant.* By William Cullen Bryant. 2 vols. New York: D. Appleton and Co., 1884.

Hollander, John. Introduction. *William Cullen Bryant.* By John Bigelow. New York: Chelsea House, 1980. xi–xx.

Leonard, William Ellery. "Bryant and the Minor Poets." *Cambridge History of American Literature.* Eds. William Peterfield Trent, et al. Vol. 1. New York: Macmillan, 1946. 260–83.

McDowell, Tremaine. Preface. *William Cullen Bryant: Representative Selections, with Introduction, Bibliography, and Notes.* New York: American Book Company, 1935. v–vii.

McLean, Albert F., Jr. *William Cullen Bryant.* Updated ed. New York: Twayne, 1989.

Moore, Charles Leonard. "Our Pioneer American Poet." *Dial* 1 April 1905: 223–26.

Parrington, Vernon Louis. *Main Currents in American Thought: An Interpretation of American Literature from the Beginnings to 1920.* Vol. 2. New York: Harcourt, Brace, 1930.

Phelps, William Lyon. *Howells, James, Bryant and Other Essays.* New York: Macmillan, 1924.

Phillips, Willard. "Bryant's Poems." *North American Review* October 1821: 380–84.

Poe, Edgar Allan. "Bryant." *Southern Literary Messenger* January 1837: 41–49.

Sedgwick, Henry D., Jr. "Byrant's Permanent Contribution to Literature." *Atlantic Monthly* April 1897: 539–49.

Sillen, Samuel, ed. *William Cullen Bryant: Selections from His Poetry and Prose.* New York: International Publishers, 1966.

Spiller, Robert E. *The Cycle of American Literature: An Essay in Historical Criticism.* New York: Free Press, 1955.

BIBLIOGRAPHY

Works by William Cullen Bryant

Verse

The Embargo; or, Sketches of the Times. A Satire. 2nd ed. Boston: E. G. House, 1809.

Poems, New York: E. Bliss, 1832.

The Fountain and Other Poems. New York: Wiley and Putnam, 1842.

The White-Footed Deer and Other Poems. New York: I. S. Platt, 1844.

A Forest Hymn. New York: W. A. Townsend & Co., 1860.

The Little People of the Snow. New York: D. Appleton, 1863.

Hymns. New York: n.p., 1864.

Thirty Poems. New York: D. Appleton, 1864.

Among the Trees. New York: G. P. Putnam's Sons; Boston: Lee & Shepard, 1874.

Godwin, Parke, ed. *The Poetical Works of William Cullen Bryant.* By William Cullen Bryant. 2 vols. New York: D. Appleton and Co., 1883.

The Poetical Works of William Cullen Bryant. Roslyn ed. New York: D. Appleton and Co., 1903.

Prose

Letters of a Traveller; or, Notes of Things Seen in Europe and America. New York: G. P. Putnam, 1850.

Discourse on the Life and Genius of James Fenimore Cooper. New York: G. P. Putnam, 1852.

Letters of a Traveler. Second Series. New York: D. Appleton & Co., 1859.

A Discourse on the Life, Character and Genius of Washington Irving. New York: G. P. Putnam, 1860.

Letters from the East. New York: G. P. Putnam and Son, 1869.

Some Notices on the Life and Writings of Fitz-Greene Halleck. 1869.

A Discourse on the Life, Character, and Writings of Gulian Crommelin Verplanck. New York: Printed for the New-York Historical Society, Evening Post, 1870.

Orations and Addresses by William Cullen Bryant. New York: G. P. Putnam's Sons, 1873.

Godwin, Parke, ed. *Prose Writings of William Cullen Bryant.* By William Cullen Bryant. 2 vols. New York: D. Appleton and Co., 1884.

Bryant, William Cullen II, and Thomas G. Voss, eds. *The Letters of William Cullen Bryant.* By William Cullen Bryant. 4 vols. New York: Fordham University Press, 1975–84.

Selections

McDowell, Tremaine, ed. *William Cullen Bryant: Representative Selections, with Introduction, Bibliography, and Notes.* New York: American Book Company, 1935.

Sillen, Samuel, ed. *William Cullen Bryant: Selections from His Poetry and Prose.* New York: International Publishers, 1966.

Translations

The Iliad of Homer. Translated into English Blank Verse. 2 vols. Boston: Fields, Osgood & Co., 1870.

The Odyssey of Homer. Translated into English Blank Verse. 2 vols. Boston: James R. Osgood & Co., 1871–72.

Studies of William Cullen Bryant

Allen, Gay Wilson. "William Cullen Bryant." *American Prosody.* New York: American Book Co., 1935. 27–55.

Arms, George Warren. *The Fields Were Green: A New View of Bryant, Holmes, Lowell, and Longfellow; with a Selection of Their Poems.* Stanford: Stanford University Press, 1953.

Bellows, Henry W. "Address at the Funeral of William Cullen Bryant." *New York Evening Post* 14 June 1878: 1.

Bigelow, John. *William Cullen Bryant.* American Men and Women of Letters Series. Boston: Houghton, Mifflin Co., 1890. New York: Chelsea House, 1980.

Blackwood, A. "Wordsworth and Bryant." *New York Times Saturday Review of Books and Art* 7 January 1899: 8.

Brown, Charles H. *William Cullen Bryant: A Biography.* New York: Charles Scribner's Sons, 1971.

Collins, L. C., ed. *The Posthumous Essays of John Churchton Collins.* By John Churchton Collins. London: J. M. Dent and Sons Ltd., 1912.

Curtis, George W. "Bryant, Father of Song—Commemorative Address and De Peyster Reception." *New York Times* 31 December 1878: 1.

Godwin, Parke. *A Biography of William Cullen Bryant, with Extracts from His Private Correspondence.* New York: D. Appleton and Co., 1883.

Hollander, John. Introduction. *William Cullen Bryant.* By John Bigelow. New York: Chelsea House, 1980. xi–xx.

Leonard, William Ellery. "Bryant and the Minor Poets." *Cambridge History of American Literature.* Eds. William Peterfield Trent, et al. Vol. 1. New York: Macmillan, 1946. 260–83.

McDowell, Tremaine. Preface. *William Cullen Bryant: Representative Selections, with Introduction, Bibliography, and Notes.* New York: American Book Company, 1935. v–vii.

McLean, Albert F., Jr. *William Cullen Bryant.* Updated ed. New York: Twayne, 1989.

Moore, Charles Leonard. "Our Pioneer American Poet." *Dial* 1 April 1905: 223–26.

Parrington, Vernon Louis. *Main Currents in American Thought: An Interpretation of American Literature from the Beginnings to 1920.* Vol. 2. New York: Harcourt, Brace, 1930.

Phelps, William Lyon. *Howells, James, Bryant and Other Essays.* New York: Macmillan, 1924.

Phillips, Willard. "Bryant's Poems." *North American Review* October 1821: 380–84.

Poe, Edgar Allan. "Bryant." *Southern Literary Messenger* January 1837: 41–49.

Sedgwick, Henry D., Jr. "Byrant's Permanent Contribution to Literature." *Atlantic Monthly* April 1897: 539–49.

Sillen, Samuel. Introduction. *William Cullen Bryant: Selections from His Poetry and Prose.* Ed. Samuel Sillen. New York: International Publishers, 1966. 7–28.

Spiller, Robert E. *The Cycle of American Literature: An Essay in Historical Criticism.* New York: Free Press, 1955.

ALICE CARY (1820–1871)

Rebecca R. Saulsbury

BIOGRAPHY

Alice Cary was born on April 26, 1820, on a farm in Hamilton County, Ohio, just eight miles north of Cincinnati. Mt. Healthy, the closest village to the family estate, became the Clovernook of her later sketches. Cary was the fourth of nine children born to her parents, Elizabeth Jessup Cary and Robert Cary. Alice's younger sister, Phoebe, who would become her lifelong companion and fellow writer, was born four years later. During her childhood, Alice was especially devoted to her older sister Rhoda, who told "wonderful" stories on their way home from school and encouraged her to write poetry.

Cary's education was sporadic at best. Although her parents were literate people, "poverty and the hard exigencies of pioneer life" left them little time for intellectual pursuits or for ensuring their own children's education (Ames 5). Later describing her efforts to educate herself as "a long struggle" (Ames 19), Alice and her sisters occasionally attended the district schoolhouse and devoured the few books housed in the family's meager library, including the Bible, Lewis and Clark's *Journal,* Pope's "Essay on Man," and Susanna Rowson's best-seller *Charlotte Temple.* Alice's only regular source of reading was the Boston-based Universalist magazine *The Trumpet.*

Cary and her family moved into a new house in 1832, marking the beginning of personal loss throughout Alice's life. Her beloved sisters Rhoda and Lucy died in 1833, and when Cary was just 15, her mother died. Two years later her father remarried a utilitarian woman who forced Alice and Phoebe to toil on the farm during the day, leaving them to study and write poetry at night, supposedly by the light of a "saucer of lard with a bit of rag for wick" (Ames 21). Yet Cincinnati's transformation into a thriving "literary center of the West" in the 1830s also provided the conditions for Alice to begin "her career as a serious writer" (Fetterley, Introduction xv).

At the age of 18, Cary published her first poem, "The Child of Sorrow," in the *Sentinal,* a Cincinnati periodical. For the next 10 years, Alice published poetry and short stories in local periodicals and newspapers without pay, but she secured a solid literary reputation in Cincinnati, one that helped pave the way to establishing a national reputation and earning her living as a writer. In 1847, Alice was introduced to Gamaliel Bailey, who founded the abolitionist weekly *The National Era,* the periodical that published Harriet Beecher's *Uncle Tom's Cabin* four years later. Writing under the pseudonym "Patty Lee," she wrote poetry and short stories and earned her first literary payment. Her writing soon attracted the attention of John Greenleaf Whittier, a contributing editor to the *Era.*

Cary's poetry also impressed Rufus Griswold, who in 1848 published several of her poems in his anthology *The Female Poets of America.* He became her most ardent supporter, arranging for the publication of her first volume of poetry, *Poems of Alice and Phoebe Cary,* by a Philadelphia publisher, for which she and Phoebe received $100. In 1849, Horace Greeley, editor of the *Herald Tribune,* visited Alice and Phoebe in Mt. Healthy.

Encouraged by their early literary successes, Alice and Phoebe made a trip to New York and Boston in the summer of 1850. On the way they visited John Greenleaf Whittier in Amesbury, Massachusetts, who later memorialized their visit in a poem called "The Singer." Cary moved to New York in November, determined to make her living as a writer, a bold move for an unmarried, 30-year-old woman. Although Cary's biographers speculate that Cary moved to get over the pain of a romantic breakup or to pursue a romantic relationship with Griswold, Fetterley concludes that New York offered to Alice most of all a literary and social community (Introduction xvii–xviii). Phoebe and Elmina joined their sister in the spring of 1851.

Once in New York, Cary published widely and regularly in several eastern periodicals and newspapers, including the *National Magazine,* the *New York Ledger, Harper's Monthly, Graham's Magazine, Sartain's Union Magazine,* the *Overland Monthly,* and the prestigious *Atlantic Monthly.* She also published several volumes of poetry, short fiction, juvenile literature, and novels. After six years of frugal and industrious living, Alice had saved enough money to purchase a house on Twentieth Street, which "became the center of one of the choicest and most cosmopolitan circles in New York" (Ames 38). For over 15 years, Alice and Phoebe held Sunday evening receptions that made them famous, attended by figures such as Greeley, Whittier, James T. Fields, Gail Hamilton, Richard Henry Stoddard, Robert Bonner, Elizabeth Cady Stanton, Anna Dickinson, and P. T. Barnum.

Cary's rigorous and tireless work schedule likely ruined her health. She died on February 12, 1871, after spending the last 18 months of her life as an invalid, paralyzed and in excruciating pain. Two days later, she was buried in Brooklyn's Greenwood Cemetery. She was 50 years old.

MAJOR WORKS AND THEMES

Alice Cary considered herself a poet first and foremost, publishing four volumes of poetry in her lifetime. Although her poetry may be too sentimental and moralistic for modern readers, Cary was considered a better poet than many of her peers, as evinced by Poe's and Whittier's general praise for her work. Cary's poetic themes were varied: often religious ("Hymn of a True Man," "Palestine," and "The Two Missionaries), didactic, and certainly dark. Her best poems, however, were those that observed nature, displaying a romantic sensibility akin to Wordsworth, and that portrayed women's lives, usually blighted by poverty, pregnancy, and unhappy marriages. "Working" describes a young bride of three months saddened and lonely by her husband's long absences. In poems such as "The Bridal Veil," Cary celebrates the independent woman who vows to maintain her identity within marriage.

Cary's three volumes of sketches and short stories—*Clovernook; or, Recollections of Our Neighborhood in the West* (1852), *Clovernook, Second Series* (1853), and *Pictures of Country Life* (1859)—feature her true artistic prowess. Resisting romantic descriptions of the region, Cary portrays the inescapable cultural, psychological, and physical deprivation that women in particular experienced in rural, frontier Ohio. In the preface to *Clovernook,* Cary explains her purpose in writing the sketches: to claim "the regional perspective and the regional subject as the truly American" (Fetterley, Introduction xxxiv). Rich in specific and realistic detail, Cary's sketches show the inherent value of describing the country's pastoral life and "incidents for the most part of so little apparent moment or significance that they who live in what is called the world would scarcely have marked them had they been detained with me while they were passing . . . " (*Clovernook Sketches* 7). Cary's stories offer a powerful and moving perspective of life in the West and merit inclusion in America's literary history.

CRITICAL RECEPTION

Near the end of her career, Cary confessed to biographer Mary Clemmer Ames, " 'I am ashamed of my work. The great bulk of what I have written is poor stuff. Some of it, maybe, indicates ability to do better—that is about all' " (Ames 100). Her evaluation notwithstanding, Alice Cary was a popular writer in the nineteenth century whose name had become a household word by as early as 1855. John Greenleaf Whittier dubbed Alice and her sister Phoebe the "sweet singers of the West," (Ames 372) while Rufus Griswold gushed about Alice, "We have perhaps no other author, so young, in whom the poetical faculty is so largely developed" (372). Reviewing Griswold's anthology in the *Southern Literary Messenger,* Poe pronounced Cary's poem "Pictures of Memory" as "decidedly the noblest poem in the collection" written by "the most imaginative poet" (Schultz 66). Despite such praise, contemporary critics often attacked Cary's poetry for its maudlin sentimentality and somber mood. A reviewer for *Putnam's Monthly* declared *Lyra and Other Poems* a "sob in three hundred and ninety-nine parts. . . . It is a parish register of funerals rendered into doleful rhyme" (Venable 494).

Critics were more universal in their praise for Cary's Clovernook sketches. *Clovernook; or, Recollections of Our Neighborhood in the West* (1852) was a minor best-seller in the United States and Britain, going through five pirated editions there and meriting the publication of a second series in 1853. Whittier reviewed *Clovernook* in *The National Era,* asserting that the sketches "evince a keen sense of the humor and pathos of the comedy and tragedy of life in the country" (Ames 372). Of her *Pictures of Country Life* (1859), a reviewer for the London *Literary Gazette,* not known for its praise of American authors, admired the volume for its "American richness of color and vigor of outline" (Ames 35). By the late nineteenth century, W. H. Venable believed that Cary's "exact truthfulness and felicitous local-coloring . . . [will be] appreciated by every reader who has seen or studied farm-life in the Ohio Valley" (490).

In the twentieth century, however, Alice Cary "disappeared from popular view," all but erased from America's literary history, with Mary Clemmer Ames' biography the only in-depth record of Cary's life to date (Fetterley, Introduction xii). Over the past 15 years or so, Judith Fetterley has single-handedly revived interest in Cary's sketches, publishing several articles about her and editing a collection of her Clovernook fiction in 1987. Cary's Ohio sketches merit an important place in American literary history, Fetterley argues, because they "establish [her] as one of the earliest regional writers to fictionalize what the Eastern magazines would call 'local color,' and which, twenty years later, would begin to define a new genre in the short story" ("Alice Cary" 2).

WORKS CITED

Ames, Mary Clemmer. *A Memorial of Alice and Phoebe Cary, with Some of Their Later Poems.* New York: Hurd and Houghton, 1873.

Cary, Alice. *Clovernook Sketches and Other Stories.* Ed. Judith Fetterley. New Brunswick, N. J.: Rutgers UP, 1987.

Fetterley, Judith. "Alice Cary: 1820–1971." *Legacy* 1.1 (Spring 1984): 1–3.

———. Introduction to *Clovernook Sketches and Other Stories* by Alice Cary. New Brunswick, N. J.: Rutgers UP, 1987. xi–xlii.

Griswold, Rufus Wilmot. "Alice and Phoebe Carey." *The Female Poets of America with Additions by R. H. Stoddard.* New York: James Miller, 1874. 372–79.

Schultz, Heidi M. "Alice Cary." *Dictionary of Literary Biography.* Vol. 202. Ed. Kent P. Ljungquist. Detroit: Gale Group, 1999. 65–68.

Venable, W. H. *Beginnings of Literary Culture in the Ohio Valley.* Cincinnati: Robert Clark & Co., 1891.

BIBLIOGRAPHY

Works by Alice Cary

Poetry

Poems of Alice and Phoebe Cary. Philadelphia: Moss and Brother, 1850.

Lyra and Other Poems. New York: Redfield, 1852.

Poems by Alice Cary. Boston: Ticknor & Fields, 1855.

Ballads, Lyrics, and Hymns. New York: Hurd & Houghton, 1866.

Early and Late Poems of Alice and Phoebe Cary. Boston and New York: Houghton & Mifflin, 1887.

Fiction

Clovernook; or, Recollections of Our Neighborhood in the West. New York: Redfield, 1852.

Hagar: A Story of To-Day. New York: Redfield, 1852.

Clovernook, Second Series. New York: Redfield, 1853.

Married, Not Mated; or, How They Lived at Woodside and Throckmorton Hall. New York: Derby & Jackson; Cincinnati: Derby, 1856.

Pictures of Country Life. New York: Derby & Jackson, 1859.

The Bishop's Son: A Novel. New York: Carleton; London: Low, 1867.

Clovernook Sketches and Other Stories. Ed. Judith Fetterley. New Brunswick, N. J.: Rutgers UP, 1987.

Juvenile Literature

Clovernook Children. Boston: Ticknor & Fields, 1854.

Snow-Berries: A Book for Young Folks. Boston: Ticknor & Fields, 1867.

Ballads for Little Folk. Ed. Mary Clemmer Ames. New York: Houghton & Mifflin, 1874.

Studies of Alice Cary

Ames, Mary Clemmer. *A Memorial of Alice and Phoebe Cary, with Some of Their Later Poems.* New York: Hurd and Houghton, 1873.

Fetterley, Judith. "Entitled to More than 'Peculiar Praise': The Extravagance of Alice Cary's *Clovernook.*" *Legacy* 10.2 (1998): 103–19.

———. Introduction to *Clovernook Sketches and Other Stories* by Alice Cary. New Brunswick, N.J.: Rutgers UP, 1987.

Kolodny, Annette. *The Land Before Her: Fantasy and Experience of the American Frontiers, 1630–1860.* Chapel Hill: University of North Carolina Press, 1984. 178–99.

Pulsifer, Janice G. "Alice and Phoebe Cary, Whittier's Sweet Singers of the West." *Essex Institute Historical Collections* 109 (January 1973): 9–59.

PHOEBE CARY (1824–1871)

MaryBeth Short Page

BIOGRAPHY

Phoebe Cary was born on September 4, 1824, into a poor rural family in a small farm-house in the Miami Valley of Ohio, eight miles north of Cincinnati. Phoebe, the sixth of nine children, was the daughter of Robert and Elizabeth Jessup Cary. Despite being poor and uneducated, both Phoebe and her older sister Alice were bright children and soon began to read and write prolifically. The sisters lost their mother and two older siblings to tuberculosis in the 1830s. Robert Cary remarried in 1837 and his new wife was a hard, cold, uncultured, and utilitarian woman who saw no justification in wasting candle wax to read and write at night. She strictly enforced the ideal that farm work and housework were more important than writing.

When Phoebe was 14, she published her first poem. By 1850, both Phoebe and Alice had published their poetry in both *Female Poets of America,* compiled by Rufus Griswold, and in an independent edition of their own, *Poems of Alice and Phoebe Cary*. In 1850, Alice moved to New York City. Shortly after, Phoebe followed, and the two worked for six years publishing books and magazines, living in a home on Twentieth Street purchased by Alice. Their home became a regular gathering place for the literary community and the sisters held regular salons.

Throughout her life, Phoebe refused many marriage proposals and chose to live the life of a writer and devotee to her sister Alice. Of the two sisters, Phoebe was far more concerned with stylish clothes and jewels and was driven by emotion more than Alice was. One biographer referred to Phoebe as "the Sensibility to Alice's Sense" (Walker 198). Despite her emotional and stylish personality, Phoebe, like Alice, was shy and self-conscious in public. Both Cary women were actively involved in the feminist world. Phoebe worked for a short time on the staff of Susan B. Anthony's *Revolution* but never again actively involved herself in reform programs due to a fear of public life. Alice Cary succumbed to tuberculosis in February 1871. After Alice's death, Phoebe retreated to Newport, Rhode Island, to recover from her loss. She died there from hepatitis on July 31, 1871, thus ending the poetic careers of both Cary women. In an 1873 memorial to

Phoebe Cary, Mary Clemmer Ames stated that "It is impossible to estimate either sister without reference to the other" (Walker 199).

MAJOR WORKS AND THEMES

Phoebe Cary devoted her writings to poetry. Unlike Alice, she never branched out into prose. As a result, Phoebe was able to fine-tune and perfect her poetic voice and style. Much of Phoebe's poetry focused on religion and nature. Her most noted poem, "Nearer Home," was widely favored as a religious hymn. Phoebe's poems tend to be naturalistic, but they often contain a hint of the supernatural. She was far from pantheistic and did not believe in the soul of nature but only in its importance to human events. Her poetry reflected the way life had molded her and demonstrated a cheerful philosophy and faith.

Aside from religious themes, much of Phoebe's poetry centered on feminist themes. Her feminist poems often examined the inequalities between men and women in all aspects of life, including the sexual and domestic realms. In her poem "Advice Gratis to a Certain Woman," Phoebe never makes the supposition that all women are saintly or pious. A surprising voice in the feminist world, Phoebe refuses to support the view that all women are faultless and pure. In another of her poems, "A Woman's Conclusion," she supports her unmarried status. A strong element of parody is evident in many of Phoebe's poems, including "Was He Henpecked?" and "Dorothy's Dower."

Phoebe's views on the feminist life were obvious in many of her poems. Her poems often discussed married life and the life of single women. Phoebe was not opposed to marriage as an institution but found that it did not suit her life. She held the ideal that marriage to the wrong man was far worse than remaining single. In "Dorothy's Dower," she discusses that issue by presenting a wastrel and violent husband who blames his wife for the lack of money. Phoebe does not overlook the isolated and lonely life of a single woman. She wrote "The Christian Woman" to emphasize that feeling of solitude.

CRITICAL RECEPTION

Although Alice's work was the subject of much acclaim and celebration during her life, Phoebe's work was not fully recognized for its value until after her death in 1871. Because Phoebe confined herself to poetry writing, Alice's work had a broader audience and was held in greater esteem during their lifetime. However, after Phoebe's death, the passion, pathos, and tenderness of her poetry were acknowledged. Phoebe was also praised for her wittiness and depth of feeling in her poetry. One biographer states that "No singer was ever more thoroughly identified with her own songs than Phoebe Cary" (Clemmer 59).

Many prominent writers of the time were attracted to the sisters' work. John Greenleaf Whittier, Rufus W. Griswold, Edgar Allan Poe, and Horace Greeley were just a few who took notice of the young women. The Cary home was the center of the literati community during their lives and many published and acclaimed poets and writers visited them there to share their work.

Phoebe Cary's poetry, once widely anthologized and revered, is rarely seen in modern-day texts. Often, one will find only brief mention of her in texts about Alice. Phoebe is still viewed as a minor figure, taking a back-row seat to the more popular Alice.

WORKS CITED

Clemmer, Mary. *The Poetical Works of Alice and Phoebe Cary With a Memorial of Their Lives.* New York: Houghton, Mifflin and Company, 1865.

Walker, Cheryl. *American Women Poets of the Nineteenth Century.* New Jersey: Rutgers University Press, 1992.

BIBLIOGRAPHY

Works by Phoebe Cary

Music

Our Old Homestead. Louisville, KY: Brainard, 1850.

One Sweetly Solemn Thought. New York: Lovell, 1900.

Poetry

Poems. New York: Hurst, n.d.

Poems of Alice and Phoebe Cary. Philadelphia: Moss and Brother, 1850.

Poems and Parodies. Boston: Ticknor, Reed, and Fields, 1854.

The Josephine Gallery. Edited with Alice Cary. Philadelphia: Lippincott, 1858.

The Poetical Works of Alice and Phoebe Cary. Household edition. Boston: Houghton Mifflin, 1865.

Poems of Faith, Hope, and Love. New York: Hurd and Houghton, 1867.

Ballads for Little Folks. Edited by Mary Clemmer. Boston: Houghton Mifflin, 1873.

The Last Poems of Alice and Phoebe Cary. Edited by Mary Clemmer Ames. New York: Hurd and Houghton; Cambridge: Riverside, 1873.

The Poems of Alice and Phoebe Cary. Edited by Mary Clemmer Ames. New York, 1873; Edited by Katherine Lee Bates. New York: Crowell, 1903.

The Poetical Works of Alice and Phoebe Cary with a Memorial of Their Lives by Mary Clemmer Ames. New York: Hurd and Houghton, 1876.

Early and Late Poems of Alice and Phoebe Cary. Boston and New York: Houghton Mifflin, 1887.

Flowers from Alice and Phoebe Cary. Boston: DeWolfe and Fiske, 1906.

Studies of Phoebe Cary

Ames, Mary Clemmer. *A Memorial of Alice and Phoebe Cary*. New York: Hurd and Houghton, 1873.

Clemmer, Mary. *The Poetical Works of Alice and Phoebe Cary With a Memorial of Their Lives.* New York: Houghton, Mifflin and Company, 1865.

Fife, Ernelle. "Phoebe Cary." *Nineteenth-Century American Women Writers: A Bio-Bibliographical Critical Sourcebook.* Ed. Denise D. Knight. Westport, CT: Greenwood, 1997. 32–35.

Griswold, Rufus Wilmot. *The Female Poets of America.* 2nd ed. Philadelphia: Parry and McMillan, 1859.

Hoeweller, Diane Long. "Phoebe Cary." *American Women Writers: A Critical Reference Guide from Colonial Times to Present.* Ed. Lina Mainiero and Langdon Lynne Faust. Vol. 1. New York: Frederick Ungar, 1979.

May, Caroline. *The American Female Poets with Biographical and Critical Notices.* New York: The World Publishing House, 1875.

Walker, Cheryl. *American Women Poets of the Nineteenth Century.* New Jersey: Rutgers University Press, 1992.

Watts, Emily Stipes. *The Poetry of American Women from 1632 to 1945.* Austin: University of Texas Press, 1977.

WILLIAM ELLERY CHANNING (1780–1842)

John J. Han

BIOGRAPHY

It is almost impossible to discuss American church history without mentioning Channing. A theologian, philanthropist, and Congregationalist-turned-Unitarian minister, William Ellery Channing was the preeminent voice of nineteenth-century American Unitarianism. Channing—often confused with William Ellery Channing II (1810–1884), our author's nephew and a Unitarian minister—played a crucial role in codifying Unitarian theology. He was an advocate of various sociopolitical causes, including antislavery, temperance, public education, pacifism, prison reforms, and labor reforms. A prolific pamphleteer, Channing also was one of the first literary critics in the United States.

Channing was born in Newport, Rhode Island, on April 7, 1780, to William and Lucy Ellen Channing. He entered Harvard College at age 14, in 1794. Upon graduation from college in 1798, Channing worked as a tutor in Richmond, Virginia, for 18 months and then studied theology at the Harvard Divinity School. On June 1, 1803, he was installed as pastor of the Federal Street (Congregational) Church in Boston, a position he held for the remainder of his life. In 1814 he married Ruth Gibbs, who bore him four children.

Averse to controversy by nature, Channing reluctantly became the spokesperson of the Unitarian movement. The Congregational churches of Massachusetts in his time were engulfed in warfare between the Calvinists and the anti-Calvinists. When Channing was attacked by the orthodox Calvinist periodical *The Panoplist,* he replied in *A Letter to the Rev. Samuel C. Thacher, on the Aspersions Contained in a Late Number of the Panoplist, on the Ministers of Boston and the Vicinity.* During the next few years he defended liberal and rationalist Christianity through various apologias, including "Unitarian Christianity" (1819) and "The Moral Argument against Calvinism" (1820). In 1820 Channing established the Berry Street Conference of Ministers, a conference of liberal Congregational clergy; the conference was reorganized in May 1825, when the Unitarians separated from the Congregational Church, as the American Unitarian Association. In 1821, he delivered a Dudleian Lecture, "The Evidences of Revealed Religion: Discourse before the University in Cambridge." From 1821 he also was associated with the *Christian Register,* the Unitarian magazine.

In 1822 and 1823, Channing traveled in Europe, meeting several literary celebrities including William Wordsworth, Samuel Taylor Coleridge, and Robert Southey. In 1824 Channing's church appointed Ezra Stile as his co-pastor, which allowed Channing to spare more time for writing. Among the works published after 1824 are "Remarks on the Character of John Milton" (1826), "Remarks on the Life and Character of Napoleon Bonaparte" (1827–28), "Remarks on the Character and Writings of Fénelon" (1829), "Remarks on National Literature" (1830), "Slavery" (1835), and "The Abolitionist" (1836). During this period he also preached important sermons and addresses which were later included in *The Works of William E. Channing, With an Introduction. New and Complete Edition, Rearranged. To Which Is Added the Perfect Life:* "Likeness to God: Discourse at the Ordination of the Rev. F. A. Farley" (1828), "The Union" (1829), "Spiritual Freedom" (1830), "Self-Culture" (1838), "Elevation of the Laboring Classes" (1840), "Emancipation in the British West Indies" (1840), and "Duty of the Free State" (1842).

Channing died of typhoid fever in Bennington, Vermont, on October 2, 1842. Most of his manuscripts were destroyed by fire, but his works are collected in *The Works of William E. Channing,* a 1,060-page volume originally published in 1841 and reprinted in 1886.

MAJOR WORKS AND THEMES

In his "Introductory Remarks" for *The Works of William E. Channing,* Channing stated that two ideas dominate his writing: "a respect for the human soul" and "reverence for liberty, for human rights" (1; 7). Indeed, these two ideas run through his dozens of essays of theological, literary, and sociopolitical criticism. Among the most highly regarded theological works are "Unitarian Christianity" (also known as the "Baltimore Sermon"), "The Moral Argument against Calvinism," and "Likeness to God: Discourse at the Ordination of the Rev. F. A. Farley." In these works, Channing reacted against New England's Calvinist inheritance and celebrated the freedom of the human will. His messages were those of optimism and hope.

A sermon originally delivered at the ordination of the Reverend Jared Sparks in Baltimore in 1819, "Unitarian Christianity" is a systematic statement of the Unitarian creed. According to Channing, Unitarian religion is chiefly based on the New Testament; the unity of God is incompatible with the doctrine of the Trinity; Christ is distinct from and inferior to God; God is benevolent rather than mean-spirited; the doctrines of election, original sin, and eternal damnation of sinner are unbiblical; and the highest object of Christ's mission was to help humans regain "virtue, or holiness" ("Unitarian Christianity," *Works,* 380).

In "The Moral Argument against Calvinism" and "Likeness to God," Channing further elaborates on his opposition to Calvinism and on his faith in human potential. In the former work, Channing asserts that Calvinistic belief in a jealous God, in inherited sin, and in the absence of free will contradicts the divine perfections as revealed in Scripture. God is merciful, humans are essentially good and potentially redeemable, and God has given humans the ability to distinguish between good and evil. In "Likeness to God," Channing contends that humans are capable of conforming themselves to God due to their potential divinity; Christ came to restore God's image in humanity—to "give an everlasting impulse and life to what is divine within us." To Channing, God is synonymous with "human intelligence raised above all error and imperfection, and extended to all possible truth" ("Likeness," *Works,* 300, 293).

In "Remarks on National Literature," Channing's most important essay of literary criticism, the author explains why America needs a national literature and how the nation should develop a literature that is uniquely American. Observing that literature is "plainly among the most powerful methods of exalting the character of a nation, of forming a better race of men," Channing stresses that American writers must produce works filled with the soul of the American rather than slavishly imitating British models ("Remarks on National Literature," *Works,* 126). In "Remarks on the Character and Writings of John Milton," Channing praises Milton's poetry for its excellence in spiritualizing human nature; good poetry, according to him, "lifts the mind above ordinary life, gives it a respite from depressing cares, and awakens the consciousness of its affinity with what is pure and noble" ("John Milton," *Works,* 498). "Remarks on the Life and Character of Napoleon" is a review of Sir Walter Scott's biography of Napoleon Bonaparte. Using the French general-turned-emperor as a bad example, Channing discusses why moral power is the noblest human greatness. In "Remarks on the Character and Writings of Fénelon" (1829), Channing discusses the literary merits of the seventeenth-century French writer and mystic. Fénelon's greatness lies, according to Channing, in his ability to think originally and independently.

Many of Channing's works advocate sociopolitical reform. "Slavery," his earliest important work on slavery, was written after his trip to the West Indies, where he had observed the cruelty of slave labor. In this work, the author points out that human beings, who are made in the image of God, should not be held and used as property. Other notable works on slavery include "Emancipation in the British West Indies" and "The Duty of the Free States." Channing espouses the cause of pacifism in *Letter to the Hon. Henry Clay, on the Annexation of Texas to the United States;* the cause of education in "Self-Culture"; and the cause of temperance in "Address on Temperance."

CRITICAL RECEPTION

William Ellery Channing has always been recognized as a highly important Unitarian preacher, theologian, and philanthropist. In 1830 the anonymous critic for *The Westminster Review* applauded Channing as "an incarnation of the intellectual spirit of Christianity" and "the tenth Avatar of the principle of reformation" (478). In his *Makers of Literature* (1900), George Edward Woodberry lists "rectitude, sensibility, and enthusiasm" as the three predominant qualities of Channing's personality, adding that "there are few in the same walk of life who attain to equal sincerity, charity, and purity, or equal serviceableness to the world" (292–301). The author of *The Clergy in American Life and Letters* (1900), Daniel Dulany Addison, declares that Channing was "one of the spiritual forces of his time, and his watchwords are everywhere incorporated into life" (228). Arthur W. Brown, writing in *Always Young for Liberty* (1956), sees Channing as a man of moral vision whose story "should be an inspiration to the thoughtful reader of mid-twentieth century America" (vii). In his 1965 essay on Channing as a literary critic, Robert S. Ward lists Joseph Story and William Ellery Channing as the two most important figures who "furthered our national literature" during the half century after the Revolution (363). Meanwhile, in *Channing, the Reluctant Radical* (1971), Jack Mendelsohn calls the author one of the "historical figures of genuine distinction," adding, "There is often an unaccountable oscillation in the repute of a genius" (3). Among Unitarians today Channing is regarded as "the single most important figure in the history of American Unitarianism" (Robinson 229). Finally, in his book *America's God: From Jonathan Edwards to Abraham Lincoln* (2002), Mark A. Noll observes that Channing played the pivotal role in the rise of American Unitarianism: "When Unitarians skillfully augmented the inheritance of English rationalism with conservative versions of Real Whig politics and Hutchesonian moral philosophy, they became a greatly disorienting force. No Unitarians carried out these tasks as skillfully as Channing . . . whom, despite his gentle mien and frail physique, orthodox leaders like Jedidiah Morse, Lyman Beecher, and N. W. Taylor feared the most" (285).

Although Channing's moral vision has elicited admiration even from his detractors, some critics have found shortcomings in his logic and writing style. William Hazlitt, in his 1829 review of Channing's works, accuses the author of oversimplifying issues, lacking original ideas, and writing in a stilted style (125–44). In "Review of Channing's Works" (1834), the Reverend Leonard Withington declares that Channing as a critic, ethicist, and theologian is eloquent but incompetent. According to David P. Edgell in his *William Ellery Channing: An Intellectual Portrait* (1955), Channing was a moralist rather than a literary critic. Channing's position in American literary history has been unjustifiably inflated: "He lived at a time when good writers were few . . . and he achieved a literary reputation greater, perhaps, than would have been his in any other period of our country's history" (224).

WORKS CITED

Addison, Daniel Dulany. *The Clergy in American Life and Letters.* New York: Macmillan Company, 1900.

Brown, Arthur W. *Always Young for Liberty: A Biography of William Ellery Channing.* Syracuse: Syracuse University Press, 1956.

Channing, William E. The Works of William E. Channing, With an Introduction. New and Complete Edition, Rearranged. To Which Is Added the Perfect Life. Boston: American Unitarian Association, 1886.

"Dr. Channing's Works." *Westminster Review* 12 (1830): 472–91.

Edgell, David P. *William Ellery Channing: An Intellectual Portrait.* Boston: Beacon Press, 1955.

Hazlitt, William. "American Literature—Dr Channing." *Edinburgh Review* October 1829: 125–44.

Mendelsohn, Jack. *Channing, the Reluctant Radical: A Biography.* Boston: Little, Brown, 1971.

Noll, Mark A. *America's God: From Jonathan Edwards to Abraham Lincoln.* New York: Oxford University Press, 2002.

Robinson, David. *The Unitarians and the Universalists.* Westport, CT: Greenwood Press, 1985.

Ward, Robert S. "The American System in Literature." *New England Quarterly* 38 (1965): 363–74.

Withington, Leonard. "Review of Channing's Works." *Literary and Theological Review* 1 (1834): 304–35.

Woodberry, George Edward. *Makers of Literature: Being Essays on Shelley, Landor, Browning, Byron, Arnold, Coleridge, Lowell, Whittier, and Others.* New York: Macmillan Company, 1900.

BIBLIOGRAPHY

Works by William Ellery Channing

Collection

The Works of William E. Channing, With an Introduction. New and Complete Edition, Rearranged. To Which Is Added the Perfect Life. Boston: American Unitarian Association, 1886.

Prose

Channing, William Henry, ed. *Memoir of William Ellery Channing, with Extracts from His Correspondence and Manuscripts.* 3 vols. Boston: Crosby, Nichols, 1848.

Memoir of William Ellery Channing: with Extracts from His Correspondence and Manuscripts. Boston: Crosby, Nichols, 1850.

Le Breton, Anna Letitia, ed. *Correspondence of William Ellery Channing and Lucy Aikin, from 1826–1842.* Boston: Roberts, 1874.

Channing, Grace Ellery, ed. *Dr. Channing's Note-Book, Passages from the Unpublished Manuscripts of William Ellery Channing, Selected by His Granddaughter, Grace Ellery Channing.* Boston: Houghton, Mifflin and Company, 1887.

Discourses on War. Boston: Ginn & Company, 1903.

Studies of William Ellery Channing

Addison, Daniel Dulany. *The Clergy in American Life and Letters.* New York: Macmillan Company, 1900.

Brown, Arthur W. *Always Young for Liberty: A Biography of William Ellery Channing.* Syracuse: Syracuse University Press, 1956.

"Dr. Channing's Works." *Westminster Review* 12 (1830): 472–91.

Edgell, David P. *William Ellery Channing: An Intellectual Portrait.* Boston: Beacon Press, 1955.

Hazlitt, William. "American Literature—Dr Channing." *Edinburgh Review* October 1829: 125–44.

Mendelsohn, Jack. *Channing, the Reluctant Radical: A Biography.* Boston: Little, Brown, 1971. Reprinted 1980.

Noll, Mark A. *America's God: From Jonathan Edwards to Abraham Lincoln.* New York: Oxford University Press, 2002.

Robinson, David. *The Unitarians and the Universalists.* Westport, CT: Greenwood Press, 1985.

Ward, Robert S. "The American System in Literature." *New England Quarterly* 38 (1965): 363–74.

Withington, Leonard. "Review of Channing's Works." *Literary and Theological Review* 1 (1834): 304–35.

Woodberry, George Edward. *Makers of Literature: Being Essays on Shelley, Landor, Browning, Byron, Arnold, Coleridge, Lowell, Whittier, and Others.* New York: Macmillan Company, 1900.

CAROLINE CHESEBRO' (1825–1873)

Lucy M. Freibert

BIOGRAPHY

Born in Canandaigua, New York, on March 30, 1825, the fifth of Betsey Kimball and Nicholas Goddard Chesebrough's eight children, Caroline Chesebro', as she chose to spell her name, came by the bold, unorthodox strain of her writing naturally. Her ancestors Anne Stevenson and William Chesebrough, who came from England to the Massachusetts Bay Colony in 1630, helped found Braintree and Rehoboth, Massachusetts, and, in 1649, Stonington, Connecticut. Her father, a hatter, wool dealer, and postmaster, held strong convictions and acted upon them. In 1826 Nicholas Chesebrough served a one-year jail sentence for joining in a conspiracy to thwart publication of a book revealing the secrets of Freemasonry.

After completing her education at the Canandaigua Seminary, Chesebro' continued to live with her family, reading widely among British and American authors. Her mother, whom the writer honored in the dedicatory poem of her first book, and her sister Catharine, to whom she dedicated her second novel, formed the core of the community of women who encouraged Chesebro'.

In 1848, Chesebro' sold her first story to *Graham's American Monthly Magazine*. Over the next three years, while continuing to write for *Graham's,* she contributed to *Holden's Dollar Magazine, Knickerbocker, Sartain's, Peterson's,* and *Godey's Lady's Book.* In 1851, J. S. Redfield published 19 of her magazine pieces and 5 new stories in *Dream-Land by Daylight, A Panorama of Romance.*

Thereafter, Chesebro' placed stories chiefly in *Harper's New Monthly Magazine,* but wrote also for *Appleton's, Beadle's, Continental, Galaxy, Lippincott's,* and *Putnam's Monthly.* When *Atlantic Monthly* began in 1857, her story "The Pure Pearl of Diver's Bay" appeared in the initial volume; she continued writing for *Atlantic.* Chesebro's published stories exceeded 80. Few of her poems reached print; some of them appeared in her fiction.

While building her reputation as a short fiction writer, Chesebro' also wrote novels. In 1852, when Redfield brought out the second edition of *Dream-Land,* he also published Chesebro's first novel, *Isa, a Pilgrimage,* and the following year *The Children of Light.* Subsequent novels included *Getting Along, Victoria, Peter Carradine,* and *The Foe in the Household.*

Chesebro' also produced juvenile fiction. Her collections of moralistic stories include *The Little Cross-Bearers, The Beautiful Gate and Other Tales,* and *Blessings in Disguise,* and her novels, *Philly and Kit; or, Life and Raiment,* and *Amy Carr; or, The Fortune-Teller.*

Personal correspondence preserved at the New York Public Library indicates that Chesebro' was still living in Canandaigua in 1859. In 1865, she became director of composition at Packard Collegiate Institute in Brooklyn, New York, a position she held until her death on February 16, 1873. During this period, she lived at 120 West 22nd Street in New York, but also spent time with her sister and brothers who resided at Piermont, north of the city. To provide her students with an outlet for their creative work, Chesebro' initiated *The Packard Quarterly.* Shortly before her death, she proofread the issue that would carry her obituary.

MAJOR WORKS AND THEMES

Unique insights into the ambiguity of woman's status, woman's potential for independence, the importance of spirituality and education, and the bonding of women rather than competition between them pervade Chesebro's writing. Her choice of allusions, quotations, and symbols and the grave tone of much of her work resemble those of her contemporaries Edgar Allan Poe and Herman Melville. Themes that would inform her later works emerged in the stories collected in *Dream-Land:* the power of love, spirituality versus materialism and/or skepticism, class distinction, the relation of the artist (genius) to nature, dreams as instructive, and the evils of ambition.

Isa, a Pilgrimage (1852), Chesebro's first novel—a dense and somber work—treats the power of wealth, the liberating effects of education on women, and the difference between spirituality and formal religion. Reared by a pious and wealthy foster mother, Isa espouses atheistic socialism. She aligns herself, outside the bonds of marriage, with an atheist philosopher committed to demonstrating the power of the human will. The novel evolves through the combination of journal entries, autobiography, and dream sequences with the basic narrative.

Multiple subplots enhance *The Children of Light* (1853), merging thematic exploration of class and gender conflicts, differences between Christianity and Transcendentalism, liberating effects of education and art, and the potential benefit of lesbianism. As protagonist Asia Phillips rises from uncertain origins and poverty through education and theatrical ability, her childhood friendship with the wealthy Maderon sisters takes diverse turns. When Blanche wins Aaron Gregorias from Asia, Vesta pledges lifelong love and support of Asia's career.

Although her next two novels *Getting Along* (1855) and *Victoria* (1856) did not further Chesebro's reputation, they enabled her to clarify her thinking about the effects on women of a male-focused curriculum. By the time she wrote *Peter Carradine; or, the Martindale Pastoral* (1863), Chesebro's writing skills had improved and her social views had moderated. The title aside, the novel focuses primarily on the community and the interactive lives of the village in which Carradine holds political eminence. When Carradine replaces the schoolteacher Miranda Roy with Mercy Fuller from Brighton, the friendship that develops between the two women, Miranda's subsequent religious conversion, and Mercy's influence on Carradine leave few villagers untouched.

The Foe in the Household (1871), Chesebro's last and, arguably, her best novel, interweaves themes of the power of love, danger of secret marriage, breakdown of communication, and evils of religious orthodoxy. Defying the inflexible Mennonite tenet that a member might not marry outside the sect, Delia, the bishop's daughter, secretly weds a nonsectarian, thereby becoming the "foe" in the household, not only of her father but also, later, of the man whom she marries after her first husband's death.

CRITICAL RECEPTION

Although Chesebro' did not attain best-seller status during her 25-year career, she received steady support from magazine editors, book publishers, and critics who appreciated her imagination. By the time *Dream-Land* appeared, she had, according to *Sartain's* reviewer, "won an enviable reputation" through her contributions to magazines. The writer praised her avoidance of "false sentimentality" and her fearlessness in protesting "conventional prejudices of education, that would forever distort and repress the finer impulses of the soul" (*Dream-Land*, 10, 196). *Harper's* critic admired her "originality of mind . . . the liveliness of her fancy and the intensity of her thought," as well as her energy, but noted her "want of proportion, of harmony, of artistic modulation" (*Dream-Land*, 4, 274). Sales of the collection justified a second edition in 1852.

When her novel *Isa* came out that same year, *Harper's* reviewer saw in it "a deeper power of reflection, a greater intensity of passion" than in her earlier work (*Isa*, 4, 853). *Sartain's* critic described its style as "terse and vigorous, yet rhetorical and brilliant" (*Isa*, 10, 515).

Like *Isa, The Children of Light* received mostly positive reviews. Although *The Literary World* complained that the characters "talk like a book" (11, 392), *Putnam's* saw it as vigorous and fresh as *Isa* (1, 106).

Not until the publication of *Peter Carradine*, more traditional than its predecessors, did Chesebro' gain wide popular appeal. *Harper's* labeled it "the best American novel which has been written for years" (27, 850). Likewise, when *The Foe in the Household* came out in book form, the reviewer for the *Atlantic Monthly*, where it had first appeared serially, ranked it "with the very best of American fictions, . . . surpassed only by Hawthorne's romances and Mrs. Stowe's greatest work" (28, 126).

In *A Manual of American Literature*, published in the year of Chesebro's death, John Seely Hart describes her as "rising steadily in favor" (502), and in 1906, William Dean Howells, reviewing his years as *Atlantic Monthly* editor, placed Chesebro' among the "favorites" whose outstanding work he recalled (100, 594) and cited the "singular excellence" of "The Foe of the Household" (100, 604).

WORKS CITED

Hart, John Seely. *A Manual of American Literature.* Philadelphia: Eldredge and Brother, 1873.
Howells, W[illiam] D[ean]. "Recollections of an Atlantic Editorship." *Atlantic Monthly* 100 (November 1907): 594–606.
Review of *The Children of Light. The Literary World* 11 (December 1852): 392.
Review of *The Children of Light. Putnam's Monthly Magazine* 1 (January 1853): 106.
Review of *Dream-Land by Daylight. Harper's New Monthly Magazine* 4 (January 1852): 274–75.
Review of *Dream-Land by Daylight. Sartain's Magazine of Literature and Art* 10 (February 1852): 196–97.
Review of *The Foe in the Household. Atlantic Monthly* 28 (July 1871): 126.
Review of *Isa, a Pilgrimage. Harper's New Monthly Magazine* 4 (May 1852): 853.

Review of *Isa, a Pilgrimage. Sartain's Magazine of Literature and Art* 10 (June 1852): 515.
Review of *Peter Carradine. Harper's New Monthly Magazine* 27 (November 1863): 850.

BIBLIOGRAPHY

Works by Caroline Chesebro'

Novels

Isa, a Pilgrimage. Clinton Hall, NY: Redfield, 1852.
The Children of Light: A Theme for the Time. New York: J. S. Redfield, 1853.
Getting Along. A Book of Illustrations. New York: J. C. Darby; Boston: Phillips, Sampson & Co., 1855. [In two volumes. See *Susan* below.]
Susan, the Fisherman's Daughter; or, Getting Along. A Book of Illustrations. New York: J. C. Derby; Boston: Phillips, Sampson & Co., 1855. [Two volumes in one. See *Getting Along:* above.]
Victoria; or, The World Overcome. New York: Derby & Jackson; Cincinnati: H. W. Derby & Co., 1856.
Peter Carradine; or, The Martindale Pastoral. New York: Seldon & Co.; Boston: Gould & Lincoln, 1863.
The Fisherman of Camp's Island; or, Ye Are not Your Own. New York: Carlton & Porter, 1865.
The Glen Cabin; or, Away to the Hills. New York: American Tract Society, 1865.
The Foe in the Household. Boston: J. R. Osgood & Company, 1871.

Short Stories

Dream-Land By Daylight, A Panorama of Romance. Clinton Hall, NY: Redfield, 1851.
"The Compensation." *In The Coronal and Young Lady's Remembrancer,* edited by Rev. Frederic Janes. New York: James H. Pratt & Co., 1853.
"The Enigma." In *The Coronal and Young Lady's Remembrancer,* edited by Rev. Frederic Janes. New York: James H. Pratt & Co., 1853.
"The Prince at Land's End." In *Gifts of Genius: A Miscellany of Prose and Poetry, by American Authors.* New York: C. A. Davenport, 1860.
"Victoria and Jacqueline." In *Atlantic Tales. A Collection of Stories from the Atlantic Monthly.* No. 1. Boston: Ticknor and Fields, 1866.
"The Record of Dorcas Bently," In *Short Stories for Spare Moments. Selected from Lippincott's Magazine,* 2nd ser. Philadelphia: J. B. Lippincott and Co., 1869.
"In Honor Bound." In *Short Stories,* edited by Constance Cary Harrison. Distaff ser. New York: Harper & Brothers Publishers, 1893.
"The Short Stories of Caroline Chesebro'." By Marjorie Jane Hunt. Master's thesis. George Washington University, 1970. Contains a list of Chesebro's stories published in magazines.

Juvenile Literature

The Little Cross-Bearers. Auburn, NY: Derby & Miller; Buffalo: Derby, Orton & Mulligan, 1854.
The Beautiful Gate and Other Tales. New York and Auburn: Miller, Orton & Mulligan, 1855.
Philly and Kit; or, Life and Raiment. New York: J. S. Redfield, 1856.
Blessings in Disguise; or, Pictures of Some of Miss Haydon's Girls. New York: Carlton & Porter, 1863.
The Sparrow's Fall; or, Under the Willow. And Other Stories. New York: Carlton & Porter, 1863.
Amy Carr; or, The Fortune-Teller. New York: M. W. Dodd, Publisher, 1864.

Studies of Caroline Chesebro'

Baym, Nina. *Woman's Fiction: A Guide to Novels by and about Women in America 1820–1870.* Ithaca: Cornell University Press, 1978. 208–30.

Blain, Virginia, Patricia Clements, and Isobel Grundy. *The Feminist Companion to Literature in English: Women Writers from the Middle Ages to the Present.* New Haven and London: Yale University Press, 1990. 201.

Fleenor, Julianne E. "Caroline Chesebro'." In Vol. 1 of *American Women Writers: A Critical Reference Guide from Colonial Times to the Present,* edited by Lina Mainiero. New York: Frederick Ungar, 1979. 346–48.

Freibert, Lucy M. "Caroline Chesebro'." In *Nineteenth-Century American Women Writers: A Bio-Bibliographical Critical Sourcebook,* edited by Denise D. Wright. Westport, Connecticut and London: Greenwood Press, 1997. 36–41.

Hart, John Seely. *The Female Prose Writers of America with Portraits, Bibliographical Notices, and Specimens of their Writings.* Philadelphia: E. H. Butler and Co., 1852. 512–16.

Meyering, Sheryl L. "Caroline Chesebro'." In *The Oxford Companion to Women's Writing in the United States,* edited by Cathy N. Davidson and Linda Wagner-Martin. New York: Oxford University Press, 1995. 164.

LYDIA MARIA CHILD (1802–1880)

Valerie D. Levy

BIOGRAPHY

Lydia Maria Francis Child was born on February 11, 1802, to Convers Francis and Susannah Rand Francis in the shipyard village of Medford, Massachusetts. The youngest of five surviving children, Child rejected her father's strict ideas about womanly avocations and, instead, found herself drawn to intellectual pursuits. Her close ties to her brother Convers Francis Jr., who was six years her senior and a graduate of the Harvard Divinity School, solidified not only the humanitarian impulses her whole family shared, but also Child's keen interest in reading and education. Her parents, by contrast, lived by simple values. Convers Francis was a baker by trade and owned his own shop while Susannah Rand Francis was in charge of teaching her daughters their domestic duties. More successful than his father, weaver Benjamin Francis, Convers Francis was able to provide modestly for his children and even sent his youngest two, Convers Jr. and Lydia, to a dame school for their early education. After Susannah died from a form of tuberculosis in May 1814, Child, at 12, found herself lonely with only her father's austere companionship in the home. Soon after, however, Convers Francis sent his daughter to Norridgewock, Maine, where she joined her sister Mary and Mary's new husband Warren Preston. Although Convers Francis hoped that living with Mary would instill in his youngest a sense of domestic responsibility, Child continued to be an avid reader of the classics and to develop her own ideas about what was befitting a woman. While in Norridgewock, she trained to be a teacher at a local academy staffed by student-teachers from Bowdoin College. In 1820, she asserted her independence by moving to Gardiner, Maine, where she taught school and continued to read Milton, Shakespeare, and English poetry of the sixteenth and seventeenth centuries.

The next 10 years proved to be pivotal in Child's life, for she established herself as the humanitarian, social critic, and popular writer she seemed destined to become. In 1821 she moved in with her brother Convers and his wife in Watertown, Massachusetts. Convers Jr. was by now an ordained minister of First (Unitarian) Church, and his place of residence was stimulating for Child because it attracted such progressive thinkers as

Ralph Waldo Emerson, John Greenleaf Whittier, George Ripley, and others. While there, Child was baptized in her father's Congregational church in Medford, joined the Swedenborgian Society of the New Jerusalem in Boston, and adopted the name Lydia Maria, Lydia being her paternal grandmother's name. She also opened a girls' school and taught physical education, domestic administration, and other more conventional subjects. Her greatest enterprise during these years, however, was inspired by an article in the *North American Review* in which the author claimed that New England's past would make an ideal subject for a story. Provoked by the challenge, Child wrote her first novel, the historical romance *Hobomok, a Tale of Early Times* (1824). Set in the Colonial times, *Hobomok* surprised readers with a heroine who, against her father's wishes, marries an Indian chief, bears his child, then leaves him for another. To Child's delight, her first novel immediately established her as a writer of tremendous ability. Child's next novel, *The Rebels; or, Boston before the Revolution* (1825), dealt with the turmoil in Boston leading up to the American Revolution, and, though not nearly as well-received as *Hobomok*, it further confirmed her reputation as a literary reformer interested in American nationalism. In 1828, Child's third novel, *The First Settlers of New-England*, broached Indian affairs once again but with a more forthright attack against the dispossession of the American Indian than that presented in *Hobomok*.

Child had many other interests as well, not the least of which was providing practical advice for women and commenting on her ideas about women's "proper" place. In 1826 she founded a bimonthly children's magazine, the successful *Juvenile Miscellany*, and edited it for eight years. She added to that with the 1829 publication of the influential domestic advice book, *The Frugal Housewife;* just two years later, *The Mother's Book* (1831) and *The Little Girl's Own Book* (1831). During her writing of these projects, Child used the all-male Boston Athenaeum as her library and was the only woman, aside from Boston historian Hannah Adams, granted access to its shelves. Such a privilege allowed her to add to her repertoire of writing with the publication of *Ladies' Family Library*, a five-volume collection that offered biographies of famous women and more domestic advice, grounded in some of the earliest feminist theory. She also spent much of the 1820s and 1830s writing short fiction for popular giftbooks of the day. Her first short story, "The Rival Brothers," appeared in the 1827 volume of *The Token*. Later stories, such as "Charity's Bowery," published in *The Liberty Bell*, became platforms for Child to voice her political views and to redefine the standards for short fiction.

It was also during her stay in Watertown that Child met her future husband, David Lee Child, in 1824. They shared many common interests—from a love of classic literature to liberal political and social views—and although some friends warned her that David was neither practical nor established, they wed on October 19, 1928. On some levels, her friends' predictions came true: David's career as a sometime lawyer, activist, writer, and editor was unpredictable, and, within a year of marriage, the couple found themselves shouldering mounting debts. Nonetheless, they cared deeply for each other and continued to support each other's philanthropic and political endeavors. A protégé of William Lloyd Garrison, David Lee Child helped to form the American Anti-Slavery Society in Boston, in January 1832, and introduced Child to more leading abolitionists of the day. Until that time, she had remained fairly subversive with the antislavery sentiments she had held since a child living in a household that opposed slavery. In 1833, however, she shocked her admirers with *An Appeal in Favor of That Class of Americans Called Africans,* which was the first abolitionist work to be published in book form in America and which strongly urged for immediate emancipation and an end to racial prejudice.

While Child explored different avenues of antislavery protest, she continued to champion women's rights, the sister cause of abolition. In 1835 she published *The History of the Condition of Women, in Various Ages and Nations,* a research-laden project that both satisfied her interest in women's issues and earned her a nominal amount of money to help support her husband's newest venture: to go to Belgium to study the process of converting beets into sugar. To deflect the costs David needed for this undertaking, Child also turned to fiction once again with the publication of *Philothea, a Romance* (1836). Set in the time of Pericles, the story featured a strong female character, Aspasia, and addressed the conflict between public law and private values. Child used some of the profits from her novel to pay off a portion of the debt she owed to her father. After a year and a half in Belgium, David returned to New England in 1837, at the height of the financial panic, with dreams of using beet sugar as a substitute for the cane sugar produced by slave labor. His undertaking was great; not only did it fail as an enterprise because the 100 acres he purchased in Northampton, Massachusetts, did not yield soil conducive to beet growing, but his project forced him and Child to live in separate places for a few years. Child hesitantly accepted the charity of her friends, the Lorings, who offered her a temporary home after she and David lost theirs at Cottage Place.

So passionate was David about growing beets that he rejected a position as editor of the *National Anti-Slavery Standard,* the Anti-Slavery Society's New York-based newspaper. The more practical Child took up the offer and moved to New York, where she stayed with Quaker Isaac T. Hopper and his family. She served as the *Standard's* editor from 1841 to 1843. Forswearing the more aggressive tactics of her peers such as Garrison and Maria Weston Chapman and appeasing the newspaper's mission to produce "family-friendly" abolitionism, Child developed her own antislavery voice and originated the genre of the journalistic sketch in her column, "Letters from New-York." These essays on her impressions of New York and views on women's rights, poverty, temperance, nature, music, and other timely topics appealed to readers even beyond her immediate audience and were frequently reprinted in such papers as the *Boston Courier.* So successful were her essays, in fact, that Child was encouraged to collect them in book form, and in 1843 and 1845, she came out with two exceptionally popular volumes of *Letters from New-York.*

With the increasing realization that she could not rely on her husband for security, Child decided to make her own security by separating her finances from David's and settling more permanently in New York, always with the hope that he would join her there and help assume their ever-growing debt. For her own part, Child continued to produce popular literary fare, including the various anthologies of her verse and stories, such as *Flowers for Children* (1844, 1846) and *Autumnal Leaves* (1856), as well as articles and occasional essays for *Columbian Lady's and Gentleman's Magazine* and Edgar Allan Poe's *Broadway Journal.* In 1845 she reviewed friend Margaret Fuller's *Woman of the Nineteenth Century,* a veritable manifesto that well expressed the philosophical underpinnings of Child's more practical work in feminist reform.

In 1852 Child and her husband were able to make a life together in Wayland, Massachusetts. They lived there modestly, caring for the now ailing Convers Sr. and reaffirming their commitment to each other. Child's newest project was a book, *The Progress of Religious Ideas, through Successive Ages* (1855), which took her eight years to write and much help from David, whose command of languages aided her in translations. The book was not a monetary success, but it effectively articulated Child's commitment to the Spirit of God and to the convergence of all world religions. It may be said, however, that the most apparent manifestation of her religious beliefs came in the form of philanthropy and humanitarianism. Child felt it to be both her will and her destiny to provide service to those in need.

Perhaps it was this ideology that helped Child to sustain her abolitionist work long after she grew weary of the politics that went along with it. Instead of abandoning the cause, she became creative with her literary options, and in 1858 published a dramatic play in *The Liberty Bell* entitled *The Stars and Stripes. A Melo-Drama,* in which she appeals for racial integration and for the abolishing, not just of slavery, but of slavery's derivation, racism. As the Civil War proved imminent, Child became even more inspired by the contagion of antislavery passion. In her correspondence with Governor Henry A. Wise of Virginia, Child defended John Brown despite his disagreeable tactics by offering to care for him in prison. Horace Greeley's *Tribune* ran a reprint of the letters in 1860, affirming to the public Child's reputation as a prominent abolitionist and the fear evoked by being associated with such a strong figure for the antislavery cause. By this time, Child supported the impending war; in her view, "a holy war was better than an unholy Union" (Osborne 34). She saw it as the North's duty not just to preserve the Union but to preserve the ideal of freedom.

In direct contrast to the war raging outside their doors, Child and her husband found themselves financially stable after Convers Francis Sr. passed away and left them his estate. David concentrated on earning money as a lawyer and writer, while Child continued to take on a variety of roles, including the editorship of the now-ubiquitous slave narrative, Harriet Jacobs's *Incidents in the Life of a Slave Girl: Written by Herself* (1861). Child's challenges with this project were threefold. Not only did she have to make sure that Jacobs's life story had literary appeal, but she had to convince readers that the story was indeed true and that it was indeed Jacobs's. In her Introduction, Child states, "I believe those who know her will not be disposed to doubt her veracity, though some incidents in her story are more romantic than fiction" (3). When Child says that some of the incidents are "more romantic than fiction," she suggests that Jacobs is not merely recounting the facts of her life, but is consciously composing her story and revising her past. Although today Jacobs's authorship is well established, Jacobs's and Child's contemporaries were wary of the authenticity of slave narratives. It was Child's faith in Jacobs as a person of dignity and talent that heightened people's awareness of the especial oppression that slave women faced and of the literary skill of which they were capable.

After the war ended, Child focused on the education of the newly freed blacks and published *The Freedmen's Book* (1865), a textbook for ex-slaves that included poems, hymns, essays in conduct, and stories praising the achievements of the black race. With uplift in mind, her future efforts likewise sought to eliminate what she felt to be the root of the American conflict: racial prejudice. As Child explains of her 1867 novel, *A Romance of the Republic,* "I wanted to do something to undermine *prejudice;* and there is such a universal passion for novels, that more can be done in that way, than by the ablest arguments, and the most serious exhortations" (qtd. in Karcher, "Lydia Maria Child's *A Romance*" 82). However, there were some things over which she found she had little control. By this time, David's health began to suffer, and in 1874, Child was devastated by his death. After David passed away, she led a somewhat Bohemian existence, visiting friends but remaining relatively reclusive. She sought companionship in her old friend, literature, and occasionally wrote articles and letters. She also began to collect religious writings of the ages that exemplified her liberal beliefs, and in May 1878, she published the collection as *Aspirations of the World.* Her last article was a tribute to Garrison, published in *Atlantic* in 1879. The following year Child returned home to Wayland, but an acute attack of rheumatism in June kept her bedridden. On October 20, 1880, she felt well enough to leave her bedroom but a sudden heart attack ended her life. At the private funeral service in her home, abolitionist and friend Wendell Phillips gave a eulogy that praised Child's ability to merge the feminine and masculine in order to stand up for the humanitarian principles in which she believed.

MAJOR WORKS AND THEMES

Child's first novel, *Hobomok* (1824), is evocative of the spirit that guided her future projects and of her basic ideology as a woman author. Not only did *Hobomok* portray a female strength and conviction fresh to American literature but it expressed one of Child's recurring themes as a writer, the belief that antimiscegenation and racial discrimination are the antithesis of democracy and freedom. As her narrator states, "Spiritual light, like that of the natural sun, shines from one source, and shines alike upon all; but it is reflected and absorbed in almost infinite variety; and in the moral, as well as the natural world, the diversity of the rays is occasioned by the nature of the recipient" (69). Indeed, Child's writing became a prism reflecting the myriad ways of seeing American history and contemporary American life. Not only did *Hobomok* revolutionize the historical novel popularized by *Ivanhoe,* but it placed American literature in a class of its own by drawing upon the specifically American topics of Indian rights and Puritan values.

Although *Hobomok* stands out as Child's most well-received novel and continues to be a popular work of study with scholars today, it would be misleading to assess her literary career by that work alone, for Child advocated on behalf of many causes and drew from many different genres of literature in order to do so. Her domestic advice books—*The Frugal Housewife, The Mother's Book,* and *The Girl's Own Book*—for instance, offered female readers educational and useful advice for everyday life. They earned Child the monetary success of a popular writer and also showed that she was not always radical in her views on women's rights and that she could embrace the more "genteel" idea of a woman's proper sphere. Never satisfied with remaining palatable to the masses, however, Child simultaneously continued to support the less popular ideas with respect to women's rights.

In her abolitionist work, too, Child was unafraid of being bold. Her *Appeal in Favor of That Class of Americans Called Africans,* for example, was so radical for its times that public reaction was, for the most part, one of antipathy. Readers of her popular *The Juvenile Miscellany* withdrew their subscriptions, the Athenaeum revoked her privileges, sales of *The Frugal Housewife* and *The Mother's Book* dropped, and Child's reputation as a woman writer suffered dramatically. Nonetheless, Child prevailed in her new role as political protester and journalist, and her abolitionist principles led her in a variety of directions: she created her own abolitionist giftbook, *The Oasis,* in 1834, organized the first antislavery fair in America in Boston that same year, and served on various committees, including the Boston Female Anti-Slavery Society and the New England Anti-Slavery Society. A frequent contributor to the top giftbooks such as *The Liberty Bell,* Child often expressed her antislavery sentiments in short stories that capitalized upon the sentimental tradition. In due course, however, Child developed a distaste for the infighting that went on amongst abolitionists. She complained in a letter to Ellis Gray Loring of "the bad *spirit* which [she saw] everywhere manifested, and the increasing tendency to *co-erce* individual freedom" (qtd. in Whittier, *Letters* 194). Though Child never abandoned the cause, she rallied on behalf of slaves and black rights under her own terms and in her own way, helping her to become one of the nation's leading activists.

CRITICAL RECEPTION

Lydia Maria Child was the quintessential overnight success. Completing her first novel, *Hobomok,* in just six weeks, she was hailed as one of the best women authors in the nation. Most of her early work, in fact, from *Hobomok* and *The Frugal Housewife* to her many antislavery pieces, only furthered her reputation as an innovator of the historical novel and the short story as well. In 1833, *North American Review* praised her contributions to American literature, stating, "We are not sure that any woman in our country would outrank Mrs. Child. Few female writers, if any, have done more or better things for our literature" (37: 139; qtd. in Karcher, Introduction to *Hobomok* xi).

Although one could say that Lydia Maria Child's success as a professional writer was to be expected after the encouraging reception of *Hobomok,* her journey as an author was riddled with obstacles and setbacks, due sometimes to her weaknesses as a writer and, more often, to her determination to speak for those groups of people who were hitherto silenced or otherwise oppressed. In general, the more forthright her attacks, the less popular her works. *Hobomok,* for example, imbued the topics of women's and Native Americans' rights with the palatability of the romance and the excitement of the historical novel. In contrast, the literary craftsmanship of *The Rebels; or, Boston before the Revolution* was not as refined and, accordingly, received a lukewarm reception. *The First Settlers of New-England,* another early novel, was also criticized for its weak construction as well as for its vociferous tone and blunt political message.

In contrast to her novels, Child's juvenile miscellany, short stories, and journalistic sketches proved to be sure-fire ways to both hone her skills and appeal to the masses. So popular were her children's stories that she was able to publish them in the successful bimonthly *The Juvenile Miscellany* (1826–34). Even her politicized short stories earned her the respect of her peers and the attention of her more mainstream audience. Among her most celebrated stories were "The Quadroons" (1842) and "Slavery's Pleasant Homes. A Faithful Sketch" (1843), two tales that popularized the tragic quadroon figure.

WORKS CITED

Child, Lydia Maria. *Hobomok, A Tale of Early Times.* Boston: Cummings, Hilliard, 1824.
Child, Lydia Maria, ed. Introduction to *Incidents in the Life of a Slave Girl. Written by Herself.* Harriet A. Jacobs. 1861.
Child, Lydia Maria. *Letters of Lydia Maria Child.* Ed. John Greenleaf Whittier. Boston: Houghton, 1882. 194.
Karcher, Carolyn L. "Lydia Maria Child's A Romance of the Republic: An Abolitionist Vision of America's Racial Identity." *Slavery and the Literary Imagination: Selected Papers from the English Institute, 1987.* Eds. McDowell, Deborah E., and Arnold Rampersad. Baltimore and London: The Johns Hopkins UP, 1989. 81–103.
Osborne, William S. *Lydia Maria Child.* Boston: Hall-Twayne, 1980.

BIBLIOGRAPHY

Works by Lydia Maria Child

Novels
Hobomok, A Tale of Early Times. Boston: Cummings, Hilliard, 1824.
The Rebels; or, Boston before the Revolution. Boston: Cummings, Hilliard, 1825.

The First Settlers of New-England: or, Conquest of the Pequods, Narragansets and Pokanokets: as Related by a Mother to Her Children, and Designed for the Instruction of Youth. Boston: Munroe and Francis, 1828.

Philothea, A Romance: Otis, Broaders; New York: George Dearborn, 1836.

A Romance of the Republic. Boston: Ticknor and Fields, 1867.

Dramatic Play

The Stars and Stripes. A Melo-Drama. The Liberty Bell (1858): 122–85.

Short Stories and Sketches

The Coronal. A Collection of Miscellaneous Pieces, Written at Various Times. Boston: Carter and Hendee, 1831.

"Charity Bowery." *The Liberty Bell* (1839): 26–43.

"The Emancipated Slaveholders." *The Liberty Bell* (1839): 71–74.

"The Black Saxons." *The Liberty Bell* (1841): 19–44.

"The Quadroons." *The Liberty Bell* (1842): 115–41.

"Slavery's Pleasant Homes. A Faithful Sketch." *The Liberty Bell* (1843): 147–60.

Fact and Fiction: A Collection of Stories. New York: C. S. Francis, 1846.

"Jan and Zaida." *The Liberty Bell* (1856): 41–93.

Nonfiction

The Juvenile Miscellany. Boston: John Putnam, 1826–1836.

The Frugal Housewife. Boston: Marsh & Capen, and Carter & Hendee, 1829.

The Little Girl's Own Book. Boston: Carter, Hendee, and Babcock, 1831.

The Mother's Book. Boston: Carter, Hendee and Babcock, 1831.

The Biographies of Madame de Staël, and Madame Roland. Vol. 1 of *Ladies' Family Library.* Boston: Carter, Hendee, 1832.

An Appeal in Favor of That Class of Americans Called Africans. Boston: Allen and Ticknor, 1833.

The Oasis. Boston: Allen & Ticknor, 1834.

The History of the Condition of Women, in Various Ages and Nations. Vols. 4 and 5 of *Ladies' Family Library.* Boston: John Allen, 1835.

Letters from New-York, First Series. New York: Charles S. Francis, 1843.

Letters from New-York, Second Series. New York: C. S. Francis, 1845.

The Progress of Religious Ideas, through Successive Ages. 3 vols. New York: C. S. Francis, 1855.

Correspondence between Lydia Maria Child and Gov. Wise and Mrs. Mason, of Virginia. Boston: American Anti-Slavery Society, 1860.

Ed. *Incidents in the Life of a Slave Girl. Written by Herself.* By Harriet A. Jacobs. 1861.

Ed. *Jean Fagan Yellin.* Cambridge and London: Harvard UP, 1987.

Ed. *Looking toward Sunset.* Boston: Ticknor and Fields, 1865.

The Freedmen's Book. Boston: Ticknor and Fields, 1865.

An Appeal for the Indians. New York: William P. Tomlinson, 1868.

Ed. *Aspirations of the World. A Chain of Opals.* Boston: Roberts, 1878.

Letters

Letters of Lydia Maria Child. Ed. John Greenleaf Whittier. Boston: Houghton, 1882.

The Collected Correspondence of Lydia Maria Child, 1817–1880. Ed. Patricia G. Holland, Milton Meltzer, and Francine Krasno. Millwood, NY: Kraus, 1980.

Lydia Maria Child: Selected Letters, 1817–1880. Ed. Milton Meltzer, Patricia G. Holland, and Francine Krasno. Amherst: U of Massachusetts P, 1982.

Miscellaneous

Flowers for Children, I, II, III. New York: C. S. Francis, 1844, 1846.

Autumnal Leaves. New York: C. S. Francis, 1856.

Studies of Lydia Maria Child

Clifford, Deborah Pickman. *Crusader for Freedom: A Life of Lydia Maria Child.* Boston: Beacon P, 1992.

Holland, Patricia G. "Lydia Maria Child as Nineteenth-Century Professional Author." *Studies in the American Renaissance* (1981): 157–67.

Kaplan, Amy. "Manifest Domesticity." *American Literature* 70.3 (September 1998): 581–606.

Karcher, Carolyn L. *The First Woman in the Republic: A Cultural Biography of Lydia Maria Child.* Durham and London: Duke UP, 1994.

———. Introduction to *Hobomok & Other Writings on Indians* by Lydia Maria Child. New Brunswick: Rutgers UP, 1986.

———. "Lydia Maria Child's *A Romance of the Republic:* An Abolitionist Vision of America's Racial Identity." *Slavery and the Literary Imagination: Selected Papers from the English Institute, 1987.* Eds. McDowell, Deborah E., and Arnold Rampersad. Baltimore and London: The Johns Hopkins UP, 1989. 81–103.

Kerber, Linda K. "The Abolitionist Perception of the Indian." *Journal of American History* 62 (1875): 271–95.

Meltzer, Milton. *Tongue of Flame: The Life of Lydia Maria Child.* New York: Crowell, 1965.

Mills, Bruce. *Cultural Reformations: Lydia Maria Child and the Literature of Reform.* Athens and London: U of Georgia P, 1994.

Osborne, William S. *Lydia Maria Child.* Boston: Hall-Twayne, 1980.

JAMES FENIMORE COOPER (1789–1851)

Annette Jael Lehmann

BIOGRAPHY

James Fenimore Cooper was born in September 1789 in Burlington, New Jersey; his father Judge William Cooper was a representative to the 4th and 6th Congress and was a prominent Federalist who gained great wealth by developing land. Cooper spent more than half his life in the thriving frontier village of Cooperstown, New York. He arrived there as a small child, shortly after the town was founded by his father, a nouveau-riche speculator in land. In 1806, Cooper was sent to sea by his father after being dismissed from Yale College for misconduct. Cooper had used his energy for the invention of campus pranks, such as teaching a donkey to sit in a professor's chair. In 1808 he began a naval career and received a warrant as a midshipman in the Navy, which he left upon marrying the wealthy Susan DeLancey in 1811. Cooper took up the comfortable life of a country gentleman on a farm in Cooperstown, overlooking Lake Otsego. For about 10 years he dabbled in agriculture, politics, the American Bible Society, and the Westchester militia. Under his mismanagement the Cooper estate yielded little. Cooper began writing at the age of 30, when the economic foundations of his life as a conservative farmer collapsed. Inspired by best-selling novels and a need for cash, he wrote his first novel *Precaution* in 1820, which was a failure. One year later he published *The Spy,* a tale of revolution, a notable success but not yet his break-through as a best-selling author. In 1823 when the first of the *Leather-Stocking Tales* was published, his household goods were seized by a sheriff at the request of creditors. Only the sudden flow of money from 3,000 sold copies of *The Pioneers* saved Cooper from bankruptcy. Cooper spent the years from 1822 to 1826 as a well-known writer in New York. There, for example, Cooper joined an organization of talented men called "The Bread and Cheese Club," which sponsored dinners for hosts of notable and famous men. In 1826 he added his name "Fenimore" to perpetuate his mother's family name, threatened with extinction. Between 1826 to 1833 he spent time traveling on Grand Tour in Europe, which carried him through France, Switzerland, Italy, and Germany. The large Cooper family—six children and a nephew—spent their days sightseeing and enjoyed entertainment in the evenings. Their journeys are reported in vivid detail in his five books on European travels. He published *The Prairie* while living in Paris in 1828 and was no longer the darling of New York society when he returned to the United States in 1833. He received harsh criticism in the American press for educating his countrymen on their cultural deficiencies and attacking the oligarchical party of his day according to the gentlemanly tradition of Jefferson and Lafayette. In *The American Democrat* (1838), Cooper presented to the public a defense of his Jeffersonian political and social philosophy and maintained, until late in his life, the landlords' position in the Anti-Rent Wars in New York State. His 1840 and 1841 published volumes *The Pathfinder* and *The Deerslayer,* the final novels in the Leatherstocking series, established Cooper as the first great professional author in the New World. Because of various conflicts with his old New York friends he spent the rest of his life in his home in Cooperstown. Cooper succumbed to illness on September 14, 1851, a day before his 62nd birthday.

MAJOR WORKS AND THEMES

Cooper produced a large and heterogeneous body of work. By 1850 he had written 30 novels, more than a dozen nonfiction books including several biographies, a play, and five travel books. His fictional work included not only historical novels, but also novels of manners grouped into multivolume family sagas, satires, and a utopian-dystopian novel. Cooper's first novel, *Precaution* (1820), was a rather unconvincing imitation of Jane Austen, but *Spy* (1821) brought him commercial success as a marine novelist. In *Spy,* Cooper transplanted Sir Walter Scott's model of the historical novel to the context of the American revolutionary wars. The American past, from Columbus via the English colonial period to Cooper's present day, is his most important historical subject, though contemporary issues and social values are often addressed as well. Cooper was a defender of democracy and became an advocate of the landowners. In novels such as *Homeward Bound* and *Home as Found* (1838), he gave a fictional defense of the landowners' claims; in the *Littlepage* trilogy (1845–46) he explicitly took up the cause of the old-established large landowners of New York state. Though famous for his genre of the frontier tale, Cooper invented with *The Pilot* (1824) the genre of the sea romance, which includes *The Red Rover* (1827), *The Two Admirals* (1842), and *The Sea Lions* (1849). He also wrote the monumental *History of the Navy of the United States of America* (1839).

The question of the rightful occupation and settling of land is approached from a different perspective in the stories that made Cooper famous, the *Leatherstocking Tales.* During his entire life, Cooper regarded the European settlers' acquisition of land as deeply problematic. The Leatherstocking series consists of five novels: *The Pioneers* (1823), *The Last of the Mohicans* (1826), *The Prairie* (1827), *The Pathfinder* (1840), and *The Deerslayer* (1841). Their main protagonist is the eighteenth-century frontiersman Natty Bumppo. In *The Pioneers,* Natty Bumppo, alias Leatherstocking, is an aged man who ineffectually opposes Judge Temple and his idea of progress. The frontier exemplifies the possibilities, peculiarities, and problems of the new civilized order: the genesis of the American nation is inseparably linked with the occupation and settling of land and the transformation of wilderness into civilization. Cooper gives detailed descriptions of the social structures of Templeton, its inhabitants, buildings, social relationships, and cultural practices. The reader is offered accounts of the Christmas turkey shoots, fishing, and bird hunting, while the values and hierarchies typical of the novel of manners are also prominent. In the novel's second part, descriptions of the new form of society are increasingly overlaid with elements of adventure. This is typical of the cycle as a whole: all of Cooper's novels span the entire spectrum from the novel of manners at one end to pure adventure and romance at the other. Following the conventions of the novel of manners, a stable core of society claiming to form civilization is surrounded by a cluster of eccentric figures, usually conspicuous by their comic deviation from the ideal. Natty Bumppo, too, basically fulfills the role of the deviant. At the same time, however, he bears traits of a strong and autonomous individual that accord with the clichés of adventure story fantasies. The resulting space generates a typical dynamic for the series hero: an initially disregarded and marginalized individual experiences imaginary exaltation and idolization through the alternation of threat and heroic success.

Throughout the series, Leatherstocking remains an unalterable figure who is, from the start, identified with the vanishing wilderness and its native inhabitants. In the novels, private property and progress stand in opposition to an almost mythically drawn world of harmony between man and nature. This mythical world is drawn most distinctly in *The Last of the Mohicans,* set in the period of the colonial wars. It is the best-known and most popular of the Leatherstocking novels. The theme of betrayal is central to this novel, in which the Native American tribes are manipulated by the British and French in shifting alliances. Cooper depicts the whites passing through the wilderness as lost. In the adventure story, the social hierarchies and conventions cultivated by civilization give way to other characteristics: qualities such as physical agility, strength, capacity for learning and adaptation, and warrior-like survival strategies receive special weight. Only the Mohicans, portrayed in the mold of the "noble savage," Natty, and hostile Indian tribes such as the Iroquois can successfully negotiate this reality. The plot is dominated by flight and pursuit and includes a failing love affair between a Mohican man and a white woman. The plot structure of the novel is marked by a gradually intensifying sequence that builds its tension through the dichotomies of threat and flight, anxiety and relief, pursuit and last-minute rescue. The characters are either stylized as rescuers or made the objects of threat, as in the cases of the rather undefined blonde heroine Alice or the Indian villain Magua. The adventure begins at the point when these characters enter and begin to wander through the forests of the Indian territory. In those forests, where the novel's plot unfolds, there is no longer any significant chance of mediation between civilization and the wild.

In *The Last of the Mohicans,* reality is unstable: buildings and settlements are destroyed, temporary resting places have to be hastily abandoned, and caves fail to offer lasting protection from pursuers. These settings are matched by a range of characters that can be typologically summarized in two groups: hunters and hunted, threats and threatened. They provide the basis for the staging of melodramatic patterns of experience. The pioneer scout and his Indian companions represent the principle of guardianship. They are the new representatives of civilization's values, and in this battle for survival their heroic qualities lend them great authority. The motif of the shooting contest, recurring in almost all the Leatherstocking novels, also establishes a symbolic ranking among the male characters. The novel is an early form of the Western, featuring key elements such as the hero incapable of integration into white society and the division of the Indians into "good" and "bad" groups. At the core of the adventure discourse, which runs through all the Leatherstocking novels, is the imagination and the desire for individual strength, self-assertion, and heroism. The capacity for self-control and control of the emotions is made the most important goal of masculine autonomy and strength. At the same time, however, the series idealizes a sentimental male camaraderie and its homosocial ties. Civilized society is often figured as a threat to individual independence.

The fact that the Indians are often represented in a positive and exemplary role arises from this idealization of independence, self-assertion, and the shared social ties of the male heroes.

The Pathfinder follows Natty Bumppo's early maturity, and *The Deerslayer* his youth. Here the idealization of the series' key character is carried further. In *The Pathfinder* he appears as an American Adam; in *The Deerslayer* he is a kind of warrior saint living in the Lake Otsego region. Cooper places the pioneer, a figure previously marginalized by history, in a central and idealized role—yet ironically one isolated in the wilderness. The character of Leatherstocking is a new mythological figure in American culture. He functions as a noble helper and rescuer; as a mediator between whites and Indians, he shares the Indians' closeness to nature while also embodying the values of the Christian occident. The books in the Leatherstocking series pursue a fundamental theme of mediation between civilization and the wild. They exemplify the symbolic reintegration of all the characters with the potential to be civilized and the elimination of all forces that might disrupt this model of civilization. This developmental model, in Cooper's view, mirrors the process of human development from childhood to adulthood. His new civilizational synthesis succeeds against the backdrop of the adventure discourse and its heroic male identity images. Leatherstocking offered the reading public in the United States a figure and legend that served as a culturally binding force in a period of transition. The myth-making power of Cooper's novels played a significant role in the formation of America's national consciousness.

CRITICAL RECEPTION

Cooper was America's first author to achieve both commercial success and an international reputation as a respected novelist. At his death, Cooper was the most successful American author of his day. He gained his popularity through the *Leatherstocking Tales,* but over the last decade of his life profits from publishing diminished. The public showed little interest in his political treatises, such as *The American Democrat* (1838), or the political satire *Home As Found* (1838). Later readers of Cooper, too, restricted their attention to the Leatherstocking stories—in fact, for D. H. Lawrence, in his influential *Studies in Classic American Literature* (1923), it is Cooper's Leatherstocking novel *The Pioneers* that marks the beginning of a distinctive American literature. Mark Twain ridiculed Cooper's literary failures and the quality of his intellectual writing in the essay "Fenimore Cooper's Literary Offenses" (1895). On the other hand, Herman Melville and Joseph Conrad learned from his sea stories, particularly *The Red Rover* (1827) and *The Sea Lions* (1849).

The full recognition of Cooper as a serious writer has begun only in the past 30 years. Critics generally agree that Cooper created one of the major nineteenth-century myths with its own set of values about America. The genre of the American Western—as seen in novels and films—is the most striking example of his continued presence. Cultural historians also recognize Cooper's widely scattered social commentaries as an encyclopedic barometer of his time, and they value his power of observation despite its precipitated and biased class associations.

Until recently, the Cooper criticism has been centered along two main lines: first, the analysis of his political, social, and philosophical thought and writing; second, the interpretation of his *Leatherstocking Tales* in their historical and literary contexts. In 1931 Robert Spiller wrote his illuminating biography *Fenimore Cooper: A Critic of His Times;* and Steven Railton's *Fenimore Cooper: A Study of His Life and Imagination* (1978) summarizes Cooper's life from a more contemporary perspective. Lawrence Buell, in *New England Literary Culture: From Revolution through Renaissance* (1986), offers a general introduction to the literature of this period. As for Cooper's poetics, specially significant for single studies are Leon Howard's introduction to *The Pioneers* (1965), Ross Pudaloff's "Cooper's Genres and American Problems" (1983), Heinz Ickstadt's "Instructing the American Democrat: Cooper and the Concept of Popular Fiction in Jacksonian America" (1986), and Daniel H. Peck's, "James Fenimore Cooper and the Writers of the Frontier" (1988). James D. Wallace, *Early Cooper and His Audience* (1986), and Warren Motley, *The American Abraham: James Fenimore Cooper and the Frontier Patriarch* (1987), provide insights into the development of Cooper's career. Jay S. Kasson explores in *Artistic Voyagers: Europe and the American Imagination in the Works of Irving, Allston, Cole, Cooper and Hawthorne* (1982) how Cooper portrayed the common man. For decades the research has centered around questions on the sources and motivations of Cooper's historical fiction, on his construction of the Jacksonian democrat, or on the modes of representing the American Indian. Mary E. Cunningham's edition of essays in the volume *James Fenimore Cooper: A Re-Appraisal* (1954) is one of the first significant essay collections of Cooper research, later followed by Robert Clark's *James Fenimore Cooper: New Critical Essays* (1985) and W. M. Verhoeven's *James Fenimore Cooper: New Historical and Literary Contexts* (1993). Verhoeven's volume presents a wide range of perspectives including Cooper's relationship within his contemporary social context and his construction of a mythical America from the viewpoints of deconstruction and New Historicism.

BIBLIOGRAPHY

Works by James Fenimore Cooper

Novels
Precaution: A Novel. New York: A. T. Goodrich & Co., 1820.
The Spy: A Tale of the Neutral Ground. New York: Wiley and Halstead, 1821.
The Pilot: A Tale of the Sea. New York: Charles Wiley, 1824.
The Pioneers; or, The Source of the Susquehanna: A Descriptive Tale. New York: Charles Wiley, 1823.
Lionel Lincoln; or, The Leaguer of Boston. New York: Charles Wiley, 1825.
The Last of the Mohicans: A Narrative of 1757. Philadelphia: Carey and Lea, 1826.
The Prairie: A Tale. Philadelphia: Carey, Lea, and Carey, 1827.
The Red Rover: A Tale. Philadelphia: Carey, Lea, and Carey, 1827.
The Wept of Wish-ton-Wish: A Tale. Philadelphia: Carey, Lea, and Carey, 1829.
The Water-Witch; or, The Skimmer of the Seas: A Tale. Philadelphia: Carey and Lea, 1830.
The Bravo: A Tale. Philadelphia: Carey and Lea, 1831.
The Heidenmauer; or, The Benedictines: A Legend of the Rhine. Philadelphia: Carey, Lea, and Blanchard, 1832.
The Headsman; or, The Abayye des Vigerons: A Tale. Philadelphia: Carey, Lea, and Blanchard, 1833.
The Monikins. Philadelphia: Carey, Lea, and Blanchard, 1835.
Homeward Bound; or, The Chase: A Tale of the Sea. Philadelphia: Carey, Lea, and Blanchard, 1838.
Home as Found. Philadelphia: Lea and Blanchard, 1838.
The Pathfinder; or, The Inland Sea. Philadelphia: Lea and Blanchard, 1840.
The Deerslayer; or, The First War-Path: A Tale. Philadelphia: Lea and Blanchard, 1841.

The Two Admirals: A Tale. Philadelphia: Lea and Blanchard, 1842.

The Wing-and-Wing: or Le Feu-Follet: A Tale. Philadelphia: Lea and Blanchard, 1842.

Wyandotté; or, The Hutted Knoll: A Tale. Philadelphia: Lea and Blanchard, 1843.

Afloat and Ashore; or, The Adventures of Miles Wallingford. Philadelphia: Published by the author, 1844.

Afloat and Ashore, second series (later retitled *Miles Wallingford*). New York: Burgess, Stringer, 1844.

Satanstoe; or, The Littlepage Manuscripts: A Tale of the Colony. New York: Burgess, Stringer, 1845.

The Chainbearer; or, The Littlepage Manuscripts. New York: Burgess, Stringer, 1845.

The Crater; or, Vulcan's Peak: A Tale of the Pacific. New York: Burgess, Stringer, 1846.

The Redskins; or, Indian and Injin: Being the Conclusion to the Littlepage Manuscripts. New York: Burgess, Stringer, 1846.

Jack Tier; or, The Florida Reef. New York: Burgess, Stringer, 1848.

The Oak Openings; or, The Bee-Hunter. New York: Burgess, Stringer, 1848.

The Sea Lions; or, The Lost Sealers. New York: Stringer, Townsend, 1849.

The Ways of the Hour: A Tale. New York: G. P. Putnam, 1850.

Nonfiction Prose

Tales for Fifteen; or, Imagination and Heart. New York: Charles Wiley, 1823.

Notions of the Americans: Picked Up by a Travelling Bachelor. Philadelphia: Carey, Lea, and Carey, 1823.

A Letter to His Countrymen. New York: John Wiley, 1834.

Sketches of Switzerland: Part I. Philadelphia: Carey, Lea, and Blanchard, 1836.

Sketches of Switzerland: Part II. Philadelphia: Carey, Lea, and Blanchard, 1837.

Gleanings in Europe: France. Philadelphia: Carey, Lea, and Blanchard, 1837.

Gleanings in Europe: England. Philadelphia: Carey, Lea, and Blanchard, 1838.

The American Democrat; or, Hints on the Social and Civic Relations of the United States of America. Cooperstown, NY: H. & E. Phinney, 1838.

The Chronicles of Cooperstown. Cooperstown, NY: H. & E. Phinney, 1838.

The History of the Navy of the United States of America. Philadelphia: Lea and Blanchard, 1839.

Le Mouchoir: An Autobiographical Romance. New York: Wilson & Co., Brother Jonathan Press, 1843 (also published as *Autobiography of a Pocket Handkerchief*).

Ned Myers; or, A Life before the Mast. Philadelphia: Lea and Blanchard, 1843.

The Battle of Lake Erie. Cooperstown, NY: H. & E. Phinney, 1843.

The Cruise of the Somers. New York: J. Winchester, 1844.

Lives of Distinguished American Naval Officers. Philadelphia: Carey and Hart, 1846.

New York. New York: William Farquhar Payson, 1930.

The Lake Gun. New York: William Farquhar Payson, 1932.

Early Critical Essays (1820–1822), with introduction and headnotes by James F. Beard. Gainesville, FL: Scholar's Facsimiles & Reprints, 1955 (Cooper's book reviews, originally published in *The Literary and Scientific Repository* between 1820 and 1822).

Collected Editions

J. Fenimore Cooper's Works. Household Edition, with an introduction by Susan Fenimore Cooper to fifteen of the volumes. 32 vols. New York and Cambridge, MA: Hurd and Houghton, 1876–84.

The Works of James Fenimore Cooper. Mohawk Edition. 33 vols. (includes *Ned Myers*). New York: G. P. Putnam's Sons, 1895–96.

Correspondence of James Fenimore Cooper. Edited by James Fenimore Cooper, grandson of the author. 2 vols. New Haven, CT: Yale University Press, 1922; reissued 1971.

The Letters and Journals of James Fenimore Cooper. Edited by James F. Feard. 6 vols. Cambridge: Harvard University Press, 1960, 1964, 1968.

Studies of James Fenimore Cooper

Buell, Lawrence. *New England Literary Culture: From Revolution through Renaissance.* New York: Cambridge Univ. Press, 1986.

Clark, Robert. *History and Myth in American Fiction 1823–1852.* New York: St. Martin's, 1984.

———, ed. *James Fenimore Cooper: New Critical Essays.* New York: Vision, Barnes & Nobel, 1985.

Cunningham, Mary E., ed. *James Fenimore Cooper: A Re-Appraisal.* Cooperstown, NY: New York State Historical Association, 1954.

Darnell, Donald. *James Fenimore Cooper: Novelist of Manners.* Newark: University of Delaware Press, 1993.

Dekker, George. *James Fenimore Cooper: The Novelist.* London: Routledge & Kegan Paul, 1967.

Fields, Wayne, ed. *James Fenimore Cooper: A Collection of Critical Essays.* Englewood Cliffs, NJ: Prentice-Hall, 1979.

Franklin, Wayne. *The New World of James Fenimore Cooper.* Chicago: The University of Chicago Press, 1982.

Harbert, Earl N., and Robert A. Rees, eds. *Fifteen American Authors before 1900: Bibliographical Essays on Research and Criticism.* Madison: University of Wisconsin Press, 1984.

Howard, Leon. Introduction to *The Pioneers* by James Fenimore Cooper. New York: Holt, Rinehart, Winston, 1965. V–XVIII.

Ickstadt, Heinz. "Instructing the American Democrat: Cooper and the Concept of Popular Fiction in Jacksonian America," *Amerikastudien/American Studies.* 31.1 (1986): 17–30.

Kalter, Susan. "The Last of the Mohicans as Contemporary Theory: James Fenimore Cooper's Philosophy of Language," *James Fenimore Cooper Society Miscellaneous Papers* 11 (Aug. 1999): 1–14.

Kasson, Jay S. *Artistic Voyagers: Europe and the American Imagination in the Works of Irving, Allston, Cole, Cooper and Hawthorne.* Westport, CT: Greenwood Press, 1982.

Kelly, William P. *Plotting America's Past: Fenimore Cooper and the Leatherstocking Tales.* Carbondale & Edwardsville: Southern Illinois University Press, 1983.

Lawrence, D. H. *Studies in Classic American Literature.* 1923; rpt. Harmondsworth: Penguin, 1971: 60–69.

Motley, Warren. *The American Abraham: James Fenimore Cooper and the Frontier Patriarch.* Cambridge: Cambridge University Press, 1987.

Peck, Daniel H. "James Fenimore Cooper and the Writers of the Frontier," *Columbia Literary History of the United States.* Emory Elliott, ed. New York: Columbia University Press (1988): 240–61.

Pudaloff, Ross J. "Cooper's Genres and American Problems." *ELH* 50 (1983):711–27.

Railton, Stephen. *Fenimore Cooper: A Study of His Life and Imagination.* Princeton: Princeton University Press, 1978.

Redekop, Ernest H. "Real versus Imagined History: Cooper's European Novels," *Mosaic: A Journal for the Interdisciplinary Study of Literature* 22.4 (Fall 1989): 81–97.

Ringe, Donald A. *James Fenimore Cooper.* New York: Twayne Publishers, 1962.

Spiller, Robert E. *Fenimore Cooper: A Critic of His Times.* New York: Minton, Balch & Co., 1931.

Spiller, Robert E., and Philip C. Blackburn. *A Descriptive Bibliography of the Writings of James Fenimore Cooper.* New York: Bowker, 1934.

Shulenberger, Arvid. *Cooper's Theory of Fiction His Prefaces and Their Relation to His Novels.* Lawrence: Univ. of Kansas Press, 1955.

Starobin, Christina. "Reading Cooper," *James Fenimore Society Miscellaneous Papers.* 6 (Aug. 1995): 10–12.

Summerlin, Mitchell Eugene. *A Dictionary to the Novels of James Fenimore Cooper.* Greenwood, FL: Penkevill, 1987.

Swann, Charles. "James Fenimore Cooper: Historical Novelist," Richard Gray; ed. & intro. *American Fictions: New Readings.* London: Barnes & Noble, 1983.

Test, George A., ed. *James Fenimore Cooper: His Country and His Art. Papers from the Bicentennial Conference, 1989.* Oneonta: State University of New York at Oneonta, 1991.

Twain, Mark. "Fenimore Cooper's Literary Offenses." *North American Review* (July) 1895. (published in: Twain, Mark. *How to Tell a Story and Other Essays.* New York: Harper & Brothers, 1897).

Verhoeven, W. M., ed. *James Fenimore Cooper: New Historical and Literary Contexts.* Amsterdam: Rodopi, 1993.

Walker, Warren S. *James Fenimore Cooper: An Introduction and Interpretation.* New York: Barnes & Noble, 1962.

Wallace, James D. *Early Cooper and His Audience.* New York: Columbia University Press, 1986.

CHRISTOPHER PEARSE CRANCH
(1813–1892)

Todd Richardson

BIOGRAPHY

Christopher Pearse Cranch published hundreds of poems and articles, four collections of poetry, a popular translation of Virgil's *Aeneid,* two children's books, and countless landscape paintings. He was easily the most versatile of the Transcendentalists, yet scholars have consistently judged him to be a mere dilettante, in part because Cranch's playful and free-spirited oeuvre has been evaluated by the same standards as have the works of his austere cohorts.

Cranch, the youngest of 13 children, was born on March 8, 1813, in Alexandria, Virginia. William Cranch, the boy's father, was a staunch Federalist who had been appointed by his uncle, John Adams, to a federal judgeship in the District of Columbia. Also a steadfast Boston Unitarian, the elder Cranch required that his wife and children kneel around him for their daily prayers. Christopher Cranch attended what is now George Washington University and the Harvard Divinity School, from which he graduated in 1835. It was there that Cranch first came in contact with radical Unitarian theology through such friends as Theodore Parker and John Sullivan Dwight. Upon graduation, Cranch's idealism prompted him to go west to promote liberal theology, and he served as an itinerant preacher in such cities as Peoria, St. Louis, and Cincinnati. In Louisville, Cranch supplied James Freeman Clarke's pulpit and served as an editor for the *Western Messenger.* In that capacity, he supported Ralph Waldo Emerson's criticism of institutional religion. Revealing his playful demeanor, Cranch also began drawing his outlandish caricatures of Emerson and other Transcendentalists.

Disillusioned with the harsh realities of the West, Cranch returned to Boston in 1839, where he further immersed himself in Transcendentalist activity. Emerson became a mentor of central importance to Cranch; he encouraged the young minister's artistic interests while he discouraged his pursuit of a career in the ministry. Like Emerson, Cranch ultimately experienced a vocational crisis, and by 1842, he confessed to his mentor that "I became more and more inclined to sink the minister into the man, and abandon my present calling *in toto* as a profession. . . . A clergyman's life is the life of a slave.

He cannot be a man. He cannot own a soul, and a mouth of his own" (Scott 60). Cranch ultimately abandoned the ministry for good in favor of a career in the arts. For his friendship at this crucial time, Cranch dedicated his first collection of poems to Emerson.

By this time, Cranch had begun painting landscapes in the style of the Hudson River school, a pursuit encouraged by his wife, Elizabeth De Windt. Although he never attained fame as an artist, he was quite prolific. In order to develop his craft, he spent most of the next 20 years in Italy and France. While abroad, he continued to write professionally for numerous periodicals, and he penned and illustrated two children's books, *The Last of the Huggermuggers* and a sequel, *Kobboltozo.* The books were quite popular, and they remained in print well into the twentieth century. The Cranch family returned to America in 1863 when Christopher's son George enlisted in the Union army; the young man was killed shortly thereafter.

Cranch spent the last decades of his life in Cambridge, Massachusetts, where he resumed his active engagement in New England cultural life with his old Transcendentalist friends. In addition to writing for such popular magazines as *Harper's,* the *Atlantic, Putnam's,* and *Lippincott's,* he produced three volumes of poetry: *Satan: A Libretto, The Bird and the Bell,* and *Ariel and Caliban.* Cranch died quietly at home in 1892.

MAJOR WORKS AND THEMES

Since his boyhood, Cranch had an interest in the arts, but it took the permission granted by radical Unitarianism for him to pursue these interests professionally. His struggle against the restrictive old school Unitarianism of his father is particularly apparent in his passionate apologies for the "New School" in the *Western Messenger.* In his "Specimens of Foreign Standard Literature" (1838), for example, Cranch promoted the work of new thinkers such as Victor Cousin, Théodore Simon Jouffroy, and G. W. F. Hegel over and against the old Lockean philosophy which had so strongly influenced Unitarianism. In "Transcendentalism" (1841), Cranch further argued that "the friends of truth cannot but rejoice in these signs of progress: to see obstinate prejudices wearing down—old errors falling away by piecemeal—the spirit of bigotry subsiding—and the spirit of liberality extending" (405).

That Cranch never lost his charming sense of humor even in the midst of theological controversy is particularly evident in his caricatures of his Transcendentalist friends. For example, parodying the line from Emerson's *Nature,* "I expend and live in the warm day, like corn and melons," Cranch drew a large figure, half man, half melon, reposing comfortably in his melon patch. Most famously, Cranch parodied the infamous line from *Nature,* "Standing on the bare ground, my head bathed in blithe air, and uplifted into infinite space, all mean egotism vanishes. I become a transparent eyeball." Cranch's depiction of a giant eyeball on long spindly legs dressed in a swallow-tailed coat is now a standard feature in many high school textbooks.

After Cranch returned to Boston, the hotbed of Transcendentalism, he began to write poetry for the *Dial,* the brainchild of Emerson and Margaret Fuller. His contributions to this endeavor have become his most prominent, partly because they express the movement's philosophical tenets with a refreshing and sometimes playful enthusiasm. In "To the Aurora Borealis" (1840), for example, the natural phenomenon becomes a metaphor for the brilliant power of the human soul which can uncover itself only when the powers of convention, represented by the daylight, are extinguished. "Correspondences" (1841) exults in Swedenborg's theory of that name, which argues that all natural facts stand for those spiritual. In the poem, Cranch suggests that the mysteries of heaven are to be discovered only by those with eyes to see. He also contributed darker musings to the *Dial,* such as "Enosis" (1840) and "Outworld" (1842), which reveal frustration with the limitations of human understanding. "What [is] our wise philosophy / But the glancing of a dream?" he asks in "Enosis." In "Outworld," a spirit dictates that the poetic persona will be forever imprisoned within the confines of time and space, rendering him forever unable to attain the truths which he "pinest for." When Cranch returned to poetry after a moderately successful career as a painter, he revived his poetic interest in the limits of knowledge and communication in numerous poems including "The American Pantheon" (1873), "Luna through a Lorgnette" (1875), and "The Poet's Soliloquy" (1885). Even though these later efforts reveal much greater technical ability than do the earlier poems, they are typically understood to be steeped in a Transcendental philosophy that had grown unfashionable, and are therefore ignored.

CRITICAL RECEPTION

Cranch's modern-day reputation has rested primarily upon his amusing caricatures, particularly the transparent eyeball. The persistence of this outrageous image has led to its adaptation in some contexts of popular culture. Members of a performance art band known as The Residents, for example, have appeared in concert for three decades dressed in tails and bulging eyeball masks.

Cranch himself, however, had reason to believe that his posthumous reputation would rest on his poetry. "Enosis" and "Correspondences" were collected in dozens of anthologies in the nineteenth century, and his works were sometimes well received. For example, Edgar Allan Poe, notorious for his hostile reviews aimed especially at Transcendentalists, found much to praise in Cranch. For Poe, *Poems* (1844) offered "an unusual vivacity of fancy and dexterity of expression, while his versification is remarkable for its accuracy, vigor, and even for its originality of effect" (*Godey's* 18). Two years later, he referred to Cranch as "One of our finest poets" (*Messenger* 673).

In recent years, however, his works have largely dropped out of circulation, except when they have been referenced to throw cross lights on Emerson or Transcendentalism generally. Perhaps the article most responsible for defining Cranch's status as a secondary poet in academic circles has been J. C. Levenson's "Christopher Pearse Cranch: The Case History of a Minor Artist in America." Taking his cue from Henry James, who blandly noted that Cranch "left verses that the American compiler sometimes includes" (1:110), Levenson offered a critical assessment that insists on the "unrelieved ordinariness of Cranch's mind" (423). Levenson concluded that Cranch "deserves remembrance as a private in the ranks of those who struggled for the birth of American art" (426). Scholars working to enhance Cranch's reputation in the past 25 years have been compelled to address Levenson's stingy praise; they have not been particularly successful, however, given the fact that the most comprehensive study of Cranch's life and works remains Frederick DeWolfe Miller's unpublished dissertation "Christopher Pearse Cranch: New England Transcendentalist." Additionally, much of Cranch's work remains in manuscript and his voluminous contributions to periodicals have never been collected. Nevertheless, excellent monographs have appeared on Cranch's artistic endeavors, including David Robinson's "Christopher Pearse Cranch," which argues that Cranch's poetry has been underrated; Julie M. Norko's "Christopher Pearse Cranch's Struggle with the Muses," which shows that Cranch was motivated by a sense of vocational duty more than a directionless aestheticism as is typically charged; and Shelley Armitage's "Christopher Pearse Cranch: The Wit as Poet," which provides solid analyses of some much-neglected later poems. Although such serious scholarly attention has been sporadic, its high quality suggests that Cranch's oeuvre will, in its own right, continue to sustain critical inquiry in the coming decades.

WORKS CITED

Cranch, Christopher Pearse. "Transcendentalism." *Western Messenger* 8 (January 1841): 405–09.
———. "Enosis" 1840.
———. "Outworld" 1842.
James, Henry. *William Wetmore Story.* 2 vols. London: Thames and Hudson, 1957.
Levenson, J. C. "Christopher Pearse Cranch: The Case History of a Minor Artist in America." *American Literature* 21 (1949–50): 415–26.
Poe, Edgar Allan. "Literati of New York City." *Godey's Lady's Book* 33 (September 1846): 18–19.
———. "The Rationale of Verse." *Southern Literary Messenger* 14 (November 1848): 673–82.
Scott, Lenora Cranch. *The Life and Letters of Christopher Pearse Cranch.* Boston: Houghton, Mifflin: 1917.

BIBLIOGRAPHY

Works by Christopher Pearse Cranch

Poetry
A Poem Delivered in the First Congregational Church in the Town of Quincy, May 25, 1840, the Two Hundredth Anniversary of the Incorporation of the Town. Boston: James Munroe, 1840.
Poems. Philadelphia: Carey and Hart, 1844.
Satan: A Libretto. Boston: Roberts, 1874.
The Bird and the Bell, with Other Poems. Boston: James R. Osgood, 1875.
Ariel and Caliban with Other Poems. Boston: James R. Osgood, 1875.
Collected Poems of Christopher Pearse Cranch. Edited by Joseph M. De Falco. Gainsville: Scholars' Facsimiles and Reprints, 1971.

Essays
"To My Sister M., with Wordsworth's Poems." *Western Messenger* 4 (February 1838): 376–76.
"Specimens of Foreign Standard Literature." *Western Messenger* 5 (June 1838): 197–202.
"Transcendentalism." *Western Messenger* 8 (January 1841): 405–09.
Address Delivered before the Harvard Musical Association. Boston: S. N. Dickinson, 1845.
"Ralph Waldo Emerson." *Unitarian Review* 20 (July 1883): 1–19.
"Personal Reminiscences." *In Memoriam. Memorial to Robert Browning.* Cambridge, England: Browning Society, 1890. 48–53.
"Emerson's Limitations as a Poet." *Critic* (New York) n.s. 17 (27 February 1892): 129.

Translation
The Aeneid *of Virgil Translated into English Blank Verse.* Boston: James R. Osgood, 1872.

Juvenile Literature
The Last of the Huggermuggers. Boston: Phillips, Sampson, 1856.
Kobboltozo: A Sequel to the Last of the Huggermuggers. Boston: Phillips, Sampson, 1857.
Three Children's Novels by Christopher Pearse Cranch. Edited with a critical introduction by Greta D. Little and Joel Myerson. Athens: University of Georgia Press, 1993.

Studies of Christopher Pearse Cranch

Armitage, Shelley. "Christopher Pearse Cranch: The Wit as Poet." *American Transcendental Quarterly* n.s. 1, no. 1 (1987): 33–47.

Carpenter, Hazen C. "Emerson and Christopher Pearse Cranch." *New England Quarterly* 37 no. 1 (1964): 18–42.

Levenson, J. C. "Christopher Pearse Cranch: The Case History of a Minor Artist in America." *American Literature* 21 (1949–50): 415–26.

Miller, Frederick DeWolfe. "Christopher Pearse Cranch and his Caricatures of New England Transcendentalism." Cambridge: Harvard University Press, 1951.

———. "Christopher Pearse Cranch: New England Transcendentalist." Diss., University of Virginia, 1942.

Norko, Julie M. "Christopher Pearse Cranch's Struggle with the Muses." *Studies in the American Renaissance* (1992): 209–27.

Robinson, David. "Christopher Pearse Cranch." *The Transcendentalists.* Edited by Joel Myerson. New York: the Modern Language Association of America, 1984.

Scott, Lenora Cranch. *The Life and Letters of Christopher Pearse Cranch.* Boston: Houghton, Mifflin: 1917.

Williams, Paul O. "The Persistence of Cranch's 'Enosis.'" *ESQ: A Journal of the American Renaissance* 57, no. 4 (1969): 41–46.

MARIA SUSANNA CUMMINS (1827–1866)

Theresa J. Flowers

BIOGRAPHY

Born on April 9, 1827, Maria Susanna Cummins was the daughter of David Cummins and Mehitable Cave Cummins. David Cummins had four children from his first two marriages, and three children were born after Maria. He was a Dartmouth graduate of the class of 1806, a lawyer and judge. Mehitable Cave was descended from a long line of physicians and was the granddaughter of Dr. Thomas Kittredge. Maria Cummins's earliest years were spent in Salem, Massachusetts, where her father was the judge of the court of common pleas in Norfolk County. The family later moved to Dorchester where Cummins spent the rest of her life. Her father educated her at home and was very interested in her literary career. She studied the classics with her father and was later sent to the fashionable Young Ladies School of Mrs. Charles Sedgwick in Lennox, Massachusetts, where Cummins met Mrs. Sedgwick's sister-in-law, Catherine Sedgwick. Some critics have suggested that perhaps the young Cummins was inspired by Sedgwick's literary career and adopted her as a role model for her own literary aspirations. After finishing at the Sedgwick school, Cummins remained unmarried and spent the rest of her life at the family residence. In her early twenties she published short stories that appeared in the *Atlantic*. Like most other women writing at that time, Cummins published her novels anonymously. However, Cummins's reluctance to place her name on her work was probably also due to an apprehension of becoming a public spectacle. This unease was emphasized by her shy, secluded life in Dorchester and the fact that she never married. After her father's death, she lived a quiet existence, devoting her life to writing and working in the church. In spite of her low-key existence, in 1854 she published *The Lamplighter,* which sold 40,000 copies in the first two months and 100,000 copies in the first decade. Maria Susanna Cummins died on October 1, 1866, at the age of 39.

MAJOR WORKS AND THEMES

The Lamplighter tells the story of an orphan girl, Gerty, who is mistreated by her caretaker and subsequently adopted by an old lamplighter, Trueman Flint. Through his love and the assistance of a prosperous blind woman who teaches Gerty about God and helps her to control her emotions, Gerty grows to be a virtuous young woman by the end of the novel. After much suffering, Gerty is rewarded by being married to her childhood friend and confidant and by being reunited with the father she thought was dead. *The Lamplighter* was frequently translated and published as a children's book. Cummins's motive for writing *The Lamplighter* is not clear. Accounts from the nineteenth century suggest that she was not aware of her gift for writing and that she wrote the novel without a concern for publication. She may have written the novel to entertain her nieces by reading it to them in installments (Williams 184). *The Lamplighter* is known for its sentimentality and devotion to home and family. Cummins leads Gerty through domestic problems and then allows her to find true love, thus providing a happy ending—the stock characteristics of the domestic or sentimental novel of the nineteenth century.

Besides *The Lamplighter*, Cummins wrote three novels before her death in 1866: *Mabel Vaughan* (1857), *El Fureidis* (1860), and *Haunted Hearts* (1864). The second novel, *Mabel Vaughan*, does not feature an orphan as does *The Lamplighter*. Instead Cummins creates a young girl who is beset by a series of misfortunes. The once affluent young woman finds herself cast into poverty with a melancholy father, an alcoholic brother, and two hopeless nephews. Much of the novel is set in the West. As with *The Lamplighter*, *Mabel Vaughan* incorporates calamities, long-lost relatives, and the reform of rogue characters. *El Fureidis*, Cummins's third novel, is a story set in Palestine and Syria. This is a tale of romance between an Englishman and an Arab woman. Because she is free of the inhibitions known to the women of Cummins's reading audience, the woman, Havilah, expresses her feelings and desires in a very unconventional manner by nineteenth-century standards. Cummins's fourth and final novel, *Haunted Hearts*, is a historical work set during the War of 1812. This work revolves around the heroine, Angela Cousins, who is blamed for the suicide of her lover who ultimately reappears and saves her reputation.

CRITICAL RECEPTION

Cummins's best known work, *The Lamplighter*, was outsold only by *Uncle Tom's Cabin*, which was published two years earlier. *The Lamplighter* also outsold *The Wide, Wide World*, Susan Warner's best-selling novel. The success of *The Lamplighter* prompted Nathaniel Hawthorne's famous protest about the "damned mob of scribbling women" to his publisher William Ticknor in 1855 (*Letters* 75). *The Lamplighter* was also published in England and translated into French, German, Danish, and Italian. The success of *The Lamplighter* has been attributed to Cummins's reliance on the styles of Dickens and the Brontë sisters. Because it expressed values of self-sacrifice and maternal power that were inherent in the middle-class society of the time, *The Lamplighter* was approved reading for women. Reading was seen as a fruitful exercise for women in their leisure time, and the novel provided entertainment while immersing women in thoughts and ideas of virtue. Women enjoyed the story while husbands enjoyed the virtuous influence. Interestingly enough, the success of the novel was based on as many sales in England as in America. At least 13 different British firms published *The Lamplighter*, some in multiple editions. The novel appeared by name in James Joyce's *Ulysses* when he commented, "Soon the lamplighter would be going his rounds . . . like she read in that book *The Lamplighter* by Miss Cummins, author of *Mabel Vaughan* and other tales" (Joyce 298). *The Lamplighter* was also popular in Europe. In 1854 a German publisher published the novel as part of his Collections of British Authors series (Williams 198).

Despite the critical comments of Nathaniel Hawthorne, Cummins was in great demand by her reading public. The editor of the *Boston Gazette* wanted to pay her $50 for another story, and the *American Union* was willing for Cummins to state her own terms for another work (Saulsbury 82). When Cummins published *Mabel Vaughan* in 1857, many critics felt that it was a better novel than *The Lamplighter.* This new work was widely read but did not approach *The Lamplighter* in sales. Neither of the two additional novels, *El Fureidis* or *Haunted Hearts,* achieved the popularity of *The Lamplighter.*

WORKS CITED

Joyce, James. *Ulysses.* New York: Vintage, 1986.

Letters of Hawthorne to William D. Ticknor, 1851–1864. Vol. 1. Newark, NJ: Carteret Book Club, 1910. Reprint, NCR/Microcard Editions, Washington, D.C., 1972.

Saulsbury, Rebecca. "Maria Susanna Cummins." *Nineteenth-Century Women Writers: A Bio-Bibliographical Sourcebook.* Ed. Denise D. Knight. Westport, Conn.: Greenwood Press, 1997. 81–87.

Williams, Susan S. " 'Promoting an Extensive Sale'—The Production and Reception of *The Lamplighter.*" *New England Quarterly* 69 (1996): 179–200.

BIBLIOGRAPHY

Works by Maria Susanna Cummins

The Lamplighter. Boston: John P. Jewett & Co.; Cleveland: Jewett, Proctor and Worthington, 1854.

Mabel Vaughan. Boston: John P. Jewett & Co.; Cleveland: Henry P.B. Jewett; London: Sampson Low, Son & Co., 1857.

El Fureidis. Boston: Ticknor and Fields, 1860.

Haunted Hearts. Boston: J. E. Tilton and Co., 1864.

Studies of Maria Susanna Cummins

Bauermeister, Erica R. "*The Lamplighter, The Wide, Wide World,* and *Hope Leslie:* Reconsidering the Recipes for Nineteenth-Century Women's Novels." *Legacy: A Journal of Nineteenth-Century Women Writers* 8.1 (1991): 17–28.

Baym, Nina. *A Guide to Novels by and About Women in America 1820–1870.* Ithaca: Cornell UP, 1978. 2nd ed. Urbana and Champaign: U of Illinois P, 1993.

———. *Novels, Readers, and Reviewers: Responses to Fiction in Antebellum America.* Ithaca: Cornell UP, 1984.

Brown, Herbert Ross. *The Sentimental Novel in America, 1789–1860.* Durham, N.C.: Duke UP, 1940.

Cooper, Allene. "Maria Susanna Cummins." *The Oxford Companion to Women's Writing in the United States.* Eds. Cathy N. Davidson and Linda Wagner-Martin. New York: Oxford UP, 1995. 230–31.

Cowie, Alexander. *The Rise of the American Novel.* New York: American Book Company, 1951.

Dobson, Joanne. "The Hidden Hand: Subversion of a Cultural Ideology in Three Mid-Nineteenth-Century Women's Novels." *American Quarterly* 38 (1986): 223–42.

Ginsberg, Elaine K. "Maria Susanna Cummins." *American Women Writers: A Critical Reference Guide From Colonial Times to the Present.* Ed. Lina Mainiero. Vol. 1. New York: Frederick Unger, 1979. 436–37.

Harris, Susan K. *19th Century American Women's Novels: Interpretive Strategies.* Cambridge: Cambridge UP, 1990.

Kelley, Mary. *Private Women, Public Stage: Literary Domesticity in Nineteenth-Century America.* New York: Oxford UP, 1984.

Mott, Frank Luther. *Golden Multitudes: The Story of Best Sellers in the United States.* New York: Macmillan Co., 1947.

Papashvily, Helen Waite. *All the Happy Endings.* New York: Harper, 1956.

Saulsbury, Rebecca. "Maria Susanna Cummins." *Nineteenth-Century Women Writers: A Bio-Bibliographical Sourcebook.* Ed. Denise D. Knight. Westport, Conn.: Greenwood Press, 1997. 81–7.

Schueller, Malini Johar. *U.S. Orientalisms: Race, Nation, and Gender in Literature, 1790–1890.* Ann Arbor: U of Michigan P, 1998.

Williams, Susan S. " 'Promoting and Extensive Sale': The Production and Reception of *The Lamplighter.*" *New England Quarterly* 69 (1996): 179–200.

REBECCA HARDING DAVIS (1831–1910)

Terry Novak

BIOGRAPHY

Rebecca Harding Davis was born Rebecca Blaine Harding on June 24, 1831, in Washington, Pennsylvania. She was the oldest of five children born to Rachel Wilson Harding and Richard W. Harding, parents who were considered financially prosperous. When Rebecca was five, the family moved to Wheeling, Virginia, a river and border town teeming with possibilities and home to steel mills. Here Mr. Harding became a successful businessman as well as a public official. Both of Davis's parents were great storytellers; her father spun fictional tales while her mother told stories of her own life. In addition, Davis heard family tales of the American Revolution and the Indian Wars from relatives. As a young child, Davis was tutored at home by her mother, who herself was well educated and highly intellectual. Mrs. Harding instilled a love of history and literature in her daughter while Mr. Harding kept political and social debates going in the home. Later in her childhood Davis was supplied with a hired tutor to take over the mother's former teaching duties. At age 14 she was sent to the Washington Female Seminary back in her own birthplace and her mother's hometown of Washington, Pennsylvania. Three years later, in 1848, Rebecca Harding graduated from the seminary with honors and returned to her parents' home. There she continued her education on her own, with the help of her brother, with whom she had a close intellectual bond and who had a more advanced formal education than she, and with the help of his old textbooks. The young Rebecca Harding was determined to fill and use her mind.

Rebecca Harding did not marry Lemuel Clarke Davis until 1863, when she was almost 33 and nearly 15 years after she had returned home from Washington Female Seminary. Such a time span between formal education and marriage would have caused many other women of Rebecca Harding's social class great consternation, but this does not appear to have been the case with Rebecca. During this 15-year time span Rebecca Harding was hard at work on her craft of writing, working occasionally for the *Wheeling Intelligencer,* and immersing herself in the best kind of real-life experience she could manage for a woman of her standing in her time: she had the habit of taking long walks about Wheeling in order to see a bit of life firsthand. It is presumed that she ventured far enough into the bowels of the mining town to see a variety of depths of despair from which she had long been sheltered by her family. In her work for the *Intelligencer* she wrote satirical editorials for a column called "Women and Politics." It is here that Davis had her writing apprenticeship, and it is here that she first learned to tone down her writing for the sake of appeasing a male editor.

All of Davis's life experiences—the family stories, the educational means, the walks through the mill town, the teeth-cutting at the newspaper—brought her the ability to write on the social topics she tackles often in her writing. In 1861 her story "Life in the Iron-Mills" was published in the *Atlantic Monthly,* a widely respected vehicle of literary mastery then as it is now. From the beginning, Davis learned that in order to be successful she was going to have to abide by editorial judgments in which she did not necessarily believe. She battled with *Atlantic Monthly* editor James T. Fields on the title of "Life in the Iron-Mills," a battle that she ultimately won. That same year she submitted the manuscript "The Deaf and the Dumb" to Fields, who advised her to change both the name of the title and the ending of the story. Davis conceded to the changes and "A Story of Today" was accepted for serialization in Fields's publication. The following year, 1862, the story was published as the novel *Margret Howth: A Story of Today* by the publishing house Ticknor and Fields.

In 1862 Rebecca Harding also traveled to Boston to meet James T. Fields and his wife Annie, with whom she struck up a long-lasting friendship. She also visited Nathaniel and Sophia Hawthorne in Boston, then traveled to Philadelphia to meet with Lemuel Clarke Davis, who had been writing to her for some time and who had traveled earlier in the year to visit her in Wheeling. It was during this visit of Rebecca's to Philadelphia that Harding and Davis became engaged. The two were married on March 5, 1863, and Rebecca moved to Philadelphia. That same year Davis became pregnant and suffered from a serious depression, perhaps complicated by the fact that she and her husband were living in the home of his sister. The following spring Davis lost her father; a month later, in April, Rebecca Harding Davis gave birth to a son, Richard Harding Davis. Later that year the family moved into their own home. By the end of the year Rebecca's depression had lifted.

Rebecca continued her writing and publishing. In 1866 she gave birth to a second son, Charles Belmont Davis. The following year her Civil War novel, *Waiting for the Verdict,* was published. Her third and last child, Nora, was born in 1872, again amidst a flurry of publishing activity. Rebecca produced a tremendous amount of writing, including five more novels, a collection of short fiction, an autobiography, and countless newspaper pieces, before her life began to wind down in 1904 with the death of her husband. She herself lived six more years, though there is no evidence of writing productivity in these years. In fact, by this time the literary career of her son Richard had become more important to the reading public. Rebecca Harding Davis died on September 29, 1910, at the home of her son Richard, after having suffered a stroke.

MAJOR WORKS AND THEMES

The work of Rebecca Harding Davis largely came to the attention of the reading public with the publication of "Life in the Iron-Mills," which remains an important work. "Life" is a remarkable example of both realism and naturalism, especially considering the fact that Davis led a fairly sheltered life. Davis writes of class struggles, poverty, and the unfairness of society in setting the haves against the have-nots. In many ways, she is preaching to her own social class in this story and attempting to make them see the humanity and the suffering of the poor working class. "Life" is very much about labor issues, but it is also about survival and creation. The protagonist Hugh Wolfe is an artist, but he has none of the advantages of the higher classes, and so he remains trapped in a frustrating life. Even so, Davis allows his creativity to come through. Themes of immigrant workers and women laborers also predominate this story. Both Hugh and the character Deborah are immigrants. Davis uses Deborah to shed light on the differences in society's treatment of women of different classes.

Davis continues with her themes of social consciousness in her first novel, *Margret Howth* (1862). The character Margret Howth is a young woman who grows up in a middle class society but who ends up, through no fault of her own, a member of the working class. Margret's job is in the office, not in the factory, and she does find her way out through marriage—an ending Davis did not originally plan for—but she still serves the purpose of attempting to enlighten the upper classes on labor issues. Even more important to this theme is the mulatta character Lois. A visible symbol of the destruction with which factory life often leaves the lives of the poor, Lois is also a symbol of the forgiving, gentle woman who attempts to see the best in others as a means of helping to make the world a better place. Lois is largely silenced by society in the novel, but the reader cannot miss the points that Davis is trying to make with her. Both Margaret and Lois possess nineteenth-century feminist qualities, qualities of quiet strength and perseverance through all odds.

"Life in the Iron-Mills" and *Margret Howth* are Davis's premarriage works. As she entered into a new phase of her life, she continued to focus on realism and social issues in her writing. *Waiting for the Verdict* (1867) tackles Civil War issues, including the ramifications of one's race. As Jean Pfaelzer puts it, "*Waiting for the Verdict* goes beyond freedom—the ending of most slave narratives—and considers the meaning of the freedom that has already been gained, using the novel's conventions empirically to explore the difficult future of race relations in the North" (140). In an often sentimental style, the novel explores the intertwined lives of plantation owner Garrick Randolph and the surgeon Dr. John Broderip, a mulatto passing as white. Davis examines the complexities of post–Civil War race issues, including the hypocrisy of some white abolitionists as well as the deep-seated issues of miscegenation and passing.

Davis followed *Waiting for the Verdict* with the political novel *John Andross* (1874). *John Andross* preaches against the corruption of politicians, something at the forefront of the news at the time, and in many ways argues for women's suffrage, the idea being that with women's higher moral standing—a popular nineteenth-century belief—infused into the world of politics, acts of corruption would surely lessen. Davis presents the character John Andross as the morally weak and corrupt politician and the character Anna Maddox as the morally superior but powerless woman who becomes a bystander in life.

Davis continued her themes of social justice throughout all of her works. Both *Kitty's Choice* (1873) and *A Law Unto Herself* (1878), for example, explicitly use themes of women's issues. Such themes are also evident in many of her shorter works. Rebecca Harding Davis had a deep sense of spirituality, although she did not necessarily believe in all that her Episcopalian upbringing had attempted to teach her. Still, one notices a definite sense of the urgent need for justice and for respect of all peoples in her writing. One also notices, of course, some themes that fit handily into the nineteenth century's views on women. Davis did allow her editors to convince her that certain endings—i.e., the tidy marriage of the heroine—would satisfy readers more than would endings of blatant female independence. Davis was without a doubt a product of her times. She also shows in her writings, however, that she was well aware of the need for social reform on many levels.

CRITICAL RECEPTION

The publication of Rebecca Harding's "Life in the Iron-Mills" garnered her much popular as well as critical attention. Not only was her initial editor, James T. Fields, impressed with her work, but so were Nathaniel Hawthorne, Louisa May Alcott, and Ralph Waldo Emerson. "Life" became—and continues to be—the driving force behind any discussion of Rebecca Harding Davis's work, even though she wrote literally hundreds of pieces in the nearly 50 years following the publication of "Life." Her writing sold tolerably well during most of her lifetime, but as she came to the end of her life, the work of her sons, particularly that of Richard Harding Davis, far outshadowed Rebecca's own work. Indeed, even her own obituary makes more of her relationship to her then-famous son than it does to her own literary work. And so it stands to reason that this slow but steady silencing of Davis led author Tillie Olsen to devote a large section of the 1972 edition of her book *Silences* to Rebecca Harding Davis, using the same long essay she wrote for the 1972 Feminist Press reprint of "Life in the Iron-Mills" as a "rediscovered classic." Davis, who had often been silenced by her male editors and whose words were long silenced by the male-dominated literary establishment, was given a renewed voice through Olsen's scholarship. Subsequently, Olsen's work led to an even closer and more carefully accurate study of Davis and all of her writing through the scholarship of Sharon M. Harris in the early 1990s. Other critics have followed suit, bringing Davis ever closer to the attention and acceptance due her work.

Sharon M. Harris acknowledges the debt of literary history to Tillie Olsen's work, but also strongly disagrees with Olsen on three main points concerning Davis: Harris persuasively demonstrates Davis's life as a reclusive one; Harris proves that Davis did not "fade away" after "Life in the Iron-Mills"; and Harris asserts that Davis was *intentionally* a social historian. Such work has led to an array of contemporary scholarship and criticism on Davis's work. Most of this work continues to be from a feminist perspective, combined with discussions of social and cultural history.

As Cecelia Tichi notes, " Most readers agree that *Life in the Iron-Mills* is Davis's best work. . . . [T]he issues Davis brought before the public—class conflict, work conditions, gender identity, art education and production, immigration, technological change, and spiritual values—remain compelling because they constitute some of the nation's most crucial, contemporary, and intractable concerns even at the turn of the twenty-first century" (25). Others, such as Jean Pfaelzer, believe that *Margret Howth* and *Waiting for the Verdict* are most important in our particular period of time. Still others, like Sharon M. Harris, have begun to focus on Davis's other writings, including her short stories, which are often extremely important to an understanding of her life at the moment of writing.

There is little current negative criticism of Davis's work. Much attention is given to her use of sentimentalism and to her relenting to the demands of editors to change scenes and endings of her books. For the most part, though, these criticisms are couched in rhetoric that excuses Davis from any culpability in the matters. By and large Davis is seen as a feminist writer of the nineteenth century who dared to touch upon the important, critical issues of the day.

WORKS CITED

Pfaelzer, Jean. *Parlor Radical: Rebecca Harding Davis and the Origins of American Social Realism.* Pittsburgh: University of Pittsburgh Press, 1996.

Tichi, Cecelia, ed. Introduction to *Life in the Iron-Mills* by Rebecca Harding Davis. Boston: Bedford Books, 1998.

BIBLIOGRAPHY

Works by Rebecca Harding Davis

Novels
Margret Howth: A Story of Today. 1862. Rpt. New York: Feminist Press, 1990.
Waiting for the Verdict. 1867. Rptd. Upper Saddle River, NJ: Gregg, 1968.
Dallas Galbraith. Philadelphia: Lippincott, 1868.
Kitty's Choice, or Berrytown and Other Stories. Philadelphia: Lippincott, 1873.
John Andross. New York: Orange Judd, 1874.
A Law Unto Herself. Philadelphia: Lippincott, 1878.
Natasqua. New York: Cassell, 1886.
Kent Hampden. New York: Scribner's, 1892.
Doctor Warrick's Daughters. New York: Harper, 1896.
Frances Waldeaux. New York: Harper, 1897.

Short Stories
"Life in the Iron-Mills." *Atlantic Monthly* 7 (April 1861): 430–51.
"John Lamar." *Atlantic Monthly* 9 (April 1862): 411–23.
"David Gaunt." *Atlantic Monthly* 10 (September–October 1862): 259–71; 403–21.
"The Wife's Story." *Atlantic Monthly* 14 (July 1864): 1–19.
"In the Market." *Peterson's Magazine* 53 (January 1868):49–57.
"Marcia." *Harper's New Monthly* 53 (November 1876): 925–28.
"Anne." *Harper's New Monthly* 78 (April 1889): 744–50.

Nonfiction
"The Middle-Aged Woman." *Scribner's Monthly* 10 (July 1875): 345–47.
"A Word to the Colored People." *Independent* 41 (September 1889): 1169.
"Women in Literature." *Independent* 43 (May 1891): 612.
"The Curse of Education." *North American Review* 168 (May 1899): 609–14.
Bits of Gossip. Boston: Houghton, 1904.

Studies of Rebecca Harding Davis

Davis, Rebecca Harding. *Life in the Iron-Mills.* Bedford Cultural Editions. Ed. Cecelia Tichi. Boston: Bedford Books, 1998.

Harris, Sharon M. *Rebecca Harding Davis and American Realism.* Philadelphia: University of Pennsylvania Press, 1991.

———. "Redefining the Feminine: Women and Work in Rebecca Harding Davis's 'In the Market.' " *Legacy* 8 (Fall 1991): 118–121.

Lasseter, Janice Milner, and Sharon M. Harris, eds. *Rebecca Harding Davis: Writing Cultural Autobiography.* Nashville: Vanderbilt UP, 2001.

Olsen, Tillie. *Silences.* New York: Delacorte Press, 1972.

Pfaelzer, Jean. *Parlor Radical: Rebecca Harding Davis and the Origins of American Social Realism.* Pittsburgh: University of Pittsburgh Press, 1996.

———. "Rebecca Harding Davis." *Legacy* 7 (Fall 1990): 39–45.

Rose, Jane Atteridge. *Rebecca Harding Davis.* New York: Twayne Publishers, 1993.

Scheiber, Andrew J. "An Unknown Infrastructure: Gender, Production, and Aesthetic Exchange in Rebecca Harding Davis's 'Life in the Iron-Mills.' " *Legacy* 11 (1994): 101–17.

Schocket, Eric. "'Discovering Some New Race': Rebecca Harding Davis's 'Life in the Iron Mills' and the Literary Emergence of Working Class Whiteness." *PMLA* 115 (January 2000): 46–59.

MARTIN ROBISON DELANY (1812–1885)

Edward Whitley

BIOGRAPHY

Born in what is now Charleston, West Virginia, on May 6, 1812, Martin Robison Delany moved to Pennsylvania in 1822 with his mother, a free black seamstress who was forced to leave Charleston after she broke the law by teaching her five children to read. His father, then a slave, purchased his freedom 10 years later and joined the family. In 1843, after having lived and studied in Pittsburgh for over a decade, Martin Delany founded *The Mystery,* the first abolitionist paper west of the Alleghenies. When lack of funding brought *The Mystery* to an end in 1847, Delany began working with Frederick Douglass as co-editor of *The North Star,* leaving two years later due to political differences with Douglass and the paper's own financial difficulties. After being admitted to and subsequently dismissed from Harvard Medical School in 1850 following protests from white students, Delany returned to politics as an advocate for black emigration. Under Delany's leadership, this controversial movement, which suggested that African Americans establish independent black settlements outside of the United States in either Africa or the Americas, held three major conventions in the United States and Canada during the 1850s. In 1859 Delany traveled to the Niger Valley to investigate the possibility of a colony for free blacks, but with the outbreak of the Civil War, Delany tabled his hopes for emigration to serve as a recruiter for the Union army, ultimately earning the rank of major in the U.S. Army. During Reconstruction, he lived in Charleston, South Carolina, where he worked at the Freedmen's Bureau, the Bureau of Agriculture, a customshouse, a newspaper, and a courthouse, and where, in 1874, he unsuccessfully ran for the office of lieutenant governor as an Independent Republican. In 1878 he became involved in a short-lived Liberian emigration plan that never materialized and in the same year applied for a diplomatic appointment that would have given him the opportunity to return to Africa, which similarly fell through. He died in Ohio on January 24, 1885.

MAJOR WORKS AND THEMES

Martin Delany's major works espouse an Afrocentric world view designed to encourage black self-determination. Delany dedicated much of his adult life to studying the African culture and history he was introduced to by his African grandparents as a youth, and texts such as *The Origin and Objects of Ancient Freemasonry* (1853) and *Principia of Ethnology* (1879) reflect this study as they argue for the primacy of Africa in the development of world civilization. While Delany praised Africa in these texts and elsewhere, he did not feel that people of African descent were necessarily bound to live on that continent. In *The Condition, Elevation, Emigration, and Destiny of the Colored People of the United States* (1852), the major political and philosophical text of his career, Delany counters the American Colonization Society's mission of returning all African Americans to Africa by saying that African physical superiority enables them not only to adapt to any climate in the world, but also to do so more successfully than people of other races. Delany also hated the paternalism of the American Colonization Society and hoped that black-directed emigration, particularly to locations in the Americas, would serve as a more empowering alternative for African Americans. One of the earliest novels written by an African American and Delany's only novel, *Blake; or, The Huts of America,* appeared serially in *The Anglo-African Magazine* and *The Weekly Anglo-African* between 1859 and 1862 (the issues containing the conclusion of the novel have never been recovered). The hero of the novel is the Cuban-born, pure-blood African Henrico Blacus, or Henry Blake, who is taken as a slave to the United States. In the first part of the novel, Blake travels through the South as a fugitive slave inciting other slaves to revolt. In the second part of the novel, he travels to Cuba to rescue his wife and liberate the island as an independent black republic, a mission that involves taking a trip to and from Africa on a slave ship. Showing that both strong black leadership and collective effort are essential to enact change, *Blake* drives home Delany's beliefs in black self-determination and the capability of people of African descent.

CRITICAL RECEPTION

Delany felt that *The Condition* would set the political agenda for the 1850s and was frustrated when *Frederick Douglass' Paper* gave more attention to Harriet Beecher Stowe's *Uncle Tom's Cabin* than to his book. Feeling that Delany's call to emigrate would jeopardize emancipation and eventual integration into white society, Douglass and other abolitionists were critical of the proposals Delany set out in *The Condition.* No one saw Delany as the visionary he imagined himself, other than committed supporters of the emigration movement, such as poet James M. Whitfield, who dedicated *America and Other Poems* (1853) to Delany. *Blake* received even less attention than *The Condition,* in part because its release coincided with the outbreak of the Civil War. After the war, Frank A. Rollin (the pseudonym of Frances E. Rollin Whipper) wrote a hagiographic biography with Delany's personal assistance. Delany received relatively little notice by twentieth-century scholars and activists until the 1970s when he gained prominence as an early voice of black nationalism. Delany's major works were reprinted in this period and a number of major books and articles were published on his life and politics. Following a lull in the 1980s, scholars in the 1990s found Delany's works to be rich sources for exploring the dynamics of the African diaspora, as well as for exploring African American attitudes toward class, gender, and sexuality. Despite this recent attention, though, Delany is conspicuously absent from the major anthologies of American and African American literature.

BIBLIOGRAPHY

Works by Martin Robison Delany

Fiction

Blake; or, The Huts of America: A Tale of the Mississippi Valley, the Southern United States. 1970. Ed. Floyd Miller. Boston: Beacon, 1989.

Nonfiction

Elegy on the Life and Character of the Rev. Fayette Davis. Pittsburgh: Benjamin Franklin Peterson, 1847.

The Condition, Elevation, Emigration, and Destiny of the Colored People of the United States. Philadelphia, 1852.

The Origin and Objects of Ancient Freemasonry: Its Introduction into the United States, and Legitimacy among Colored Men. Pittsburgh: W. S. Haven, 1853.

Official Report of the Niger Valley Exploring Party. New York: T. Hamilton, 1861.

"Political Destiny of the Colored Race on the American Continent." In *Life and Public Services of Martin R. Delany.* Frank A. Rollin. Boston: Lee and Shephard, 1868. 327–67.

A Series of Four Tracts on National Policy: To the Students of Wilberforce University, Being Adapted to the Capacity of the Newly Enfranchised Citizens, First Series. Charleston, SC: Republican Book and Job Office, 1870.

Principia of Ethnology: The Origin of Races and Color, with an Archeological Compendium of Ethiopian and Egyptian Civilization, from Years of Careful Examination and Enquiry. Philadelphia, 1879.

Studies of Martin Robison Delany

Adeleke, Tunde. "Black Biography in the Service of a Revolution: Martin R. Delany in Afro-American Historiography." *Biography* 17, no. 3 (1994): 248–67.

Austin, Allan D. "The Significance of Martin Robison Delany's *Blake; or, The Huts of America.*" Ph.D. diss, University of Massachusetts, 1975.

Bienvenu, Germain J. "The People of Delany's *Blake.*" *College Language Association Journal* 36, no. 4 (1993): 406–29.

Crane, Gregg D. "The Lexicon of Rights, Power, and Community in *Blake:* Martin R. Delany's Dissent from Dred Scott." *American Literature* 68, no. 3 (1996): 527–53.

Ellison, Curtis W., and E. W. Metcalf, Jr. *William Wells Brown and Martin R. Delany: A Reference Guide.* Boston: G. K. Hall, 1978.

Ernest, John. *Resistance and Reformation in Nineteenth Century African American Literature: Brown, Wilson, Jacobs, Delany, Douglass and Harper.* Jackson: University Press of Mississippi, 1995.

Griffith, Cyril E. *The African Dream: Martin R. Delany and the Emergence of Pan-African Thought.* University Park: Pennsylvania State University Press, 1975.

Hite, Roger W. " 'Stand Still and See the Salvation': The Rhetorical Design of Martin Delany's *Blake.*" *Journal of Black Studies* 5, no. 2 (1974): 192–202.

Khan, Robert. "The Political Ideology of Martin Delany." *Journal of Black Studies* 15, no. 4 (1984): 415–40.

Levine, Robert S. *Martin Delany, Frederick Douglass, and the Politics of Representative Identity.* Chapel Hill: University of North Carolina Press, 1997.

Miller, Floyd J. *The Search for a Black Nationality: Black Emigration and Colonization, 1787–1863.* Urbana: University of Illinois Press, 1975.

Painter, Nell. "Martin R. Delany: Elitism and Black Nationalism." *Black Leaders of the Nineteenth Century.* Ed. Leon Litwack and August Meier. Chicago: University of Illinois Press, 1988. 149–71.

Reid-Pharr, Robert. *Conjugal Union: The Body, the House, and the Black American.* New York: Oxford University Press, 1999.

Rollin, Frank A. *The Life and Public Services of Martin R. Delany.* Boston: Lee and Shepard, 1868.

Sterling, Dorothy. *The Making of an Afro-American: Martin Robison Delany, 1812–1885.* Garden City, NY: Doubleday, 1971.

Sundquist, Eric J. *To Wake the Nations: Race in the Making of American Literature.* Cambridge: Harvard University Press, 1993.

Ullman, Victor. *Martin R. Delany: The Beginnings of Black Nationalism.* Boston: Beacon, 1971.

Wallace, Maurice. *Constructing the Black Masculine: Identity and Ideality in African American Men's Literature and Culture, 1775–1995.* Durham: Duke University Press, 2002.

Whitfield, J[ames]. M. *America and Other Poems.* Buffalo: James S. Leavitt, 1853.

Whitlow, Roger. "The Revolutionary Black Novels of Martin R. Delany and Sutton Griggs." *MELUS* 5, no. 3 (1978): 26–36.

Zeugner, John. "A Note on Martin Delany's *Blake* and Black Militancy." *Phylon* 32 (March 1971): 98–105.

EMILY DICKINSON (1830–1886)

Annette Jael Lehmann

BIOGRAPHY

Emily Dickinson was born the second of three children in Amherst, Massachusetts, a New England college town where her father was a prominent lawyer. Her father was one of the wealthiest and most respected citizens of the town and a conservative leader of the church. Dickinson grew up in a period of intense religious activity in New England's Calvinist churches and regularly attended the services at the Congregational First Church of Christ. She studied a modern curriculum of English and the sciences at Amherst Academy, including Latin, mathematics, and botany. Apart from one school year at the Mount Holyoke Female Seminary (1847–48) and a trip to Washington, D.C., where she visited her father, Dickinson spent her life exclusively in Amherst. Amherst was a country town remote from the intellectual scene of Boston or Concord, but in her family's home were not only religious books but also works by Emerson and current magazines. Around 1850 she began to write verse, which she sent to a circle of friends. Her "Sic transit gloria mundi" appeared in 1852 in the *Springfield Daily Republican.* Dickinson spent sociable evenings in the company of guests such as Samuel Bowles, editor of the *Springfield Daily Republican,* and Kate Scott Anthon. Dickinson also enjoyed dancing, buggy rides, parlor games, and other forms of entertainment until she began to seclude herself from the world outside her family's home. Around 1860 she ceased visits to other people and gradually became a recluse. In 1862 "Safe in their alabaster chambers" was published in the *Springfield Daily Republican* and Dickinson started her correspondence with Thomas Wentworth Higginson, asking him for advice on her poems. In the following years her reclusiveness became more habitual, though her poetic output and her correspondence with various friends intensified. In 1864 and 1865 she suffered from persistent eye trouble, for which she sought treatment in Cambridge, Massachusetts. The last 12 years of her life were spent in self-imposed isolation in her parental home, a Federal-style homestead on Main Street in Amherst. Dickinson is alleged to have dressed entirely in white, and communicated only indirectly with visitors and friends, from behind a folding screen or via notes and gifts in a basket she let down from her window into the garden. In those years her chief occupations were reading books—which her father bought for her while simultaneously advising her not to read them—and writing poems, without the knowledge of almost everyone around her. During this period, which coincided with the Civil War, Dickinson produced more than 800 poems. Her real business, as she put it, was writing poetry: "My Business is Circumference" (Nos. 268, 269), "circumference" being a term she borrowed from Emerson to mean poetry. Between 1860 and 1865 Dickinson was especially prolific and copied almost 300 poems into booklets or "fascicles" and sent those sewn packets to friends and family as poetic gifts. One of the most intriguing questions about her life—the mystery of her seclusion—remains unanswered.

Like her sister Lavinia, Dickinson never married, although several men played a role in her life. She kept up a lively correspondence with Benjamin Franklin Newton on contemporary literature and philosophy, especially on the topic of Ralph Waldo Emerson. Samuel Bowles, of the *Springfield Republican,* published a few of her poems, while Thomas Wentworth Higginson, whom she asked for advice in publishing her work, did not recognize her qualities. A close emotional bond tied her to Charles Wadsworth, whom she had met on her journey home from Washington. Dickinson had a special, though sometimes strained, relationship with her sister-in-law Susan Gilbert, who, as some passages from their correspondence suggest, was apparently the object of her desire in such homoerotic poems as "Her face was in a bed of hair" (No. 1722). In her later years Dickinson mourned the loss of many of the friends with whom she had entertained an almost lifelong relationship and correspondence.

When Dickinson died of Bright's disease in May 1886, friends and family were surprised at the amount of work she left behind. Her sister Lavinia found 40 notebooks and loose poems in a locked box in her bedroom. The poems were unarranged and only 24 were titled.

MAJOR WORKS AND THEMES

All in all, Dickinson wrote 1,775 poems. They brought her posthumous recognition as one of America's most important poets. In her style and themes, Dickinson draws on initially familiar patterns and topics: the formal basis of her poems is "common meter," the hymnal or ballad stanza with four iambic lines, alternating four and three stresses, and a rhyming scheme of abcb. However, this conventional framework is ruptured by experiments in the use of rhythm, rhyme, and enjambment. Dickinson's poems challenge the reader with their ellipses, syntactical and grammatical innovations, and irregular punctuation, which functions as a rhythmic and rhetorical tool. The poems are the fruit of a conscious process of experimentation that established Dickinson's distinctive stylistic habits. Among the primary aspects of her poems are their colloquialism, obliqueness, and a private or idiosyncratic use of language. Dickinson's fondness of ellipsis or a private diction manifested itself in specific meanings attached to words like "Etruscan" or "purple." Although for the most part Dickinson takes colloquial language as her starting point, her choice of words is innovative and full of variation. Syntactically, she makes much use of the dash, contributing to the condensation of associations she strives for.

The unsystematic arrangement of Dickinson's stanzas makes it difficult to identify a coherent thematic spectrum for her work, which defies easy classification. In the 1890s, Dickinson's first editors divided her poems into four categories: Life; Love; Nature; Time and Eternity. However, this and other groupings remain unsatisfactory. Some thematic lists collect almost 40 different subjects, ranging from poets and poetry itself, nature and the Amherst region, to God and faith, the soul's society, Eden and other faraway places, immortality and love. In fascicle 23, for example, one finds "Because I could not stop for Death" (No. 712) next to "He fought like those Who've nought to lose" (No. 759) and "Fame of Myself, to justify" (No. 713). Despite the incoherence in the oeuvre and the broad variety of themes, the poems concentrate on exploring the lyrical persona, through the topics of love, despair, and pain, as well as nature, life and death, time and eternity, God and immortality. Ecstatic emotions and metaphysical meditations are tied to precise observations of nature and everyday life. Love, death, and eternity seem to be the most significant of these themes. The brevity of Dickinson's verse enhances the effect of several subjects appearing simultaneously, and many of her poems refer to an occasion. Recent editions arrange Dickinson's poems according to conventional categories of her time, such as life, nature, and eternity. In Thomas H. Johnson's edition, the index is 13 pages long and includes every possible keyword from "Action," "Death of the Year," and "Fence" to "Fly," "Worm," and "Yesterday." This arrangement indicates that most of Dickinson's best poems refuse to be confined to a single subject and that none of the various classifications can serve as an interpretative tool.

Dickinson works through elements of the Metaphysical poets and the New England Puritan tradition. Her early years were shaped by her reception of orthodox Puritanism, with notions of hellfire, damnation, and a merciless God, which, however, she later managed to leave behind her; see, for example, "That odd old man is dead a year" (No. 1130). Characteristic though of all her poetry is the idiosyncratic employment of religious vocabulary, especially sacramental terminology, creating a unique tonality. Under the influence of Emerson and Transcendentalism, as well as Shakespeare, she turned her attention to "Eternity" and "Immortality" (No. 1231). The metaphysical qualities of her work are almost everywhere apparent, signified by the frequent use of the word "Eden" and the expression of infinite desires or immortal longings. Various poems are preoccupied with the moment of transition from earth to eternal life and a place imagined as heaven. The loss of certainty in her faith and the need to preserve an inner freedom leave thematic marks in Dickinson's work, yet the domain of religious and metaphysical experience remained decisive for her (see "Those dying then," No. 1551)—if often with an ironic and skeptical touch (see "Lightly stepped a yellow star," No. 1672).

An important vehicle of her personal definitions of spiritual joy and expression of desire are the so-called Master poems and letters. In these lyrics the unreachable Master is described as her lover for eternity and she creates a substantial narrative with metaphors drawn from paintings and various literary works of her time. Painting and its nineteenth-century traditions also influenced Dickinson's choice of symbols, visual images, and verbal arrangements of her verse. She sometimes compared her writing to the landscape paintings of artists such as Thomas Cole, Fredric Edwin Church, Sanford Gifford, or John Ruskin.

In Dickinson's poetry a modern self replaces the romantic self, enlarging and expanding its existence and experience. Her poetry is a territory for the self-exploration of an unfinalized identity and its inventions, testing the boundaries of self-transformation. It displays a range of personae, such as child, girl, madwoman, lover, or performing actress—yet it does not permit an autobiographical reading. Instead, the verse allows the reader to participate in a lyrical self of astonishing variety, which engages in dialogic encounters with the "You" so frequently addressed in the verse. In one of her famous statements, she explained to Higginson in a letter that the chosen person of her verse means a supposed person and not herself as the representative of the verse. Dickinson's concentrated, elliptical diction, with its paradoxes and graphic quality, anticipates elements of twentieth-century Imagist poetry, with which she also shares thematic preoccupations. Her confrontation with fundamental existential and borderline states, such as longing, loneliness, pain, and death, prove her a modern poet.

CRITICAL RECEPTION

Dickinson was unknown in her lifetime: a mere seven of her poems were published with her consent. The three-volume *Poems* appeared posthumously in 1890–96 and *The Complete Poems* in 1924; not until 1955 and 1958 were complete editions of her works published. Yet she had sent hundreds of poems to literary friends and family, and tried to self-publish groups of her poems in fascicles. Dickinson produced these booklets for seven years, starting at the age of 27. She copied more than 800 of her poems into 40 small booklets made of folded letter paper and bound each one herself using string passed through holes at the left edge.

For Dickinson, the lack of interest and comprehension shown by the critic Thomas W. Higginson, whom she had sent four poems in April 1862, was a particularly heavy blow. Higginson asked for the poems to be revised and for the grammar, meter, and rhyme to be adapted to the norms of contemporary lyric poetry. Dickinson responded to this, and other, lack of comprehension with the light irony of the poem "I'm Nobody! Who are you?" (No. 288) or "Publication—is the Auction / Of the Mind of Man" (No. 709). She justified her radical retreat from the outside world in "The Soul selects her own Society" (No. 303). After 1890, a selection of her poems—in a revised and some-times smoothed-out form—was published by M. L. Todd and Thomas W. Higginson. While the edition was a commercial success, it attracted mainly negative responses from the critics. Her 1,775 poems, and a great number of her letters, were appreciated only much later. Not until the twentieth century was Dickinson accorded a significant place in the history of American literature. Once R. Hillyer (in 1922) and, somewhat later, C. Aiken in his edition *Selected Poems* (1924) had whetted both biographical and schol-arly interest, M. Todd and M. Todd Bingham presented another 668 poems and frag-ments to the public. Only in 1955 did Thomas H. Johnson's three-volume critical edition of the poems appear, laying the foundation for an extensive reception. In this edition Dickinson's readers learned for the first time of her pleasure in dashes, irregular orthog-raphy, and unrelated words. For Dickinson's poetry, it is important to remember that all the published versions of her poems are the result of editorial revision. Since the early 1960s, Dickinson has been considered not only an equal counterpart to Walt Whitman but also the initiator of a new female line of tradition. She is judged the most important American woman poet of the nineteenth century. In *The Western Canon* (1994), Harold Bloom even credits her with "more cognitive originality than any other Western poet since Dante" (291).

Biographical studies of Dickinson can make a valuable contribution to under-standing the context of her poetry. The 1890s mark the beginning of such studies. Bianchi's *Emily Dickinson Face to Face* and *The Life and Letters of Emily Dickinson* mix information on the poet's family history, extracts from correspondence, and per-sonal memories. In the subsequent years the biographies of Dickinson spin a tale of a romantic and obscure figure, blurring the line between the subjects of her poetry and of her life. Even today, the central question for biographers is the reason for her later seclusion. Did she withdraw out of disappointed love? Was she acting in a drama invented to call attention to herself, or was she a hermit totally dedicated to art? Was she agoraphobic, or a victim of her father's repression?

All these questions remain much discussed but still unanswered. In the 1930s George Frisbie Whicher's *This Was A Poet* (1938) was the first work to study the intellectual and cultural influences of New England society on Dickinson's life and work. Between the 1950s and the 1960s three important biographies were written: Rebecca Patterson's *The Riddle of Emily Dickinson* (1951), which focuses on the importance of a woman poet's life; Thomas H. Johnson's *Emily Dickinson: An Interpretive Biography* (1955), accompanying his edition of poems and letters; and Jay Leyda's *The Years and Hours of Emily Dickinson* (1960), a two-volume collection of detailed life-records and raw material on the poet's life. In 1974, Richard B. Sewall produced the most comprehensive biography so far, *The Life of Emily Dickinson,* which portrays her through her involvement with ideas and individuals. In the following years biographical essays from a feminist perspective dominate the biographies. They try to critique the cliché of Dickinson as a lonely, childlike, fragile, and timid person. Most prominent are Elsa Green's "Emily Dickinson Was a Poetess" (1972) and Adrienne Rich's " 'Vesuvius at Home': The Power of Emily Dickinson" (1976). The feminist approach to biographical studies has stressed the importance of issues concerned with gender and Dickinson's relationships with women. Cynthia Griffin Wolff's *Emily Dickinson* (1986), for example, offers an interpretation based on her sociohistorical context, regarding her life as a struggle with religious beliefs against the gender conventions of her time. The growth of strictly biographical accounts has slowed down in the past 25 years. William H. Shurr's *The Marriage of Emily Dickinson: A Study of the Fascicles* (1983) links specific events of her life and relationships to lines of her poetry, speculating on unlocking the enigmatic nature of her verses. Shurr's biography proves, however, that there is no essentially biographical key to decoding Dickinson's poetry and that it is not helpful to reduce her poetry to autobiographical clues. Useful biographical studies of Dickinson concentrate on the creative interplay between the poet's life—her familial, historical, religious, and economic environment—and the development of her poetry. The emphasis here is on the importance of particular documents or details of Dickinson's family life. Polly Longsworth's *Austin and Mabel: The Amherst Affair and Love Letters of Austin Dickinson and Mabel Loomis Todd* (1984) or Vivian Pollak's *A Poet's Parents: The Courtship Letters of Emily Norcross and Edward Dickinson* (1988) pay tribute to those aspects. Longsworth's *The World of Emily Dickinson* (1990) provides a brief selection of photographic documents of Dickinson's environment.

Most manuscript scholars distinguish between Dickinson's holographic originals and the print translations. From the beginning of editorial work, her handwriting was considered peculiar, cultivated, quaint, and generally unique. Facsimiles were therefore included in some early editions. Dickinson's poems are frequently left with variant lines or stanzas and mostly with variant words marked and placed beside or above the poem's last line. Consequently the question has been raised many times about the most convincing or "authoritative" version for printing. Only 65 years after the first printed editions, Thomas H. Johnson included in *The Complete Poems of Emily Dickinson* (1955) her variant word choices. Ralph W. Franklin's facsimile edition *The Manuscript Books of Emily Dickinson* (1981) provides a comprehensive insight into her visual poetic sensibilities. Susan Albertine, editor of *A Living of Words: American Women in Print Culture* (1995), and Marta Werner, *Emily Dickinson's Open Folios: Scenes of Reading, Surfaces of Writing* (1995), reflect on various aspects of the value of editions and alterations in reading practices.

Most of the Dickinson manuscripts are in the possession of the Houghton Library, at Harvard University. But in the past decade the Dickinson Editing Collective (Martha Nell Smith, Ellen Louise Hart, and Marta Werner, editors) has developed a hypermedia archive of Dickinson's documents at http://jefferson.village.virginia.edu/dickinson/. A CD-ROM by Marta Werner, *Radical Scatters: An Electronic Archive of Emily Dickinson's Late Fragments* (1998), is also available.

The critical reception of Dickinson has become the focus of a variety of perspectives in literary theory, such as cultural criticism, feminism, studies in experiments in language, or audience studies. An overview can be found in Joseph Duchac, *The Poems of Emily Dickinson: An Annotated Guide to Commentary Published in English, 1890–1989* (1979, 1993). From the 1970s onward, critics began to concentrate on Dickinson's place within wider cultural traditions and to investigate her literary background. Karl Keller's *The Only Kangaroo Among the Beauty: Emily Dickinson and America* (1979) gives her work an approximate location within the American literary context. In *The Landscape of Absence* (1974), Inder Nath Kher connects Dickinson's verse to Kierkegaard, Aurobindo, and Buber. Barton Levi St. Armand has collected a wide range of cultural materials (women's scrapbooks, journals, folk art) to build up a biography of American Victorian culture in his study *Emily Dickinson and her Culture: The Soul's Society* (1984). Judith Farr's book *The Passion of Emily Dickinson* (1992) very profoundly contextualizes Dickinson's work within her American and European culture and reevaluates her artistic self-image. Jack Capps's *Emily Dickinson's Reading, 1836–1886* (1966) includes rich material on the books and authors Dickinson refers to in her poems and letters. In *The Years and Hours of Emily Dickinson,* Jay Leyda has chronologically arranged letters, diaries of the Dickinson family, and newspapers and magazines that circulated in the Amherst household. A special field of inquiry is Dickinson's dialogue with the visual arts, especially for the case of Thomas Cole and Fredric Church.

A substantial number of publications on Dickinson have come from the perspective of feminist theory and gender studies. In the final chapter of their well-known study *The Madwoman in the Attic* (1979), Sandra Gilbert and Susan Gubar demonstrate how Dickinson escaped and subverted the limits and norms of her patriarchal cultural environment. The conditions of a woman writer in Victorian America are the focus of studies like Margaret Homans's *Bearing the Word: Language and Female Experience in Nineteenth-Century Women's Writing* (1986) and *Women Writers and Poetic Identity: Dorothy Wordsworth, Emily Brontë, and Emily Dickinson* (1980). The role of female authorship is also examined in Barbara Antonina Clarke Mossberg's book *Emily Dickinson: When a Writer is a Daughter* (1982). Suzanne Juhasz's collection of essays *Feminist Critics Read Emily Dickinson* (1983) follows a similar line. In Mary Loeffelholz's collection *Dickinson and the Boundaries of Feminist Theory* (1991), the emphasis is on the intersections between feminism, deconstruction, and psychoanalysis. Martha Nell Smith's *Rowing in Eden: Rereading Emily Dickinson* (1992) stresses Dickinson's originality in overthrowing conventional notions of femininity and shows how she subverts and criticizes these clichés. Essays continue to appear in various journals dealing with the impact of the privileges, pressures, and experiences of race, class, gender, and sexual orientation on Dickinson's writing. A significant number of studies have concentrated on Dickinson's experiments in language, analyzing in detail her diction, use of semantic contrasts, variation in punctuation, patterns of rhetoric, and aspects of her style, especially the effect of the use of informal speech in her verse. Brita Lindberg-Seyersted's *Voice of the Poet* (1968) and Cristanne Miller's *Emily Dickinson: A Poet's Grammar* (1987) both examine Dickinson's work on all levels of language. The primary critical focus of the last years lies on the materiality of Dickinson's poetry and the affinities of her work with contemporary arts, such as adaptions in music or theater. Most contemporary approaches are reflected in the *Emily Dickinson Journal,* which in the mid-1990s was, for example, focused on issues such as writing practices and their impact on the editions of her work.

WORK CITED

Bloom, Harold. *The Western Canon.* New York: Harcourt Brace & Co., 1994.

BIBLIOGRAPHY

Works by Emily Dickinson

Poems by Emily Dickinson. 3 vols. Mabel Loomis Todd and Thomas Wentworth Higginson, eds. Boston: Roberts Brothers, 1890, 1891, 1896.
Letters of Emily Dickinson. 2 vols. Mabel Loomis Todd, ed. Boston: Roberts Brothers, 1894.
The Complete Poems of Emily Dickinson. Martha Dickinson Bianchi, ed. Boston: Little, Brown, 1924.
Selected Poems of Emily Dickinson. Conrad Aiken, ed. London: Cape, 1924.
Bolts of Melody: New Poems by Emily Dickinson. Millicent Todd and Millicent Todd Bingham, eds. New York: Harper, 1945.
The Complete Poems of Emily Dickinson. 3 vols. Thomas H. Johnson, ed. Boston & Toronto: Little, Brown, and Company, 1955.
The Poems of Emily Dickinson: Including Variant Readings Critically Compared with All Known Manuscripts. 3 vols. Thomas H. Johnson, ed. Cambridge: Belknap-Harvard University Press, 1955.
The Letters of Emily Dickinson. 3 vols. Thomas H. Johnson and Theodora Ward, eds. Cambridge: Belknap-Harvard University Press, 1958.
The Manuscript Books of Emily Dickinson. 2 vols. R. W. Franklin, ed. Cambridge: Belknap Press of Harvard University Press, 1981.
The Master Letters of Emily Dickinson. R. W. Franklin, ed. Amherst: Amherst College Press, 1986.
Selected Letters: Emily Dickinson and Her Family. Thomas H. Johnson, ed. Cambridge: Belknap Press of Harvard University Press, 1986.
The Diary of Emily Dickinson. Jamie Fuller, ed.; Marlene McLouglin, illus. San Francisco: Mercury House, 1993.

Studies of Emily Dickinson

Albertine, Susan, ed. *A Living of Words: American Women in Print Culture.* Knoxville, TN: University of Tennessee Press, 1995.
Anderson, Charles R. *Emily Dickinson's Poetry: Stairway to Surprise.* New York: Holt, 1960.
Barker, Wendy. *Lunacy of Light: Emily Dickinson and the Experience of Metaphor.* Carbondale: Southern Illinois University Press, 1987.
Bennett, Fordyce R. *A Reference Guide to the Bible in Emily Dickinson's Poetry.* Lanham, Md.: Scarecrow, 1977.
Bennett, Paula. *My Life a Loaded Gun: Female Creativity and Feminist Poetics.* Boston: Beacon, 1986.
Bianchi, Martha Dickinson. *Emily Dickinson Face to Face: Unpublished Letters with Notes and Reminiscences.* Boston: Houghton Mifflin, 1932.
———, ed. *The Life and Letters of Emily Dickinson.* Boston: Houghton Mifflin, 1924.

Cameron, Sharon. *Choosing Not Choosing: Dickinson's Fascicles.* Chicago: University of Chicago Press, 1992.

Capps, Jack. *Emily Dickinson's Reading, 1836–1886.* Cambridge: Harvard University Press, 1966.

Cody, John. *After Great Pain: The Inner Life of Emily Dickinson.* Cambridge: Belknap Press of Harvard University Press, 1971.

Dickinson Editing Collective. *Dickinson Electronic Archives.* Available at http://jefferson. village.virginia.edu/dickinson/.

Diehl, Joanne Feit. *Dickinson and the Romantic Imagination.* Princeton: Princeton University Press, 1981.

———. *Women Poets and the American Sublime.* Bloomington: Indiana University Press, 1990.

Dobson, Joanne. *Dickinson and the Strategies of Reticence: The Woman Writer in Nineteenth-Century America.* Bloomington: Indiana University Press, 1989.

Duchac, Joseph. *The Poems of Emily Dickinson: An Annotated Guide to Commentary Published in English, 1890–1989.* Boston: Hall, 1979 (vol. 1) and 1993 (vol. 2).

Eberwein, Jane Donahue. *Dickinson: Strategies of Limitation.* Amherst: The University of Massachusetts Press, 1985.

———, ed. *An Emily Dickinson Encyclopedia.* Westport: Greenwood, 1998.

Farr, Judith. *The Passion of Emily Dickinson.* Cambridge: Harvard University Press, 1992.

———, ed. *Emily Dickinson: A Collection of Critical Essays.* Englewood Cliffs: Prentice, 1996.

Ferlazzo, Paul J. *Critical Essays on Emily Dickinson.* Boston: G. K. Hall & Co., 1984.

Frank, Adam. "Emily Dickinson and Photography." *Emily Dickinson Journal* 10.2 (2001): 1–21.

Franklin, Ralph W. *The Editing of Emily Dickinson.* Madison: University of Wisconsin Press, 1967.

Gelpi, Albert J. *Emily Dickinson: The Mind of the Poet.* Cambridge: Harvard University Press, 1965.

Gilbert, Sandra M., and Susan Gubar, eds. *The Madwoman in the Attic: The Woman Writer and the Nineteenth-Century Literary Imagination.* New Haven & London: Yale University Press, 1979.

Grabher, Gudrun, Roland Hagenbüchler, and Cristanne Miller, eds; Richard B. Sewall, introd. *The Emily Dickinson Handbook.* Amherst: University of Massachusetts Press, 1998.

Green, Elsa. "Emily Dickinson Was a Poetess." *College English* 34 (1972): 63–70.

Guthrie, James R. " 'Before I got my eye put out': Dickinson's Illness and Its Effect on Her Poetry." *Dickinson Studies* 42.1 (1982): 16–25.

———. *Emily Dickinson's Vision: Illness and Identity in Her Poetry.* Gainesville, Fla.: University Press of Florida, 1998.

Hart, Ellen Louise, and Martha Nell Smith, eds. *Open me Carefully: Emily Dickinson's Intimate Letters to Susan Huntington Gilbert.* Ashfield, Mass.: Paris, 1998.

Higgins, David. *Portrait of Emily Dickinson: The Poet and Her Prose.* New Brunswick: Rutgers University Press, 1967.

Hillyer, Robert. "Emily Dickinson." *Freeman* 6 (18 Oct. 1922).

Homans, Margaret. *Bearing the Word: Language and Female Experience in Nineteenth-Century Women's Writing.* Chicago: University of Chicago Press, 1986.

———. *Women Writers and Poetic Identity: Dorothy Wordsworth, Emily Brontë, and Emily Dickinson.* Princeton: Princeton University Press, 1980.

Howe, Susan. *My Emily Dickinson.* Berkeley: North Atlantic Books, 1985.

Johnson, Greg. *Emily Dickinson: Perception and the Poet's Quest.* Tuscaloosa: The University of Alabama Press, 1985.

Johnson, Thomas H. *Emily Dickinson: An Interpretive Biography.* Cambridge: Harvard University Press, 1955.

Juhasz, Suzanne, ed. *Feminist Critics Read Emily Dickinson.* Bloomington: Indiana University Press, 1983.

———. *Naked and Fiery Forms: Modern American Poetry by Women: A New Tradition.* New York: Harper and Row, 1976.

————. *The Undiscovered Continent: Emily Dickinson and the Space of Mind.* Bloomington: Indiana University Press, 1983.

Juhasz, Suzanne, Cristanne Miller, and Martha Nell Smith. *Comic Power in Emily Dickinson.* Austin: University of Texas Press, 1993.

Keller, Karl. *The Only Kangaroo among the Beauty: Emily Dickinson and America.* Baltimore: John Hopkins University Press, 1979.

Kelly, Barbara. "Current Bibliography." *Dickinson Studies: Emily Dickinson (1830–1886), U.S. Poet* 86 (1993): 1–31.

Kher, Inder Nath. *The Landscape of Absence: Emily Dickinson's Poetry.* New Haven: Yale University Press, 1974.

Kirkby, Joan. *Emily Dickinson.* Women Writers Series. Gen. eds. Eva Figes and Adele King. Houndmills, Basingstoke & London: Macmillan Education Ltd., 1991.

Lease, Benjamin. *Emily Dickinson's Reading of Man and Books: Sacred Soundings.* New York: St. Martin's Press, 1990.

Leyda, Jay. *The Years and Hours of Emily Dickinson.* 2 vols. New Haven: Yale University Press, 1960.

Lilliedahl, Ann Martha. *Emily Dickinson in Europe: Her Literary Reputation in Selected Countries.* Washington, D.C.: University Press of America, 1981.

Lindberg-Seyersted, Brita. *Emily Dickinson's Punctuation.* Oslo: University of Oslo, 1976.

————. *Voice of the Poet: Aspects of Style in the Poetry of Emily Dickinson.* Cambridge: Harvard University Press, 1968/Uppsala: Almquist and Wiksells, 1968.

Loeffelholz, Mary. *Dickinson and the Boundaries of Feminist Theory.* Urbana and Chicago: University of Illinois Press, 1991.

Longsworth, Polly. *Austin and Mabel: The Amherst Affair and Love Letters of Austin Dickinson and Mabel Loomis Todd.* New York: Farrar, Straus and Giroux, 1984.

————. *The World of Emily Dickinson.* New York: Norton, 1990.

McRee, Ruth. "The Protected Voice: Playwriting as Craft, Not Therapy." *Emily Dickinson International Society Bulletin* 11.1 (1999 May/June): 11–12, 24–25.

Miller, Cristanne. *Emily Dickinson: A Poet's Grammar.* Cambridge: Harvard University Press, 1987.

Miller, Ruth. *The Poetry of Emily Dickinson.* Middletown: Wesleyan University Press, 1968.

Mossberg, Barbara Antonina Clarke. *Emily Dickinson: When a Writer is a Daughter.* Bloomington: Indiana University Press, 1982.

Myerson, Joel. "Supplement to Emily Dickinson: A Descriptive Bibliography." *The Emily Dickinson Journal* 4.2 (1995): 87–128.

Nathan, Rhoda B., ed. *Nineteenth-Century Women Writers of the English-Speaking World.* New York: Greenwood, 1986.

Orzeck, Martin, and Robert Weisbuch, eds. *Dickinson and Audience.* Ann Arbor: University of Michigan Press, 1996.

Paglia, Camille. *Sexual Personae: Art and Decadence from Nefertiti to Emily Dickinson.* New Haven: Yale University Press, 1990.

Patterson, Rebecca. *The Riddle of Emily Dickinson.* Boston: Houghton, 1951.

Phillips, Elizabeth. *Emily Dickinson: Personae and Performance.* University Park & London: The Pennsylvania State University Press, 1988.

Pollak, Vivian. *A Poet's Parents: The Courtship Letters of Emily Norcross and Edward Dickinson.* Chapel Hill: University of North Carolina Press, 1988.

Rich, Adrienne. " 'Vesuvius at Home': The Power of Emily Dickinson." *Parnassus* 5 (1976): 49–74.

Sewall, Richard B. *The Life of Emily Dickinson.* 2 vols. London: Faber and Faber, 1974.

————, ed. *Emily Dickinson: A Collection of Critical Essays.* Englewood Cliffs: Prentice Hall, 1963.

Shurr, Williams H. *The Marriage of Emily Dickinson: A Study of the Fascicles.* Lexington: University Press of Kentucky, 1983.

Sielke, Sabine. *Fashioning of the Female Subject: The Intertextual Networking of Dickinson, Moore, and Rich.* Ann Arbor: University of Michigan Press, 1997.

Small, Judy Jo. *Positive as Sound: Emily Dickinson's Rhyme.* Athens: University of Georgia Press, 1990.

Smith, Martha Nell. *Rowing in Eden: Rereading Emily Dickinson.* Austin: University of Texas Press, 1992.

St. Armand, Barton Levi. *Emily Dickinson and Her Culture: The Soul's Society.* Cambridge: Cambridge University Press, 1984.

Stocks, Kenneth. *Emily Dickinson and the Modern Consciousness: A Poet of our Time.* New York: St. Martin's Press, 1988.

Todd, John E. *Emily Dickinson's Use of the Persona.* The Hague: Mounton, 1973.

Turco, Lewis. *Emily Dickinson: Woman of Letters. Poems and Cantos from Lines in Emily Dickinson's Letters.* New York: State University of New York Press, 1993.

Ward, Theodora van Wagenen. *The Capsule of the Mind: Chapters in the Life of Emily Dickinson.* Cambridge: Harvard University Press, 1961.

Wells, Henry W. *Introduction to Emily Dickinson.* Chicago: Packard, 1947.

Werner, Marta L. *Emily Dickinson's Open Folios: Scenes of Reading, Surfaces of Writing.* Ann Arbor: University of Michigan Press, 1995.

————. *Radical Scatters: An Electronic Archive of Emily Dickinson's Late Fragments.* CD-ROM, Ann Arbor: University of Michigan Press, 1998.

Whicher, George Frisbie. *This Was a Poet: A Critical Biography of Emily Dickinson.* Ann Arbor: University of Michigan Press, 1965. (first published 1938)

Wolff, Cynthia Griffin. *Emily Dickinson.* New York: Knopf, 1986.

Wolosky, Shira. "Emily Dickinson's Manuscript Body: History/Textuality/Gender." *The Emily Dickinson Journal* 8.2 (1999): 87–99.

Woodress, James. "Emily Dickinson." *Fifteen American Authors before 1900: Bibliographical Essays on Research and Criticism.* Ed. Earl N. Harbert and Robert A. Rees. Madison: University of Wisconsin Press, 1984. 184–229.

Wylder, Edith. *The Last Face: Emily Dickinson's Manuscripts.* Albuquerque: University of New Mexico Press, 1971.

FREDERICK DOUGLASS (1818–1895)

William J. Scheick

BIOGRAPHY

Frederick Augustus Washington Bailey, the slave son of Harriet Bailey, was born in February 1818, at Holme Hill Farm in eastern Maryland. Raised by his grandmother, he remembered seeing his mother, who was hired out by her master, on only five occasions. Although Frederick Douglass, as he later named himself, never learned the identity of his father, early in his life he believed the person to be a white man, possibly his master Aaron Anthony.

Initially unaware of his status as a slave, Douglass enjoyed the first six years of his life. After his grandmother suddenly left him at the master's plantation, however, his life drastically changed. At the age of 8 he was sent to Fells Point, Baltimore (a place of personal importance to him throughout his life), to live with Thomas and Sophia Auld. At first Sophia treated him like the little child he was and even enthusiastically granted his wish that she teach him to read. Her husband, however, chastised her in a tirade against slave literacy. His angry comments had an ironic countereffect on Douglass, for whom Auld's harangue seemed an "anti-slavery lecture," a "special revelation," an intellectual epiphany demystifying "the white man's power" over slaves (*My Bondage and My Freedom* 218).

Douglass improved his reading skills by trading bread for lessons from fellow children, and at the age of 12 he also taught himself to write by tracing carpenter letters at the Auld & Harrison shipyard and by copying from books, including the Bible. About a year later, after joining the Bethel African Methodist Episcopal Church, he clandestinely studied the Bible with the help of a free black man, Charles Lawson. Douglass was especially influenced by a used copy of *The Columbian Orator* (1797), Caleb Bingham's collection of "freedom" speeches ranging from classical times to the American early national period. "Dialogue between a Master and a Slave" particularly attracted Douglass's interest. After Aaron Anthony's death, Douglass unhappily returned to Thomas Auld's household by the age of 15, Douglass was caught teaching other slaves to read during Sunday school. As a result, he was rented as a field hand to Edward Covey, a notoriously brutal "slave-breaker."

Following a failed attempt at escape, Douglass was apprenticed at William Gardner's shipyard, but was forced to surrender his income to Hugh Auld, his master. He joined a debating club, where he met Anna Murray, a free slave five years his senior. Within a year they were engaged, after which Douglass borrowed a retired black seaman's protection papers to enable him to board a Philadelphia-bound steamer in Delaware. While in hiding in New York under the name of Frederick Johnson, he married Anna on September 15, 1838, and together they traveled to New Bedford, Massachusetts, where he adopted the name Douglass, derived from his reading of Sir Walter Scott's *The Lady of the Lake* (1810).

William Lloyd Garrison's *Liberator,* an abolitionist weekly, impressed Douglass, who became an outspoken member of the Bristol County Anti-Slavery Society and a licensed Methodist preacher. His speeches against racial segregation and his skill in impromptu argument secured him a paid job as a regular agent for the Massachusetts Anti-Slavery Society, and on one occasion as an agent he received permanent injuries at the hands of an angry mob. While Douglass was abroad for the Society, Anna supported herself and their several children on a very modest seamstress's income supplemented by the earnings of Douglass's best-seller autobiography in 1845. While abroad, Douglass's freedom was purchased for him by English friends, who paid Hugh Auld $711.66.

Douglass established a newspaper, *North Star* (later renamed *Frederick Douglass' Paper*) in Rochester, New York. The first issue appeared in December 1847, the final issue in July 1860. Although its circulation reached 4,000 within two years, the newspaper ended in debt. Douglass also aided the Underground Railroad (designed to facilitate the escape of fugitive slaves to Canada), and he vigorously participated in debates concerning slavery in the decade preceding the Civil War. These debates unfortunately caused a rift between him and several abolitionists (William Lloyd Garrison, for example) who once thought of him as their ally. During the 1850s Douglass met several times with the firebrand John Brown, who did not receive Douglass's support for a plan for the violent overthrow of southern slavery by capturing the federal weapons at Harper's Ferry, Virginia. When Brown was defeated—he was hanged on December 2, 1859—Douglass was implicated, fled to Canada, and in subsequent lectures in Britain spoke of Brown as an abolitionist martyr. Although Douglass was ambivalent on the subject of abolitionist violence, his usually muted sympathy for slave insurrection sometimes became apparent in his comments: "If [the slave] kills his master, he imitates only the heroes of the [American] revolution"; "every hour [the slaveholder is] silently whetting the knife of vengeance for his own throat" (*My Bondage and My Freedom* 248, 301–2).

Back home in the 1860s, Douglass was hopeful about Abraham Lincoln's presidency, advocated Union intervention in the South, applauded the outbreak of the War between the States, and recruited soldiers (including two of his sons) for the first northern black infantry regiment. Douglass served Lincoln in a number of ways, not all successful, and after the assassination of the president, he received Lincoln's walking stick in acknowledgment of his assistance. In his lectures and writings (the primary sources of his income) during post-war reconstruction, Douglass remained a fierce critic of President Andrew Johnson's policies and a staunch advocate of the constitutional enfranchisement of African Americans. In 1872, he was awarded an honorary LL.D. degree during the first graduation ceremony at Howard University.

Two years after the death of his wife in 1882, Douglass married women's-rights activist Helen Pitts, an interracial union disconcerting to both her parents and his children. From 1889 to 1891, Douglass served as consul general to Haiti and later wrote and lectured on behalf of Haitian independence. The last years of Douglass's life were spent advocating controversial civil rights causes. It was after such an address at a meeting of the National Council of Women that Douglass suddenly died from a heart condition on February 20, 1895.

MAJOR WORKS AND THEMES

Although Douglass was well known in his time as a lecturer, his autobiographies have been the primary focus of literary critics. Many prefer and in fact most editors reproduce the *Narrative* (1845), the earliest and shortest account of his life. As the book closest in time to Douglass's youthful experiences, the *Narrative* is valued for its relatively unembellished, seemingly more spontaneous representation. Many critics, however, prefer *My Bondage and My Freedom* (1855), in which Douglass vaguely configures himself as both a latter-day Moses and Revolutionary War patriot (309). This second account of Douglass's life is appreciated for its more controlled, enhanced and reflective presentation. In contrast, it is rare indeed to meet the critic who sings the praises of either edition of *Life and Times* (1881), which strikes many readers as disappointingly overblown. In the course of these various versions there is a progression in Douglass's self-awareness, as the focus on the role of divine providence in the *Narrative* yields to an emphasis on the narrator's personal intellectual development in *My Bondage and My Freedom,* which in turn gives way to a stress on the protagonist's personal achievements in *Life and Times.*

All autobiography is the product of what memory recalls, edits, emphasizes, and either accidentally or conveniently forgets. So it is not surprising that in the course of four versions of Douglass's life he alters certain details, such as his steady retreat from his initial claims about the white identity of his father. In fact, over time Douglass's autobiographies increasingly dramatize his life as the product of self-fathering. And in this regard his personal narratives not only elicit comparisons to Benjamin Franklin, the cultural hero of self-reliance, but also tap into the Transcendentalist regard for a Manifest Destiny of personal and cultural self-expansion.

This similarity notwithstanding, most of Douglass's experiences hardly conformed to Transcendentalist notions. Consider, for example, the matter of universal meanings. In *Nature* (1836) Ralph Waldo Emerson, a leading spokesman for Transcendentalism, argued that words are symbols (signs) of natural facts and that these natural facts are symbols (signs) of spiritual truths. Although Emerson (later an abolitionist) certainly was not then thinking of the word "slave" when he made this claim, his argument was unfortunately applicable to a defense of slavery. That is, in terms of Emerson's claims for universal truths informing language, the word "slave" and the idea behind this word must be authorized by nature and by the spiritual truth informing nature. Douglass had certainly encountered a similar claim every time he heard slavery defended, as it commonly was, on the basis of both natural and biblical authority.

Douglass reverses the Transcendentalist understanding of words as the embodiment of natural and universal truths. In *My Bondage and My Freedom,* for instance, he introduces two pertinent details from his childhood not found in the earlier *Narrative*—a ladder and a windmill. Both objects are usually defined by their utility, their useful function in human labor, and as such neither object is threatening to the slaveholder. But Douglass indicates that the meaning, the sign-implication, of these objects is not stable, not necessarily restricted to the master's utilitarian sense of them. On the contrary, to his child's mind the ladder "was a really high invention, and possessed a sort of charm as [he] played with delight upon the rounds of it." The windmill likewise was one of those "wondrous things" that "a child cannot well look upon . . . without *thinking*" (142, 161). The master might look with approval at a slave child's interest in such objects because he expects that the child's familiarity with them will eventually make a better worker. But Douglass here intimates that a slaveholder cannot count on such fixed (universal) meanings for words or the objects represented by language. A slave's body may not be free, but his or her mind is beyond the slaver's reach and freely fashions its own associations in response to objects and words.

That words do not necessarily signify in absolute terms what the slaveholder believes them to mean is indicated in Douglass's observations about slave songs. These songs, Douglass explains, seem to "flatter the pride of the owner, and, possibly, draw a favorable glance from him," but they also simultaneously include "improvising—jargon to others, but full of meaning" to the slaves (184). Moreover, sometimes in these songs certain conventionally understood words become doubly encoded. When, for instance, slaves sing of Canaan as the promised land, "something more than a hope of reaching heaven" is indicated (308). What the slaveholder does not know is that on such occasions Canaan represents the northern states and Canada, a promised land for runaway and emancipated slaves.

In still another pertinent episode, when Hugh Auld scolds his wife for giving young Douglass reading lessons, the meaning of his words is not the same for the wife and the slave child. Auld's defense of slavery ironically becomes Douglass's "first decidedly antislavery lecture" (217). In fact, it becomes something of an unintended sermon occasioning "a special revelation, dispelling a painful mystery" (218). The mystery of the slaveholder's power, Douglass now understands, is based on nothing more than words, words said to be authorized by nature and the Bible. For Douglass, however, the meaning of words (like the meaning of objects represented in language) is humanly invented (as he saw in slave songs); their meaning is not based on absolute universal truths, as Transcendentalists like Emerson claimed. And so, Douglass concludes, the word "slave" has no authority in nature; "nature . . . [does not] prepare men and women to be either slaves or slaveholders" (222). Slavery is "conventional" rather than "constitutional" (164)—that is, the word "slave" and the institution of slavery are merely human constructions (conventions), the result of "rigid training" passed off as universal truths (222).

The indeterminacy of language—its origin in the mind's inventiveness and its variable signification of meaning—is also suggested in Douglass's management of animal imagery in *My Bondage and My Freedom*. Slaves were routinely likened to chattel, their status equated to that of farm animals. Speaking of oxen, for example, Douglass reports: "they were property, so was I"; "like a wild young working animal, I [was] to be broken to the yoke of a bitter and life-long bondage" (259, 263). Douglass reverses the pattern, however, when he indicates that Covey, the vicious slave-breaker, growls from the side of his mouth like a dog and sneaks up on slaves in the field like a snake (261, 265). Of slaveholders generally, Douglass writes, "like the fangs of the rattlesnake, his malice retains its poison long" (338).

As his adopted surname and many other literary allusions in *My Bondage and My Freedom* indicate, Douglass was well acquainted with Transcendentalist and other Romantic writers (e.g., William Cullen Bryant and Henry Wadsworth Longfellow). Besides inverting the Transcendentalist theory of the universal signification of language, Douglass also made ironic use of the Romantic catalog. This literary device, later a prominent feature of Walt Whitman's Transcendentalist poetry, is derived from early advertisement literature pertaining to the New World. The catalog is designed to suggest that abundant natural resources are readily and beneficently available to enable self-reliant people to realize the highest ideals of self-fulfillment. Chapter 7 of *My Bondage and My Freedom* opens at length with such commodity listings. One list includes the "teeming riches of the Chesapeake bay" region, where each "fertile garden, many acres in size," sprout "the tender asparagus, the succulent celery, and the delicate cauliflower; egg plants, beets, lettuce, parsnips, peas, and French beans, early and late; radishes, cantelopes, melons of all kinds; the fruits and flowers of all climes and of all descriptions" (191). Yet, in Douglass's ironic use of the catalog, none of the splendor of this natural abundance is available to the slave, who lives and works in this very region but who barely subsists on "coarse corn-meal and tainted meat" (190). Douglass uses the Romantic device to create an instructive duality. His presentation of the Romantic catalog highlights the complete deprivation of slaves in a land of plenty, an image designed to provoke thought about why slaves have been disfranchised from the Romantic promise of self-improvement through nature's abundance.

There is another scene in *My Bondage and My Freedom* quoted, not quite verbatim, from the *Narrative* that recalls, perhaps fortuitously, the Romantic prospect convention. The prospect device, dramatically represented in Asher Durand's painting *Kindred Spirits* (1849), presents the majesty of nature's immensity from an uncommon height that yields an unusual perspective designed to inspire personal confidence in individual and human destiny. Such a scene occurs when young Douglass stands "all alone" on "the lofty banks" of the Chesapeake Bay and "trace[s] . . . the countless number of sails moving off to the mighty ocean." Instead of feeling uplifted, this prospect encounter leads to "saddened heart and tearful eye": "You are loosed from your moorings, and free; I am fast in my chains, and am a slave. . . . You are freedom's swift-winged angels that fly around the world; I am confined in bands of iron" (268). Young Douglass has a vision upon his prospect, but it is a far cry from the inspiration typical of a Romantic encounter.

The power of language, especially the capacity to shape language to one's own advantage, is an important theme in Douglass's autobiographies. No matter how many times he retold the story of his life, the episodes detailing his learning to read and write are highlighted as major events, turning points in his life. Everything for him depended on the achievement of literacy as the means of overthrowing his abject condition and forming a personal identity based on his feelings and thoughts. Literacy enabled him to focus and to act. It enabled him first to demystify the universal claims made for the culturally constructed meanings imposed on him and second, as with his new surname, to invent his own meaning, to create the pattern of his own life.

CRITICAL RECEPTION

Douglass's *Narrative,* priced at 50 cents, sold 13,000 copies in 1845 and another 17,000 copies by 1850. This influential best-seller also appeared in Britain and was translated into French and Dutch. Although there was some objection in the *Christian Examiner* to its depiction of violence and its passionate manner of expression, most reviewers praised the book. In her *New York Tribune* report, reprinted in *Liberator,* Transcendentalist Margaret Fuller spoke for many others when she noted, "we have never read [a narrative] more simple, true, coherent, and warm with genuine feeling" (2).

The appearance 10 years later of an expanded version of Douglass's autobiography, entitled *My Bondage and My Freedom,* likewise found a happy reception. There were three printings (18,000 copies) between 1855 and 1858, and a German translation in 1860. Reviewers for the *New York Tribune* and the *Ohio State Journal* enthusiastically recommended the book, while an anonymous commentator for *Putnam's Monthly* favorably compared the autobiography to Harriet Beecher Stowe's popular abolitionist novel *Uncle Tom's Cabin* (1852). The success of Douglass's book on the eve of the Civil War assured him of a lecture career as a spokesman for African American liberation and justice.

But if his career was assured, not so his ability to sell two still-more-expanded editions of his autobiography. The nation had changed, and neither the 1881 nor the 1892 edition of *Life and Times of Frederick Douglass* sold well. The former edition sold fewer than 500 copies between 1881 and 1888, and the latter edition sold fewer than 400 copies between 1892 and 1893. There were few reviews, too, and they were not all that friendly even when they reported something positive about the work.

From 1900 to 1970 Douglass received very little attention as a writer. It is characteristic of these times that his name does not appear in any of the five editions of the *Literary History of the United States* published between 1948 and 1963. However, it is noteworthy that Benjamin Quarles's scholarly biography of Douglass (the first of its kind) appeared in 1948 and Philip S. Foner's five-volume collection of Douglass's works appeared in 1950. The effect of the civil rights movement of the 1960s raised interest in African American authors, including Douglass, whose autobiography underwent serious reevaluation during the 1970s. His writings were now praised for their stress on communal rather than strictly individualistic values and for their rhetorical sophistication (especially their ironic and satiric elements) in the context of the tradition of black ministerial oratory. In a particularly apt essay Albert E. Stone read the *Narrative* for its dichotomies, the most prominent being the unresolved and instructive juxtaposition of two points of view—that of a slave and that of a freeman.

Douglass's autobiographies, rather than his speeches, remained the primary interest of critics during the 1980s, which commenced with the publication of Dickson J. Preston's substantial *Young Frederick Douglass.* Preston focused on the difference between Douglass's personal experiences (which were relatively fortunate for a slave) and his public persona as presented in his lectures and books. A related rhetorical construction, Robert B. Stepto reported, can be observed in the parallel between southern Revolutionary War heroes and the black protagonist of "The Heroic Slave," Douglass's only known work of fiction. In one way or another much of the work of the 1980s, including Waldo E. Martin Jr.'s *The Mind of Frederick Douglass,* Houston Baker's *The Journey Back,* and William L. Andrews's *To Tell a Free Story,* featured considerations of Douglass's various narrative strategies and shortcomings in self-representation. Baker particularly stressed Douglass's inability to fathom how his Anglo linguistic and ideological options limited his self-expression.

Such considerations continued during the 1990s as well, though there were critics who searched specifically for ways in which Douglass revised Anglo-cultural conventions. He was now said to have recast the southern view of the garden, reworked the southern tradition of sentimentality, derived a unique stance within Christianity, played the trickster in transgressing cultural barriers, undermined America's cultural myth of unity, asserted an urban ideal opposed to the nineteenth-century preference for the pastoral, and reinvented the pattern of American cultural heroes. In a particularly challenging essay Lisa Brawley argued that in his second autobiography Douglass revised travel description away from conventional patterns because these patterns subtly reinforced racism.

During the 1990s more attention was paid to Douglass's speeches. Several articles and books identified the formal and informal (oral) rhetorical features of his writings.

Some consideration was given to Douglass's increasingly violent rhetoric, while several scholars specifically investigated the effect of his oratory on reform movements abroad. By the turn of the twentieth century several critics declared Douglass to be the foremost African American of the nineteenth century and, as Wilson J. Moses indicated, there is much scholarly work yet do be done concerning Douglass.

WORKS CITED

Douglass, Frederick. *My Bondage and My Freedom*. In *Autobiographies*. Ed. Henry Louis Gates Jr. New York: Library of America, 1994. 105–452.

Fuller, Margaret. *New York Tribune* 10 June 1845. p. 2.

BIBLIOGRAPHY

Works by Frederick Douglass

Contemporary Editions

The Frederick Douglass Papers. Ed. John R. Blassingame et al. New Haven: Yale UP, 1979–92. 5 vols.

Autobiographies. Ed. Henry Louis Gates Jr. New York: Library of America, 1994.

The Oxford Frederick Douglass Reader. Ed. William L. Andrews. New York: Oxford UP, 1995.

The Frederick Douglass Papers: Series Two: Autobiographical Writings: Volume I. Ed. John R. Blassingame et al. New Haven: Yale UP, 1999.

Books

Narrative of the Life of Frederick Douglass. Boston: Anti-Slavery Office, 1845.

My Bondage and My Freedom. Auburn, N.Y.: Miller, Orton and Mulligan, 1855.

Life and Times of Frederick Douglass. Hartford: Park Publishing Company, 1881.

Life and Times of Frederick Douglass. Boston: DeWolfe, Fiske, and Company, 1892.

Select Pamphlets

Address by Frederick Douglass, Formerly a Slave to the People of the United States of America. Edinburgh: H. Armour, 1852?

The Anti-Slavery Movement. Rochester, N.Y.: Lee, Mann & Co., 1855.

The Claims of the Negro Ethnologically Considered. Rochester, N.Y.: Lee, Mann & Co., 1854.

The Constitution of the United States: Is It Pro-Slavery or Anti-Slavery? Halifax, England: T. and W. Birtwhistle, 1860.

Lessons of the Hour. Baltimore: Thomas & Evans, 1894.

Oration Delivered in Corinthian Hall. Rochester, N.Y.: Lee, Mann & Co. 1852.

Two Speeches by Frederick Douglass. Rochester, N.Y.: C. P. Dewey, 1857.

Select Articles

"Reconstruction." *Atlantic Monthly* 18 (December 1866): 761–65.

"The Negro Exodus from the Gulf States." *Journal of Social Science* 11 (May 1880): 1–21.

"Lynch Law in the South." *North American Review* 155 (July 1892): 17–24.

Fiction

"The Heroic Slave." *Autographs for Freedom*. Ed. Julia Griffiths. Boston: John P. Jewett, 1853. 174–239.

Studies of Frederick Douglass

Andrews, William L., ed. *Critical Essays on Frederick Douglass.* Boston: G. K. Hall, 1991.
———. *To Tell a Free Story: The First Century of Afro-American Autobiography, 1760–1865.* Urbana: U of Illinois P, 1996.
Baker, Houston. *The Journey Back.* Chicago: U of Chicago P, 1980.
Blight, David W. *Frederick Douglass' Civil War.* Baton Rouge: Louisiana State UP, 1989.
Bloom, Harold (ed.). *Modern Critical Interpretations: Frederick Douglass's Narrative of the Life of Frederick Douglass.* New York: Chelsea House, 1988.
Brawley, Lisa. "Frederick Douglass's *My Bondage and My Freedom* and the Fugitive Tourist Industry." *Novel* 30 (1996): 98–128.
Chesebrough, David B. *Frederick Douglass: Oratory from Slavery.* Westport, Conn.: Greenwood, 1998.
Foner, Philip S. *The Life and Writings of Frederick Douglass.* New York: International, 1950.
Hall, James C., ed. *Approaches to Teaching: Narrative of the Life of Frederick Douglass.* New York: Modern Language Association, 1999.
Huggins, Nathan Irvin. *Slave and Citizen: The Life of Frederick Douglass.* Boston: Little, Brown, 1980.
Lampe, Gregory P. *Frederick Douglass: Freedom's Voice, 1818–1845.* East Lansing: Michigan State UP, 1998.
Martin, Waldo E., Jr. *The Mind of Frederick Douglass.* Chapel Hill: U of North Carolina P, 1984.
McAndrews, William L. *To Tell a Free Story: The First Century of Afro-American Autobiography, 1760–1865.* Urbana: U of Illinois P, 1986.
McFeely, William F. *Frederick Douglass.* New York: W. W. Norton, 1990.
Moses, Wilson J. "Prospects for the Study of Frederick Douglass." *Resources for the Study of American Literature* 23 (1997): 1–18.
Preston, Dickson J. *Young Frederick Douglass: The Maryland Years.* Baltimore: Johns Hopkins UP, 1980.
Quarles, Benjamin. *Frederick Douglass.* Washington, D. C.: Associated Publishers, 1948.
Rice, Alan J., and Martin Crawford, eds. *Liberating Sojourn: Frederick Douglass and Transatlantic Reform.* Athens: U of Georgia P, 1999.
Stepto, Robert. "Storytelling in Early Afro-American Fiction: Frederick Douglass's 'The Heroic Slave.' " *Georgia Review* 36 (1982): 355–68. Rptd. in *Critical Essays,* 108–19.
Stone, Albert E. "Identity and Art in Frederick Douglass's *Narrative.*" *College Language Association Journal* 17 (1973): 191–213.
Sundquist, Eric J., ed. *Frederick Douglass: New Literary and Historical Essays.* Cambridge: Cambridge UP, 1990.

EMMA CATHERINE EMBURY (1806–1863)

Amy L. Burtner

BIOGRAPHY

The eldest child of Dr. James R. Manley and Elizabeth Post, Emma Catherine was born in 1806, the exact month and day unknown. Well-educated and economically privileged, Emma began publishing poetry in her twenties, under the pseudonym "Ianthe." On May 10, 1828, she married Daniel Embury, a banker who subsequently became president of the Atlantic Bank in Brooklyn.

Although Embury "denied having a literary career" (Gomes 118), she eventually abandoned the pseudonym and published with regularity under her full name: as Emma C. Embury or Mrs. E. C. Embury. Throughout the 1830s and 1840s, Embury was visible in New York City literary circles, hosting, with Anne Lynch Botta, literary salons in Brooklyn whose members included Edgar Allan Poe and Frances Sargent Locke Osgood, among others.

The symptoms of an unnamed, chronic illness shortened her publishing career sometime between 1848 and 1851. An invalid for the last two years of her life, Embury died on February 10, 1863, at her home in Brooklyn.

MAJOR WORKS AND THEMES

Embury's first book of poetry, *Guido, a Tale; Sketches from History and Other Poems,* was published in 1828; her first book of prose, *Pictures of Early Life,* appeared in 1830; and in 1831, at a celebration at the Brooklyn Collegiate Institute for Young Ladies, she gave a speech that came to be known in print as "Female Education." Two collections of stories that gathered attention were *Constance Latimer, or, The Blind Girl, with Other Tales,* released in 1838, and *Glimpses of Home Life* published 10 years later. Much of Embury's work appeared first in popular magazines such as *Ladies' Companion* and *Godey's Lady's Book, and Ladies' American Magazine.* A full collection of her poetry and a collection of selected prose were published posthumously. One poem, "The Maiden's Story," was set to music by Sir Arthur Sullivan in 1867.

Called "idealized sentiments of her day" (Rosenberg 595), themes of love, loss, and virtue pervade Embury's work. Often, tones and messages of poems will collide with those of stories that center around similar themes. While an "old régime" speaker in the poem "Lament" delivers a rhetorically charged eulogy for a male-dominated "world [that] will never be again" (Walker 90), some of Embury's prose is critical of feminism, for she sees the value of women's education mainly as preparation for marriage and motherhood (Rosenberg 596; Walker 79). In the poem "Stanzas," the speaker bids a tearful goodbye to her "precious gem" of a friend who is getting married. However, throughout *Glimpses of Home Life,* most of the husbands are "victims of discontent" (*Glimpses* 287), exasperated by wives who are slovenly, childish, and materialistic.

Regardless of subject matter, Embury's style takes the reader inside the minds of speakers and characters, who vary in gender, nationality, and age from one poem and story to the next. Settings in Embury's work fluctuate between rural and urban: in *American Wild Flowers,* Embury's descriptions of "native haunts" complement color engravings by Edwin Whitefield; while in much of her fiction, Embury depicts the confines of houses and sickrooms to complement the inner struggles of her characters.

CRITICAL RECEPTION

Embury's writing has inspired a mixture of contemporary praise and posthumous dismissal. However, both sides share a common ground for criticism: Embury's thematic focus on domesticity and "womanly" virtue. In 1847, a writer for *The United States Democratic Review* praised *Pictures of Early Life* as "highly interesting and instructive; and of a character which should place it in the hands of youth, as well to instruct as to interest and amuse" (191). Edgar Allan Poe devotes a section of his text "The Literati" to Embury, whom he praises as a kindred "writer of tales," and whose style is, according to Poe, "pure, earnest, and devoid of verbiage and exaggeration" (84). Poe is quick to add, "She is noted for her domestic virtues no less than for literary talents and acquirements" (85).

Posthumous criticism focuses differently on many of the same qualities. George Harvey Genzmer, writing for the *Dictionary of Literary Biography* in 1931, scolds, "Book reviewers habitually confused Mrs. Embury's literary achievements with her virtues as a wife and mother and her charm as a hostess" (125). Genzmer blames Poe's praise of Embury on regional manners: "Southern chivalry was the weak spot in his critical armor" (125). According to Genzmer, Embury's writing "has the vagueness of imagery, conventionality of theme, and unimpassioned fluency of all bad verse" (125). The 1995 edition of the *Oxford Companion to American Literature* notes, vaguely, that Embury's "conventional feminine novels . . . were popular in her time" (97).

Attention to the double standards imposed on many women writers, especially those of the nineteenth century, helps to evaluate the contradictions. Barbara Welter frames Embury in terms of a gender-based "anti-intellectualism" in which women had "to reconcile their gifts and their womanly natures" (79). Julia Rosenberg regrets that Embury "often does her best work when she takes on a male persona or when a man is the protagonist" (595), concluding, "E[mbury] is typical of a time when women writers were exalting and perpetuating the values and ideas that limited them most" (596).

WORKS CITED

"Embury, Emma Catherine (1806–63)." *Oxford Companion to American Literature.* 6th ed. Ed. James D. Hart. New York: Oxford UP, 1995. 97.

Genzmer, George Harvey. "Embury, Emma Catherine." *Dictionary of American Biography.* Vol. 6. Ed. Allen Johnson and Dumas Malone. New York: Charles Scribner's Sons, 1931. 124–25.

Gomes, Janette M. "Emma Embury (1806–1863)." *Nineteenth Century American Women Writers: A Bio-Bibliographical Critical Sourcebook.* Ed. Denise D. Knight. Westport, CT: Greenwood, 1997. 118–22.

"Notices of New Books." *The United States Democratic Review.* Vol. 20. New York: J. & H. G. Langley, 1847. 191. Available at <http://cdl.library.cornell.edu/cgi-bin/moa/moa-cgi?notisid = AGD1642–0020–73>

Poe, Edgar Allan. "Emma C. Embury." *The Works of the Late Edgar Allan Poe.* Vol. 3. New York: J. S. Redfield, 1850. 84–6.

Rosenberg, Julia. "Emma Catherine Manley Embury." *American Women Writers: A Critical Reference Guide from Colonial Times to the Present.* Vol. 1. Ed. Lina Mainiero. New York: Frederick Ungar, 1979. 594–96.

Walker, Cheryl, ed. "Emma Embury." *American Women Poets of the Nineteenth Century: An Anthology.* New Brunswick, NJ: Rutgers UP, 1992. 78–92.

Welter, Barbara. *Dimity Convictions: The American Woman in the Nineteenth Century.* Athens, OH: Ohio UP, 1976.

BIBLIOGRAPHY

Works by Emma Catherine Embury

Poetry

Guido, a Tale; Sketches from History and Other Poems. New York: G. and C. Carvill, 1828.
Love's Token Flowers. New York: J. C. Riker, 1846.
The Poems of Emma C. Embury. New York: Hurd and Houghton, 1869.

Poetry and Prose

American Wild Flowers in Their Native Haunts. New York: D. Appleton and Co., 1845. Alternate title: *Nature's Gems.* Republished as *American Wildflowers;* engravings by Edwin Whitefield; edited by Alice Radt. New York: Hastings House, 1946.

Prose

Pictures of Early Life, or, Sketches of Youth. New York: Harper, 1830.
An Address on Female Education, Read at the Anniversary of the Brooklyn Collegiate Institute for Young Ladies. 1831. Published as "Female Education." *Woman and the Higher Education.* Ed. Anna C. Brackett. New York: Harper and Bros., 1893. 47–64.
Constance Latimer, or, The Blind Girl, with Other Tales. New York: Harper and Bros., 1838.
The Ladies' Companion: A Monthly Magazine Embracing Every Department of Literature; Embellished with Original Engravings and Music Arranged for the Piano-forte [Harp and] Guitar. New York: W. W. Snowden, 1838–39.
"Life, of Fashion." *Godey's Lady's Book, and Ladies' American Magazine* 22 (1841): 22.
"Rights of Children." *Godey's Lady's Book, and Ladies' American Magazine* 28 (1844): 80.
Glimpses of Home Life, or, Causes and Consequences. New York: J. C. Riker, 1848.
"Little Mary–The Lover's Appeal, or The Double Error." *Household Narratives for the Family Circle.* Philadelphia: H. C. Peck and Theo Bliss, 1854. Reprinted as *Home Made Happy, or, Pictures of Every-day Life for the Family Circle.* Philadelphia: H. C. Peck and Theo Bliss, 1858.
The Greek Slave: A Story. San Francisco: A. Roman and Co., 1864. Published under the pseudonym Ianthe, with V. L. Mendenhall and Maude Ernest.
Selected Prose Writings of Mrs. Emma C. Embury. New York: DeVinne Press, 1893.

Studies of Emma Catherine Embury

Baym, Nina. *Woman's Fiction: A Guide to Novels by and about Women in America 1820–1870.* Ithaca: Cornell UP, 1978. 73.

Cleveland, Charles D. *A Compendium of American Literature.* Philadelphia: J. H. Bancroft and Co., 1859. 614–16.

"Embury, Emma Catherine (1806–63)." *Oxford Companion to American Literature.* 6th ed. Ed. James D. Hart. New York: Oxford UP, 1995. 97.

Gomes, Janette M. "Emma Embury (1806–1863)." *Nineteenth Century American Women Writers: A Bio-Bibliographical Critical Sourcebook.* Ed. Denise D. Knight. Westport, CT: Greenwood, 1997. 118–22.

Griswold, Rufus Wilmot. *The Female Poets of America.* 2nd ed. Philadelphia: Parry and McMillan, 1856. 143–48.

Hale, Sarah Josepha. *Woman's Record: or, Sketches of All Distinguished Women from the Creation to A.D. 1854.* New York: Harper and Bros., 1855. 653–57.

Hart, John S. *Female Prose Writers of America.* Philadelphia: E. H. Butler and Co., 1866. 139–40.

Genzmer, George Harvey. "Embury, Emma Catherine." *Dictionary of American Biography.* Vol. 6. Ed. Allen Johnson and Dumas Malone. New York: Charles Scribner's Sons, 1931. 124–25.

"Notices of New Books." *The United States Democratic Review.* Vol. 20. New York: J. & H. G. Langley, 1847. 191. Available at <http://cdl.library.cornell.edu/cgi-bin/moa/moa-cgi?notisid = AGD1642–0020–73>

Poe, Edgar Allan. "Emma C. Embury." *The Works of the Late Edgar Allan Poe.* Vol. 3. New York: J. S. Redfield, 1850. 84–6.

Read, Thomas Buchanan. *The Female Poets of America.* 9th ed. Philadelphia: E. H. Butler and Co., 1867. 87–98.

Robbins, J. Albert. *Mrs. Emma C. Embury's Account Book: A Study of Some of Her Periodical Contributions.* New York: New York Public Library, 1947.

Rosenberg, Julia. "Emma Catherine Manley Embury." *American Women Writers: A Critical Reference Guide from Colonial Times to the Present.* Vol. 1. Ed. Lina Mainiero. New York: Frederick Ungar, 1979. 594–96.

Walker, Cheryl, ed. "Emma Embury." *American Women Poets of the Nineteenth Century: An Anthology.* New Brunswick, NJ: Rutgers UP, 1992. 78–92.

Welter, Barbara. *Dimity Convictions: The American Woman in the Nineteenth Century.* Athens, OH: Ohio UP, 1976.

RALPH WALDO EMERSON (1803–1882)

Sharon L. Gravett

BIOGRAPHY

Born in Boston on May 25, 1803, Ralph Waldo Emerson was one of eight children of the Reverend William Emerson, pastor of the First Church of Boston, and his wife, Ruth. The family faced a series of losses, including the deaths of two daughters, one son, and the Reverend Emerson. Emerson was eight when his father died, leaving his mother to support the family largely on her own, with occasional help from her independent, intellectual, and deeply religious sister-in-law, Mary Moody Emerson. Despite these obstacles, the young Emerson received a fairly good education, first at the Boston Public Latin School and then at Harvard, entering in 1817 at age 14. However, of the three sons in the Emerson family educated at Harvard, he was considered the least promising.

While his younger brothers, Edward and Charles, were at the head of their respective classes at Harvard, Emerson's performance was not similarly distinguished. However, his unexceptional record seemed due less to ability than to interest. Even while a grammar school student, he had discovered other activities to interest him, including exploring the outdoors and writing verse. When he reached Harvard, finding the traditional course of study intellectually unsatisfying, Emerson began reading outside of the established curriculum, particularly in more contemporary literature, even forming his own informal book club; he also initiated his lifelong habit of keeping a journal. Thus, in small ways, he began to forge his own path outside of traditional expectations. During this time, for example, he asked his family members to call him "Waldo" rather than "Ralph," a name he shared with six cousins, thereby asserting his own identity more definitively.

Upon graduating from college, Emerson had few vocational options. Like many Harvard students of the time, he had supplemented his college income by teaching school, a practice he continued after his graduation. However, as he approached his twenty-first birthday, he wanted to establish a more permanent vocation. In spite of doubts about his facility for such a career, he decided to follow the family custom of entering the ministry, enrolling in the Harvard Divinity School in 1825. He did not spend much time in formal study; after an eye operation, he returned to teaching school. Despite his lack of formal training, he was approbated to preach in the fall of 1826. Because he continued to be plagued by health problems, his career started slowly.

After a trip south to avoid the harsh Massachusetts winter, he was well enough to return home and launch a sporadic preaching career by the spring of 1827. In 1829, he was ordained as the junior minister of the Second Church in Boston, soon assuming the position of senior minister. That same year, he married Ellen Tucker. Although seeming to settle into a routine, Emerson showed signs of intellectual restlessness, continuing to read widely. At the same time, personal tragedy began to take its toll. His 19-year-old wife died of tuberculosis after a mere 16 months of marriage. Perhaps her death, and the inheritance she left him gave Emerson the confidence (and the means) to finally reject his vocation. Although he resigned his pastorate over a specific incident (his refusal to administer the sacrament of the Last Supper), he had obviously been struggling with his vocation for some time.

After his resignation, he traveled to Italy, France, and England in 1832–33 where he met a number of the writers—such as Thomas Carlyle, William Wordsworth, Samuel Taylor Coleridge, Walter Savage Landor, and John Stuart Mill—who had been the objects of his voracious reading. Returning home in 1833, Emerson still had not settled on a permanent vocation, but he continued to preach occasionally, and, more important, he also began to lecture in the Boston area. The growing lyceum movement in the United States provided him with the perfect venue in which to continue to preach, albeit in the secular arena. As he wrote to his friend Thomas Carlyle, "I find myself so much more and freer on the platform of the lecture-room than in the pulpit . . ." (Slater 171).

He started his life over again not only professionally but also personally, marrying Lydia Jackson in 1835 and moving to Concord, Massachusetts. This marriage lasted until Emerson's death. The union produced four children, the eldest of whom, Waldo, died at the age of five, much to his father's long-lasting grief. Other family losses during this period included the deaths of Emerson's talented younger brothers Edward and Charles (in 1834 and 1836). However, despite these troubles, Emerson was slowly evolving his own thought, publishing his first work, *Nature,* in 1836.

Not only was he beginning to articulate a new creed at variance with the orthodoxies in which he was raised, but he had also begun to find others who were similarly inclined. Only a week or so after publishing *Nature,* he met for the first time with a group of like-minded thinkers. This first meeting of the group, which eventually came to be known as the Transcendental Club, was composed mainly of fellow Unitarian ministers. This new club met again in August 1837 after Emerson's Phi Beta Kappa address at Harvard. The number attending had swelled to 17, including female members such as Elizabeth Hoar, Sarah Bradford Ripley, and Margaret Fuller.

Emerson was also coming into even greater demand as a lecturer, first giving talks around Boston but then slowly enlarging his circuit to include areas such as New York, Philadelphia, Baltimore, and Washington. However, he was also interested in endeavors other than his own lecturing/publishing. He helped to found the *Dial,* a Transcendentalist magazine, published from 1840 to 1844, dedicated to reflecting the new thought of the time. This journal provided a publishing venue for many of his circle, including Henry David Thoreau. When Margaret Fuller relinquished the editorship in 1842, Emerson took over for the remaining two years of publication. While many of his fellow members in the Transcendental group participated in a number of social causes—such as Brook Farm—Emerson became seriously involved in only one of the issues of the day: abolitionism. He began speaking directly on that issue in 1844, and his activities intensified after the passage of the Fugitive Slave Act in 1850.

Although he did not often participate in the social causes his colleagues espoused, Emerson was a helpful friend, colleague, and mentor. For example, recognizing in his Concord neighbor and fellow Harvard graduate Henry David Thoreau some of the same vocational struggles he had faced, Emerson assisted the younger man in a variety of ways. For example, he provided a home to Thoreau for a couple of extended periods, during which Thoreau served as a general handyman and helped to take care of the Emerson property; he aided Thoreau's desire to begin a career in New York by securing him a position in New York City as tutor to his brother's son; and he even provided the plot of land at Walden Pond on which Thoreau built his cabin. Among the other friends he aided were Bronson Alcott, the father of novelist Louisa May Alcott, as well as the Scottish writer, Thomas Carlyle. After meeting him on his first trip abroad, Emerson initiated a correspondence with Carlyle, which lasted from May 14, 1834, to April 2, 1872. For Carlyle, he arranged the U.S. publication of his works such as *Sartor Resartus* (1836), *The French Revolution* (1837), and *Critical and Miscellaneous Essays* (1838–39).

With increasing fame came expanded opportunities as Emerson returned to England on a lecture tour in 1847–48. On this trip abroad, Emerson reunited with some of those he met on his first trip, including Carlyle, and he also met with Charles Dickens; Alfred, Lord Tennyson; Coventry Patmore; and Arthur Hugh Clough. Of course, on this trip, he was not a former minister looking for a vocation but an established writer and lecturer. Upon his return, he also increasingly journeyed farther away from home on his lecture tours, first crossing the Alleghanies in the 1850s and beginning regular tours of the Midwest.

His growing respectability was marked by Harvard's acceptance of him after a long estrangement because of the repercussions from his 1838 Divinity School address. In 1866, Harvard awarded him an honorary degree, and he was also elected to the Board of Overseers. A year later, 30 years after his first address to the Phi Beta Kappa Honor Society, he was invited back to lecture on the same occasion.

Even as his health declined with increasing age, Emerson continued to lecture, although largely repeating his earlier talks. He also traveled, undertaking a trip to California in 1871. The following year, when his house burned, his friends collected money to completely rebuild his house as well as send him on a tour of Europe and Egypt. On his final trip to England, he met again with his old friend Carlyle as well with John Ruskin and Charles Dodgson. When he finally returned to Concord, he was touched by the crowd that turned out to welcome him home. In 1876, hoping to heal some of the rifts from the Civil War, he traveled to Charlottesville to speak at the University of Virginia's commencement. His last years, marked by the gradual loss of his memory, were quiet ones. His last public lecture, on February 10, 1881, was to mark the death of his friend Carlyle. Emerson himself died on April 27, 1882, and was buried in Concord's Sleepy Hollow Cemetery, near the graves of Henry David Thoreau and Nathaniel Hawthorne.

MAJOR WORKS AND THEMES

While he produced two volumes of poetry, *Poems* in 1847 and *May-Day and Other Poems* in 1860, most of Emerson's publications evolved from his lectures. *Essays: First Series* was published in 1841, *Essays: Second Series* in 1844, and *Nature: Addresses and Lectures* in 1849. As his writing career progressed, he focused increasingly on practical topics as well as the ideal, in works such as *Representative Men* (1850), *English Traits* (1856), *The Conduct of Life* (1860), *Society and Solitude* (1870), and *Letters and Social Aims* (1874).

In his first published work, *Nature* (1836), Emerson delineates many of the themes important to his subsequent work. Most prominently, he insists that his readers focus on the present and future rather than fixate on the past. He reminds them, "The sun shines to-day also. There is more wool and flax in the fields. There are new lands, new men, new thoughts. Let us demand our own works and laws and worship" (1: 3). Such an emphasis on the present rather than the past was relevant not only to his own situation as a young man still searching for a viable vocation but also to a young nation still struggling to develop its own intellectual independence. Emerson's injunction at the end of the essay, "Build therefore your own world" (1: 76) could appeal both to a young and uncertain country and to many struggling young men and women.

Repeating this theme in the annual Phi Beta Kappa Address at Harvard on August 31, 1837, he declares, "we have listened too long to the courtly muses of Europe" ("The American Scholar" 1: 114). In this address, he stresses the importance of the scholar's attention to a number of influences, including nature, the past, and action, but he also warns against a mechanical adherence to any of them, emphasizing the scholar's need to face squarely his own times.

Emerson applies these principles to yet another arena in his talk to the graduating seniors at the Harvard Divinity School on July 15, 1838. The resulting talk, published as "The Divinity School Address" (1838), critiques the current state of organized religion. In front of the faculty and students, he chastised the ministry for neglecting God in the present, exclaiming, "Men have come to speak of the revelation as somewhat given long ago and done; as if God were dead. The injury to faith throttles the preacher; and the goodliest of institutions becomes an uncertain and inarticulate voice" (1: 134). Perhaps Emerson's best-known statement of this theme is "Self-Reliance." In this essay, he reiterates his steady refrain of living in the present, insisting that individuals should rely on themselves, not take refuge in external norms and expectations.

While Emerson's essays seem relatively straightforward and unambiguous, they are actually considerably more challenging than they may at first appear. Readers often use Emerson's imminently quotable pronouncements to summarize his philosophy. However, one statement may often directly conflict with another equally adamant assertion. For example, while Emerson, in *Nature,* instructs readers to build their own world, he also proclaims, with equal authority, "Every spirit makes its own house; but afterwards the house confines the spirit" ("Fate" 6: 9). These oppositional statements occur even in the same work. In "Self-Reliance," for example, he berates his contemporary society, exclaiming, "Man is timid and apologetic, he is no longer upright; he dares not say 'I think,' 'I am,' but quotes some saint or sage" (2: 67). However, while critiquing society's reliance on external norms, in this same essay, he continually quotes a host of others, including the Caliph Ali, Las Cases, Zoroaster, Fletcher, and Milton.

Surprisingly, this American prophet of self-reliance, who said "envy is ignorance [. . .] imitation is suicide" ("Self-Reliance" 2: 46), also constantly insists that no such thing as originality even exists. He writes, "The history of literature—take the net result of Tiraboschi, Warton, or Schlegel—is a sum of very few ideas and of very few original tales; all the rest being variation of these" ("Experience" 3: 47). Therefore, since no true originality can exist, the best authors are the best borrowers. "The greatest genius," according to him, "is the most indebted man" ("Shakespeare," *Representative Men* 4: 190).

Emerson even critiques his own mode of expression. "Words," he notes, "are finite organs of the infinite mind. They cannot cover the dimensions of what is truth. They break, chop, and impoverish it" (*Nature* 1: 44–45). Is Emerson's writing and lecturing thus a futile endeavor? No, but Emerson's method, particularly its strategy of contra-dictions, demands a great deal from his readers. Emerson demands that readers, as well as writers, must be creators. However, risks are inherent in this process. Emerson explains, "You have observed a skilful man reading Virgil. Well, that author is a thou-sand books to a thousand persons. Take the book into your two hands, and read your eyes out, you will never find what I find" ("Spiritual Laws" 2: 149). Yet, the compensa-tions are equally as great: "Art should exhilarate, and throw down the walls of circum-stance on every side, awakening in the beholder the same sense of universal relation and power which the work evinced in the artist and its highest effect is to make new artists" ("Art" 2: 363). This creation of vital and active readers is as important to the United States' fledging democracy as it is to its nascent intellectual life. Yet, at the same time that Emerson encourages and demands readers' active participation, he also presents himself as the passive receptacle of the divine spirit, most notably in *Nature*'s famous transparent eyeball passage where the narrator describes, "[. . .] the currents of the Uni-versal Being circulate through me; I am part or parcel of God" (1: 10).

The complications in Emerson's work grow even more acute as he gradually tem-pers his early idealism. In "Experience," written after the death of his six-year old son Waldo, Emerson questions some of the assumptions that had governed his thought up to that point. The essay even starts with the query, "Where do we find ourselves?" (3: 45). In "Experience," he describes a world where people are always separated from each other, unable to break through the prisons of self and mood that surround them. Ultimately, he concedes that he prefers to live in the middle range, not seeking out the giddying transcendental heights he had earlier proclaimed. He even claims that direct sight is impossible; instead, one must accept the contrary tendencies and live life. In "Illusions," he asserts, "Life is a series of lessons which must be lived to be under-stood. All is riddle, and the key to a riddle is another riddle" (6: 313). Emerson pre-sents a world where no truth is ultimate, no assertion unopen to question.

However, in a way, he constructs this more mature philosophy on his enduring idea that life is predicated on change. In his essay, "Circles," he maintains, "In Nature every moment is new; the past is always swallowed and forgotten; the coming only is sacred. Nothing is secure but life, transition, the energizing spirit" (2: 319–20). He expresses the same sentiment in "Self-Reliance," claiming, "Life only avails, not the having lived. Power ceases in the instant of repose; it resides in the moment of transition from a past to a new state; in the shooting of the gulf, in the darting to an aim" (2: 69). While Emer-son celebrates the possibilities of organic dynamism, at the same time he is also keenly aware of the drawbacks of this state, knowing that this never-ending becoming ensures that no standards can ever be permanent. "This surface," he observes, "on which we now stand is not fixed, but sliding" ("Circles" 2: 314). The circle is thus the perfect symbol of his world vision, indicating both totality and completion as well as partiality and incompleteness. This message of a continuing newness and revelation is part of the phi-losophy he shared with the British and German romantics, yet it also has a particular relevancy to Americans seeking a place in a world filled with a variety of rich, and at times overwhelming, traditions.

Emerson reflects the world's variety in his essays, constructing his world view out of a dialectic—Nature and Soul, the Me and Not-Me, Nature and Art—that he recon-figures in each of them. These dualities, first articulated in *Nature,* pervade all of his writings and, as he argues, all of human existence; he observes, "The value of the uni-verse contrives to throw itself into every point. If the good is there, so is the evil; if the affinity, so the repulsion; if the force, so the limitation" ("Compensation" 2: 102). These dualities operated everywhere, even the political arena: "The two parties which divide the state, the party of Conservatism and that of Innovation, are very old, and have disputed the possession of the world ever since it was made. It is the opposition of Past and Future, of Memory and Hope, of the Understanding and the Reason. It is the primal antagonism, the appearance in trifles of the two poles of nature" ("The Conservative" 1: 295–96).

In Emerson's eyes, difficulties arise when only one part of the dialectic functions; according to him, society is full of halves rather than wholes. In "The American Scholar," he asserts, "The state of society is one in which the members have suffered amputation from the trunk, and strut about so many monsters,—a good finger, a neck, a stomach, an elbow, but never a man" (1: 83). He even needs to enumerate the qualities of at least two different men in *Representative Men* to describe his turbulent century, "I described Bonaparte as a representative of the popular external life and aims of the nineteenth century. Its other half, its poet, is Goethe" (4: 270).

Yet, despite continuing to insist on the irremediable duality of his age, Emerson paradoxically holds the abiding faith that all this diversity will one day reveal its underlying unity. Beginning in *Nature,* he writes, "Herein is especially apprehended the unity of Nature,—this unity in variety,—which meets us everywhere. All the endless variety of things make an identical impression" (1: 43). For this lapsed minister, the conduit to this unity is still religious. In "The Over-Soul," he remarks, "In all conversation between two persons tacit reference is made, as to a third party, to a common nature. That third party or common nature is not social; it is impersonal; is God" (2: 277). Nonetheless, while maintaining his hope in the ultimate unity of the cosmos, he is forced to admit, "We are incompetent to solve the times. Our geometry cannot span the huge orbits of prevailing ideas, behold their return and reconcile their opposition. We can only obey our own polarity" ("Fate" 6: 31). Again, Emerson manages to hold contrary positions simultaneously. On the one hand, he maintains that "Life is not dialectics" ("Experience" 3: 58); on the other, he asserts that "there is a science of sciences,—I call it Dialectic" ("Plato" 4: 62).

Despite all, Emerson, throughout his career, continues to hope for a reconciliation, an apprehension of unity. For example, at the close of "The Divinity School Address," he looks for "the new Teacher that shall follow so far those shining laws that he shall see them come full circle . . ." (1: 151). However, in "The Poet," Emerson doubts that the ideal he seeks could exist. "I look in vain," he mourns, "for the poet whom I describe. We do not with sufficient plainness or sufficient profoundness address ourselves to life. . . . Time and nature yield us many gifts, but not yet the timely man, the new religion, the reconciler, whom all things await" (3: 37).

Emerson's whole volume on representative men does not celebrate the greatness of these men per se but hopes that soon these partial men may play their part in the creation of a greater whole. He proclaims, "No man, in all the procession of famous men, is reason or illumination or that essence we are looking for; but is an exhibition, in some quarter, of new possibilities. Could we one day complete the immense figure which these flagrant points compose!" (4: 32–33). Emerson's gaze remains resolutely fixed on the promise of the future, not the past.

CRITICAL RECEPTION

From an uncertain and inauspicious beginning, Emerson came to be revered as one of the seminal figures in American literature. His first essay, *Nature,* originally printed anonymously in a limited edition, sold moderately well, attracting the attention of like-minded thinkers. His second essay, *The American Scholar,* fared better, selling out its edition of 500 within a month. Later, Dr. Oliver Wendell Holmes pronounced the lecture "our intellectual Declaration of Independence" (qtd. in Allen 300). However, his early career also aroused controversy, particularly his talk to a small audience at the Harvard Divinity School in 1838. The Reverend Henry Ware Jr. responded in a way typical of many of the day when he wrote of Emerson's ideas that "their prevalence would tend to overthrow the authority and influence of Christianity" (qtd. in Allen 320). The public outcry against the address was so severe that Emerson worried it would affect his lecturing career.

Nonetheless, enhanced by the opportunities available on the American Lyceum circuit, his popularity increased in the 1830s and 40s. By the 1850s, he was giving as many as 70 lectures a year (Wilson 79). Despite his success on the lecture platform, his two volumes of *Essays* received mixed reviews, praise from those who admired his new thought and objections from the more conservative elements. Yet, his reputation spread beyond the United States. His friend Thomas Carlyle wrote the introduction to the English edition of *Essays,* which proved popular throughout Europe. One testament to his growing reputation was his invitation to return to England in 1847; this time, though, he did not return as a seeker, but as a guest of honor, invited to lecture around the country. In fact, the first biography of Emerson, published in 1855, was by an Englishman, George Searle Phillips.

One of the signs of his growing influence was the number of people he affected, both personally and professionally. In his inner circle, he personally aided in the publishing careers of Henry David Thoreau and Margaret Fuller. However, eventually his influence spread so far that an aspiring young poet, Walt Whitman, sent his first volume of poetry, *Leaves of Grass* (1855), to the writer he admired.

At his death, the *New York Times* wrote, "His influence has in all likelihood been greater upon the American, and in less degree upon the English, mind than any other writer in the Nation" (qtd. in Allen 669–70). After his death, his critical reputation continued to grow, not only with further editions of his work but also with various critical appraisals. The beginning of the new century brought further recognition: his election into the American Hall of Fame in 1900 and the celebration of the centenary of his birth in 1903. The latter event elicited yet more criticism and the beginning of the publication of his *Complete Works.* His journals were published in 1909, and Bliss Perry's *The Heart of Emerson's Journals* was a best-seller in 1926. Emerson's reputation probably reached its high-water mark in the 1920s.

His influence was profoundly felt among writers and thinkers in his own generation and in subsequent ones. Among the philosophers, he was read and admired by William James, John Dewey, and George Santayana. Among the poets who admired him were James Russell Lowell, Oliver Wendell Holmes, John Greenleaf Whittier, Emily Dickinson, Edward Arlington Robinson, Robinson Jeffers, Hart Crane, and Robert Frost. Emersonian ideas and characters have appeared in fiction as well. While his Concord neighbor, Nathaniel Hawthorne, often disagreed with him, his work utilizes and questions a number of Transcendentalist ideas in works such as *The Scarlet Letter* (1850), *The Blithedale Romance* (1852), and "The Celestial Railroad" (1846). Herman Melville also frequently satirized Emersonian ideas through characters such as Plotinus Plinlimmon in *Pierre* (1852) and Mark Winsome in *The Confidence-Man* (1857). Other Emerson-influenced characters include Miss Birdseye in Henry James' *The Bostonians* (1886) and Jim Casy in John Steinbeck's *The Grapes of Wrath* (1939). Not only Americans were affected by

Emerson; he influenced a number of British writers including Thomas Carlyle, Arthur Hugh Clough, Matthew Arnold, John Ruskin, and George Eliot. Among the Europeans the French poet Charles Baudelaire, the Belgian writer Maurice Maeterlinck, the French philosopher Henri Bergson, the Russian writer Ivan Turgenev, and the German philosopher Friedrich Nietzsche were all admirers. Even today, the extent and scope of his influence continue to be debated.

WORKS CITED

Allen, Gay Wilson. *Waldo Emerson: A Biography.* New York: Penguin, 1982.

Emerson. Ralph Waldo. *The Complete Works of Ralph Waldo Emerson.* Centenary Edition, Volumes 1–12. Ed. Edward Waldo Emerson. Boston: Houghton Mifflin, 1883–1904.

Slater, Joseph, ed. *The Correspondence of Emerson and Carlyle.* New York: Columbia UP, 1964.

Wilson, R. Jackson. "Emerson as Lecturer: Man Thinking, Man Saying." *The Cambridge Companion to Ralph Waldo Emerson.* Eds. Joel Porte and Sandra Morris. Cambridge: Cambridge UP, 1999. 76–96.

BIBLIOGRAPHY

Works by Ralph Waldo Emerson

The Complete Works of Ralph Waldo Emerson. Centenary Edition. Ed. Edward Waldo Emerson. 12 vols. Boston and New York: Houghton Mifflin, 1903–1904.

The Letters of Ralph Waldo Emerson. Ed. Ralph L. Rusk and Eleanor M. Tilton. 9 vols. New York: Columbia UP, 1939–94.

The Early Lectures of Ralph Waldo Emerson. Ed. Stephen E. Whicher, Robert E. Spiller, and Wallace E. Williams. 3 vols. Cambridge: The Belknap P of Harvard UP, 1959–72.

The Journals and Miscellaneous Notebooks of Ralph Waldo Emerson. Ed. William H. Gilman et al. 16 vols. Cambridge: Harvard UP, 1960–82.

The Correspondence of Emerson and Carlyle. Ed. Joseph Slater. New York: Columbia UP, 1964.

The Collected Works of Ralph Waldo Emerson. Ed. Robert E. Spiller et al. 5 vols. to date. Cambridge: Harvard UP, 1971.

Ralph Waldo Emerson: Essays and Lectures. Ed. Joel Porte. New York: Library of America, 1983.

The Poetry Notebooks of Ralph Waldo Emerson. Ed. Ralph H. Orth et al. Columbia: U of Missouri P, 1986.

Complete Sermons of Ralph Waldo Emerson. Ed. Albert J. von Frank et al. 4 vols. Columbia: U of Missouri P, 1994.

Emerson: Collected Poems and Translations. Ed. Harold Bloom and Paul Kane. New York: Library of America, 1994.

Emerson's Antislavery Writings. Ed. Len Gougeon and Joel Meyerson. New Haven: Yale UP, 1995.

Studies of Ralph Waldo Emerson

Allen, Gay Wilson. *Waldo Emerson: A Biography.* New York: Penguin, 1982.

Baker, Carlos. *Emerson Among the Eccentrics.* New York: Viking, 1996.

Barish, Evelyn. *Emerson: The Roots of Prophecy.* Princeton: Princeton UP, 1989.

Bishop, Jonathan. *Emerson on the Soul.* Cambridge: Harvard UP, 1964.

Bloom, Harold, ed. *Ralph Waldo Emerson.* Modern Critical Views Series. New York: Chelsea House, 1985.

Bode, Carl, ed. *Ralph Waldo Emerson: A Profile.* New York: Hill and Wang, 1969.

Brooks, Van Wyck. *The Life of Emerson.* New York: The Literary Guild, 1932.

Brown, Lee R. *The Emerson Museum: Practical Romanticism and the Pursuit of the Whole*. Cambridge: Harvard UP, 1997.

Buell, Lawrence. *Literary Transcendentalism: Style and Vision in the American Renaissance*. Ithaca: Cornell UP, 1973.

———. *Ralph Waldo Emerson: A Collection of Critical Essays*. Englewood Cliffs, NJ: Prentice-Hall, 1993.

Burkholder, Robert E., and Joel Meyerson, eds. *Ralph Waldo Emerson: An Annotated Secondary Bibliography*. Pittsburgh: U of Pittsburgh P, 1985.

———. *Critical Essays on Ralph Waldo Emerson*. Boston: G. K. Hall, 1983.

Cabot, James Elliot. *A Memoir of Ralph Waldo Emerson*. Boston: Houghton Mifflin, 1887.

Cadava, Eduardo. *Emerson and the Climates of History*. Stanford: Stanford UP, 1997.

Cady, Edwin, and Louis J. Budd, eds. *On Emerson*. Durham: Duke UP, 1988.

Carpenter, F. I. *Emerson Handbook*. New York: Hendricks House, 1953.

Cayton, Mary Kupiec. *Emerson's Emergence: Self and Society in the Transformation of New England, 1800–1845*. Chapel Hill: U of North Carolina P, 1983.

Cheyfitz, Eric. *The Trans-Parent: Sexual Politics in the Language of Emerson*. Baltimore: Johns Hopkins UP, 1981.

Donadio, Stephen, Stephen Railton, and Ormond Seavey, eds. *Emerson and His Legacy: Essays in Honor of Quentin Anderson*. Carbondale: Southern Illinois UP, 1986.

Duncan, Jeffrey. *Power and Form in Emerson's Thought*. Charlottesville: U of Virginia P, 1973.

Ellison, Julie. *Emerson's Romantic Style*. Princeton: Princeton UP, 1984.

Firkins, O. W. *Ralph Waldo Emerson*. Boston: Houghton Mifflin, 1915.

Garvey, T. Gregory. ed. *The Emerson Dilemma: Essays on Emerson and Social Reform*. Athens: U of Georgia P, 2000.

Gelpi, Donald. *Endless Seeker: The Religious Quest of Ralph Waldo Emerson*. Lanham, MD: UP of America, 1991.

Gougeon, Len. *Virtue's Hero: Emerson, Antislavery and Reform*. Athens: U of Georgia P, 1990.

Harding, Walter. *Emerson's Library*. Charlottesville: UP of Virginia, 1967.

Harris, Kenneth Marc. *Carlyle and Emerson: Their Long Debate*. Cambridge: Harvard UP, 1978.

Hednut, Robert K. *The Aesthetics of Ralph Waldo Emerson: The Materials and Methods of His Poetry*. Lewiston, NY: Mellen, 1996.

Hodder, Alan D. *Emerson's Rhetoric of Revelation*. University Park: Pennsylvania State UP, 1989.

Holmes, Oliver Wendell. *Ralph Waldo Emerson*. Boston: Houghton Mifflin, 1884.

Hopkins, Vivian C. *Spires of Form: A Study of Emerson's Aesthetic Theory*. Cambridge: Harvard UP, 1951.

Howe, Irving. *The American Newness: Culture and Politics in the Age of Emerson*. Cambridge: Harvard UP, 1986.

Hubbell, George S. *Concordance to the Poems of Ralph Waldo Emerson*. New York: H. W. Wilson, 1932.

Hughes, Gertrude Reif. *Emerson's Demanding Optimism*. Baton Rouge: Louisiana UP, 1984.

Ihrig, Mary Alice. *Emerson's Transcendental Vocabulary: A Concordance*. New York: Garland, 1981.

Irey, Eugene F. *A Concordance to Five Essays of Ralph Waldo Emerson*. New York: Garland, 1981.

Konvitz, Milton R., ed. *The Recognition of Ralph Waldo Emerson: Selected Criticism Since 1937*. Ann Arbor: U of Michigan P, 1972.

Konvitz, Milton R., and Stephen E. Whicher, eds. *Emerson: A Collection of Critical Essays*. Englewood Cliffs, NJ: Prentice-Hall, 1962.

Leary, Lewis. *Ralph Waldo Emerson: An Interpretive Essay*. Boston: Twayne Publishers, 1980.

Levin, David, ed. *Emerson: Prophecy, Metamorphosis, Influence*. New York: Columbia UP, 1975.

Levin, Jonathan. *The Poetics of Transition: Emerson, Pragmatism & American Literary Modernism*. Durham: Duke UP, 1999.

Lopez, Michael. *Emerson and Power: Creative Antagonism in the Nineteenth Century*. DeKalb, IL: Northern Illinois UP, 1996.

Matthiessen, F. O. *American Renaissance: Art and Expression in the Age of Emerson and Whitman.* New York: Oxford UP, 1941.

McAleer, John. *Ralph Waldo Emerson: Days of Encounter.* Boston: Little, Brown, 1984.

Michael, John. *Emerson and Skepticism: The Cipher of the World.* Baltimore, MD: Johns Hopkins UP, 1988.

Mitchell, Charles E. *Individualism and its Discontents: Appropriations of Emerson, 1880–1950.* Amherst: U of Massachusetts P, 1997.

Mott, Wesley T. *"The Strains of Eloquence": Emerson and His Sermons.* University Park: Pennsylvania State UP, 1988.

Mott, Wesley T., and Robert E. Burkholder. eds. *Emersonian Circles: Essays in Honor of Joel Myerson.* Rochester, NY: U of Rochester P, 1996.

Myerson, Joel. ed. *A Historical Guide to Ralph Waldo Emerson.* NY: Oxford UP, 1999.

———. *Ralph Waldo Emerson: A Descriptive Bibliography.* Pittsburgh: U of Pittsburgh P, 1982.

Neufeldt, Leonard. *The House of Emerson.* Lincoln: U of Nebraska P, 1982.

Newfield, Christopher. *The Emerson Effect: Individualism and Submission in America.* Chicago: U of Chicago P, 1996.

Packer, B. L. *Emerson's Fall: A New Interpretation of the Major Essays.* New York: Continuum, 1982.

———. "Origin and Authority: Emerson and the Higher Criticism." *Reconstructing American Literary History.* Ed. Sacvan Bercovitch. Cambridge: Harvard UP, 1986. 67–92.

Paul, Sherman. *Emerson's Angle of Vision: Man and Nature in American Experience.* Cambridge: Harvard UP, 1952.

Poirier, Richard. *The Renewal of Literature: Emersonian Reflections.* New York: Random House, 1987.

Pommer, Henry F. *Emerson's First Marriage.* Carbondale: Southern Illinois UP, 1967.

Porte, Joel. *Emerson and Thoreau: Transcendentalists in Conflict.* Middletown, CT: Wesleyan UP, 1966.

———, ed. *Emerson, Prospect and Retrospect.* Cambridge: Harvard UP, 1982.

———. *Representative Man: Ralph Waldo Emerson in His Time.* New York: Oxford UP, 1979; rev. ed. New York: Columbia UP, 1988.

Porte, Joel, and Saundra Morris. eds. *The Cambridge Companion to Ralph Waldo Emerson.* Cambridge UP, 1999.

———. *Emerson's Prose and Poetry: A Norton Critical Edition.* NY: W. W. Norton & Co., 2001.

Porter, David. *Emerson and Literary Change.* Cambridge: Harvard UP, 1978.

Richardson, Robert D. *Emerson: The Mind on Fire.* Berkeley: U of California P, 1995.

Roberson, Susan L. *Emerson in His Sermons: A Man-Made Self.* Columbia: U of Missouri P, 1982.

Robinson, David. *Apostle of Culture: Emerson as Lecturer.* Philadelphia: U of Pennsylvania P, 1982.

———. *Emerson and The Conduct of Life.* New York: Cambridge UP, 1993.

Rosenwald, Lawrence. *Emerson and the Art of the Diary.* New York: Oxford UP, 1988.

Rowe, John Carlos. *At Emerson's Tomb: The Politics of Classical American Literature.* NY: Columbia UP, 1997.

Rusk, Ralph L. *The Life of Ralph Waldo Emerson.* New York: Columbia UP, 1949.

Scudder, Horace. *The Lonely Wayfaring Man: Emerson and Some Englishmen.* London: Oxford UP, 1936.

Sealts, Merton M. *Emerson on the Scholar.* Columbia: U of Missouri P, 1992.

Sealts, Merton M., and Alfred R. Ferguson. *Emerson's Nature; Origin, Growth, Meaning.* Carbondale: Southern Illinois UP, 1979.

Sowder, William J. *Emerson's Impact on the British Isles and Canada.* Charlottesville: The UP of Virginia, 1966.

Van-Cromphour, Gustaaf. *Emerson's Ethics.* Columbia: U of Missouri P, 1999.

von Frank, Albert J. *An Emerson Chronology.* New York: G. K. Hall, 1994.

Van Leer, David. *Emerson's Epistemology: The Argument of the Essays.* New York: Cambridge UP, 1986.

Wagenknecht, Edward. *Ralph Waldo Emerson: Portrait of a Balanced Soul.* New York: Oxford UP, 1974.

Waggoner, Hyatt H. *Emerson as Poet.* Princeton: Princeton UP, 1974.

Weisbuch, Robert. *Atlantic Double-Cross: American Literature and British Influence in the Age of Emerson.* Chicago: U of Chicago P, 1987.

Whicher, Stephen. *Freedom and Fate: An Inner Life of Ralph Waldo Emerson.* Philadelphia: U of Pennsylvania P, 1953.

Yannella, Donald. *Ralph Waldo Emerson.* Boston: Twayne Publishers, 1982.

Yoder, R. A. *Emerson and the Orphic Poet in America.* Berkeley: U of California P, 1978.

Zwang, Christina. *Feminist Conversations: Fuller, Emerson, and the Play of Reading.* Ithaca: Cornell UP, 1995.

FANNY FERN [SARA WILLIS PARTON] (1811–1872)

Terry Novak

BIOGRAPHY

Sara Payson Willis Parton was born in Portland, Maine, on July 9, 1811, to Nathaniel and Hannah Willis, parents with distinctly opposite personalities. Nathaniel Willis was a devout Calvinist who preached the doctrine of a harsh, punishing God from the pulpit as Deacon Willis. His beliefs permeated his life and set the tone for his parenting style. Hannah Willis, on the other hand, was a much more cheerful and lighthearted person who did not necessarily adhere to the same religious doctrine as did her husband. It was to her mother that Sara looked for religious inspiration and character modeling. Sara Willis was the fifth of nine children born to Hannah and Nathaniel. Her siblings included Nathaniel Parker Willis, six years her senior, who himself became a writer and powerful publisher.

At only six weeks of age, Sara Willis moved with her family to Boston. There the elder Nathaniel Willis became deacon of the Park Street Church and founded the first religious newspaper in the United States, *The Recorder.* Eleven years later he founded the first newspaper exclusively for children, *The Youth's Companion.* Mr. Willis was concerned about his daughter Sara's free spirit and lack of seriousness about religion—at least in his estimation. Sara was sent to two boarding schools in an effort to help her improve her outlook before being sent to Catharine Beecher's famous Hartford Female Seminary in Hartford, Connecticut. As was common with female seminaries, Beecher's school placed a heavy emphasis on Christianity and the proper role of women in a Christian society. Beecher failed to tame the mischievous girl, however, though she and her sister, Harriet Beecher Stowe, who taught at the school while Sara was a student there, both later remembered Sara Willis as a remarkable albeit undisciplined girl. It was while a student at the Hartford Female Seminary that Sara's writing first came to public attention, with her essays finding their way into print in the local newspaper. Her satiric style was already firmly in place.

Sara left the school in 1830 and returned to her family in Boston where, besides her domestic duties, she did some writing and editing work for her father's newspaper. On

May 4, 1837, at the age of 26, Sara Willis married Charles Harrington Eldredge, a banker, and left her family home again. By all accounts, this was a happy marriage. The Eldredges' happiness did not last long, though. Their daughter Mary was born in 1838; daughter Grace's birth followed in 1841. Three years after Grace's birth hardships began for Sara and her husband. Within a six-week period both Sara's youngest sister Ellen and her mother died. Sara's time of sorrow was tempered for a bit by the birth of a third daughter, Ellen. Six months after baby Ellen's birth, though, the Eldredges faced the unimaginable tragedy of losing their firstborn, Mary, to brain fever. Sara's troubles were further compounded a year later by the death of her husband Charles, who succumbed to typhoid fever.

Charles's death left Sara in dire straits. Eldredge had been far from financially successful and left Sara with an indebted estate. With two young daughters for whom to care and no inherited financial comforts, Sara found herself in the midst of an ugly and disgraceful battle between her father, Deacon Nathaniel Willis, and her in-laws over how much money each party could—or, more accurately, could not—afford to contribute to the livelihood of the widow and her fatherless children. This argument was somewhat settled in 1849 when Sara agreed to marry Samuel P. Farrington purely for the sake of financial security. Farrington was a widower with two children who married Sara despite her confession that she bore no love for him. The marriage was ill fated from the beginning and became more miserable with each passing day. In early 1851, Sara left her husband, which spurred him to rumor spreading before he left town and began divorce proceedings against his wife, on the grounds of desertion. The act of a wife leaving her husband was almost unheard of in the nineteenth century. There were very few opportunities for women to make their own living; hence, marriage was seen as largely the only option for women. Add to this the Cult of True Womanhood that existed during the time, urging women to be good Christian stewards and obedient to society's laws, and the contemporary reader can begin to understand how shocking and distressing Sara's actions would have been to her family and friends. Because Sara's act of leaving her second husband was an embarrassment to her family's nineteenth-century sensibilities, she received no further assistance from her family. Instead, she was left to her own devices in order to earn a living for herself and her children. Unsuccessful at her attempts to gain a teaching job, Sara took a job as a seamstress, but this was a job that paid far too little for her to support her family. Sara was forced to allow the Eldredge family to take in Grace, a move that proved especially miserable for Grace, who was not treated especially well by her grandparents. Sara and Ellen, meanwhile, lived in poverty. Sara's desperation led her to begin writing for newspapers in mid-1851. She managed to eke out a small living at first and adopted the pseudonym Fanny Fern, the name by which she is best known today. Realizing that her brother Nathaniel had helped other women writers by publishing their work in his *Home Journal,* Sara sent her brother several samples of her work. Her brother refused to help her, citing his shame at her choice of article topics, which were for the most part biting satires. One might also presume that he, like his father, was still ashamed that Sara had left her second marriage and did not wish to condone what would have been deemed a sinful way of life.

As she had been accustomed to, Sara continued to toil without assistance. She began writing several articles a week for both the *Olive Branch* and the *True Flag.* Though she worked hard and produced much, Sara was still not paid very well. Her work, however, was gaining notice and admiration, to the point that other publications were also reprinting her articles, though without any remuneration to the author. Even a member of her brother's editorial staff, James Parton, began publishing Sara's work, which led to his loss of a position at the *Home Journal* once Nathaniel Willis discovered what was happening. In 1852 the publisher of the New York periodical *Musical World and Times* offered Fanny Fern a job writing exclusively for his publication at a salary double that which she was at the time earning from the other two papers. The publisher soon discovered that Fern was in fact the sister of his editor, Sara's brother Richard Willis. Richard, unlike Nathaniel, was delighted to have Fanny Fern's column in his paper. With this job, Fanny Fern became the first true woman columnist in the history of publishing in the United States. She also became extremely popular. The editors of the papers for which she had ceased writing begged her to come back to them, at much more attractive financial terms. *Musical World*'s publisher, Oliver Dyer, agreed to allow Fern to write for other publications as well.

By 1853 Fern had been approached with an offer to compile some of her writings in a book. Wisely, Fern chose to take royalties rather than outright payment for the book, *Fern Leaves from Fanny's Portfolio,* which became a best-seller in both the United States and England. A second collection, *Little Ferns for Fanny's Little Friends,* was published later in 1853, and a third collection, *Fern Leaves from Fanny's Portfolio, Series Two,* was published the following year. In the middle of 1853 Fern and her daughter Ellen were able to move to New York; Grace was finally able to rejoin her family.

Soon after Fern was contracted to write a novel. *Ruth Hall* was published in late 1855. Although the autobiographical work sold well, Fern's true identity was revealed to the public by a former employer who recognized himself in one of the unflattering character descriptions. His determination to "get back" at Sara led to much castigation from people who found it difficult to accept that a woman could write so harshly—and truthfully—about her family. Fern persevered, however, and continued with her successful writing career. In 1855 she became the highest paid newspaper writer of the time when she signed a contract to write an exclusive regular column for the *New York Ledger.* Her columns began in early 1856, as did her marriage to James Parton, the former employee of her brother Nathaniel and her friend since her arrival in New York. Ever the woman beyond her time, Fern had Parton sign a prenuptial agreement that made it clear that her property and her earnings were hers and would revert to the ownership of her children upon her death.

Fern also published a second novel, *Rose Clark,* in 1856. This novel also contained autobiographical elements and was followed by the publication of several more collections of her articles. In addition, Fern continued writing her newspaper column until her death from cancer on October 10, 1872. Ever the strong and independent spirit, Fern hid the severity of her illness from others and compensated handily when her body began to fail her. Her last columns were published posthumously.

MAJOR WORKS AND THEMES

Without a doubt Sara Willis Parton's/Fanny Fern's most significant work is her autobiographical novel *Ruth Hall.* Elizabeth Cady Stanton found it easy in the nineteenth century to declare that "*Ruth Hall* marked the beginning of a genuine female literature, because it was the first book by a woman to give an honest account of her life" (Huf 19). Fern, writing under the comfort of anonymity, does indeed honestly write of her struggles in this novel. The reader understands exactly how life was for the young wife and mother as she lost her daughter, her husband, and nearly her faith in others. Along with the autobiographical elements, however, are the striking bits of satire for which Fanny Fern is so well known. Fern deals with hypocrisy among the so-called religious, with the inequities of society, with the callousness of those who have much, and with the pitiful struggles of the desperately poor in this novel. She also deals with issues that seem much more attuned to our own time: the struggles of the single mother, the fight for fair wages for women, the feminist philosophy of how women should lead their lives. Also deeply ingrained in the novel is the exercise of hearty attention to one's passions, for the character Ruth Hall is nothing if not passionate. So deeply ingrained into her personhood are Ruth's passions that they formulate the crux of Ruth's soul and of her sense of spirituality.

Ruth Hall can also be read as a primer of women's issues in the mid-nineteenth century. Fern shows the reader how society fit women into the role of wife; there was not much beyond that. When Ruth Hall becomes a widow, she also becomes a misfit in her society. The bulk of the novel deals with Ruth's widowhood and her struggle to support her two young children and to become financially independent. Fern shows the reader how difficult it was for a woman to earn a decent wage; more often than not she was seen as a hard worker who would work for low wages. When Ruth does indeed achieve financial security, it is against all odds. Even Fern's contemporary readers, who were aware of the link between Ruth Hall and Fanny Fern, realized that such a situation was far from the norm.

Parton's second novel, *Rose Clark*, published in 1856, is less biting than the first novel. Parton had learned a hard lesson when her true identity was revealed shortly after the publication of *Ruth Hall*. She was not going to lay herself so bare again. Still, *Rose Clark* does draw upon Parton's life, particularly her bad second marriage. The character Gertrude Dean is a widow who marries a widower with children and has to endure emotional abuse from him. Gertrude also finds herself with a nonsupportive family, in every sense of the word. Also like her creator, Gertrude Dean strives to be her own person, strong and independent. Rose Clark, on the other hand, is much more the stereotypical nineteenth-century woman. Fern draws upon the style of sentimentalism in her portrayal of Rose and distances herself from her character. The reader is left with a much less satisfying experience than can be had with Fern's first novel, although the work fits more handily into the general canon of nineteenth-century American women's fiction.

Fern's collected newspaper writings are a major part of her individual canon as well. Most of her articles focus on the condition of women in the nineteenth century. In her chatty, matter-of-fact way, Fern tackles the subjects of women's rights, women's suffrage, and women's independence (or lack thereof) deftly and expertly. She also shows a commitment to general issues of social justice, class structure, and the plight of the poor. Many of her articles are also pieces of sentimental literature, following closely the expectations of women of the day. The contemporary reader may find these less provocative and useful, but they served Fern's purposes well. Always her articles are interesting and pointed and provide an accurate glimpse into nineteenth-century society.

CRITICAL RECEPTION

Fanny Fern was highly paid during her writing career for good reason: she was extremely popular. Even when her contemporary critics were lambasting her for being indelicate and unwomanly, they were at the same time delighting in her fine-tuned craft. There were discussions about whether or not Fanny Fern could actually be a woman or if this were not simply the pseudonym of a clever man, but there were no arguments about the quality of Fern's work or the interest in her subjects. Even Nathaniel

Hawthorne, well known for his derogatory comments on nineteenth-century women writers, found *Ruth Hall* noteworthy. In her work, Joyce W. Warren quotes from a letter Hawthorne wrote to his publisher shortly after reading *Ruth Hall:*

I have since been reading "Ruth Hall"; and I must say I enjoyed it a good deal. The woman writes as if the devil was in her; and that is the only condition under which a woman ever writes anything worth reading. Generally women write like emasculated men, and are only distinguished from male authors by greater feebleness and folly; but when they throw off the restraints of decency, and come before the public stark naked, as it were—then their books are sure to possess character and value. (xxxv)

While Fern's writings remained popular through her own century, many twentieth-century critics dismissed her as just another sentimental woman writer from the nineteenth century. Many critics tend to be unforgiving of authors who are popular successes in their own time. Some critics failed to look closely at Fern's work—especially her novel *Ruth Hall*—and many failed to consider the social implications of Fern's era when studying her work. In the 1980s critics were ready to take a new look at Fanny Fern. Joyce W. Warren took the lead in revitalizing the study of Fern. Writing about the novel *Ruth Hall,* Warren says, "It was through her experiences as a widow in a patriarchal society that Fanny Fern was brought to a realization of the need for a change in the position of women" ("Text" 68); this change was largely a woman's need for financial independence. Contemporary critics continue to see this as an important theme throughout Fern's writing.

Later twentieth-century critics have also paid attention to the unique and liberating writing style used by Fern, a style that differs drastically from that of her male contemporaries as well as from that of other nineteenth-century women who attempted to pattern themselves after the accepted style of fine writing. Fern writes as if she is chatting cozily with the reader in her kitchen over a plate of cookies and a pot of tea, unabashedly rebelling against accepted writing conventions and daring to use her own style, something that has become quite critically popular and important in more recent times. Nancy Walker writes, "By focusing on the claiming of one's own language as a precondition of autonomy, by resisting the closure of the 'marriage plot' and by establishing her heroine within the matrix of authentic nineteenth-century culture, Fanny Fern made a major contribution to the tradition of American fiction" (62). As Walker points out, Fern is also acclaimed in modern times for avoiding the idea of marriage as the answer to all a woman's dreams. Rather, Fern focuses on women's independence and strength in her writings.

By and large, current literary critics respect Fanny Fern not only for her use of language but also for the courage she exhibits in her choice of themes. While there is still some criticism concerning her occasional use of sentimentalism, most critics choose to focus on Fern's social conscience and find it captivating and praiseworthy.

WORKS CITED

Fern, Fanny. *Ruth Hall and Other Writings.* 1855. Ed. Joyce W. Warren. New Brunswick, NJ: Rutgers UP, 1986.

Huf, Linda. *A Portrait of the Artist as a Young Woman: The Writer as Heroine in American Literature.* New York: Frederick Ungar Publication Company, 1985.

Walker, Nancy A. *Fanny Fern.* New York: Twayne Publishers, 1993.

Warren, Joyce W. Introduction to *Ruth Hall and Other Writings*. By Fanny Fern. Ed. Joyce W. Warren. New Brunswick, NJ: Rutgers UP, 1986. ix–xxxix.

————. "Text and Context in Fanny Fern's *Ruth Hall: From Widowhood to Independence*." In Mink and Ward. *Joinings and Disjoinings: The Significance of Marital Status in Literature*. Ohio: Bowling Green State University Popular Press, 1991.

BIBLIOGRAPHY

Works by Fanny Fern

Novels
Ruth Hall. New York: Mason Brothers, 1855.
Rose Clark. New York: Mason Brothers, 1856.

Collected Nonfiction
Fern Leaves from Fanny's Portfolio. Auburn: Derby and Miller, 1853.
Little Ferns for Fanny's Little Friends. Auburn: Derby and Miller, 1853.
Fern Leaves from Fanny's Portfolio, Series Two. Auburn and Buffalo: Miller, Orton, & Mulligan, 1854.
Fresh Leaves. New York: Mason Brothers, 1857.
The Play-Day Book. New York: Mason Brothers, 1857.
A New Story Book for Children. New York: Mason Brothers, 1864.
Folly As It Flies. New York: G. W. Carleton, 1868.
Ginger-Snaps. New York: G. W. Carleton, 1870.
Caper-Sauce. New York: G. W. Carleton, 1872.

Studies of Fanny Fern

Baym, Nina. *Woman's Fiction: A Guide to Novels by and about Women in America*. Ithaca: Cornell UP, 1978.
Harker, Jaime. " 'Pious Cant' and Blasphemy: Fanny Fern's Radicalized Sentiment." *Legacy* 18 (2001): 52–64.
Kelley, Mary. *Private Women, Public Stage: Literary Domesticity in Nineteenth Century America*. New York: Oxford UP, 1984.
Walker, Nancy A. *Fanny Fern*. New York: Twayne Publishers, 1993.
Warren, Joyce W. *Fanny Fern: An Independent Woman*. New Brunswick: Rutgers UP, 1992.
————. "Fanny Fern's *Rose Clark*." *Legacy* 8 (1991): 92–103.
Wood, Ann Douglas. "Scribbling Women and Fanny Fern: Why Women Wrote." *American Quarterly* 23 (September 1971): 3–14.

MARGARET FULLER (1810–1850)

Anne Baker

BIOGRAPHY

Sarah Margaret Fuller (she began to call herself Margaret as a teenager) was born in her parents' home in Cambridgeport, Massachusetts, on May 23, 1810. She was the first of eight children born to Margarett Crane and Timothy Fuller; two of her siblings did not survive infancy. As a child, the most significant factor in Margaret's life was her father's strong influence on her education and development. Timothy Fuller, a lawyer and later a representative to Congress for four terms, gave his daughter a rigorous classical education that began when she was only three years old. At six years old Margaret was reading and translating Latin, and by the time she was 10 she was well read in Latin classics. At 11 she moved on to a serious study of French and Italian. While her father's enlightenment regard for the intellect and reason enabled her to receive an education that was nearly unheard of for girls, his high standards also placed a considerable strain on her. Later in life she blamed her father's exacting love and his valuation of accuracy and precision above all other aspects of education for her childhood nightmares and sleepwalking. And there is no doubt that Fuller's unusual education and the intellectual ambitions her father encouraged led to a difficult adolescence.

Margaret began attending the Port School in Cambridgeport in 1819, and later studied for a year and a half at the Boston Lyceum for Young Ladies, which was highly unusual in holding female students to high academic standards. But though her classmates at both schools were the children of Cambridge's intellectual elite, Margaret stood out as a prodigy. She preferred adults to her classmates, and apparently the lack of interest and sympathy was mutual. Alarmed by her difficulties with her peers and by her aggressive socializing with Harvard students and professors at the balls and parties she began attending at age 13, her father altered his views about Margaret's education and sent her for a year to a country boarding school for girls. At Miss Prescott's Seminary, Margaret was expected to accustom herself to more traditional feminine behavior.

Despite the close attachment she developed to the headmistress, this final year of Fuller's formal education was not an easy one. (She later recorded some of the details in the autobiographical sketch "Mariana," which she included in *Summer on the Lakes in 1843*.) In 1825, however, she returned home with her intellectual curiosity intact, and happily reentered Cambridge society. There, at a time when European Romantic ideas and Harvard Unitarianism were mingling to create an unusually vibrant intellectual atmosphere, she spent eight years meeting important literary figures of the period and developing close friendships with Harvard students—all male in those days—who shared her literary and philosophical interests. The most significant development in Margaret's continuing process of self-education at this time was her discovery of German writers such as Novalis, Schiller, and Goethe, and she taught herself German in order to read them.

This period of intellectual growth and cameraderie ended when Margaret was 23 and her father decided to retire from political life to a farm in Groton, Massachusetts. Cut off from the intellectual life of Cambridge, which she loved, and now responsible for the education of her siblings, her unhappiness during this period was exacerbated by the fact that the male friends she had made in recent years were beginning careers and, in many cases, getting married. Keenly aware that the careers her male peers pursued were closed to women, she also became increasingly aware that her male friends—though they valued her intellect and lively conversation—preferred more conventional, less bookish young women as wives. At a crossroads, Fuller turned to writing as a potential means of creating a meaningful life for herself, publishing several reviews and a short story, and beginning to work on a translation of Goethe's play *Torquato Tasso*.

These early efforts to launch a literary career became more urgent when her father died suddenly of cholera in 1835. Fuller continued to publish and to work on her writing, but, in need of a steady income, she also began teaching. The next few years saw her teaching at some of the most progressive schools in New England—Bronson Alcott's Temple School in Boston and the Greene Street School in Providence. Fuller was by all accounts a successful teacher, and, at the latter school in particular, her interactions with her female students played an important role in shaping views about gender and education that would figure prominently in her writing. She found, however, that teaching left her little time to write, and in 1839 she resigned from her teaching position and returned to Boston. There she initiated a series of "Conversations"—essentially a kind of private adult education class for well-to-do women who paid for the rare opportunity to participate in intellectually challenging discussion on subjects such as art and Greek mythology. A year later, she also accepted the position of editor for the *Dial*, which became the most important periodical of the Transcendentalist movement. Her friendship with Emerson—the chief spokesman of Transcendentalism—blossomed during this time, and in 1842, Fuller published both "Bettine Brentano and Her Friend Günderode" and her translation of *Correspondence of Fraulein Günderode with Bettine von Arnim*. Both works were the product of Fuller's fascination with German Romanticism and with gender.

During the early 1840s, then, Fuller attained the livelihood and the intellectual community that she had longed for during her exile in Groton. But she soon began to chafe at the narrowness of life in the Transcendentalist milieu of Boston, Cambridge, and Concord, and in 1843, she joined her friend Sarah Freeman Clarke on the trip to the West that would mark the beginning of her break from New England. In a letter to Emerson written during that trip, Fuller weighed the intellectual life back East against the rough life of the frontier and found both wanting: "Truly there is no place for me to live. . . . I like not the petty intellectualities, cant, and bloodless theory there at home, but this merely instinctive existence . . . pleases me no better" (*Letters* 3:143). In response to this dilemma, Fuller, after publishing *Summer on the Lakes in 1843*—an account of her journey to the West—moved to New York City and took a position as writer for Horace Greeley's *New-York Tribune.*

As a newspaper writer, Fuller maintained her interest in literature and the arts, often writing book and theater reviews. But she also had the opportunity to expand her subjects to include social issues such as immigration and prison reform and to reach a much wider audience. In 1846, after a year and a half of newspaper work and the publication of *Woman in the Nineteenth Century* and *Papers on Literature and Art,* Fuller took the opportunity to travel to Europe as foreign correspondent for the *Tribune.*

After visiting England, Scotland, and Paris, she traveled on to Italy in 1847, where she became intensely sympathetic to the Italian nationalist movement, which was rising up against the Austro-Hungarian Empire and attempting to found an Italian state. While in Italy, Fuller also met Giovanni Ossoli, an impoverished nobleman. Despite the fact that Ossoli was considerably younger than she and did not share her intellectual interests, the two became romantically involved and Fuller became pregnant, giving birth to a son, Angelo, in September 1848. The question of when, or even whether, Fuller and Ossoli were married has never been satisfactorily answered. In 1850, however, Fuller sailed for America with Ossoli and their child. All three were drowned when their ship broke up in a storm off Fire Island, New York.

MAJOR WORKS AND THEMES

Upon meeting her in England in 1846, Thomas Carlyle observed in Fuller "a predetermination to *eat* this big universe as her oyster or her egg . . . " (qtd. in Capper x). Although Carlyle was referring to her conversation, the voracious quality can be seen in her writings as well. For Fuller took on an astonishing range of subjects over the course of her truncated career, including European literature, gender theory, Westward expansion, and Italian nationalism (to name only a few). Her approach to these wide-ranging interests, however, was almost always shaped by the Transcendentalist sensibility that Fuller had absorbed in her Cambridge youth. She was a firm believer in the primacy of the individual and in the necessity of seizing opportunities for the expansion of individual consciousness. And this meant also resisting social norms that militated against the possibility of "self-culture."

Fuller's first original work, published in 1844, was *Summer on the Lakes in 1843,* a record of a trip she took to the Great Lakes region. At first glance, the subject matter suggests that this first book is to be a radical departure from her previous literary work in Cambridge. Those essays, reviews, and translations had focused on European literary materials, particularly on the German Romantic writers that she had begun to study when she was in her early twenties. *Summer on the Lakes,* by contrast, is about recently settled American territory and focuses on her reactions to "the new scene" (80). A careful look, however, reveals Fuller bringing a decidedly Romantic perspective to her musings on the West. She is fascinated, for example, by her own emotional reactions to the natural world, particularly the novel landscape of the prairie and Niagara Falls, which for nineteenth-century viewers epitomized the "sublimity" to be found on the North American continent. She is also curious about whether the settlers establishing new lives for themselves on the frontier will be better positioned than Easterners—living in longer established communities—to heed the Romantic call for a life based on the inner directives of the soul rather than on stale tradition and social expectations.

Fuller is largely disappointed in this hope. She finds most settlers focused on material gain and slavishly devoted to attitudes and social customs they have imported from the East. She is appalled, moreover, by the settlers' treatment of Indians. Despite her sympathy for the Indians' plight, however, she shares the view—common at the time—that their eventual extinction is inevitable. Nevertheless, her depiction of the Indians prefigures a lifelong sympathy for underdogs and indignity at injustice that appears in all of her later work.

In *Woman in the Nineteenth Century,* published in 1845 and based on an earlier essay called "The Great Lawsuit," Fuller explored the subordinate status of women in society. She was by no means the first American woman of her generation to address the issue. Elizabeth Cady Stanton and Lucretia Mott were already laying the groundwork for the Seneca Falls Convention on women's rights that would take place in 1848. But where those activists were largely concerned with women's legal rights, Fuller took a very different approach, bringing Transcendentalist ideals to bear on the question of women's position. For Fuller, the basis of the problem was that women "are taught to learn their rule from without, not to unfold it from within" (*Woman* 40). The solution, in other words, was for women to achieve a kind of Emersonian self-reliance and to allow their minds and souls to develop more freely than current custom allowed.

In taking this view, and insisting that men as well as women would benefit if women were acknowledged as men's equals, Fuller took issue with the domestic ideology of the time. Adherents of that worldview regarded the home as a sanctuary from the market forces that increasingly dominated American culture during the nineteenth century. And the home, according to this view, was the proper sphere of women. By restricting themselves to the home and leaving public affairs to men, the reasoning went, women were able to remain free from the corrupting influences of politics and the market. They could then function as moral and ethical touchstones for society by exerting a gentle and benevolent influence on their husbands and children. In *Woman in the Nineteenth Century,* Fuller often seems to agree with the basic premise underlying domestic ideology: that there are natural, essential differences between men and women. But where many in the nineteenth century saw those differences as a justification for "separate spheres," Fuller saw in them grounds for her belief that women had an important part to play outside the home and that both men and women were being unjustly restricted to particular social roles, to the detriment of their society.

The articles that Fuller wrote for the *New-York Tribune* during 1845 and 1846— on topics such as immigration, insane asylums, and poverty—reflect Fuller's growing interest in politics and social reform even as she continued to pursue her interest in literature and the arts in reviews written for the same newspaper. Her trip to Europe in 1846 and the "Dispatches" that her editor commissioned her to write for the *Tribune* offered even greater scope for Fuller's expansive mind and enabled her to combine her interest in art and politics. Her early dispatches often focus on her meetings with writers or musicians such as George Sand and Chopin, and they also recall her travel writing about the West in their attempts to paint a vivid European landscape for American readers. But once she begins writing from Italy—having been caught up in the ferment of the revolutionary attempt to establish a Roman Republic—she turns her attention to history itself. As in *Woman in the Nineteenth Century,* Fuller uses verbal sketches of exemplary individuals to convey her ideas. And the central idea linking her dispatches from Italy is that the actions—and ultimate failure—of the Italian patriot make up a grand, historical tragedy almost Shakespearean in tone. A manuscript history of the short-lived Roman republic was lost in the shipwreck in which Fuller lost her life.

CRITICAL RECEPTION

Fuller's writings were modestly successful during her lifetime: her work received considerable attention in the press and, as a consequence of her newspaper writing, reached a wider audience than many of her now better known contemporaries such as Thoreau or Hawthorne. Critical appraisals of her work were mixed, however. Many reviewers praised her work for its originality and ambitious scope, but others found fault with her Transcendentalist premises and with "a certain stiffness, an unnaturalness, in the style of the work" (Stetson 37, 276).

Her first book, *Summer on the Lakes in 1843,* sold fairly well and was considered sufficiently marketable by English publishers to merit a pirated edition. Many reviewers were intrigued by her fresh perspective on important subject matter. James Freeman Clarke, for example, saw the West as "our American Romance, our unwritten Poetry" (Clarke), and was delighted to see Fuller bringing her "faculties of keen perception . . . and constructive imagination" (Clarke) to bear on it. On the other hand, Fuller's role as editor of the *Dial* and her well-known friendship with Emerson and his circle seem to have prejudiced other reviewers against her work. Orestes Brownson, who disdained Fuller as "the high priestess of American Transcendentalism," declared that her observations of the West "lie fermenting in her intellectual stomach, and generate all manner of strange and diseased fancies" (546–7).

Brownson's review of *Summer on the Lakes* was also typical of negative commentaries on Fuller's work in its invocation of gender. For Brownson, who condemned Transcendentalism as sacrilegious and encouraged his readers to hold fast to more traditional theological doctrine, Fuller was "a melancholy instance of the fate which awaits a gifted woman in an age of infidelity." In order to be "the ornament of her sex," he insisted, Fuller must abandon "heathen" ideas imported from Germany and embrace "the firm, old-fashioned . . . faith in the Gospel" (Brownson 546–7). This focus on gender naturally increased in critical responses to *Woman in the Nineteenth Century.* While many reviewers saw it as a courageous attempt to explore the issue of women's role in society, others saw it as an impious effort to overthrow women's divinely ordained relation to men and to call into question the sacred institution of marriage. Although many of the negative reviewers seem to have woefully misunderstood Fuller's argument in the book, the lively critical debate over *Woman in the Nineteenth Century* led to good sales; the American edition (1,500 copies) sold out, and a pirated English edition also increased awareness of Fuller in England.

Fuller began her New York journalism career, then, with a well-established literary reputation. Though her essays for the *New-York Daily Tribune* dealt with a wide variety of subjects, including social issues such as immigration, poverty, and prison reform, her literary reviews were regarded as her most significant writing during this period. Her collection of those essays, *Papers on Literature and Art,* generally received positive reviews and was popular enough to make a second printing profitable. But some authors were offended by Fuller's assessment of them in "American Literature, Its Position in the Present Time, and Its Prospects for the Future," an essay she had written especially for the collection. In *A Fable for Critics* (1848), James Russell Lowell created a thinly disguised portrait that represented her as spiteful, vain, and untalented. Edgar Allan Poe, offended at not having been included in the essay at all, described her in a letter as "an ill-tempered . . . old-maid" (qtd. in Albrecht 172). Regrettably, such unflattering pictures were sometimes taken too seriously by later literary historians who ignored the immediate context.

After Fuller's death, the tendency of critics, reviewers, and editors was to focus on Fuller's personality and private life more often than on her work. This trend was inaugurated by her friends Ralph Waldo Emerson, James Freeman Clarke, and William Henry Channing, who were concerned that the scandal surrounding her final years in Italy might tarnish her reputation. Accordingly, they edited portions of her diaries and letters, solicited reminiscences of her from her friends, and collected the results in a book they called *Memoirs of Margaret Fuller Ossoli* (1852). The book was enormously popular and 13 editions of it had appeared by the end of the century. But it overshadowed her published writings, which her brother Arthur, in the decade following her death, published in stripped-down versions that deviated sharply from Fuller's own intentions.

The result was that Fuller's writings were misunderstood and underappreciated for over a century after her death. Even as other mid-nineteenth-century writers were rediscovered in the 1920s and the period as a whole began to receive sustained critical attention during the 1940s and 50s, Fuller was usually seen as a marginal figure. The subtitle of Mason Wade's 1940 biography, *Margaret Fuller: Whetstone of Genius,* is highly revealing of the general attitude toward her: she was seen as an associate of Emerson, Hawthorne, and other male literati of the period, rather than as an important literary figure in her own right.

The "women's liberation" movement of the 1970s, and the corresponding interest among academic historians and literary critics in women's history and the work of nineteenth-century women writers, led to a new awareness of Fuller's historical and literary significance. The publication of Bell Gale Chevigny's *The Woman and the Myth: Margaret Fuller's Life and Writings* in 1976 by the newly founded Feminist Press was a pivotal moment in the history of Fuller scholarship. Chevigny's book enabled scholars to see Fuller as a rich subject for study, and, in its focus on tracing Fuller's "struggle to conceive and act out of free womanhood" (Chevigny 9), also shaped the feminist approach that the first generation of Fuller scholars would take toward their subject.

In the wake of Chevigny and her fellow groundbreaking scholars, the 1980s and 90s have seen a genuine Fuller revival in the academy, as well as proliferating approaches to her work. The republication of Chevigny's *The Woman and the Myth* by Northeastern University Press in 1994 attests to the broader appeal Fuller now holds. Although there is no question that gender issues color nearly everything Fuller writes about, she is no longer seen as of interest exclusively to feminist scholars. Accordingly, more attention has been paid in recent years to works other than *Woman in the Nineteenth Century,* such as *Summer on the Lakes,* her translations from the German, and her *Dispatches from Europe,* which some critics now regard as her best writing. Greater awareness of the range of Fuller's work has, in recent years, secured her a prominent place in nineteenth-century literary history.

WORKS CITED

Albrecht, James. "Margaret Fuller." *The American Renaissance in New England, Second Series.* ed. Wesley T. Mott. *Dictionary of Literary Biography,* Vol. 223. Detroit, MI: Bruccoli Clark Layman, 2000.

Brownson, Orestes A. Review of *Summer on the Lakes. Brownson's Quarterly Review* 6 (October 1844), 546–7.

Capper, Charles. *The Private Years.* New York: Oxford University Press, 1992. Vol. 1 of *Margaret Fuller: An American Romantic Life.* 2 vols. 1992–.

Clarke, J[ames]. F[reeman]. Review of *Summer on the Lakes. Christian World* 2 (6 July 1844).

The Letters of Margaret Fuller. Ed. Robert N. Hudspeth. 6 vols. Ithaca, NY: Cornell University Press, 1983–94.

Summer on the Lakes in 1843. Boston: Little & Brown, 1844.

Fuller, Margaret. *Woman in the Nineteenth Century.* New York: Greeley & McElrath, 1845.

Stetson, Caleb. "Notice of Recent Publications." *Christian Examiner* 37 (September 1844), 274–6.

BIBLIOGRAPHY

Works by Margaret Fuller

Translations
Johann Peter Eckermann, *Conversations with Goethe.* Boston: Hilliard, Gray, 1839.

Bettine von Arnim, *Günderode* [*The Correspondence of Fraulein Günderode with Bettine von Arnim*]. Boston: Elizabeth Peabody, 1842.

Books
Summer on the Lakes in 1843. Boston: Little & Brown, 1844.

Woman in the Nineteenth Century. New York: Greeley & McElrath, 1845.

Papers on Literature and Art. New York: Wiley and Putnam, 1846; London: Wiley & Putnam, 1846.

Selected Periodical Publications
"The Great Lawsuit. Man *versus* Men. Woman *versus* Women." *Dial* 4 (July 1843): 1–47.

"Emerson's Essays." *New-York Daily Tribune,* 7 December 1844, pp. 1:1–3.

"St. Valentine's Day—Bloomingdale Asylum for the Insane." *New-York Daily Tribune,* 22 February 1845, pp. 1:1–2.

"Our City Charities. Visit to Bellevue Alms House, to the Farm School, the Asylum for the Insane, and Penitentiary of Blackwell's Island." *New-York Daily Tribune,* 19 March 1845, pp. 1:1–3.

"Prevalent Idea that Politeness is too Great a Luxury to be given to the Poor." *New-York Daily Tribune,* 31 May 1845, p. 2:2.

"The Irish Character." *New-York Daily Tribune,* 28 June 1845, p. 1:1.

"German Opera at Palmo's Opera House." *New-York Daily Tribune,* 11 December 1845, p. 1:1.

"What Fits a Man to be a Voter? Is it to be White Within, or White Without?" *New-York Daily Tribune,* 31 March 1846, pp. 1:1–2.

Modern Editions of Articles, Essays, and Letters
"These Sad But Glorious Days": Dispatches from Europe: 1846–1850. Ed. Larry J. Reynolds and Susan Belasco Smith. New Haven: Yale University Press, 1991.

The Letters of Margaret Fuller. Ed. Robert N. Hudspeth. 6 vols. Ithaca, NY: Cornell University Press, 1983–94.

Margaret Fuller's New York Journalism: A Biographical Essay and Key Writings. Ed. Catherine C. Mitchell. Knoxville: University of Tennessee Press, 1995.

Margaret Fuller, Critic, Writings from the New York Tribune. Ed. Judith Mattson Bean and Joel Myerson. New York: Columbia University Press, 2000.

Studies of Margaret Fuller

Adams, Stephen. " 'That Tidiness We Always Look for in Woman': Fuller's *Summer on the Lakes* and Romantic Aesthetics." *Studies in the American Renaissance 1987*. Ed. Joel Myerson. Charlottesville: University Press of Virginia, 1987.

Albrecht, James. "Margaret Fuller" in *The American Renaissance in New England, Second Series*. ed. Wesley T. Mott. *Dictionary of Literary Biography,* Vol. 223. Detroit, MI: Bruccoli Clark Layman, 2000.

Baker, Anne. " 'A Commanding View': Vision and the Problem of Nationality in Fuller's *Summer on the Lakes*." ESQ 44 (1998): 61–77.

Bean, Judith Mattson. " 'A *Presence* among Us': Fuller's Place in Nineteenth-Century Oral Culture." *ESQ* 44 (1998): 79–123.

Capper, Charles. *The Private Years*. New York: Oxford University Press, 1992. Vol. 1 of *Margaret Fuller: An American Romantic Life*. 2 vols. 1992–.

Chevigny, Bell Gale. *The Woman and the Myth: Margaret Fuller's Life and Writings*. 1976. Rev. ed. Boston: Northeastern University Press, 1994.

Cole, Phyllis. "The Nineteenth-Century Women's Rights Movement and the Canonization of Margaret Fuller." *ESQ* 44 (1998): 1–33.

Fleischmann, Fritz, ed. *Margaret Fuller's Cultural Critique: Her Age and Legacy*. New York: Peter Lang, 2000.

Gustafson, Sandra M. "Choosing a Medium: Margaret Fuller and the Forms of Sentiment." *American Quarterly* 47 (1995): 35–59.

Kolodny, Annette. "Inventing a Feminist Discourse: Rhetoric and Resistance in Margaret Fuller's *Woman in the Nineteenth Century*." *New Literary History* 25 (1994): 355–82.

Mitchell, Thomas R. *Hawthorne's Fuller Mystery*. Amherst: University of Massachusetts Press, 1998.

Myerson, Joel. *Margaret Fuller: A Descriptive Bibliography*. Pittsburgh: University of Pittsburgh Press, 1978.

———. *Critical Essays on American Literature*. Boston: G. K. Hall & Co., 1980.

Reynolds, Larry J. "The 'Cause' and Fuller's Tribune Letters." *European Revolutions and the American Literary Renaissance*. New Haven, CT: Yale University Press, 1988. 54–78.

———. "From *Dial* Essay to New York Book: The Making of *Woman in the Nineteenth Century*." *Periodical Literature in Nineteenth-Century America*. Charlottesville: University Press of Virginia, 1995. 17–34.

Robinson, David M. "Margaret Fuller, and the Transcendental Ethos: *Woman in the Nineteenth Century*." PMLA 97 (1982): 83–98.

Rosowski, Susan J. "Margaret Fuller, an Engendered West, and *Summer on the Lakes*." *Western American Literature* 25 (1990): 125–44.

Smith, Susan Belasco. "Margaret Fuller in New York: Private Letters, Public Texts." *Documentary Editing* 18 (1996): 63–67, 80.

Steele, Jeffrey. *Transfiguring America: Myth Ideology, and Mourning in Margaret Fuller's Writing*. Columbia: University of Missouri Press, 2002.

von Mehren, Joan. *Minerva and the Muse: A Life of Margaret Fuller*. Amherst: University of Massachusetts Press, 1994.

Wade, Mason. *Margaret Fuller: Whetstone of Genius*. New York: Viking, 1940.

Watson, David. *Margaret Fuller: An American Romantic*. New York: St. Martin's, 1988.

Zwarg, Christina. *Feminist Conversations: Fuller, Emerson, and the Play of Reading*. Ithaca, NY: Cornell University Press, 1995.

WILLIAM LLOYD GARRISON (1805–1879)

Lynn Domina

BIOGRAPHY

Born on December 12, 1805, in Newburyport, Massachusetts, William Lloyd Garrison was the second son of Frances Maria Lloyd Garrison and Abijah Garrison. Before William Lloyd reached the age of five, however, his father had deserted the family, probably because of a combination of several factors: unemployment, the death of one daughter, loss of his religious faith, and alcoholism. Then, in 1811, a fire devastated much of Newburyport, an event that would eventually lead to the separation of Frances Garrison from most of her children, including William Lloyd. In 1815, William Lloyd moved to Lynn, Massachusetts, to be nearer his mother and to learn a trade. He struggled through several jobs until in 1818 he became a printer's devil, a fortuitous move that would significantly contribute to his influence and notoriety in later decades.

As a young man, Garrison edited two newspapers, the *National Philanthropist* published in Boston and the *Journal of the Times* published in Bennington, Vermont. His political perspective had already been formed, however, and he had joined the abolitionist movement at the age of 25. Initially, like many of his peers, he supported colonization—that is, he believed slaves should be freed but also transported back to Africa; like many Americans at the time, he assumed that blacks and whites could not live harmoniously together. His politics would grow progressively radical, eventually eclipsing the perspectives of even the fiercest of other abolitionists. After a brief period co-editing the *Genius of Universal Emancipation* with Benjamin Lundy, its founder, Garrison founded *The Liberator* in 1830. This abolitionist paper would become his life work, and it remains the work for which he is best known.

By this point, Garrison's abolitionist views had shifted significantly. He no longer supported colonization; rather, he held that slaves should be emancipated immediately; eventually he would also urge the northern states to secede from the Union, that is, from union with slaveholders. His views on immediatism led him to organize the New England Anti-Slavery Society in 1832 and the American Anti-Slavery Society a year later. Garrison also supported other progressive issues of the day—women's rights, temperance, pacifism—and his integration of these issues with abolitionism, as well as his increasing radicalism, contributed to a crisis in the abolition movement. In 1840, a number of less radical members resigned from the American Anti-Slavery Society in part because of Garrison's support of the membership being opened to women. Because of his strong views, Garrison was arrested, was excoriated by the more mainstream press, and received several threats against his life.

During these decades, Garrison's personal life also flourished. He married Helen Benson in 1834. They would eventually have seven children, some of whom would be named for fellow abolitionists. Helen died in 1876, as Garrison's own health was also failing.

As occurs with many crusaders, Garrison's influence declined as the views expressed in his editorials and elsewhere became more radical. Yet he eventually did witness the emancipation of slaves, if only as the result of a bloody war. At the end of the Civil War, he ceased publishing *The Liberator,* since he believed its goal had been accomplished. He remained active in public life, however, continuing to support the other causes he had long championed. Garrison died in 1879 in New York. At his funeral, mourners numbered in the thousands, and flags across Massachusetts flew at half-mast. Garrison is buried in Boston's Forest Hills Cemetery.

MAJOR WORKS AND THEMES

William Lloyd Garrison became a writer from political and moral necessity rather than from a compelling need in his personality to produce great literature. He responded directly to the issues of his day rather than attempting to populate a fictive world through his imagination. In this sense, he may be more easily compared to Henry David Thoreau than to many of the other writers whose work comprises the American Renaissance. His themes consist of responses to the political issues of the early- to mid-nineteenth century: the need to redefine relationships between slave and free, woman and man, laborer and capitalist.

Although Garrison had earlier espoused support for the idea of African colonization, by 1832, when he published *Thoughts on African Colonization,* he had reversed that stance. Garrison situated his response in the Christian gospel. He criticized members of the American Colonization Society for misleading the public about the advantages of such a proposal to freed slaves and white Americans alike. Yet, even if freed slaves could lead positive and productive lives after being returned to Africa, Garrison argued, the cause would remain immoral. Garrison defined slaves as his brothers and sisters; hence, they could not justifiably be excluded from the American family. After the question of colonization became moot, Garrison would continue to express his views in terms of their consistency with the Bible, or at least his reading of it.

Garrison's major life work was *The Liberator,* which he edited for over 30 years. In his editorials for that publication, he addressed virtually all of the major incidents and issues of the time, especially as they related to slavery. After the Nat Turner insurrection in 1831, Garrison referred to it as a prophecy fulfilled—and the prophet was Garrison himself and like-minded abolitionists. He expected that this rebellion was but the first of many, and blood would be demanded not only of additional slaveholders, but also of New Englanders who permitted themselves to be citizens of a nation that tolerated slavery. While Garrison did not fully support the actions of Turner and his followers, he did argue that the slaves were no more guilty than American colonists who had killed British soldiers during the Revolution 55 years before. Shortly thereafter, Garrison described abolition as a woman's issue because half of all slaves were women and because a female slave could not exercise her proper role as a woman; she could not, especially, maintain her own chastity or protect her own children. These arguments were among those Garrison used to urge the inclusion of women as members in the American Anti-Slavery Society. In 1860, Garrison endorsed John A. Andrew, the Republican candidate for governor of Massachusetts, in part because Andrew had provided financial support to John Brown when Brown attempted to capture the arsenal at Harper's Ferry. Finally, on December 29, 1865, Garrison published the last issue of *The Liberator,* writing a valedictory editorial that stated that the object for which the newspaper had been founded—the eradication of slavery—had been achieved. While the tone of this editorial is somewhat triumphant, Garrison also used this forum to express appreciation for those who had labored with him and regret that the regular communication *The Liberator* had permitted among abolitionists across the country would cease.

CRITICAL RECEPTION

Because Garrison was a crusading journalist rather than primarily a poet or novelist, his popularity rose and fell with the popularity of his ideas—not simply the popularity of abolition itself but of the particular approaches and interpretations Garrison espoused. Not surprisingly, his work was most popular among like-minded people. As Garrison's ideas became increasingly radical, fewer and fewer of his peers were able to accompany him politically. While abolition itself obviously remained a powerful cause, the ideas of immediate emancipation, of the North seceding from the Union, and of women achieving equal authority with men in the movement became unpalatable to many members of the American Anti-Slavery Society and subscribers to *The Liberator.*

As one would expect, Garrison's writing was from the beginning extremely unpopular in the South. Since he generally wrote from the most extreme perspective, even among abolitionists, few people attempted to distinguish between the writing and the man. While he was still working with Benjamin Lundy, he was jailed in Baltimore; he had been found guilty of libeling a Newburyport, Massachusetts, merchant, Francis Todd, by accusing him of connections with the slave trade. And Garrison was accused of inciting Nat Turner's rebellion, for instance, rather than merely predicting such an event and supporting it after the fact. Responses to Garrison's editorials on this incident included assassination threats from North and South. In 1835, a mob in Boston attempted to lynch him after publicity surrounding an antislavery meeting.

As the attendance at his funeral will testify, Garrison was, a generation after the Civil War, seen as a prophet. Yet, his reputation quickly faded, and in later decades of the nineteenth century and early decades of the twentieth, he was regarded as an extremist driven as much by his ego as by his ideology, a minor player in a major event. This evaluation is certainly unfair. Today, Garrison remains too little known. Scholars exhibit a much greater tendency to focus on his life than on his writing. As such, the small home he has found in the academy tends to be in departments of history rather than literature.

BIBLIOGRAPHY

Works by William Lloyd Garrison

The Liberator. Boston, 1831–65.
Thoughts on African Colonization. 1832. Reprint, New York: Arno P, 1968.

"Preface." *Narrative of the Life of Frederick Douglass.* 1845. Reprint, Mineola, NY: Dover, 1995. vii–xiii.

Documents of Upheaval: Selections from William Lloyd Garrison's The Liberator, 1831–1865. Truman Nelson, ed. New York: Hill and Wang, 1966.

Letters of William Lloyd Garrison. Walter M. Merrill and Louis Ruchames, eds. 6 vols. Cambridge: Harvard UP, 1971–81.

William Lloyd Garrison and the Fight Against Slavery: Selections from the Liberator. William E. Cain, ed. New York: Bedford / St. Martins, 1995.

Studies of William Lloyd Garrison

Chapman, John Jay. *William Lloyd Garrison.* Boston: The Atlantic Monthly Press, 1921.

Garrison, Wendell P., and Francis J. *William Lloyd Garrison, 1805–1879: The Story of His Life Told by His Children.* 4 vols. New York: The Century Co., 1885–89.

Grimké, Archibald Henry. *William Lloyd Garrison: The Abolitionist.* 1891. Reprint, New York: AMS Press, 1974.

Johnson, Oliver. *William Lloyd Garrison and His Times.* Boston: Houghton Mifflin, 1881.

Korngold, Ralph. *Two Friends of Man.* Boston: Little Brown, 1950.

Kraditor, Aileen S. *Means and Ends in American Abolitionism: Garrison and His Critics on Strategy and Tactics, 1834–1850.* Chicago: Ivan R. Dee, Inc., 1989.

Martineau, Harriet. *The Martyr Age of the United States of America.* 1839. Reprint, New York: Arno Press, 1969.

May, Samuel J. *Some Reflections of Our Antislavery Conflict.* Boston: Fields, Osgood, and Co., 1869.

Mayer, Henry. *All on Fire: William Lloyd Garrison and the Abolition of Slavery.* New York: St. Martin's, 1998.

Merrill, Walter B. *Against Wind and Tide: A Biography of William Lloyd Garrison.* Cambridge: Harvard UP, 1963.

Nye, Russell B. *William Lloyd Garrison and the Humanitarian Reformers.* Oscar Handlin, ed. Boston: Little, Brown, 1955.

Rogers, William B. *"We Are All Together Now": Frederick Douglass, William Lloyd Garrison and the Prophetic Tradition.* New York: Garland, 1995.

Stewart, James Brewer. *William Lloyd Garrison and the Challenge of Emancipation.* Arlington Heights, IL: Harlan Davidson, 1992.

Thomas, John L. *The Liberato: William Lloyd Garrison, a Biography.* Boston: Little Brown, 1963.

Villard, Fanny Garrison. *William Lloyd Garrison on Non-Resistance.* New York: The Nation Publishing Co., 1924.

CAROLINE HOWARD GILMAN (1794–1888)

Dorothy J. Rumenik

BIOGRAPHY

Born to a prominent New England couple, Caroline Howard Gilman, a forerunner to the genre of "domestic novelists," provided the literary world with an authentic history of the nineteenth century. Her prolific writings include a large collection of personal letters, poems, novels, and essays that span a 70-year period. Her parents died when she was very young, and she grew up in New England living with her older sister and brothers. She recollects in her autobiography that her early education was a "dark age" (Hart 51). Fortunately, she was exposed to the library of a neighbor, Governor Elbridge Gerry, which she visited often to read the great works of literature. She was motivated by her own desire to learn and took it upon herself to expand her education by independent study.

She began writing as a young girl; however, when at age 16 her poem, "Jephthah's Rash Vow," was printed without her permission, she was very upset. Years later, she recalled in a letter to her sister that she "cried half the night with a kind of shame" as if she had been "detected in man's apparel" (qtd. in Kelley 180). However, in 1817 she allowed her second biblical poem, "Jarius's Daughter," to be printed in the prestigious *North American Review.* Shortly afterward, at a party, she met her future husband Samuel Gilman, a Harvard theological student and writer who later distinguished himself by writing "Fair Harvard," the University's present-day alma mater. Two years later, in 1819, they married and traveled to Charleston, South Carolina, when Samuel was appointed minister of the First Unitarian Church. The young couple adjusted quickly to life in the South, even acquiring house slaves to help raise their children. Over time they became sympathetic to the southern cause and as the Civil War approached, Caroline's writings reflected her desire to bring harmony to the country by promoting domestic tranquility.

Her literary career was slow to develop, but it began in earnest when she was 38 with the publication of *The Rose-Bud* (1832), a periodical for children. *The Rose Bud* matured into *The Southern Rose,* but in 1839, with the death of her infant son, she ceased publication. Henceforth, she concentrated on the publication of her novels, which had been serialized in her *Rose* magazines, and writing giftbooks, moral stories, and poems for children.

After the death of her husband in 1858, Caroline remained in Charleston, maintaining her loyalty to the southern cause in spite of her New England background. Stirred by the danger of the Civil War, she moved to Greenville, South Carolina, in 1862, where she helped the war effort by supplying food and medical aid to Confederate soldiers. After the War, she returned to Charleston until 1873, when she moved back to New England. She died September 15, 1888, in Washington, D.C., at the age of 94. Her remains are with her husband's in the Unitarian Churchyard, Charleston, South Carolina.

MAJOR WORKS AND THEMES

Gilman's love of God, children, and family life are the major themes of her works. Even as the strife of the Civil War disrupted her peaceful existence, she maintained her theme of a tranquil home, guided by a "good wife," as the means for not only family happiness, but national unity. Her earliest poems were of a biblical nature: "Jephthah's Rash Vow," based on Judges 11, and "Jarius's Daughter." Her giftbooks of verse for children, *The Little Wreath of Stories and Poems for Children* (1846), *Verses of a Lifetime* (1849), and *A Gift Book of Stories and Poems for Children* (1850), emphasize proper manners and behavior. Poems, such as "The Little Girl who Bites her Nails" and "Lucy Dash in School," show her desire to guide children in a gentle way to correct behavior. She uses common-day occurrences such as celebration of holidays, vacations at Sullivan's Island, and learning the multiplication tables in rhyme to reach the "youthful heart."

Gilman's formal career as a writer and publisher began in 1832 when she founded *The Rose Bud,* or *Youth's Gazette,* perhaps the first children's periodical in the South. By 1834 *The Rose Bud* was renamed *The Southern Rose,* expanding its contents to include literary reviews and short stories for adults. She published Nathaniel Hawthorne's "Lily's Quest," later published in "*Twice-Told Tales*"; political commentaries of Thomas Paine and Ralph Waldo Emerson; short stories of Harriet Martineau, Elizabeth F. Ellett, and William Gilmore Simms; and critical analyses of articles in various British journals.

Gilman and her husband Samuel were major contributors to the magazine. Her first novel, *Recollections of a Housekeeper* (1834), written under the pseudonym of Mrs. Clarissa Packard, tells the story of a New England bride and her efforts at training her housemaids and cooks. Two years later she wrote a companion piece, *Recollections of a Southern Matron,* (1838), which paints a happy picture of southern plantation life showing the mistress working side by side with the slaves. She underlines the prevailing philosophy of her era in espousing the belief that the wife must practice "self-control, almost to hypocrisy" (*Southern Matron* 297) in order to do her job required by God and her husband. This theme is carried to a national level in *The Poetry of Travelling in the United States* (1838) written, as she remarks in the preface, "to increase a good sympathy between different portions of the country" (n.p.) by striving to show that the bonds of family life can overcome political differences. She hoped to offset the tension growing between the North and South. Her third novel, *Love's Progress* (1840), continues the theme of submission of women, in this case, a daughter, to her demented and patriarchal father. Ironically, as Gilman was writing her definition of a good wife, she was asserting herself into the business world, dealing with the financial matters of publishing a magazine, and espousing articles that promoted more rights for women, not only on the home front but educationally as well.

After she ceased the publication of *The Southern Rose* in 1839, Gilman rarely wrote. Some of her later poems and verses were compiled into her giftbooks. She wrote her *Oracles* (1844), which reference over 100 American and English poets and writers. "Household Woman," a significant poem she wrote in 1872, at 72 years of age, was dedicated to the Ladies Sewing Circle of the Unitarian Church in Charleston; in it she speaks out against submissiveness to domesticity, all the while defending it as well, maintaining that "the life of woman in the home has not been idle, useless, wasted, or without redeeming value" (Kelley 334). With her daughter, Caroline Howard Jervey, she collaborated on *Stories and Poems by Mother and Daughter* (1872). In 1874 she commemorated her father's participation in the Boston Tea Party with the publication of a long poem, *Recollections of the Private Centennial Celebration of the Overthrow of the Tea at Griffin's Wharf, in Boston Harbour.* The popularity she experienced before the Civil War never returned, however, more than likely because of her undying support for the southern cause.

CRITICAL RECEPTION

In the mid-1800s, Gilman was on the best-sellers list, and she was a favorite throughout the country. After the first edition of *The Rose Bud,* "thanks and congratulations" poured upon her "from every quarter," her books went through several editions, and she herself ascribed her popularity to the fact that she had made "the first attempt to enter into the recesses of American homes and hearths" (Baym 67). Mary Kelley classifies Gilman as among the nineteenth-century female sentimentalists responsible for making private conflict public. Gilman assessed herself in a letter to her sister at age 60 that she was "somewhat of a patriarch in the line of American female authors—a kind of Past Master in the Order" (Gilman Letters).

R. W. Griswold wrote in 1852 that her works will be valued for the "spirit and vitality with which she has painted a warm domestic affection, and pure religious feeling." He goes on to say that "her wit, unaffected pathos, and vividly drawn characters drew to her a host of readers" (qtd. in Hart 52). J. A. Wauchope praises her skill in character writing, such as use of the Negro dialect, especially prevalent in *The Southern Matron,* her "artist-like power of grouping," and her love of nature and good sense. He gave her the title of the "most eminent woman writer of her time" (qtd. in Hoole 127).

Archibald Rutledge, in the foreword to Mary Scott Saint-Amand's book *A Balcony in Charleston,* praises Gilman's works, declaring her writings to be "rarely gifted with an insight that might well be called genius, sensitive alike to reality and to the mystery of life," and that she "holds a secure place in American literature" (n.p.). Indeed, Gilman has given modern readers a clear, educated view of what life was like for women of class and stature during the nineteenth century.

WORKS CITED

Baym, Nina. *Woman's Fiction: A Guide to Novels by and about Women in America, 1820–70,* 2nd edition. Urbana and Chicago: Univ. of Illinois Press, 1993.

Gilman Letters. A collection of Gilman's letters, written between 1810 and 1880, is located at the South Carolina Historical Society in Charleston, South Carolina.

Hart, John S., ed. *Female Prose Writers of America.* Philadelphia: E. H. Butler and Co., 1852.

Hoole, William Stanley. "The Gilmans and 'The Southern Rose.'" *North Carolina Historical Review.* Vol. 11, April 1934, 116–28.

Gilman, Caroline. *Recollections of a Southern Matron.* New York: Harpers, 1838.

Kelley, Mary. *Private Woman, Public Stage: Literary Domesticity in Nineteenth-Century America.* New York: Oxford University Press, 1984.

Saint-Amand, Mary Scott. *A Balcony in Charleston.* Richmond, VA: Garrett and Massie, 1941.

BIBLIOGRAPHY

Works by Caroline Howard Gilman

Periodicals

The Rose-Bud or *Youth's Gazette.* Charleston, SC: J. S. Burgess, 1832–35.

The Southern Rose. Charleston, SC: J. S. Burgess, 1835–39.

Books

Recollections of a Housekeeper as Mrs. Clarrissa Packard. New York: Harpers, 1834.

Recollections of a Southern Matron. New York: Harpers, 1838.

Recollections of a New England Bride and of a Southern Matron. New York: G. P. Putnam, 1852.

The Poetry of Travelling in the United States. New York: S. Colman, 1838.

Tales and Ballads. New York: S. Colman, 1839.

Love's Progress. New York: Harper's, 1840.

The Rose-Bud Wreath. Charleston, SC: S. Babcock, 1841.

Oracles from the Poets: A Fanciful Diversion for the Drawing Room. New York & London: Wiley & Putnam, 1844.

Verse

The Little Wreath of Stories and Poems for Children. New York: C. S. Francis/Boston: J. H. Francis, 1846.

The Sibyl, or New Oracles from the Poets. New York: Wiley & Putnam, 1848.

Verses of a Life Time. Boston & Cambridge: J. Munroe, 1849.

A Gift Book of Stories and Poems for Children. New York: C. S. Francis/Boston: J. H. Francis, 1850.

Oracles for Youth: A Home Pastime. New York: Putnam, 1852.

Vernon Grove or *Hearts as They Are.* New York: Rudd & Carleton, 1859.

Stories and Poems by Mother and Daughter, by Gilman and Caroline Howard Jervey. Boston: Lee & Shepard, 1872.

The Poetic Fate Book, New Oracles from the Poets. Boston: Lee & Shepard/New York: Lee, Shepard & Dillingham, 1874.

Recollections of the Private Centennial Celebration of the Overthrow of the Tea at Griffin's Wharf, in Boston Harbour, Dec. 16, 1773. Cambridge, MA: Wilson, 1874.

The Young Fortune Teller, Oracles for Youth, by Gilman and Caroline Howard. Boston: Lee & Shepard, 1874.

Miscellaneous

The Ladies Annual Register and Housewife's Memorandum Book for 1838. 1839.

Letters of Caroline Gilman (1810–1880). South Carolina Historical Society, Charleston, SC.

Letters of Eliza Wilkinson During the Invasion and Possession of Charleston, SC by the British in the Revolutionary War, compiled by Gilman. New York: S. Colman, 1839.

Record of Inscriptions in the Cemetery and Building of the Unitarian, Formerly Denominated the Independent Church, Archdale Street, Charleston, SC from 1777 to 1860, compiled by Gilman. Charleston, SC: Walker, Evans, 1860.

Gilman, Caroline Howard, "My Autobiography." *The Female Prose Writers of America*. Ed. John S. Hart. Philadelphia: E. H. Butler, 1852. 49–57.

Studies of Caroline Howard Gilman

Bakker, Jan. "Another Dilemma of an Intellectual in the Old South: Caroline Gilman, the Peculiar Institution and Greater Rights for Women in *The Rose Magazine*." *Southern Literary Journal,* Fall 1984, pp. 12–25.

_____. "Caroline Gilman and the Issue of Slavery in the *Rose* Magazines, 1832–1839." *Southern Studies,* 1985, vol. 24, pp. 273–83.

Baym, Nina. *Woman's Fiction: A Guide to Novels by and about Women in America, 1820–70,* 2nd edition. Urbana and Chicago: U of Illinois P, 1993. 5–85.

Beasley, Maurice H. "Caroline Howard Gilman," *Literature Resource Center.* http://www.galenet.com. 06/26/00.

Chielens, Edward E., ed. "The Southern Rose," *American Literary Magazines.* New York: Greenwood Press, 1986. 413–5.

Clinton, Catherine. *The Other Civil War: American Women in the Nineteenth Century.* New York: Hill & Wang, 1984. 48.

Griswold, R. W. *Female Poets of America.* Philadelphia: Carey & Hart, 1848.

Hart, John S., ed. *Female Prose Writers of America.* Philadelphia: E.H. Butler and Co., 1852. 55.

Hoole, William Stanley. "The Gilmans and "The Southern Rose," *North Carolina Historical Review.* Vol. 11, April 1934, pp. 116–28.

Kelley, Mary. *Private Woman, Public Stage: Literary Domesticity in Nineteenth-Century America.* New York: Oxford University Press, 1984.

Kennedy, Fronde. "The Southern Rose-Bud and The Southern Rose." *The South Atlantic Quarterly,* Vol. 23, Jan. 1924, pp. 10–9.

Micheletti, Ellen. "Popular Fiction in the 19th Century," http://www.likesbooks.com.fiction.html. Accessed: 6/10/02.

Moss, Elizabeth. *Domestic Novelists in the Old South: Defenders of Southern Culture.* Baton Rouge: Louisiana State U P, 1992.

Pease, Jane H. *Ladies, Women, and Wenches, Choice and Constraint in Antebellum Charleston and Boston.* Chapel Hill and London: U of North Carolina P, 1990.

Saint-Amand, Mary Scott. *A Balcony in Charleston.* Richmond, VA: Garrett and Massie, Inc., 1941.

Wauchope, G. A. *Writers of South Carolina.* Columbia, SC: The State Co., 1910. 65.

Waugh, Charles G., and Martin H. Greenberg, ed. *The Women's War in the South: Recollections and Reflections of the American Civil War.* Nashville, TN: Cumberland House, 1999.

GRACE GREENWOOD [SARA JANE CLARKE LIPPINCOTT] (1823–1904)

Fredrica Bearg Glucksman

BIOGRAPHY

A great-granddaughter of Puritan minister Jonathan Edwards, Sara Jane Clarke was born on September 23, 1823, in Pompey, New York. The youngest of 11 children in the culturally rich household of Dr. Thaddeus and Deborah Baker Clarke, Sara left school in 1843. However, her work appeared in newspapers in Rochester, New York, when she was 16; at 19, her poems appeared in antislavery journals.

In 1843, the family moved to rural New Brighton, Pennsylvania. Under the pseudonym of Grace Greenwood, Sara wrote poems, moral tales, and columns for *Home Journal* and *National Press*. Her popular "Heart Histories" and novellas appeared in *Godey's Lady's Book, Graham's Magazine, Sartain's,* and *Neal's Gazette.* Parodies of Melville and Poe appeared in *The Saturday Evening Post. The History of My Pets,* her first stories for children, was printed in 1851. *Poems* was published in the same year.

At Gamaliel Bailey's invitation, Greenwood moved to Washington, in 1850, where she wrote for his liberal *National Era* and lived with the family, enjoying its patronage and salons. Theodore Parker, poets John Greenleaf Whittier and Alice and Phoebe Cary, and President Lincoln were counted among her friends and readers. The second female Washington correspondent (after Jane Swisshelm), Greenwood wrote for the *Saturday Evening Post* (1850–1897). During this time, Greenwood also proofread *Uncle Tom's Cabin* and served as a foreign correspondent for Bailey from 1852 to 1853.

With Leander K. Lippincott, whom she married in 1853, Greenwood published a popular children's magazine, *The Little Pilgrim,* from 1853 through the mid-1870s. These works, too, were published in books. Another Washington correspondent disclosed the financial extravagances that, in 1876, led to a grand jury's indictment of Lippincott for fraud. Lippincott fled the country to escape punishment. Earlier, sources had revealed Lippincott's marital infidelity.

In the 1850s, Greenwood lectured on abolition, prison reform, comfortable clothing for women, and universal suffrage, and, in the 1860s, she spoke in support of the Union Army. Later, Greenwood wrote about America's western frontier, the settlers,

Native Americans, the landscape, and the cities, helping her eastern readership visualize the territory. In 1875, Greenwood traveled to Europe with Annie, her daughter. Annie studied music, and the multilingual Greenwood reported on scientific breakthroughs, Communist demonstrations, the death of Garibaldi, and American artists abroad. On her return, Greenwood resided in Washington and New York. She died on April 20, 1904, at her daughter's home in New Rochelle, New York.

MAJOR WORKS AND THEMES

Spanning six decades and two continents, Greenwood's articles, poems, and stories reflect her era's morality and her view of its issues, and are compiled in hardcover volumes. Both series of *Greenwood Leaves* highlight rural living and women left home during war, "light romances," reviews of poetry and lyceum speakers, support for Irish patriotism, and prison reform. "Washington Letters" discusses politicians' appearances and rhetoric more than the debates (Daniel Webster and Henry Clay on the Missouri Compromise). In 1850, her pro-abolition article for Bailey's *Era* jettisoned her from editorial positions on the conservative *Godey's Lady's Book* and *Lady's Dollar Magazine.* "An American Salon," published in *Cosmopolitan* in 1890, reflects on this era. *Records of Five Years* compiles Civil War stories and profiles.

Greenwood's juvenilia describe farming, homemaking, and foreign sights, legends, and customs. Her underlying ideology always is Federal patriotism, faith as a salve to death, and Christian morality. Queen Victoria's biography stresses the monarch's domesticity.

Interestingly, Greenwood's domestic and foreign travelogues—anthologized anecdotes and vivid descriptions and opinions of landscape, architecture, society, and people, including regional legends and histories—are expressively written (foreign governments compare unfavorably to America's democracy), but she wrote nothing about her marriage; however, "Zelma's Vow," written in 1859 for *The Atlantic,* fictionalizes an actor's infidelity to his long-suffering wife (Thorp 159).

CRITICAL RECEPTION

Editions of *Greenwood Leaves* anthologize Greenwood's early pieces. All critics acknowledge Greenwood's keen observations of nature, lively writing, and historical and literary knowledge. Contemporary reviewers recognize her "vigorous pen" and "lively and earnest thoughts" about religion, art, and government (*Christian Examiner* 156); charm and humor belie her moral purpose and concern for humanity (*Holden's Dollar Magazine* 501–2). Lyman's rococo praise of her early work resembles Greenwood's style: "[her writings have] the dew of youth, the purple light of love, the bloom of young desire" (152). Nathaniel Hawthorne contradicted laudatory letters to Greenwood in letters and notebooks disparaging the popular, widely read work of female writers (Baym 25). A popular writer, Greenwood could negotiate the timing of publication and sales of her books (Thorp 154), compiling a second collection of *Greenwood Leaves* only when sales of the first edition sold out. Today, Greenwood's oeuvre sounds "pietistic, domestic, and sentimental," but the author advanced feminism, abolitionism, and opposition to capital punishment (Baym 29–32).

While Greenwood's letters from Europe and the American West in the late 1800s are moderate in style—"good reading today" (Thorp 175–6), unattributed facts are undifferentiated from opinions. Her travelogues present callous and incorrect stereotypes of

Jews and Catholics; however compassionate, those of Native Americans and African Americans (emancipation and colonization) are condescending. Considering Greenwood's progressive stance on many topics, empathy for the downtrodden, and extensive exposure to American and world cultures, her work carries the imprimatur of the republican, millennial spirit of nineteenth-century America.

WORKS CITED

Baym, Nina. "Again and Again, The Scribbling Women." *Hawthorne and Women: Engendering and Expanding the Hawthorne Tradition*. Ed. John L. Idol Jr. and Melinda M. Ponder. Amherst: University of Massachusetts Press, 1999. 20–35.

Lyman, Joseph B. "Grace Greenwood—Mrs. Lippincott." *Eminent Women of the Age*. Hartford, Conn.: S. M. Betts & Co., 1869. 147–63.

"Review of *Greenwood Leaves*." *Holden's Dollar Magazine* (Aug 1850): 501–2.

"Review of *Greenwood Leaves. Second Series*." *The Christian Examiner* (Jan. 1852): 156.

Thorp, Margaret Farrand. "Greenwood Leaves." *Female Persuasion: Six Strong-Minded Women*. New Haven: Yale UP, 1949; New York: Archon Books, 1971. 143–78.

BIBLIOGRAPHY

Works by Grace Greenwood

Poems. Boston: Ticknor, Reed and Fields, 1851.

Greenwood Leaves. Boston: Ticknor, Reed and Fields, 1850.

Greenwood Leaves: A Collection of Sketches and Letters. Second Series. Boston: Ticknor, Reed and Fields, 1852.

Recollections of My Childhood and Other Stories. Boston: Ticknor, Reed and Fields, 1853.

Europe: Its People and Princes—Its Pleasures and Palaces. Philadelphia: Burlock & Co., 1853.

Haps and Mishaps of a Tour in Europe. Boston: Ticknor, Reed and Fields, 1854.

A Forest Tragedy and Other Tales. Boston: Ticknor and Fields, 1856.

Records of Five Years. Boston: Ticknor and Fields, 1867.

Stories and Sights of France and Italy. Boston: Ticknor and Fields, 1867.

New Life in New Lands: Notes of Travel. New York: J. B. Ford & Co., 1873.

Stories for Home Folks, Young and Old. New York: J. B. Alden, 1884.

"An American Salon." *Cosmopolitan* (Feb 1890): 437–47.

Stories and Sketches. New York: Tait, Sons & Company, 1892.

Juvenile Literature

The History of My Pets. Boston: Ticknor, Reed, and Fields, 1851.

Merrie England: Travels, Descriptions, Tales and Historical Sketches. Boston: Ticknor and Fields, 1855.

Old Wonder Eyes: and Other Stories for Children. With Leander K. Lippincott. New York: J. Miller, 1857.

Stories & Legends of Travel and History for Children. Boston: Ticknor and Fields, 1857.

Stories from Famous Ballads. Boston: Ticknor and Fields, 1860.

Bonnie Scotland: Tales of her History, Heroes, and Poets. Boston: Ticknor and Fields, 1861.

Nellie, the Gypsy Girl. New York: General Protestant Episcopal Sunday School Union and Church Book Society, 1863.

Stories of Many Lands. New York: Hurst, 1866.

Heads and Tails: Studies and Stories of Pets. New York: The American News Co., 1874.

Treasures from Fairy Land. With Rossiter W. Raymond. *Treasures from Fairy Land*. New York: The American News Co., 1879.

Queen Victoria: Her Girlhood and Womanhood. New York: John R. Anderson and Henry S. Allen, 1883.

Studies of Grace Greenwood

Baym, Nina. "Again and Again, The Scribbling Women." *Hawthorne and Women: Engendering and Expanding the Hawthorne Tradition.* Ed. John L. Idol Jr. and Melinda M. Ponder. Amherst: University of Massachusetts Press, 1999.

"Critical Notices." *Southern Quarterly Review* (July 1854): 242–3.

Greene, Carol Marie. "Letters Home: Newspaper Travel Writing of Kate Field, Mary Elizabeth McGarth Blake, and Grace Greenwood." Ph.D. diss., Indiana University of Pennsylvania, 2001.

Guilbert, Juliette. "Rewriting the Republic: American Women's Historical Fiction, 1824–1869." Ph.D. diss., Yale University, 1999.

Hayes, Kevin J. "Grace Greenwood (Sara Jane Clarke Lippincott)." *Nineteenth Century American Women Writers.* Ed. Denise D. Knight. Westport, CT: Greenwood Press, 1997.

Lyman, Joseph B. "Grace Greenwood—Mrs. Lippincott." *Eminent Women of the Age.* Hartford, Conn.: S. M. Betts & Co., 1869. 147–63.

Pattee, Fred Lewis. *The Feminine Fifties.* New York: D. Appleton-Century Company, 1940. 66, 85, 277–82.

"Review of *Greenwood Leaves.*" *Graham's American Monthly Magazine of Literature, Art and Fashion* (April 1850): 286.

"Review of *Greenwood Leaves.*" *Holden's Dollar Magazine* (Aug. 1850): 501–2.

"Review of *Greenwood Leaves. Second Series.*" *The Christian Examiner* (Jan. 1852): 156.

"Review of *Haps and Mishaps.*" *Graham's American Monthly Magazine of Literature, Art, and Fashion* (Feb. 1854): 234.

Thorp, Margaret Farrand. "Greenwood Leaves." *Female Persuasion: Six Strong-Minded Women.* New York: Archon Books, 1971. 142–78.

Whittier, J. G. "Review of *Greenwood Leaves.*" *The National Era* (Dec 13., 1849): 197.

ANGELINA GRIMKÉ (1805–1879)

Robert A. Russ

BIOGRAPHY

The abolitionist and feminist writer and orator Angelina Grimké was born February 20, 1805, the fourteenth child (the second daughter) of Judge John Faucheraud Grimké and Mary Smith Grimké, prominent members of wealthy, aristocratic Charleston, South Carolina, society. She and older sister Sarah were unique in being the only white Southern women prominent in the abolition movement, and as women who sought to have a voice in public affairs, they were drawn to connect their interest in abolition with the rights of women. When Angelina was born, her older sister Sarah, 13 at that time, requested, and was permitted, to become godmother to the newborn Angelina. When their father's ill health led to a trip to Philadelphia, Sarah accompanied him there, where he died, and two years later, after being drawn to Quakerism, she returned to Philadelphia to live. In 1829, after much personal anguish over slavery and public speaking against it, Angelina followed sister Sarah both into Quakerism and to Philadelphia.

Although Angelina and Sarah had already long been concerned about slavery and had read abolitionist newspapers and attended abolitionist meetings, the sisters' public work against slavery began, almost by chance, in 1835, with Angelina's letter to William Lloyd Garrison, encouraging him in his abolitionist work and his recent criticism of mob violence in Boston. "The ground upon which you stand," she wrote, "is holy ground: never—never surrender it" (qtd. in *Public Years* 25). Garrison immediately published it in *The Liberator,* without her consent, and though Quaker friends appealed to her to retract or modify the letter, and though the association with Garrison would be perceived as a disgrace on her family name, she would not. As the Grimké sisters' biographer Gerda Lerner states, "It was a symbolic act, a public gesture of commitment from one world to another" (*Grimké Sisters* 125). That symbolic gesture was the beginning of Angelina's notoriety, but it was followed quickly by the publication of her first major work, *Appeal to the Christian Women of the Southern States* (1836).

Shortly thereafter, the sisters attended a training convention of the American Anti-Slavery Society, began lecturing in parlors and a Baptist church in New York, and after

Angelina's *Appeal to the Women of the Nominally Free States* (1837) was published, the sisters went on a 23-week lecture tour, during which they spoke to over 40,000 people in more than 80 meetings in 67 towns. The demands of this tour took their toll. Exhausted, both sisters fell ill, Angelina taking to her bed for weeks to recover.

The following year, 1838, was the culmination of the sisters' "public life" and brought enormous changes in their personal lives. In February, Angelina delivered a speech before the legislative committee of the Massachusetts State Legislature, becoming the first woman to speak before a legislative body. In May, she married the infamous abolitionist Theodore Dwight Weld, who was called "the most mobbed man in America" (qtd. in Lerner 208), whom she had met at the abolitionist training convention the previous year. Due to the marriage, both sisters were disowned by the Quakers, Angelina for marrying a non-Quaker, and Sarah for attending the wedding. Two days after the wedding, Angelina was a featured speaker at the dedication of Pennsylvania Hall, in Philadelphia. It was the largest building of its kind, built by reformers to answer the problems of renting halls for a cause that drew such violent protests, but it was destroyed by fire the night after the dedication.

Following the brief, bright spark of their few intense public years of writing and speaking, the Grimké sisters led a more private, retired life with Angelina's husband. Though they were now out of the limelight, they were still actively involved in progressive causes. Their research for Theodore Weld's book *American Slavery As It Is* (1839), which became one of the sources for Harriet Beecher Stowe's novel *Uncle Tom's Cabin,* required them to examine literally thousands of newspapers for news stories, trial records and decisions, records of punishment, speeches, advertisements for runaway slaves, and other items pertaining to the conditions of slaves. On their Belleville farm, the Welds' involvement in their own children's education and their need for money led them to take in boarding children/students until they had an actual boarding school (Belleville School), with Weld as teacher and principal, and with Sarah and Angelina helping out with instruction as well as doing all the cooking, washing, and other household chores. Weld, Angelina, and Sarah were even more involved in education and social "progress" when they later joined the utopian Raritan Bay Union, home of the Eagleswood School, where they lived and worked until 1863, when they moved to Hyde Park, a south Boston suburb. Angelina Grimké died on October 26, 1879, at age 74. Her husband lived another 15 years.

MAJOR WORKS AND THEMES

Angelina Grimké's *Appeal to the Christian Women of the Southern States* was immediately famous, or infamous, and copies that reached the South were often destroyed by southern postmasters. In its simple, direct, and personal language, the *Appeal* exposes how the institution of slavery violates human law, the teachings of Jesus, and the Declaration of Independence, and calls on Christian women of the South to read and educate themselves about slavery, to speak out against it, and to free their own slaves, who, if they chose to remain with their former masters, should be paid and educated.

Throughout her work—whether in writing, or speaking, or personal involvement—Grimké was guided by a sense of responsibility and a sense of ability. When she urged the women of the South to take action, she was urging them, in spite of social customs, to accept their status as moral agents, as both able to make moral choices and responsible for doing so. It was a daunting task to oppose the given conditions of society—both the conditions regarding slaves and those regarding women—even opposing abolitionists who disapproved the linking of the slave issue with that of women's rights, but Grimké's actions and messages grew out of a spiritual commitment that gave her the assurance to defy all social barriers. In a letter to her sister, she wrote of the *Appeal:* "I feel as if He directed and helped me to write it" (qtd. in Lerner 141). The depth of that personal commitment strengthened her to do the work that resulted in various levels of exclusion, isolation and rejection—from family, from church, from "decent" society, from her native region.

Grimké's sense of anguish in perceiving the evils of slavery and her sense of personal responsibility for taking action are vividly conveyed in her 1838 speech at Pennsylvania Hall:

As a Southerner I feel that it is my duty to stand up here tonight and bear testimony against slavery. I have seen it—I have seen it. I know it has horrors that can never be described. I was brought up under its wing: I witnessed for many years its demoralizing influences, and its destructiveness to human happiness. It is admitted by some that the slave is not happy under the *worst* forms of slavery. But I have *never* seen a happy slave. I have seen him dance in his chains, it is true; but he was not happy. There is a wide difference between happiness and mirth. Man cannot enjoy the former while his manhood is destroyed, and that part of the being which is necessary to the making, and to the enjoyment of happiness, is completely blotted out. The slaves, however, may be, and sometimes are, mirthful. When hope is extinguished, they say, "let us eat and drink, for to-morrow we die." (qtd. in *Public Years* 319)

This speech, which provoked yelling and stone-throwing from those present, was one of the shining moments in her public career, for the disruptions provided her with the opportunity to depart from her prepared message and to spontaneously and sincerely address the moral basis of the "mob" that opposed her: "What is a mob?" she fearlessly exclaimed. "What would the breaking of every window be? What would the leveling of this Hall be? Any evidence that we are wrong or that slavery is a good and wholesome institution?" (qtd. in *Public Years* 319–20) The next night, Pennsylvania Hall was destroyed by fire.

The sisters' ideas, values, and activism acquired a truly personal connection when they learned of their nephews Francis, Archibald, and John, sons of their brother Henry by the slave Nancy Weston, and developed a long and supportive relationship with them. Lerner calls this connection "remarkable and probably unique among the complexities of race relations in this country . . . the acid test of the sisters' convictions" (361).

Given the sisters' depth of commitment to the abolition cause and the social constraints upon women's involvement in public affairs, the linkage between the abolitionist cause and that of women's rights was perhaps inevitable. In response to criticism, Angelina wrote, "If we surrender the right to speak to the public this year, we must surrender the right to petition next year and the right to write the year after and so on. What then can woman do for the slave when she is herself under the feet of man and shamed into silence?" (*Letters of Theodore Dwight Weld* 430)

But Angelina's convictions precluded silence, not only in her written and spoken works, but in her life's actions as well. In 1863, 25 years after her last previous public speech, Angelina addressed the 1863 Women's Convention in a resolution supporting the Union soldiers ("Soldiers of Our Second Revolution"), who would bring about "the victory of free government, sacred rights, justice, liberty, and law" (qtd. in Lerner 390). In 1870, at the age of 65, she and Sarah (then 77) became the first women to go to the polls in Massachusetts. Though they were publicly derided, and though their ballots were not counted, they still made a statement against the political exclusion of women.

CRITICAL RECEPTION

During their own time, the reception of the Grimké sisters work was dependent more on the ideological stance of the readers or audience than on the quality of the work itself, as high as that may have been. As women from a slaveholding family, the sisters' unique background was enough to ensure the notoriety of their work, and the "radical" ideas expressed in their writings and speeches overshadowed the literary qualities of the works. At Angelina's death, the old abolitionists gathered and spoke in her memory and in praise of her strength, her courage, her fortitude, her eloquence, and her principles. And though Angelina may not have approved of the display, as Katherine Du Pre Lumpkin observes, "Here was the stuff of which her greatness was made, and because these friends knew it, even after long years, they could still hold in memory the moving power of her voice" (230).

Though the Grimké sisters' public career lasted but four years, their impact was enormous. While they may now be accorded only a minor place in American history, there is a significant current interest in their work, not only as abolitionists and advocates of women's rights, but as writers and speakers using carefully crafted rhetoric to express a vision of a possible world. And contemporary scholarship, being more removed from the immediacy of the issues Angelina addressed, may more dispassionately consider those qualities that made her speeches and her writings so effective. Stephen Howard Browne, for example, maintains that Angelina "*so managed the resources of her art as to create from the limitations of her world new possibilities for collective moral action*" (16, emphasis in original). What artist could ask for a better tribute?

WORKS CITED

Lerner, Gerda. *The Grimké Sisters from South Carolina: Rebels Against Slavery.* Boston: Houghton Mifflin, 1967.

Letters of Theodore Dwight Weld, Angelina Grimké Weld, and Sarah Grimké. 2 vols. Ed. Gilbert H. Barnes and Dwight L. Dumond. New York: D. Appleton-Century Co., 1934.

BIBLIOGRAPHY

Works by Angelina Grimké

Slavery and the Boston Riot: A Letter to Wm. L. Garrison. Philadelphia: August 30, 1835. Broadside.

Appeal to the Christian Women of the Southern States. New York: American Anti-Slavery Society, 1836.

An Appeal to the Women of the Nominally Free States. New York: W. S. Dorr, 1837.

Letters to Catherine E. Beecher, in Reply to an Essay on Slavery and Abolitionism, Addressed to A. E. Grimké. Revised by the Author. Boston: Isaac Knapp, 1838.

Letter from Angelina Grimké Weld, to the Woman's Rights Convention, held at Syracuse, September, 1852. Syracuse: Master's print, 1852.

The Public Years of Sarah and Angelina Grimké: Selected Writings, 1835–1839. Ed. Larry Ceplair. New York: Columbia UP, 1989.

Letters of Theodore Dwight Weld, Angelina Grimké Weld, and Sarah Grimké. 2 vols. Ed. Gilbert H. Barnes and Dwight L. Dumond. New York: D. Appleton-Century Co., 1934.

Studies of Angelina Grimké

Birney, Catherine H. *The Grimké Sisters: Sarah and Angelina Grimké, The First American Women Advocates of Abolition and Woman's Rights,* 1885; rpt. Westport, CT: Greenwood Press, 1969.

Browne, Stephen Howard. *Angelina Grimké: Rhetoric, Identity, and the Radical Imagination.* East Lansing: Michigan State UP, 1999.

Lerner, Gerda. *The Grimké Sisters from South Carolina: Rebels Against Slavery.* Boston: Houghton Mifflin, 1967.

Lumpkin, Katharine Du Pre. *The Emancipation of Angelina Grimké.* Chapel Hill: U of North Carolina P, 1974.

Perry, Mark. *Lift Up Thy Voice: The Grimké Family's Journey from Slaveholders to Civil Rights Leaders.* New York: Viking, 2001.

CHARLOTTE L. FORTEN GRIMKÉ (1837–1914)

Theodore R. Hovet

BIOGRAPHY

The major events of Charlotte L. Forten Grimké's life are quite well known because her personal journals still exist as does some of her correspondence. She was born in Philadelphia into a prominent African American family. Her father was the son of James Forten who made a fortune as a sail maker and became an influential supporter of abolition, helping to finance William Lloyd Garrison's activities and the publication of the *Liberator.* After the death of her mother, Mary Woods Forten, when she was three, her grandmother (Charlotte) and three aunts—Margaretta, Sarah, and Harriet—became the dominant female influences in her life. These women were educated, energetic, and dedicated to abolition and women's rights. The husbands of Sarah and Harriet, Joseph and Robert Purvis, were well-to-do sons of an English cotton trader and were dedicated to antislavery and improving the condition of free African Americans. In 1854, Forten's father sent her to Salem, Massachusetts, for schooling rather then having her attend the segregated Philadelphia schools. That year she began keeping a journal as she became an intimate member of the family of Charles Lenox Remond, a noted abolitionist and reformer. Forten graduated from the Higginson Grammar School in 1855 and from the Salem Normal School in 1856. She then began her teaching career, which was frequently interrupted by a pulmonary ailment and severe headaches.

The year 1862 brought a major change in Forten's life. John Greenleaf Whittier, whom she had known for some time, urged her to volunteer for the "Port Royal Experiment," an attempt to educate freed slaves on the South Carolina Coast. After initially being turned down, she was accepted by the Port Royal Relief Association on Port Royal Island and assigned to a one-room schoolhouse where she served from October 1862 to May 1864. At first put off by the seeming strangeness of the culture, particularly the Gullah language, a Creole blend of English and African languages spoken by the freed slaves, Forten soon learned to love the people and the culture, which she described in letters and two articles in the *Atlantic Monthly.* As Edmund Wilson has discussed, she formed several close relationships with prominent white men, most notably Thomas

Wentworth Higginson and Dr. Seth Rogers, both of whom left testimonials to her intelligence and attractiveness. If Forten's entries in her journal are to be trusted, the relationship with Rogers, married and white, clearly verged on the romantic. However, her relationships with white men in South Carolina also elicited one of her typically understated but devastating comments on her countrymen when she dismissed a rumor that an officer was in love with her with the observation that this could not be true since he was a white American.

After returning North, Forten worked in Boston from 1865 to 1871 for the Freedmen's Union Commission and taught at the Shaw Memorial School. She then moved to Washington, D. C., where she taught and served in the U.S. Treasury Department. In 1878 she married Francis Grimké, the son of a slave woman and the brother of the famed Grimké sisters. By all accounts, the marriage of Charlotte and Francis, the younger by 13 years, was a happy one, marred only by the death of an infant daughter. She was bedridden for a year before her death in 1914.

MAJOR WORKS AND THEMES

Charlotte Forten Grimké's published work during her lifetime is scant, consisting of about 15 poems and 15 essays (the count varies slightly from one study to the next) which appeared in publications such as the *Atlantic, Liberator, New England Magazine, National Anti-Slavery Standard, Christian Recorder,* and *Anglo-American Magazine.* Today her journals, not published until 1953, are considered her major accomplishment.

Her poems deal with national figures and events ("Charles Sumner," "The Slave Girl's Prayer"); personal feelings ("The Angel's Visit," "The Two Voices"); and responses to nature ("Flowers"). The essays address people and events connected to the antislavery movement and to personal experiences, such as her life on the South Carolina coast.

The journals are an engrossing account of the many famous reformers and writers she met when she lived in New England (e. g., Garrison and Whittier who became friends and mentors, Ralph Waldo Emerson, William Wells Brown); Civil War luminaries such as Robert Shaw and Higginson; her insightful responses to a wide range of literature from the classical to the contemporary period (she read Charlotte Brontë, Elizabeth Barrett Browning, and Nathaniel Hawthorne with enthusiasm); and responses to some of her personal problems such as her lifelong feelings of homelessness, her mixed feelings toward her father whom she felt had abandoned her during her Salem years, her rage at northern racism, and her discouragement over her poor health.

CRITICAL RECEPTION

Her poems are today generally dismissed as weak derivatives of nineteenth-century sentimentality and English romanticism, but some critics point out that they are much like a great deal of the verse written in the middle decades of the nineteenth century. In her own day a few writers like William Wells Brown extravagantly praised what he considered to be her beautiful diction and unerring sense of rhythm. Also Joan R. Sherman argues that Forten displayed considerable development as a poet considering her lack of sustained publication.

Her essays and letters on Port Royal are much more highly regarded, particularly for her keen and sympathetic observations of an African American culture much different from her own. She is convincing in her praise of the hymns of the ex-slaves, which she considers superior to those heard in the mainstream churches, vivid in her accounts of "shouts" and dances, and eloquent in her praise of the bearing and manners of a people only recently freed from slavery.

Her place in American literature, however, is based on the *Journals,* which consist of five volumes containing entries from May 1854 to July 1892 (only a few from 1865 to 1885 and none between 1885 and 1892). The first edition of the *Journals* published in 1953, edited by Ray Allen Billington, ended in 1864. The complete edition was published in 1988 by Oxford University Press as part of the Schomburg Library's Nineteenth-Century Black Women's Writer Series.

The *Journals* have been the subject of several recent provocative studies. In keeping with the recent vogue of culture studies, these analyses are more concerned with what Forten's life tells us about American society in the nineteenth century than with her literary accomplishments. For example, studies by Joanne M. Braxton, Emma Jones Lapansky, Lisa A. Long, and Carla L. Peterson speculate on how her upbringing in a wealthy and educated family complicated efforts of an African American and a woman to find a convincing voice and an audience. Also several commentators, most extensively Lisa M. Koch and Diane Price Herndl, speculate on the significance of Forten's frequent descriptions of her bouts with illness, suggesting that they can be viewed, like those of Alice James, as a performance which helped her to define a literary persona. In Forten's case, they may have enabled her literary voice to subvert the belief widely held by whites that the identity of African American women was primarily shaped by physical vitality and sexuality rather than by intellect and emotional sensitivity.

Recent criticism exemplified by Nellie Y. McKay's essay on "Les Lieux de Memoire" indicates a shift toward an evaluation of the *Journals* as a literary document. First of all, analysis of the rhetoric indicates that Forten, like Alice James or Mary Chesnut, used a journal to explore her narrative voice and to envision a potential audience. Thus it should be considered a literary document of unusual interest because of the light it casts on individuals attempting to develop an authentic identity in a culture that either ignores or oppresses them. Second, the current attitude in the United States that memoirs and "life writing," even by people with no public identity, constitute a legitimate literary genre greatly alters, as McKay's analysis indicates, the way Forten's journals are read. She becomes an exemplar of the many individuals who attempt without regard for publication to make sense of their lives through literary expression.

WORKS CITED

Braxton, Joan M. "Charlotte Forten Grimké and the Search for a Public Voice." *The Private Self: Theory and Practice of Women's Autobiographical Writings.* Ed. Shari Benstock. Chapel Hill, NC: U of North Carolina P, 1988: 254.

Gates, Henry Louis, Jr. "Forward: In Her Own Write." *The Journals of Charlotte Forten Grimké.* Ed. Brenda Stevenson. New York: Oxford UP, 1988: vii.

Herndl, Diane Price. "The Invisible (Invalid) Woman: African-American Women, Illness, and Nineteenth-Century Narrative." *American Studies: An Interdisciplinary Journal* 24.6 (1995): 553.

Koch, Lisa M. "Bodies as Stage Props: Enacting Hysteria in the Diaries of Charlotte Forten." *Legacy* 15.1 (1998): 59.

Lapansky, Emma Jones. "Feminism, Freedom, and Community: Charlotte Forten and Women Activists in Nineteenth-Century Philadelphia." *The Pennsylvania Magazine of History and Biography* CXIII. 6 (Jan. 1989): 3.

Long, Lisa A. "Charlotte Forten's Civil War Journals and the Quest for 'Genius, Beauty, and Deathless Fame.' " *Legacy* 16.1 (1999): 37.

McKay, Nellie Y. "The Journals of Charlotte Forten Grimké: Les Lieux de Memoire in African-American Women's Autobiography." *History and Memoirie in African-American Culture.* Eds. Genevieve Fahr and Robert O'Meally. New York and Oxford: Oxford UP, 1994: 261.

Peterson, Carla L. "Seeking the 'Writable': Charlotte Forten and the Problem of Narration." *Doers of the Word: African-American Speakers and Writers in the North (1830–1880).* New York and London: Oxford UP, 1995: 176.

Sherman, Joan R. Ed. *African-American Poetry of the Nineteenth Century: An Anthology.* Champaign-Urbana: U of Illinois P, 1992: 211.

Stevenson, Brenda. "Introduction." *The Journals of Charlotte Forten Grimké.* Ed. Brenda Stevenson. New York: Oxford UP, 1988: 3.

Wilson, Edmund. Patriotic Gore: Studies in the Literature of the American Civil War. New York and London: Oxford UP, 1962: 239.

BIBLIOGRAPHY

Works by Charlotte L. Forten Grimké

Selected Poems

"A Parting Hymn." (1856). Printed in *The Norton Anthology of African-American Literature,* Ed. Henry Louis Gates Jr. and Nellie Y. McKay. New York and London: W. W. Norton and Co., 1997: 472.

"Poem for Normal School Graduation." *Liberator* (August 1856).

"To W. L. G. on Reading His 'Chosen Queen." *Liberator* (March 1855).

"Flowers." *Christian Recorder* (May 20 1858).

"The Angel's Visit." Submitted to *Anglo-African Magazine* (July 26 1858). Reprinted in *African-American Poetry of the Nineteenth Century.* Ed. Joan R. Sherman. Champaign-Urbana: U of Illinois P, 1992: 213–215.

"Two Voices." *National Anti-Slavery Standard* (January 15 1859).

"The Wind Among the Poplars." *Liberator* (May 27 1859).

"The Slave Girl's Prayer." *National Anti-Slavery Standard* (January 14 1860).

"Charles Sumner." (1874). Printed in *African-American Poetry of the Nineteenth Century.* Ed. Joan R. Sherman. Champaign-Urbana: U of Illinois P, 1992: 216–17.

"The Gathering of the Grand Army." (1890). Printed in *African-American Poetry of the Nineteenth Century: An Anthology.* Ed. Joan R. Sherman. Champaign-Urbana: U of Illinois P, 1992: 218–219.

"Wordsworth." (c. 1890). Printed in *African-American Poetry of the Nineteenth Century: An Anthology.* Ed. Joan R. Sherman. Champaign-Urbana: U of Illinois P, 1992.

Selected Essays, Sketches, and Published Letters

"Glimpses of New England." *National Anti-Slavery Standard* (June 18 1858).

Letters from South Carolina Sea Islands. *Liberator* (December 12 and 19 1862 and January 23 1863).

"Life on the Sea Islands," Parts I and II. *Atlantic Monthly* (May/June 1864).

"Personal Recollections of Whittier." *New England Magazine* (1893).

Miscellaneous

Translation of French novel *Madame Therese; or, the Volunteers of '92.* New York: Scribners, 1869.

Studies of Charlotte L. Forten Grimké

Bolden, Tanya. "Charlotte Forten Grimké." In *And Not Afraid to Dare: The Stories of Ten African-American Women.* New York: Scholastic P, 1998: 30–47.

———. "The Forten Women." In *The Book of African-American Women: Crusaders, Creators, and Uplifters.* Holbrook, MA: Adams Media Corporation: 1996: 39–44.

Braxton, Joan M. "Charlotte Forten Grimke and the Search for a Public Voice." *The Private Self: Theory and Practice of Women's Autobiographical Writings.* Ed. Shari Benstock. Chapel Hill, NC: U of North Carolina P, 1988: 254–71.

Chittenden, Elizabeth F. *Profiles in Black and White: Stories of Men and Women Who Fought Against Slavery.* New York: Charles Scribner's Sons, 1973: 107–24.

Gates, Henry Louis, Jr. "Forward: In Her Own Write." *The Journals of Charlotte Forten Grimke.* Ed. Brenda Stevenson. New York: Oxford UP, 1988: vii–xii.

Harris, Trudier. "Charlotte L. Forten." In *Afro-American Writers Before the Harlem Renaissance,* Ed. Trudy Harris. Vol. 50 of *Dictionary of Literary Biography.* Detroit: Gale Research Co., 1986: 130–9.

Herndl, Diane Price. "The Invisible (Invalid) Woman: African-American Women, Illness, and Nineteenth-Century Narrative." *American Studies: An Interdisciplinary Journal* 24.6 (1995): 553–71.

Koch, Lisa M. "Bodies as Stage Props: Enacting Hysteria in the Diaries of Charlotte Forten." *Legacy* 15.1 (1998): 59–64.

Lapansky, Emma Jones. "Feminism, Freedom, and Community: Charlotte Forten and Women Activists in Nineteenth-Century Philadelphia." *The Pennsylvania Magazine of History and Biography* CXIII. 6 (Jan. 1989): 3–20.

Long, Lisa A. "Charlotte Forten's Civil War Journals and the Quest for 'Genius, Beauty, and Death- less Fame.' " *Legacy* 16.1 (1999): 37–48.

McKay, Nellie Y. "The Journals of Charlotte Forten Grimké: Les Lieux de Memoire in African- American Women's Autobiography." *History and Memoirie in African-American Culture.* Eds. Genevieve Fahr and Robert O'Meally. New York and Oxford: Oxford UP, 1994: 261–71.

Peterson, Carla L. "Seeking the 'Writable': Charlotte Forten and the Problem of Narration." *Doers of the Word: African-American Speakers and Writers in the North (1830–1880).* New York and London: Oxford UP, 1995: 176–95.

Rodier, Katharine. "Charlotte L. Forten." In *American Women Prose Writers, 1820–70.* Ed. Amy Hudock and Katharine Rodier. Vol. 239 of *Dictionary of Literary Biography.* Detroit: Gale Research Co., 1986: 107–17.

Sherman, Joan R. Ed. *African-American Poetry of the Nineteenth Century: An Anthology.* Champaign-Urbana: U of Illinois P, 1992: 211–20.

Sterling, Dorothy. *We are Your Sisters.* New York and London: W. W. Norton, 1984: 279–86.

Stevenson, Brenda. "Introduction." *The Journals of Charlotte Forten Grimké.* Ed. Brenda Steven- son. New York: Oxford UP, 1988: 3–56.

Thomas, Gwendolyn A. "Charlotte L. Forten." In *American Women Writers: A Critical Reference Guide from Colonial Times to the Present,* Vol. 2. Ed. Lina Mainero. New York: Fred Ungar Pub. Co., 1980: 69–71.

Wilson, Edmund. *Patriotic Gore: Studies in the Literature of the American Civil War.* New York and London: Oxford UP, 1962: 239–56.

SARAH GRIMKÉ (1792–1873)

Robert A. Russ

BIOGRAPHY

The abolitionist and feminist writer and orator Sarah Grimké was born November 26, 1792, the sixth child (the second daughter) of Judge John Faucheraud Grimké and Mary Smith Grimké, prominent members of wealthy, aristocratic Charleston, South Carolina, society. She and her younger sister Angelina were unique in being the only white southern women prominent—even "notorious"—in the abolition movement, and as women who sought to have a voice in public affairs, they were drawn to connect their interest in abolition with the rights of women. Various issues that would be important lifelong concerns are conspicuous in Sarah Grimké's childhood. She was deeply anguished over the treatment of blacks under the system of slavery, and she was likewise personally touched by the injustice under which women lived. Despite the southern laws and customs, as well as her father's explicit orders, Sarah secretly taught her waiting-maid to read. And as a sign of her lifelong tendency to link the spiritual life with social concerns, Sarah already expected religious institutions to show leadership in addressing the injustices in secular society, and was disappointed when they did not.

Although she received a "proper" education for a young woman of her time and place, it was inadequate for the desire that she held, to become a lawyer, nor was such line socially acceptable. Even at the end of her life she was bitter of such injustice and pondered what she could have made of her life in a world of sexual equality. In 1805, the last child in the family was born, a sister, and Sarah Grimké, now 13, requested, and was permitted, to become godmother to the newborn Angelina Emily Grimké. When their father's health led to a trip to Philadelphia, Sarah accompanied him there, where he died, and two years later, after being drawn to Quakerism, she returned to Philadelphia to live.

In Philadelphia she struggled with herself over her perceived calling into Quaker ministry, and she struggled with the influential Orthodox Quaker leaders for acceptance of her abolitionist and feminist views. She also struggled with her personal relationship with Israel Morris, the widowed Quaker whom she had met on her original return from Philadelphia and whose encouragement and spiritual guidance had led her to Quakerism.

She loved him, and he repeatedly proposed marriage, but she repeatedly rejected him, perhaps because of the opposition of his children, perhaps because of her apprehension over her ability to combine the roles of Quaker minister and wife.

After sister Angelina followed her, both into Quakerism and to Philadelphia, it was there that the women's public work began, almost by chance, in 1835, with Angelina's letter to William Lloyd Garrison, encouraging him in his abolitionist work and his recent criticism of mob violence in Boston. Following the publication of Angelina's *Appeal to the Christian Women of the Southern States* (1836), which was burned in the South, the sisters attended a training convention of the American Anti-Slavery Society and began a 23-week lecture tour, during which they spoke to over 40,000 people in more than 80 meetings in 67 towns. Both sisters fell ill, exhausted from the demands of this tour, by the end of 1837, but before they completely retired from public life in 1838, Angelina did speak before the legislative committee of the Massachusetts State Legislature, becoming the first woman to speak before a legislative body, and then, two days after her marriage to abolitionist Theodore Dwight Weld, she spoke at the dedication of Philadelphia's new Pennsylvania Hall, which was burned by protestors the following night.

With her sister Angelina, Sarah Grimké had only a few intense public years of writing and speaking, but those years were a bright and shining moment in noble causes. Following Angelina's marriage to Weld in 1838, Sarah was disowned by the Quakers, simply for attending the wedding (Angelina had been disowned for marrying a non-Quaker), and Sarah lived with the couple in the same household.

Though they were now out of the limelight, the sisters were still actively involved in progressive causes. Their research for Weld's book *American Slavery As It Is* (1839), which became one of the sources for Harriet Beecher Stowe's novel *Uncle Tom's Cabin,* required them to examine literally thousands of newspapers for news stories, trial records and decisions, records of punishment, speeches, advertisements for runaway slaves, and other items pertaining to the conditions of slaves. On their Belleville farm, the Welds' involvement in their own children's education and their need for money led them to take in boarding children/students until they had an actual boarding school (Belleville School), with Weld as teacher and principal, and with Sarah and Angelina helping out with instruction as well as doing all the cooking, washing, and other household chores. Weld, Angelina, and Sarah were even more involved in education and social "progress" when they later joined the utopian Raritan Bay Union, home of the Eagleswood School, where they lived and worked until 1863, when they moved to Hyde Park, a south Boston suburb. Sarah Grimké died on December 23, 1873, at age 81. Her sister Angelina lived another six years.

MAJOR WORKS AND THEMES

Although both Angelina and Sarah Grimké wrote and spoke about both abolition and women's rights, Angelina concentrated more on the abolition issue and Sarah more on women's issues. Her antislavery pamphlet *Epistle to the Clergy of the Southern States* (1836) appears to have been strongly influenced by her brother-in-law Theodore Weld's *The Bible Against Slavery* (1837), although Sarah's own work appeared first. However, in contrast to the generally logical, detached argument of Weld's work, Sarah's message is passionate, exhortative, and marked with the tone and language of Biblical prophecy:

For you the midnight tear is shed, for you the daily and the nightly prayer ascends that God in his unbounded mercy may open your hearts to believe his awful enunciations against those who "rob the poor because he is poor." (1)

In its daring and righteous message to the supposed spiritual leaders of the South, Sarah issued a moral challenge to Christians to put principles into practice. Grimké biographer Gerda Lerner states: "Her boldness in directly challenging the church, to which she had felt hopelessly subject for so many years, was a sign of her intellectual and personal growth" (*Grimké Sisters* 156).

The attack on the oppression of the privileged and comfortable position of Christian orthodoxy was repeated in relation to women's rights in Sarah's *Letters on the Equality of the Sexes and the Condition of Woman* (1838), published 10 years before the Seneca Falls convention. In this landmark document in the history of women's rights, Sarah attacked the biblical argument for the inferior position of women and held that God had created woman as a companion equal in all respects.

The sisters' ideas, values, and activism acquired a truly personal connection when they learned of their nephews Francis, Archibald, and John, sons of their brother Henry by the slave Nancy Weston, and developed a long and supportive relationship with them. Lerner calls this connection "remarkable and probably unique among the complexities of race relations in this country . . . the acid test of the sisters' convictions" (*Grimké Sisters* 361).

Given the sisters' depth of commitment to the abolition cause and the social constraints upon women's involvement in public affairs, the linkage between the abolitionist cause and that of women's rights was perhaps inevitable. It is certainly consistent with Sarah's other work and indicative of her spiritual/social activism that she produced an English translation of Lamartine's *Joan of Arc* (1867). In 1870, at the age of 77, she and Angelina (then 65) became the first women to go to the polls in Massachusetts. Though they were publicly derided, and though their ballots were not counted, they still made a statement against the political exclusion of women.

CRITICAL RECEPTION

While the Grimké sisters are now accorded only a minor place in American history, there is a significant current interest in their work, both as abolitionists and advocates of women's rights. During their own time, the reception of the Grimké sisters work was dependent on the ideological stance of the readers or audience, not on the quality of the work itself, as high as that may have been. The "radical" ideas expressed in their writings and speeches made the artistic qualities of their work relatively insignificant, and as women from a slaveholding family, the Grimké sisters' unique background was enough to ensure the notoriety of their work, and during their years of public speaking on abolition, the malicious commented about their motivation for speaking, characterizing them as spinsters who might find Negro husbands if "amalgamation" became "fashionable." But not only the malicious opposed them: the Congregational ministers of Massachusetts issued a "Pastoral Letter" condemning them; the Quakers, the American Anti-Slavery Society, and even Theodore Weld sought to restrain them, especially in linking the abolitionist activism with issues of women's rights.

During their lifetimes, Angelina was noted as a more effective public speaker, and her reputation far exceeded her sister's; however, current scholarship is now more willing to recognize in Sarah's writing the work of a major feminist thinker. Over 30 years after writing her impressive biography of the Grimké sisters, Lerner admits that, at the time, she herself did not fully understand and appreciate Sarah's religious language and could not fully enter into her mind. Sarah was a pioneer, a revolutionary, in feminist theory and expression, and she was difficult to understand because her "feminist thought had leaped far ahead of her generation, even her century." But the significance of Sarah's

rhetorical and theoretical contributions to the foundations of the women's rights movement may now be a little better appreciated:

She offered the best and most coherent Bible argument for woman's equality yet offered by a
woman; she identified and characterized the distinction between sex and gender; she took class and
race into consideration; and she tied the subordination of women both to educational deprivation
and sexual oppression. She identified men, individually and as a group, as having benefited from
the subordination of women. Above all, she understood that women must acquire feminist consciousness by conscious effort and that they must practice asserting their rights in order to think
more appropriately. (*Feminist Thought* 40)

Seen from this perspective, Sarah Grimké contributed to the women's movement
not only through her bold public appearances in a few years in the public eye, but also
through planting the seeds of modern feminist thought.

BIBLIOGRAPHY

Works by Sarah Grimké

An Epistle to the Clergy of the Southern States. New York, 1836.
The Feminist Thought of Sarah Grimké. Ed. Gerda Lerner. New York: Oxford UP, 1998.
*Letters on the Equality of the Sexes and the Condition of Woman; Addressed to Mary Parker, Pres-
     ident of the Boston Female Anti-Slavery Society.* Boston: Isaac Knapp, 1838.
Trans. Lamartine, Alphonse M. L. de Prat de. *Joan of Arc: A Biography.* Boston: Adams & Co.,
     1867.
The Public Years of Sarah and Angelina Grimké: Selected Writings, 1835–1839. Ed. Larry Ceplair.
     New York: Columbia UP, 1989.

Studies of Sarah Grimké

Birney, Catherine H. *The Grimké Sisters: Sarah and Angelina Grimké, The First American Women
     Advocates of Abolition and Woman's Rights,* 1885; rpt. Westport, CT: Greenwood Press, 1969.
Lerner, Gerda. *The Grimké Sisters from South Carolina: Rebels Against Slavery.* Boston: Houghton
     Mifflin, 1967
Perry, Mark. *Lift Up Thy Voice: The Grimké Family's Journey from Slaveholders to Civil Rights
     Leaders.* New York: Viking, 2001.

SARAH JOSEPHA HALE (1788–1879)

Aleta Cane

BIOGRAPHY

Sarah Josepha was born on October 24, 1788, the third child of Gordon and Martha Whittlesey Buell. That was the year Washington assumed the presidency of the United States. Sarah was educated at home, in Newport, New Hampshire, with her older brothers Charles and Horatio. When Horatio went off to Dartmouth, he shared his notes and texts with Sarah, thus affording her more education than most women of her time. She conducted a dame school for six years until her marriage to David Hale in 1813. An ambitious lawyer and a Freemason, Hale encouraged Sarah to continue her studies and to write. Several of her poems were published by *The New Hampshire Spectator,* Newport's weekly newspaper. Sarah Hale bore five children during her happy nine-year marriage. David died suddenly, in 1822, and Sarah tried the millinery trade to support herself and her children while continuing to write stories and poems. David's Freemason lodge paid for the publication of Sarah's first book of poems, *The Genius of Oblivion and Other Original Poems* (1823). Although not a critical success, the book sold well, allowing Hale to write full-time. The *Atlantic Monthly, The Literary Gazette,* and *The Spectator and Ladies' Album* published her poems and stories. She submitted winning entries to several poetry contests. In 1826, *The Spectator and Ladies' Album* published 17 of Hale's poems, 2 short stories, and 1 literary review. Four other poems appeared in the fashionable giftbook *The Memorial* in 1827.

Hale's novel, *Northwood,* was published that same year to enthusiastic reviews launching her national literary career. John Lauris Blake invited her to edit his new publication, *The Ladies' Magazine.* Although she tried editing the journal from Newport, she had to move to Boston to continue her work. Leaving her four older children to continue their educations in the homes of their aunts and uncles, Hale vowed to earn enough money to support and educate all of them. She succeeded.

Hale envisioned a magazine containing only well-written, original materials. She particularly encouraged women authors to submit their writings. Desire for originality forced Hale to write many of the stories and poems for the first issues of the magazine herself. Later contributors included Lydia Sigourney, Elmira Hunt, and Sarah Whitman. Hale's magazine encouraged the education of women, published American authors writing about American scenes and themes, and promoted the good works of its readers.

The Ladies' Magazine supported the Perkins School, the first school for the blind; organized a mammoth fair that raised the funds to complete the Bunker Hill Monument; founded the Seaman's Aid Society; and promoted a school for the children of poor working women as good works.

Although Hale supported poor women who had to work, she publicly espoused the notion that men and women belonged in separate spheres of influence and that women, the morally purer of the two sexes, would be polluted by entering into the public sphere that men inhabited. In the February 1832 issue of *The Ladies' Magazine,* she opined, "I consider every attempt to induce women to think they have a right to participate in the public duties of government as injurious to their best interests and derogatory to their character. Our empire is purer, more excellent and spiritual" (87). Thirty-seven years later she denounced the woman's suffrage movement on the same grounds.

In 1830, Marshall Lowell, a composer and a friend of Hale's, asked her to write verses for children, which he then set to music, thus making them easy to learn and remember. *Poems for Our Children* (1830) were metrically regular poems with a different moral message as the theme of each one. "Mary Had a Little Lamb" was one of these poems.

Louis Godey's *Lady's Book* and *The Ladies' Magazine* merged in 1836. Hale and Godey made the new magazine, which kept the name *Lady's Book,* the most influential and most widely circulated periodical of its era. The magazine's hand-tinted fashion plates and sentimental poems and stories raised the number of subscribers to 150,000 just prior to the Civil War.

In 1841 Hale moved to Philadelphia to be close to the publisher of the *Lady's Book.* Philadelphia was the home of many well-known magazines such as *Graham's Magazine.* Both Godey and Graham realized the value of publishing original works by well-known authors. In 1854, both magazines took out copyrights on their contents. Newspapers and publishers of giftbooks railed against their actions, but Hale defended the copyrights as protection for American authors and publications.

During the 1840s and 1850s, Hale championed daily bathing; psychologically sound child-rearing practices; playgrounds for city children; the career of the first female doctor, Elizabeth Blackwell; healthful clothing styles for women; and the rehabilitation of Washington's home at Mt. Vernon, which became a national monument. She advised Matthew Vassar on the creation of Vassar College and lobbied the college's trustees to hire female faculty members. In 1863, Hale encouraged President Lincoln to declare the third Thursday of November to be a day of national thanksgiving.

When arguments concerning slavery rent the Union, Hale published *Northwood* (1852), reminding abolitionists in her introduction that "the master is their brother as well as the servant" (Finley 175). Her novel *Liberia* (1853) makes the case for educating slaves before their liberation and subsequent repatriation in Liberia.

The year 1853 was a prolific one for Hale. She published the encyclopedic *Woman's Record; or Sketches of All Distinguished Women.* It was revised twice, in 1855 and 1876. In December 1877, Hale retired from *Godey's Lady's Book,* writing in her final editorial column, "I must bid farewell to my countrywomen, with the hope that this work of half a century may be blessed to the furtherance of the happiness and usefulness in their Divinely appointed sphere" (254). Sixteen months later, at the age of 90, she died peacefully.

MAJOR WORKS AND THEMES

Hale's novels *Northwood* (1827, 1852) and *Liberia* (1853) dealt with the differences in life and industry between the northern and southern states and the question of slavery. Hale sought to teach her readers that there were more similarities than differences among Americans. She supported education and liberation of slaves and their repatriation in Africa.

In her editorial writings in *The Ladies' Magazine* and the subsequent *Lady's Book,* Hale presented her most repeated theme: the differentiation of the sexes. Men are physically stronger, and women show greater moral and religious strength. That these two spheres of influence are of equal importance, she had no doubt. To Hale they were also divinely designated as separate. She reiterated this theme in *Woman's Record* (1853, 1855, 1876), which *Notable American Women* characterizes as "an ambitious biographical encyclopedia containing 2500 entries and an early effort to remedy the neglect of women in most such works" (114). Nina Baym describes the book as "a conflation of the progress of Christianity with that of women. The Christian message is precisely the superiority of women" ("Onward Christian Women" 253).

Hale's other major themes are the encouragement of women's education and the support of organizations for social improvement. She declared that women's education and the promotion of women as teachers were her favorite themes. She argued that women are natural teachers and that they would happily work for lower wages which would make universal education affordable to all.

Hale supported Godey's policy that forbid political or religious issues from appearing in the pages of their magazine. Godey feared alienating any reader, and Hale concurred. When the Civil War broke out, Hale wrote that she wanted to make the *Lady's Book* "an oasis in the desert" (December 1862).

Stating that women at home wielded moral suasion, which would help to end the war, she elided her conservative social ideology and editorially neutral position in the wartime pages of the *Lady's Book.* She promoted the moral education of children, which she believed was a mother's most important task. Her etiquette, homemaking, and recipe books also demonstrate her interest in making woman's work at home more scientific and more praiseworthy.

CRITICAL RECEPTION

Critically, Hale has been viewed more as an important social force than as a prominent author. When *Northwood* was first published, it received positive reviews including one in the *United States Review and Literary Gazette* by William Cullen Bryant, who wrote that the book was "another proof to many already existing that neither talents nor materials were wanting in the United States" (Finley 38).

The *New Englander and Yale Review* (1853) declared that *Woman's Record* was unbalanced, in that, of the four sections, the section on contemporary women and their writings was too long and the other sections too brief. The anonymous writer also takes issue with Hale's inclusion of snippets of writings by women, which the writer felt was not in keeping with the encyclopedia's genre. As to woman's moral superiority, the same reviewer takes exception, noting that "will and conscience [are] common to both sexes" (150). Like *The Genius of Oblivion* (1823), *Woman's Record* may not have received critical acclaim, but both were well received by the book-buying public.

Contemporary scholarship questions whether Hale was a proto-feminist, through the example of her own life, or a negative influence due to her conviction that separate spheres for the sexes were divinely ordained. While early biographers, such as Ruth Finley (1931) and Isabelle Webb Entrikin (1946), argue that Hale was the consummate feminist, Ann Douglas, Nina Baym, and Patricia Okker agree that Hale's ideology marked her as an adherent of Victorian womanhood that sought to keep women out of the public realms of politics, commerce, and ideas. Hale's strong antisuffrage rhetoric is also seen by contemporary critics as evidence of her valorization of an ideology that limited, rather than liberated, her loyal readers.

WORKS CITED

Anonymous. "Literary Notices." *New Englander and Yale Review* 11. 41 (Feb. 1853) 149–53.

Baym, Nina. "Onward Christian Women: Sarah J. Hale's History of the World." *New England Quarterly* 63 (June 1990): 249–70.

Finley, Ruth. *The Lady of Godey's: Sarah Josepha Hale.* Philadelphia: J. B. Lippincott, 1931.

Godey's Lady's Book. Vols. 14–95.Philadelphia: Godey, January 1837–December 1877.

"Sarah Josepha Hale." *Notable American Women, 1607–1950.* Ed. Edward T. James. Cambridge, Mass.: Belknap Press, 1971.

BIBLIOGRAPHY

Works by Sarah Josepha Hale

Books

The Genius of Oblivion and Other Original Poems. Concord, N. H.: Jacob B. Moore, 1823.

Northwood: A Tale of New England. 2 vols. Boston: Bowles and Dearborn, 1827.

Sketches of American Character. Boston: Putnam and Hunt, 1829.

Poems for Our Children. Boston: R. W. Hale, 1830.

Flora's Interpreter: or the American Book of Flowers and Sentiments. Boston: Marsh, Capen and Lyon, 1832.

The Ladies Wreath: A Selection from the Poetic Writers of England and America. Boston: Marsh, Capen and Lyon, 1837.

Northwood or Life North and South Showing the Character of Both. 2nd ed. New York: H. Long and Parather, 1852.

Woman's Record; or Sketches of All Distinguished Women from "The Beginning" till A.D. 1850. New York: Harper and Brothers, 1853.

Manners: or Happy Homes and Good Society All the Year Round. Boston: J. E. Tilton and Co., 1867.

Liberia: or Mr. Peyton's Experiments. New York: Harper and Brothers, 1853. Reprint, Upper Saddle River, N.J.: Gregg Press, 1968.

Love: or A Woman's Destiny, a Poem. Philadelphia: Duffield Ashmead, 1870.

Edited Periodicals

The Ladies' Magazine. Vols. 1–3. Boston: Putnam and Hunt 1828–1830. Vol. 4. Boston: Marsh, Capen and Lyon, 1831.

The Ladies' Magazine and Literary Gazette. Vols. 5–6. Boston: Marsh, Capen and Lyon, 1832–1833.

The American Ladies' Magazine. Vols. 7–9. Boston: James B. Dow, 1834–1836.

Godey's Lady's Book. Vols. 14–95. Philadelphia: Godey, January 1837–December 1877.

Studies of Sarah Josepha Hale

Aronson, Amy. "Domesticity and Women's Collective Agency: Contribution and Collaboration in America's First Successful Women's Magazine." *American Periodicals* 11 (2001):1–23.

Baym, Nina. "At Home with History: History Books and Women's Sphere before the Civil War." *Proceedings of the American Antiquarian Society* 101 (1991): 275–95.

———. "Onward Christian Women: Sarah J. Hale's History of the World." *New England Quarterly* 63 (June 1990): 249–70.

Douglas, Ann. *The Feminization of American Culture.* New York: Alfred A. Knopf, 1977.

Entrikin, Isabelle Webb. *Sarah Josepha Hale and "Godey's Lady's Book."* Lancaster, Pa.: Lancaster Press, 1946.

Finley, Ruth. *The Lady of Godey's: Sarah Josepha Hale.* Philadelphia: J. B. Lippincott, 1931.

Hoffman, Nicole Tonkovich. "*Legacy* Profile: Sarah Josepha Hale." *Legacy: A Journal of 19th Century American Women* 7 (Fall 1990): 47–55.

Kaplan, Amy. "Manifest Domesticity." *American Literature* 70:3 (1998): 581–606.

Maida, Patricia. "Breaking Ground: The Legacy of an American Female Editor." *CEA Magazine* 11 (1998): 47–56.

Okker, Patricia. *Our Sister Editors: Sarah J. Hale and the Tradition of Nineteenth Century American Women Editors.* Athens: University of Georgia Press, 1995.

Rogers, Sherbrooke. *Sarah Josepha Hale: A New England Pioneer 1788–1879.* Grantham, N.H.: Tompson and Rutter, 1985.

"Sarah Josepha Hale." *Notable American Women, 1607–1950.* Ed. Edward T. James. Cambridge, Mass.: Belknap Press, 1971.

Scott, Ernest L., Jr. "Sarah Josepha Hale's New Hampshire Years, 1788–1828." *Historical New Hampshire* 49 (1994): 59–96.

FRANCES ELLEN WATKINS HARPER (1825–1911)

Hildegard Hoeller

BIOGRAPHY

Frances Ellen Watkins Harper, "the best known and best loved African-American poet prior to Paul Laurence Dunbar" (Foster 4), had a long and remarkable career and life. Born as a free black in Maryland on September 24, 1825, she published her first book of poems in 1845 and lived and wrote until 1911, when she died of heart failure on February 22. Harper was orphaned as a three-year-old and raised by her aunt and uncle, Reverend William Watkins; she attended her uncle's school for free blacks until she was 13 years old. The school's "[well-known] emphasis upon biblical studies, the classics, and elocution" seems as important an influence on Harper's formation as a thinker, writer, and speaker as her uncle's evangelical fervor and commitment to abolition, education, and the moral improvement of the world (Foster 7). Frances Foster furthermore speculates that "since William Watkins frequently contributed to papers such as the *Liberator,* it is also possible that he assisted her in her first efforts to publish" (7).

After her formal schooling ended at the age of 13, Harper "was hired to sew and care for children" (Foster 8). Since her employers owned a bookstore, Harper continued her education on her own and in her spare time. In 1845 she published her first volume of poetry, *Forest Leaves,* of which no copy is known to exist. In 1854 the next volume *Poems on Miscellaneous Subjects* appeared. The Watkins' had in the meantime relocated to Canada under the pressure of the Fugitive Slave Law and the difficulties of living as free blacks in a slave state. For unknown reasons, Harper moved to Ohio instead to "become the first female teacher at Union seminary, a school near Columbus, Ohio, which had been founded a few years earlier by the [African Methodist Episcopal] Church" (Foster 9). She left the school in 1852 to become a teacher in Little York, Pennsylvania, then an Underground Railroad worker, and later a public lecturer for the Maine Anti-Slavery Society. Her letters of those times indicate a hectic schedule of travels throughout the nation, and all her writings, like her life, speak of a ceaseless energy to devote her life to the cause of abolition as well as women's rights and temperance; a devoted Christian, Harper saw—and preached—Christianity as the religion to address and further these causes, which would remain the political focal points of her work throughout her life.

In 1860 Frances Ellen Watkins married Fenton Harper, a farmer, with whom she had a daughter, Mary. Four years later her husband died and left his family impoverished. Harper returned to her public career. As the bibliography of her work below indicates, Harper's literary production never ceased and made her a tremendously powerful public presence. She used a variety of genres: poetry, fiction, lectures and essays, and the public letter. Her art is best understood when one realizes that her oratory skills were legendary as well and that she reached both a white and black audience through her speaking and writing.

When Harper died in 1911, her writings had, in some ways, become outdated; her work is clearly that of a nineteenth-century writer, with its astute use of sentimental forms in both her poetry and fiction, its ballad form and regular meter, its fervent Christianity, its use of the public lecture format, and even its causes. With the advent of modernism and a new group of (predominantly male) black public intellectuals with new concerns, Harper was slowly forgotten. Famously, W. E. B. DuBois wrote in his eulogy to her: "She was not a great writer, but she wrote much worth reading. She was above all, sincere" (qtd. in Foster, Introduction to *Iola Leroy* xxxv). Harper suffered the fate of so many prominent nineteenth-century women writers whose art was judged by modernism's preference for irony and formal experimentation and thus found lacking. Yet, as discussed below, with shifts in critical interests and criteria Harper is slowly regaining her status as one of the foremost voices of nineteenth-century America.

MAJOR WORKS AND THEMES

The most crucial theme and guiding principle of Harper's life was the devotion of one's private life to public causes. This theme connects all of her writings, which invariably urge the reader to take responsibility for the world around them, to see, hear, reflect, help, and devote themselves both to alleviate the miseries of others and to embrace Christianity as a way to improve the world. The specific causes—abolition, women's rights, temperance—for which Harper fought may be seen as manifestations of this central belief; both the form *and* content of her art can best be understood in terms of the transformation, or conversion, of the reader from a private and self-interested person to a public, socially engaged—and truly Christian—person. For example, in her 1854 poem "The Slave Mother," Harper begins with a question to the reader: "Heard you that shriek?" (Foster 58). Her poems are like her speeches in that regard, appealing to the reader to end the blindness and deafness that allows oppression to continue and to connect their private worlds with public realities. In the same spirit, Harper's letters are private and public documents at the same time; many of them were sent to her friend and fellow-abolitionist William Still, for example, as apparently personal communications but always with magazine publication in mind. Harper's writings elicit sentimental sympathy as a form of political responsibility, a way to transform the private into the public and to respond and become politically active—hence her deeply felt tributes to Harriet Beecher Stowe's writing.

Harper's most well-known work is her novel *Iola Leroy* (1892), named after its mulatta heroine who lives the life of a white person, being educated in the North, until she is brought back to the South to learn that she is a slave; unbeknownst to her, her mother was her father's slave and her father neglected to free them lawfully. Set in the

Civil War, the novel depicts Iola as a nurse in a hospital who has devoted her life to the African American community. Emblematic of this choice is her refusal of a marriage to the white Dr. Gresham, who offers her a life as a white person in comfortable circumstances. Instead, Iola insists on her blackness—despite having been raised in the false belief that she is white. She searches for and reunites with her family, becomes a teacher, and finally marries a black man. Harper here employs the "tragic mulatta" plot for her own purposes: not so much to dwell on her character's victimization but on her *choices* to live a socially responsible life devoted to the cause of African Americans. Equally the plot serves to involve all audiences, including a white audience who gets implicated in the discovery that each one of them could be black. As well, Iola's brother marries the admirable figure of Ms. Delaney, a woman significantly darker than he is. Finally, the novel is remarkable not only for this redirection of the tragic mulatta plot but also for its use of dialect and regionalism in its respectful depiction of African American characters of all hues and classes.

Three further novels by Harper, *Minnie's Sacrifice* (1869), *Sowing and Reaping* (1876–77), and *Trial and Triumph* (1888–89), rediscovered by Frances Smith Foster, were republished in 1994. In *Minnie's Sacrifice* Harper portrays the conflicts of two characters, Minnie and Louis, who, like Iola, are mistakenly assumed to be white. *Sowing and Reaping* is a persuasive and programmatic temperance novel, which stresses—as does some of Harper's other temperance writing—the dangers women face from drunken husbands. *Trial and Triumph* is a *kuenstlerroman* of kinds, describing the education of the impetuous Annette who finds little support for her poetic ambitions but finally, after a romantic disappointment, becomes a teacher. The illegitimate child of a "fallen woman," Annette is a misfit in both her character and her ambitions. Harper uses Annette to reflect on the importance of heritage, or "ante-natal history" as she calls it.

Harper's short story "The Two Offers" (1859) is regarded to be the first short story written by an African American writer; it combines two important concerns in Harper's work: temperance and female autonomy. In this story, Harper compares the lives of two cousins: Laura Lagrange, who faces the choice of two marriage offers, and Janette Alston, an "old maid." Laura accepts the offer of a husband who turns out to be a drunk; she dies in misery. In Janette, Harper offers us a significant revision of the old maid figure; her old maid is passionate, artistic, and ultimately successful as a public speaker and writer.

Harper's poetry relies heavily on the ballad form and regular rhyme and meter. It skillfully gives voice to the plight of slaves in moving poems such as "The Slave Mother" or "The Tennessee Hero." Remarkable are also the Aunt Chloe poems, which are revolutionary in their celebration of an older African American woman's vision and speech. Some of Harper's poetry—like her fiction—revises biblical stories, such as the long poem *Moses: A Story of the Nile* (1869). Her temperance poetry provides vivid depictions of alcoholism; Harper's thoughts on heredity make her depictions of alcoholism as a form of addiction (or metaphorical slavery) appear quite contemporary.

Harper's essays and speeches make strongly visible her feminist consciousness as well. They highlight her courage as a political thinker as well as her scope—she saw slavery in the system of slavery itself, and also in the racism of Reconstruction America, in the dependence on alcohol, and in the patriarchal oppression and abuse of women. Her writing was devoted to the abolition of all of those forms of slavery. Her final poems, perhaps in response to Harper's own aging, are predominantly about Christian salvation and the hope for uplift.

CRITICAL RECEPTION

Harper criticism has come a long way since W. E. B. Dubois's emblematic dismissal of her art as "sincere." It has occurred in the stages rather typical of nineteenth-century American women writers: recovery and republication, attempts at canonization, and gradually a detailed criticism exploring more and more of Harper's considerable oeuvre. As the bibliography shows, Frances Smith Foster is one of the foremost critics responsible for much of the rediscovery, republication, and reconsideration of Harper's work. Critics initially concentrated their critical attention on *Iola Leroy,* predominantly debating the merits of Harper's use of the mulatta figure; then, Harper was considered mostly in a feminist and black feminist context. But since then critical work on Harper has greatly expanded; as the bibliography indicates, studies have moved from offering introductions and discussing the literary merit of Harper's work to discussion of issues of race and gender, to more specific discussions of individual short stories, relation to other writers, both black and white, and even composition studies. Melba Joyce Boyd has published the only book-length study of Harper so far, written as a response by a contemporary poet to Harper as an "artist-activist" (11). While the ongoing reconsideration of sentimental writing in the nineteenth-century American canon has done much to enhance our understanding of Harper's use of that powerful tradition, critics have also pointed to the realism and regionalism in her writing. Hence interesting studies linking Harper to Howells or Chesnutt have emerged. Careful historicization and close readings of Harper's work characterize the most recent phase of Harper criticism and hopefully define its future; particularly insightful in this regard are essays by Carolyn Sorisio and Elizabeth Young.

These studies show how much Harper's work offers when read closely and historically. Finally, Harper should be considered much more in connection to other American Renaissance writers, and, indeed, as this volume implies, should be habitually considered one of the American Renaissance writers. Her concerns and the urgencies of her writing connect her clearly to those of Emerson, Thoreau, Stowe, Jacobs, Child, Douglass, and others, and it is up to critics to elucidate these connections further.

WORKS CITED

Boyd, Melba Joyce. *Discarded Legacy: Politics in the Life of Frances E.W. Harper 1825–1911.* Detroit: Wayne State UP, 1994.

Foster, Frances Smith. "Gender, Genre, and Vulgar Secularism: The Case of Frances Ellen Watkins Harper and the AME Press." *Recovered Writers/Recovered Texts.* Ed. Dolan Hubbard. Knoxville: U of Tennessee P, 1997. 46–59.

BIBLIOGRAPHY

Works by Frances Ellen Watkins Harper

Forest Leaves. Baltimore, ca. 1845. No copy extant.

Poems on Miscellaneous Subjects. Boston: J.B. Yerrington & Son, 1854. Reprinted Kraus 1971. Enlarged edition Philadelphia, PA, 1855. 2nd enlarged edition Philadelphia: Merrihew & Thompson 1857. Reprinted with new introduction by Maxwell Whiteman, Historic Publications 1969. 20th Edition Philadelphia: Merrihew & Son, 1871.

Eventide (poem and tales). Under pseudonym Effie Afton. Boston: Ferridege & Co., 1854.

"The Two Offers." *Anglo-African Magazine* 1 (1859): 288–91, 339–45.

Moses: A Story of the Nile. Philadelphia: Merrihew & Son, Printers, 1869.

Sketches of Southern Life (poems). Philadelphia: George S. Ferguson, 1872.

Light Beyond the Darkness. Chicago: Donohue & Henneberry, 1890?

Iola Leroy or Shadows Uplifted (novel). Philadelphia: Garrigues Brothers, 1892. 2nd edition, introduced by William Still, James H. Earle, 1893. Reprinted with introduction by Hazel Carby, Boston: Beacon P, 1987. Reprinted with introduction by Frances Smith Foster, New York: Oxford UP, 1988.

Atlanta Offering: Poems. George S. Ferguson, 1895. Reprinted Mnemosyne, 1969.

Poems. George S. Ferguson, 1895. 2nd enlarged edition, Philadelphia 1900. Reprint Books for Libraries, 1970.

The Poems of Frances E. W. Harper. Books for Libraries, 1970.

Poems. AMS P, 1975.

Complete Poems of Frances E. W. Harper. Ed. Maryemma Graham. New York: Oxford UP, 1988.

A Brighter Day Coming: A Frances Ellen Watkins Harper Reader. (Contains Foster's Speeches, Essays, short fiction, and letters as well as poetry.) Ed. and introd. Frances Smith Foster. New York: Feminist P at the City U of New York, 1990.

Minnie's Sacrifice; Sowing and Reaping; Trial and Triumph; Three Rediscovered Novels. Ed. and introd. Frances Smith Foster. Boston: Beacon P, 1994.

Studies of Frances Ellen Watkins Harper

Ammons, Elizabeth. "Frances Ellen Watkins Harper." *Legacy* 2 (1985): 61–66.

Bennett, Michael. "Frances Ellen Watkins Harper Sings the Body Electric." *Recovering the Black Female Body: Self-Representations by African-American Women.* Ed. Michael Bennett and Carla Peterson. New Brunswick, NJ: Rutgers UP, 2000. 19–40.

Berlant, Lauren. "The Queen of America Goes to Washington City: Harriet Jacobs, Frances Harper, Anita Hill." *American Literature* 65.3 (September 1993): 549–74.

Birnbaum, Michele. "Racial Hysteria: Female Pathology and Race Politics in Frances Harper's *Iola Leroy* and W. D. Howells's *An Imperative Duty.*" *African-American Review* 33.1 (Spring 1999): 7–23.

Bizzell, Patrizia. " 'Stolen Literacies' in *Iola Leroy.*" *Popular Literacy: Studies in Cultural Practices and Poetics.* Pittsburgh, PA: U of Pittsburgh P, 2001. 143–150.

Bost, Suzanne. "Fluidity Without Post-Modernism: Michelle Cliff and the 'Tragic Mulatta' Tradition." *African American Review* 32.4 (Winter 1998): 673–89.

Boyd, Melba Joyce. *Discarded Legacy: Politics in the Life of Frances E. W. Harper 1825–1911.* Detroit: Wayne State UP, 1994.

Campbell, Jennifer. " 'The Great Something Else': Women's Search for Meaningful Work in Sarah Orne Jewett's *A Country Doctor* and Frances E. W. Harper's *Trial and Triumph.*" *Colby Quarterly* 34.2 (June 1998): 83–98.

Carby, Hazel V. *Reconstructing Womanhood: The Emergence of the Afro-American Woman Novelist.* New York: Oxford UP, 1987.

Christman, James. "Raising Voices, Lifting Shadows: Competing Voice-Paradigms in Frances E. W. Harper's *Iola Leroy.*" *African-American Review* 34.1 (Spring 2000): 5–18.

Engle, Anna. "Depictions of the Irish in Frank Webb's *The Gairies and Their Friends* and Frances E. W. Harper's *Trial and Triumph.*" *Melus* 26.1 (Spring 2001): 151–71.

Ernest, John. "From Mysteries to Histories: Cultural Pedagogy in Frances E. Harper's *Iola Leroy.*" *American Literature* 64.3 (September 1992): 497–518.

Fabi, M. Guilia. "Reconstructing Literary Genealogies: Frances E. W. Harper's and William Dean Howells's Race Novels." *Soft Canons: American Women Writers and Masculine Tradition.* Ed. Karen Kilcup. Iowa City, IA: U of Iowa P, 1999. 48–66.

Foreman, P. Gabrielle. " 'Reading Aright': White Slavery, Black Referents, and the Strategy of Histotextuality in *Iola Leroy.*" *Yale Journal of Criticism* 10.2 (Fall 1997): 327–54.

Foster, Frances Smith. "Gender, Genre, and Vulgar Secularism: The Case of Frances Ellen Watkins Harper and the AME Press." *Recovered Writers/Recovered Texts*. Ed. Dolan Hubbard. Knoxville: U of Tennessee P, 1997. 46–59.

Gerzina, Gretchen Holbrook. "Frances E. W. Harper (1825–1911)." *Nineteenth-Century American Women Writers: A Bio-Bibliographical Critical Sourcebook*. Ed. Denise D. Knight. Westport CT: Greenwood, 1997. 213–19.

Griffin, Farah Jasmine. "Frances Ellen Watkins Harper in the Reconstruction South." *Sage* Supp. (1988): 45–47.

Knittel, Janna. " 'Songs for the People': Politics and Poetics in the Career of Frances Harper." *MAWA Review* 12.1 (1999): 30–43.

Lauter, Paul. "Is Frances Ellen Watkins Harper Good Enough to Teach?" *Legacy* 5.1 (Spring 1988): 27–32.

Logan, Shirley Wilson. " 'What's Rhetoric Got to Do With It?': Frances E. W. Harper in the Writing Class." *Composition Forum: A Journal of the Association of Teachers of Advanced Composition* 7.2 (Fall 1996): 95–110.

Novak, Terry. "Frances Ellen Watkins Harper (1825–1911)." *African American Authors, 1745–1945: A Bio-Bibliographical Critical Sourcebook*. Westport, CT: Greenwood, 2000. 213–9.

Peterson, Carla L. " 'Further Lifting of the Veil': Gender, Class, and Labor in Frances E. W. Harper's *Iola Leroy*." *Listening to Silences: New Essays in Feminist Criticism*. Ed. Elaine Hedges and Shelley Fisher Fishkin. New York: Oxford UP, 1994. 97–112.

Pollard, Leslie J. "Frances Harper and the Old People: Two recently Discovered Poems." *Griot* 4.1–2 (Winter–Summer 1985): 52–56.

Riggins, Linda N. "The Works of Frances E. W. Harper: An 18th Century Writer." *Black World* 22.2 (1972): 30–36.

Rosenthal, Debra J. "Deracialized Discourse: Temperance and Racial Ambiguity in Harper's 'The Two Offers' and *Sowing and Reaping*." *The Serpent in the Cup: Temperance in American Literature*. Ed. David Reynolds and Debra Rosenthal. Amherst, MA: U of Mass. P, 1997. 153–64.

Scheick, William J. "Strategic Ellipses in Harper's 'The Two Offers'." *Southern Literary Journal* 23.1 (Spring 1991): 14–18.

Sorisio, Carolyn. "The Spectacle of the Body: Torture in the Antislavery Writing of Lydia Maria Child and Frances E. W. Harper." *Modern Language Studies* 30.1 (Spring 2000): 45–66.

Still, William. *The Underground Railroad*. Philadelphia: Porters and Coates, 1872.

Toohey, Michelle Campbell. " 'A Deeper Purpose' in the Serialized Novels of Frances Ellen Watkins Harper." *"The Only Efficient Instrument": American Women Writers and the Periodical 1837–1916*. Ed. Aleta Feinsod Cane and Susan Alves. Iowa City: U of Iowa P, 2001. 202–15.

Warren, Joyce W. "Fracturing Gender: Woman's Economic Independence." *Nineteenth-Century American Women Writers: A Critical Reader*. Ed. Karen Kilcup. Malden, MA: Blackwell, 1998. 146–63.

Wilson, Kimberly A. C. "The Function of the 'Fair' Mulatto: Complexion, Audience, and Mediation in Frances Harper's *Iola Leroy*." *Cimarron Review* 106 (January 1994): 104–13.

Young, Elizabeth. "Warring Fictions: *Iola Leroy* and the Color of Gender. *American Literature* 64.2 (June 1992): 273–97.

Zackodnik, Teresa. "Little Romances and Mulatta Heroines: Passing for a 'True' Woman in Frances Harper's *Iola Leroy* and Pauline Hopkins's *Contending Forces*." *Nineteenth Century Feminisms* 2 (Spring-Summer 2000): 103–24.

GEORGE WASHINGTON HARRIS (1814–1869)

Samuel I. Bellman

BIOGRAPHY

A very controversial nineteenth-century writer, George Washington Harris was a man of many parts and intense political convictions. He was born on March 20, 1814, in Allegheny City, Pennsylvania, to George Washington Harris and Margaret Glover Bell Harris. Of his early life only basic facts are known. At age five, Harris was taken by his half brother, Samuel Bell (the son of Harris's mother and her first husband), to live with him and his wife in the village of Knoxville, Tennessee. Here Bell, an accomplished metalworker, set up his machine shop. Because of the boy's access to the shop and his response to the work done there, the next 15 years were a formative period for Harris. Though his formal education was slight by today's standards—at most, a year and a half of reading, writing, and arithmetic—he would become a skilled technician, versatile in numerous areas of mechanical arts and crafts.

At age 12 he began an apprenticeship under his half brother and built a functional model of a steamboat, winning praise from the local citizenry. At 15 he was a jockey in quarter horse races. After his seven-year apprenticeship, he became captain of a commercial steamboat, the *Knoxville,* on the Tennessee River. (He would again serve as a steamboat captain in 1854 on the *Alida.*) In 1835 he married Mary Nance. Three years later, as steamboat captain, he participated in the forced relocation of the Cherokee Indians from their ancient lands, across the Mississippi to the western territory. In 1839, like a gentleman farmer, he purchased a sizable tract of farm land near the Great Smoky Mountains. The elegant lifestyle that he and his family enjoyed on their "Tennessee Land" lasted only about four years, owing to Harris's failure as a farmer and inability to keep up his loan payments. Having returned to Knoxville with his family, Harris again became the masterly artisan (metalworking and making jewelry) in his own shop.

Later Harris, staunch Presbyterian and secessionist, extended his range of activities. New endeavors included superintendent of a glass works, overseer of copper mines surveyors, Knoxville postmaster, political activist, railroad conductor and freight agent, elder in Knoxville's First Presbyterian Church, sawmill operator, and Knoxville alderman. From the 1843 until his death in 1869 Harris wrote a sizable number of imaginative articles and stories: sporting epistles, backwoods yarns, sketches and satires, political and otherwise. His earliest pieces appeared in the New York sporting periodical, *Spirit of the Times,* edited by William T. Porter. Harris wrote under the pseudonym of "Mr. Free," then adopted the pen name "Sugartail" for a while. Southern papers (mostly in Tennessee) became the outlets for his salty, often antisocial material: the Nashville *Union & American,* the Chattanooga *Daily American Union,* and others. Among his political satires were three vitriolic spoofs of Abraham Lincoln, printed in the Nashville *Union & American* in 1861, shortly before the start of the Civil War.

Harris did not fight in the Civil War; his two sons fought with the Confederates. When the War ended, Harris, having left Nashville several years before, made his home in Chattanooga, Tennessee. Here he worked for the Wills Valley Railroad and resumed writing polemical attacks on the North, lambasting in the Nashville *Union & American* northerners, Yankees, and Negroes. In 1867 his one and only book published during his lifetime appeared, *Sut Lovingood. Yarns Spun by a "Nat'ral Born Durn'd Fool."* During that year his wife Mary Nance died. In 1869 he married a woman named Jane Pride. Two months later that year, returning from Lynchburg, Virginia, where he had gone on business for the railroad and to seek publication for the manuscript of another book, *High Times and Hard Times,* Harris died of a sudden mysterious illness.

MAJOR WORKS AND THEMES

There is a curious aspect of Harris's life and work. While his country background and political sentiments might help explain what he is best known for, his journalistic career seems at odds with his religious upbringing and upright way of life. Harris's scenes of ordinary life in the Tennessee backwoods are filled with feuding, fighting, troublemaking, frolicking, and lovemaking. The focus of most of Harris's (presumably) comic tales is a wild backwoods "natural"—Sut Lovingood—apparently based on a local countryman Harris knew, a corn farmer named Sut Miller. Lovingood relates in his rude, illiterate country dialect a series of personal anecdotes to a formal, well-spoken gentleman he addresses as "George" (Harris, presumably).

"George" might represent Harris's prim and proper façade, contrasting the vulgar, uninhibited, mayhem-causing Sut, symbolizing Harris's shadowy secret self that would discredit him if he went public. Sut brags about his wild exploits, vents his personal animosities, and reiterates his self-loathing. There might have been an additional reason for Sut's regarding himself as an unsightly "natral-born durn'd fool," and worse. Depicting such a ridiculous figure as one who considers himself soulless and worthless, who is at odds with respectable society, and (in the manner of a fool) who doesn't know any better, would be another means for concealing Harris's true feelings from the public. But in reality, as one Harris scholar points out, people in Knoxville identified Harris with Sut and his friends called him Sut. Harris apparently "delighted in being associated with his literary creation" (Bain 141).

Harris's 1867 collection, *Sut Lovingood. Yarns Spun by a "Nat'ral Born Durn'd Fool,"* contained 24 of his pieces dealing with Sut Lovingood, only a sampling of the numerous stories, sketches, satires, and other writings published to date. An expanded collection of his writings, *High Times and Hard Times,* for which he had unsuccessfully sought publication just before his sudden death in 1869, appeared in 1967, edited with introductory essays by M. Thomas Inge. Aside from Harris's four sporting epistles, which introduced him to the newspaper public, and a scattering of other pieces not dealing with

Sut Lovingood, the collection is largely devoted to Sut and includes three derogatory satires (dated 1861) about the newly elected president. Abraham Lincoln, whose politics (Republican, Unionist) was anathema to the reactionary Sut, was making his railroad journey to Washington, D.C., to assume his duties. Southern states were seceding, feelings against Lincoln were running high, the Civil War was in the offing. In these lampoons, the endangered president was being managed by his confidential friend and advisor, Sut Lovingood.

One of Harris's best-known pieces is an early sketch, "The Knob Dance—A Tennessee Frolic" (1845). Narrated by "Sugartail," a pen name of Harris's, it describes a wild fun extravaganza of fiddling and dancing, fighting, laughing, and drinking in Tennessee's Knox County. Another tale of the wild goings-on at a backwoods fiddle frolic, "Bart Davis's Dance" (n.d.), describes the hairpulling and routing of a whiskey-loving hard-shell preacher who broke up the festivities. In "Parson John Bullen's Lizards" (1867) Sut played a nasty trick with the reptiles on a parson who divulged a girl's guilty secret he had promised to keep, thereby subjecting her—after she had cooked him a meal—to a beating by her mother. In a sadistic tale, "Mrs. Yardley's Quilting" (1867), the amoral Sut disrupted a quilting party by destroying all the ladies' quilts, causing Mrs. Yardley's death when she realized that her prize quilt was lost too.

Among other Harris writings are the following. "Sut Lovingood Reports What Bob Dawson Said, After Marrying A Substitute" (1867) recounts the ancient, hardy folktale about what the naïve groom discovered (to his distress) on his wedding night. Nathaniel Hawthorne used it in his story "Mrs. Bullfrog" (1837), omitting the shocking punch line. Here, the startled groom watched in horror as his disrobing bride removed one artificial body part after another, until the ultimate remaining possibility was left, and before she could finish the job he fled in fear, never to return. Three of Harris's stories, "Sut Lovingood's Daddy, 'Acting Horse' " (1854), " 'Well! Dad's Dead' " (1868), and "Dad's Dog-School" (n.d.), reveal Sut's father degraded beyond restoration. The first and last reduce Dad to animal status, at his behest—he assumes the character of a horse in the first story, and a yearling calf in the second, in order to do an animal's job around his farm. In the middle story Sut's Dad *is* dead, and as a corpse he is reduced to the level of debris that must be summarily shoved below ground.

Sut as "nat'ral born durn'd fool"—so important a claim in many of Harris's writings—is a major theme. But with all his pranks, cruelties, crudities, acts of revenge, and barbarisms, Sut doesn't *act* the fool, he *talks* the fool. When he is made into a political advocate or a man of affairs, he ceases to be Sut, and Harris appears not to take his character seriously. Sut as fool whose comic mask permits criticism of society's foibles seems untenable, given his brutish personal and family life. However, Sut's assuming the mantle of fool implies a ploy by Harris, a "mouthpiece," given Harris's beliefs and commitments. Sut in his utterances and deeds is filled with hate and contempt for individuals and groups, backward looking and fearful of new discoveries and ideas. His exuberant comic freedom, praised by certain writers and literature professors, suggests liberty becoming license, resulting from the "loser" mentality of a pro-slavery secessionist doing little to alleviate his large family's poverty, besides abetting his Dad's "acting plowhorse" scheme.

This "profile" of Sut evokes a secondary thematic pattern. Paraphrasing Puck in Shakespeare's *A Midsummer Night's Dream,* "What fools, hateful and contemptible, these mortals be!" Remarks scattered throughout Harris's writings indicate that not only are Sut and his Daddy natural fools, but this "fool" condition is widespread. Among the targets of Sut's hatred and contempt are innkeepers, Yankees, circuit riding preachers, Sut himself, Sut's Daddy, Negroes, New York Dandies, Jews, Abraham Lincoln, Joseph Smith, Horace Greeley, strong-minded women and the woman suffrage movement, progressive thinking, and so on.

CRITICAL RECEPTION

Harris's writings, given his secessionist, pro-slavery stand, the Confederacy's defeat, and his intense prejudices and hatreds, offer a tentative litmus test of readers' sympathies for "human rights." During his lifetime Harris's writings enjoyed popular, if not critical, success. Mark Twain, reviewing *Sut Lovingood Yarns* (1867), praised its handling of dialects but expressed misgivings about its appeal to Easterners. Some of Harris's pieces were reprinted in *Mark Twain's Library of Humor* (1888) and in a few other contemporaneous anthologies. Critical interest in Harris began to develop during the 1930s as scholars, such as Franklin J. Meine, Bernard DeVoto, and Walter Blair, studied regional writers of what was then called the Southwest. For them, and F. O. Matthiessen (*American Renaissance* 1941), Harris's illiterate rustic speech was praised for its local color, regional humor, and storytelling power. The sharpest critic to reject *Yarns* was Edmund Wilson, who in his 1962 *Patriotic Gore* wrote that he was far more repelled by that book than by any other American literary book of genuine literary quality. Since the mid-1900s Harris's work has elicited increased scholarly research and criticism.

WORK CITED

Bain, Robert. "George Washington Harris." In *Dictionary of Literary Biography 3,* ed. Joel Myerson. Detroit, MI: Gale Research Company/A Bruccoli Clark Book, 1979. 138–43.

BIBLIOGRAPHY

Works by George Washington Harris

Sut Lovingood: Yarns Spun by a "Nat'ral Born Durn'd Fool." New York: Dick & Fitzgerald, 1867.
The Lovingood Papers. 4 volumes. Ed. Ben Harris McClary. Knoxville: University of Tennessee Press, 1962–1965.
High Times and Hard Times. Ed. M. Thomas Inge. Nashville: Vanderbilt University Press, 1967.

Studies of George Washington Harris

Bain, Robert. "George Washington Harris." In *Dictionary of Literary Biography 3,* ed. Joel Myerson. Detroit, MI: Gale Research Company/A Bruccoli Clark Book, 1979. 138–43.
Rickels, Milton. *George Washington Harris.* New York: Twayne Publishers, Inc., 1965.
———. "George Washington Harris." In *Dictionary of Literary Biography 11, Part 1,* ed. Stanley Trachtenberg. Detroit, MI: Gale Research Company/A Bruccoli Clark Book, 1979. 180–89.

NATHANIEL HAWTHORNE (1804–1864)

Monika Elbert

BIOGRAPHY

Nathaniel Hawthorne was born in Salem on July 4, 1804, to Nathaniel and Elizabeth Manning Hathorne, the only son and the second of three children. After his graduation from Bowdoin College, Hawthorne added the "w" to his name—conceivably as an attempt to break with his puritanical past, as represented in his forebear, Judge John Hathorne, who presided over the Salem Witch Trials. When Nathaniel was only three, his father, a sea captain, died of yellow fever in Surinam. Hawthorne's family was dependent on the Manning relatives after his father's death and moved into the parental home of Elizabeth, where Hawthorne lived mainly among women: grandmother Manning, aunts, his mother, and his sisters. Hawthorne's early education in Salem was disrupted in 1813 when he sustained a foot injury while playing ball, and he was forced to receive home schooling for almost two and a half years. During this time, Hawthorne spent much of his time isolated—and reading. In 1818 the Hawthornes moved to family property in Raymond, Maine, where Hawthorne passed an idyllic time romping in nature and living in the country with his immediate family—his mother and his two sisters. From 1819 to 1821, Hawthorne went to school in Salem and resided with his Manning relatives; his mother and sisters stayed on in Raymond during these two years. There may have been a harsh influence from an uncle on his mother's side, Uncle Robert Manning, who tried to instill a business sense into the young Hawthorne, but as a letter (March 13, 1821) to his mother testifies, Hawthorne had no intention of doing anything practical. The position of lawyer or doctor did not appeal to him, because there were too many of the former, and the latter profession preyed upon the diseased to make a living. He also had reservations about becoming a writer, since writers were, by tradition, horribly underpaid.

From 1821 to 1825 Hawthorne attended Bowdoin College in Brunswick, Maine, where his classmates included the young Henry W. Longfellow and Franklin Pierce, who would become the fourteenth president and remain lifelong friends with Hawthorne (indeed, Hawthorne wrote a campaign biography for Pierce in 1852 and died on an excursion he undertook with Pierce in 1864). Though Hawthorne did not have an illustrious college career, graduating eighteenth in a class of 35, his interest in the literary profession was developed, and he began writing his first novel, *Fanshawe,* which was published in 1828. Unhappy with his first attempt at literary fame, Hawthorne was able to obtain most of the copies before they were sold (an action that later prompted him to write "The Devil in Manuscript"). Ironically, in 1831, the unsold copies of *Fanshawe* were lost in a fire at a Boston bookstore. Hawthorne's first success as a writer can be seen in his earliest works for the *Salem Gazette,* in 1830, among them "The Hollow of the Three Hills" and "An Old Woman's Tale."

Though the famed publisher Samuel Goodrich rejected Hawthorne's idea for "The Story Teller" in 1834, many of the sketches and stories, such as the famous "Young Goodman Brown," appeared in journals and annuals, including Goodrich's annual *The Token,* from 1834 to 1835. In 1836, Hawthorne served as editor of the *American Magazine of Useful and Entertaining Knowledge,* and this foray into the publishing world forced him to move to Boston from January to June, when the publishing house met with bankruptcy. In 1836, with his sister Elizabeth, he edited *Peter Parley's Universal History, on the Basis of Geography.* In 1837, *Twice-told Tales,* his first collection of stories was published, for which he received positive reviews. During this same year, he met his wife-to-be, Sophia Peabody, while visiting the Peabodys in Salem. The elder sister, Elizabeth Peabody, would try to mentor Hawthorne and encourage his literary efforts for the rest of his life. In 1838 Hawthorne was a frequent contributor to *The Democratic Review* and became good friends with the editor, John L. O'Sullivan.

In 1839, the Peabodys became very important in his life: Elizabeth helped him obtain a post at the Custom House in Boston, and Sophia became his fiancée. In 1840 and 1841, Hawthorne published three collections of children's stories, the most famous one being *The Whole History of Grandfather's Chair.* In 1841 he left his post at the Boston Custom House and spent eight months at the utopian community, Brook Farm, in West Roxbury, Massachusetts, an experience that would lead to his penning *The Blithedale Romance.* Disillusioned, he left Brook Farm and told Sophia that his plans to live in the utopia were misguided. Married on July 9, 1842, they settled into the Old Manse, in Concord, Massachusetts.

In March 1844, Hawthorne celebrated the birth of his first child, Una. As demonstrated in Hawthorne's notebooks, Una served as the model for Pearl in *The Scarlet Letter* (1850). Leaving the Manse in 1845, Hawthorne took his family to live briefly with his mother and sisters in Salem, where he soon received appointment by President Polk to the post of Surveyor of the Custom House. The year 1846 marked two important events: the birth of his son, Julian, and the publication of *Mosses from an Old Manse,* which included 21 previously uncollected stories and sketches, in addition to the introductory sketch, "The Old Manse." In 1849 Hawthorne suffered two traumatic events: he was ousted from his post at the Custom House by the incoming political party, the Whigs, and his mother died, an experience that Hawthorne called the darkest hour of his life. The magnitude of these events can be discerned in *The Scarlet Letter,* which he began writing in 1849. In "The Custom-House" introduction, he vents his scorn upon the narrowness of Salemites and proclaims that he and his children will free themselves from Salem once and for all. The narrative proper, which makes Hester Prynne's motherhood larger than life, is a tribute to his now-deceased mother, who, like Hester, had to make ends meet as a widow with children.

Shortly after *The Scarlet Letter* appeared in March 1850, the Hawthornes moved to Lenox, Massachusetts. Here Hawthorne met James Russell Lowell, Oliver Wendell

Holmes, the actress Fanny Kemble, and, most significantly, Herman Melville, who would later write a glowing review about Hawthorne's literary genius in "Hawthorne and His Mosses" (published 17 and 24 August 1850 in *Literary World*). This was a prolific period for Hawthorne: in 1851, he published *The House of the Seven Gables* and *A Wonder-Book for Girls and Boys*. He added a preface to a new edition of *Twice-told Tales,* which was reissued in March 1851. His third and last child, Rose, was born in May 1851; and in December, Hawthorne's *The Snow-Image, and Other Twice-told Tales* was released, a collection that included 17 previously uncollected stories. In 1852, Hawthorne published *The Blithedale Romance* and returned to live in Concord. The following year he also published a children's book, *Tanglewood Tales,* one of the last major (new) publications of the decade, though the second edition of *Mosses from an Old Manse* appeared in 1854.

As a reward for his campaign biography of Franklin Pierce, who was elected president in 1852, Hawthorne was appointed American Consul to Liverpool, serving from 1853 to 1857. While in England, he kept a detailed journal of his experiences and travels, which would later be published as *The English Notebooks.* In 1858, Hawthorne traveled to Paris and Marseilles in January, and then made his way to Rome, where he and his family stayed from January until May and where he began work on *The Ancestral Footstep,* a Gothic novel he would never finish. During the summer, the Hawthornes spent time in Florence, returning to Rome in the fall. Hawthorne kept notebooks of observations of people and places during this time period, later published as *The French and Italian Notebooks.* In 1858, he also visited Villa Borghese and observed the Fauns; and he also saw the Faun of Praxiteles at the Capitol. These sculptures served as an inspiration for the faunlike Donatello in *The Marble Faun,* a novel he embarked upon during this period. Unfortunately, Hawthorne's daughter, Una, contracted malaria in October 1858 and almost died. The Hawthornes returned to England in June 1859. The literary culmination of this period of travel in the 1850s was the last novel published in Hawthorne's lifetime, appearing first in England in 1860 as *Transformation* and then shortly after in the United States as *The Marble Faun.*

In June 1860, the Hawthornes returned to Massachusetts. Hawthorne was depressed by the outbreak of the Civil War and would not live long enough to see its conclusion. The years are marked by abortive attempts at Gothic romances. Hawthorne's final literary work was a collection of essays, most of them previously published in *The Atlantic Monthly* (between 1860 and 1863), recalling his impressions of England, entitled *Our Old Home* (1863).

On the morning of May 19, 1864, Hawthorne died in Plymouth, New Hampshire, while traveling for his health with Franklin Pierce. He was buried in Concord on May 23 at Sleepy Hollow Cemetery, with the intellectual circle of Concord and Boston in attendance. A small, simple headstone, with only his last name, marks Hawthorne's final resting place, but like Hester in *The Scarlet Letter,* his dust was not to mingle with his partner's. Sophia died in London in 1871 and lies buried in the cemetery at Kensal Green.

MAJOR WORKS AND THEMES

Hawthorne's work mostly focused on three themes: alienation, especially of the artist figure, within a community marked by hypocrisy and bourgeois values; the poisonous effects of secret sin and guilt on an individual's psyche and the burden of the past weighing upon the present; and unfortunate love triangles, in which all three characters often suffer, even if one seems ultimately redeemed by suffering. Hawthorne often drew his materials from his notebooks, which he regularly penned. His observation of the quotidian details in everyday life made him a realistic Romancer.

In *Fanshawe* (1828), Hawthorne uses a Gothic backdrop and creates a semi-autobiographical setting, Harley College, a fictionalized version of Bowdoin College, to explore the feelings of two students (Fanshawe and Walcott) vying for the affection of Ellen Langton, whom they try to save after she has been kidnapped. The solitary Fanshawe, though he saves Ellen, foregoes his love for her to devote himself to a life of study. Fanshawe dies and Walcott gets the girl. In many ways, Fanshawe foreshadows the long line of intellectuals and scientists in the Hawthorne canon who will live in their intellect rather than feel with their hearts; Hawthorne would later refer to this preponderance of intellect over heart as the "Unpardonable Sin."

In Hawthorne's first major phase of story-writing, from 1830 to 1837, the period of the *Twice-told Tales,* Hawthorne has a number of male initiates (like Fanshawe) who try to become masters of themselves. These protagonists often confront a world bereft of fathers, with avuncular figures amounting to sorry surrogates, as was the case in Hawthorne's own life. On a psychological level, the protagonists rebel against oppressive authority figures. Hawthorne often locates young men in historical settings, usually in America's colonial past, so that they are seen rebelling against patriarchs of the government and the church. In "My Kinsman, Major Molineux," for example, Robin Molineux is forced to leave his paternal country home and make a life in the city with the help of his father's cousin. Robin ultimately has to give up his kinsman, whom the American colonists tar and feather in the last scene, and also has to deny the validity of his father's simple country faith. He must look to himself for the future, and the ensuing manic sense of liberation shows the pitfalls of new-found independence for Robin as a character and as a representative of Young America. In early stories like this one, Hawthorne shows not only the necessity of breaking away from the old but also the dangers and follies of independence and, in some ways, he also shows some allegiance to America's parent country, England. He would forever remain ambivalent in his attitude toward progress and change and in his relationship with the past and with tradition. This problematic attitude toward historical change would later be explored fully in *The House of the Seven Gables* (1851), where both the past (in the shape of dead men's houses) and the present (in terms of technological advances, like the railroad) are attacked.

"Roger Malvin's Burial" is another tale of initiation that depicts a young Reuben Bourne, who is also struggling to achieve manhood without a male mentor. Hawthorne's ambiguity is best expressed in Reuben's moral decision to abandon his wounded father-in-law-to-be in order to return to civilization and marry Malvin's daughter, Dorcas. Once he is home, Reuben's inner conflict with a mythologized image of heroic/frontier manhood causes him to lie to Dorcas and tell her that he had been with her father when he died. Thus, he breaks his promise with the father to return and give him a proper burial. In keeping with Hawthorne's penchant for exploring the theme of the "sins of the fathers," the story ends quite tragically: Reuben and Dorcas's son, Cyrus, while out hunting, is shot by Reuben, who mistakes him for a deer. In this fashion, Reuben's sin and guilt seem to be expiated, and Cyrus dies becoming a sacrifice at the exact spot where Roger Malvin had died.

In the allegorical "Young Goodman Brown" (1835) Hawthorne once again resorts to the colonial past and shows his distrust of Puritan religious authority. Seeming to expose the hypocrisy of the Puritan community, Hawthorne actually makes Goodman Brown the hypocrite for he continues to attend Sunday meeting and to have intimate relations with his wife, even as he has cursed the treachery of the Church fathers and doubted his allegorized wife's faith. Moreover, a theme that would interest Hawthorne throughout his career is apparent in this story—the "Unpardonable Sin," or hubris, in which a man holds himself so superior to the community that his individualism isolates him and finally damns him.

In another significant allegorical story, "The Minister's Black Veil" (1835), Hawthorne shows the corrosive effect of secret sin on the Reverend Hooper. Based upon a real minister who hung a handkerchief over his face so that his congregation could no longer see it, the story is more concerned with the consequences of the unknown sin on the conjecturing community than on the nature of the sin itself. The predilection of Hawthorne to analyze the interpretations and the reactions of this audience and a community would be further developed in *The Scarlet Letter.*

In the 1830s Hawthorne also experimented with the "sketch," which was popular in journals, especially attracting women readers, even though later he would write acerbically about the "damned mob of scribbling women," whom he most likely saw as competition in the literary marketplace, which catered to a majority of women readers. Hawthorne writes three distinct kinds of sketches: the historical sketch, which profiles an important personage in tableauesque form (e.g., "Mrs. Hutchinson" and "Sir William Pepperell"), the travel sketch, which is based upon his own travels (e.g., "My Visit to Niagara," and "Sketches from Memory"), and the sketch drawn from everyday life.

In his second phase of story-telling, the Old Manse period of the early 1840s, Hawthorne is less interested in colonial history and more intent upon writing allegorical parodies about contemporary reform movements or about apocalyptic sects (such as the Millerites) in such stories as "The Celestial Railroad," "Earth's Holocaust," "The Procession of Life," "The Hall of Fantasy," and "The New Adam and Eve." He would also critique the Transcendentalist movement in "The Artist of the Beautiful" and misguided or overreaching scientists in two of his most memorable and frequently anthologized stories, "The Birth-mark" (1843) and "Rappaccini's Daughter" (1844). These stories stem from Hawthorne's earlier preoccupation with scientist figures who suffer from the sin of hubris in "Dr. Heidegger's Experiment" (1837). For Hawthorne, the wisdom of the heart, or of intuition, affords greater enlightenment than the facts of science.

"The Birth-mark" depicts Aylmer, who falls out of love with science for a short time to fall in love with Georgiana; but his love for Georgiana lacks depth. Having fallen in love with her physical beauty, he became obsessed with the tiny hand-shaped birthmark on her cheek, a mark which other suitors have found lovely. Aylmer, who has a poor record of trying to outsmart Mother Nature, returns to his scientific studies to figure out a way to remove this one imperfection from his wife. The experiment is a failure. At the moment he removes the birthmark, Georgiana dies, with the moral message that, though Aylmer has aimed loftily, he has failed miserably. A strange combination of alchemist and empirical scientist, Aylmer could have known the perfection of earthly life had he accepted his wife as part of a perfect alchemical union.

Another story that uses the conflict between empirical science and medieval science is "Rappaccini's Daughter" (1844), in which three men vie over Beatrice. Rappaccini, who holds a professorship in Padua, relies primarily on empirical science to create a perfect woman in his daughter. Giovanni, an unassuming young student, rents out a room that overlooks Rappaccini's garden, a veritable scientific laboratory. He unwittingly becomes Rappaccini's pawn as he falls in love with Beatrice. Though true love might save Beatrice, Giovanni begins to question her purity when he observes her ability to destroy life. Baglioni, a rival of Rappaccini, sees Beatrice as a rival because of her superior intellect and thus gives Giovanni an antidote to offer to her. A medieval concoction of sorts, the antidote has its desired effect for Baglioni; it kills his rival's creation, his daughter. Beatrice has the last word, though it is with her dying breath; she chastises her father for endowing her with deadly gifts, and she admonishes Giovanni for having had more poison in his nature than in hers. The story offers a tragic parable about the erosion of faith with the advent of Baconian science, which was so prevalent in early nineteenth-century America.

The Scarlet Letter (1850), Hawthorne's masterpiece about a torturous love triangle, continues the themes of his early works—innate depravity, artistic alienation, historical collective evil, and communal hypocrisy. Character types also reappear: Dimmesdale, the miscreant minister, who is tormented by the struggle between the spirit and the flesh; Chillingworth, the monomaniacal scientist, whose ego exceeds his love for his wife; and Hester, the woman wronged, who is morally superior to her suitors. Hawthorne creates for the first time a full-blooded woman who possesses a great emotional and intellectual nature. In effect, Hawthorne presents Hester as a woman of the nineteenth century, even as he depicts her in a seventeenth-century Puritan setting. Hester, like Hawthorne, could not escape the past, and so continues to wear her scarlet "A" until her dying day. Hawthorne, a man wronged by the Salemites, with his political fall from grace in the Custom House, embroiders his personal vendetta against Salem in this novel. Though he declares in the introduction that for him Salem is no longer a reality, and that he is henceforth "a citizen of somewhere else," Hawthorne could never escape the feeling of guilt surrounding the acts of his oppressive and judgmental Puritan forebears of Salem.

The burden of the past as a theme is prominent in Hawthorne's next novel, *The House of the Seven Gables* (1851), in which two feuding families, the oppressive aristocratic Pyncheons and the victimized artisan Maules, ultimately reconcile in the manner of a true Gothic novel—with the marriage of Phoebe Pyncheon and Holgrave (a Maule). As in *The Scarlet Letter,* where the outsider figure who might disrupt the status quo is often deemed suspect or diabolical, so too in *The House of the Seven Gables,* in which Matthew Maule accuses Colonel Pyncheon of wrongfully claiming his land and is finally executed as a witch so that the Pyncheons might seize the Maule land. Borrowing devices from the Gothic, Hawthorne invests the setting with magical elements. The patriarchs of the Pyncheon family, especially the cruelest ones, are accursed and fated to die of apoplexy. The class conflict is not resolved in the next few generations, as the grandson of Matthew Maule hypnotizes and destroys the unwitting Alice Pyncheon. Following the Gothic tradition, the conflict is resolved when Phoebe, because she is not a pure Pyncheon, enters the house and literally sweeps up the old cobwebs to make things new. She is a perfect delight to the brother and sister, Clifford and Hepzibah, who are deeply imprisoned in the past, though Hepzibah tries to become modern, breaking her bonds with her aristocratic past and entering the working class, by setting up a cent-shop. The current Maule, Holgrave, jack-of-all-trades, is a daguerreotypist, whose reform activities frighten the old Hepzibah. As a tenant of the Pyncheon House of the Seven Gables, he is supposed to serve in the same capacity as his forebear—to seduce and destroy Phoebe—but he chooses instead the path of love and marriage. The apparently happy conclusion has a less-than-happy implication, for the newlyweds will simply move out of one oppressive Pyncheon mansion into another, the country estate of the now-deceased Judge Pyncheon. This move does not suggest any progress forward, especially considering that Holgrave and Clifford have repeatedly cursed the past in the shape of dead men's houses.

In his next novel, *The Blithedale Romance* (1852), the first-person narrator, Coverdale, bears some resemblance to Hawthorne during his stay at the utopian Brook

Farm community in 1841. Like Hawthorne, Coverdale tires of the physical labor and of being sociable with fellow utopians. He retreats to his womblike treehouse from which he observes the others voyeuristically. More dilettante than artist, Coverdale does not correspond with Hawthorne in every respect, but he does show Hawthorne's reclusive side and need for solitude. Coverdale is more like the detached intellectuals of Hawthorne's earlier works who cannot bond with others and who fabricate relationships in their head; he can easily switch his love and allegiance from Zenobia to Priscilla, because in his fictionalizing, he can never really see either woman as she is. Hollingsworth is interested in prison reform, not for the sake of mankind, but for his own sense of self; as Zenobia proclaims to Coverdale, Hollingsworth is cold hearted. Like Westervelt, the mesmerist who toys with Zenobia's affection and attempts to victimize Priscilla in the Veiled Lady Show, Hollingsworth is one of the long line of intellectuals and reformers whom Hawthorne critiques. However, there are no perfect models of manhood in this book, as Coverdale, the effete bachelor, cannot save Zenobia from her suicide. Instead, he dreams about the days of patriarchy to come, when he will live on heroically in his epic poem as "Father Hollingsworth and Uncle Coverdale." And Zenobia's and Priscilla's father (they are half-sisters), Old Moodie, is also a specimen of failed manhood, as he has succumbed to drink and destroyed his business dealings. The women, though strong in different ways, Zenobia as a feminist orator, and Priscilla as the epitome of True Woman, capture the attention and maintain the energy in this romance. Hawthorne is keenly aware of his cultural milieu, as he recognizes that the time for strong women like Zenobia has not arrived, even though he sees her as admirable.

Although the autobiographical impulse in *The Marble Faun* (1860) is not as strong as in *Blithedale,* one can tell from his notes in *The French and Italian Notebooks* that his observations of everyday life in Rome and of Florence as well as of the extraordinary events enter into his romance: for example, the role of the Catholic Church, the hedonistic rituals of Carnival, and the artwork and architecture of Rome. Though to the end a good New England Protestant, like his protagonist, Hilda, Hawthorne (always obsessed with secret sin) nonetheless notes the cathartic value of the Roman Catholic sacrament of confession in this novel. Moreover, his descriptions of the famous locations, such as the Coliseum or the Catacombs, and his knowledge of the art world, such as Praxiteles' Faun at the Capitol Gallery and Guido Reni's portrait of Beatrice Cenci at the Barberini Palace enter the text. The novel reads like a tour guide of Rome, as the four friends, Hilda, Kenyon, Miriam, and Donatello, take a personal odyssey through Rome and the Italian landscape.

The impending sense of doom in this final romance is exacerbated by Hawthorne's comments to the reader in his preface, which captures Hawthorne's darkening vision about the literary man in the marketplace. He also begins to think America is not conducive to romance-writing. In his abortive romances that follow, Hawthorne tried to make the Old World his setting, and the books were never completed.

CRITICAL RECEPTION

Early famous critics of Hawthorne in the nineteenth century, namely Poe, Melville, and James, paved the way for future critics with their varying interests in Hawthorne's psychology and knowledge of history. Melville, in his review essay, "Hawthorne and His Mosses," saw Hawthorne as a genius whose artistic innovations and whose understanding of the dark side of humanity would garner him laurels in the blossoming American literary landscape; he admired Hawthorne's fiction for its "blackness" stemming from "that Calvinistic sense of Innate Depravity and Original Sin" (406). Poe was also intrigued by the darkness in Hawthorne, as expressed in his reviews. He initially praised Hawthorne as "a man of the truest genius" in his review in *Graham's Magazine* in 1842 and found his use of the single effect in his tales impressive. But in a later review in *Godey's* (1847), Poe was less generous, claiming Hawthorne's allegorizing monotonous and his use of German Romantics like Tieck tiresome. In his study of Hawthorne, James speaks less effusively than Melville of Hawthorne's genius, but, for the most part, he is complimentary. He is especially impressed by Hawthorne's ability to convey the history and capture the local color of New England. If at times James seems impatient with the simplicity of Hawthorne's style, he nevertheless concludes that Hawthorne "combined in a singular degree the spontaneity of the imagination with a haunting care for moral problems" (145). In the twentieth century, D. H. Lawrence is the first important modern critic to recognize gender issues in Hawthorne, as he explores relationships between men and the undoing of men by strong female characters. Though Lawrence is often dramatic and extravagant in his assertions, many of the finest gender critics today simply remark upon gender issues more politely, but they are still concerned about the unmanning of Hawthorne's male protagonists.

There have been many biographies of Hawthorne, starting with those by his son-in-law George Parsons Lathrop and by his son Julian Hawthorne, and reminiscences by his daughter, Rose. Early twentieth-century biographers, such as Newton Arvin, made Hawthorne seem far more reclusive than he really was, but Randall Stewart rectified this problem by making Hawthorne appear more sociable and extroverted. Though recent biographers have continued to correct the problems of early biographers, some, such as T. Walter Herbert, are far too speculative to be truly helpful. If Julian Hawthorne painted a picture of Hawthorne's domestic life as too unrealistic and sweet, Herbert presents Hawthorne as a dysfunctional father. Margaret Moore's account of Hawthorne's early years in Salem has excellent historical information and presents a work of solid scholarship. Edwin Haviland Miller's study is even-tempered and fair, offering a poignant description of Hawthorne's last painful years as an ill and discouraged man. The most brilliant biography on Hawthorne is James R. Mellow's *Nathaniel Hawthorne in His Times* (1980). A skillfully nuanced biographer, Mellow delves to the heart and soul of Hawthorne and places him accurately in his cultural milieu.

F. O. Matthiessen's ground-breaking study of Hawthorne and other American Renaissance writers focuses on the interplay between history, psychology, and Hawthorne's cultural/intellectual milieu, and most studies have followed his example by emphasizing either history, psychology, or, more recently, gender studies. In the past 30 years, too, there have been studies analyzing Hawthorne from a linguistic or philosophical perspective.

In the 1950s and 1960s, many critics focused on the moral world that Hawthorne creates or on his aesthetic values (e.g., Hyatt Waggoner). Seminal psychological perspectives were offered by Roy Male and by Frederick Crews, who later recanted his Freudian approach to Hawthorne in the introduction of a reissued edition; Millicent Bell's theme-based study looked at artists in Hawthorne's work. In the 1970s and 1980s, many studies focused on Hawthorne as artist, on Hawthorne's aesthetics, or on Hawthorne's notion of the romance versus the novel (Claudia D. Johnson, John Caldwell Stubbs, Michael Davitt Bell, Richard Brodhead, Elissa Greenwald). Michael Gilmore explored Hawthorne as a writer who had to make himself marketable in the growing business of literary production. Richard Millington's study in the 1990s showed a renewed interest in Hawthorne's innovations as a romance-writer, expanding the definition of romance to include a historical perspective. In the 1980s, a plethora of books appeared offering a linguistic and/or a deconstructionist perspective of Hawthorne. Such studies include those by Edgar Dryden, Kenneth Dauber, and J. Hillis Miller. David Leverenz's oft-cited essay on "Mrs. Hawthorne's Headache" explores the tensions wrought in a reader-response analysis of *The Scarlet Letter*. Studies dealing with Hawthorne's philosophical approach to life include those by Melinda Ponder, who analyzes the influence of the Scottish school of thinkers on Hawthorne, and by John Dolis, who considers Hawthorne's relationship to continental philosophers of his time and to Jacques Lacan. Detailed studies about Hawthorne as a sketch-writer have also appeared (e.g., Thomas R. Moore; and Alfred Weber, Beth Lueck, Dennis Berthold) and about Hawthorne's structural and dialogical narrative structures (G. R. Thompson).

Nina Baym's ground-breaking study of Hawthorne in 1976 (and her many essays on Hawthorne) offers literary critics a more personal look at Hawthorne and his emotional life. Taking their cue from Baym, many critics who followed focused on personal relationships in Hawthorne's family (Gloria Erlich), or on gender dynamics within his fiction (Monika Elbert, Leland Person, Joel Pfister). Feminist critics, starting with Judith Fetterley, have been especially interested in Hawthorne's depiction of strong and weak women in his fiction or in his relationship to female authors (Jane Tompkins, Joyce Warren, Louise DeSalvo, Emily Budick, Melinda Ponder and John Idol, and Jamie Barlowe). Gender critics focusing on masculine dynamics in Hawthorne's fiction include David Leverenz and Leland Person. Many of these gender studies are, by extension and of necessity, also historicist in nature. For example, Pfister is also very interested in the study of class dynamics in Hawthorne's works.

Historicism was redefined in the 1980s so that old historicism gave way to New Historicism. Exemplary new historicist perspectives are offered by Michael Colacurcio, whose study explores Hawthorne's deep knowledge of colonial history, and Frederick Newberry, who examines Hawthorne's divided loyalties to England and America. Equally important is Sacvan Bercovitch's historicist approach to the role of both the seventeenth and the nineteenth century in the cultural myth-making invested in *The Scarlet Letter*. Bercovitch sees Hawthorne as an exponent of liberal, moderating tradition, whereas Charles Swann also looks at Hawthorne's contemporary historiography but reinvents Hawthorne as an ardent supporter of American patriotism. Lauren Berlant's work on the National Symbolic in Hawthorne evinces an interest in cultural mythmaking and redefinitions of America in Hawthorne's work. Recently written were more specific studies of a historical nature, such as Nancy Bentley's and Jean Fagan Yellin's explorations of Hawthorne's views of slavery, or Robert S. Levine's or Janny Franchot's study of tensions toward Catholicism in the fiction of Hawthorne. Explorations of the role of children and of changing attitudes toward children or children's literature highlight the studies by Laura Laffrado and Gillian Brown.

More esoteric studies of Hawthorne include those by Samuel Coale, who examines the symbolism of mesmerism in Hawthorne's fiction, and by Taylor Stoehr, who focuses on Hawthorne's mad scientists. Rita Gollin has written a compelling study of the influence of dreams in Hawthorne's fiction, and Luther Luedtke has written an absorbing study of Hawthorne's fascination with the Other, in terms of the Orient. Carol Marie Bensick has convincingly shown the influence of Hawthorne's knowledge of Renaissance thinking and Renaissance culture in her historicist approach to backgrounds in "Rappaccini's Daughter."

Hawthorne scholars have profited from source studies, such as Hawthorne's correspondence (Centenary edition, Thomas Woodson), annotated bibliographies (C. E. Frazier Clark), Hawthorne's reading list (Marion L. Kesselring), critical histories of Hawthorne's tales (Lea Newman), and contemporary reviews (John L. Idol and Buford Jones; Gary Scharnhorst). In the future, it would do scholars well to look at such source studies carefully.

WORKS CITED

James, Henry. *Hawthorne.* English Men of Letters Series. London: Macmillan, 1879. (Rpt. 1997, foreword Dan McCall, Cornell UP.)

Melville, Herman. "Hawthorne and His Mosses." *The Portable Melville.* Ed. Jay Leyda. New York: Penguin, 1978. 400–21.

Poe, Edgar Allan. *Essays and Reviews.* Ed. G. R. Thompson. New York: Library of America, 1984.

BIBLIOGRAPHY

Works by Nathaniel Hawthorne

Authoritative editions of Hawthorne's works are in *The Centenary Edition of the Works of Nathaniel Hawthorne,* ed. William Charvat et al. 23 vols. Columbus: Ohio State UP, 1962–1997.

Novels

Fanshawe. Boston: Marsh and Capen, 1828.

The Scarlet Letter. Boston: Ticknor, Reed, and Fields, 1850.

The House of the Seven Gables. Boston: Ticknor, Reed, and Fields, 1851.

The Blithedale Romance. Boston: Ticknor, Reed, and Fields, 1852.

The Marble Faun. Boston: Ticknor and Fields, March, 1860; published in February with the title *Transformation,* London: Smith, Elder, and Co.

Short Story Collections

Twice-told Tales. Boston: American Stationers' Co., 1837, and Boston: James Monroe and Co., 1842.

Mosses from an Old Manse. New York: Wiley and Putnam, 1846, and Boston: Ticknor and Fields, 1854.

The Snow Image, and Other Twice-told Tales. Boston: Ticknor, Reed, and Fields, 1851.

Children's Books

The Whole History of Grandfather's Chair. Boston: Elizabeth Peabody, 1841; New York: Wiley and Putnam, 1841.

Famous Old People. Boston: E. P. Peabody, 1841.

Liberty Tree. Boston: E. P. Peabody, 1841.

(These previous three works were formally collected and published together in *True Stories from History and Biography* in Boston: Ticknor, Reed, and Fields, 1851.)

A Wonder-Book for Boys and Girls. Boston: Ticknor, Reed, and Fields, 1851.

Tanglewood Tales. Boston: Ticknor, Reed, and Fields, 1853.

Other Works—Miscellaneous

Life of Franklin Pierce. Boston: Ticknor, Reed, and Fields, 1852.

"Chiefly About War Matters," *Atlantic Monthly,* July 1862.

Our Old Home, essay collection, Boston: Ticknor and Fields, 1863; London: Smith, Elder, & Co., 1863.

American Notebooks. Boston: Fields, Osgood, & Co., 1868 (pub. posthumously).

English Notebooks, Boston: Osgood & Co., 1870 (pub. posthumously).

French and Italian Notebooks. London: Strahan & Co. 1871; Boston: James R. Osgood & Co., 1872 (pub. posthumously).

Studies of Nathaniel Hawthorne

Arvin, Newton. *Hawthorne.* Boston: Little, Brown, 1929.

Barlowe, Jamie. *The Scarlet Mob of Scribblers: Rereading Hester Prynne.* Carbondale, Ill.: Southern Illinois UP, 2000.

Baym, Nina. *The Shape of Hawthorne's Career.* Ithaca, N.Y.: Cornell UP, 1976.

Bell, Michael Davitt. *Hawthorne and the Historical Romance of New England.* Princeton, N.J.: Princeton UP, 1971.

Bell, Millicent. *Hawthorne's View of the Artist.* New York: State Univ. Press of N.Y., 1962.

Bensick, Carol Marie. *La Nouvelle Beatrice: Renaissance and Romance in "Rappaccini's Daughter."* New Brunswick, N.J.: Rutgers UP, 1985.

Bentley, Nancy. *The Ethnography of Manners: Hawthorne, James, Wharton.* New York: Cambridge Univ. P., 1995.

Bercovitch, Sacvan. *The Office of "The Scarlet Letter."* Baltimore: Johns Hopkins UP, 1991.

Berlant, Lauren. *The Anatomy of National Fantasy: Hawthorne, Utopia, and Everyday Life.* Chicago: U of Chicago P, 1991.

Brodhead, Richard. *Hawthorne, Melville, and the Novel.* Chicago: Univ. of Chicago P, 1976.

———. *The School of Hawthorne.* N.Y.: Oxford UP, 1986.

Brown, Gillian. "Hawthorne and Children in the Nineteenth Century: Daughters, Flowers, Stories." In Reynolds, Larry J., ed. *A Historical Guide to Nathaniel Hawthorne.* New York: Oxford UP, 2001. 79–108.

Budick, Emily Miller. *Engendering Romance: Women Writers and the Hawthorne Tradition, 1850–1990.* New Haven, Conn.: Yale UP, 1994.

Clark, C. E. Frazier, Jr. *Nathaniel Hawthorne: A Descriptive Bibliography.* Pittsburgh, Pa.: Univ. of Pittsburgh P, 1978.

Coale, Samuel Chase. *Mesmerism and Hawthorne: Mediums of American Romance.* Tuscaloosa, Ala.: Univ. of Alabama P, 1998.

Colacurcio, Michael. *The Province of Piety: Moral History in Hawthorne's Early Tales.* Cambridge, Mass.: Harvard UP, 1984.

Crews, Frederick. *The Sins of the Fathers: Hawthorne's Psychological Themes.* New York: Oxford UP, 1966.

Dauber, Kenneth. *Rediscovering Hawthorne.* Princeton, N.J.: Princeton UP, 1977.

DeSalvo, Louise. *Nathaniel Hawthorne.* Atlantic Highlands, N.J.: Humanities P, 1987.

Dolis, John. *The Style of Hawthorne's Gaze: Regarding Subjectivity.* Tuscaloosa: Univ. of Alabama P., 1993.

Dryden, Edgar. *Nathaniel Hawthorne: The Poetics of Enchantment.* Ithaca, N.Y.: Cornell UP, 1977.

Elbert, Monika M. *Encoding the Letter "A": Gender and Authority in Hawthorne's Early Fiction.* Frankfurt, Germany: Haag & Herchen, 1990.

Erlich, Gloria C. *Family Themes and Hawthorne's Fiction: The Tenacious Web.* New Brunswick, N.J.: Rutgers UP, 1984.

Fetterley, Judith. *The Resisting Reader: A Feminist Approach to American Fiction.* Bloomington, Ind.: Indiana UP, 1978.

Franchot, Jenny. *Roads to Rome: The Antebellum Protestant Encounter with Catholicism.* Berkeley, Calif.: Univ. of California P, 1994.

Gilmore, Michael T. *American Romanticism and the Marketplace.* Chicago: Univ. of Chicago P, 1985.

Gollin, Rita K. *Nathaniel Hawthorne and the Truth of Dreams.* Baton Rouge, La.: Louisiana State UP, 1979.

Greenwald, Elisa. *Realism and the Romance: Nathaniel Hawthorne, Henry James, and American Fiction*. Ann Arbor: Univ. of Michigan P, 1989.

Hawthorne, Julian. *Nathaniel Hawthorne and His Wife: A Biography*. 2d ed., 2 vols. Boston: James Osgood, 1885.

Herbert, T. Walter. *Dearest Beloved: The Hawthornes and the Making of the Middle-Class Family*. Berkeley, Calif.: Univ. of California Press, 1993.

Idol, John L., Jr., and Buford Jones, eds. *Nathaniel Hawthorne: The Contemporary Reviews*. New York: Cambridge UP, 1994.

Idol, John L., Jr., and Melinda Ponder, eds. *Hawthorne and Women: Engendering and Expanding the Hawthorne Tradition*. Amherst, Mass.: U of Mass. P, 1999.

James, Henry. *Hawthorne*. English Men of Letters Series. London: Macmillan, 1879. (Rpt. 1997, foreword Dan McCall, Cornell UP)

Johnson, Claudia Durst. *The Productive Tension of Hawthorne's Art*. Tuscaloosa, Ala.: Univ. of Alabama P, 1981.

Kesselring, Marion L. *Hawthorne's Reading, 1828–1850*. N.Y.: N.Y. Public Library, 1949.

Kesterson, David B., ed. *Critical Essays on Hawthorne's "The Scarlet Letter."* Boston: G. K. Hall, 1988.

Laffrado, Laura. *Hawthorne's Literature for Children*. Athens, Ga.: Univ. of Ga. Press, 1992.

Lawrence, D. H. *Studies in Classical American Literature*. New York: Penguin, 1978. (Rpt. 1923)

Lathrop, George Parsons. *A Study of Hawthorne*. Boston: James R. Osgood and Co., 1876.

Lathrop, Rose Hawthorne. *Memories of Hawthorne*. Boston: Houghton Mifflin, 1923.

Leverenz, David. "Mrs. Hawthorne's Headache: Reading *The Scarlet Letter*." *Nineteenth-Century Fiction* 37.4 (1983): 552–75.

Levine, Robert S. *Conspiracy and Romance: Studies in Brockden Brown, Cooper, Hawthorne, and Melville*. N.Y.: Cambridge UP, 1989.

Luedtke, Luther S. *Nathaniel Hawthorne and the Romance of the Orient*. Bloomington, Ind.: Indiana UP, 1989.

Male, Roy. *Hawthorne's Tragic Vision*. Austin, Texas: Univ. of Texas P, 1957.

Matthiessen, F. O. *American Renaissance: Art and Expression in the Age of Emerson and Whitman*. N.Y.: Oxford UP, 1974. (Rpt. from 1941)

Mellow, James. *Nathaniel Hawthorne in His Times*. Boston: Houghton Mifflin, 1980.

Melville, Herman. "Hawthorne and His Mosses." *The Portable Melville*. Ed. Jay Leyda. New York: Penguin, 1978. 400–21.

Miller, Edwin Haviland. *Salem is My Dwelling Place: A Life of Nathaniel Hawthorne*. Iowa City: Univ. of Iowa P, 1991.

Miller, J. Hillis. *Hawthorne and History: Defacing It*. Cambridge: Basil Blackwell, 1991.

Millington, Richard H. *Practicing Romance: Narrative Form and Cultural Engagement in Hawthorne's Fiction*. Princeton, N.J.: Princeton UP, 1988.

Moore, Margaret B. *The Salem World of Nathaniel Hawthorne*. Columbia, Mo.: Univ. of Missouri P, 1988.

Moore, Thomas R. *A Thick and Darksome Veil: The Rhetoric of Hawthorne's Sketches, Prefaces, and Essays*. Boston: Northeastern UP, 1994.

Newberry, Frederick. *Hawthorne's Divided Loyalties: England and America in His Works*. Rutherford, N. J.: Fairleigh Dickinson UP, 1987.

Newman, Lea Bertani Vozar. *A Reader's Guide to the Short Stories of Nathaniel Hawthorne*. Boston: G. K. Hall, 1979.

Person, Leland S. *Aesthetic Headaches: Women and a Masculine Poetics in Poe, Melville, and Hawthorne*. Athens, Ga.: Univ. of Georgia P, 1988.

Pfister, Joel. *The Production of Personal Life: Class, Gender, and the Psychological in Hawthorne's Fiction*. Stanford, Calif.: Stanford UP, 1991.

Poe, Edgar Allan. *Essays and Reviews*. Ed. G. R. Thompson. N.Y.: Library of America, 1984.

Ponder, Melinda M. *Hawthorne's Early Narrative Art*. Lewiston, Maine: Edwin Mellen, 1990.

Reynolds, Larry J., ed. *A Historical Guide to Nathaniel Hawthorne*. New York: Oxford UP, 2001.

Scharnhorst, Gary, ed. *Nathaniel Hawthorne: An Annotated Bibliography of Commentary and Criticism before 1900*. Metuchen, N.J.: Scarecrow Press, 1988.

Stewart, Randall. *Nathaniel Hawthorne: A Biography*. New Haven, Conn.: Yale UP, 1948.

Stoehr, Taylor. *Hawthorne's Mad Scientists: Pseudoscience and Social Science in Nineteenth-Century Life and Letters*. Hamden, Conn.: Shoe String, 1978.

Stubbs, John Caldwell. *The Pursuit of Form: A Study of Hawthorne and the Romance*. Urbana: Univ. of Illinois P, 1970.

Swann, Charles. *Nathaniel Hawthorne: Tradition and Revolution*. New York: Cambridge UP, 1991.

Thompson, G.R. *The Art of Authorial Presence: Hawthorne's Provincial Tales*. Durham, N.C.: Duke UP, 1993.

Tompkins, Jane. *Sensational Designs: The Cultural Work of American Fiction, 1790–1860*. New York: Oxford UP, 1985.

Waggoner, Hyatt H. *The Presence of Hawthorne*. Baton Rouge: Louisiana State UP, 1979.

Warren, Joyce. *The American Narcissus: Individualism and Women in Nineteenth-Century American Fiction*. New Brunswick, N.J.: Rutgers UP, 1984.

Weber, Alfred, Beth L. Lueck, and Dennis Berthold, eds. *Hawthorne's American Travel Sketches*. Hanover, N.H.: UP of New England, 1989.

Yellin, Jean Fagan. "Nathaniel Hawthorne's *The Scarlet Letter*." *Women and Sisters: The Anti-Slavery Feminists in American Culture*. New Haven: Yale UP, 1989.

CAROLINE LEE WHITING HENTZ
(1800–1856)

Theresa J. Flowers

BIOGRAPHY

Born on June 1, 1800, Caroline Lee Whiting was the eighth and youngest child of John and Orpah Danforth Whiting. The Whitings were an old New England family who had been in Massachusetts since 1626 and were directly descended from the Reverend Samuel Whiting. John Whiting served as a colonel in the Revolutionary War. At the age of 24, Caroline married Nicholas Marcellus Hentz, a political refugee from France who held a professorship in modern languages at the University of North Carolina. In 1830 the couple left the university and jointly supervised a number of schools for girls, the first in Covington, Kentucky. In 1832, the Hentzes opened another academy in Cincinnati where Caroline's literary ambitions prompted her to join the Semi-Colon Club. At the time, Harriet Beecher Stowe was a member, and it seems likely that Hentz knew her. Later in *The Planter's Northern Bride* (1854), Hentz would provide a southern answer to Stowe's famous *Uncle Tom's Cabin*. Hentz bore five children, losing the oldest son when he was only two years old. In addition to rearing the children, running her household, supervising the boarding school, and helping her husband with his scholarly work, Hentz wrote verse, drama, tales, and novels. Although Hentz began writing at an early age, she did not gain public attention until the *Philadelphia Saturday Courier* published a domestic story in 1844 as a series. It was later published in book form as *Aunt Patty's Scrap Bag* (1846). Her novel *Linda; or, The Young Pilot of the Belle Creole* (1850) became a best-seller. Seven more domestic novels and six collections of stories were published in a swift progression. Because of her husband's extended illness and eventual death, profits from Hentz's novels were the means of support for her family. Her books remained popular after her death until the end of the century.

MAJOR WORKS AND THEMES

Though she was born in Massachusetts, Hentz began writing in 1846 after living 20 years in the South. Her most profitable novel was *Linda* (1850). This novel introduced a heroine who was bold in thought and deed, a concept that would become embedded in all of her writing. *Linda* also introduced a basic distrust of jealous men, which can be traced to problems in Hentz's relationship with her own husband. Today Hentz's best-known work is *The Planter's Northern Bride* (1854). Although it was not typical of her other fiction, at the time it was considered an effective answer to *Uncle Tom's Cabin.* This work presented a defense for the southern attitude toward slavery. Hentz insisted that slaves were children of an inferior society who profited from the white Christian civilization. It is true that Hentz did not live on a plantation herself and her novels are not a strict representation of plantation life; however, they do illustrate how the economic and social systems of the South differ from those of the North. Her work gives insight into the feelings of many southern white women on the eve of the Civil War. However, Hentz deserves to be remembered for more than her impractical views of slavery. Her long fiction exhibits a strong moral and religious framework that demonstrates her under-standing of right and wrong. The majority of her narratives center on young lovers who are united, separated, tested, and eventually reunited. In addition, four of Hentz's eight novels set the heroine against another woman: in *Linda,* a stepmother; in *Rena,* a jeal-ous rival; in *The Planter's Northern Bride,* a former wife; and, in *Helen and Arthur,* an older sister. Hentz preferred to create active, strong-willed women rather than passive and delicate heroines. Although Hentz wrote in the romantic tradition, she was often critical of the standard romantic patterns of the day and of patriarchy. Even so, in each of her novels she provided a mate for her heroine who appreciated her and "ruled" her in a benevolent manner. Hentz combined feminine self-expression and self-development with the traditional hierarchical view of relations between men and women (Baym 138–39).

CRITICAL RECEPTION

Hentz's work was mostly well accepted by the critics in her lifetime. Those who found fault with her writing almost always pointed to her use or overuse of sentimen-tality. The critics who were impressed by Hentz looked to her willingness to step beyond the ordinary, especially with her female characters. An early review published in the *Southern Review Quarterly* in 1851 described Hentz's "novelettes" as "unusually pleas-ant and piquant—full of the sweetest caprices, that usually end happily at last, with one or more marriages, and to the satisfaction of the spectators" (Tracey, "Little Counter-plots" 2). A reviewer for the *Southern Literary Messenger* describes Hentz's popular audience in 1855 as a "great mass of readers" for whom "the lines between right and wrong, vice and virtue cannot be too plain" (Tracey, *Plots* 51). In just two years *Linda* was printed in 13 editions. Hentz's novels reportedly sold 93,000 copies in three years and remained popular well into the 1890s (53). Hentz was praised for her wit and humor. One critic observed that hers was a "merry muse" (Baym 127). Fortunately for Hentz, the real appeal of her books did not lie in their propaganda. She sold as well or better in the North, and a generation after emancipation, the Boston Public Library counted her among three of the most popular authors on their shelves (Papashvily 89).

Although Hentz was once among the most prominent writers of her era, like so many others she has been forgotten over time. However, her work is worthy of critical attention. Her longer works in particular closely follow the general tradition of romance. Her characterizations are vivid and bold, and her use of fairy tales and folklore as well as her sometimes pointed feminism emphasize her talent for character and narrative development (Wimsatt 162). Recent criticism has focused on Hentz's feminist heroines and her support of slavery. Her work is now generally placed in the tradition of the sentimental novel.

WORKS CITED

Baym, Nina. *Women's Fiction: A Guide to Novels by and about Women in America, 1820–1870.* Ithaca: Cornell UP, 1978.

Papashvily, Helen Waite. *All the Happy Endings.* New York: Harper & Brothers, 1956.

Tracey, Karen. "Little Counterplots in the Old South: Narrative Subterfuge in Caroline Hentz's Domestic Fiction." *The Journal of Narrative Technique* 28.1 (1998): 1–20.

———. *Plots and Proposals: American Women's Fiction, 1850–90.* Urbana: U of Illinois P, 2000.

Wimsatt, Mary Ann. "Caroline Hentz's Balancing Act." *The Southern Tradition in Southern Literature.* Ed. Carol S. Manning. Urbana: U of Illinois P, 1993. 161–75.

BIBLIOGRAPHY

Works by Caroline Lee Whiting Hentz

Lovell's Folly. Cincinnati: Hubbard and Edmands, 1833.

DeLara; or, The Moorish Bride. Tuscaloosa, AL: Wodruff & Olcott, 1843.

Aunt Patty's Scrap Bag, Philadelphia: Carey & Hart, 1846.

The Mob Cap; and Other Tales. Philadelphia: T. B. Peterson, 1848.

Linda; or, The Young Pilot of Belle Creole. Philadelphia: A. Hart, 1850.

Rena; or, The Snow Bird. Philadelphia: T. B. Peterson, 1851.

Eoline; or, Magnolia Vale. Philadelphia: T. B. Peterson, 1852.

Marcus Warland; or, The Long Moss Spring, a Tale of the South. Philadelphia: A. Hart, 1852.

Helen and Arthur; or, Miss Thusa's Spinning Wheel. Philadelphia: T. B. Peterson, 1853.

The Planter's Northern Bride. 2 vols. Philadelphia: Parry & McMillian, 1854.

Robert Graham. Philadelphia: Parry & McMillian, 1855.

Ernest Linwood. Boston: J. P. Jewett, 1856.

Courtship and Marriage; or, The Joys and Sorrows of American Life. Philadelphia: T. B. Peterson, 1856.

Love After Marriage, and Other Stories of the Heart. Philadelphia: T. B. Peterson, 1857.

Studies of Caroline Lee Whiting Hentz

Bakker, Jan. " . . . The Bold Atmosphere of Mrs. Hentz and Others: Fast Food and Feminine Rebelliousness in Some Romances of the Old South." *Journal of American Culture* 21.2 (1998): 1–9.

———. "Twists of Sentiment in Antebellum Southern Romance." *The Literary Southern Journal* 26.1 (1993): 3–13.

Barnes, Elizabeth. "Mirroring the Mother Text: Histories of Seduction in the American Domestic Novel." *Anxious Power: Reading, Writing, and Ambivalence in Narrative By Women.* Eds. Carol J. Singley and Susan Elizabeth Sweeney. Albany: U of New York P, 1993. 157–72.

Baym, Nina. *Women's Fiction: A Guide to Novels by and about Women in America, 1820–1870.* Ithaca, N.Y.: Cornell UP, 1978.

Brown, Lynda W. "Caroline (Lee) Whiting Hentz." *American Women Writers: A Critical Reference Guide from Colonial Times to the Present.* Vol. 2, E–K, 2nd ed. Ed. Taryn Benbow-Pfalzgraf. Detroit: St. James Press, 2000. 203–4.

Davis, Thadious. "Women's Art and Authorship in the Southern Region: Connections." *The Female Tradition in Southern Literature.* Ed. Carol S. Manning. Urbana: U of Illinois P, 1993. 15–36.

Hunt, Robert. "A Domesticated Slavery: Political Economy in Caroline Hentz's Fiction." *The Southern Quarterly* 34.4 (1996): 25–35.

Kelley, Mary. *Private Women, Public Stage: Literary Domesticity in Nineteenth-Century America.* New York: Oxford UP, 1984.

Levinson, Melanie. "Caroline Lee Whiting Hentz (1800–1856)." *Nineteenth-Century Women Writers: A Bio-Bibliographical Sourcebook.* Ed. Denise D. Knight. Westport, Conn.: Greenwood Press, 1997. 220–223.

Moss, Elizabeth. *Domestic Novelists in the Old South.* Baton Rouge: Louisiana State UP, 1992.

Papashvily, Helen Waite. *All the Happy Endings.* New York: Harper & Brothers, 1956.

Shillingsburg, Miriam. "Caroline Lee (Whiting) Hentz." *Antebellum Writers in New York and the South.* Ed. Joel Myerson. Detroit: Gale Research Company, 1979. 148.

Stanesa, Jamie. "Caroline Hentz's Rereading of Southern Paternalism; or, Pastoral Naturalism in *The Planter's Northern Bride.*" *Southern Studies* 3.4 (1992): 221–52.

Tracey, Karen. "Little Counterplots in the Old South: Narrative Subterfuge in Caroline Hentz's Domestic Fiction." *The Journal of Narrative Technique* 28.1 (1998): 1–20.

———. *Plots and Proposals: American Women's Fiction, 1850–90.* Urbana: U of Illinois P, 2000.

Wimsatt, Mary Ann. "Caroline Hentz's Balancing Act." *The Southern Tradition in Southern Literature.* Ed. Carol S. Manning. Urbana: U of Illinois P, 1993. 161–75.

OLIVER WENDELL HOLMES (1809–1894)

Denise D. Knight

BIOGRAPHY

Oliver Wendell Holmes was born in Cambridge, Massachusetts, on August 29, 1809. His father, the Reverend Abiel Holmes, was a historian and Congregationalist minister, and his mother, Sarah Wendell, was a descendent of the Puritan poet Anne Bradstreet. Despite the fact that Holmes's father was harshly dogmatic in his religious views, he was, by all accounts, a good father. By the time Holmes enrolled in Harvard at the age of 16, however, he had rejected his father's religious conservatism and pursued a degree in science rather than religion. For a short time after graduating from Harvard in 1829, Holmes pursued law, but he soon enrolled in Harvard Medical School, where he studied for three years.

During his years at Harvard Medical School, Holmes began publishing poetry, primarily in newspapers. Several of his works, "The Height of the Ridiculous" (1830), "Old Ironsides" (1830), "My Aunt" (1831), and "The Last Leaf" (1831) were well received. He viewed his poetry writing as a hobby for idle hours, however, rather than a serious endeavor. In 1833, Holmes traveled to France, where he continued his medical education; in 1836, he received his M. D. from Harvard and opened a private practice in Boston. His first book, *Poems,* was published in 1836. Holmes also published medical essays, for which he won the Boylston Prize in 1836 and 1837. His achievements caught the attention of the Board of Trustees at Dartmouth College, where he was offered a professorship in anatomy and physiology. He accepted the position but remained there for only two years before returning to private practice.

In 1840, Holmes married Amelia Lee Jackson, the daughter of a Boston judge. Together they parented three children: Oliver Wendell Jr. (a future Supreme Court justice), Amelia Jackson Holmes, and Edward Jackson Holmes. From 1840 to 1847, Holmes continued his private practice but also found time to lecture and publish. In 1843 he published a controversial essay on the contagiousness of puerperal fever, which marked his most significant contribution to medical science. In 1847, he accepted an appointment as the Parkman professor of anatomy and physiology at Harvard Medical school, a post he held until he retired in 1882. His passion for teaching made him an effective and popular teacher. He also enjoyed participating in one of Boston's proudest traditions—the dinners of the Saturday Club, which were also attended, among others, by Emerson, Longfellow, Whittier, and Lowell.

Throughout Holmes's medical career, and following his retirement, he continued to write. The *Atlantic Monthly* published his series of witty essays titled *The Autocrat of the Breakfast-Table* (1858), in which he discoursed on topics including New Englanders, human behavior, faulty logic, and religion. That sequence was followed in 1860 by *The Professor at the Breakfast-Table* and in 1872 by *The Poet at the Breakfast-Table.* In the interim, Holmes produced three novels, *Elsie Venner* (1861), *The Guardian Angel* (1867), and *A Mortal Antipathy* (1885). In 1885, he published a biography on Ralph Waldo Emerson.

The following year, Holmes traveled to Europe, accompanied by his daughter. During his visit, he received honorary doctorates from Cambridge, Edinburgh, and Oxford Universities. In 1887, he published an account of his travels, *Our Hundred Days in Europe.* His wife Amelia died the following year. Holmes himself succumbed suddenly on October 7, 1894, at his home in Boston. The funeral service, held at King's Chapel, was conducted by the Reverend Edward Everett Hale. Holmes was 85 years old.

MAJOR WORKS AND THEMES

As a writer, Holmes was not only prolific, but also versatile. He was a poet, humorist, medical essayist, fiction writer, and a biographer, who discoursed on a wide range of topics from the dangers of homeopathy in "Homeopathy and Its Kindred Delusions" (1842) to the philosophical reflections inspired by observing "The Chambered Nautilus" (1858), a rare sea mollusk. It is for his poetry, however—and his identification as one of the famed New England "Fireside Poets" (along with Bryant, Longfellow, Lowell, and Whittier)—that he is best remembered today.

Over the course of his lifetime, Holmes published nearly 400 poems. His first book-length volume of poetry, titled *Poems* (1836), was a collection of previously published works. The edition featured occasional poetry, elegies, and witty verse, along with his most famous poem, "Old Ironsides," a protest against the U. S. Navy's plan to dismantle the frigate *Constitution,* perhaps the nation's most renowned Navy vessel. The poem won Holmes national acclaim when it was published in 1830, and the publicity it generated was instrumental in saving the ship from destruction.

Also noteworthy among Holmes's early poems is "The Last Leaf," originally published in 1831. A blend of humor and pathos, "The Last Leaf, " was inspired by the unorthodox appearance of Major Thomas Melville (Herman Melville's grandfather), whom Holmes had observed on the streets of Boston. It was praised by Poe and Lincoln. Another popular satirical poem, "My Aunt," was originally published in 1831 and is still occasionally anthologized today. Also significant is the 1846 work, *Urania: A Rhymed Lesson,* a didactic yet satirical rejection of Calvinist doctrine.

Among Holmes's prose works, *The Autocrat of the Breakfast-Table*—a series of humorous essays that appeared in the *Atlantic Monthly*—won Holmes immediate popularity. Based on a simple premise—residents of a boarding house discussing various matters at the breakfast table—the series showcases Holmes's gift as a witty and spirited conversationalist who relished verbal sparring. The work depicts the urbane and genial banter of a group of Boston intellectuals including such characters as the Autocrat, the Professor, the Landlady, the Schoolmistress, and the Divinity Student. Two sequels followed: *The Professor at the Breakfast-Table* appeared in 1860 and *The Poet at the Breakfast-Table* was published in 1872.

Holmes also published three novels: *Elsie Venner,* the best known of the three, appeared in 1861 and was followed by *The Guardian Angel* in 1867 and *A Mortal Antipathy* in 1885. The three novels are loosely connected by their pre-Freudian examination of various psychiatric conditions. Subtitled *A Romance of Destiny, Elsie Venner* centers on a young New England woman whose mother, while pregnant with Elsie, was bitten by a rattlesnake; hence, Elsie is born with "reptilian" qualities stemming from the pre-natal influence. As a result, she is doomed to a life of sorrow and misfortune. Holmes used the idea of a poisoned embryo to explore the connection between physiological conditions and mental aberrations.

The Guardian Angel focuses on a psychological theme similar to that of *Elsie Venner.* Holmes proclaimed that he wanted to show "how in the normal order of things a series of inborn instincts and propensities" might influence one's will (qtd. in Tilton 287). Myrtle Hazard, the orphaned heroine, is a runaway from the New England home of her stern and pious relatives. Disguising herself as a boy, she escapes down river. After nearly drowning, she returns home, experiences a bout of hysteria, and is unsuccessfully treated. She is eventually "cured" by Gridley, a wise and sympathetic tutor, who insists that leaving the narrow confines of the village for a city environment would prove therapeutic. Holmes suggests that Myrtle's emotional instability is connected to childhood trauma and that she has to work through the heredity and environmental forces that conspire against her.

The humorous plot of *A Mortal Antipathy* centers on Maurice Kirkwood, who suffers from a paralyzing fear of beautiful women. Kirkwood's phobia has its origins in his childhood, after he is snatched from his mother's arms at the age of two and dropped into a thorny bush by an attractive young cousin. He eventually overcomes his phobia after undergoing shock therapy.

In addition to fiction writing, Holmes also penned a biography of Emerson, which he published in 1885 at the request of Emerson's family. Two years later, he published a travel narrative titled *Our Hundred Days in Europe,* based on his sojourn to Europe with his daughter in 1886. His final book, *Over the Teacups,* written in a similar vein to the "Breakfast-Table" series, appeared in 1891, when Holmes was 81 years old. Despite his advanced age, his wit and shrewdness of expression remained intact.

CRITICAL RECEPTION

Holmes was a beloved figure in his day, and, with few exceptions, his occasional poetry was well received. Critic John Gorham Palfrey wrote of Holmes's 1836 edition, *Poems,* "the author is a man of genius. . . . His manner is entirely his own, manly and unaffected; generally easy and playful, and sinking at times into 'a most humorous sadness'" (275, 276). After hearing Holmes read one of his poems at a function in 1839, an anonymous reporter for the *Boston Daily Atlas* remarked, "I have ever regarded Holmes as one of the very first poets in the country, and [his latest] performance . . . will raise him higher in public estimation" (qtd. in Tilton 155). In a posthumous tribute, Henry Cabot Lodge noted that Holmes "was very much more than a writer of occasional poems" and that "his extraordinary success" as an occasional poet "tended to obscure his much higher successes, and to cause men to overlook the fact that he was a true poet in the best sense" (669). Not all critics were as kind, however. An anonymous reviewer for *The Yale Literary Magazine* opined that Holmes had compromised the quality of his edition by allowing several "*mediocre* poems to fill out the volume" (122).

The "Breakfast-Table" works have drawn the most consistently positive praise. Rowland E. Prothero's characterization is typical of the acclaim accorded the series:

Holmes discovered in the *Autocrat* the form of expression which was most perfectly fitted for the display of his gifts. . . . [His] rambling, discursive series [is] his own best title to immortality. . . . Its charm lies in the lightness and ease of its flow, the crispness and pungency of its reflections, the freshness and pertinence of its observations. Good conversation is, like occasional verse, a patrician art which Holmes inherited. In his hands it is the instrument by which he can teach without being didactic, preach without sermonising, and amuse without offending the most fastidious taste. (202)

Reviews of Holmes's novels were far less favorable. Prothero noted that *Elsie Venner, The Guardian Angel,* and *A Mortal Antipathy* "are singularly deficient" in construction and "show little dramatic power." Rather, "the author is always on the stage directing the movements of his puppets, and . . . the minor figures are coarsely drawn and harshly coloured; the chief actors are anatomical puzzles, concrete problems in heredity, examples of mental states, psychological instances scientifically, but not dramatically, constructed" (203). Frank H. Hill agrees, writing that *Elsie Venner* is merely a form of " 'sensation writing;' the object is to startle. The best proof of this is that Dr. Holmes's serpent-woman does not excite awe, pity, or terror, but simply incredulity. *Elsie Venner* . . . has neither the verisimilitude of a story of real life, nor the instructiveness of avowed parable or allegory (371). Clarence P. Oberndorf, M. D., author of *The Psychiatric Novels of Oliver Wendell Holmes,* concurs: "His three [novels] are poor fiction when judged by modern criteria. . . . Their plots are simple, almost juvenile and, in two of them, the reader is not disappointed in the customary thwarting of the villain and the coming of true love to its own" (13–14).

Of his Emerson biography one critic wrote that "except for the chapter on Emerson's poetry, the book is of little use to Emersonian's today. . . . Holmes had little understanding" of Emersonian philosophy (Wortham 316). Eleanor M. Tilton agrees, remarking that "the biography of Emerson is chiefly notable for Holmes's careful study of Emerson's poems and appreciation of their success in uniting idea and form" (138). An anonymous critic writing in *The Nation* offers a mixed review: while the biography "leaves us almost wholly uninformed as to two of the most important aspects of Emerson's earlier life—his relations to the anti-slavery agitation and to the so-called transcendental movement"—its "detailed review of . . . one man of genius by another, with running annotations, grave, gay, learned, and witty," makes it "both valuable and attractive" (99–100).

Today, Holmes is a casualty of the ongoing movement to revise the literary canon. His work is the least likely of the Fireside Poets to find its way into American literature anthologies.

WORKS CITED

Hill, Frank H. "Dr. Oliver Wendell Holmes and 'Elsie Venner.' " *The National Review,* London, Vol. XIII, no. XXVI (Oct. 1861): 359–72.
"Holmes's *Emerson.*" *The Nation,* Vol. XL, no. 1022 (January 29, 1885): 99–100.
Lodge, Henry Cabot. "Dr. Holmes." *The North American Review.* Vol. CLIV, no. 457. (Dec. 1894): 669–77.

Palfrey, John Gorham. "Holmes's Poems." *The North American Review.* Vol. XLIV, no. 94 (Jan. 1837): 275–77.

Oberndorf, Clarence P. *The Psychiatric Novels of Oliver Wendell Holmes.* Revised ed. New York: Columbia University Press, 1946.

Prothero, Rowland E. "A Review of *The Writings of Oliver Wendell Holmes.*" *The Quarterly Review.* Vol. CLXXIX, no. CCCLIX. (Jan. 1895): 189–206.

"A review of 'Poems.' " *The Yale Literary Magazine.* Vol. 2, no. 4 (Feb. 1837): 113–24.

Tilton, Eleanor M. *Amiable Autocrat: A Biography of Dr. Oliver Wendell Holmes.* New York: Schuman, 1947.

Wortham, Thomas. "Oliver Wendell Holmes." *American Writers.* Supp. 1, Vol. 1. New York: Charles Scribner's Sons, 1979. 299–319.

BIBLIOGRAPHY

Works by Oliver Wendell Holmes

Poems. Boston: Otis, Broaders, 1836.

Boylston Prize Dissertations for the Years 1836 and 1837. Boston: Little and Brown, 1838.

Urania: A Rhymed Lesson. Boston: Ticknor, 1846.

The Autocrat of the Breakfast-Table. Boston: Phillips, Sampson, 1858.

The Professor at the Breakfast-Table. Boston: Ticknor and Fields, 1860.

Currents and Counter-Currents in Medical Science. Boston: Ticknor and Fields, 1861.

Elsie Venner: A Romance of Destiny. Boston: Ticknor and Fields, 1861; rev. ed. Boston: Houghton, Mifflin, 1883.

Songs in Many Keys. Boston: Ticknor and Fields, 1862.

The Guardian Angel. Boston: Ticknor and Fields, 1867.

The Poet at the Breakfast-Table. Boston: Osgood, 1872.

Songs of Many Seasons. 1862–1874. Boston: Osgood, 1875.

The Iron Gate, and Other Poems. Boston: Houghton, Mifflin, 1880.

Medical Essays 1842–1882. Boston: Houghton-Mifflin, 1883.

Pages from an Old Volume of Life. Boston: Houghton, Mifflin, 1883.

A Mortal Antipathy. Boston: Houghton, Mifflin, 1885.

Ralph Waldo Emerson. Boston: Houghton, Mifflin, 1885.

Our Hundred Days in Europe. Boston: Houghton, Mifflin, 1887.

Before the Curfew and Other Poems. Boston: Houghton, Mifflin, 1888.

Over the Teacups. Boston: Houghton, Mifflin, 1891.

Collected Editions

The Writings of Oliver Wendell Holmes. Riverside edition. 13 vols. Boston: Houghton, Mifflin, 1891.

The Complete Poetical Works of Oliver Wendell Holmes, edited by H. E. Scudder. Cambridge Edition. Boston: Houghton, Mifflin, 1895.

Oliver Wendell Holmes: Representative Selections, edited by S. I. Hayakawa and Howard Mumford Jones. American Writers Series. New York: American Book Company, 1939.

The Autocrat's Miscellanies, edited by Albert Mordell. New York: Twayne, 1959.

Bibliographies

Currier, Thomas Franklin. *A Bibliography of Oliver Wendell Holmes,* edited by Eleanor M. Tilton. New York: New York University Press, 1953.

Menikoff, Barry. "Oliver Wendell Holmes." In *Fifteen American Authors Before 1900: Bibliographical Essays on Research and Criticism,* edited by Robert A. Rees and Earl N. Harbert. Madison: University of Wisconsin Press, 1971. 207–28.

Studies of Oliver Wendell Holmes

Arms, George. *The Fields Were Green.* Stanford, CA: Stanford University Press, 1953. 97–114.

Clark, Harry Hayden. "Dr. Holmes: A Reinterpretation." *New England Quarterly* 12: (1939) 19–34.

Gibian, Peter. *Oliver Wendell Holmes and the Culture of Conversation.* Cambridge: Cambridge University Press, 2001.

Gougeon, Len. "Holmes's *Emerson* and the Conservative Critique of Realism." *South Atlantic Review* 59, no. 1 (1994 Jan): 107–25.

Hallissy, Margaret. "Poisonous Creature: Holmes's *Elsie Venner. Studies in the Novel.*" 17, no. 4 (1985 Winter): 406–19.

Hill, Frank H. "Dr. Oliver Wendell Holmes and 'Elsie Venner.' " *The National Review,* London, Vol. XIII, no. XXVI (Oct. 1861): 359–72.

"Holmes's *Emerson.*" *The Nation,* Vol. XL, no. 1022 (January 29, 1885): 99–100.

Howe, M. A. DeWolfe. *Holmes of the Breakfast-Table.* London and New York: Oxford University Press, 1939.

Hoyt, Edwin P. *The Improper Bostonian: Dr. Oliver Wendell Holmes.* New York: Morrow, 1979.

Leary, Lewis. "Oliver Wendell Holmes." In *The Comic Imagination in American Literature,* edited by Louis D. Rubin Jr. New Brunswick, New Jersey: Rutgers University Press, 1973. 113–26.

Lodge, Henry Cabot. "Dr. Holmes." *The North American Review.* Vol. CLIV, no. 457 (Dec. 1894): 669–77.

Martin, John Stephen. "The Novels of Oliver Wendell Holmes: A Re-Interpretation." In *Literature and Ideas in America: Essays in Memory of Harry Hayden Clark,* edited by Robert Falk. Athens: Ohio University Press, 1975. 111–27.

Morse, John T. *Life and Letters of Oliver Wendell Holmes.* 2 vols. Boston: Houghton, Mifflin, 1896.

Oberndorf, Clarence P. *The Psychiatric Novels of Oliver Wendell Holmes.* Revised ed. New York: Columbia University Press, 1946.

Palfrey, John Gorham. "Holmes's Poems." *The North American Review.* Vol. XLIV, no. 94 (Jan. 1837): 275–77.

Prothero, Rowland E. "A Review of *The Writings of Oliver Wendell Holmes." The Quarterly Review.* Vol. CLXXIX, no. CCCLIX (Jan. 1895): 189–206.

"A review of 'Poems.' " *The Yale Literary Magazine.* Vol. 2, no. 4 (Feb. 1837): 113–24.

Small, Miriam Rossiter. *Oliver Wendell Holmes.* New York: Twayne, 1962.

Tilton, Eleanor M. *Amiable Autocrat: A Biography of Dr. Oliver Wendell Holmes.* New York: Schuman, 1947.

Wortham, Thomas. "Oliver Wendell Holmes." *American Writers.* Supp. 1, Vol. 1. New York: Charles Scribner's Sons, 1979. 299–319.

ELLEN STURGIS HOOPER (1812–1848)

Cecile Anne de Rocher

BIOGRAPHY

Ellen Sturgis, born in Boston, lived with her brother and five sisters, one of them poet Caroline Sturgis. Her wealthy, cultured parents came from old, prominent families: William Sturgis, the father, a legislator, had signed on shipboard as a youth and within a few years owned a very successful Boston company trading with China; and Elizabeth Marston Davis, the mother, was the daughter of a high-ranking Boston judge. With parents known for their learning, the young Sturgises lived and studied in an environment well suited to education and dedicated to progressive values, and at home, Ellen also met such illustrious household guests as the young Ralph Waldo Emerson.

Critic Eugenia Kaledin explains that the children's mother, a very independent woman for the times, spent considerable time apart from her husband, modeling for her daughters a value in seeking "self-fulfillment as many women do today" (19–20). In 1837, Sturgis married Robert Hooper, a physician of good family, making a match that disappointed her associates who considered the doctor his wife's intellectual inferior. Margaret Fuller, for example, described her friend as "that perfume . . . wasted on the desert wind" (175). The couple had three children: Edward, Ellen, and Marian, nick-named Clover, future wife of Henry Adams. Although a doting mother, Hooper remained, like her own mother, one of her family's many "assertive female personalities" (Kaledin 20). Through her sister Caroline, Hooper gained entrée into the Boston and Concord intelligentsia, including the Transcendentalist circle. She participated in her friend Margaret Fuller's famous conversations, exploring with other educated women such topics as the nature of femininity and masculinity, morality and selfhood, and obligations imposed by society on the sexes. Hooper contributed unsigned poems to *The Dial* and earned the esteem of her friends and acquaintances in the literati.

Ellen Sturgis Hooper died at age 36 of tuberculosis, the disease that had sickened her throughout adult life. Learning of her friend's untimely death, Margaret Fuller eulogized her: "[S]he was a woman of my years, of the most precious gifts in heart and genius. She had also beauty and fortune. She died at last of weariness and inanition. She never, to any of us, her friends, hinted her sufferings. But they were obvious in her poems, which, with great dignity, expressed a resolute but most mournful resignation" (193).

MAJOR WORKS AND THEMES

Under the editorship of Fuller and Emerson and in collections by friends, Hooper published her best-known poems, many of them untitled except by editors: "I slept and dreamed that life was Beauty," "Heart, heart, lie still," and "Better a sin which purposed wrong to none." True to her parenting and her group of friends, Hooper wrote indictments of the materialism rampant in her culture and time, and she criticized the emotional coldness that she found alarming and contrary to Romantic ideals. She grew close, however, despite his aloofness, to Emerson, whom she celebrated as a "[d]ry-lighted soul" in a poem, "To R. W. E." Elizabeth Peabody's *Aesthetic Papers* featured Hooper's poem "Hymn of a Spirit Shrouded," and Henry David Thoreau included her poem "The Wood-Fire" in his chapter of *Walden* titled "Economy." Ten of her poems appear in James Freeman Clarke's 1855 work, *The Disciples' Hymn Book,* and ten in John M. Forbe's *An Old Scrap-Book* (Cooke 55).

CRITICAL RECEPTION

Most scholars describe Hooper as one of few women in the Transcendentalist movement, with the exception of Myerson, who considers her an associate rather than an adherent (167). Cooke describes her poetry as "some of the best [*The Dial*] gave to the public" and her poem on beauty as "one of the finest poetical expressions of transcendentalism" (54). While any reader of the famed periodical could read the poems, only Hooper's acquaintances knew who wrote them. Her life as a poet remained private, restricted to her own circle.

After Hooper's death, Margaret Fuller wrote to Sarah Clarke about printing the poems, which Fuller had admired and published only a few years before in *The Dial* (172). The publication would not take place, however, until decades later, when Hooper's son, Edward, printed her poems in an untitled collection of at least 105 loose leaves and distributed the portfolios to his mother's old friends and associates. Boston Public Library, Brown University, and the Houghton Library all house copies. While few readers today know Hooper's name, they can find her most famous couplet on life, beauty, and duty in Bartlett's *Familiar Quotations.*

WORKS CITED

Cooke, George Willis. *An Historical and Biographical Introduction to Accompany* The Dial. Vol. II. New York: Russell and Russell, 1961.

Familiar Quotations. Comp. John Bartlett. 10th ed. rev. and enl. by Nathan Haskell Dole. Boston: Little Brown, 1919.

Fuller, Margaret. *Letters of Margaret Fuller.* Vol V. Ed. Robert N. Hudspeth. Ithaca: Cornell UP, 1988.

Kaledin, Eugenia. *The Education of Mrs. Henry Adams.* Philadelphia: Temple UP, 1981.

Myerson, Joel. *The New England Transcendentalists and the* Dial: *A History of the Magazine and Its Contributors.* Rutherford: Fairleigh Dickinson UP, 1980.

Thoreau, Henry David. *Walden and Resistance to Civil Government.* 2nd ed. Ed. William Rossi. New York: Norton, 1992.

BIBLIOGRAPHY

Works by Ellen Sturgis Hooper

"I slept and dreamed that life was Beauty." *The Dial* 1.1 (1840): 123.
"The Poor Rich Man." *The Dial* 1.2 (1840): 187.
"The Wood-Fire." *The Dial* 1.2 (1840): 193.
"The Poet." *The Dial* 1.2 (1840): 194.
"Wayfarers." *The Dial* 1.2 (1840): 216.
"To the Ideal." *The Dial* 1.3 (1841): 400.
"The Out-Bid." *The Dial* 1.4 (1841): 519.
"Farewell." *The Dial* 1.4 (1841): 544.
"The Hour of Reckoning." *The Dial* 2.3 (1842): 358.
"Sweep Ho!" *The Dial* 4.2 (1843): 245.
Clarke, James Freeman. *The Disciples' Hymn Book: A Collection of Hymns for Public and Private Devotion*. Boston: Horace B. Fuller, 1852.
Forbes, J. M. *An Old Scrap-Book*. Cambridge, MA: University Press, 1884.

Studies of Ellen Sturgis Hooper

The American Transcendentalists: Their Prose and Poetry. Ed. Perry Miller. Garden City: Doubleday, 1957.
Cooke, George Willis. *An Historical and Biographical Introduction to Accompany* The Dial. Vol. II. New York: Russell and Russell, 1961.
Kaledin, Eugenia. *The Education of Mrs. Henry Adams*. Philadelphia: Temple UP, 1981.
Myerson, Joel. *The New England Transcendentalists and the* Dial*: A History of the Magazine and Its Contributors*. Rutherford, NJ: Fairleigh Dickinson UP, 1980.
Notable American Women 1607–1950: A Biographical Dictionary. Vol II. Ed. Edward T. James. Cambridge, MA: Belknap, 1971.
Sturgis, Roger Faxton, ed. *Edward Sturgis of Yarmouth, Massachusetts 1613–1695 and His Descendants*. Boston: Stanhope, 1914.
Wider, Sarah Ann. "Ellen Sturgis Hooper." *Biographical Dictionary of Transcendentalism*. Ed. Wesley T. Mott. Westport, CT: Greenwood, 1996.

JULIA WARD HOWE (1819–1910)

Lori N. Howard

BIOGRAPHY

Julia Ward Howe was born on May 27, 1819, in New York City. Her father Samuel Ward descended from two colonial governors of Rhode Island and a Revolutionary War colonel. A successful partner in the banking firm Prime and Ward, Howe's father helped found New York University. Her mother, Julia Cutler Ward, was the grandniece of the American Revolutionary soldier, General Francis Marion, nicknamed the Swamp Fox. Julia Cutler Ward was a bright woman who wrote religious poetry. After marrying the much older Samuel Ward, her health quickly declined; she died in 1824 after the birth of her seventh child.

After their mother's death, the Ward children found themselves hemmed in by their father's sorrow and the solace he found in evangelical Christianity. Samuel Ward devoted himself to educating his children and protecting them from the outside world. As a result, Howe's education surpassed the standards for mid-nineteenth-century women. After approximately seven years of formal schooling, she decided she would learn more at home, where her father provided excellent tutors. Her subjects included the Romance languages, philosophy, history, literature, religion, chemistry, and math. Howe was an accomplished musician and wrote poetry and plays from a young age. When she was 14, a selection of her poetry appeared in the *American* magazine, and while still a teen she knew that writing would be her future (Clifford 23, 32).

Samuel Ward died in 1839 when Howe was 20. Although Howe entered two years of mourning, her world expanded immensely after the loss of her father's confining influence. She met a range of people with whom she shared literary, philosophical, and religious interests, including Henry Wadsworth Longfellow, Margaret Fuller, Ralph Waldo Emerson, Elizabeth Peabody, and Charles Dickens. Howe also attracted the romantic interest of several men. After a difficult courtship, in 1843 she married the respected doctor and philanthropist Samuel Gridley Howe, the director of the Perkins Institute for the Blind, who was 18 years her senior and would prove to be as restrictive as her father and considerably less supportive of her intellectual endeavors. Howe bore him six children over 16 years, suffering intense bouts of depression during the first decade of their marriage (Wurzel 248).

Samuel Howe disapproved of his wife's literary aspirations except when they found outlet in his projects. She contributed essays and editorials to the abolitionist journal the *Commonwealth,* which he edited (Wurzel 248). By the mid-1850s, Howe managed to balance her responsibilities at home and her interest in writing. Ticknor, Reed, and Fields published her first volume of verse, *Passion Flowers,* in 1854. Howe followed *Passion Flowers* with more poetry as well as travel narratives, plays, memoirs, and essays.

Howe composed her most beloved lyric, "The Battle Hymn of the Republic," when she accompanied her husband to Washington for a medical examination of the Union troops. On the slow journey home from a troop review interrupted by a Confederate attack, the Howes and their companions, including James Freeman Clarke, sang songs to pass the time. When they sang the popular "John Brown's Body," the troops on the road sang along. Freeman encouraged Howe to write a more inspiring set of lyrics to accompany the rousing ballad. When she woke at dawn, the new words began to form and she immediately wrote them down (*Reminiscences* 274–75). She was pleased with the song, and the lyrics appeared in the *Atlantic Monthly* as "The Battle Hymn of the Republic" in February 1862.

In 1863, Howe's youngest child died, and she sank into a depression followed by a renewed interest in philosophy and religion. Howe joined the Unitarian Church and started to lecture. She attended her first suffrage meeting in 1868; by the convention's end, she was president of the New England Woman Suffrage Association (Clifford 169–71, 178). She helped found the American Woman's Suffrage Association and edited its weekly *Woman's Journal.* She served as president of several additional organizations, including the New England Woman's Club, the American chapter of the Women's International Peace Organization, and the Association for the Advancement of Women (Wurzel 249).

Samuel Howe did not approve of his wife's public life but did support the suffrage cause. They managed to put their differences aside before his death, after which Howe depended on her speaking tours for income. She lectured internationally on suffrage, the plight of working women, and less frequently on literature (Wurzel 250). In 1908, she was the first woman elected to the American Academy of Arts and Letters. Howe died in her beloved Newport on October 17, 1910.

MAJOR WORKS AND THEMES

Howe's *Passion Flowers,* written in the sentimental and romantic mode, deals with a range of subject matter from slavery in America and political turbulence in Italy to more personal subjects reflecting her difficult life and intellectual and religious interests. Her next verse collection, *Words for the Hour* (1857), conveys her personal sorrows and addresses topical subjects such as Florence Nightingale's heroism. The play *Leonora, Or The World's Own* (1857) details the heroine's violent revenge on the Lothario who dishonored her. Howe's most popular work, the "Battle Hymn of the Republic," moves from the personal to the universal, calling for action in support of the righteous cause of the Union. Her biography of Margaret Fuller (1883) and her *Reminiscences* (1899) allow Howe to put forth independent, intellectual, and moral female role models in a time of great social change.

CRITICAL RECEPTION

By her early twenties, Howe had published two anonymous review articles written in a knowledgeable, authoritative voice that impressed the small circle who knew her identity, including family friends in publishing and Longfellow. *Passion Flowers,* by far her most popular and best-selling verse collection, garnered acclaim more for depth of feeling than for poetic skill. The New York *Tribune*'s George Ripley praised its emotional authenticity: "Nothing but the profound experience of a rarely endowed nature could give such an air of reality to such impassioned wails of suffering" (6). In a congratulatory letter, Emerson focused on the work's confessional nature rather than its poetic prowess.

Howe's editor found her second volume of verse, *Words for the Hour,* superior to *Passion Flowers,* but correctly predicted it would be less successful. *Later Lyrics* (1866) fared poorly; the *North American Review* faulted Howe for the repeated "introduction of some recondite fancy or some transcendental allusion" (644). The mixed reactions continued with *Leonora,* which shocked audiences with sexual content. One reviewer wrote that it was "full of literary merits and of dramatic defects" (quoted in *Reminiscences* 230). Her greatest renown followed the timely publication of "Battle Hymn of the Republic," which inspired and galvanized soldiers and civilians alike. Her later works of nonfiction, including the biography *Margaret Fuller* and her memoir *Reminiscences,* were respected and well received.

WORKS CITED

"Review of *Later Lyrics.*" *North American Review* 104 (April 1867): 644–46.
Clifford, Deborah Pickman. *Mine Eyes Have Seen the Glory: A Biography of Julia Ward Howe.* Boston: Little Brown, 1979.
Howe, Julia Ward. *Reminiscences.* 1899. Reprint, New York: New American Library, 1969.
Ripley, George. Review of *Passion Flowers.* [New York] *Tribune,* January 10, 1854.
Wurzel, Nancy R. "Julia Ward Howe (1819–1910)." *Nineteenth-Century American Women Writers: A Bio-Bibliographical Critical Sourcebook.* Ed. Denise D. Knight. Westport, CT: Greenwood, 1997. 247–53.

BIBLIOGRAPHY

Works by Julia Ward Howe

Passion Flowers. Boston: Ticknor, Reed & Fields, 1854.
Leonora, Or The World's Own: A Tragedy in Five Acts. New York: Baker & Godwin, 1857.
Words for the Hour. Boston: Ticknor & Fields, 1857.
A Trip to Cuba. 1860. New York: Praeger, 1969.
Later Lyrics. Boston: J. E. Tilton, 1866.
From the Oak to the Olive: A Plain Record of a Pleasant Journey. Boston: Lee & Shepard, 1868.
Margaret Fuller. 1883. Reprint, Westport, CT: Greenwood, 1970.
Is Polite Society Polite? And Other Essays. Boston: Lamson, Wolffe, 1895.
From Sunset Ridge: Poems Old and New. Boston: Houghton, 1898.
Reminiscences. 1899. New York: New American Library, 1969.

Work Edited by Julia Ward Howe

Sex and Education: A Reply to Dr. E. H. Clarke's "Sex in Education." 1874. Reprint, New York: Arno, 1972.

Studies of Julia Ward Howe

Bean, Judith Mattson. "Margaret Fuller and Julia Ward Howe: A Woman-to-Woman Influence." *Margaret Fuller's Cultural Critique: Her Age and Legacy.* Edited by Fritz Fleischmann. NY: Peter Lang, 2000. 91–108.

Clifford, Deborah Pickman. *Mine Eyes Have Seen the Glory: A Biography of Julia Ward Howe.* Boston: Little Brown, 1979.

Grant, Mary H. *Private Woman, Public Person: An Account of the Life of Julia Ward Howe from 1819–1868.* Brooklyn: Carlson, 1994.

Richards, Laura E. *Two Noble Lives: Samuel Gridley Howe and Julia Ward Howe.* Boston: Dana, 1906.

Williams, Gary. *Hungry Heart: The Literary Emergence of Julia Ward Howe.* Amherst: U of Massachusetts P, 1999.

Wurzel, Nancy R. "Julia Ward Howe." *Nineteenth-Century American Women Writers: A Bio-Bibliographical Critical Sourcebook.* Ed. Denise D. Knight. Westport, CT: Greenwood, 1997. 247–53.

WASHINGTON IRVING (1783–1859)

Joseph Rosenblum

BIOGRAPHY

The eleventh and youngest child of William and Sarah (Sanders) Irving, Washington Irving, named for the Revolutionary War hero, was born on April 3, 1783, at 131 William Street, New York City. At the age of 16 Irving began studying law, first with Henry Masterton and then with Josiah Hoffman. Irving fell in love with Hoffman's daughter Matilda, and he attempted for her sake to pursue a career in law. Though Irving was admitted to the bar on November 21, 1806, he never practiced. Matilda's death on April 26, 1809, was a terrible blow to Irving, but it freed him to pursue his other love, literature. At the age of 19 he had appeared in print for the first time in his brother Peter's *Morning Chronicle,* signing his letters "Jonathan Oldstyle, Gent."

In 1807 Irving, together with his brother William and James Kirke Paulding, created the magazine *Salmagundi.* Patterned after the early eighteenth-century British *Tatler* and *Spectator,* it ran for 20 issues (January 24, 1807–January 25, 1808). In it Irving coined the term "Gotham" for New York. With his brother Peter, Irving began a parody of Samuel Latham Mitchell's *A Picture of New York* (1807), which grew into *A History of New York* by "Dietrich Knickerbocker" after Peter left for Europe.

During the war of 1812 Irving edited and wrote for the *Analectic Magazine,* but when the conflict ended he joined his brother Peter in England (1815). When Irving's three-year effort to save the family business failed in 1818, he turned to his pen to earn a living. The first result was *The Sketch Book* (1819–20), which includes his two best-known stories, "Rip Van Winkle" and "The Legend of Sleepy Hollow." *The Sketch Book* concludes with a fictional visit to Bracebridge Hall, Yorkshire, for a traditional Christmas, anticipating Charles Dickens' evocation of the holiday by two decades. Irving's next book, *Bracebridge Hall* (1822), details the rural life of Squire Bracebridge, his family, and his neighbors. Both works enjoyed popular and critical acclaim. For *Tales of a Traveller* (1824), the London publisher John Murray II paid Irving £1,500. This title was not as well received as his earlier writings.

An invitation to serve in the American legation in Madrid and to translate documents relating to Columbus that had been collected by Don Martín Fernández de Navarette took Irving to Spain in 1826. Murray was not interested in publishing a mere translation, but he paid Irving 3,000 guineas for *A History of the Life and Voyages of Christopher Columbus* (1828) that Irving forged from these materials. Spain gripped Irving's fancy, figuring in about a third of his work. He was especially enchanted by Grenada, the last Moorish stronghold in the country. He first saw the city in 1828, and the following year he lived in the Alhambra for two and a half months, soaking up the atmosphere and legends of the palace and beginning work on *The Alhambra.*

Much as Irving loved Spain, he yearned to return to the United States. As a first step in that direction he accepted the appointment as secretary to the American legation in London (1829). During this period he received a gold medal from the Royal Society of Literature for his historical writings (1830) and an honorary Doctor of Civil Laws from Oxford University (1831). From June 1831 through April 1832 he was acting chargé d'affaires. In the latter part of April, he sailed to America, arriving in New York on May 21, 1832. Except for the four years he spent abroad as American minister to Spain, he remained in his native land for the rest of his life.

Back home, Irving quickly plunged into the nation's heartland, joining Indian Commissioner Henry Leavitt Ellsworth on a trip to Fort Gibson, Arkansas. Irving participated in a one-month side trip to Oklahoma to hunt buffalo. This expedition served as the basis for *A Tour of the Prairies* (1835), Irving's first contribution to the literature of western America. At the urging of his friend John Jacob Astor, Irving wrote an account of the fur-trader's abortive attempt to establish a colony in the Pacific Northwest, *Astoria,* published in 1836. Using the diaries of Benjamin Bonneville, Irving produced yet another work about the west detailing Bonneville's adventures in the Rockies.

In 1835 Irving bought a cottage near the Hudson River north of New York City. Calling it Sunnyside, he remodeled it in the neo-Gothic style he had admired at Sir Walter Scott's Abbotsford, which Irving had visited in 1817. In 1848 George Putnam published a complete edition of Irving's writings, an enterprise that made both men rich. Though Irving's productivity declined in his later years, he managed to write a five-volume biography of his namesake, George Washington. The fifth and final volume appeared a few months before Irving's death on November 28, 1859. On December 1, 1859, he was buried in the Tarrytown cemetery overlooking his beloved Hudson River.

MAJOR WORKS AND THEMES

In his first letter to appear in the *Morning Chronicle* (November 15, 1802), Irving contrasted the formality of ballroom behavior in the eighteenth century with the lack of contemporary manners. In both the letters of Jonathan Oldstyle and *Salmagundi,* Irving's praise of former times is to a large extent a mockery of the past and of those who admire it. Yet in the tradition of eighteenth-century burlesque to which these pieces belong, they accommodate what they mock. So, too, does Knickerbocker's *History of New York.* In part the work satirizes historians and current political affairs. William Kieff can be seen as Thomas Jefferson, with his wars by proclamation. The halcyon days of Wouter Van Twiller recall those of John Adams' administration. The burghers Olaffe Van Kortland, Abraham Hardenbroek, Jacobus Van Zandt, and Weinant Ten Broek are thinly disguised New York City politicos. Wynant Van Zandt, for example, served as an alderman in 1807, the year Irving began the book. Nonetheless, even the first version of the history casts a kindly nostalgic look backwards, not just to the Federalist era but more remotely to Dutch New Amsterdam. When Irving revised the text in the 1840s he intensified this sympathy for a bygone age.

In *The Sketch Book* this love of the past predominates. In "The Author's Account of Himself" Irving explained why he crossed the Atlantic. While granting America great natural beauty, he wrote that "Europe was rich in the accumulated treasures of age. Her very ruins told the history of times gone by, and every mouldering stone was a chronicle. I longed to wander over the scenes of renowned achievement—to tread as it were in the footsteps of antiquity—. . . to escape in short, from the common-place realities of the present, and lose myself among the shadowy grandeurs of the past" (4). Irving's pseudonymous Geoffrey Crayon therefore visits Little Britain, Westminster Abbey, and the Boar's Head Tavern in London, and he revels at Bracebridge Hall, where the squire attempts to preserve the customs of old England.

Irving's two most famous stories in this collection, though set in America, embody this nostalgia. "Rip Van Winkle" represents the transformation of America from pastoral innocence to "bustling" and "disputatious" commercialism. Standing in the Catskill mountains, Rip sees to the east a serene, pleasant world, while to the west lies "a deep mountain glen, wild, lonely and shagged, the bottom filled with fragments from the impending cliffs and scarcely lighted by the reflected rays of the setting sun" (33). The east represents the happy past, the west the ominous future. At the end of the story Rip returns to a world ruled by mutability, where one's very identity can be lost.

"Rip Van Winkle" is a tale of paradise lost. In "The Legend of Sleepy Hollow" paradise is regained. In Sleepy Hollow "population, manners, and customs, remain fixed, while the great torrent of migration and improvement, which is making such incessant changes in other parts of this restless country, sweeps by unobserved" (274). In "Rip Van Winkle" the Dutch burgher Nicholaus Vedder gives way to the entrepreneur Yankee; the giant oak that shaded the villagers has been replaced by the leafless liberty pole. Sleepy Hollow resists such change. Ichabod Crane is the only discordant element in this rustic Eden. In the midst of the farmers he is the entrepreneur, who wants the Van Tassel farm so he can mortgage it to speculate on other lands. But the past asserts itself in the guise of the legend of the headless horseman to drive out this interloper. Crane allegedly settles in New York City, a fitting place for one of his commercial bent.

Though Irving allowed the past to triumph in "The Legend of Sleepy Hollow," he recognized that Sleepy Hollow itself is the legend. The story's epigraph, drawn from James Thomson's *The Castle of Indolence,* reveals the ephemeral nature of the village:

A pleasing land of drowsy head it was,
Of dreams that wave before the half-shut eye;
And of gay castles in the clouds that pass,
Forever flushing round a summer sky. (272)

The land "was"; like any other dream, it could not endure.

Repeatedly Crayon in *The Sketch Book* discovers the impossibility of returning to the past. Westminster Abbey is decaying. Already moss obscures inscriptions and monuments, and Crayon recognizes that in time the Abbey will be no more than a pile of rubble. Little Britain, Crayon initially believes, "is a fragment of London as it was in its better days, with its antiquated folks and fashions" (198). However, after one of the Lambs attends a ball, the family rejects their former ways, and the Trotters ape their example. Soon "[t]he old games of Pope-Joan and Tom-come-tickle-me are entirely discarded; there is no such thing as getting up an honest country dance" (208).

In *The Sketch Book* Bracebridge Hall resembles Sleepy Hollow as "one of the few tolerable specimens that can now be met with, of the establishment of an English country gentleman of the old school"(15), where one can still enjoy old Christmas games in "their original form," old Christmas songs and old Christmas fare, and where the gardens exhibit "obsolete finery" (161). Yet the sketches here demonstrate that the unattractive present is making inroads into even this remote corner of England. In "English Gravity" Mr. Faddy has grown rich through steam engines and spinning jennies. His name and source of wealth expose him as an embodiment of the modern. With no respect for the past, he remodels his house and prosecutes representatives of the colorful old ways, such as Gypsies, whom Squire Bracebridge would protect. In another sketch, Dudley Castle has been converted into dark, satanic mills. Other tales show how the squire's attempts to revive hawking and preserve the rites of May-Day end in chaos. Nothing gold can stay.

This longing for and inability to hold on to the past inform the books that Irving wrote in Spain. His biography of Columbus recounts the fall of both the explorer himself and the Eden he discovered. Like Columbus, Boabdil, the last Moorish emperor, loses his paradise when Grenada falls to Ferdinand and Isabella. On May 23, 1829, Irving wrote to his friend Henry Brevoort that the Alhambra was "one of the most remarkable, romantic, and delicious spots in the world" (*Letters* 424), but it, too, was a monument to a lost world that was itself subject to time. Irving noted that in the garden of Lindaraxa "the alabaster had lost its whiteness, and the basin beneath overrun with weeds, had become the nestling-place of the lizard" (*Letters* 57–58). In "The Mysterious Chamber" Irving recalls Elizabetta of Farnese and her court. "Here was the scene of their transient gaiety and loneliness: . . . but what and where were they? Dust and ashes! Tenants of the tomb! Phantoms of the memory!" (59). At the end of *The Alhambra* Irving, like Boabdil, must leave his paradise to confront a less attractive present.

On one level Irving's books about the west celebrated America's expansion and introduced his readers to a region as unfamiliar and exotic to them as Moorish Spain. On another level, though, he was again seeking to preserve in literature a vanishing way of life. After returning east from Arkansas and Oklahoma, he explained to his brother Peter why he had undertaken this expedition.

The offer was too tempting to be resisted: I should have an opportunity of seeing the remnants of those great Indian tribes, which are now about to disappear as independent nations, or to be amalgamated under some new form of government. I should see those fine countries of the "far west," while still in a state of pristine wilderness, and behold herds of buffaloes scouring their native prairies, before they are driven beyond the reach of a civilized tourist. (letter of December 18, 1832, pp. 733–4)

The intent of *A Tour of the Prairies* is consistent with that of the other two volumes of *The Crayon Miscellany.* The second volume recounts Irving's visits to Abbotsford in 1817 and Newstead Abbey in 1831 and 1832. The piece on Abbotsford is a tribute to the recently deceased Sir Walter Scott; Newstead Abbey is a meditation on the dead George Gordon, Lord Byron. Visiting Annesley Hall, the home of Mary Ann Chaworth, Byron's first love, Irving finds the garden and house in ruins. When he goes to Parliament Oak, where he imagines that Robin Hood may have hidden, he hears the sound of the axe. "A noble agriculturalist; a modern utilitarian, who had no feeling for poetry or forest scenery" is destroying yet another part of the past (219). *Legends of the Conquest of Spain,* which completes the *Miscellany,* recalls the vanished Moorish kingdom.

The theme of a lost Eden informs even Irving's biography of Washington. As the nation drifted toward civil war, Irving dramatized the struggle that had forged the country: three of the five volumes focus on the Revolutionary War period. Irving emphasized Washington's rejection of sectionalism; he showed the general visiting all parts of the new nation. The life concludes with the hope that the memory of Washington will serve as a force to unite North and South as the colonies had joined in the eighteenth century in their quest for freedom.

CRITICAL RECEPTION

In 1863 Christian Schussele painted *Washington Irving and His Literary Friends at Sunnyside.* The illustration is a pleasant fiction, since it includes people Irving never met, and such a group never assembled at Irving's home. Nonetheless, the picture demonstrates the central place that Irving held in American letters at the time of his death.

In the *Edinburgh Monthly Review* in 1820 Sydney Smith sneered, "In the four corners of the globe, who reads an American book?" (79). The question was ill-timed, since in that year Irving's *Sketch Book* appeared in England to great praise. The *Quarterly Review* concluded its favorable review by stating, "We take leave of [Irving] with the highest respect for his talents, and a warm feeling of regard for those amiable and benevolent qualities of heart and mind which beam through every page of his book" (67). Francis Jeffrey in the *Edinburgh Monthly Review* and John Lockhart in *Blackwood's Edinburgh Magazine* joined the chorus of praise. Irving's contemporary admirers included Sir Walter Scott, Henry Wadsworth Longfellow, Nathaniel Hawthorne, and Charles Dickens. In 1841 Dickens wrote to Irving, "There is no living writer, and there are very few among the dead, whose approbation I should feel so proud to earn" (267). Hotels, steamboats, wagons, and cigars were named for him. Dearman, New York, changed its name to Irvington. Irving's funeral procession included 150 carriages; Napoleon III made a pilgrimage to Sunnyside.

After the Civil War Irving fell from favor. The rise of realism and naturalism made Irving's stories seem sentimental and old-fashioned. Stanley Williams's 1935 biography described his subject's work as "often trivial" and "outmoded" (xiii). Critics on the left in the first half of the twentieth century had no sympathy for Irving's elegance, gentility, and Federalist sympathies. In 1962 Edward Wagenknecht summarized the decline in Irving's reputation:

Irving's position in American literature is a rather odd one. So far as his name goes, he is still one of the most famous American authors. There is also a conventional honor paid to him as the Father of American Literature. Yet the living body of his work is small, and in the critical estimate generally placed upon his effort as a whole, he now ranks below any of the others who enjoy a comparable fame. (ix)

Yet the 1960s witnessed a revival of critical appreciation of America's first professional man of letters. Daniel G. Hoffman credited Irving with introducing myth, folklore, and history into the mainstream of American literature. William L. Hedges pointed out the darker tones in the work, stressing the themes of alienation, mutability, and loss, and Hedges linked Irving to the literary trends and concerns of the Romantic movement. Henry A. Pochmann's "Washington Irving: Amateur or Professional" in *Essays on American Literature in Honor of Jay B. Hubbell* rejected the notion that Irving was a lucky, talented amateur and emphasized his dedication to his craft. Eugene Current-Garcia confirmed in "Irving Sets the Pattern: Notes on Professionalism and the Art of the Short Story" that Irving deserves the credit, often given to Edgar Allan Poe, for inventing the American short story. In "'Soundings and Alarums': The Beginning of the Short Story in America" Current-Garcia added that Irving's sketches possess a realism previously lacking in the genre.

Irving has also regained a prominent position as a writer of nonfiction. John Harmon McElroy's "The Integrity of Irving's *Columbus*" defended Irving's accuracy as a biographer. Earl N. Harbert's "The Manuscripts of *A Chronicle of the Conquest of Grenada:* A Revised Census with Commentary" similarly noted that Irving was committed to historical accuracy. Richard H. Cracroft credits Irving with introducing the trans-Mississippi west as a literary subject. Allan Nevin called Irving's *Life of George Washington* "the first great American biography" (355). Douglas Sothall Freeman's standard *George Washington* (1948–1957) draws heavily on Irving's account. Andrew B. Myers' "The New York Years in Irving's *The Life of George Washington*" praised the biographer for presenting his subject as a human being rather than a saint. Irving's resurgence since the appearance of Hedges's seminal book is reflected in James W. Tuttleton's observation that despite Irving's limitations as a writer, "the wheat survives the separation of the chaff, because of the true greatness of a number of his stories which generations of readers would not willingly let die. . . . [T]he verdict of readers has been decisive, and [Irving] remains a presence not to be dismissed by accusations of 'gentility,' 'elegance,' 'sexism,' and 'old-fashionedness'" (11).

WORKS CITED

Dickens, Charles. *The Letters of Charles Dickens. Volume Two: 1840–1841.* Eds. Madeline House and Graham Storey. Oxford: Clarendon Press, 1969.

Irving, Washington. *The Crayon Miscellany.* Ed. Dahlia Kirby Terell. Boston: Twayne, 1979.

———. *Letters. Volume II, 1823–1838.* Eds. Ralph M. Aderman, Herbert L. Kleinfield, and Jenifer S. Banks. Boston: Twayne, 1979.

———. *The Sketch Book of Geoffrey Crayon, Gent.* Ed. Haskell Springer. Boston: Twayne, 1978.

Jeffrey, Francis. Review of *The Sketch Book. Edinburgh Monthly Review* 34 (August 1820): 160–176.

Nevin, Allan. *The Gateway to History.* Chicago: Quadrangle Books, 1963.

Review of *The Sketch Book. Quarterly Review* 25 (April 1821): 50–67.

Smith, Sydney. Review of Adam Seybert's *Statistical Annals of the United States of America. Edinburgh Monthly Review* 33 (January 1820): 69–80.

Tuttleton, James W., ed. *Washington Irving: The Critical Reaction.* New York: AMS Press, 1993.

Wagenknecht, Edward. *Washington Irving: Moderation Displayed.* New York: Oxford University Press, 1962.

Williams, Stanley T. *The Life of Washington Irving.* 2 vols. New York: Oxford University Press, 1935.

BIBLIOGRAPHY

Works by Washington Irving

Salmagundi; or, the Whim-whams and Opinions of Launcelot Langstaff, Esq. & Others (with William Irving and James Kirke Paulding). New York: D. Longworth, 1807–1808.

A History of New York, from the Beginning of the World to the End of the Dutch Dynasty . . . . New York & Philadelphia: Inskeep & Bradford; Boston: M'Ilhenny; Baltimore: Coale & Thomas; Charleston: Morford, Willington, 1809.

The Sketch Book of Geoffrey Crayon, Gent. New York: C. S. Van Winkle, 1819–1820; London: John Murray, 1820.

Bracebridge Hall, or the Humourists. A Medley. New York: C. S. Van Winkle; London: John Murray, 1822.

Tales of a Traveller. London: John Murray, 1824.

The Miscellaneous Works of Oliver Goldsmith, with an Account of His Life and Writings. Paris: Galignani/Didot, 1825. Biography revised in *The Life of Oliver Goldsmith, with Selections from His Writings.* New York: Harper, 1840; revised and enlarged again as *Oliver Goldsmith: A Biography.* New York: Putnam; London: John Murray, 1849.

A History of the Life and Voyages of Christopher Columbus. London: John Murray; New York: G & C. Carvill, 1828.

A Chronicle of the Conquest of Granada. Philadelphia: Carey, Lea & Carey; London: John Murray, 1829.

Voyages and Discoveries of the Companions of Columbus. London: John Murray; Philadelphia: Carey & Lea, 1831.

The Alhambra. London: Colburn & Bentley; Philadelphia: Carey & Lea, 1832.

A Tour of the Prairies, number 1 of *The Crayon Miscellany.* London: John Murray; Philadelphia: Carey, Lea & Blanchard, 1835.

Abbotsford and Newstead Abbey, number 2 of *The Crayon Miscellany.* London: John Murray; Philadelphia: Carey, Lea & Blanchard, 1835.

Legends of the Conquest of Spain, number 3 of *The Crayon Miscellany.* London: John Murray; Philadelphia: Carey, Lea & Blanchard, 1835.

Astoria, or, Enterprise Beyond the Rocky Mountains. London: Bentley, 1836; *Astoria, or Anecdotes of an Enterprise Beyond the Rocky Mountains.* Philadelphia: Carey, Lea & Blanchard, 1836.

Adventures of Captain Bonneville, or Scenes beyond the Rocky Mountains of the Far West. London: Bentley, 1837; *The Rocky Mountains: Or, Scenes, Incidents, and Adventures in the Far West. . . .* Philadelphia: Carey, Lea & Blanchard, 1837.

Biography and Poetical Remains of the Late Margaret Miller Davidson. Philadelphia: Lea & Blanchard, 1841.

Mahomet and His Successors. New York: Putnam; London: John Murray, 1850.

Chronicles of Wolfert's Roost and Other Papers. Edinburgh: Constable, Low; London: Hamilton, Adams; Dublin: M'Glashan, 1855; *Wolfert's Roost and Other Papers.* New York: Putnam, 1855.

Life of George Washington. New York: Putnam; London: Bohn, 1855–1859.

Spanish Papers and Other Miscellanies, Hitherto Unpublished or Uncollected. Ed. Pierre M. Irving. New York: Putnam/Hurd & Houghton; London: Low, 1866.

Studies of Washington Irving

Aderman, Ralph, ed. *Critical Essays on Washington Irving.* Boston: G. K. Hall, 1990.

Antelyes, Peter. *Tales of Adventurous Enterprise: Washington Irving and the Poetics of Western Expansion.* New York: Columbia University Press, 1990.

Bowden, Mary Weatherspoon. *Washington Irving.* Boston: Twayne, 1981.

Browdin, Stanley, ed. *The Old World and New World Romanticism of Washington Irving.* Westport, CT: Greenwood Press, 1986.

Cracroft, Richard H. *Washington Irving: The Western Works.* Boise, ID: Boise State University, 1974.

Current-Garcia, Eugene. "Irving Sets the Pattern: Notes on Professionalism and the Art of the Short Story." *Studies in Short Fiction* 10 (1973): 327–41.

———. " 'Soundings and Alarums': The Beginning of the Short Story in America." *Midwest Quarterly* 17 (1976): 311–28.

Egan, Hugh. "The Second-Hand Wilderness: History and Art in Irving's *Astoria.*" *American Transcendental Quarterly* 2 (1988): 253–70.

Harbert, Earl N. "The Manuscripts of *A Chronicle of the Conquest of Grenada:* A Revised Census with Commentary." *Bulletin of Research in the Humanities* 82.1 (1979): 124–9.

Hedges, William L. *Washington Irving: An American Study, 1802–1832.* Baltimore: Johns Hopkins University Press, 1965.

Hoffman, Daniel G. *Form and Fable in American Fiction.* New York: Oxford University Press, 1961.

Lockhardt, John. "On the Writings of Charles Brockden Brown and Washington Irving." *Blackwood's Edinburgh Magazine* 6 (February 1820): 554–61.

McElroy, John Harmon. "The Integrity of Irving's *Columbus.*" *American Literature* 50 (1978): 1–16.

Myers, Andrew B. "The New York Years in Irving's *The Life of George Washington.*" *Early American Literature* 11 (1976): 68–83.

Pochmann, Henry A. "Washington Irving: Amateur or Professional." In *Essays on American Literature in Honor of Jay B. Hubbell.* Ed. Clarence Gohdes. Durham, NC: Duke University Press, 1967. 63–76.

Rubin-Dorsky, Jeffrey. *Adrift in the Old World: The Psychological Pilgrimage of Washington Irving.* Chicago: University of Chicago Press, 1988.

Tuttleton, James W., ed. *Washington Irving: The Critical Reaction.* New York: AMS Press, 1993.

Wagenknecht, Edward. *Washington Irving: Moderation Displayed.* New York: Oxford University Press, 1962.

Williams, Stanley T. *The Life of Washington Irving.* 2 vols. New York: Oxford University Press, 1935.

HARRIET ANN JACOBS (c. 1813–1897)

Terry Novak

BIOGRAPHY

Although Harriet Ann Jacobs was born a slave around the year 1813 in Edenton, North Carolina, she was not consciously aware of her status as a slave until she was left an orphan at age six after her mother's death. For those first years of her life, though, Jacobs experienced the highly unusual condition of living as if she were a free child at the home of her legally free grandmother, Molly Horniblow, a woman who had worked to pay for her own freedom and who had a decidedly entrepreneurial spirit. Jacobs's removal from her grandmother's home to that of her mistress, Margaret Horniblow, was not altogether traumatic. Margaret Horniblow taught Jacobs to read and sew, and there is no evidence that Horniblow was a harsh mistress. It would have made a tremendous difference to Jacobs's life, however, if Margaret Horniblow had set her free upon Horniblow's death; instead, Margaret Horniblow willed the slave girl to three-year-old Mary Matilda Norcom. Consequently, the 11-year-old Jacobs was sent to the home of Mary's father, Dr. James Norcom. Though she remained in her hometown, Jacobs soon found herself in a world that compromised the high sense of morality her grandmother had instilled in her.

At the home of Dr. Norcom, Jacobs was subjected to repeated sexual harassment by Dr. Norcom. In a desperate attempt to save herself from being sexually abused, Jacobs, at age 16, took the drastic measure of beginning a sexual affair with Samuel Tredwell Sawyer, a white lawyer and neighbor of Dr. Norcom's. Jacobs believed that her involvement with Sawyer would protect her from further advances from Norcom; she also showed the determination to exercise some choice in that horrendous practice of slavery: the sexual control of a black woman by a white man.

Sawyer fathered Jacobs's two children, Joseph, who was born around 1829, and Louisa Matilda, who was born around 1833. Rather than stop Dr. Norcom's desire to control Jacobs sexually, her affair with Sawyer and the birth of her children only further enraged Norcom, who vowed always to remain her master. Jacobs feared that Norcom would sell her children in retaliation. To stop this from happening, she took another desperate measure. In 1835 Harriet Ann Jacobs ran away from the Norcom household, hoping that Norcom would find Jacobs's children a nuisance and sell them to their father. Norcom did indeed sell Joseph and Louisa to Sawyer, who did not, however, fulfill Jacobs's hope that he would in turn set them free. The children did, though, remain under the care of their great-grandmother, Molly Horniblow, at her home. Jacobs, in the meantime, spent seven years secretly watching over them from her hiding place in a tiny upper crawlspace in her grandmother's home. The children were unaware of their mother's whereabouts and so were unable to unwittingly give her away to Dr. Norcom, who continued to pursue her and visited Molly Horniblow in the hopes of finding the runaway slave.

Finally in 1842, after seven long years in a crawlspace that did not allow her to stand or freely move about, Jacobs escaped north. Her body bore the physical strain of her seven years of hiding, but her spirit remained strong and determined. It was Jacobs's plan to travel to New York and find her daughter Louisa, who had been taken North by Sawyer, then to send for her son Joseph. Jacobs found employment as a nanny in the New York home of the editor Nathaniel Parker Willis and resumed contact with her children. Dr. Norcom heard of Jacobs's whereabouts and traveled north more than once in pursuit of her. Jacobs confessed her fugitive slave status to her employer, Mary Stace Willis, who assisted both Jacobs and her daughter in fleeing to Boston in the fall of 1844. Shortly thereafter, Mrs. Willis died and Mr. Willis asked Jacobs to travel to England with him and his child to visit the family of his late wife. Jacobs spent nearly a year in England. Upon her return to America, she settled for a time in Rochester, New York, working with her brother in the abolitionist movement. For several months Jacobs lived in the home of the famous abolitionist and writer Amy Post. Jacobs became very close to Post, who convinced Jacobs of the importance of making her own story of slavery public.

Shortly after the enactment of the Fugitive Slave Law in 1850, Jacobs returned to New York and once again joined the Willis household as a nanny, this time for the second Mrs. Willis. Jacobs continued her friendship with Amy Post, who suggested Jacobs approach Harriet Beecher Stowe about helping her write her story. This advice yielded poor results. Stowe found Jacobs's story hard to believe and turned to Mrs. Willis for confirmation of the facts, much to Jacobs's mortification, as she had never shared her story with Mrs. Willis. At the same time Jacobs was dealing with Stowe, the now grown and married Mary Norcom was taking up where her father had left off. Mary Norcom Messmore came to New York confident that she would be able to take possession not only of Jacobs but of Jacobs's children as well. Mrs. Willis came to Jacobs's rescue and in 1852 purchased Jacobs and her children from Mary and her husband. Bitter that she could still be bought and sold, but also grateful to Mrs. Willis for granting her the freedom she could not have gained for herself, Jacobs became more determined to put her story to print.

This time Jacobs found help from the abolitionist Lydia Maria Child, who edited the book and wrote its preface. She also vouched for the veracity of the tale and the actual existence of its author, as was common with nineteenth-century slave narratives. After some problems with publishers, Jacobs saw her narrative, *Incidents in the Life of a Slave Girl, Written by Herself,* published in 1861. Although the title page of the book listed only Child as editor, it was widely acknowledged that Jacobs was the author of the book.

In the almost 10-year lapse between gaining her freedom and seeing *Incidents* published, Jacobs's life was far from uneventful. She published letters and accounts of her work in publications such as the *Freedmen's Record* and the *New York Tribune;* continued written correspondence with Amy Post and Lydia Maria Child; began a school for free blacks called Jacobs Free School in Alexandria, Virginia; lived in Georgia for a couple of years; traveled to England twice, once seeking publication of her book and once seeking donations for an orphanage; moved to Massachusetts and ran a boarding house there; and in the early 1880s moved to Washington, D.C., where she died on March 7, 1897.

MAJOR WORK AND THEMES

Harriet Ann Jacobs wrote only one piece of literature in her lifetime, her autobiographical *Incidents in the Life of a Slave Girl, Written by Herself.* Jacobs's work is an important contribution to the slave narrative genre. Before Jacobs's narrative, themes of sexual abuse and appropriation by white male slaveholders over their black female slaves had been largely ignored not only in the genre but also as a topic of discussion among abolitionists. Jacobs broke new ground in recounting with candor the details of her experience.

Incidents in the Life of a Slave Girl recounts Jacobs's life from childhood to the gaining of her freedom through the help of Mrs. Willis. Although the title page does not specifically list Jacobs as the author, Jacobs does take it upon herself to include her own preface to the narrative, in which she assures readers of the truth of her tale, asks pardon for her self-perceived incompetence, and reveals her purpose in writing the tale: " . . . I do earnestly desire to arouse the women of the North to a realizing sense of the condition of two millions of women at the South, still in bondage, suffering what I suffered, and most of them far worse" (1). As was her intent, Jacobs's major theme of sexual abuse in slavery predominates the book and makes it an especially interesting study when paralleled to the slave narratives of African American men such as Frederick Douglass.

Incidents is written in a style popular with nineteenth-century American women writers. The didacticism and sentimentalism of the day are easily found in Jacobs's work, illustrating both her knowledge of the contemporary literature and her familiarity with the philosophies of true Christian womanhood that pervaded the time period. And although Jacobs is careful to cover all of the major personalities of her life in the work, she is equally careful to protect their identities, giving each person a new name. Even Jacobs herself receives a new name, becoming Linda Brent in the narrative. For this reason one may sometimes find Brent, not Jacobs, listed as the author of the work.

Jacobs's slave narrative includes an introduction by her editor, Lydia Maria Child, the white abolitionist and writer, in which she vouches for Jacobs's talent and truthtelling. Child also provides an appendix with letters further corroborating the truth of Jacobs's work and speaking for the character of Jacobs herself. One letter is written by the white Amy Post, the other by George W. Lowther, whom Child describes as "a highly respectable colored citizen of Boston" (205).

Although the writing and the publishing of *Incidents* were not easy ventures—the narrative was not published until 1861, 19 years after Jacobs's escape from the South— Jacobs succeeded in leaving a work that has made an indelible mark on the canon of American literature in general and on the genre of the slave narrative in particular.

CRITICAL RECEPTION

Incidents in the Life of a Slave Girl, referred to popularly in Jacobs's time as simply *Linda,* with the longer title serving as a subtitle, enjoyed favorable reviews and good sales upon its first publication. Certainly the fact that the book was published the same year that the Civil War began added to its popularity, especially among northern abolitionists. By the time Jacobs died in 1897, however, the book had been all but forgotten. It wasn't until late in the twentieth century that Jacobs's narrative was resurrected and once again began to excite critics and scholars. This resurrection was initiated by Jean Fagan Yellin, who labored in the early 1980s to authenticate the facts of Jacobs's story and life. The 1987 edition of *Incidents*, edited and introduced by Yellin, began the resurgence of interest in the slave narrative. Yellin explains some of the difficulties encountered in the search for authorship over the years: "Some thought it a narrative dictated by a fugitive slave, Jacobs, to Child; others thought it an antislavery novel that Child had written in the form of a slave narrative" (xxv). One can see, given the particulars of the narrative's publication, how such theories could have been very popular. In any case, since 1987 much interest and attention have been given to the narrative, to the point where Jacobs has become the central figure in discussions of the woman's slave narrative and *Incidents* a popular choice in the classroom.

Much attention has been given to feminist issues and discussions of voice and empowerment in the narrative as well as to its place in the canon of slave narratives. Notable scholars such as Jean Fagan Yellin, Frances Smith Foster, and Martha Cutter, to name a few, have written much on these subjects in conjunction with *Incidents*, laying a solid foundation to future scholarship on the novel. Other scholars have continued the strands begun in the 1980s and have initiated new discussions of *Incidents*. Jennifer Rae Greeson describes the book as " . . . representative of a major shift in Northern conceptions of U.S. slavery in the antebellum period" (277), citing an antebellum interest in sexuality and slavery. Greeson also discusses at length Jacobs's identity as a writer: Is she truly a southern writer, as some have claimed her to be, or is she much more a northern, specifically, a New York, writer? Patricia Felisa Barbeito also focuses on sexuality and identity in the slave narrative, writing that "Jacobs's narrative repeatedly returns to what can be seen as the repressed and unarticulated primal scene of racial identity—the black female sexual and procreative body—and locates it at the heart of slavery's denial of personhood" (370).

Other scholars have been troubled by the role Lydia Maria Child played in the publication of *Incidents*. Bruce Mills, for instance, questions Child's editorial suggestion about the end of the book, a suggestion which Jacobs agreed to follow. Jacobs had originally ended the manuscript with a chapter on John Brown, the extremist abolitionist who was hanged for his violent efforts. Child urged Jacobs instead to end the book with a chapter on Jacobs's grandmother. Child preferred that Jacobs confine her discussion of violent acts against slavery to her chapter on the aftereffects of Nat Turner's Rebellion, just as she preferred Jacobs confine her most explicit chapters concerning her sexual abuse to one chapter. As Mills explains, Child was most likely wishing to avoid offending the sensibilities of the nineteenth-century reader, sensibilities that included an aversion to talk of violent rebellions against white people as well as to talk of white Christian men sexually abusing black women.

Many other scholars continue to examine and discuss *Incidents*. Jacobs's slave narrative by now enjoys a solid—perhaps even a pivotal—place in the canon of American literature. As more information about the culture and history of American slavery is revealed and as more pieces of slave literature are discovered, Harriet Ann Jacobs's *Incidents in the Life of a Slave Girl* promises to continue to be an important tool of comparison and information.

WORKS CITED

Barbeito, Patricia Felisa. " 'Making Generations' in Jacobs, Larsen, and Hurston: A Genealogy of Black Women's Writing." *American Literature* 70.2 (1998): 366–95.

Greeson, Jennifer Rae. "The 'Mysteries and Miseries' of North Carolina: New York City, Urban Gothic Fiction, and *Incidents in the Life of a Slave Girl.*" *American Literature* 73.2 (2001): 277–309.

Jacobs, Harriet Ann. *Incidents in the Life of a Slave Girl, Written by Herself.* Ed. Jean Fagan Yellin. Cambridge: Harvard UP, 1987.

Mills, Bruce. "Lydia Maria Child and the Endings to Harriet Ann Jacobs's *Incidents in the Life Of a Slave Girl.*" *American Literature* 62.2 (1992): 255–72.

Yellin, Jean Fagan. "Introduction." *Incidents in the Life of a Slave Girl, Written by Herself.* Cambridge: Harvard UP, 1987. vii–xxxiv.

BIBLIOGRAPHY

Work by Harriet Ann Jacobs

Incidents in the Life of a Slave Girl, Written by Herself. Boston, 1861. Reprint, Cambridge: Harvard UP, 1987.

Studies of Harriet Ann Jacobs

Accomando, Christina. " 'The Laws were Laid Down to Me Anew': Harriet Jacobs and the Reframing of Legal Fictions." *African American Review* 32.2 (1998): 229–45.

Barbeito, Patricia Felisa. " 'Making Generations' in Jacobs, Larsen, and Hurston: A Genealogy of Black Women's Writing." *American Literature* 70.2 (1998): 365–95.

Cutter, Martha J. "Dismantling 'The Master's House': Critical Literacy in Harriet Jacobs's *Incidents in the Life of a Slave Girl.*" *Callaloo* 19.1 (1996): 209–25.

Ferguson, SallyAnn H. "Christian Violence and the Slave Narrative." *American Literature* 68.2 (1996): 297–320.

Foreman, P. Gabrielle. "The Spoken and the Silenced in *Incidents in the Life of a Slave Girl* and *Our Nig.*" *Callaloo* 13.2 (1990): 313–24.

Foster, Frances Smith. *Written by Herself: Literary Production by African-American Women, 1746–1892.* Bloomington: Indiana UP, 1993.

Garfield, Deborah M., and Rafia Zafar, eds. *Harriet Jacobs and Life in the Incidents of a Slave Girl: New Critical Essays.* New York: Cambridge UP, 1996.

Greeson, Jennifer Rae. "The 'Mysteries and Miseries' of North Carolina: New York City, Urban Gothic Fiction, and *Incidents in the Life of a Slave Girl.*" *American Literature* 73.2 (2001): 278–309.

Kaplan, Carla. "Narrative Contracts and Emancipatory Readers: *Incidents in the Life of a Slave Girl.*" *The Yale Journal of Criticism* 6.1 (1993): 93–119.

Mills, Bruce. "Lydia Maria Child and the Endings to Harriet Jacobs's *Incidents in the Life of a Slave Girl.*" *American Literature* 62.2 (1992): 255–72.

Scorisio, Carolyn. " 'There is Might in Each': Conceptions of Self in Harriet Jacobs's *Incidents In the Life of a Slave Girl, Written by Herself.*" *Legacy* 13.1 (1996): 1–18.

Yellin, Jean Fagan. "Harriet Jacobs's Family History." *American Literature* 66.4 (1994): 765–67.

SYLVESTER JUDD (1813–1853)

John J. Han

BIOGRAPHY

Sylvester Judd III was born in Westhampton, Massachusetts, on July 23, 1813, the second son of Sylvester and Apphia Hall Judd. In 1822 the family moved to nearby Northampton, where Judd's father worked as proprietor and editor of a newspaper, the *Hampshire Gazette.* At age 13 Judd accepted Calvinistic Christianity during a religious revival. After attending Westfield and Hopkins academies in Massachusetts, he entered Yale College in 1832 to prepare himself for the Congregational ministry.

By the time he graduated from college in 1836, however, Judd had become increasingly skeptical about Calvinist doctrines. The following year, he broke with the Calvinism of his ancestors and embraced Unitarian faith; he declined the offer of a professorial position at Miami College, Ohio, because it was a Presbyterian institution. From 1836 to 1840 he studied theology at the Harvard Divinity School. After receiving his Bachelor of Divinity degree, he was installed as pastor of the East Parish (later Christ Church) in Augusta, Maine, a Unitarian church that he was to serve until his death. In 1841, Judd married Jane Elizabeth Williams by whom he had three daughters.

Judd dedicated himself to the advancement of sociopolitical causes such as pacifism, abolition, and temperance; he condemned capital punishment, mistreatment of the Native Americans and prisoners, and the American government's military intervention in foreign countries. One of the ideas that he advanced as a clergyman was a "birthright church," in which all people would automatically become church members by birth.

Judd was also a man of letters. The body of his writings encompasses such genres as religious discourse, novel, short story, and poetry. Most of Judd's works reached the public between 1844 and 1854. He published his most well-known work, the novel *Margaret,* in 1845. *Philo: An Evangeliad,* an eschatological epic, appeared in 1850. Also published in that year was Judd's second novel, *Richard Edney and the Governor's Family.*

Judd died at his home in Augusta, January 20, 1853, several weeks after he had developed a sudden illness on his way to Boston. He left behind a manuscript of a drama in five acts, *The White Hills, An American Tragedy.*

MAJOR WORKS AND THEMES

The four major writings by Sylvester Judd include *Margaret, Philo: An Evangeliad, Richard Edney and the Governor's Family,* and the unpublished *The White Hills, An American Tragedy.* All of them embody the author's Unitarian ideals: the innate goodness of humanity, sociopolitical reform, and construction of a utopian society. *Margaret* was written "to promote the course of liberal Christianity, or, in other words, of a pure Christianity" (qtd. in Hall 353). The protagonist is an orphan raised by a backwoods Maine family. She encounters a Unitarian, Mr. Evelyn, who teaches her that Christ came to this world to save humanity from all kinds of social evils. Eventually the two characters fall in love, are married, and transform their village into a Christian Utopian community.

The protagonist of *Philo: An Evangeliad,* a Christian, visits various places under the guidance of the Archangel Gabriel. The Devil informs Philo that literal hell is nonexistent and that evil originates in the human heart, not in the Devil himself. The work culminates in a vision in which human hearts regain Christian love and all forms of injustice vanish from society.

The hero of *Richard Edney and the Governor's Family* is a well-bred Christian who models righteous living. He rebukes a dishonest fellow worker, Clover, and defends moral imperatives such as the abolition of slavery, temperance, and charity work. At the end of the novel, Richard marries Melicent, a Christian woman, and the unrepentant Clover is killed by lightning.

The White Hills, An American Tragedy focuses on Normand who resents his poverty. Mammon, the evil spirit of riches, introduces him to Vafer, the witch-mother, whose daughter Normand marries. On the steps of a church, however, the protagonist is touched by the mercy of God and gains a Christian perspective on material wealth.

CRITICAL RECEPTION

Twentieth-century criticism of Judd's literature is scarce. Upon publication, however, *Margaret* received a fair amount of critical attention. Some of the prominent literary figures praised it highly. James Russell Lowell, for instance, viewed *Margaret* as "the most emphatically *American* book ever written" in its theme, setting, plot, characterization, style, and structure. According to Lowell, the novel was "the first Yankee book/With the *soul* of Down East in't" (Smith 129, 200). Margaret Fuller called the novel "a work of great power and richness, a genuine disclosure of the life of mind and the history of character" (Wade 370). In contrast, W. B. O. Peabody found problems with the novel's artistic faults and misguided didacticism; the kind of utopian society Judd envisioned was "not only dreary and disgusting, but one-sided and unjust" (W. B. O. Peabody 103, 107).

Reviews of Judd's other works were scant and at best lukewarm. According to A. P. Peabody, the author of *Margaret* and *Philo: An Evangeliad* "personates alternately the copyist and the poet." The author of *Philo: An Evangeliad* "is too familiar with the best literature of all times, not to have the canons of good taste at his easy command" (A. P. Peabody 434, 440). *Richard Edney and the Governor's Family* received an even harsher criticism. A reviewer, A. W. Abbott, noted the disturbing presence of "constant shocks and distractions, occasioned by prevalent bad taste in style, and by many dramatic absurdities" (494).

Several book-length studies of Judd have appeared since his death. Among the most useful are Arethusa Hall's *Life and Character of the Rev. Sylvester Judd* (1854; reprinted in 1971), Francis B. Dedmond's *Sylvester Judd* (1980), and Richard D. Hathaway's *Sylvester Judd's New England* (1981). Hall's work, the earliest biography of the author, is an excellent source of information on Judd's life and writing. *Sylvester Judd* is perhaps the best introductory book which combines detailed description and analysis of Judd's works. Hathaway's book examines Judd's literary world in connection with his New England heritage.

WORKS CITED

Abbott, A. W. Rev. of *Richard Edney and the Governor's Family. North American Review.* April 1851: 493–505.

Hall, Arethusa. *Life and Character of the Rev. Sylvester Judd.* Port Washington, NY: Kennikat Press, 1971.

Peabody, A. P. Rev. of *Philo: An Evangeliad. By the Author of "Margaret: A Tale of the Real and Ideal." North American Review.* April 1850: 433–43.

Peabody, W. B. O. Rev. of *Margaret, a Tale of the Real and the Ideal, Blight and Bloom; Including Sketches of a Place Not before Described, Called Mons Christi. North American Review* Jan. 1846: 102–41.

Wade, Mason, ed. *The Writings of Margaret Fuller.* By Margaret Fuller. New York: Viking Press, 1941.

BIBLIOGRAPHY

Works by Sylvester Judd

Novels

Margaret. A Tale of the Real and Ideal, Blight and Bloom; Including Sketches of a Place Not before Described, Called Mons Christi. Boston: Jordan and Wiley, 1845. Republished as *Margaret: A Tale of the Real and the Ideal, Blight and Bloom.* Upper Saddle River, NJ: Gregg Press, 1968.

Richard Edney and the Governor's Family. A Rus-Urban Tale, Simple and Popular, Yet Cultured and Noble, Of Morals, Sentiment, and Life, Practically Treated and Pleasantly Illustrated . . . By the Author of "Margaret," and "Philo." Boston: Phillips, Sampson and Company, 1850.

Short Stories

"The Outlaw and His Daughter." *Yale Literary Magazine* 1 (June 1836): 155–61.

Prose

"What Is Truth?" *Yale Literary Magazine* 1 (June 1836): 129–31.

A Young Man's Account of His Conversion from Calvinism. A Statement of Facts. Boston: James Munroe & Co., 1838.

The Little Coat: A Sermon. No. 9. Cincinnati: American Reform Tract and Book Society, 1840.

The Beautiful Zion: A Sermon Preached July 4, 1841. Augusta, ME: Severance and Dorr, Printers, 1841.

A Moral Review of the Revolutionary War, Or Some of the Evils of That Event Considered. A Discourse Delivered at the Unitarian Church, Augusta, Sabbath Evening, March 13ᵗʰ, 1842. With an Introductory Address, and Notes. Hallowell, ME: Glazier, Masters & Smith, Printers, 1842.

A Discourse Touching the Causes and Remedies of Intemperance. Preached February 2, 1845. Augusta, ME: William T. Johnson, Printer, 1845.

"Worth of the Soul." *Sermons on Christian Communion, Designed to Promote the Growth of the Religious Affections, by Living Ministers.* Ed. T. R. Sullivan. Boston: William Crosby and H. P. Nichols, 1848. 24–37.

The True Dignity of Politics. A Sermon . . . Preached in Christ Church, Augusta, May 26, 1850. Augusta, ME: William T. Johnson, Printer to the State, 1850.

Williams, Joseph H., ed. *The Birthright Church: A Discourse by the Late Rev. Sylvester Judd . . . Designed for "Thursday Lecture" in Boston, Jan. 6, 1853.* By Sylvester Judd. Boston: Crosby, Nichols, and Company, 1853.

Williams, Joseph H., ed. *The Church: In a Series of Discourses.* By Sylvester Judd. Boston: Crosby, Nichols, and Company, 1854.

"The Dramatic Elements in the Bible." *Atlantic Monthly* August 1859: 137–53.

Verse

Philo: An Evangeliad. By the Author of "Margaret: A Tale of the Real and Ideal." Boston: Phillips, Sampson and Company, 1850.

Drama: Unpublished Manuscript

The White Hills, An American Tragedy.

Studies of Sylvester Judd

Brockway, Philip Judd. *Sylvester Judd (1813–1853): Novelist of Transcendentalism.* Orono, ME: University [of Maine] Press, 1941.

Dedmond, Francis B. *Sylvester Judd.* Boston: Twayne, 1980.

Hall, Arethusa. *Life and Character of the Rev. Sylvester Judd.* Port Washington, NY: Kennikat Press, 1971.

Hathaway, Richard D. *Sylvester Judd's New England.* University Park: Pennsylvania University Press, 1981.

Peabody, A. P. Rev. of *Philo: An Evangeliad. By the Author of "Margaret: A Tale of the Real and Ideal."* April 1850: 433–43.

Peabody, W. B. O. Rev. of *Margaret, a Tale of the Real and the Ideal, Blight and Bloom; Including Sketches of a Place Not before Described, Called Mons Christi. North American Review* Jan. 1846: 102–41.

Smith, Herbert F., ed. *Literary Criticism of James Russell Lowell.* By James Russell Lowell. Regents Critics Series. Lincoln, NE: University of Nebraska Press, 1969.

Wade, Mason, ed. *The Writings of Margaret Fuller.* By Margaret Fuller. New York: Viking Press, 1941.

CAROLINE M. KIRKLAND (1801–1864)

Jana A. Bouma

BIOGRAPHY

On January 11, 1801, in New York City, Samuel Stansbury and Elizabeth Alexander Stansbury celebrated the birth of a daughter, Caroline Matilda Stansbury. Caroline, the eldest of eight surviving children, joined a family that often enjoyed prosperity but also experienced the economic turmoil so characteristic of the nineteenth century United States. As a young man, Samuel Stansbury had struggled to establish himself in business; he eventually obtained a lucrative post with an insurance company. Then, after Caroline's eighth birthday, having purchased a business that failed, Samuel found himself confined for his debts for nearly a year. Soon after his release, he obtained a position with a New York bank and the family enjoyed a long stretch of comfort and security. Samuel Stansbury despised pretension but also harbored his own class sensitivities; Caroline would share those traits.

Samuel's letters suggest that he was an affectionate, genial father, attentive to his children's education and proud especially of his precocious eldest daughter. Samuel's father had been a satiric poet; as a letter writer, Samuel himself exhibited wit and a flair for metaphor.

Elizabeth Stansbury was the busy, competent head of a large household that often sheltered extended family members. Her single surviving letter reveals a touch of irreverence for the ideal of feminine submissiveness. In her snatches of spare time, Elizabeth was also a writer.

Young Caroline studied at several private schools, most notably that of her Quaker aunt, Lydia Philadelphia Mott. A widow, a noted teacher, and a preacher and leader within the Quaker movement, Mott provided a model for Caroline of independent, actively engaged womanhood. As the founder of a girls' school in remote Skaneateles, New York, Mott may also have given Caroline an early taste of frontier life. Caroline probably apprenticed as a teacher under her aunt's supervision. From Mott, Caroline (who eventually became a Unitarian) also gained a lifelong sense of the Christian God as an accessible, merciful creator. She would emulate her aunt's dedication to education and to social service.

In 1821, Caroline became engaged to William Kirkland, a tutor in the classics at Hamilton College in Clinton, New York. In 1822, Caroline's father died. Elizabeth Stansbury soon moved her large family to Clinton, where Caroline, who likely postponed her marriage to assist her family, could be near her fiancé. Four of Caroline's brothers attended college; Caroline did not. Nonetheless, she succeeded in acquiring a broad knowledge of Latin, French, German, and English literature.

In 1823, William Kirkland was rendered nearly deaf by a cannon explosion. Unsure of his future, William eventually departed for graduate study in Europe. Upon his return in 1828, William and Caroline finally wed. They moved to Geneva, New York, and founded a boarding school for boys—the first in a series of professional partnerships that characterized an unusually egalitarian marriage. In Geneva, Caroline also gave birth to three daughters and a son. One daughter died in infancy.

In 1836, with Caroline expecting another child, the Kirklands moved to the frontier town of Detroit, Michigan, to direct the new Detroit Female Seminary. In Detroit, William served in the Underground Railroad and became a leader in the state antislavery movement. Within a year, the Kirklands began purchasing frontier lands in Putnam Township, 60 miles (three days' travel) west of Detroit. William platted a new village—Pinckney—and built a grist mill and a tavern. By the fall of 1837, the Kirklands and their extended family (including two of Kirkland's brothers), having accumulated some 1,300 acres of land, moved to Pinckney. As she began her frontier adventure, Caroline mourned the recent death of yet another daughter and the death of her mother. Around this time, she also gave birth to her second son.

The struggles of a genteel woman seeking her place in a rough-and-tumble frontier community provided both the impetus and the material for Kirkland's first book, *A New Home, Who'll Follow? or, Glimpses of Western Life* (1839), published under the pseudonym, "Mrs. Mary Clavers, an actual settler." The book achieved instant celebrity, and *Forest Life* followed in 1842. Kirkland's stories also began appearing in East Coast periodicals, and she abridged and edited Jonathan Dymond's *Principles of Morality* for use as a school text. While busy with these projects, Kirkland gave birth to a son. Within a few months the baby sickened, and soon Kirkland mourned the loss of a third child. Meanwhile, Kirkland bore the wrath of neighbors incensed at her satiric depiction of their community.

After six years in Pinckney, their fortunes devastated by swindle, by the national economic panic of 1837, by a statewide monetary crisis, and by catastrophic weather, the Kirklands abandoned the frontier and moved to New York City. William Kirkland sought work as a writer and editor, and Caroline continued writing while she conducted a girls' school in her home. (Her third frontier book, *Western Clearings,* appeared in 1845.) The Kirklands also joined New York's literary and publishing circles, attending the salon of Anne Lynch and becoming lifelong friends with editor Evert Duyckink, poet William Cullen Bryant, writers Catharine Sedgwick and Nathaniel P. Willis, and publisher George Palmer Putnam. Kirkland also formed a deep friendship with the influential Unitarian minister the Rev. Henry Bellows. Plunging into social activism, Caroline joined the prison reform movement. At a time when "fallen women" were generally shunned and abandoned to their fate, she helped to found the Women's Prison Association of New York and the Home for Discharged Female Convicts. In 1845, Kirkland published her most outspoken statement on women's rights, her introduction to the American edition of Marion Reid's *A Plea for Woman*. Kirkland used satire, pathos, and vivid metaphor to argue for women's property rights and to disparage men's tyrannical anxieties about women's sphere.

In 1846, William Kirkland died in an accidental drowning. Kirkland, left to support herself and four children, continued teaching and writing and also took on the editorships of two new periodicals: the *Christian Inquirer* (an organ of the New York Unitarian movement) and the *Union Magazine of Literature and Art*. Similar to many of its contemporaries, the *Union* advocated a distinctly American body of literature and art. Frustrated by the obstacles to creating a quality literary magazine, Kirkland scrambled for "name" contributors (herself contributing editorial columns, western sketches, and book reviews) and advocated a broad range of reading, rejecting the idea of separate reading lists for men and women.

In 1848, Kirkland arranged to tour Europe as a correspondent for the *Union*. She spent six months visiting Europe's cities and monuments, sending back reflections upon its people, places, cultures, and artistic masterpieces, and upon her own adventures as a woman traveler.

After Philadelphian John Sartain purchased the *Union* in 1848, Kirkland played a smaller role at the magazine, finally departing in 1851. Between 1849 and 1854, she published her collected travel essays (*Holidays Abroad*) and three more volumes of collected periodical pieces.

In the 1850s, Kirkland continued publishing in magazines, though at a slowed pace, most notably producing review essays on literature and culture for the *American Review*. In 1853, she published *The Helping Hand: Comprising an Account of the Home for Discharged Female Convicts* to raise funds for the halfway house. Responding to growing dissention over the slavery question, she became more intensely interested in national history, and turned to the genre of biography. Inspired by the work of historian Elizabeth Ellet, Kirkland set out to revise biography's exclusive focus upon the public— particularly the military—lives of American heroes. Her biography of George Washington (1857), marketed as a school text, emphasized Washington's domestic and personal character and incorporated a chapter on Washington's views concerning slavery. Kirkland also published three antislavery magazine essays during this period.

In 1857, Kirkland built a spacious home for herself in Perth Amboy, New Jersey, near her friends, associationists Marcus and Rebecca Spring and abolitionists Sarah Grimké and Angelina Grimké Weld. As civil war approached in 1860, Kirkland moved back to New York City and worked for the Union cause. She joined a grassroots women's movement that led to the formation of the United States Sanitary Commission, a quasi-governmental agency that regularized the supplying and medical care of the Union Army. Kirkland visited Washington, D. C., and various Army camps, as well as operated a sewing room that produced thousands of shirts and linens for the troops.

During 1864, Kirkland organized, traveled, sewed, and wrote in support of the Metropolitan Sanitary Fair, an exposition that would raise more than one million dollars for the Union cause. On April 6, 1864, on the second full day of the Fair, Kirkland died of a stroke at age 64. An obituary in William Cullen Bryant's *Evening Post* praised Kirkland as "among the most original and vigorous of all our female authors" ("Death of Mrs. Kirkland" 237), while also praising her power of conversation and her devotion to social causes. Kirkland's eulogist, Dr. S. K. Lothrop, praised the "originality and freshness" and "masculine grasp of . . . theme" ("Death of Mrs. Kirkland" 316) in Kirkland's writings, but reserved his highest praise for Kirkland as an influential and devoted educator.

MAJOR WORKS AND THEMES

Kirkland wrote from the privileged position of a well-to-do, educated white woman who deputed to herself both the duty and the privilege of guiding an emergent national culture. Though Kirkland retained her allegiance to the white middle class, she is most notable for the ways in which her writings probe the collisions, discontinuities, and hypocrisies of American culture. In *Forest Life,* for example (as in many of Kirkland's works), both genres and cultures collide: the village sketch meets the courtship tale, the epistolary narrative, the essay, and the poem, creating a multivocal examination of frontier landscape, culture, and politics that anticipates Margaret Fuller's *Summer on the Lakes.* In *Holidays Abroad,* Kirkland narrates her own collisions with European life. An encounter with an English nun jars Kirkland's complacent, middle-class Protestantism, while Kirkland's physical adventures on the sea and in the mountains contradict Victorian notions of feminine weakness and vulnerability.

Most sophisticated of all, perhaps, was Kirkland's deployment of humor and satire. At a time when critics often set strict limits of feminine delicacy and demureness, Kirkland sharpened her satiric pen. She took aim at ignorance, corruption, and hypocrisy, whether those vices appeared at a village sewing party or in a public debate over women's rights. Lacing her critiques with charming self-deprecation, Kirkland lampooned frontier land sharks and racist Indian traders. If she was sometimes smug in caricaturing her uncouth western neighbors, she also satirized her own smugness and frontier incompetence. Kirkland seldom spoke out directly on political issues, but when she addressed women's rights in her introduction to *A Plea for Woman,* her anger erupted in satiric metaphor. She likened repressed womanhood to a gaggle of hens confined to a basket, and the Victorian ideal woman to "'The Good Woman' . . . aptly pictured upon sundry signposts in England, as a woman without a head," an ideal that produced "mere machines of habit and instinct, fit for drudgery, but not companionship" (Hamilton viii).

Despite strong personal feelings about racial injustice, Kirkland wrote relatively little on issues of race. This silence is especially significant given Kirkland's experiences on the interracial Michigan frontier, and her privately expressed antislavery sentiments. *A New Home,* with the exception of several brief but significant passages, elides the presence of Native Americans in Michigan. As the Civil War approached, Kirkland did publish three brief antislavery pieces, and *Forest Life,* though not an antislavery text, was serialized in 1842 in Lydia Maria Child's *Anti-Slavery Standard.* But Kirkland's most extended treatment of African American issues, "Liberia College," advocated voluntary emigration of free African Americans to Liberia. By emigrating, Kirkland argued, African Americans would escape America's insurmountable racism and achieve full development. Kirkland failed to acknowledge that such separation would also protect whites from the conflicts of an interracial society. Kirkland chastised herself for her own lack of courage in speaking out on controversial issues. Her reluctance to speak publicly on race may have reflected her own sense of vulnerability, especially after William's death. It also reflected her own ambivalence: Though she critiqued whiskey traders' exploitation of Native Americans, for example, she and William were among the thousands of settlers who rushed into Michigan, displacing, farm by farm, the Native Americans who still lived on Michigan lands.

Kirkland was a resourceful and creative writer. Aware of reader sensibilities, skillful at negotiating the marketplace, she often shaped her writing to fit the narrow limits of nineteenth-century publishing. She did not, however, bow thoughtlessly to such pressures. Rather, she explored multiple avenues of expression, blending and expanding genres, interweaving satire and self-deprecation. Whether she wrote as a frontier adventurer, a social critic, or a magazine editor, she always acted out of the sentiment that she expressed to a friend: "I shall try to do some good with my pen" (letter to Henry Bellows 27 May 1849; *Letters*).

CRITICAL RECEPTION

Upon its publication in 1839, *A New Home* created an "undoubted sensation" in both the United States and England (Poe 1181), gaining praise for its racy humor, its vividness, its perceived authenticity in portraying frontier life, and the author's "intellectual power" (Conway 206). By 1855, the book had gone through five editions in the United States and numerous editions (many unauthorized) in England. Critics also praised Kirkland's sequel, *Forest Life*. In 1847, the *Literary World* named Kirkland, along with N. P. Willis, Edgar Allan Poe, William Cullen Bryant, and James Fenimore Cooper, as the "splendid exceptions"—writers who could command 50 dollars for a single magazine contribution ("Pay of Authors" 221).

Kirkland remained a respected figure in New York literary circles, but her later New York writings gained less critical attention, in part because she was often required to write quick, saleable magazine pieces—often, conventional romances and sketches—to support her family. As her fictional writing became more conventional, however, Kirkland continued to speak out through essays on literature, American history, and social issues. Critics ignored her most daring cultural critiques—her introduction to *A Plea for Woman* and her *The Helping Hand*. At Kirkland's death, her eulogists acknowledged her literary contributions, but her work was already subsiding into obscurity.

During the twentieth century, a thesis by Louise Knudsen and a dissertation by Langley Keyes unearthed important primary materials while presenting Kirkland as a frontier writer and as a minor realist. Audrey Roberts's 1976 edition of Kirkland's letters, with detailed notes and a substantial introduction, provides an invaluable resource in reconstructing Kirkland's career. William Osborne's dismissive study of Kirkland's career, published in 1972, served mostly to obscure Kirkland's significance.

In the 1980s, Kirkland returned to the attention of literary scholars through such critics as Annette Kolodny, who in *The Land Before Her: Fantasy and Experience of the American Frontier, 1630–1820*, examined women writers' struggles to find a voice within the gendered imagery of the frontier. Kolodny credited Kirkland with producing the "first sustained expression of American literary realism," a realism that "derived from a *woman's* need to reject . . . the available *male* fantasies" (157). An edition of *A New Home* edited by Sandra Zagarell appeared in 1990 as part of Rutgers' American Women Writers series. Excerpts of *A New Home* have been included in major anthologies, and the book is widely taught in college courses on American literature, women's literature, frontier writing, and nature writing.

A New Home (the only Kirkland book currently in print) has received significant critical attention in studies of frontier writing and women's writing. In her introduction to *A New Home*, Sandra Zagarell highlights Kirkland's critique of masculine frontier values, and the way in which Kirkland's narrator comes to embody a "genuinely bicultural stance" (xxxvii), identifying with both her western community and her middle-class, eastern audience. Brigitte Georgi-Findlay, in her discussion of women's frontier writing, characterizes *A New Home* as an "anti-conquest" (35) tale—one that denies the protagonist's goal of conquest and dominance while portraying the achievement of that goal. Kristie Hamilton has analyzed Kirkland's deployment of the sketch, a genre that marked the transition from romanticism to modernity, expressing the "psychological and social fragmentation" that characterized nineteenth-century life (31).

Scattered attention has been given to other aspects of Kirkland's career, particularly her magazine pieces and her European travel writings. Erika Kreger has produced a nearly comprehensive bibliography of works by and about Kirkland.

Jana Bouma's dissertation, "Caroline M. Kirkland: A Literary Life," provides the first thorough discussion of Kirkland's 25-year literary career. Bouma highlights Kirkland's complex engagement with her culture through her writing, her editing, her membership in New York literary and publishing circles, and her benevolent activism.

Kirkland continues to be known almost exclusively as a frontier writer, but *A New Home* was only the beginning of a productive, 25-year literary career. Scholars who explore Kirkland's work as a satirist and a magazinist, her connections to the men and women of New York's publishing world, and the intersections between Kirkland's writing and activism will add to our knowledge not only of Kirkland's career, but of mid-nineteenth-century American life and culture.

WORKS CITED

[Conway, Cornelius]. "Clavers's Glimpses of Western Life." *North American Review* 50 (1840): 206–13.

"Death of Mrs. Kirkland." *New York Evening Post* 6 April 1864. Reprint, *Littel's Living Age* 81 (30 April 1864), 237.

Georgi-Findlay, Brigitte. *The Frontier of Women's Writing: Women's Narratives and the Rhetoric of Westward Expansion.* Tucson: U of Arizona P, 1996.

Hamilton, Kristie. *America's Sketchbook: The Cultural Life of a Nineteenth-Century Literary Genre.* Athens: Ohio UP, 1998.

Kirkland, Caroline M. "Introduction. By the American Editor." *A Plea for Woman.* By Mrs. Hugo [Marion] Reid. New York: Farmer and Daggers, 1845. v–xxv.

———. "The Letters of Caroline M. Kirkland." Ed. Audrey J. Roberts. Dissertation. University of Wisconsin-Madison, 1976.

Kolodny, Annette. *The Land Before Her: Fantasy and Experience of the American Frontier, 1630–1820.* Chapel Hill: The U of North Carolina P, 1984.

"Pay of Authors." *Literary World* 1 (10 April 1847): 221.

Poe, Edgar Allan. "The Literati of New York City." *Edgar Allan Poe: Essays and Reviews.* Ed. G. R. Thompson. New York: The Library of America, 1984.

Untitled. *New York Evening Post* (11 April 1864). Reprinted in Keyes, Langley Carleton, dissertation, "Caroline M. Kirkland: A Pioneer in American Realism." Harvard University, 1935. 314–16.

Zagarell, Sandra. Introduction. *A New Home, Who'll Follow? or, Glimpses of Western Life.* By Caroline M. Kirkland. New Brunswick: Rutgers UP, 1990. xi–xlvi.

BIBLIOGRAPHY

Selected Works by Caroline M. Kirkland

Books

A New Home, Who'll Follow? or, Glimpses of Western Life, by Mrs. Mary Clavers, an actual settler. New York: C. S. Francis, 1839. Reprint, New Brunswick: Rutgers UP, 1990.

Forest Life. New York: C. S. Francis, 1842.

Editor, *The Principles of Morality and the Private and Political Rights and Obligations of Mankind.* By Jonathan Dymond. New York: C. S. Francis, 1842.

Western Clearings. New York: Wiley and Putnam, 1845.

The Helping Hand, Comprising an Account of the Home for Discharged Female Convicts and an Appeal in Behalf of that Institution. New York: Charles Scribner, 1853.

Holidays Abroad, or, Europe from the West. New York: Baker and Scribner, 1849.

The Book of Home Beauty. New York: G. P. Putnam, 1852.

The Evening Book, or, Fireside Talk on Morals and Manners, with Sketches of Western Life. New York: Charles Scribner, 1852.

A Book for the Home Circle; or, Familiar Thoughts on Various Topics, Literary, Moral, and Social. A Companion for the Evening Book. New York: Charles Scribner, 1853.

Autumn Hours and Fireside Reading. New York: Charles Scribner, 1854.

Memoirs of Washington. New York: D. Appleton, 1857.

A Few Words on Behalf of the Loyal Women of the United States. By One of Themselves. New York: W. Bryant and Company, 1863.

Short Stories and Essays

Kirkland collected many of her nearly 200 short stories and essays in *Western Clearings, Holidays Abroad, The Evening Book, A Book for the Home Circle,* and *Autumn Hours.* Other pieces of particular interest are noted here.

"A Lady-Sufferer on 'Domestic Servitude.' " *The Knickerbocker* August 1842: 141–3.

"An Intercepted Letter to Dickens." *Graham's* February 1843: 144.

"Introduction. By the American Editor." *A Plea for Woman.* By Mrs. Hugo [Marion] Reid. New York: Farmer and Daggers, 1845. v–xxv.

"Notes for the Biography of a Distinguée." 3 parts. *Yankee Doodle* 17 Oct. 1846: 15; 24 Oct. 1846: 27; 31 Oct. 1846: 45–6.

"Recollections of Anti-Slavery at the West." *The Liberty Bell* 1846: 195–203.

"George Sand and the Journeyman Joiner." *Union Magazine of Literature and Art* Nov. 1847: 221–3.

Preface to *Dahcotah, or, Life and Legends of the Sioux around Fort Snelling,* by Mrs. Mary Eastman. New York: John Wiley, 1849.

"Ellet's *Women of the Revolution.*" *North American Review* Apr. 1849: 362–88.

"Thoughts on Education No. 1." *Sartain's Union Magazine* July 1849: 40–3.

"Thoughts on Education No. 2." *Sartain's Union Magazine* Oct. 1849: 236–9.

"Literary Women." *Sartain's Union Magazine* Feb. 1850: 150–4.

"The Household." *Sartain's Union Magazine* July 1850: 42–6.

"Mahomet and His Successors." *North American Review* October 1850: 273–307.

"Momma Charlotte." *Autographs for Freedom.* Vol. 1. n.p.: John P. Jewett and Co., 1853. 13–17. Reprint, Miami: Mnemosyne Publishing Co., 1969.

"Modern Saints, Catholic and Heretic." *North American Review* July 1853: 145–73.

"A Wish." *Autographs for Freedom.* Ed. Julia Griffiths. Auburn: Alden, Beardsley and Co., 1854. 209.

"The Great Prairie State." *The Continental Monthly* May 1863: 513–9.

"Liberia College." *North American Review* July 1863: 102–32.

Studies of Caroline M. Kirkland

Bailey, Brigitte. "Gender, Nation, and the Tourist Gaze in the European 'Year of Revolutions': Kirkland's *Holidays Abroad.*" *American Literary History* 14 (2002): 60–82.

Bouma, Jana A. "Caroline M. Kirkland: A Literary Life." Diss., University of Nebraska-Lincoln. 2000.

Keetley, Dawn. "Unsettling the American Frontier: Gender and Racial Identity in Caroline Kirkland's *A New Home, Who'll Follow?* and *Forest Life.*" *Legacy* 12 (1995): 17–37.

Keyes, Langley Carleton. "Caroline M. Kirkland: A Pioneer in American Realism." Diss. Harvard University, 1935.

Knudsen, Louise N. "Caroline Kirkland, Pioneer." Thesis. Michigan State College, 1934.

Kreger, Erika M. "A Bibliography of Works by and about Caroline M. Kirkland." *Tulsa Studies in Women's Literature* 18 (1999): 299–350.

Lewis, Nathaniel. "Penetrating the Interior: Recontextualizing Caroline Kirkland's *A New Home, Who'll Follow?*" *American Literary Realism* 31, no. 2 (1999): 63–71.

Merish, Lori. " 'The Hand of Refined Taste' in the Frontier Landscape: Caroline Kirkland's *A New Home, Who'll Follow?* and the Feminization of American Consumerism." *American Quarterly* 45 (1993): 485–523.

Osborne, William S. *Caroline M. Kirkland.* New York: Twayne, 1972.

Peeples, Scott. " 'The Servant Is as His Master': Western Exceptionalism in Caroline Kirkland's Short Fiction." *ATQ* December 1999, 305–16.

Walker, Nancy. *The Disobedient Writer: Women and Narrative Tradition.* Austin: U of Texas P, 1995.

Letters and Archival Materials

"The Letters of Caroline M. Kirkland." Ed. Audrey Roberts. Diss. University of Wisconsin-Madison, 1976.

Hill-Kirkland Papers. Chicago Historical Society.

Kirkland, Caroline M. Letters to Samuel Kirkland Lothrop and others. University of Wisconsin-Madison Libraries.

ABRAHAM LINCOLN (1809–1865)

William Etter

BIOGRAPHY

Abraham Lincoln was born in Hardin County, Kentucky, on February 12, 1809. At the age of seven he moved with his parents, Thomas and Nancy, to Indiana. A year after Lincoln's mother died in 1818, Thomas married Sarah Bush, the woman credited with recognizing Abraham's promising intellect. Despite his stepmother's support, however, Lincoln was able to attend school only intermittently between 1816 and 1824; historians estimate the time he spent in the classroom did not total a year. After the 21-year-old Lincoln moved with his family to Illinois, he worked at diverse occupations: hired hand, store clerk, miller, postmaster, surveyor, and lawyer. He also became celebrated for his wrestling prowess and was chosen a captain by popular election when he served for five weeks in the Black Hawk War. Though he fell into debt and handily lost his bid for a seat in the Illinois General Assembly in 1832, Lincoln earned his first elected political position two years later by winning a seat in the Assembly. Serving from 1834 to 1842, Lincoln voted for internal improvements to bolster the state's economy and promoted Whig candidates for local, state, and national offices.

During this period his personal life followed a similarly uncertain path. As early as 1836 Lincoln expressed feelings of depression (which he termed "hypochondria") in letters to close friends. Mary Owens's rejection of his marriage proposal in 1837 only exacerbated his despair. After he left the Assembly, however, his public and private life improved. He married Mary Todd—nine years his junior and daughter of a Whig banker from Kentucky—on November 4, 1842. The couple's first child, Robert Todd, was born August 1, 1843. An affectionate father, Lincoln, by all accounts, was emotionally devastated when two of his other sons died young, one in 1850 and the other in 1862. Lincoln also established a law practice, working primarily in Springfield where his new family lived from 1844 until they moved into the White House.

Election to the U.S. House of Representatives in 1846 marked Lincoln's entrance into national politics. While serving his term Lincoln resisted the extension of slavery into newly formed states and territories and opposed the Mexican War. In 1848, he delivered a long speech to the House, supporting Zachary Taylor's candidacy for president and asserting that the chief executive should not veto congressional bills if he were unsure of their constitutionality, thereby allowing the will of the people, through their elected representatives, to be realized. There was sufficient displeasure with these positions among his Illinois constituents, however, to prevent Lincoln from being nominated for a second term. He returned to his successful legal practice, taking on cases of property litigation and acting as a criminal defense attorney.

Lincoln was elected again to the Illinois state legislature in 1854. He stridently opposed the Kansas-Nebraska Bill (which repealed antislavery provisions of the Missouri Compromise) proposed by Stephen Douglas, Lincoln's longtime political nemesis. He ran for the U.S. Senate and, despite being defeated, remained politically active. In May 1856, Lincoln participated in the creation of the Republican party and concluded its first convention by delivering his "House Divided" speech, charging Democrats, a pro-slavery Supreme Court, and the southern states with conspiring to legalize slavery throughout the nation. The following year Douglas defeated Lincoln in another Senate campaign marked by the seven "Lincoln-Douglas Debates" held between August and October. In 1860, now a recognized spokesman for the Republican party, Lincoln delivered an aggressive address to New York's Cooper Union stating that the Constitution permitted the federal government "to control . . . Slavery in our Federal Territories" and accusing the South of threatening to "rule or ruin in all events" (*Speeches and Writings 1859–1865,* 117, 126).

That same year Lincoln was elected president of the United States. As commander-in-chief during the Civil War, he earnestly sought victory while remaining true to the conservative spirit of concession and compromise he had lauded in his early writings. Sometimes criticized for his slow response to military and political crises, Lincoln delayed public announcement of the Emancipation Proclamation, declaring all Confederate slaves free, until he could make it after a northern victory at Antietam. On March 4, 1865, with Union victory in the war assured, Lincoln delivered his Second Inaugural Address, urging all Americans to reunite "With malice toward none; with charity for all" (*Speeches and Writings 1859–1865,* 687) and to understand the war as God's punishment for the sin of slavery. He gave his last public speech, on Reconstruction, on April 11, 1865. Three days later he was shot in the head by John Wilkes Booth while attending the comedy *Our American Cousin* at Ford's Theater in Washington, D. C. Lincoln died the following morning.

MAJOR WORKS AND THEMES

The volume and diversity of Lincoln's writings are formidable. The most comprehensive edition of them—the nine-volume *Collected Works* edited by Roy P. Basler—includes letters, satirical pieces, editorials, speeches, and legal documents. Three central themes are, however, dominant in the Lincoln canon: the relationship of the general public to its government, slavery, and the preservation of a United States founded on the principles of the Declaration of Independence.

Lincoln's early political writing expresses a virtually utilitarian conviction that the voice of the majority, legally expressed through citizens' elected representatives, should determine the direction of governmental policy to achieve the greatest good and least evil for the most people. Yet at times he viewed democratic society with suspicion, fearing its potential to degenerate into what he termed "mobocracy" in an address entitled "The Perpetuation of our Political Institutions" (1838). As president, Lincoln conceived of the federal government as a repository of national ideology and the institution responsible for realizing the nation's will.

While a state representative in the 1830s, Lincoln asserted that slavery should be regulated by state governments and later won a case before the Illinois Supreme Court using this argument in 1841. When the United States Supreme Court issued the Dred Scott decision in 1857, Lincoln delivered an address against it. Even as he argued slavery was a "universal" injustice and voted for antislavery measures, Lincoln repeatedly railed against abolitionists for aiming to "shiver [the nation] into fragments" and asserted the federal constitution gave Congress "no power . . . to interfere with the institution of slavery in the different states." Lincoln believed in gradual emancipation and the preservation of racial hierarchies and suggested the emigration of slaves and free blacks to Africa or simple "toleration and protection" of southern slavery as resolutions to the nation's racial problems. Adopting antebellum racial conventions, he told the audience of the fourth Lincoln-Douglas debate (September 18, 1858): "there is a physical difference between the white and black races which I believe will for ever forbid the two races living together on terms of social and political equality."

Lincoln always emphasized the necessity of preserving the Union, as indicated in his 1862 comment to newspaper editor Horace Greeley: "If I could save the Union without freeing any slave, I would do it." Perhaps his most enduring contribution to American letters and ideology was his recasting of the United States as a nation founded in the Declaration of Independence (even more so than the Constitution) while simultaneously maintaining a commitment to a strong federal government. Though these positions appear in Lincoln's pre-war writings, like his 1854 speech against the Kansas-Nebraska Act, they achieved their most developed form during the Civil War. Ultimately, Lincoln sought to portray the federal government as "the vehicle of a strong nationalism" and "a regulative force" (Arieli 316). In the Gettysburg Address (1863), delivered at the dedication of Gettysburg's national cemetery, Lincoln seized an opportunity to present this view publicly, encourage morale in the face of recent Union defeats, and strategically advance a war for reunification by literary means. Only 272 words long, this complex address is structured around rhetorical contrasts, especially those of life versus death and union versus dissolution, but it never mentions slavery, the South, Gettysburg, or the Union (Wills 58–59, 90). Instead, it presents a reunified nation which "shall not perish from the earth," a theme Lincoln had expounded upon two years earlier in his First Inaugural Address.

Lincoln's literary influences included texts familiar to antebellum Americans: the Bible, Weems's biography of Washington, *Robinson Crusoe,* and *The Pilgrim's Progress.* Shakespeare, Robert Burns's poetry, and the works of Thomas Jefferson were also part of the small collection of texts from which Lincoln quoted in his writings. He enjoyed eighteenth-century English poets and on occasion wrote original compositions in the vein of the popular sentimental poetry of his day. In contrast, Lincoln read little prose fiction, though he did know work by Stowe, Hawthorne, and Poe (Edwards and Hankins 52).

When he delivered a eulogy for Henry Clay in 1852, Lincoln expressed great admiration for Clay's oratorical talents and his ability to advance a political cause or inspire legislative compromise by rhetorical means. Lincoln composed his own public addresses carefully, revising them repeatedly while searching for effective means of employing rigorous logic as well as self-deprecation and sarcasm, some of his favorite rhetorical tools. He appreciated the value of inserting a maxim or joke into an argument and could be bitterly insulting. Speaking before Congress in 1848 Lincoln attacked presidential candidate Lewis Cass for wasting federal funds while serving as a government official: "we have all heard of the animal standing in doubt between two stacks of hay, and starving to death. The like of that would never happen to Gen. Cass." Later works like the "Cooper Union Address" (1860) exhibit Lincoln's use of historical analysis to ground his arguments in the ideals of the "Founding Fathers."

CRITICAL RECEPTION

Lincoln's orations and writings most familiar and esteemed among readers today, such as the Lincoln-Douglas Debates and "House Divided" speech, were similarly recognized in the nineteenth century. When first composed, these works were also controversial, alternately attacked as despotic and as unreasonably conciliatory to the South. Multivolume works by John Nicolay and John Hay, Lincoln's private secretaries and later his editors and biographers, initially established his historical and literary reputation. Readers of the later nineteenth century often praised Lincoln's ability to write in the "language of humanity." Joseph Kirkland, a father of the Western novel, admired Lincoln's ability to relate yarns and jokes in frontier vernacular language. James Russell Lowell, in his poem "The Commemoration Ode," celebrated Lincoln as "the first American." In a 1903 essay, "The Frontier in American History," historian Frederick Jackson Turner quoted this line and argued that Lincoln was the first national icon to emerge from the untamed West. Indeed, many modern scholars believe Lincoln's political views were formed amidst the spirit of novelty, "equality of opportunity," and independence cherished by "self-made" Westerners (Arieli 316).

These honorific views have been countered by more critical statements, like those made by Frederick Douglass in his speech at the dedication of the Freedman's Lincoln Monument in 1876. The ex-slave's statement that Lincoln's "prejudices" prevented him from truly being "our man or our model" (Arieli 492) encourages scholars to appreciate Lincoln's influence, for good and ill, on the history and literature of African America. As Eric Sundquist argues, recent efforts "to reconfigure the American Renaissance from an African American perspective" must incorporate Lincoln's writings into the analysis (29).

Mid- to late-twentieth-century scholars of Lincoln's writing further examine the rhetorical strategies he employed during the Civil War to constitute the Union imaginatively even as it was shaped on the battlefield. The texts typically examined in these studies are the Gettysburg and Second Inaugural Addresses. Priscilla Wald understands the imagination of "the metaphysical self rather than the body as the symbol of . . . Union" to be a crucial element of Lincoln's wartime speeches as he strove to portray the "disintegration" of the nation as an attack on American identity (66). At the same time, as Lisa A. Long and Garry Wills point out, in his wartime orations Lincoln rhetorically "transfigures the 'tragedy of macerated bodies' " on the battlefield into a struggle for a politically and spiritually reunified nation, thereby "erasing" the war's horrific physical carnage (Long 794). In doing so, Wills contends, speeches like the Gettysburg Address figure the war and the principles of the Declaration of Independence as agents of "spiritual rebirth" (Wills 77–78). Some scholars have also interpreted this address (and Lincoln's thought in general) as grounded in Transcendentalist philosophy. It remains the most widely read testament to Lincoln's historical and literary legacy.

WORKS CITED

Arieli, Yehoshua. *Individualism and Nationalism in American Ideology*. Cambridge: Harvard UP, 1964.

Douglass, Frederick. *Life and Times of Frederick Douglass*. Facsimile Edition. New York: Citadel Press, 1983.

Edwards, Herbert J., and John E. Hankins. *Lincoln the Writer: The Development of His Style*. Orono: University of Maine Press, 1962.

Lincoln, Abraham. *Speeches and Writings 1832–1858*. Ed. Don E. Fehrenbacher. New York: Literary Classics of the United States, 1989.

————. *Speeches and Writings 1859–1865*. Ed. Don E. Fehrenbacher. New York: Literary Classics of the United States, 1989.

Long, Lisa A. " 'The Corporeity of Heaven': Rehabilitating the Civil War Body in The Gates Ajar." *American Literature* 69:4 (December 1997): 781–811.

Lowell, James Russell. "The Commemoration Ode." 15 Oct. 2003. <http://www.bartleby.com/102/130.html>.
Sundquist, Eric. *To Wake the Nations: Race in the Making of American Literature.* Cambridge: Belknap, Harvard UP, 1993.
Wald, Priscilla. *Constituting Americans: Cultural Anxiety and Narrative Form.* Durham: Duke UP, 1995.
Wills, Garry. *Lincoln at Gettysburg: The Words that Remade America.* New York: Simon and Schuster, 1992.

BIBLIOGRAPHY

Works by Abraham Lincoln

Basler, Roy P., ed. *Collected Works of Abraham Lincoln* 9 vols. New Brunswick: Rutgers UP, 1955.
Letter to Mary S. Owens, May 7, 1837.
"The Perpetuation of our Political Institutions," Address to the Young Men's Lyceum of Springfield, January 27, 1838.
"Remarkable Case of Arrest for Murder," Quincy *Whig,* April 15, 1846.
Speech in the U.S. House of Representatives on the Mexican War, January 12, 1848.
Speech in the U.S. House of Representatives on Zachary Taylor's Candidacy, July 27, 1848.
Eulogy for Henry Clay, July 6, 1852.
Speech on the Kansas–Nebraska Act, October 16, 1854.
Speech on the Dred Scott Decision, June 26, 1857.
Lincoln–Douglas Debates, August 21, 1858, to October 15, 1858.
Cooper Union Address, February 27, 1860.
First Inaugural Address, March 4, 1861.
Address on Colonization to a Committee of Colored Men, August 14, 1862.
Letter to Horace Greeley, August 22, 1862.
Emancipation Proclamation, Final Draft, January 1, 1863.
Speech to Indian Chiefs at Washington, D.C., March 27, 1863.
Address Delivered at the Dedication of the Cemetery at Gettysburg, November 19, 1863.
Second Inaugural Address, March 4, 1865.
Speech on Reconstruction, April 11, 1865.

Studies of Abraham Lincoln

Collins, Bruce W. "The Lincoln–Douglas Contest of 1858 and the Illinois Electorate." *Journal of American Studies* 20 (1986): 391–420.
Donald, David Herbert. *Lincoln.* New York: Simon and Schuster, 1995.
Einhorn, Lois J. *Abraham Lincoln the Orator: Penetrating the Lincoln Legend.* Westport: Greenwood Press, 1992.
Fehrenbacher, Don E. *Lincoln in Text and Context.* Stanford: Stanford UP, 1987.
Frederickson, George M. "A Man but Not a Brother: Abraham Lincoln and Racial Equality." *Journal of Southern History* 41 (1975): 39–58.
Hurt, James. "All the Living and the Dead: Lincoln's Imagery." *American Literature* 52 (1980): 351–80.
Keckley, Elizabeth. *Behind the Scenes. Or, Thirty Years a Slave, and Four Years in the White House.* (1868) New York: Oxford UP, 1988.
Klingaman, William K. *Abraham Lincoln and the Road to Emancipation, 1861–1865.* New York: Viking Penguin, 2001.
McPherson, James M. *Abraham Lincoln and the Second American Revolution.* New York: Oxford UP, 1990.
Nicolay, John G., and John Hay. *Abraham Lincoln: A History.* 10 vols. New York: Century Company, 1890.
White, Ronald. *Lincoln's Greatest Speech: The Second Inaugural.* New York: Simon and Schuster, 2002.
Wilson, Edmund. *Patriotic Gore: Studies in the Literature of the American Civil War.* New York: Oxford UP, 1962.

GEORGE LIPPARD (1822–1854)

Paul J. Erickson

BIOGRAPHY

George Lippard was born in Chester County, Pennsylvania, on April 10, 1822. In 1824, his father, Daniel Lippard, a former school teacher descended from German immigrants, sold the family farm and moved with his wife to Philadelphia. George and his sisters went to live with their grandfather and two maiden aunts in nearby Germantown. A frail and intense boy, Lippard attended the Concord School in Germantown for several years. Falling on hard times, George's aunts sold the family homestead in Germantown in 1832 and took the children to live in Philadelphia. They continued to live apart from their father; their mother had died in 1831. George was sent to a private school in upstate New York at the age of 15, purportedly to prepare for the Methodist ministry, but he feuded with the school's director and left after several months.

Returning to Philadelphia in October 1837, George found his father near death; sharpening the blow, George received nothing from his father's estate. Penniless and homeless at the height of a terrible economic depression, Lippard wandered the streets, eventually finding work as a lawyer's assistant, during which time he tried his hand at writing fiction. Disillusioned with the law, in 1842 Lippard started working for a Philadelphia newspaper, the *Spirit of the Times,* where he distinguished himself as a police-court reporter and the author of numerous satires on local literary luminaries. In July 1842, the *Saturday Evening Post* published one of his stories, and in the fall it serialized his novel *Herbert Tracy.*

In 1843, Lippard began writing for a Philadelphia weekly, the *Citizen Soldier,* eventually becoming its editor. Along with his popular satirical columns, the paper published several of the "Legends of the American Revolution" that would help make him famous, along with two Gothic novellas. In the fall of 1844 he began serial publication of what would be his best-seller, *The Quaker City; or, The Monks of Monk-Hall,* an exposé of corruption in Philadelphia society whose racy content and local color turned the city on its ear. During the winter, a proposed theatrical version of the novel nearly caused a riot outside the Chesnut Street Theater, when the person on whom one of the characters was based threatened to disrupt the performance.

In May 1845, *Quaker City* was published as a single volume, selling 60,000 copies the first year. How many copies were sold overall is unclear, but it was enough to make it the second-biggest antebellum novel, behind *Uncle Tom's Cabin.* Pirated editions appeared in England and Germany. In 1846, the *Saturday Courier* started publishing Lippard's series of Revolutionary War legends, including one about the ringing of the Liberty Bell that was long accepted as historical fact. In 1847, Lippard married Rose Newman in a moonlight ceremony overlooking Wissahickon Creek; the couple would have two children, Mima and Paul, both of whom died at a young age. The following years would see Lippard publishing novels set in America's teeming cities, on the battlefields of the Revolution, in the wilds of colonial Pennsylvania, and on the front lines of the Mexican-American War. His unconventional appearance—long hair and Byronic attire—made him an easily recognizable figure on the streets of Philadelphia, and both his commercial success and radical politics made him a frequent target for critics.

In 1848 Lippard started his own newspaper, the *Quaker City Weekly,* in which he published reformist essays and several serial novels, including *Memoirs of a Preacher,* its sequel *The Man with the Mask, The Empire City,* and *The Killers,* about a Philadelphia race riot. Lippard continued the paper until 1850. In 1849, Lippard formed a fraternal labor organization called the Brotherhood of the Union, which consumed much of his energy and took him on numerous lecture tours. Lippard's primary concern was with the rights of laborers, and in 1850 he helped to found a cooperative for Philadelphia seamstresses. These political activities, combined with his overheated prose style, earned him the derision of the literary elite but made him a favorite of the mass audience.

In 1851, following the deaths of his wife and infant son, Lippard reportedly attempted suicide. After a brief term as literary editor of the *New York National Democrat* in 1852, Lippard published *The Midnight Queen* and *New York: Its Upper Ten and Lower Million,* two more city-mysteries narratives, the latter being the sequel to *The Empire City.* Lippard died of tuberculosis in Philadelphia on February 9, 1854.

MAJOR WORKS AND THEMES

Lippard's major works, for which he was best known both in his time and today, fall into the categories of historical fiction and the sensational urban exposé. While many of Lippard's books enjoyed large sales, by far his most famous works were *Washington and His Generals* and *Quaker City; or, the Monks of Monk-Hall,* and the latter overshadowed the former. In all his works, however, Lippard fused his unique brand of radical republicanism to a sensational prose style in order to forcefully convey his political and social ideas. His style was compared to Poe's and is held up as an example of American Gothicism as well as for its surrealist qualities. His primary themes were an intense patriotism and idealization of the heroes of the Revolution, a passionate concern with the condition of the laboring classes, a fascination with early Christianity, and a profound distrust of institutions, organized religion, political parties, and the rich. In delineating conditions in America's cities, Lippard also dealt with themes of racial and ethnic diversity, in the process proving himself adept at vernacular humor. Having witnessed firsthand the dislocations caused by the processes of urbanization and America's economic boom-and-bust cycles, Lippard's most consistent theme was the relationship of labor to capital and the danger that accumulated wealth posed to American democracy.

CRITICAL RECEPTION

Apart from a few sympathetic readers of literary standing, like his friend Edgar Allan Poe, Lippard was disdained by the literary establishment of antebellum America, a situation that was not helped by his frequent and vituperative attacks on the literati. In large part, these literary elites and their descendents were successful in marginalizing Lippard as a hack sensationalist who was popular with the masses (a popularity Lippard avidly pursued) but was ignored by discerning readers. Following a reissue of his best-known works in 1876, his reputation faded into obscurity in this country, and by the 1920s and 30s he was largely forgotten. Since the mid-twentieth century, however, with increasing scholarly attention being given to all aspects of popular culture, Lippard's work has been rediscovered. It is now widely accepted that *Quaker City* was one of the first (and most successful) American novels to incorporate the radical egalitarian politics sweeping the world in the 1840s, and that it set the tone for an outburst of popular American city fiction. Its sensational style and its deliberate parodying of the conventions of domestic fiction have contributed to an overly simplified view of Lippard's work as representing the male inverse of popular antebellum sentimental fiction by women. A study of Lippard's works can offer literary critics important insights into antebellum popular culture, especially as a counterpoint to the standard works of the American Renaissance, as well as into the heritage of the novel of social protest, the culture of labor radicalism, and a crucial moment in the practice of authorship.

BIBLIOGRAPHY

Works by George Lippard

The Battle-Day of Germantown. Philadelphia: Diller, 1843.
Herbert Tracy. Philadelphia: Berford, 1844.
The Ladye Annabel; or, The Doom of the Poisoner. Philadelphia: Berford, 1844.
The Quaker City; or, The Monks of Monk-Hall. Philadelphia: Zieber, 1844–45.
Blanche of Brandywine; or, September the Eleventh, 1777. Philadelphia: Zieber, 1846.
The Nazarene. Philadelphia: Lippard, 1846.
Legends of Mexico. Philadelphia: Peterson, 1847.
Washington and His Generals; or, Legends of the Revolution. Philadelphia: Zieber, 1847.
'Bel of Prairie Eden. A Romance of Mexico. Philadelphia: Peterson, 1848.
Paul Ardenheim, The Monk of Wissahikon. Philadelphia: Peterson, 1848.
The Memoirs of a Preacher. Philadelphia: Severns, 1849.
The Man with the Mask. Philadelphia: Severns, 1849.
Washington and His Men. Philadelphia: Severns, 1849.
The Empire City; or, New York by Night and Day. New York: Stringer and Townsend, 1850.
The Killers. Philadelphia: Hankinson and Bartholomew, 1850.
The Midnight Queen; or, Leaves from New-York Life. New York: Garrett, 1853.
New York: Its Upper Ten and Lower Million. Cincinnati: Rulison, 1853.

Studies of George Lippard

Ashwill, Gary. "The Mysteries of Capitalism in George Lippard's City Novels." *ESQ* 40:4 (1994): 293–317.
Butterfield, Roger. "George Lippard and His Secret Brotherhood." *PMHB* 74 (July 1955): 291–309.

De Grazia, Emilio. "The Life and Works of George Lippard." Ph.D. diss., Ohio State University, 1969.

Denning, Michael. *Mechanic Accents: Dime Novels and Working Class Culture in America.* London: Verso, 1982.

Ehrlich, Heyward. "The 'Mysteries' of Philadelphia: Lippard's *Quaker City* and 'Urban' Gothic." *ESQ* 66 (1972): 50–65.

Fiedler, Leslie. "The Male Novel." *Partisan Review* 37 (1970): 74–89.

Reynolds, David S. *Beneath the American Renaissance.* Cambridge: Harvard University Press, 1988.

———. *George Lippard.* Boston: Twayne Publishers, 1982.

———, ed. *George Lippard, Prophet of Protest: Writings of an American Radical, 1822–1854.* New York: Peter Lang, 1986.

Streeby, Shelley. "Opening Up the Story Paper: George Lippard and the Construction of Class." *Boundary 2* 24:1 (Spring 1997): 177–203.

———. "Haunted Houses: George Lippard, Nathaniel Hawthorne, and Middle-Class America." *Criticism* 38:3 (Summer 1996): 443–72.

HENRY WADSWORTH LONGFELLOW (1807–1882)

Patrick M. Erben

BIOGRAPHY

Henry Wadsworth Longfellow was born on February 27, 1807, in Portland, Maine. Henry was the second son of the lawyer and Harvard graduate Stephen Longfellow and Zilpah Wadsworth Longfellow, the daughter of a Revolutionary War general. His mother named Henry after her brother Henry Wadsworth, who had died during the Barbary Wars in North Africa. Growing up in the historic town of Portland as well as imbibing the family's storytelling traditions provided Longfellow with inspirations reflected throughout his literary work. Henry and his brother Stephen received a privileged private school education to prepare them to attend Bowdoin College in New Brunswick, Maine. Longfellow published his first poem, "The Battle of Lovell's Pond," in the local *Portland Gazette* on November 17, 1820.

In 1822, Longfellow began his studies at Bowdoin, where he participated avidly in literary clubs such as the Peucinian Society. Although his father hoped to direct him toward a legal career, Longfellow endeavored to become a poet, literary scholar, and linguist. He contributed numerous poems, reviews, and essays to local newspapers throughout his college career, rivaling his classmate Nathaniel Hawthorne. Upon his graduation in 1825, Bowdoin College offered Longfellow a newly created professorship in modern languages under the condition that he prepare for the position by studying the Romance languages during an extended visit to Europe. Longfellow spent three years on the Continent perfecting his command of French, Italian, and Spanish, as well as developing a new interest in German. His meeting with literary celebrity Washington Irving in Spain strengthened his desire to pursue a literary career alongside his academic duties.

In 1829, Longfellow returned to Maine and commenced his professorship at Bowdoin. He took his assignment seriously and, besides his regular teaching duties, developed a plethora of didactic materials in the modern languages, an academic discipline only recently introduced to the United States. His numerous critical essays on European literatures and languages as well as translations of literary works advanced the appreciation of his contemporaries for the cultural and intellectual ideals of nineteenth-century Europe.

Shortly after his return to the United States, Longfellow began to court Mary Potter of Portland, and they married on September 14, 1831. Finding the intellectual atmosphere at Bowdoin stifling and provincial, Longfellow continuously sought new opportunities and challenges. In 1835, Harvard University proposed that Longfellow replace George Ticknor as Smith Professor of Modern Languages. Longfellow accepted and embarked on another trip to Europe to prepare for his new position. While staying at Amsterdam, his wife Mary died of complications from a miscarriage on November 29, 1835. Though grief-stricken, Longfellow intensified his studies, particularly of the German Romantics, including Schiller, Goethe, and Novalis. While traveling through the Alps, he met the wealthy Appleton family of Boston and fell in love with the 17-year-old daughter Frances (Fanny). Upon his return to the United States in 1836, Longfellow began his professorship at Harvard as well as a courtship of Fanny Appleton.

When Fanny rejected Longfellow's marriage proposal in 1837, he again sought consolation in his work. He wrote numerous critical essays, among them a review of Hawthorne's *Twice-Told Tales.* Concomitantly, Longfellow's literary career began to flourish. Numerous poems, first published in *Knickerbocker Magazine,* were collected in the successful volume *Voices of the Night* (1839), which included "A Psalm of Life," one of Longfellow's most famous and most widely anthologized poems. His prose romance *Hyperion* (1839) and a second volume of poetry, *Ballads and Other Poems* (1842) followed briefly thereafter. Surprising the public with an emphatic sentiment for social causes, Longfellow published a volume of abolitionist poetry, *Poems on Slavery* (1842). The fast pace of his academic and literary endeavors took a toll on Longfellow's health, and, to recuperate, he embarked on a third journey to Europe. Upon his return to the United States, Longfellow renewed his courtship of Fanny Appleton, who finally accepted his proposal. Their wedding on July 13, 1843, initiated the happiest and most productive period in Longfellow's life. Henry and Fanny's harmonious marriage resulted in six children and a household open to local and foreign visitors alike.

Longfellow's literary fame soon increased with volumes of poetry such as *The Belfry of Bruges and Other Poems* (1845) and his long narrative poem *Evangeline, A Tale of Acadie* (1847). Besides his poetic endeavors, Longfellow published a novel, *Kavanagh* (1849), and he edited *Poets and Poetry of Europe* (1845), which first introduced many Americans to the literary currents and tastes of Europe. Longfellow's professorial duties at Harvard, however, curtailed the amount of time he could invest in his writing, and he resigned his position in 1854. One of the few American writers at the time who could support himself exclusively through his literary talent, Longfellow sold as many as 300,000 copies of his poetry and prose by his fiftieth birthday.

With the tragic death of his wife in 1861, Longfellow's personal and marital happiness came to a sudden end. Fanny suffered severe burns when a candle caught fire and died a few days later. In his attempt to extinguish the flames, Longfellow suffered extensive burns on his face, which he subsequently covered with the white beard familiar from his later portraits. Weighed down by grief, he again sought refuge in his work. In 1863, he completed his collection *Tales of a Wayside Inn* and embarked on the translation of Dante's *Divine Comedy,* published in three volumes from 1865 to 1867. During the 1870s, Longfellow edited the monumental, 31-volume collection, *Poems of Places.* He enjoyed literary fame throughout the rest of his life. A final visit to Europe in 1868–69 culminated in honorary degrees from Oxford and Cambridge University, as well as meetings with Queen Victoria and famed British authors such as Charles Dickens and Alfred Lord Tennyson. Longfellow's work was translated into numerous languages, and he enjoyed a reputation as a national poet in his own country. He died on March 24, 1882.

MAJOR WORKS AND THEMES

Although Longfellow is today known chiefly for a small number of short, anthologized poems including "A Psalm of Life," "Excelsior," and "The Village Blacksmith," his oeuvre comprises long narrative poetry and verse dramas, as well as prose works, including a novel. Many of these works reflect his childhood fascination with the folklore and legends of the colonial and early national period of American history. Longfellow persistently strove to establish specifically American themes as the appropriate topic matter for a national literature. His academic career as professor of foreign languages at Bowdoin and Harvard, however, provided a second and not altogether separate impetus for his literary work. While he felt that his teaching obligations distracted him from his writing, the lengthy periods of European travel provided him with a singular perspective on the romantic literary currents of nineteenth-century Europe, particularly Germany. In many of his works, therefore, Longfellow wedded the romantic literary sensibilities and poetic techniques of German romanticism with distinctively American subjects. Literary and cultural historians, overall, credit Longfellow with the enhancement of an American taste for poetry and the creation of an American literary tradition beyond the imitation of European, specifically English, models. Though often concerned with local themes and images, Longfellow's work clearly represents a cosmopolitan impulse in American literary history.

The quick succession of happy and tragic personal events in Longfellow's life, moreover, yielded the most widely recognizable feature of his work, especially with respect to his poetry. Longfellow turned the grief of losing his two wives into an outpouring of creative energy that did not project despondency and gloom but a fundamental assurance of the triumph of the human spirit. Many of his poems, therefore, place a strong emphasis on the importance of living an active, virtuous, and optimistic life free from regret or the defiance of spiritual and moral principles. Instead of leaving his readers with a self-conscious doubt about the meaning and purpose of the human condition, Longfellow strove to provide others with the consolation he frequently sought for himself.

Longfellow's early work, specifically his prose romances *Outre-Mer: A Pilgrimage Beyond the Sea* and *Hyperion,* adapted personal experience to established literary precedents such as Washington Irving's *Sketch Book. Hyperion,* for instance, retraces Longfellow's wanderings through Europe and features a heroine closely modeled after his second wife Fanny Appleton. The work is interspersed with translations of German romantic poetry. Longfellow found his poetic voice, as well as his first public recognition, with the poetry collected in *Voices of the Night* and *Ballads and Other Poems.* The emphatically didactic poem "Psalm of Life," for instance, epitomizes the *carpe diem* sentiment of making the most of one's lifespan rather than surrendering to self-doubt or regret. In "The Village Blacksmith," Longfellow chooses a familiar scene—a nearby blacksmith shop and its honest and hardworking owner—as a symbol for the man of action and a life of moral rectitude.

With his marriage to Fanny and another trip to Europe in 1842, Longfellow entered the most harmonious period in his life. Fanny collaborated on Longfellow's volume of poetry *The Belfry of Bruges,* which was heavily influenced by his last European journey. The title poem, for instance, recalls the medieval aura of the Belgian city of Bruges. Published in the same year, *Poems on Slavery* revealed Longfellow's social concerns and his forebodings for the divisive effects of slavery on the nation. While his antislavery poems garnered little attention outside of abolitionist circles, his poem "The Building of the Ship," collected in *The Seaside and the Fireside,* voiced a widely heard plea for the preservation of the Union during the heightened political tensions of pre–Civil War America.

During the 1840s and 50s, Longfellow further turned to historical themes emphasizing colonial and Native American subject matters. His popular narrative poem *Evangeline* dramatizes the expulsion of the Acadians from Nova Scotia by British troops during the French and Indian War. The poem focuses on the fate of one central couple, Evangeline and her beloved Gabriel. The sentimental plot concludes with the lovers' final reunion in death. In *Hiawatha,* Longfellow joined his long-standing interests in Native American mythology and a general American fascination with a culture that was disappearing rapidly under the pressure of territorial expansion and Indian warfare in the West. During a junior exhibition at Bowdoin College, Longfellow had presented a dialogue between a "North American Savage" and an English settler. For his epic poem *Hiawatha,* Longfellow merged oral traditions about an Ojibwa culture hero and accounts of an historical Iroquois figure contributing to the founding of the Iroquois Confederacy in a single, central character. Longfellow derived most of his information from the writings of ethnologist Henry Rowe Schoolcraft, particularly his *Algic Researches* (1839). For the poem's characteristic meter, however, Longfellow turned to the Finnish epic *Kalevala.* In the context of Indian removal and cultural genocide, Longfellow's poem—specifically in Hiawatha's admonition to his people to welcome the white missionaries and embrace their new religion—portrays a vanishing mode of life to ultimately affirm or accommodate political doctrine. His popular collection *Tales of a Wayside Inn* uses the literary convention of a group of travelers exchanging stories—based on Boccaccio's *Decameron* and Chaucer's *Canterbury Tales*—and transfers it to a familiar New England setting, an actual inn located near Sudbury, Massachusetts.

After the death of Longfellow's second wife in 1863, his grief remained both explicit and implicit throughout his literary works. Found in his portfolio after his death, Longfellow's poem "The Cross of Snow" compares his mourning to a cross-shaped field of snow that is neither touched nor changed by a warming ray of sunlight. His 1871 poem *The Divine Tragedy* seeks affirmation in Christianity, as it follows the impact of Christ's suffering on different characters of the Bible. While the poetry written during the latter part of his life did not find the popular acclaim of his earlier work, his translation of Dante's *Divine Comedy* and his work as editor of the multivolume *Poetry of Places* testify to Longfellow's ongoing contribution to the literary life of nineteenth-century America.

CRITICAL RECEPTION

Longfellow is the only American in whose honor a bust was erected in Poet's Corner of London's Westminster Abbey. In spite of this honor, his reputation quickly declined after his death, and his work has only recently undergone a critical resurgence. During his lifetime, Longfellow enjoyed celebrity status, and he was one of the few nineteenth-century American poets who could support himself exclusively through his writing. Indeed, recent critic Clarence Wolfshohl uses the poet as a case study for the permutations of American literary taste and the cultural politics of canon formation.

After the publication of Longfellow's first volume of poetry, *Voices of the Night,* Nathaniel Hawthorne praised his former Bowdoin classmate as one of the foremost poets in the Western hemisphere, if not the entire world. Even the British public agreed in awarding Longfellow laurels of poetic greatness while regarding most other American writers as inferior. His English admirers ranged from art critic John Ruskin to Queen Victoria. In the United States, Longfellow's burgeoning reputation was reflected in the rising sales of his works. While he received $15 for the publication of "The Village Blacksmith" in the 1830s, his monetary worth increased to $3,000 for the poem "The Hanging of the Crane" in 1873. Readers in the United States and abroad valued his moral themes, his affirmation of human endurance, and the comforting, sympathetic, and sincere tone of his poetry. Only a few detractors, including Edgar Allan Poe and Margaret Fuller, criticized Longfellow for the derivative nature of his poetry—specifically its reliance on European models—and his openly didactic messages.

Toward the end of his life, Longfellow's poetry could be found in any literature textbook in the United States, and the news of his death was met with public mourning and school closings across the country. With the advent of literary modernism in the 1910s and 1920s, as well as sociopolitical upheavals ranging from rapid industrialization and urbanization to the cataclysms of World War I and II, Longfellow's poetry came into disrepute. Critics began to blame Longfellow for those attributes that nineteenth-century readers had admired, especially his sentimentalism and moral clarity. Popular and critical tastes alike favored reflections of the inner and outer conflicts of the times and dismissed Longfellow's Victorian gentility.

While early twentieth-century readers primarily rejected the values and the background Longfellow represented, the New Critics of the 1930s, 40s, and 50s denounced his work for its apparent lack of complexity, imagination, and ambiguity. From John Crowe Ransom to F. O. Matthiessen, literary scholars sought to exclude Longfellow from a new canon of American literature that championed Whitman and Melville. In the 50s and 60s, biographers Cecil Williams and Edward Wagenknecht criticized the fact that the inclusion of formerly unappreciated writers had become contingent upon the dismissal of household names such as Longfellow. In spite of these sympathetic appraisals, Longfellow's share in literary anthologies remains small, relegating him to the status of "minor poet."

In recent years, however, some scholars have come to reexamine Longfellow's contribution to the cultural and intellectual history of nineteenth-century America. Longfellow's tireless work as a translator now appears as a major contribution to the multilingual and multicultural formation of American society. In a time when most white, Anglo-Saxon Americans feared that immigration from non-English-speaking countries, particularly from southern Europe, would bring about cultural and social decline, Longfellow introduced U.S. readers to the cultural achievements of Germany, France, Spain, and Italy. Directed by Marc Shell and Werner Sollors, the Longfellow Institute at Harvard University paradigmatically refers to its namesake's work in promoting the mission "to pull together past efforts to study the non-English writings in what is now the United States and to reexamine the English-language tradition in the context of American multilingualism" (*Longfellow Institute*).

WORKS CITED

The Longfellow Institute. Marc Shell and Werner Sollors. Department of English and American Language and Literature. Harvard University. 23 Nov. 2002 http://www.fas.harvard.edu/~lowinus/.

BIBLIOGRAPHY

Works by Henry Wadsworth Longfellow

Selected Poetry and Prose
Outre-Mer: A Pilgrimage Beyond the Sea. 2 vols. New York: Harper, 1835.
Voices of the Night. Cambridge, MA: John Owen, 1839.
Hyperion, A Romance. New York: Samuel Colman, 1839.
Poems on Slavery. Cambridge, MA: John Owen, 1842.
Ballads and Other Poems. Cambridge, MA: John Owen, 1842.
The Belfry of Bruges and Other Poems. Cambridge, MA: John Owen, 1845.
Evangeline, A Tale of Acadie. Boston: William D. Ticknor, 1847.
Kavanagh, A Tale. Boston: Ticknor, Reed & Fields, 1849.
The Seaside and the Fireside. Boston: Ticknor, Reed & Fields, 1850.
The Golden Legend. Boston: Ticknor, Reed & Fields, 1851.
The Song of Hiawatha. Boston: Ticknor & Fields, 1855.
The Courtship of Miles Standish and Other Poems. Boston: Ticknor & Fields, 1858.
Tales of a Wayside Inn. Boston: Ticknor & Fields, 1863.
The Divine Tragedy. Boston: Osgood, 1871.
The New England Tragedies. Boston: Ticknor & Fields, 1868.
Christus, A Mystery. 3 vols. Boston: Osgood, 1872.
Kéramos and Other Poems. Boston: Houghton, Osgood, 1878.
Ultima Thule. Boston: Houghton, Mifflin, 1880.
In the Harbor, Ultima Thule, Part II. Boston: Houghton: Mifflin, 1882.
Michael Angelo. Boston: Houghton, Mifflin, 1883.

Translations, Editions, and Letters
The Poets and Poetry of Europe. Edited by Longfellow. Philadelphia: Carey & Hart, 1845.
The Divine Comedy of Dante Alighieri. 3 vols. Translated by Longfellow. Boston: Ticknor &
    Fields, 1865–1867.
Poems of Places. Edited by Longfellow. Vols. 1–19. Boston: Osgood, 1876–1877. Vols. 20–31.
    Boston: Houghton, Osgood, 1878–1879.
The Letters of Henry Wadsworth Longfellow. 6 vols. Ed. Andrew Hilen. Cambridge, Mass.:
    Belknap Press of Harvard University Press, 1966–1983.

Studies of Henry Wadsworth Longfellow

Arvin, Newton. *Longfellow: His Life and Work.* Boston: Little, Brown, 1963.
Boswell, Jeanetta. *The Schoolroom Poets: A Bibliography of Bryant, Holmes, Longfellow, Lowell,*
    and Whittier. Metuchen, N.J.: Scarecrow Press, 1983.
Carr, Helen. *The Myth of Hiawatha. Literature & History* 12 (1986): 58–78.
Eberwein, Jane Donahue. "Henry Wadsworth Longfellow." *DLB 235.*
Fletcher, Angus. "Whitman and Longfellow: Two Types of the American Poet." *Raritan* 10 (1991):
    131–45.
Gartner, Matthew. "Becoming Longfellow: Work, Manhood, and Poetry." *American Literature* 72
    (2000): 59–86.
———. "Longfellow's Place: The Poet and Poetry of Craigie House." *New England Quarterly* 73
    (2000): 32–57.
Gruesz, Kirsten Silva. "Feeling for the Fireside: Longfellow, Lynch, and the Topography of Poetic
    Power." *Sentimental Men: Masculinity and the Politics of Affect in American Culture.* Eds.
    Mary Chapman and Glenn Hendler. Berkeley: U of California Press, 1999. 43–63.
Haralson, Eric L. "Mars in Petticoats: Longfellow and Sentimental Masculinity." *Nineteenth-*
    Century Literature 51 (1996): 327–56.
Harris, Janet. "Longfellow's Poems on Slavery." *Colby Library Quarterly* 14 (1978): 84–92.

Higginson, Thomas Wentworth. *Henry Wadsworth Longfellow.* Boston and New York: Houghton, Mifflin, 1902.

Hovey, Kenneth. " 'A Psalm of Life' Reconsidered: The Dialogue of Western Literature and Monologue of Young America." *American Transcendental Quarterly* 1 (1987): 3–19.

Jackson, Virginia. "Longfellow's Tradition: Or, Picture-Writing a Nation." *Modern Language Quarterly* 59 (1998): 471–96.

———. "Poe, Longfellow, and the Institution of Poetry." *Poe Studies* 33 (2000): 23–28.

Osborn, Chase S., and Stellanova Osborn. *Schoolcraft, Longfellow, Hiawatha.* Lancaster, PA: Jaques Cattell Press, 1942.

Pauly, Thomas H. "*Outre-mer* and Longfellow's Quest for a Career." *New England Quarterly* 50 (1977): 30–52.

Robichaud, Deborah. "Images of Evangeline: Continuity of the Iconographic Tradition." *River Review/La Revue Riviere: a Multidisciplinary Journal of Arts & Ideas/Revue Multidisciplinaire D'Arts et D'Idees* 3 (1997): 97–107.

Scharnhorst, Gary. "Longfellow as a Translator." *Translation Review* 12 (1983): 23–7.

Wagenknecht, Edward. *Henry Wadsworth Longfellow: His Poetry and Prose.* New York: Ungar, 1986.

———. *Henry Wadsworth Longfellow: Portrait of an American Humanist.* New York: Oxford University Press, 1966.

Williams, Cecil B. *Henry Wadsworth Longfellow.* New York: Twayne, 1964.

Wolfshohl, Clarence. "Blown Out of the Canon: The Rise and Fall of the Critical Reputation of Henry Wadsworth Longfellow." *West Virginia University Philological Papers* 42–43 (1997–1998): 115–20.

AUGUSTUS BALDWIN LONGSTREET (1790–1870)

Joan Wylie Hall

BIOGRAPHY

Augustus Baldwin Longstreet was born in Augusta, Georgia, on September 22, 1790, to Hannah Randolph Longstreet and William Longstreet, who had moved to the southern frontier from New Jersey about five years earlier. His father was a farmer, businessman, and inventor with a special interest in the new steam technology. Gus—as the child was nicknamed—was a quick learner at Richmond Academy in Augusta, but he developed a reputation for mischief in Edgefield District, South Carolina, where the family relocated temporarily. Near the end of his life, Longstreet recalled that his boyhood goal was to trounce every challenger, whether at racing, shooting, or barehanded fighting—behavior mirrored in the rowdies of his *Georgia Scenes* (1835), the first major work in the southwestern humor tradition.

Between 1808 and 1811, a more studious Augustus Baldwin displayed a talent for mathematics and the classics in Willington, South Carolina, at the Reverend Moses Waddel's academy. The legendary teacher—feared and idolized by his students—was the namesake of the headmaster in Longstreet's only novel, *Master William Mitten* (1864). Like the future senator John C. Calhoun, another Waddel scholar, Longstreet entered Yale in New Haven, Connecticut, as a junior. Known for relating hilarious stories about the South, he graduated with honors and then studied the law under Judge Tapping Reeve and Judge James Gould in Litchfield, Connecticut.

After passing the Georgia bar exam in 1815, Longstreet rode a seven-county circuit each spring and fall, lodging in rustic quarters with other young attorneys, some of whom became his lifelong friends. On March 3, 1817, he married Frances Eliza Parke, from a wealthy family in Greensboro, Georgia, where the couple first settled; only two of their eight children lived to adulthood. As a Georgia assemblyman, circuit court judge, and criminal trial lawyer, Longstreet was outspoken in his defense of states' rights. From 1834 to 1836, he edited the Augusta *State Rights Sentinel,* for which he wrote scores of pseudonymous political satires, as well as a series of realistic and comic sketches of town and country life that he collected in the volume *Georgia Scenes, Characters, Incidents, &c. in the First Half Century of the Republic.*

Longstreet resumed his legal career after selling the newspaper, but in 1838 he also became a Methodist preacher and the next year was elected to the presidency of Emory College, founded in 1836 by the Methodist Church. As a teacher and chief administrator at the Georgia school, he published the pro-slavery pamphlets *Letters on the Epistle of Paul to Philemon, or the Connection of Apostolical Christianity with Slavery* (1845) and *A Voice from the South: Comprising Letters from Georgia to Massachusetts, and to the Southern States* (1847). Between 1848 and the start of the Civil War in 1861, Longstreet served as president of three other colleges: Centenary in Louisiana, the University of Mississippi, and South Carolina College.

During Longstreet's brief term at Centenary in 1849, a local press serialized the first few chapters of his *Master William Mitten: Or, A Youth of Brilliant Talents, Who Was Ruined by Bad Luck.* Most of his writings at the University of Mississippi were theological and political in nature, but he continued to develop the novel when one of his former law partners solicited material for a new paper after Longstreet moved to South Carolina College. Fans of *Georgia Scenes* might have been disappointed by *William Mitten*'s didacticism yet the tone was consistent with the stern essays Longstreet wrote in 1860 and 1861 supporting slavery and secession. Confederate General James Longstreet was his nephew, and his son-in-law L. Q. C. Lamar helped draft Mississippi's ordinance of secession.

After the Civil War, Judge Longstreet (as he was commonly called) and his wife returned to Oxford, Mississippi, home of both their daughters. Mrs. Longstreet died in 1867, not long after the couple's fiftieth anniversary. Longstreet published four essays in the journal *The Nineteenth Century* between 1869 and 1870; his last major work before his death in Oxford on July 9, 1870, was a manuscript about biblical interpretation, which was destroyed in a fire along with many of his other papers.

MAJOR WORKS AND THEMES

Longstreet's literary fame rests on 19 pieces he collected in 1835 as *Georgia Scenes,* the first book in the popular antebellum genre known as southwestern humor. Newspapers were the usual venue for such comedy, and most of Longstreet's tales of horse-swaps, bloody fights, fox-hunts, and oratorical bombast first appeared in two Georgia papers, the Milledgeville *Southern Recorder* and the Augusta *State Rights Sentinel.* He began writing the short fictions in 1830 to preserve the speech, manners, and folkways of the Old Southwest (which stretched from Georgia to Arkansas) for his own descendents. Longstreet tells his "gentle reader" that the morality of rural Georgians has improved in the decades following a rude encounter he describes in "Georgia Theatrics," the opening sketch of *Georgia Scenes.* Yet Longstreet evokes the past much more nostalgically in longing for the pastoral pleasures of youth in the next piece, "The Dance."

These sketches introduce Longstreet's two narrators, Lyman Hall and Abraham Baldwin—articulate travelers who journey from town to country, always on the alert for a good story. (Timothy Crabshaw, narrator of "The Shooting Match," is the pseudonym of Oliver Hillhouse Prince, who contributed the single Georgia scene Longstreet did not write himself.) Although the collection was published anonymously, Longstreet's narrators reflect his experience as a peripatetic lawyer and itinerant pastor; and both raconteurs are named after famous politicians from Georgia history. In the preface, Longstreet explains that Baldwin's six narratives feature women as important characters, while men are the usual focus of Hall's 12 tales. The Latinate diction of both narrators contrasts with the vernacular speech of the rustics they meet on their travels, including the pugnacious Ransy Sniffle, the conniving horsetrader Yellow Blossom, and a trio of gossiping matrons.

In 1836, Edgar Allan Poe quoted extensively from *Georgia Scenes* in his long review for the *Southern Literary Messenger,* remarking on the author's ability to capture southern character and to make even a serious reader like Poe burst into laughter. Four years later, Harper and Brothers published a New York edition of the book with copperplate engravings of several characters in action, including Ned Brace at his hymn-singing antics and a schoolmaster's show-down with a group of rebellious young students. Ahmed Nimeiri has recently suggested that the central motif of *Georgia Scenes* is an emphasis on play as an exceptional feature of the antebellum South. According to Nimeiri, this focus separates Longstreet from many of his contemporaries, including not only the literary descendents of New England Puritanism but the Transcendentalists and other Romantics as well.

Play encompasses the subtle social games in sketches like "The 'Charming Creature' as a Wife" and "The Ball," but Baldwin's cynical observations on the shallow young women in these pieces is alien to the boisterous comedy of the physical games common in southwestern humor. With such names as Miss Gilt, Mr. Flirt, and Mr. Crouch, the urbane dancers in "The Ball" could take to the stage with the fops and mistresses satirized in Restoration and eighteenth-century theater. Joseph Addison's humor of manners in *The Tatler* is another antecedent of Longstreet's several town sketches, although critics more often find analogues for *Georgia Scenes* in the early American humor of Davy Crockett and Washington Irving.

Despite the great popularity of *Georgia Scenes,* Longstreet never finished the second volume of sketches that would, he proposed, expand his survey of society. "Julia and Clarissa. Severed Friendship—Village Gossip" is the longest and most interesting of eight additional pieces gathered by David Rachels in *Augustus Baldwin Longstreet's Georgia Scenes Completed* (1998). This satire of courtship and female friendship has parallels in *Master William Mitten,* Longstreet's tedious novel about a misguided youth who belatedly regrets his lust and his lies. Longstreet's most didactic fiction made no noticeable impact on the literature of the United States, but his riotous sketches of rural Georgia helped to establish a strong vernacular tradition that includes George Washington Harris, Johnson Jones Hooper, Mark Twain, several male and female local colorists, William Faulkner, and such recent humorists as Clyde Edgerton, Randall Kenan, Lee Smith, and Barry Hannah.

CRITICAL RECEPTION

Georgia Scenes was so widely read in the nineteenth century that both the author and the title quickly became household words, according to O. P. Fitzgerald, who published a sketch of Longstreet in 1891. Poe's praise of *Georgia Scenes* in the 1836 *South Literary Messenger* doubtless encouraged many amateurs to try their hand at the relatively new form of comedy represented in Longstreet's rural tall tales. Between 1835 and the Civil War, frontier humor by lawyers, planters, journalists, and pastors filled periodical columns from New Orleans to New York. William T. Porter, editor of the *New York Spirit of the Times,* went on the road in search of writers who could vividly express the Old Southwest's rapid transition from wilderness to settlement. *Georgia Scenes* was followed by many other volumes of southwestern humor, including Johnson Hooper's 1845 collection of Simon Suggs stories and Joseph Glover Baldwin's *Flush Times of Alabama and Mississippi* (1853).

Recent studies both review and advance Longstreet criticism. In his scholarly edition of *Georgia Scenes,* Rachels suggests that, by emphasizing realistic details and humor, earlier critics neglected Longstreet's artistry, his treatment of themes like politics and sexuality, and his skillful characterization of the narrators. Antebellum society is a focus of essays on *Georgia Scenes* in *The Humor of the Old South,* edited by M. Thomas Inge and Edward J. Piacentino; Piacentino's comprehensive bibliography reveals the contexts besides southwestern humor in which Longstreet's work has been discussed, from legal education to race, ethics, and gender. In *Narrative Forms of Southern Community,* Scott Romine takes a revisionist view of Longstreet and class hierarchies; his stress on narrative stylistics further reflects a growing tendency to de-emphasize Longstreet's comedy and to explore his social dynamics from the perspective of culture studies.

BIBLIOGRAPHY

Works by Augustus Baldwin Longstreet

Georgia Scenes, Characters, Incidents, &c. in the First Half Century of the Republic: By a Native Georgian. Augusta, GA: S. R. Sentinel Office, 1835. Reprint, Nashville: Sanders, 1992.

A Voice from the South: Comprising Letters from Georgia to Massachusetts, and to the Southern States. Baltimore: Western Continent Press, 1847.

Master William Mitten: Or, A Youth of Brilliant Talents, Who Was Ruined by Bad Luck. Macon, GA: Burke, Boykin, 1864.

"The Letters of Augustus Baldwin Longstreet." Ed. James R. Scafidel. Ph.D. diss., University of South Carolina, 1976.

Augustus Baldwin Longstreet's Georgia Scenes Completed: A Scholarly Text. Ed. David Rachels. Athens: University of Georgia Press, 1998.

Studies of Augustus Baldwin Longstreet

Beam, Patricia. "The Theme and Structure of *Georgia Scenes.*" *Journal of English* 15 (1987): 68–79.

Fitzgerald, O. P. *Judge Longstreet: A Life Sketch.* Nashville: Publishing House of the Methodist Episcopal Church, South, 1891.

Inge, M. Thomas, and Edward J. Piacentino, eds. *The Humor of the Old South.* Lexington: University Press of Kentucky, 2001.

King, Kimball. *Augustus Baldwin Longstreet.* Boston: Twayne, 1984.

Lenz, William E. "Longstreet's *Georgia Scenes:* Developing American Characters and Narrative Techniques." *Markham Review* 11 (1981): 5–10.

Lilly, Paul R., Jr. "Augustus Baldwin Longstreet." *American Humorists, 1800–1950.* Ed. Stanley Trachtenberg. Vol. 11. *Dictionary of Literary Biography.* Detroit: Gale Research, 1982. 276–83.

Lynn, Kenneth S. *Mark Twain and Southwestern Humor.* Boston: Little, Brown, 1959.

Meriwether, James B. "Augustus Baldwin Longstreet: Realist and Artist." *Mississippi Quarterly* 35 (1982): 351–64.

Newlin, Keith. "*Georgia Scenes:* The Satiric Artistry of Augustus Baldwin Longstreet." *Mississippi Quarterly* 41 (1987–88): 21–37.

Nimeiri, Ahmed. "Play in Augustus Baldwin Longstreet's *Georgia Scenes.*" *Southern Literary Journal* 33.2 (2001): 44–61.

Poe, Edgar Allan. "Georgia Scenes." *Southern Literary Messenger* 2 (1836): 287–92.

Romine, Scott. *The Narrative Forms of Southern Community.* Baton Rouge: Louisiana State University Press, 1999.

Wade, John Donald. *Augustus Baldwin Longstreet: A Study of the Development of Culture in the South,* 1924. Reprint ed. M. Thomas Inge, Athens: University of Georgia Press, 1969.

Wegmann, Jessica. " 'Playing in the Dark' with Longstreet's *Georgia Scenes:* Critical Reception and Reader Response to Treatments of Race and Gender." *Southern Literary Journal* 30.1 (1997): 13–26.

JAMES RUSSELL LOWELL (1819–1891)

William Pannapacker

BIOGRAPHY

Poet, essayist, editor, scholar, educator, abolitionist, and diplomat, James Russell Lowell was born in Cambridge, Massachusetts, and graduated from Harvard University (1838; LL.B., 1840; M.A., 1841). He was editor of *The Pioneer* (1843) and the *Atlantic Monthly* (1857–61), coeditor with Charles Eliot Norton of the *North American Review* (1863–72), Smith Professor of Modern Languages, Harvard University (1855–86), U.S. Minister to Spain (1877–80) and England (1880–85), and the second president of the Modern Language Association (1887–91). Considered a "Brahmin," Lowell was descended from a prominent colonial family. He was a decade or more younger than the other Fireside Poets (Holmes, Longfellow, Whittier), but Lowell shared with them the leadership of the cultural establishment of New England from the 1840s through the 1880s. Lowell was among the most versatile authors of his time, adept at many different genres: satire, dialect writing, occasional verse, oratory, political essays, literary scholarship, and criticism. His poems, particularly *The Biglow Papers, First Series* (1848), *The Vision of Sir Launfal* (1848), and the "Ode Recited at the Commemoration of the Living and Dead Soldiers of Harvard University, July 21, 1865" (usually called the "Commemoration Ode"), were among the most admired works produced by an American in the nineteenth century. Since then, Lowell's overall reputation has declined; he seldom appears in anthologies, and he is remembered primarily by specialists in American literature for his rendering of Yankee dialect in *The Biglow Papers,* his abolitionist writings, and his criticism of more recognized contemporaries in *A Fable for Critics* (1848) and other literary essays.

Lowell became a literary writer after abandoning the legal profession. Something of a genteel dilettante in his early years, Lowell published *A Year's Life, and Other Poems* (1841), contributed essays to *The Dial* and *Graham's,* and founded a short-lived journal of his own, *The Pioneer* (1843), which was a critical success but a financial failure. In 1844 he married Maria White (1821–53), a poet and abolitionist who stimulated his interest in liberal humanitarianism and his determination to become a literary professional. Lowell's *Poems* (1844) demonstrated more overt political concerns and brought him more positive attention and sales than his earlier work. His prominence increased when he became an editor and contributor to the *National Anti-Slavery Standard* (1848–52) and contributed to the *Pennsylvania Freeman*. In 1848 Lowell established his national reputation as a satirist, poet, and literary critic with the publication of *The Biglow Papers, A Fable for Critics: A Glance at a Few of Our Literary Progenies, Poems: Second Series,* and *The Vision of Sir Launfal.*

After the death of Maria in 1853, Lowell turned increasingly to editing, scholarship, and literary criticism. He succeeded Henry Wadsworth Longfellow as Smith Professor of Modern Languages at Harvard (1855–86). In this period he also became the founding editor of the *Atlantic Monthly* (1857–61) and later became co-editor with Charles Eliot Norton of the *North American Review* (1863–72). Both magazines were widely circulated and well respected; they shaped the literary status hierarchies of the United States for much of the nineteenth century, reinforcing the authority of New England writers but also launching the careers of many younger authors such as William Dean Howells and Louisa May Alcott. During his years as an academic and an editor, Lowell collected his literary essays in *Fireside Travels* (1864) and published *The Biglow Papers, Second Series* (1867). Originally serialized during the Civil War, the *Second Series* attacked the Confederacy and burlesqued the speeches of Jefferson Davis. Lowell's "Commemoration Ode," presented at the dedication of Harvard's Memorial Hall in 1865, established Lowell as one of the poet laureates of the Civil War.

Though he was respected as a teacher, scholar, and critic, Lowell's career as a literary artist declined after the 1860s. *Under the Willows* (1869) gathered together poems published during the preceding 20 years; *The Cathedral* (1870) was a blank verse meditation on science and religion. However, Lowell's pro-Union writings during and after the Civil War, and his support for Rutherford B. Hayes in the contested 1876 presidential election, resulted in his appointment as minister to Spain (1877–80) followed by his appointment as minister to Great Britain (1880–85). Increasingly conservative and Anglophile in his final decade, Lowell became part of London's literary society. After the death of his second wife, Frances Dunlap, in 1885, Lowell retired to Elmwood, his estate in Cambridge, Massachusetts, where he died in 1891.

MAJOR WORKS AND THEMES

Lowell's activities as an author were varied, and his writings are often described as lacking a specific focus or method. His "serious" poetry, such as *Sir Launfal* and *The Cathedral,* has not endured so well as his satire, literary criticism, political essays, and occasional verse.

Most critics regard *The Biglow Papers, First Series* (1848) as Lowell's major contribution to American literature. Presenting the comical observations of Hosea Biglow, a New England farmer (edited in a mock academic style by Homer Wilbur), it was one of the earliest and most notable renderings of Yankee dialect in verse; it was also a sharp critique of southern expansionism via the Mexican War and liberal racism among northern abolitionists who regarded Africans as an inferior race, however much they desired the end of slavery. Some of the political satire requires footnoting today, but the black humor of the *Biglow Papers* anticipates the later writings of Mark Twain.

A Fable for Critics (1848) documents the younger Lowell's support for the Young America movement's efforts to establish literary independence from Europe standards of taste. *A Fable* also spoofed many of the leading American literary figures of the period, including Alcott, Brownson, Bryant, Cooper, Emerson, Hawthorne, Holmes, Poe, Thoreau, and Whittier. Lowell's verse is sometimes careless, but his critical assessments of contemporary writers are perceptive and often witty.

Although Lowell's political writings receive less attention than his poetry and criticism, he was a leading voice of abolitionism. Lowell made notable attacks on the hypocrisy of institutional religious support for slavery (see "The Church and the Clergy" and its sequel "The Church and the Clergy Again" [1845], and "Politics and the Pulpit" [1849]). In an influential *Atlantic* essay, "The Election in November," Lowell argued that slavery had corrupted American democracy, North and South, and that the election of 1860 would be a referendum on the future of the institution. In another *Atlantic* essay, "E Pluribus Unum," Lowell argued against the separation of North and South because they were essentially the same culture. These essays, along with both issues of *The Biglow Papers* and Lowell's other writings on race, the Civil War, and Abraham Lincoln, are of particular interest to historians as well as literary scholars.

Many of Lowell's contemporaries praised the "Commemoration Ode" as the one of the greatest poetic tributes to the sacrifice of the Union soldiers. Lowell was unhappy with it; it was written in haste under the pressure of a deadline, and it sometimes shows. Nevertheless, the poem remains a deeply felt evocation of the mood of the time and place. Lowell's description of Lincoln, "our Martyr-Chief," is particularly memorable (Lowell xx).

CRITICAL RECEPTION

Even in the nineteenth century, Lowell was never as popular as the other Fireside Poets. He provoked contradictory reactions. Edgar Allan Poe called Lowell one of the best poets in America (despite his technical flaws), and Thomas Wentworth Higginson declared Lowell's "Commemoration Ode" "the finest single poem yet produced in this country" (qtd. in Rees 390). Yet Margaret Fuller described Lowell as "absolutely wanting in the true spirit and tone of poesy . . . his verse is stereotyped; his thought sounds no depths, and posterity will not remember him" (qtd. in Duberman 99). By the end of his life, Lowell had outlived many of the institutions and political interests that sustained his reputation. In 1892, Horace Traubel presented him as a foil for the poet Walt Whitman, whom Lowell had slighted on numerous occasions: "One man contributes preservation; another movement. One is conservative; another dynamic" (22). To populists Lowell was an elitist. To socialists he was a reactionary conservative. To modernists he was excessively traditional, an icon of the "Genteel Tradition" they wished to smash. Ironically (given his early support for the Young America movement), all of these groups came to consider Lowell an obstacle to the emergence of an "authentic" and "modern" American literature. By the mid-twentieth century the New Critics had finally reduced Lowell to a minor poet; it became a cliché to state that his voice was too diffuse, he never mastered the lyric mode, and his work is characterized by technical infelicities, didacticism, lack of clarity, and obscurity. Few critics since then have taken much of an interest in him.

Lowell is sometimes depicted as a case study in unrealized literary potential; his political commitments were more pressing than the technical demands of poetry. With the rise of historicist literary criticism and its interest in ideology and the politics of literary history, a reconsideration of Lowell's significance is long overdue.

WORKS CITED

Duberman, Martin. *James Russell Lowell.* Boston: Houghton Mifflin, 1966.

Lowell, James Russell. *The Poetical Works of James Russell Lowell.* Ed. Marjorie R. Kaufman. Boston: Houghton Mifflin, 1978.

Rees, Robert A. "James Russell Lowell." *Fifteen American Authors Before 1900: Bibliographic Essays on Research and Criticism.* Rev. ed. Eds. Earl N. Harbert and Robert A. Rees. Madison: University of Wisconsin Press, 1984. 379–401.

Traubel, Horace. "Lowell–Whitman: A Contrast." *Poet-Lore* 4 (1892): 22–31.

BIBLIOGRAPHY

Works by James Russell Lowell

Poetry

A Year's Life, and Other Poems. Boston: Little and Brown, 1841.

Poems. Cambridge, MA: John Owen, 1844.

The Biglow Papers, First Series. Cambridge, MA: George Nichols, 1848. Reprint: *The Biglow Papers (First Series): A Critical Edition.* Ed. Thomas Wortham. Dekalb, IL: Northern Illinois University Press, 1977.

A Fable for Critics: A Glance at a Few of Our Literary Progenies. New York: Putnam, 1848.

Poems: Second Series. Cambridge, MA: George Nichols, 1848.

The Vision of Sir Launfal. Cambridge, MA: George Nichols, 1848.

Ode Recited at the Commemoration of the Living and Dead Soldiers of Harvard University, July 21, 1865. Cambridge, MA: Privately Printed, 1865.

The Biglow Papers, Second Series. Boston: Ticknor and Fields, 1867.

Under the Willows and Other Poems. Boston: Fields, Osgood, and Co., 1869.

The Cathedral. Boston: Fields, Osgood, and Co., 1870.

Three Memorial Poems. Boston: James R. Osgood, 1877.

Early Poems. New York: John B. Alden, 1887.

Heartease and Rue. Boston and New York: Houghton, Mifflin and Co., 1888.

Last Poems. Ed. Charles Eliot Norton. Boston and New York: Houghton, Mifflin and Co., 1895.

The Uncollected Poems of James Russell Lowell. Ed. Thelma M. Smith. Philadelphia: University of Pennsylvania Press, 1950.

Essays and Criticism

Conversations on Some of the Old Poets. Cambridge, MA: John Owen, 1845.

A Fable for Critics: A Glance at a Few of Our Literary Progenies. New York: Putnam, 1848.

Fireside Travels. Boston: Ticknor and Fields, 1864.

Among My Books. Boston: Fields, Osgood, and Co., 1870.

My Study Windows. Boston: James R. Osgood and Co., 1871.

Among My Books, Second Series. Boston: James R. Osgood and Co., 1876.

Democracy and Other Addresses. Boston and New York: Houghton, Mifflin and Co., 1887.

Political Essays. Boston and New York: Houghton, Mifflin and Co., 1888.

Latest Literary Essays and Addresses of James Russell Lowell. Ed. Charles Eliot Norton. Boston and New York: Houghton, Mifflin and Co., 1892.

The Old English Dramatists. Ed. Charles Eliot Norton. Boston and New York: Houghton, Mifflin and Co., 1892.

Lectures on the English Poets. Cleveland, OH: The Rowfant Club, 1897.

Early Prose Writings of James Russell Lowell. Ed. Edward Everett Hale, London and New York: John Lane, 1902.

The Anti-Slavery Papers of James Russell Lowell. Ed. William Belmont Parker. 2 vols. Boston and New York: Houghton Mifflin, 1902.

The Function of the Poet and Other Essays. Ed. Albert Mordell. Boston and New York: Houghton Mifflin, 1920.

Literary Criticism of James Russell Lowell. Ed. Herbert Smith. Lincoln: University of Nebraska Press, 1969.

Letters

Letters of James Russell Lowell. Ed. Charles Eliot Norton. 2 vols. New York: Harper and Brothers, 1894.

Letters of John Holmes to James Russell Lowell and Others. Ed. William Roscoe Thayer. Boston and New York: Houghton Mifflin, 1917.

New Letters of James Russell Lowell. Ed. M. A. DeWolfe Howe. New York and London: Harper and Brothers, 1932.

The Scholar-Friends, Letters of Francis James Child and James Russell Lowell. Ed. M. A. DeWolfe Howe and G. W. Cottrell Jr. Cambridge: Harvard University Press, 1952.

Browning to His American Friends: Letters Between the Brownings, the Storys and James Russell Lowell, 1841–1890. Ed. Gertrude Reese Hudson. New York: Barnes and Noble, 1965.

Standard Editions

The Writings of James Russell Lowell. The Riverside Edition. Ed. James Russell Lowell and Charles Eliot Norton. 12 vols. Boston and New York: Houghton Mifflin, 1890–92.

The Complete Poetical Works of James Russell Lowell. The Cambridge Edition. Ed. Horace E. Scudder. Boston: Houghton Mifflin and Co., 1897. Reprint: *The Poetical Works of James Russell Lowell.* Revised with a critical introduction by Marjorie R. Kaufman. Boston: Houghton Mifflin, 1978.

Bibliography

Blanck, Jacob. "James Russell Lowell." *Bibliography of American Literature.* Vol. 6. New Haven: Yale University Press, 1973. 21–104.

Rees, Robert A. "James Russell Lowell." *Fifteen American Authors Before 1900: Bibliographic Essays on Research and Criticism.* Rev. ed. Eds. Earl N. Harbert and Robert A. Rees. Madison: University of Wisconsin Press, 1984. 379–401.

See also *American Literary Scholarship,* published annually by Duke University Press since 1963.

Selected Studies of James Russell Lowell

Altick, R. D. "Was Lowell an Historical Critic?" *American Literature* 14 (1942): 250–9.

Austin, James C. *Fields of the* Atlantic Monthly*: Letters to an Editor 1861–1870.* San Marino, CA: Huntington Library, 1953.

Bail, Hamilton Vaughan. "James Russell Lowell's *Ode Recited at the Commemoration of the Living and Dead Soldiers of Harvard University, July 21, 1865.*" *Papers of the Bibliographical Society of America* 37 (1943): 169–202.

Baker, Paul R. *The Fortunate Pilgrims: Americans in Italy 1800–1860.* Cambridge, MA: Harvard University Press, 1964.

Bell, Michael J. " 'The Only True Folk Songs We Have in English': James Russell Lowell and the Politics of the Nation." *Journal of American Folklore* 108 (1995): 131–55.

Bernard, E. G. "New Light on Lowell as Editor." *New England Quarterly* 10 (1937): 337–41.

Brooks, Van Wyck. *The Flowering of New England 1815–1865.* New York: E. P. Dutton, 1936.

Brownell, William C. "Lowell." *Scribner's* 41 (1907): 220–35.

Clark, Harry H. "Lowell—Humanitarian, Nationalist, or Humanist?" *Studies in Philology* 27 (1930): 411–41.

——. "Lowell's Criticism of Romantic Literature." *PMLA* 41 (1926): 209–28.

Duberman, Martin. *James Russell Lowell.* Boston: Houghton Mifflin, 1966.

Ehrlich, Heyward. "Charles Frederick Briggs and Lowell's *Fable for Critics.*" *Modern Language Quarterly* 28 (1967): 329–41.

Eliot, Charles W. "James Russell Lowell As a Professor." *Harvard Graduates Magazine* 27 (1919): 482–87.

Enkvist, N. E. "*The Biglow Papers* in Nineteenth-Century England." *New England Quarterly* 26 (1953): 219–36.

Gnomes, Emmanuel. "The Crackerbox Tradition and the Race Problem in Lowell's *The Biglow Papers* and Hughes *Sketches of Simple. College Language Association Journal.* 3 (1984): 254–69.

Graf, Leroy P. " 'This Clangor of Belated Mourning': James Russell Lowell on Andrew Johnson's Father." *South Atlantic Quarterly* 62 (1963): 423–34.

Greenslet, Ferris. *James Russell Lowell, His Life and Work.* Boston and New York: Houghton, Mifflin and Co., 1905.

Hale, [E]dward [E]verett. *James Russell Lowell and His Friends.* Boston and New York: Houghton, Mifflin and Co., 1899.

Henry, H. T. "Music in Lowell's Prose and Verse." *Musical Quarterly* 24 (1924): 546–72.

Howard, Leon. *Victorian Knight-Errant: A Study of the Early Career of James Russell Lowell.* Berkeley and Los Angeles: University of California Press, 1952.

Howells, William Dean. "Studies of Lowell." *Literary Friends and Acquaintance: A Personal Retrospect of American Authorship.* New York and London: Harper and Brothers, 1900. 212–50.

James, Henry. "James Russell Lowell." *Atlantic Monthly* 69 (1892): 35–50.

Jenkins, W. G. "Lowell's Criteria of Political Values." *New England Quarterly* 7 (1934): 115–41.

Klibbe, Laurence H. *James Russell Lowell's Residence in Spain 1877–1880.* Newark: Washington Irving, 1964.

Macy, John. *The Spirit of American Literature.* Garden City and New York: Doubleday, Page, and Co., 1913.

Matthews, Brander. *Introduction to American Literature.* New York: American Book Company, 1896.

McGlinchee, Claire. *James Russell Lowell.* New York: Twayne, 1967.

Nye, Russell. "Lowell and American Speech." *Philological Quarterly* 17 (1939): 249–56.

Oggel, L. Terry. "Lowell's Humor and His Other Review of Thoreau." *American Transcendental Quarterly* 43 (1979): 189–98.

Parrington, Vernon. L. *The Romantic Revolution in America.* New York: Harcourt, Brace, 1927.

Pearce, Roy Harvey. *The Continuity of American Poetry.* Middletown, CT: Wesleyan University Press, 1987.

Perry, Bliss. *The Praise of Folly, and Other Papers.* Boston: Houghton Mifflin, 1923.

Reilly, Joseph J. *James Russell Lowell as a Critic.* New York and London: G. P. Putnam's Son, 1915.

Robertson, J. M. "Lowell as a Critic." *North American Review* 209 (1919): 246–62.

Scudder, Horace E. *James Russell Lowell.* 2 vols. Boston: Houghton Mifflin, 1902.

Sedgwick, Ellery. *The Atlantic Monthly: Yankee Humanism at High Tide and Ebb.* Amherst: University of Massachusetts Press, 1994.

Thayer, William Roscoe. "James Russell Lowell As a Teacher: Recollections of His Last Pupil." *Scribner's Magazine* 68 (1920): 473–80.

Traubel, Horace. "Lowell—Whitman: A Contrast." *Poet-Lore* 4 (1892): 22–31.

Tucker, Edward. "James Russell Lowell and Robert Carter: *The Pioneer* and Fifty Letters from Lowell to Carter." *Studies in the American Renaissance* (1987): 187–246.

Underwood, Francis Henry. *The Poet and the Man: Recollections and Appreciations of James Russell Lowell.* Boston: Lee and Shepard, 1892.

Vernon, Hope Jillson, ed. *The Poems of Maria Lowell with Unpublished Letters and a Biography.* Providence: Brown University Press, 1936.

Voss, Arthur. "Background of Satire in *The Biglow Papers.*" *The New England Quarterly.* 23.1 (1950): 47–64.

Warren, Austin. "Lowell on Thoreau." *Studies in Philology* 27 (1930): 442–61.

Wagenknecht, Edward. *James Russell Lowell: Portrait of a Many-Sided Man.* New York and Oxford: Oxford University Press, 1971.

Wilson, Edmund. *Patriotic Gore: Studies in the Literature of the American Civil War.* New York: Oxford University Press, 1962.

Wortham, Thomas. "James Russell Lowell." *The Transcendentalists: A Review of Research and Criticism.* Ed. Joel Myerson. New York: Modern Language Association, 1984. 336–42.

——. "William Cullen Bryant and the Fireside Poets." *Columbia Literary History of the United States.* Ed. Emory Elliott. New York: Columbia University Press, 1988. 278–88.

MARIA JANE McINTOSH (1803–1878)

Rebecca R. Saulsbury

BIOGRAPHY

Born in 1803 in Sunbury, a coastal village and health resort in Georgia, Maria Jane McIntosh was a best-selling and prolific writer of 24 books, "one of the first of the popular women novelists of the mid-century" (Baym 86). McIntosh grew up a member of a wealthy and distinguished Georgia family, the daughter of Lachlan McIntosh, a lawyer, and his fifth wife, Mary Moore Maxwell. McIntosh's father died when she was three years old, and she was raised and educated primarily by her often-invalid mother. McIntosh attended Sunbury Academy, a coeducational institution, and in 1820 she studied at nearby Baiden's Bluff Academy.

After her mother died in 1823, McIntosh managed the family estate, selling it 12 years later and investing the profits in securities. She moved to New York City to live with her half brother, a Naval officer, and then lost her fortune in the Panic of 1837. Showing the resolve and strength later characteristic of her heroines, McIntosh turned to writing to support herself. In 1841, under the pseudonym Aunt Kitty, she penned a children's story, *Blind Alice*. Two years later, McIntosh began writing and publishing novels anonymously. Her fourth novel, *Two Lives,* was a best-seller, going through seven editions in four years, while *Charms and Counter-Charms* had eight editions, reportedly selling more than 100,000 copies. McIntosh's novels enjoyed popularity in France and England, allowing her financial independence.

In 1859, McIntosh traveled through England and France and then spent a year in Geneva with a nephew, John Elliott Ward, and his family. After her return to New York, she taught briefly at Miss Henrietta B. Haines's school and published her last novel, *Two Pictures,* in 1863.

She later moved to Morristown, New Jersey, where she made her home with her niece and namesake, Maria McIntosh Cox. After suffering a painful, yearlong illness, McIntosh died on February 25, 1878.

MAJOR WORKS AND THEMES

McIntosh began her career by writing moral tales for children modeled on Samuel Goodrich's "Peter Parley" stories. Two years after *Blind Alice* was published, she began writing moral novels for adults, *Conquest and Self-Conquest; or, Which Makes the Hero?* and *Woman an Enigma; or, Life and Its Revealings,* both appearing in 1843. In the six "woman's novels" that followed, McIntosh contrasted characters, places, and situations to depict the trials and tribulations endured by her heroines, a formula frequently employed in "woman's fiction." *Two Lives; or, To Seem and To Be,* the first novel McIntosh published under her own name, for instance, features a pair of heroines opposite in nature and appearance. Grace Elliot, fragile, diminutive, and blond, lacks self-control. In contrast, her cousin Isabel Duncan is tall, dark-haired, and analytical. She possesses the self-awareness and principle deficient in Grace. Together, Grace and Isabel serve as cautions against women's excess dependence and independence.

Baym argues, however, that McIntosh employed the elements of "woman's fiction" not merely to write moral tales, but also to explore variations in women's inner development. For example, in *Woman an Enigma,* she employs the conventional romantic setting of a convent in revolutionary France as a cover for her real purpose: to show the heroine Louise de Valière's intellectual, moral, and emotional growth in adversity. She evolves from a superficial girl to an independent, self-assured woman who inspires deep love rather than superficial passion.

In 1850, McIntosh addressed the woman question in *Woman in America: Her Work and Her Reward,* her first work of nonfiction. Echoing Catherine Beecher's conservative stance on woman's place in nineteenth-century America, she opposed the burgeoning women's rights movement. Instead, she urged her readers to "walk the narrow path of right," as "Christian gentlewomen" (Hart 72–73).

Three years later, McIntosh participated, albeit reluctantly, in the national debate on slavery. In response to "An Affectionate and Christian Address of Many Thousands of Women of Great Britain and Ireland to Their Sisters the Thousands of Women of the United States of America," an abolitionist tract entrusted to Harriet Beecher Stowe by the Duchess of Sutherland, McIntosh wrote *A Letter on the Address of the Women of England to Their Sisters of America, in Relation to Slavery,* a pamphlet that originally appeared as an essay in the editorial pages of the *New York Observer.* She argued slavery was a benevolent institution that fostered close familial relationships and slaves' happiness. Unable to ignore the power of Stowe's runaway best-seller, *Uncle Tom's Cabin,* McIntosh also wrote a pro-slavery novel, ironically titled *The Lofty and the Lowly,* in which she contrasts the pernicious, exploitative values of northern capitalism with the nurturing, communitarian and Christian ethics of the plantation system.

CRITICAL RECEPTION

Critics and readers alike praised McIntosh for her moral and Christian sensibilities, qualities highly valued in antebellum women writers. John Hart, who considered McIntosh important enough to include in his anthology *The Female Prose Writers of America* (1852), appreciated her determination to exclude "from her attention everything that did not absolutely belong to the moral life" (68). In 1855, Sarah Josepha Hale cited McIntosh in *Woman's Record,* where she celebrated McIntosh's "pure morality and religion" (742).

In her anthology *Women of the South Distinguished in Literature* (1861), Mary Forrest lauded McIntosh's abilities as a social critic, asserting that she "most skillfully dissects the artificial system of social life in America, and shows herself capable of a wide and well-linked range of logical thought" (167). In 1875, McIntosh appeared in Evert A. and George L. Duyckinck's prestigious *Cyclopaedia of American Literature,* and as late as 1888, she was cited in Phoebe Hanaford's *Daughters of America; or, Women of the Century.*

Like so many of her contemporaries, however, McIntosh's reputation and writing sank into literary oblivion. The recovery project of nineteenth-century women writers has benefited McIntosh only somewhat. Indeed, studies of her work by Nina Baym, Elizabeth Moss, and Bashar Akili, as well as two bio-bibliographical essays in the *Dictionary of Literary Biography,* have failed to revive more than passing interest in McIntosh. She remains a relatively obscure writer, remembered mostly for her flowery, sentimental prose and her pro-slavery stance, the latter no doubt explaining feminist critics' reluctance to study her writing.

WORKS CITED

Baym, Nina. *Woman's Fiction: A Guide to Novels by and about Women in America 1820–1870.* 2nd ed. Urbana and Chicago: University of Illinois Press, 1993.

Forrest, Mary. *Women of the South Distinguished in Literature.* New York: Derby & Jackson, 1861.

Hale, Sarah Josepha. *Woman's Record.* New York: Harper & Brothers, 1855.

Hart, John S. *The Female Prose Writers of America.* Philadelphia: E. H. Butler & Co., 1852.

BIBLIOGRAPHY

Works by Maria Jane McIntosh

Blind Alice; or, Do Right If You Wish to Be Happy. New York: Dayton & Saxton, 1841.

Florence Arnott; or, Is She Generous? New York: Dayton & Saxton, 1841.

Jessie Graham; or, Friends Dear, but Truth Dearer. New York: Dayton & Saxton, 1841.

Ellen Leslie; or, The Reward of Self-Control. New York: Dayton & Saxton, 1842.

Grace and Clara; or, Be Just as Well as Generous. New York: Dayton & Saxton, 1842; London: T. Nelson, 1850.

Conquest and Self-Conquest; or, Which Makes the Hero? New York: Harper, 1843.

Woman an Enigma; or, Life and Its Revealings. New York: Harper, 1843; London: T. Nelson, 1854.

The Cousins: A Tale of Early Life. New York: Harper, 1845; London: T. Nelson, 1850.

Praise and Principle; or, For What Shall I Live? New York: Harper, 1845; London: Routledge, 1850.

Two Lives; or, To Seem and To Be. New York: D. Appleton; Philadelphia: G. S. Appleton, 1846; London: Routledge, 1852.

Aunt Kitty's Tales. New York: D. Appleton, 1847.

Charms and Counter-Charms. New York: D. Appleton, 1848; London: Routledge, 1849.

Woman in America: Her Work and Her Reward. New York: D. Appleton; Philadelphia: Geo. S. Appleton, 1850.

Evenings at Donaldson Manor; or, The Christmas Guest. New York: D. Appleton, 1851; London, T. Nelson, 1845.

A Letter on the Address of the Women of England to Their Sisters of America, in Relation to Slavery. New York: T. J. Crowen, 1853.

The Lofty and the Lowly; or, Good in All and None All-Good. New York: D. Appleton, 1853; republished as *Alice Montrose; or, The Lofty and the Lowly; Good in All and None All Good.* London: R. Bentley, 1853.

Meta Gray; or, What Makes Home Happy. New York: D. Appleton, 1859.

Emily Herbert; or, The Happy Home. New York & London: D. Appleton, 1855.

Rose and Lillie Stanhope; or, The Power of Conscience. New York: D. Appleton, 1855; London: Routledge, 1855.

Violet; or, The Cross and the Crown. Boston: John P. Jewett, 1856; London: Routledge, 1856.

A Year with Maggie and Emma: A True Story. New York & London: D. Appleton, 1861.

Two Pictures; or, What We Think of Ourselves, and What the World Thinks of Us. New York: D. Appleton, 1863.

Violetta and I. Boston: Loring, 1870.

The Children's Mirror: A Treasury of Stories. New York: T. Nelson, 1887; London: T. Nelson, 1887.

Studies of Maria Jane McIntosh

Akili, Bashar. "Maria Jane McIntosh, a Woman in Her Time: A Biographical and Critical Study." Diss., University of Technology, Loughborough, United Kingdom, 1990.

Baym, Nina. *Woman's Fiction: A Guide to Novels by and about Women in America 1820–1870.* 2nd ed. Urbana and Chicago: University of Illinois Press, 1993.

Duyckinck, Evert A., and George L. Duyckinck. *Cyclopaedia of American Literature.* 2 vols. Philadelphia: William Rutter & Co., 1875.

Hanaford, Phebe A. *Daughters of America; or, Women of the Century.* Augusta, ME: True and Company, 1883.

Hynes, Jennifer. "Maria Jane McIntosh." *Dictionary of Literary Biography.* Vol. 239: *American Women Prose Writers, 1820–1870.* Eds. Amy E. Huduck and Katharine Rodier. Detroit: Gale Group, 2001. 206–12.

Lopez, Esther. "Maria Jane McIntosh." *Dictionary of Literary Biography.* Vol. 248: *Antebellum Women Writers in the South.* Ed. Kent P. Lundquist. Detroit: Gale Group, 2001. 246–51.

Moss, Elizabeth. *Domestic Novelists in the Old South: Defenders of Southern Culture.* Baton Rouge: Louisiana University Press, 1992.

HERMAN MELVILLE (1819–1891)

Steven Olsen-Smith

BIOGRAPHY

Born in New York City on August 1, 1819, to Allan and Maria Gansevoort Melvill (the *e* was added in 1833), Herman Melville was the third of eight children and the second son in the family. His paternal grandfather was a member of the Boston Tea Party, and Maria's father had served as a general in the Revolutionary War. The Melvill children enjoyed all the benefits of patrician life until 1830, when the family fell into poverty and removed to Albany after the bankruptcy of Allan Melvill, who then grew deranged and died in 1832. Herman was withdrawn from school and put to work as a clerk in the New York State Bank, where a maternal uncle served on the board of directors. Pressured by her husband's creditors and all but abandoned by most of her relatives, Maria brought the family to Lansingburgh in 1838. There Herman studied surveying and engineering but could only find work as a school teacher, first in the Berkshires outside Pittsfield, Massachusetts, where his paternal uncle ran a farm, and then in different locations along the Hudson River. During the summer of 1839 he served aboard a merchant ship between Manhattan and Liverpool, England, and in 1840 he traveled to Illinois and back in a failed effort to seek his fortune. Without prospects ashore, he returned to sea in January 1841 on a whaling voyage out of Fairhaven, Massachusetts.

Aboard the whaling ship *Acushnet* Melville rounded Cape Horn (later a symbol for life's perils in his fiction) and labored for a year and a half in the Offshore Grounds of the southern Pacific before jumping ship with crewmate Tobias Greene at Nukahiva in the Marquesas Islands. In the island's interior Melville suffered a leg injury and took refuge among the Typee tribes people with Greene, who left to find help but never returned. Melville had been with the Typees for approximately four weeks when he left them and signed on with a whaling ship that bore him to Tahiti, where he and other crewmates were imprisoned for refusing duty aboard the vessel, which was badly captained. Upon release Melville worked as a farmhand on nearby Eimeo before journeying aboard another whaler to the Sandwich (now Hawaiian) Islands, disembarking at Maui and moving on to Honolulu. Melville's prior immersion at Nukahiva among an indigenous tribe still relatively unaffected by western influence made him a thoughtful witness to profound disruptions in Tahitian and Hawaiian life and culture wrought by vigorous Protestant missionary activity and by French, English, and American imperialism. In 1843 he left Honolulu as an ordinary seaman aboard the U.S. naval warship *United States,* which toured the South American coastlines and arrived in Boston in October 1844.

Melville's sea-faring experiences provided the main catalyst for his authorship. In 1846 he achieved international fame with *Typee,* which depicts his stay among the Typee natives (extending the duration to four months) and generates suspense from their reputation as cannibals. Publicity for the book was sustained by ongoing newspaper debates about its authenticity and still more by the reemergence of Greene, who publicly vouched for its truthfulness. Melville followed up on this success with *Omoo* (1847), a similarly embellished account of his experiences in and around Tahiti. In August 1847 he married Elizabeth Shaw, the daughter of chief justice Lemuel Shaw, of the Massachusetts Supreme Court. They settled with family members in Manhattan, where their son Malcolm was born in February 1849, and where Melville completed his third book *Mardi* that same year. By necessity a resourceful autodidact since childhood, he invested much of his profits in books and studied the works of Plato, Shakespeare, Milton, and other great writers. Signaling his growing commitment to intellectual matters, Melville's *Mardi* bears the influence of ambitious reading and consists of extended philosophical speculation and political satire. Quite unlike his first two books, it failed in the marketplace and damaged his popular reputation. That summer he dutifully turned out the market-oriented *Redburn* (based on his trip to Liverpool) and *White-Jacket* (his account of life on a U.S. warship)—two "jobs," he told his father-in-law, adding that it was his "earnest desire to write those sort of books which are said to 'fail' " (*Correspondence* 139). In late 1849 he crossed the Atlantic to arrange for the publication of *White-Jacket* in London, and it was apparently on the journey back that he began planning *Moby-Dick* (1851), begun in Manhattan and finished in the Berkshires, where in October 1850 he and Elizabeth settled with Melville's mother and three of his sisters near Pittsfield on a farm they named Arrowhead.

In the Berkshires Melville cultivated a relationship with Nathaniel Hawthorne, whom he had met the previous summer and whose literary talents he had praised in an essay, "Hawthorne and His Mosses," which appeared in the New York *Literary World* in August 1850. His admiration for the older writer was probably instrumental in Melville's own bid for literary greatness with *Moby-Dick,* but the book's daring treatment of religious matters offended many readers, and it did not sell well. *Pierre* followed shortly in 1852 but fared much worse and even prompted some reviewers to question the author's sanity. Melville's reputation was now marred to the point that he was unable to publish his next work, *The Isle of the Cross* (completed in May 1853), which remains lost. For the next three years he earned an income writing anonymous stories for magazines, leading to his serialized novel *Israel Potter,* published as a book in 1855 to favorable reviews. But his *The Piazza Tales* and his last novel *The Confidence-Man* (1857) would each fail to make a profit. Deeply in debt, stricken by health problems, and now a father of four, Melville escaped bankruptcy only by the good grace of his wife's father, Judge Shaw, who paid off his debts and financed Melville's recuperative visit to the Holy Land and Europe from October 1856 to May 1857. From late 1857 to 1860 Melville earned money by lecturing, traveling as far west as Milwaukee in 1859. In 1860 he embarked for a voyage around the world aboard a merchant ship captained by his brother Thomas; but the ship was rerouted, and Melville turned back at San Francisco. By prior arrangement,

Elizabeth attempted to have a book of poems by Melville published in his absence, but the manuscript was rejected by publishers.

Melville sold Arrowhead in 1863 and lived for the rest of his life in Manhattan. In 1866 he published his first volume of poetry, *Battle-Pieces,* and obtained his first regular job as a customs inspector. Despite the modest upturn in fortune, Melville grew increasingly bitter about his career and appears to have taken out his frustrations on those nearest to him. Feeling "ill treated" by her husband (*Correspondence* 859), Elizabeth came close to leaving him in the spring of 1867, and in September of that year Malcolm died, under ambiguous circumstances, from a self-inflicted gunshot wound. Over the next two decades Melville continued to study and write. In 1876 he published *Clarel,* a book-length poem some seven or eight years in the making, exploring the crisis of religious faith in late-nineteenth-century secular society. Two more poetic works followed: *John Marr* (1888) and *Timoleon* (1891), both printed for private circulation. Melville's short masterpiece *Billy Budd, Sailor* was unfinished when he died in obscurity on September 28, 1891, survived by Elizabeth and his two daughters, Bessie and Frances (his son Stanwix had died in 1886). Newspaper obituaries commented that he had long been assumed dead, but enthusiastic readers were already laying the foundation for a sweeping revival of Melville's literary fame.

MAJOR WORKS AND THEMES

Scholars often point to the tragic reversals of Melville's childhood when accounting for preponderant themes of isolation and dispossession in his fiction. He drew from memories of his father's death and his family's abrupt descent into poverty for the background of the boy-narrator in *Redburn,* who reflects: "never can such blights be made good; they strike in too deep, and leave such a scar that the air of Paradise might not erase it" (11). Melville's personal experience with the vagaries of fate informs his characters' embattled notions of their own personal integrity and their keen sense of the arbitrariness of social privilege, which together contribute to a running theme of rebellion in his fiction. Defiance of authority precipitates narrative action in the early chapters of *Typee, Omoo,* and *Mardi,* each of which portrays the progress of independent experience through a loosely controlled, picaresque narrative structure. In *Typee* and *Omoo* Melville challenges nineteenth-century constructs of "savagery" and "civilization" by observing the effects of colonial trade, military dominance, and missionary activity on indigenous cultures—at points relying upon the writings of previous visitors to the South Seas to expand his narratives while rhetorically combating (through the appropriation and revision of source passages) their imperialist and racial viewpoints.

Melville likewise pursues social criticism in *Mardi,* yet here the purely fictive South Seas setting serves as a springboard for his ambitious expansion into matters of epistemology, psychology, and the human condition. The pivotal narrative event in *Mardi* is a spontaneous act of violence from which arise thematic issues of human impulse, remorse, and moral ambiguity. Melville addresses these themes again in *White-Jacket* with the authoritarian shipboard dynamics of flogging and the motif of impulsive, violent reaction in Chapter 67, "White-Jacket Arraigned at the Mast," where the sailor-narrator struggles with destructive impulses when his captain threatens to have him flogged. Typifying Melville's use of the "inferior-superior relationship" among characters throughout his fiction (Hayford 661), the episode depicts spontaneous violence as an instinctual reaction to intolerable treatment, with the title character reluctantly acknowledging that murder and suicide are "the last resources of an insulted and unendurable existence" (*White-Jacket* 202). The paradoxical union of crime with innocence is central to Melville's formation of character here and in the ambitious works that followed *White-Jacket.* Keenly attentive to the harmful and volatile effects of arbitrary power in institutional and social systems, Melville was no less fascinated by the individual self's imperfect authority over its own wayward tendencies.

These themes go cosmic in America's first prose epic, *Moby-Dick,* where Ahab's archetypal struggle against the white whale is at once a heroic revolt against higher powers and a tragic surrender to the mind's own pathological tyrannies. Indebted to Calvinist strains of American Protestant theology and to ancient Gnostic heresies, and likewise influenced by Melville's close study of Milton's *Paradise Lost,* the tragedies of Shakespeare, and other revered works of western literary tradition, *Moby-Dick* questions the traditional cosmological argument for a benevolent creator by underscoring the brutality of the material world. A pervasive motif of the book is mutilation, chiefly symbolized by the physical image of Ahab, whose severed leg and vivid birthmark (suggestive of original sin) illustrate the essential insecurity of human life and invoke further doubts concerning human prospects for spiritual salvation. In exploring the problem of evil in a world reputedly watched over by an all-good and all-powerful God, Melville illustrates among the crewmembers of the *Pequod* a wide spectrum of psychological reactions to the "ungraspable phantom of life" (5)—an expression linked in the opening chapter to the white whale itself—foregrounding Ahab's impulsive, monomaniacal revolt against a God he judges to be evil, but balancing his blasphemy with the piety of Starbuck, the reckless indifference of Stubb, and the shifting epistemological strategies of the narrator Ishmael, who in his own right displays an extraordinary pageant of psychological responses.

Before *Moby-Dick* appeared in print Melville began writing *Pierre; or the Ambiguities* (1852), which he had been formulating since as early as 1849. Dealing with the moral dilemmas of an idealistic youth who discovers that his deceased father had sired an illegitimate daughter (whose identity must remain hidden from Pierre's mother), *Pierre* is much indebted to Melville's close study of the Elizabethan dramatists and their depiction of family relationships. As in the work he had just completed, Melville questions the practicability of moral action in a world seemingly inimical to virtue—here illustrated by Pierre's impulsive and ill-fated decision to rescue his impoverished sister by making her his wife. As indicated by the book's alternate title, Pierre's exact motives are ambiguous, perhaps hinting of unacknowledged incestuous desire, and typifying Melville's thematic preoccupation with the overlapping boundaries of virtue and vice. Themes of imprisonment inform Melville's characterization of both Ahab and Pierre, for whom sources of psychological frustration often figure through wall imagery. The motif abounds in "Bartleby, the Scrivener," set in Wall Street, where the two earlier protagonists' strategy of violent defiance against higher powers is replaced by the forlorn title-character's passive refusal to participate in a heartless capitalistic system that mirrors the severity of human life in the world. As with many of his enigmatic short stories, the arcane qualities of "Bartleby" spring from allegorical patterns that were deeply private to Melville—perhaps never to be elucidated in adequate detail. He achieved the height of prose mastery in his last novel *The Confidence-Man* (1857), satirizing numerous forms of American optimism through a series of tightly constructed vignettes about an equally baffling swindler who manipulates the gullibility and greed of passengers aboard a Mississippi steamboat.

Melville's increasing commitment to technical artistry prompted his transition from fiction to poetry in the late 1850s, leading in 1860 to the unpublished *Poems,* and then in 1866 to *Battle-Pieces,* devoted to the American Civil War and influenced by Melville's own visit to the front in the spring of 1864. Stylistically original, Melville's verse displays a concentrated diction within a curtailed and highly controlled syntax—more like the compacted verse structures of Emily Dickinson than the overflowing lines of his other contemporary in innovation, Walt Whitman. In *Battle-Pieces* Melville applied his thematic preoccupations with the problem of evil to the national cataclysm of civil war. This major theme accumulates as uninitiated soldiers and citizens in individual poems undergo dark, mind-altering revelations about the human costs of the conflict (as in "The March into Virginia" and "On the Slain Collegians") and about its ultimate embodiment of the world's abiding evil (as in "The House-top" and "The Apparition"). Melville's poetic ambition climaxed with his long epic work *Clarel* (1876), centering upon the experiences and observations of a young American divinity student traveling with an intellectually diverse group of westerners in the Holy Land. Isolation and reminiscence dominate *John Marr and Other Sailors* (1888), and in *Timoleon* (1891) Melville meditated on the social alienation of artists and philosophers who think ahead of their times. Among numerous works left in manuscript at his death, the unfinished novella *Billy Budd, Sailor* depicts the spontaneous crime of an innocent seaman and marks Melville's return to the mystery of depravity in humanity, human impulse and the inscrutable workings of fate, and the consequent struggle of moral judgment in human life.

CRITICAL RECEPTION

With its meteoric early celebrity, near-total eclipse, and posthumous revival, Melville's reputation as an author represents one of the most significant records of critical reception in American literary history. Contemporary reviews of *Typee* (1846) and *Omoo* (1847) were nearly unanimous in recognizing the novelty of Melville's subject matter and his extraordinary talent with language, and they commonly reprinted long excerpts illustrating Melville's powers of natural description and delineation of native character. But reviews clashed in their appraisals of Melville's authenticity, his criticism of missionary activity in the South Seas, and his sensuality (*Typee* was expurgated after its initial publication). Though not roundly condemned, his third book *Mardi* (1849) convinced many reviewers that Melville had been foisting fiction upon his readers all along. Most major newspapers ridiculed the work's ambitious philosophical digressions and allegorical structures, and many berated Melville for departing from the graceful style and original subject matter of his first two books.

The market-oriented *Redburn* (1849) and *White-Jacket* (1850) each received favorable reviews, with critics observing that Melville had returned to his real talents of truthful portraiture and simplicity of description—pre-Romantic aesthetic criteria poorly suited for the appraisal of Melville's innovative genius. In his 1849 London journal Melville scoffed at the prestigious *Blackwood's Edinburgh Magazine* for its praise of *Redburn,* a book Melville knew to be "trash" that he wrote "to buy some tobacco with" (*Journals* 13). Voicing prevalent critical opinion on both sides of the Atlantic, the *Blackwood's* reviewer had insisted Melville should aim to be an "agreeable writer of nautical fictions," and warned that he would "do very well without aspiring to rival the masters of the art" (Higgins and Parker 271). The warning resonates in Melville's bold declaration the following year that "it is better to fail in originality, than to succeed in imitation"

("Hawthorne and his Mosses" 247), an attitude that was even then shaping the whaling narrative he had in progress.

Contemporary praise of *Moby-Dick* (1851) was limited primarily to Melville's powers of natural description and overall grasp of the language. Most reviewers criticized his attempt at a new form of elevated Elizabethan rhetoric, and the speeches of Ahab (modeled after the monologues of Hamlet and Lear) were singularly condemned, with some reviewers advising readers to skip the book's dialogue all together. On both sides of the Atlantic Melville was attacked for his irreverent treatment of organized religion and for the ribaldry of some passages in *Moby-Dick*. The New York *Independent* went so far as to prophesize that both writer and publisher would be punished by God for the book's injurious effects on the minds of its readers. Such censure was less severe in England, where *The Whale* (as it was there titled) had been expurgated. Contemporary reception in England was also affected by the publisher's inadvertent omission of the book's epilogue (which explains how Ishmael alone survives to tell the story of the *Pequod*), with British reviewers criticizing Melville's preposterous use of a narrator who perishes in the catastrophe he relates.

Contemporary criticism of *Pierre* (1852) was universally hostile. "Herman Melville Crazy," announced the New York *Day Book* (Higgins and Parker 436); "A bad book! Affected in dialect, unnatural in conception, repulsive in plot, and inartistic in construction," opened a notice of *Pierre* in the *American Whig Review* (Higgins and Parker 441). Still lamenting his departure from the style and subject matter of *Typee,* reviewers concluded that Melville had exhausted his literary talents and that his career was over. In 1855 and 1856 *Israel Potter* and *The Piazza-Tales* achieved favorable reviews, but the boost to Melville's declining reputation was quelled by hostile reviews of *The Confidence-Man* (1857), which many readers judged to be incomprehensible. The charge of unintelligibility would recur also in the contemporary reception of *Battle-Pieces* (1866) and *Clarel* (1876), with reviewers acknowledging Melville's talent for descriptive imagery but for the most part judging his versification to be crudely executed and unpoetic.

The obscurity of Melville's reputation was more complete in America than in England, where there was quiet but continuous recognition of Melville's fame. In the 1880s British enthusiasts from diverse social and institutional backgrounds began praising his writings in print and accusing the American critical establishment of neglect. These included the sea novelist William Clark Russell, the poet and dramatist Robert Buchanan, and the English classicist and socialist Henry Stephens Salt. All three played roles in prompting and encouraging American recognition of Melville's writings, particularly by the American critic Edmund Clarence Stedman, who alluded to Melville favorably in his *Poets of America* (1885), included him in his *Library of American Literature* (1889–90), and became a visitor at Melville's home. Stedman's son Arthur acted as Melville's literary executor after the author's death and edited a new edition of Melville's selected writings for the United States Book Company in 1892. Separate editions and reprints followed in London, Boston, and New York, generating a new posthumous transatlantic readership for Melville. In 1899 William Livingston Alden, a London correspondent for the *New York Times,* called for the formation of a Melville society. American recognition after the turn of the century was influenced by the efforts of another foreigner, Archibald MacMechan, of Dalhousie College, in Nova Scotia, who promoted Melville's writings among American colleagues in person and in print, with his essay "The Best Sea Story Ever Written."

Melville's fame was officially restored at the centenary of his birth, following Carl Van Doren's discussion of Melville in the *Cambridge History of American Literature*

(1917) and inaugurating a "Melville Revival." The revival was consecrated by a host of newspaper and magazine articles and propelled by the first book on Melville, Raymond Weaver's biography *Herman Melville: Mariner and Mystic* (1921), and by Weaver's publication of *Billy Budd* in 1924. Coinciding with the rise of Modernism, critical reception during the revival honored the very qualities of Melville's work that had been condemned by his original reviewers: his complex symbolism, unorthodox philosophical and psychological speculation, innovative rhetoric, and, most important, his thematic dichotomy of human isolation and the forces of nature. These aspects of Melville's craft and thought continued to absorb critics throughout the century, though in recent decades increasing attention has been paid to Melville's ambiguous treatments of race and gender and to the historical, social, and cultural contexts of his writings.

Though profoundly important in its time, Weaver's biography was often inaccurate and his edition of *Billy Budd* was flawed, eventually prompting concerted archival and textual investigation that continues today. The most prominent examples of this tradition are *The Melville Log* (1951), edited by Jay Leyda; *Melville's Reading* (1988) by Merton M. Sealts Jr.; the Northwestern-Newberry *Writings of Herman Melville* (1968–), edited by Harrison Hayford, Hershel Parker, and G. Thomas Tanselle; and Parker's two-volume *Herman Melville: A Biography* (1996, 2002). Marked and annotated copies from Melville's library of some 1,000 volumes (dispersed after his death among family members and secondhand book dealers) continue to resurface, facilitating generations of source and influence study. The second volume of Parker's biography informs a new surge of critical interest in Melville's verse (to be aided further by the forthcoming Northwestern-Newberry poetry volumes), and Melville's craft as a poet will soon occupy a major new phase in his critical reception.

Alden's turn-of-the-century call for a Melville society was not fulfilled until 1946, and its newsletter *Extracts* was not begun until 1969. But critical studies of Melville proliferated throughout the first half and dominated American literary scholarship in the second half of the century, with the academic journal *American Literature* reporting in 1994 that it receives more submissions on Melville than on any other writer. In 1999 the Melville Society inaugurated the peer-reviewed journal *Leviathan: A Journal of Melville Studies* and in 2003 established the Melville Society Cultural Project at the Kendall Whaling Museum in New Bedford, Massachusetts, designed to facilitate study of Melville's life and writings for educators and the general public through lyceum series, conferences, and an extensive library.

WORKS CITED

Hayford, Harrison. " 'Loomings': Yarns and Figures in the Fabric in *Moby-Dick.*" Eds. Hershel Parker and Harrison Hayford. New York: W. W. Norton & Co., 2001. 657–69.

Higgins, Brian and Hershel Parker, eds. *Herman Melville: The Contemporary Reviews.* Cambridge and New York: Cambridge University Press, 1995.

Melville, Herman. *Correspondence.* Ed. Lynn Horth. Evanston and Chicago: Northwestern University Press and The Newberry Library, 1993.

———. *Journals.* Ed. Howard C. Horsford with Lynn Horth. Evanston and Chicago: Northwestern University Press and The Newberry Library, 1989.

———. *Moby-Dick.* Ed. Harrison Hayford, Hershel Parker, and G. Thomas Tanselle. Evanston and Chicago: Northwestern University Press and The Newberry Library, 1988.

———. "Hawthorne and His Mosses" in *The Piazza-Tales and Other Prose Pieces.* Ed. Harrison Hayford, Alma A. MacDougall, and G. Thomas Tanselle. Evanston and Chicago: Northwestern University Press and The Newberry Library, 1987. 239–53.

——. *Redburn*. Ed. Harrison Hayford, Hershel Parker, and G. Thomas Tanselle. Evanston and Chicago: Northwestern University Press and The Newberry Library, 1969.
——. *White-Jacket*. Ed. Harrison Hayford, Hershel Parker, and G. Thomas Tanselle. Evanston and Chicago: Northwestern University Press and The Newberry Library, 1970.

BIBLIOGRAPHY

Works by Herman Melville

Prose Books
Typee: A Peep at Polynesian Life. New York: Wiley and Putnam, 1846. Published in England as *Narrative of a Four Months' Residence Among the Natives of a Valley of the Marquesas Islands; or, A Peep at Polynesian Life*. London: John Murray, 1846.
Omoo: A Narrative of Adventures in the South Seas. New York: Harper Brothers, 1847. London: John Murray, 1847.
Mardi: And a Voyage Thither. New York: Harper Brothers, 1849. London: Richard Bentley, 1849.
Redburn: His First Voyage. New York: Harper Brothers, 1849. London: Richard Bentley, 1849.
White-Jacket; or The World in a Man-of-War. New York: Harper Brothers, 1850. London: Richard Bentley, 1850.
Moby-Dick; or The Whale. New York: Harper Brothers, 1851. Published in England as *The Whale*. London: Richard Bentley, 1851.
Pierre; or The Ambiguities. New York: Harper Brothers, 1852.
Israel Potter: His Fifty Years of Exile. New York: G. P. Putnam, 1855.
The Piazza-Tales. New York: Dix & Edwards, 1856. London: Sampson Low, 1856.
The Confidence-Man: His Masquerade. New York: Dix & Edwards, 1857. London: Longman, 1857.

Poetry
Battle-Pieces and Aspects of the War. New York: Harper Brothers, 1866.
Clarel: A Poem and Pilgrimage in the Holy Land. New York: G. P. Putnam's Sons, 1876.
John Marr and Other Sailors. New York: De Vinne Press, 1888.
Timoleon. New York: Caxton Press, 1891.

Short Fiction
"Fragments from a Writing Desk." *Democratic Press, and Lansingburgh Advertiser* II (4 May and 18 May 1839).
"Authentic Anecdotes of Old Zack." *Yankee Doodle* II Nos. 42–49 (24 July–11 September 1847): 152, 167, 172, 188, 199, 202, 229.
"Bartleby, the Scrivener. A Story of Wall-Street." *Putnam's Monthly Magazine* II (November and December 1853): 546–57, 609–15.
"Cock-A-Doodle-Doo!" *Harper's New Monthly Magazine* VIII (December 1853): 77–86.
"The Encantadas, or Enchanted Isles." *Putnam's Monthly Magazine* III (March, April, and May 1854): 311–19, 345–55, 460–66.
"Poor Man's Pudding and Rich Man's Crumbs." *Harper's New Monthly Magazine* IX (June 1854): 95–101.
"The Happy Failure: A Story of the River Hudson." *Harper's New Monthly Magazine* IX (July 1854): 196–99.
"The Lightning-Rod Man." *Putnam's Monthly Magazine* IV (August 1854): 131–34.
"The Fiddler." *Harper's New Monthly Magazine* IX (September 1854): 536–39.
"The Paradise of Bachelors and the Tartarus of Maids." *Harper's New Monthly Magazine* X (April 1855): 670–78.
"The Bell-Tower." *Putnam's Monthly Magazine* VI (August 1855): 123–30.

"Benito Cereno." *Putnam's Monthly Magazine* VI (October, November, and December 1855): 353–67, 459–73, 633–44.

"Jimmy Rose." *Harper's New Monthly Magazine* XI (November 1855): 803–07.

"The 'Gees." *Harper's New Monthly Magazine* XII (March 1856): 507–09.

"I and My Chimney." *Putnam's Monthly Magazine* VII (March 1856): 269–83.

"The Apple-Tree Table; or, Original Spiritual Manifestations." *Putnam's Monthly Magazine* VII (May 1856): 465–75.

"The Two Temples." *The Works of Herman Melville, Standard Edition.* Vol. XIII (London 1924), 173–91.

Billy Budd, Sailor. Ed. Harrison Hayford and Merton M. Sealts Jr. Chicago: University of Chicago Press, 1962.

Reviews

"Etchings of a Whaling Cruise." *Literary World* 1 (6 March 1847): 105–06.

"Mr. Parkman's Tour." *Literary World* 4 (31 March 1849): 291–93.

"Cooper's New Novel." *Literary World* 4 (28 April 1849): 370.

"A Thought on Book-Binding." *Literary World* 6 (16 March 1850): 276–77.

"Hawthorne and His Mosses." *Literary World* 7 (17 August–24 August 1850): 125–27, 145–47.

Collected Writings

The Writings of Herman Melville. 13 volumes to date. Edited by Harrison Hayford, Hershel Parker, G. Thomas Tanselle, and others. Evanston and Chicago: Northwestern University Press and the Newberry Library, 1968–. *Typee* (1968); *Omoo* (1968); *Mardi* (1970); *Redburn* (1969); *White-Jacket* (1970); *Moby-Dick* (1988); *Pierre* (1971); *The Piazza-Tales, and Other Prose Pieces* (1987); *Israel Potter* (1982); *The Confidence-Man* (1984); *Clarel* (1991); *Correspondence* (1993); *Journals* (1989).

Studies of Herman Melville

Anderson, Charles Roberts. *Melville in the South Seas.* New York: Columbia University Press, 1939.

Bercaw, Mary K. *Melville's Sources.* Evanston: Northwestern University Press, 1987.

Bryant, John, ed. *A Companion to Melville Studies.* New York: Greenwood Press, 1986.

Cook, Jonathan A. *Satirical Apocalypse: An Anatomy of Melville's "The Confidence-Man."* Westport: Greenwood, 1996.

Davis, Merrell R. *Melville's Mardi: A Chartless Voyage.* New Haven: Yale University Press, 1952.

Dillingham, William B. *Melville's Later Novels* Athens and London: University of Georgia Press, 1986.

Garner, Stanton. *The Civil War World of Herman Melville.* Lawrence: University of Kansas Press, 1993.

Gilman, William H.. *Melville's Early Life and Redburn.* New York: New York University Press, 1951.

Hayford, Harrison. *Melville's Prisoners.* Evanston: Northwestern University Press, 2002.

Higgins, Brian, and Hershel Parker. *Essays on Herman Melville's Moby-Dick.* New York: G. K. Hall, 1992.

Howard, Leon. *Herman Melville: A Biography.* Berkeley: University of California Press, 1951.

Parker, Hershel. *Herman Melville: A Biography.* 2 vols. Baltimore: Johns Hopkins University Press, 1996 and 2002.

Robertson-Lorant, Laurie. *Melville: A biography.* New York: Clarkson Potter Publishers, 1996.

Sanborn, Geoffrey. *The Sign of the Cannibal: Melville and the Making of a Postcolonial Reader.* Durham: Duke University Press, 1998.

Sealts, Merton M., Jr. *Melville's Reading.* Columbia: University of South Carolina Press, 1988.

——. *Pursuing Melville.* Madison: University of Wisconsin Press, 1982.

Sten, Christopher, ed. *Savage Eye: Melville and the Visual Arts.* Kent: Kent State University Press, 1991.

Vincent, Howard P. *The Trying-out of Moby-Dick.* Boston: Houghton Mifflin, 1949.

Wallace, Robert K. *Melville and Turner: Spheres of Love and Fright.* Athens: University of Georgia Press, 1992.

Wright, Nathalia. *Melville's Use of the Bible.* New York: Octagon Books, 1969.

Yanella, Donald and Hershel Parker, eds. *The Endless, Winding Way in Melville: New Charts by Kring and Carey.* Glassboro: The Melville Society, 1981.

Bibliographies, Reference Guides, and Other Scholarly Resources

Bryant, John, and Haskell Springer, eds. *The Melville Electronic Library.* <http://people. hofstra.edu/faculty/John_L_Bryant/Melville/melville.html>

Higgins, Brian, ed. *Herman Melville: An Annotated Bibliography, 1846–1930.* New York: G. K. Hall, 1979.

———. *Herman Melville: A Reference Guide, 1931–1960.* New York: G. K. Hall, 1987.

Kier, Kathleen E. *A Melville Encyclopedia: The Novels.* Troy, NY: Whitston Publishing Co., 1994.

Leyda, Jay, ed. *The Melville Log: A Documentary Life of Herman Melville, 1819–1891.* New York: Harcourt Brace, 1951; reprint, with supplement, New York: Gordian Press, 1969.

ELIZABETH OAKES SMITH (1806–1893)

Veronica Margrave

BIOGRAPHY

Born in North Yarmouth, Maine, on August 12, 1806, Elizabeth Oakes Smith was the second daughter of David Cushing Prince, a sea captain, and Sophia (Blanchard) Price. At age two, Elizabeth's father died at sea, and her mother remarried and moved the family to Portland. Elizabeth loved reading during her childhood and read *The Bible* twice by the age of 12. She also wrote poetry, essays, short stories, and sketches. Excited by the knowledge she acquired in the classroom, she longed to be a school teacher. However, her mother felt Elizabeth was becoming too bookish and feared her daughter would die an old maid, so she arranged for Elizabeth to wed a man almost twice her age. Elizabeth and Seba Smith were married in 1823. Oakes Smith never forgave her mother for the marriage, an institution she saw as hypocritical.

At the time of the marriage, Seba was the editor of a newspaper, *the Eastern Argus,* in Portland, Maine, but in 1826 he sold his share in order to create two papers, *The Family Reader* and *The Portland Courier.* Oakes Smith wrote numerous pieces for both papers signing them simply "E." She bore six sons during this time, including one who died shortly after childbirth, and she became grounded in the stark realization that her life afforded her little time for her own pursuits. Around 1837, Smith was forced to sell his interest in the newspapers, and the family moved to South Carolina where they tried to gain wealth with a new type of cotton gin.

It was in the South that Oakes Smith viewed slavery first-hand, and it was an image she would not soon forget. Deep in a state of financial distress the couple traveled to New York City in 1839 where they hoped to make it as writers. This period in life proved to be the major turning point for Oakes Smith; the next two decades would be her most productive. A children's book, *Riches Without Wings, or, the Cleveland Family* (1838), was her first published work under the name Mrs. Seba Smith. By the 1840s she was being published in all of the leading periodicals, eclipsing the minor fame her husband had with his political satire, *The Jack Downing Letters* (1845). Though she experimented with Indian romance dramas, her most successful fictional piece came in the form of

"The Sinless Child," a poem published in a series bearing the same name. During this time she abandoned signing her work anonymously or with a pseudonym such as Ernest Helfstein, in favor of a name she adopted for herself: Elizabeth Oakes Smith, naming herself Oakes after a prestigious male ancestor who had been the president of Harvard in 1675 (Conrad 129). Having always felt her surname was too common, she took legal action to have her children's surnames changed to Oaksmith.

Toward the end of the 1840s Oakes Smith became interested in the women's rights movement, publishing a series of feminist articles entitled *Woman and Her Needs* (1851). By the 1850s she had joined the lyceum circuit that allowed her to travel across the county addressing issues such as feminism, abolitionism, and religion. Meeting dire financial circumstances after her husband died, she was forced to sell a large personal library in order to stay afloat. In January 1879, she delivered "Biology and Woman's Rights" at the 11th Woman's Suffrage Convention in Washington, D.C. Late in her life she was largely forgotten, and without having completed her autobiography, she died after a short illness on November 15, 1893.

MAJOR WORKS AND THEMES

Like many women writers of her time, Oakes Smith felt a literary career must "be guiltily fitted around domestic activities" (Walker 78). Her most notable poem, "The Sinless Child," first published in the *Southern Literary Messenger,* exposed the embedded Puritan values of virtue she said flowed through her blood from her paternal grandfather. "The Sinless Child" was a beautiful Wordsworth-like depiction of childhood and nature. Eva, the heroine, is a pure, almost celestial being, who communes with nature and the spirit world until she kisses a man and dies, allowing the man to be reborn from all of his sins. Oakes Smith's intentions in writing this were to let all women know they were born pure and sinless, and that even housework, sex, and other wifely duties could not deprive them of their virginal core. As Sheryl Conrad writes, "[it] expresses woman's hope that she has not been brought down to the level of her own experiences, that she is better than it seems" (Conrad 259). The unique nature of women was something Oakes Smith would continue to concentrate on in later works. As she became more involved in feminist lectures, she began to publish highly opinionated essays including a group collectively called *Woman and Her Needs.* In the essays she argued for equality in all spheres for women. She espoused her beliefs that, if women were trained only to be good wives, they will never be anything else. The works also focused on the necessity of a woman to choose marriage consciously instead of being forced into it as she was years before. In her feminist novel, *Bertha and Lily* (1854), she focused on the superiority of women and took the radical step by making the heroine, Bertha, a fallen woman. Because Bertha had given birth to a child outside of wedlock, she was marked as fallen by society, but unlike Hester Prynne in Nathaniel Hawthorne's *The Scarlet Letter,* Oakes Smith's heroine maintains a level of superiority throughout the novel.

CRITICAL RECEPTION

When Oakes Smith published "The Sinless Child," she gained the support of Edgar Allan Poe, Henry Longfellow, and Harriet Beecher Stowe. The two male authors incorporated ideas from the poem into their own poetry, and it is likely that Stowe had Oakes Smith's heroine of Eva in mind when she created her own angelic Eva in *Uncle Tom's Cabin.* Not only did she gather the support of other writers of her day, but Oakes Smith also captured the imagination of the public, who immediately saw her as the basis for the heroine. None of her poetical works would ever be as popular as "The Sinless Child," but she did become well known because of her feminist lectures later in life. Oakes Smith was "cruelly abused by the press because of her feminist lyceum lectures," even losing the respect of some fellow women writers who felt her ideas had encapsulated "dangerous fanaticism" (Walker 81). She found favor from those she considered the best thinkers of her time: Theodore Parker, Ralph Waldo Emerson, Lucretia Mott, James Freeman Clark, Wendell Phillips, William Lloyd Garrison, and many others; however, she lost more respect from her fellow writers when she stated that the majority of women writers of the time wrote nothing but drivel, which kept women in a complacent state of mind. She aligned herself with what she called "true women" who had joined her transformation from "Puritan maiden" to "woman of intellect" (Conrad 132). Through her later years as a lecturer, her words would inspire future feminists such as Christine Ladd-Franklin.

WORKS CITED

Conrad, Susan Phinney. *Perish the Thought: Intellectual Women in Romantic America, 1830–1860.* New York: Oxford University Press, 1976.

Walker, Cheryl. *The Nightingale's Burden: Women Poets and American Culture before 1900.* Bloomington: Indiana University Press, 1982.

BIBLIOGRAPHY

Works by Elizabeth Oakes Smith

Books

Riches Without Wings, or, The Cleveland Family. Boston: G. W. Light, 1838.

The Western Captive, or The Times of Tecumseh. New York: J. Winchester, 1842.

The Sinless Child and Other Poems. New York: Wiley and Putnam; Boston: W. D. Ticknor, 1843.

The Poetical Writings of Elizabeth Oakes Smith. New York: J. S. Redfield, 1845.

The Dandelion. New York: Saxton and Miles; Boston: Saxton and Kelt, 1846, republished as *The Dandelion: Stories not for good children, nor bad children, but for real children.* Buffalo: G. H. Derby & Co., 1849, republished as *The Dandelion.* Auburn: Derby and Miller; Buffalo: Derby, Orton and Mulligan, 1853.

The Moss Cup. Boston: Saxton and Kelt, 1846, republished as *The Moss Cup: Stories not for good children, nor bad children, but for real children.* Buffalo: G. W. Derby, 1849, republished as *The Moss Cup.* Auburn: Derby and Miller, 1853.

Rosebud, or The True Child. New York: Saxton and Miles; Boston: Saxton and Kelt, 1846, republished as *The Rosebud: Stories not for good children, nor bad children, but for real children.* Buffalo: G. H. Derby and Co., 1849.

The Salamander: A Legend for Christmas, found amongst the papers of the late Ernest Helfenstein, ed. E. Oakes Smith. New York: G. P. Putnam, 1848; republished as *Hugo: A Legend of Rockland Lake, found amongst the papers of the late Ernest Helfenstein,* Ed. E. Oakes Smith. New York: J. S. Taylor, 1851; republished as *Mary and Hugo: or, The Lost Angel: A Christmas Legend.* New York: Derby and Jackson; Cincinnati: H. W. Derby, 1857.

The Keepsake: A Wreath of Poems and Sonnets. New York: Leavitt and Company, 1849.

The Lover's Gift, or, Tributes to the Beautiful: American Series. Ed. E. Oakes Smith. Hartford: J. S. Parsons, 1850.

Woman and Her Needs. New York: Fowler and Wells, 1851; republished in *Liberating the Home.* New York: Arno Press, 1974.

Hints on Dress and Beauty. New York: Fowler and Wells, 1852.

Shadowland, or, the Seer. New York: Fowler and Wells, 1852.

Old New York, or Democracy in 1689: a tragedy in five acts. New York: Stringer and Towsend, 1853.

The Newsboy. New York: J. C. Derby; Boston: Phillips, Sampson, and Co., 1854.

Bertha and Lily, or The Parsonage of Beech Glen: A Romance. New York: J. C. Derby; Boston: Phillips, Sampson, and Co., 1854.

Bald Eagle, or The Last of the Ramapaughs: A Romance of Revolutionary Times. New York: Beadle and Adams, 1867.

The Sagamore of Saco. New York: Beadle and Adams, 1868.

Short Fiction

"The Lover's Tailsman, or The Spirit Bride." *Southern Literary Messenger.* July 1839: 465–69; republished in *The Mayflower for MDCCCXLVIII.* Boston: Saxton and Kelt, 1847.

"The Opal Ring," *Godey's Lady's Book.* January, February 1840.

"Gems and Reptiles," *Godey's Lady's Book.* February 1841, republished in *The New World* extra series No. 27/28. 27 Oct. 1842: 46–8.

"Leaves on the Wayside," *Godey's Lady's Book.* July–December 1842: 94, 149.

"Bud and Blossom." *Graham's Magazine.* August 1842: 61–3.

"The Christian Sisters," *The New World* extra series No. 27/28. 27 Oct. 1842: 39–46.

"The Witch of Endor," *Graham's Magazine.* April 1843: 225–27; republished in *The Rover* 2/2, 1843: 42–4; republished in *Dew Drops of the Nineteenth Century.* Ed. Seba Smith. New York: J. K. Wellman, 1845: 71–9; republished in *The Mayflower for MDCCCXLVII.* Boston: Saxton and Kelt, 1846: 282–91.

"Lunacy, or Fanny Parr," *Godey's Lady's Book.* January 1843; republished in *The Rover* 2/21, 1843: 321–4.

"Hobomok: A Legend of Maine," *The Rover* 2/2, 1843: 175–76.

 "The Sentiment of Self-Sacrifice," *Graham's Magazine.* April 1843: 225–7; republished in *The Rover* 2/2. 1843: 42–4; republished in *Dew Drops of the Nineteenth Century.* Ed. Seba Smith. New York: J. K. Wellman, 1845: 71–9; republished in *The Mayflower for MDCCCXLVII.* Boston: Saxton and Kelt, 1846: 282–91.

"The Unrequited," *Godey's Lady's Book.* May 1843.

"The Miser's Wife," *The Rover.* 1/20. 1843: 313–14.

"Coming to Get Married," *Graham's Magazine.* July 1843: 52–6.

"Not Sure About That Same," *Godey's Lady's Book.* July 1844.

 "The Interrupted Letter," *Godey's Lady's Journal.* April 1845.

"Religious Duties—The Poor Woman," *Dew Drops of the Nineteenth Century.* Ed. Seba Smith. New York: J. K. Wellman, 1845: 188–90.

"The Little Child's Philosophy," *Dew Drops of the Nineteenth Century.* Ed. Seba Smith. New York: J. K. Wellman, 1845: 202–3.

"The Defeated Life," *The Mayflower for MDCCCXLVII.* Boston: Saxton and Kelt, 1846: 36–75.

"Machinito," *The Mayflower for MDCCCXLVII.* Boston: Saxton and Kelt, 1847: 172–87.

"Beauty, Vanity, and Marble Mantles," *The Mayflower for MDCCCXLVIII.* Boston: Saxton and Kelt, 1847.

"The Sentiment of Petship," *The Mayflower for MDCCCXLVIII.* Boston: Saxton and Kelt, 1847.

"The Sagamore of Saco," *Graham's Magazine.* July 1848: 47–52.

Nonfiction

"Characterless Women," *Graham's Magazine.* October 1842: 199–200.

"A Word Upon Conceitedness," *Graham's Magazine.* October 1843: 203–4.

"A Card from Mrs. E. Oakes Smith," *New York Tribune.* December 31, 1852.

"Reply to P. T. Barnum," *New York Tribune.* May 5, 1855.

"Men and Women," *Emerson's Magazine and Putnam's Monthly.* 1857: 83–6.

"A Happy New Year," *Emerson's Magazine and Putnam's Monthly.* 1857: 87–8.

"Writing in New York," *Emerson's Magazine and Putnam's Monthly.* 1857: 88–9.

"Power and Genius," *Emerson's Magazine and Putnam's Monthly.* 1857: 312–3.

"The Weaker Vessel," *Emerson's Magazine and Putnam's Monthly.* 1857: 319–20.

"Button-Holes and Babies," *Emerson's Magazine and Putnam's Monthly.* 1857: 320–1.

"Women Voting," *Emerson's Magazine and Putnam's Monthly.* 1857: 417.

"New York State Teachers' Convention: Protest of a Lady Member," *Emerson's Magazine and Putnam's Monthly.* 1857: 517–9.

"Alice Cary," *Emerson's Magazine and Putnam's Monthly.* 1857: 520–1.

"Womanly Perception," *Emerson's Magazine and Putnam's Monthly.* 1857: 529–30.

"Books," *Emerson's Magazine and Putnam's Monthly.* 1857: 591–2.

"Who Are Our Educators?" *Emerson's Magazine and Putnam's Monthly.* 1857: 636–8.

"Bankruptcy and Dress," *Emerson's Magazine and Putnam's Monthly.* 1857: 746–7.

"Fashions and Fashion Plates," *Emerson's Magazine and Putnam's Monthly.* 1857: 764.

"The Sewing Machine," *Emerson's Magazine and Putnam's Monthly.* 1858: 101–2.

"Sarah Helen Whitman," *Emerson's Magazine and Putnam's Monthly.* 1858: 115.

"Poverty a Producer," *Emerson's Magazine and Putnam's Monthly.* 1858: 174–6.

"Private Insane Hospitals," *Emerson's Magazine and Putnam's Monthly.* 1858: 214–5.

"Burning Libraries," *Emerson's Magazine and Putnam's Monthly.* 1858: 324–5.

"Women as Physicians," *Emerson's Magazine and Putnam's Monthly.* 1858: 433–4.

"Virtue Rewarded," *Emerson's Magazine and Putnam's Monthly.* 1858: 431–3.

"The Ragpickers of New York," *The Great Republic Monthly.* January 1859: 133–9.

"The Newsboys of New York," *The Great Republic Monthly.* February 1859: 242–8.

"The Firemen of New York," *The Great Republic Monthly.* March 1859: 357–63.

"The Tombs, The Great City Prison," *The Great Republic Monthly.* March 1859: 364–8.

"The Carmen of New York," *The Great Republic Monthly.* April 1859: 486–90.

"The Sewing Girls of New York," *The Great Republic Monthly.* May 1859: 568–76.

"Autobiographic Notes," *Beadles Monthly.* 1867: 30–3, 147–56, 220–5, 325–9, 437–42, 538–49.

"The Puritan Child, Being an Autobiography," *The Phrenological Journal of Science and Health.* 72. 1881: 188–92, 304–9.

"The Puritan Child," *The Phrenological Journal of Science and Health.* 73. 1881: 72–8, 241–8.

"The Puritan Child," *The Phrenological Journal of Science and Health.* 74. 1882: 80–6.

"Reminiscences and Reflections," *The Phrenological Journal of Science and Health.* September 1890: 105–6.

Studies of Elizabeth Oakes Smith

Baym, Nina. *Woman's Fiction: A Guide to Novels by and about Women in America 1820–1870.* Ithaca and London: Cornell University Press, 1978.

Conrad, Susan Phinney. *Perish the Thought: Intellectual Women in Romantic America, 1830–1860.* New York: Oxford University Press, 1976.

Nickels, Cameron, and Timothy H. Scherman. "Elizabeth Oakes Smith: The Puritan Feminist." *Femmes de conscience: aspects du feminisme americain (1848–1875).* Eds. Susan Goodman and Daniel Royot. Paris: Presse de la Sorbonne Nouvelle, 1994.

Scherman, Timothy H. "Elizabeth Oakes Smith." *Dictionary of Literary Biography 239: American Women Prose Writers, 1820–1870.* Detroit: Gale Research, 2000. 222–30.

Walker, Cheryl. *The Nightingale's Burden: Women Poets and American Culture before 1900.* Bloomington: Indiana University Press, 1982.

Watts, Emily Stipes. *The Poetry of American Women from 1632 to 1945.* Austin and London: University of Texas Press, 1977.

Wyman, Mary Alice. *Selections from the Autobiography of Elizabeth Oakes Smith.* Lewiston, ME: Lewiston Journal Company, 1924.

FRANCES SARGENT LOCKE OSGOOD (1811–1850)

Mary G. De Jong

BIOGRAPHY

Frances Sargent Locke Osgood was born in Boston on June 18, 1811, to Joseph Locke, a successful merchant, and his second wife, Mary (Ingersoll) Foster, and spent much of her childhood in Hingham, Massachusetts. She was educated primarily at home, in part by her half-sister Anna Maria Foster (later Wells), also a poet. Encouraged to write as a child, Frances composed stories in prose and verse and addressed poems to friends and relatives. Some of her juvenilia, signed "Florence," appeared in the *Juvenile Miscellany* and *Ladies' Magazine* and in giftbooks (illustrated literary annuals).

She met Samuel Stillman Osgood, a self-educated painter, in 1834. At his request she sat for a portrait; they became engaged before it was finished. They married on October 7, 1835, and promptly went to London, where he studied art and exhibited his work while she wrote and met literary people such as Samuel Rogers and Lady Caroline Norton. A daughter, Ellen Frances, was born in July 1836. Osgood placed poems in periodicals and giftbooks on both sides of the Atlantic. Another child, May Vincent, was born in Boston in July 1839, soon after the family returned to the United States. The poet promptly became a regular contributor to the *Ladies' Companion* of New York. By the early 1840s she was steadily publishing poems, stories, and sketches in nationally circulated magazines such as *Godey's Lady's Book* and *Graham's Magazine,* the latter noted for paying established authors well. She wrote poetry with evident ease and enjoyed a wide circle of friends and admirers; unmarried men wrote her complimentary letters. Samuel, handicapped by an eye disorder, painted when he could, periodically traveling alone to find work in distant cities.

The Osgoods settled in New York City in 1842, residing in boarding houses and hotels. While meeting editors' deadlines, the poet also prepared books, befriended other women with young children, and attended soirees frequented by literary celebrities, among them Margaret Fuller, Elizabeth Oakes Smith, and Edgar Allan Poe. Her visits and correspondence with Poe and their exchange of complimentary poems in his *Broadway Journal* in 1845 prompted scandalous rumors. She felt compelled to recall her letters to Poe and stop meeting him in early 1846, but they continued to communicate by way of print. She hovered over Fanny Fay, born in June 1846, and grieved deeply after the child died in her arms in October 1847.

Osgood's husband sailed for San Francisco in February 1848, leaving her and their daughters in New York. Aware of the potential for gossip, her devoted friend, anthologist and editor Rufus W. Griswold, later explained that Samuel went to California "in pursuit of health and riches" (132). Though suffering from a racking cough by March 1848, she continued writing but eventually left it to Griswold to submit her work to editors and bargain for good pay. She spent part of the summer of 1849 in Saratoga Springs, New York, in hopes of recovering her health.

Osgood was bedridden by February 1850 when her husband returned with enough money to buy a home, their first. Consulting with Samuel about furnishings, she anticipated enjoying her home and reunited family and writing her best poems (Griswold 132, 136). However, she succumbed to tuberculosis on May 12, 1850, and was buried in the Locke plot in Mount Auburn Cemetery in Cambridge, Massachusetts. Periodicals all over the United States reported her death. Assisted by Griswold, her friend Mary E. Hewitt edited a giftbook, *The Memorial* (1851), to raise money for a graveside monument. A reprint of that volume titled *Laurel Leaves* (1854) yielded sufficient funds to erect a monument topped by a lyre—symbol of the lyric poet—crowned with laurel. Griswold's sketch "Frances Sargent Osgood," his contribution to *The Memorial,* is marred by errors and gender bias but remains the most complete biography.

MAJOR WORKS AND THEMES

Osgood wrote and edited five substantial books besides publishing widely in periodicals and giftbooks and writing for private audiences. Griswold, who helped her compile the 466-page *Poems* of 1850, stated that she had scattered her "flowers of feeling" liberally, never printing many and collecting in her last book fewer than "half of [the] printed pieces which she acknowledged" (135).

A Wreath of Wild Flowers from New England includes 37 juvenile verses and 100 more recent poems: ballads and other narratives, responses to pictures, verse letters to relatives and friends, dramatic monologues, and a "dramatic sketch" with two speakers. "Elfrida," a five-act tragedy in blank verse, portrays a woman willing to have her husband murdered so that she can marry the king of England. Skillfully employing a variety of lyric forms and voices, Osgood early demonstrated features characteristic of her work: humor and verbal playfulness, engaging portrayals of children, conventional images (blushes, dimples, curls); favorite words and phrases ("untaught by art," often rhymed with "heart"); idealization of beauty and innocence; and fluency tending toward expansiveness. Though charming, "The Spoilt Pupil of Fancy," spoken by a girl/poet who dislikes study and rules, burgeoned to 25 quatrains. In contrast, each of the 11 eight-line stanzas in "A Flight of Fancy" functions effectively. Enacting the irreconcilability of Reason and the poetic imagination, the narrative subtly celebrates "female poetry" and "the female, subversive element in the masculine-feminine dichotomy" (Watts 119).

Many lyrics in *Wreath,* as in Osgood's work generally, are about familial, friendly, and amatory relationships. Insistent that marriage should be founded on mutual love, Osgood portrays flirtations, courtships, and lovers enthralled and disenchanted. Flowers represent women and girls; gems symbolize abstractions. Some of these lyrics are less diaphanous than they appear. The women she presents sympathetically are loving and sensitive, innocent enough to blush at impropriety, clever enough to inspire admiration—and proud enough to end demeaning relationships and conceal their emotions.

Lyrics Osgood published in the 1840s also include joyous love songs and portrayals of domestic contentment, but the poet increasingly questioned social norms and explored the consequences of insincerity, betrayal, and sexual passion. Disappointed in love and friendship, her female speakers and other characters awake from romantic dreams; refuse to "stoop" to dishonorable persons and deeds; and realize that idolizing or depending on another human being damages the self. In "Alone" (1849), womanly pride, "self-reliance," and faith in God are elevated over "Love" (*Poems* [1850], 127–8). In her 1846 and 1850 collections Osgood acknowledges one of the most devastating realities of domestic sentimentalism, as of life: a mother's inability to protect her children from suffering and death. Most of her poems employ sentimental conventions, often successfully.

Yet Osgood takes more risks than most popular antebellum poets. She flirts with readers, sometimes inviting them to identify her vibrant persona with herself. She addresses women's issues in tonally complex poems that might have disturbed both advocates of women's rights and reactionaries bent on keeping them in their place. Going against the grain of sentimentalism, she treats coquettes sympathetically. The speaker of "Caprice" justifies her inconstancy because it counteracts men's power over women. Other poems and stories argue that a high-souled woman is entitled to discard a favored suitor upon discovering that he falls short of her "ideal." "Woman: A Fragment" protests social restraints and men's "tyrant power" but rejects the expanded roles advocated by "stern reformers" who fail to appreciate the sanctity of home. The final lines mischievously assert that Woman is content in her small sphere when she can "*have—her way!*" (*Poems* [1850], 71, 72). Does Osgood mean to dismiss women's rights in favor of feminine wiles? As Cheryl Walker remarks, readers must ask, "who is it that the poet is ridiculing?" (29). In Osgood's work as a whole, her voices are by turns sweet, playful, and solemn, apparently or actually sincere—but sometimes she teases.

She edited two giftbooks that explicate the language of flowers. *The Poetry of Flowers and Flowers of Poetry* (1841) associates each species with an emotion, abstraction, or message: hyacinth, grief; blue violet, modesty; Jacob's ladder, Come down to me. Each flower is also accompanied by at least one clipping of appropriate verse. Some of the numerous lines signed F. S. O. appear exclusively in this volume. *The Floral Offering* (1847) likewise features selected poems, many by the editor herself. Although Elizabeth A. Petrino writes knowledgeably about Osgood's deployment of traditional floral symbolism, these editorial projects, along with her satire *A Letter about the Lions* and three books for children, have received little scholarly notice.

CRITICAL RECEPTION

Osgood's poetry was warmly received by nineteenth-century magazine readers and by most critics. Complimented for her choice of subject matter ("the affections"), graceful prosody, and sprightliness, she ranked with the best American women poets. Mid-century anthologies of American "female poetry" edited by Caroline May, Thomas Buchanan Read, and Griswold included her. She was considered a natural, feminine "singer," not an artist, but some commentators urged her to do her talents justice by taking on weightier subjects or revising with care. By the early twentieth century she was generally forgotten, dismissed as a sentimentalist, or remembered as the charmer whose poems Poe praised for extra-literary reasons.

Emily Stipes Watts redeemed Osgood from obscurity in 1977 by calling her poetry at its best remarkably "honest" and "sophisticated," her voice "unique" (105–8). Placing her within the context of a distinctively female poetic tradition, Walker encouraged more scholars to read her. Osgood's visibility grew rapidly after Joanne Dobson discovered her "roguish" poems about heterosexual relationships, some of them unpublished or uncollected in her lifetime ("Sex, Wit, and Sentiment"). Osgood as high sentimentalist, satirist, and rogue was represented in new anthologies of American women's writing edited by Walker, Paula Bernat Bennett, and Karen L. Kilcup. She made her first appearance in the third edition (1998) of the *Heath Anthology of American Literature*. A versatile, urbane, sometimes surprising poet, Osgood slipped through some of the closed doors of antebellum culture.

WORKS CITED

Dobson, Joanne. "Sex, Wit, and Sentiment: Frances Osgood and the Poetry of Love." *American Literature* 69 (December 1993): 631–50.

Griswold, Rufus Wilmot. "Frances Sargent Osgood." *International Monthly Magazine* 2 (December 1850): 131–40.

Osgood, Frances Sargent Locke. *Poems.* Philadelphia: Carey & Hart, 1850.

Walker, Cheryl. *The Nightingale's Burden: Women Poets and American Culture before 1900.* Bloomington: Indiana UP, 1982.

Watts, Emily Stipes. *The Poetry of American Women from 1632 to 1945.* Austin: U of Texas P, 1977.

BIBLIOGRAPHY

Works by Frances Sargent Locke Osgood

Books

A Wreath of Wild Flowers from New England. London: Edward Churton, 1838; Boston: Weeks, Jordan, 1839.

The Casket of Fate. London: C. Whittingham, 1839; Boston: Weeks, Jordan, 1840.

The Poetry of Flowers and Flowers of Poetry. To Which are Added, a Simple Treatise on Botany, With Familiar Examples, and a Copious Floral Dictionary. Ed. Frances Osgood. New York: J. C. Riker, 1841.

Poems. New York: Clark & Austin, 1846.

The Cries of New-York, with Fifteen Illustrations. Drawn from Life by a Distinguished Artist. The Poetry by Frances S. Osgood. New York: John Doggett, 1846.

The Floral Offering, a Token of Friendship. Ed. Frances Osgood. Philadelphia: Carey & Hart, 1847.

A Letter about the Lions. New York: George P. Putnam; London: Putnam's American Agency, 1849.

Poems. Philadelphia: Carey & Hart, 1850.

Juvenile Literature

The Snow-Drop; A New-Year's Gift for Children. Providence: Hiram Fuller, 1842.

Puss in Boots, and the Marquis of Carabas. Rendered into Verse. New York: Benjamin & Young, 1844.

The Flower Alphabet, in Gold and Colors. Boston: S. Colman, 1845.

Studies of Frances Sargent Locke Osgood

De Jong, Mary G. "Frances Sargent Osgood." *DLB 250: Antebellum Writers in New York.* 2nd Series. Ed. Kent P. Ljungquist. Detroit: Gale Group, 2002. 275–84.

Dobson, Joanne. "Reclaiming Sentimental Literature." *American Literature* 69 no. 2 (June 1997): 263–98.

Petrino, Elizabeth A. *Emily Dickinson and Her Contemporaries: Women's Verse in America.* Hanover, NH: University P of New England, 1998.

Richards, Eliza Clark. "Poetic Attractions: Gender, Celebrity, and Authority in Poe's Circle." Diss., U of Michigan, 1997.

THEODORE PARKER (1810–1860)

John J. Han

BIOGRAPHY

William Ellery Channing (1780–1842) and Theodore Parker are commonly regarded as the two most important figures in the history of American Unitarianism. Channing codified rationalistic Unitarianism, while Parker took one step forward by blending Transcendental philosophy and Unitarian theology. Parker was born in Lexington, Massachusetts, on August 24, 1810, to John and Hannah Stearns Parker. Upon graduation from Harvard Divinity School in 1836, Parker married Lydia Dodge Cabot; the couple had no children in their married life.

From 1837 to 1846, Parker served as minister of the West Roxbury Unitarian Church, near Boston. He promoted a radical form of Unitarianism through his sermons and lectures. Influenced by such European philosophers as Immanuel Kant, Friedrich Ernst Daniel Schleiermacher, Henry Thomas Buckle, David Friedrich Strauss, Ferdinand Christian Bauer, and Wilhelm Martin Lebrecht DeWette, Parker proclaimed that the Bible is fallible, Jesus Christ is not the Savior but a supreme moral example, the human soul is innately divine, and the forms and doctrines of Christianity are provisional. His first important article, "The Previous Question between Mr. Andrews Norton and His Alumni Moved and Handled in a Letter to All Those Gentlemen" (1840), clearly signaled his conversion from rationalistic Unitarianism to transcendental Unitarianism.

Then, on May 19, 1841, Parker delivered a bombshell sermon, "Discourse of the Transient and Permanent in Christianity," at the ordination of Charles Chauncy Shackford at Hawes Place Church in South Boston. In this manifesto of transcendental Unitarianism, Parker distinguished provisional elements (dogma) from unchanging elements (moral truths) in Christianity. The sermon caused major controversy among Boston clergymen, most of whom condemned Parker as a heretic.

In 1841–42, Parker delivered a series of five lectures, in Boston, which were later printed as *A Discourse of Matters Pertaining to Religion* (1842). Commonly known as *Parker's Discourse of Religion,* this work elaborated on Parker's transcendental view of Christianity. In 1843, he was excluded from the Boston Association of (Unitarian) Ministers, of which he was a member, although he sustained membership with the Unitarians for 20 years. In 1843, he also published a two-volume work *A Critical and Historical Introduction to the Canonical Scriptures of the Old Testament*. This was his annotated translation of German theologian Wilhelm Martin Lebrecht De Wette's scientific study of the Old Testament, *Lehrbuch der historisch-kritischen Einleitung in die kanonischen und apocryphischen Bücher des Alten Testementes* (1817).

In 1846–59, Parker pastored a new free church, the Twenty-eighth Congregational Society of Boston. He was the most popular and influential preacher in Boston, his church grew to be one of the largest in the nation, and he lectured throughout the United States. During this period, especially the 1850s, Parker championed progressive sociopolitical causes, including abolitionism, prison reform, temperance, women's education, and pacifism. He helped fugitive slaves escape to the North and wrote the tract *A Letter to the People of the United States Touching the Matter of Slavery* (1848).

Parker contracted tuberculosis in 1859 and went to Europe hoping to regain his health. He died, however, on May 10, 1860, in Florence, Italy, where he was buried at the "English Cemetery." The inscription on his gravestone reads, "Theodore Parker / The Great American Preacher / . . . His Name Is Engraved in Marble / His Virtues in the Hearts of Those He / Helped to Free from Slavery / And Superstition." A voracious reader in his lifetime, Parker left behind 13,000 valuable books to the Boston Public Library. Parker's *Works* was published in 14 volumes in 1863–70; a 15-volume centenary edition came out in 1907–11.

MAJOR WORKS AND THEMES

In his lifetime Parker wrote 925 sermons and many essays of social criticism. They embody Parker's philosophy of natural religion, the transcendental existence of God, the benevolence and beneficence of God, the divinity of humanity, and social justice. In "The Previous Question between Mr. Andrews Norton and His Alumni," for instance, Parker argues that the basis of Christianity is neither *à priori* arguments nor miracles. Rather, it is the transcendental truths verifiable through intellectual and intuitive faculties.

"Discourse of the Transient and Permanent in Christianity" discusses what is provisional in Christianity and what is eternal therein. According to the author, the religious forms and doctrines—a large part of what is commonly taught as religion—are merely imperfect human expressions. At the core of Christian faith lie the divine life of the human soul, love to God, and love to humanity. Christianity is anything but pure morality—the love of God and the love of man—sublimely exemplified by Christ himself.

In *A Discourse of Matters Pertaining to Religion,* Parker expounds on the religious element and its manifestations, the relation of the religious sentiment to God, the relation of the religious element to Jesus of Nazareth, the relation of the religious element to the Bible, and the relation of the religious element to the church. The author denies the uniqueness and superiority of Christianity and, as in his previous works, claims that the permanent substance of Christianity is intuition, not church, creed, clergy, authority, or tradition.

A Critical and Historical Introduction to the Canonical Scriptures of the Old Testament is a translation of De Wette's 1817 book which, according to Parker, "imbodies the results of the critical labors of the whole world upon the Scriptures, and exhibits, in a brief space, the opinions of the great critics of past and present times" (vol. 1, vii). In addition to his translation, Parker offers extensive extracts from other writers, essays of his own, and opinions of various biblical scholars.

Finally, in *A Letter to the People of the United States Touching the Matter of Slavery,* Parker discusses the history of slavery; the conditions and treatment of slaves; slavery's effects on industry, population, education, and law and politics; and the moral objection to slavery. According to the author, slavery is a crime against the higher law, and thus resistance to the Fugitive Slave Law is morally justified.

CRITICAL RECEPTION

Although some of Parker's friends considered him a Martin Luther figure in latter-day Protestantism, he was severely denounced by numerous opponents as "infidel," "scorner," "blasphemer," "Deist," "unbeliever," "destroyer," "fanatic," "Atheist," or "enemy of mankind." His intuitional Christianity has also been repudiated by orthodox theologians. For example, in *Orthodoxy, with Preludes on Current Events* (1878), Joseph Cook lists several "self-contradictions" in Parker's idea of the intuitions of conscience: the intuitions of conscience declare man's "ill-desert" when he says "I will not" to the Divine "I ought"; the ill-desert of man is thus a self-evident fact; the intuitions were Parker's authority; the life, correspondence, and public utterances of Parker yield almost no proof that he was accustomed to confessing sin to the Supreme Being; Parker did not believe in the doctrine of inherited sin; and he did not carefully distinguish human infirmity from human iniquity (121).

Since his death, however, Parker has earned widespread support from liberal Christians and social reformers. In the introduction to *Three Prophets of Religious Liberalism: Channing—Emerson—Parker* (1961), Conrad Wright notes that Channing's Baltimore Sermon (1819), Emerson's Divinity School Address (1838), and Parker's South Boston Sermon (1841) have long been viewed as "the three great classic utterances of American Unitarianism"; all of these addresses caused great controversy, represent turning points in the history of American Unitarianism, and were influential far beyond the confines of Unitarianism (3–4). According to Jack Mendelsohn, author of *Why I Am a Unitarian Universalist* (1966), "The two colossi of religious liberalism in America were William Ellery Channing and Theodore Parker"; Channing was "the most influential figure yet produced by American Unitarianism," while Parker was "the most remarkable" (59, 62). Mendelsohn adds, "No part of my legacy as a Unitarian is more precious to me than the portion created by Theodore Parker. He was a prophet of righteousness, who believed, as I do, in the progressive development of the church" (64). Robert E. Collins, writing in *Theodore Parker: American Transcendentalist* (1973), considers Parker "one of the most outstanding transcendentalists" in New England; Parker was "the most outstanding member of the pre-Civil War group" and "had the most orderly and vigorous mind of any of the group and is the equal of any in forcefulness of expression" (iii). In *Theodore Parker: Yankee Crusader* (1960), Henry Steele Commager states, "Parker is not only one of the striking examples of the moralist in American history; he is also perhaps the most impressive example of the scholar in politics" (x).

Much scholarly attention has been focused on the nature and extent of Parker's transcendentalism. For example, Octavius Brooks Frothingham, in his *Theodore Parker: A Biography* (1874), declares that Theodore Parker was one of the true prophets of the transcendentalist gospel. John White Chadwick concurs with Frothingham in *Theodore Parker: Preacher and Reformer* (1900): transcendentalism provided Parker with "an admirable formula of his personal religion" (178). Edwin D. Mead, author of *The Influence of Emerson* (1903), maintains that Emerson and Parker are inseparable in religious ideas; they "stand for the same thing. Emerson was Parker writing books. Parker was

Emerson's truth in the pulpit" (111). William Gannett agrees with Mead: "What Emerson uttered without plot or plan, Theodore Parker elaborated to a system. Parker was the Paul of Transcendentalism" (qtd. in Mead 111). Harold Clarke Goddard's *Studies in New England Transcendentalism* (1908) addresses four major authors—Theodore Parker alongside Amos Bronson Alcott, Ralph Waldo Emerson, and Margaret Fuller—because "common consent has selected" them as "the leaders of the [transcendentalist] movement" (9). In his *Theodore Parker: Yankee Crusader* (1960), Henry Steele Commager sees Parker as one of the leaders of New England transcendentalism; Parker "[burrowed] down to the very subsoil of transcendentalism" (63). In contrast, John Edward Dirks does not consider Parker a New England transcendentalist. In *The Critical Theology of Theodore Parker* (1948), he notes, "Parker stood near, but not within, New England transcendentalism. He looked upon Emerson's as an 'extreme' viewpoint; his 'spiritual philosophy' is consequently a critical system" (136). According to Dirks, Parker was a "mediating" theologian who attempted to strike a balance between the extremes of rationalism and Evangelical orthodoxy (132).

WORKS CITED

Chadwick, John White. *Theodore Parker: Preacher and Reformer.* Boston: Houghton, Mifflin and Company, 1900.

Collins, Robert E. *Theodore Parker: American Transcendentalist.* Metuchen, NJ: Scarecrow Press, 1973.

Commager, Henry Steele. *Theodore Parker: Yankee Crusader.* 1st Beacon paperback ed. Boston: Beacon Press, 1960.

Cook, Joseph. *Orthodoxy, with Preludes on Current Events.* Boston: James R. Osgood and Company, 1878.

Dirks, John Edward. *The Critical Theology of Theodore Parker.* Westport, CT: Greenwood Press, 1948.

Goddard, Harold Clarke. *Studies in New England Transcendentalism.* New York: Columbia University Press, 1908.

Mead, Edwin D. *The Influence of Emerson.* Boston: American Unitarian Association, 1903.

Mendelsohn, Jack. *Why I Am a Unitarian Universalist.* 1st Beacon paperback ed. Boston: Beacon Press, 1966.

Parker, Theodore. A Critical and Historical Introduction to the Canonical Scriptures of the Old Testament. 2 vols. Boston: Charles C. Little and James Brown, 1843. Translation of Wilhelm Martin Lebrecht De Wette. *Lehrbuch der historisch-kritischen Einleitung in die kanonischen und apocryphischen Bücher des Alten Testementes.* 1817.

Wright, Conrad. Introduction. *Three Prophets of Religious Liberalism: Channing—Emerson—Parker.* Boston: Beacon Press, 1961. 3–46.

BIBLIOGRAPHY

Works by Theodore Parker

Collections

The Collected Works of Theodore Parker. Centenary ed. 15 vols. Boston: Beacon Press, 1907–10.

Commager, Henry Steele, ed. *Theodore Parker: An Anthology.* By Theodore Parker. Boston, 1960.

Prose

West Roxbury Sermons 1837–1848. Boston: American Unitarian Association, 1902.

Translation

A Critical and Historical Introduction to the Canonical Scriptures of the Old Testament. 2 vols. Boston: Charles C. Little and James Brown, 1843. Translation of Wilhelm Martin Lebrecht De Wette. *Lehrbuch der historisch-kritischen Einleitung in die kanonischen und apocryphischen Bücher des Alten Testementes.* 1817.

Manuscript

Letters to Convers Francis. Boston Public Library.

Studies of Theodore Parker

Chadwick, John White. *Theodore Parker: Preacher and Reformer.* Boston: Houghton, Mifflin and Company, 1900.

Collins, Robert E. *Theodore Parker: American Transcendentalist.* Metuchen, NJ: Scarecrow Press, 1973.

Commager, Henry Steele. *Theodore Parker: Yankee Crusader.* 1st Beacon paperback ed. Boston: Beacon Press, 1960.

Cook, Joseph. *Orthodoxy, with Preludes on Current Events.* Boston: James R. Osgood and Company, 1878.

Dirks, John Edward. *The Critical Theology of Theodore Parker.* Westport, CT: Greenwood Press, 1948.

Frothingham, Octavius Brooks. *Theodore Parker: A Biography.* Boston: James R. Osgood and Company, 1874.

Goddard, Harold Clarke. *Studies in New England Transcendentalism.* New York: Columbia University Press, 1908.

Hutchison, William R. *The Transcendentalist Ministers: Church Reform in the New England Renaissance.* New Haven: Yale University Press, 1959.

Mead, Edwin D. *The Influence of Emerson.* Boston: American Unitarian Association, 1903.

Mendelsohn, Jack. *Why I Am a Unitarian Universalist.* 1st Beacon paperback ed. Boston: Beacon Press, 1966.

Weiss, John. *Life and Correspondence of Theodore Parker, Minister of the Twenty-eighth Congregational Society.* 2 vols. New York: D. Appleton & Company, 1864.

Wright, Conrad. Introduction. *Three Prophets of Religious Liberalism: Channing—Emerson—Parker.* Boston: Beacon Press, 1961. 3–46.

ELIZABETH STUART PHELPS (1815–1852)

Ann Beebe

BIOGRAPHY

While many people are aware of notable father-daughter connections in American literature (James and Susan Fenimore Cooper, Bronson and Louisa May Alcott, and John and Susan Cheever), few people could readily name such distinctive mother-daughter pairs. The nineteenth-century women authors, somewhat confusedly named Elizabeth Stuart Phelps and Elizabeth Stuart Phelps Ward, were two of the most popular writers of their era. Recent critical attention indicates that their reputations are on an upsurge in the twenty-first century.

Elizabeth Wooster Stuart Phelps (1815–52) was born in Andover, Massachusetts, to Abigail Clark (1783–1855) and Moses Stuart (1780–1852), a professor of Greek and Hebrew literature at Andover Theological Seminary. Moses Stuart's family reached New England in 1650 and produced generation after generation of preachers. This atmosphere of male achievement threatened to overwhelm the women of each generation. Late in life another Stuart daughter published her recollections of childhood in Andover during the 1820s. Sarah Stuart Robbins (1817–1910) detailed the rigidity of their father's schedule and sensitive nerves that required absolute silence (Robbins 164). Elizabeth inherited her father's intellectual curiosity and desired to earn his respect. One of nine children, Elizabeth Stuart began writing stories at age 10 (Kessler 5). Although her father held what his granddaughter later called a "feudal" attitude about women's position in society (Phelps Ward 134), he did allow his daughters to have formal educations. Elizabeth went to Abbott Academy in Andover and then to Mount Vernon School in Boston for two years. She blossomed in the cultural air of the city and published her first short stories in Sunday-school periodicals under the anagram H. Trusta during this period.

Elizabeth Stuart returned to Andover in 1834 suffering from severe headaches and intermittent paralysis. Both Carol Farley Kessler, her daughter's biographer, and Judith Fetterley read this illness as partially psychosomatic (Kessler 6 and Fetterley 204). Stuart's conflict between her need to be a dutiful daughter and her repressed ambition to be a writer manifested itself in a series of illnesses that debilitated her. She officially declared her religious faith and joined the chapel at Andover Theological Seminary in this year. The 18-year-old, however, struggled to obey the accepted patriarchal interpretations of the Bible in her Calvinist household. Her husband later quoted from his wife's personal journal:

Yet, I was not happy. My soul did thirst for the beautiful and the true. Suppressed longings, and unsatisfied tastes, and despised capacities, at length took their revenge. They fretted, and chafed, and wore upon the delicate framework that enclosed them, until it gave way. Then followed four long, dreary years. (Austin Phelps 37)

By 1838 Stuart had reached an uneasy internal truce, never fully recovering her health, but also never again to repress her desires to write and publish.

Elizabeth Stuart met her future husband Austin Phelps (1820–90) while he was a student at Andover Theological Seminary. Phelps was also a descendent of New England ministers. He went into the "family business," but became a more conservative preacher than his revivalist father Eliakim Phelps (1789–1880). Elizabeth and Austin Phelps married in 1842 and settled in Boston where Austin had accepted a call from the Pine Street Church. Elizabeth Stuart Phelps gave birth to their first child, Mary Gray Phelps, in 1844. This only daughter changed her name to Elizabeth Stuart Phelps after her mother's death in 1852. Austin Phelps, an insecure man filled with self-doubt about his own abilities, was unhappy as the pastor to a congregation. The isolation from academic circles and the multiple demands upon his time wearied him. In 1848 he accepted the position of Chair of Rhetoric at Andover, thus returning his wife Elizabeth to the life and circle she had been so relieved to escape six years earlier. The Phelps household also increased in 1849 when Elizabeth gave birth to a son, Moses Stuart Phelps.

Elizabeth Stuart Phelps now had to maintain a small-town household with children on an academic salary without the cultural resources found in Boston. In the 1840s, Boston furnished beginning writers with lectures by Ralph Waldo Emerson and others, the "Conversations" of Margaret Fuller, antislavery debates and periodicals, and bookstores stocked with the works of all the key writers of the American Renaissance. Despite the physical and cultural deprivations of her Andover life, Phelps continued to write. She produced the "Kitty Brown" series for the American Sunday-School Union, and in 1851 published her first novel, *The Sunny Side; or, The Country Minister's Wife,* which sold 100,000 copies in the first year (Baym, *Woman's Fiction* 246). The work, credited to "the author of the 'Little Kitty Brown and her Bible Verses," was published by the American Sunday-School Union. These Christian publishers, carefully screening books for a Sunday audience, provided a springboard for national publication for many nineteenth-century women including Harriet Beecher Stowe, Elizabeth Stuart Phelps Ward, Anna Warner, and Susan Warner.

Elizabeth Stuart Phelps's second novel, *A Peep at 'Number Five'; or, A Chapter in the Life of a City Pastor* appeared in 1852 under the pseudonym H. Trusta. This novel also went on to sell several thousands in the 1850s. Phelps separately published as a Christmas book the short story, "The Angel over the Right Shoulder," in 1852. Her health, however, was bad. The move to Andover and her increased domestic duties, coupled with her writing, weakened her. She gave birth to a second son, Amos Lawrence Phelps (a future minister), in 1852 after the death of her father. Soon after, Elizabeth Stuart Phelps died on November 29, 1852, at age 37. Austin Phelps, her husband, made an effort to foster posthumously his wife's writing career, arranging for the publication of *The Last Leaf from Sunny Side* (1853), *The Tell-Tale; or, Home Secrets Told by Old*

Travellers (1853), and *Little Mary; or, Talks and Tales for Children* (1854). Many of the selections in these collections had been published anonymously in periodicals during her lifetime. In addition, Phelps composed "A Memorial of the Author" for inclusion in *The Last Leaf.* In his revealing essay, Phelps acknowledges the pain his wife felt at leaving Boston and returning to Andover. He writes, "she concealed in great measure the foreboding with which she anticipated the change, lest [her husband's] decision be unduly influenced by a knowledge of her feelings" (Austin Phelps 74). Phelps later gave his permission for large portions of this memorial to be quoted by the Rev. D. W. Clark in his glowing biographical sketch of the author in *The Ladies' Repository* in 1855. Austin Phelps's remorse over his wife's death may have induced him to marry her sister Mary Stuart (1822–56) in 1854 knowing that she was ill from tuberculosis. This second wife died in 1856, and Austin Phelps remarried for the last time in 1858.

Elizabeth Stuart Phelps's biography is significant for the light it sheds on the reality of married women's lives in nineteenth-century America and the obstacles they faced in their efforts to become professional writers. Furthermore, the perceived lessons of Phelps's life influenced her daughter's personal choices and fictional characters. Describing her mother in 1896, Phelps Ward remembers, "she lived one of those rich and piteous lives such as only gifted women know; torn by the civil war of the dual nature which can be given to women only" (Phelps Ward 12). Phelps Ward appeared to avoid marriage for many years, leery of the institution after her mother's experiences. Like her mother, she began writing juvenile fiction for Sunday-school publishers; her "Gypsy Breynton" series launched her publication career just as her mother's "Kitty Brown" series first introduced her to the public. In addition, many critics connect the devastation marriage wreaks on the life of Avis Dobell in the daughter's *The Story of Avis* (1877) with the life of Elizabeth Stuart Phelps. Last, the influence of Elizabeth Stuart Phelps on her daughter can be seen in her daughter's appropriation of the fictionalized diary technique in her *The Gates Ajar* (1868), a strategy partially used by her mother in *The Sunny Side.*

MAJOR WORKS AND THEMES

Phelps's early death at age 37 cut short her literary career. Nevertheless, as the author of two novels and several works of short fiction, Phelps had begun to develop a few key themes and characters in her works. Immediately noticeable is her development as a storyteller from her 1851 *The Sunny Side* to the 1852 *A Peep at 'Number Five'.* These novels fall directly into the golden era of the American Renaissance. Key novels from this time period include Hawthorne's *The Scarlet Letter* (1850) and *The House of the Seven Gables* (1851), Warner's *The Wide Wide World* (1850), Melville's *Moby-Dick* (1851), Stowe's *Uncle Tom's Cabin* (1852), and Cummins's *The Lamplighter* (1854). Phelps's fiction, to use Nina Baym's phrase, falls into the category of domestic or bourgeois realism (*Woman's Fiction* 247). Primarily concerned with the situation of the middle-class family, and more particularly with middle-class wives, Phelps questioned the idealized façade of the nineteenth-century household for women.

In her groundbreaking anthology of nineteenth-century women writers, Judith Fetterley identifies an important perspective for many of these writers. Unlike some of their male contemporaries (such as Poe or Hawthorne) nineteenth-century women writers make a conscious decision to reject the "dark, perverse, demonic side of human nature" (Fetterley 27). This exploration of the lowest denominator in humanity, however, earned the condemnation of twentieth-century critics who dismissed the works of Phelps and fellow women writers as too good for serious literature. As scholars reclaim and interpret these nineteenth-century women's texts, Fetterley demands that we take into account this long-standing gender bias on the part of critics and appreciate that "in writing as Christians, nineteenth-century American women writers aligned themselves with a different kind of power, one that they saw as essentially female. They write, not on the side of the devil, who was most definitely male, but on the side of Christ who stood for women" (Fetterley 28). In citing Phelps as an example of this consciousness, Fetterley recognizes that Phelps's works require and deserve a different approach than the works we commonly praise as masterworks of the American Renaissance. With this approach critics can analyze Phelps's portrayals of nineteenth-century marriages and the unpaid career of a minister's wife.

Phelps's adult fiction presents extended portraits of married life in antebellum America. The Edwards in *The Sunny Side,* the Holbrooks in *A Peep at 'Number Five',* and the Jameses in "The Angel over the Right Shoulder" negotiate the roles of husbands and wives and spell out their expectations for each other. The wives (Emily Edwards, Lucy Holbrook, and Mary James) are not silent automatons. They struggle to understand their roles as the "angels" in the household and occasionally subvert their husbands' expectations. Over the breakfast table (e.g., see Chapter 3 of *The Sunny Side,* "The Breakfast-Chat") these wives force the men to articulate guidelines about money and time.

All of Phelps's wives struggle with household finances. The wife in *The Sunny Side* is the most severely challenged, trying to feed and clothe a family of seven children on $500 a month with the occasional donation party. Some passages gently instruct readers to act honorably and practically when considering a minister's salary. This congregation is "remiss" in paying their minister and after a few years, Emily Edwards supports her husband in his decision to seek a dismissal from his church and find another occupation to support his growing family. The congregation becomes more diligent in paying its minister his promised salary, however, and Emily Edwards spends the rest of her life in the same parsonage cheerfully remaking clothes and going without any luxuries. The financial situation for the Holbrooks is not as dire. The novel follows this couple, loosely based on Austin and Elizabeth Phelps, through the first few years of their marriage and demonstrates the different challenges a city minister faces. He is generally granted a larger salary than a country parson usually is and has more opportunities to earn speaking fees. His congregation, moreover, is often wealthier and more accustomed to donating food, clothes, or luxuries to their minister. The recurring theme in this novel is the need to stay out of debt, a goal accomplished by the Holbrooks after careful joint budgeting. The detail these works provide about the daily management of a ministerial household has a cumulative effect. The weight of these cares on these fictional wives exposes the reality of domestic responsibilities women in the nineteenth century faced. Detailing all the small tasks necessary to place a meal on the table, clean the house, care for children, clothe a family, and maintain family and social relations, often with limited funds, validates the skills and attention of women like Emily Edwards and Lucy Holbrook.

The adult works of Phelps also emphasize the value of time for both men and women to pursue intellectual goals. For ministers like Edwards and Holbrook, the time to read, meditate, and write is too often underestimated and undervalued. These novels argue that ministers must be allowed time to refresh their minds and spirits in order to craft meaningful sermons. Phelps also shows how in these novels a minister's wife must fulfill the duties of a professional secretary. She must screen all callers and complete as many of the daily pastoring duties as possible, all without a salary or official recognition. Phelps has the ministers in the novels articulate these responsibilities so that once again the many demands on a wife's time are validated. Furthermore, Phelps makes a claim that a minister's wife, in order to fulfill these special duties, should be allowed time to pursue her own intellectual pursuits if for no other reason than that her continued reading and writing will assist her in her rounds as the minister's wife. Interestingly, Phelps is not able to sustain this vision of intellectual time for the female of a household. The last work published in her lifetime, "The Angel over the Right Shoulder," features a young wife, Mary James, whose attempts to claim two hours of each day for private use are thwarted by her husband and children. The woman's struggle to fulfill her duties as a wife and mother and still maintain her independent identity plays out in a dream of two angels. The angel over the right shoulder records all the times she comforts or guides her children while the angel over her left shoulder logs every time she neglects her parental duties. In the end, the woman relinquishes her claim for independent study time and rechannels her ambitions into the lives of her husband and children.

CRITICAL RECEPTION

There has been very little criticism of Elizabeth Stuart Phelps. During her lifetime she received a few short complimentary notices, but from the late 1850s through the 1980s, Phelps was referenced, if at all, as the mother of the more famous Elizabeth Stuart Phelps Ward. Critics of nineteenth-century American women authors have long faced the difficulties of rediscovering and republishing lost works. In Phelps's case, the attribution of works has been further hampered by her custom of unsigned works or the use of a pseudonym, H. Trusta. Furthermore, while Phelps Ward intended her assumption of her mother's name as a tribute, this appropriation has overshadowed her mother's work. In addition, since Phelps Ward did not marry until age 44, after her most popular works had been published, most twentieth-century critics (including her biographer) leave off the "Ward" when discussing her work. Judith Fetterley rather bitingly mocks critics whose sloppy research fails to properly assign authorship to the correct Elizabeth Stuart Phelps. For some scholars,

[i]t does not matter that Elizabeth Stuart Phelps, who was married to Austin Phelps, becomes Miss Phelps in the commentary of one critic, or that her daughter, who wrote under the same name and who did not marry until late in life, becomes in the commentary of another Mrs. Phelps. Nor does it matter that *The Sunny Side; or, The Country Minister's Wife,* the work of Elizabeth Stuart Phelps the elder, is ascribed by one critic to Almira Lincoln Phelps. . . . (Fetterley 21)

Thankfully, the past 20 years have witnessed a more careful recovery process for nineteenth-century American women writers, and mistakes such as those listed above are in the past.

During her brief lifetime, Phelps enjoyed the favor of a few select editors. Notices in respectable periodicals like *The New Englander and Yale Review, The Ladies' Repository,* and *Harper's New Monthly Magazine,* while short, were positive. An encouraging 1852 critic promised, "the public have their eye upon her [Elizabeth Stuart Phelps] as one able to interest and instruct them, and they will not easily suffer her pen to be idle" (*New Englander* 239). The *Christian Examiner's* review of this 1852 novel praises the character of Emily Edwards: "she appears the true pastor's wife, ready when occasion calls to be the friend and counselor to those around her, but finding her peculiar sphere of duty in her own home" (qtd. in Baym, *Novels* 102). The *Ladies' Repository* reviewer of

A Peep at 'Number Five' apparently felt Phelps had achieved an accurate depiction of life for a city pastor and gushed, "it has done our soul good in its perusal" (333). Even after her death was made known to the public, Phelps's posthumous collections earned the reviewers' praise. *Harper's* 1853 critic called her *The Tell-Tale* "delightful and instructive" (570), while the magazine's 1854 notice of the recently published *Little Mary; or, Talks and Tales for Children* explained, "few juvenile works display greater purity of sentiment or beauty of style, or can be more unhesitantly recommended for the family literary than this excellent volume" (570).

The two longer contemporary notices of Phelps's novels in *The New Englander and Yale Review* interestingly view these books as opportunities to speak on the subject of American ministers. They urge their readers to read these novels in order to gain an appreciation for the many unseen duties and sacrifices made by ministers and their families. The 1852 review is entitled "The Relation of Ministers to their People," and after three pages of commentary on Phelps's novel continues for 20 pages on the current challenges facing ministers. The periodical's 1854 article, " 'Shady Side' Literature," notes the influence Phelps's original 1851 *The Sunny Side* had on American literature, spawning several companion works. Listed among these fictionalized accounts of ministers and their wives are Phelps's own *A Peep at 'Number Five'* (1852), *The Shady Side; or, Life in a Country Parsonage* (1853, by a Pastor's Wife), and *The Prairie Missionary* (1853, Anonymous). The reach of Phelps's work can also be noted in Nehemiah Adams's allusion to her title in his 1855 proslavery work, *A South-Side View of Slavery; or, Three Months at the South in 1854*. The 1854 *New Englander* article, however, spends its remaining 15 pages discussing a congregation's treatment of its minister, clerical salaries, and recruitment.

While Carol Farley Kessler, Nina Baym, and Judith Fetterley include cogent remarks on the elder Phelps in their larger projects on nineteenth-century women writers, the single twentieth-century critical article dedicated to Phelps is Carol Holly's 1988 piece on "The Angel over the Right Shoulder" for *American Literature.* Using Fetterley's 1985 reprint of the story, Holly attempts to place the tale in the context of nineteenth-century domestic fiction. She argues that this short story

represents the experience of any and every woman—writer or otherwise—who has so internalized the patriarchal culture's prescriptions for female identity that, through the unconscious content of a dream, she shames herself for nurturing her own ambitions and, through the cheerful resolution that follows, coerces herself into reaffirming what the conduct books, the women's magazines, and a good deal of fiction in the mid-nineteenth century portrayed as woman's divinely appointed role in life, that of the submissive, self-sacrificing 'angel in the house.' (Holly 44)

Identifying herself as a feminist critic, Holly views this story as a particularly apt representation of the curtailed reality of life for a nineteenth-century woman. Clearly, there remain many opportunities for critics interested in the works of Elizabeth Stuart Phelps. Possibilities include a more in-depth analysis of her influence on her daughter's fiction, her placement in the peak years of the American Renaissance, and her contribution to the tradition of domestic realism.

WORKS CITED

Baym, Nina. *Novels, Readers, and Reviewers: Responses to Fiction in Antebellum America.* Ithaca: Cornell University Press, 1984.

———. *Woman's Fiction: A Guide to Novels by and about Women in America, 1820–1870.* 2nd ed. Urbana: University of Illinois Press, 1993.

Fetterley, Judith. "Elizabeth Stuart Phelps (1815–1852)." In *Provisions: A Reader from 19th-Century American Women,* edited by Judith Fetterley. Bloomington: Indiana University Press, 1985.

Holly, Carol. "Shaming the Self in 'The Angel over the Right Shoulder.' " *American Literature* 60.1 (March 1988): 42–60.

Kessler, Carol Farley. *Elizabeth Stuart Phelps.* Boston: Twayne, 1982.

"Literary Notice of *A Peep at 'Number Five'; or, A Chapter in the Life of a City Pastor.*" *The Ladies' Repository* 13.7 (July 1853): 333.

"Literary Notice of *Talks and Tales for Children.*" *Harper's New Monthly Magazine* 8.46 (March 1854): 570.

"Literary Notice of *The Tell-Tale.*" *Harper's New Monthly Magazine* 6.34 (March 1853): 570.

Phelps, Austin. "A Memorial of the Author." In *The Last Leaf from Sunny Side,* by Elizabeth Stuart Phelps. Boston: Phillips, Samson and Co., 1853.

Phelps (Ward), Elizabeth Stuart. *Chapters from a Life.* Boston: Houghton Mifflin, 1896.

"The Relation of Ministers to their People." *New Englander and Yale Review* 10.38 (May 1852): 236–59.

Robbins, Mrs. S[arah] S[tuart]. *Old Andover Days.* Boston: Pilgrim Press, 1909.

" 'Shady Side' Literature." *New Englander and Yale Review* 12.45 (February 1854): 54–71.

BIBLIOGRAPHY

Works by Elizabeth Stuart Phelps

Short Stories
"The Angel over the Right Shoulder." Andover: Warren F. Draper, 1852. Reprinted in *Provisions: A Reader from 19th-Century American Women,* edited by Judith Fetterley. Bloomington: Indiana University Press, 1985. 209–15.

The Last Leaf from Sunny Side. Boston: Phillips, Samson, and Co., 1853.

The Tell-Tale; or, Home Secrets Told by Old Travellers. Boston: Phillips, Sampson, and Co., 1853.

Little Mary; or, Talks and Tales for Children. Boston: Phillips, Samson, and Co., 1854.

Novels
The Sunny Side; or, The Country Minister's Wife. Philadelphia: American Sunday-School Union, 1851.

A Peep at 'Number Five'; or, A Chapter in the Life of a City Pastor. Boston: Phillips, Samson, and Co., 1852.

Juvenile Literature
Little Kitty Brown and Her Bible Verses. Philadelphia: American Sunday-School Union, 1851.

Kitty Brown and Her City Cousins. Philadelphia: American Sunday-School Union, 1852.

Kitty Brown and Her Little School. Philadelphia: American Sunday-School Union, 1852.

Kitty Brown Beginning to Think. Philadelphia: American Sunday-School Union, 1853.

Studies of Elizabeth Stuart Phelps

"Author of *Sunny Side* (engraving)." *The Ladies' Repository* 15.5 (May 1855): 320c.

Baym, Nina. *Woman's Fiction: A Guide to Novels by and about Women in America, 1820–1870.* 2nd ed. Urbana: University of Illinois Press, 1993. 246–8.

Clark, Rev. D. W. "Literary Women of America—The Author of 'Sunny-Side.' " *The Ladies' Repository* 15.6 (June 1855): 364–70.

Davis, Cynthia J. "Elizabeth Stuart Phelps (1815–1852)." In *Nineteenth-Century American Women Writers: A Bio-Bibliographical Critical Sourcebook,* edited by Denise D. Knight. Westport: Greenwood, 1997. 336–42.

Fetterley, Judith. "Elizabeth Stuart Phelps (1815–1852)." In *Provisions: A Reader from 19th-Century American Women,* edited by Judith Fetterley. Bloomington: Indiana University Press, 1985. 203–9.

Holly, Carol. "Shaming the Self in 'The Angel over the Right Shoulder.' " *American Literature* 60.1 (March 1988): 42–60.

Kessler, Carol Farley. *Elizabeth Stuart Phelps.* Boston: Twayne, 1982.

———. "A Literary Legacy: Elizabeth Stuart Phelps, Mother and Daughter." *Frontiers: A Journal of Woman's Studies* 5.3 (Fall 1980): 28–33.

"Literary Notice of *A Peep at 'Number Five'; or, A Chapter in the Life of a City Pastor.*" *The Ladies' Repository* 13.7 (July 1853): 333.

"Literary Notice of *Talks and Tales for Children.*" *Harper's New Monthly Magazine* 8.46 (March 1854): 570.

"Literary Notice of *The Tell-Tale.*" *Harper's New Monthly Magazine* 6.34 (March 1853): 570.

Phelps, Austin. "A Memorial of the Author." In *The Last Leaf from Sunny Side,* by Elizabeth Stuart Phelps. Boston: Phillips, Samson, and Co., 1853.

Phelps (Ward), Elizabeth Stuart. *Chapters from a Life.* Boston: Houghton Mifflin, 1896.

"The Relation of Ministers to their People." *New Englander and Yale Review* 10.38 (May 1852): 236–59.

" 'Shady Side' Literature." *New Englander and Yale Review* 12.45 (February 1854): 54–71.

EDGAR ALLAN POE (1809–1849)

Catherine Rainwater

BIOGRAPHY

On January 19, 1809, Edgar Poe was born to David and Eliza Poe, two aspiring young actors in Boston, Massachusetts. Unstable and alcoholic, David soon abandoned his family; not long afterward Eliza died, leaving behind not only three-year-old Edgar, but also five-year-old William Henry Leonard and one-year-old Rosalie. Although the orphaned children were sent to live with three different families, Poe maintained contact with his siblings throughout his life.

Poe himself was taken in by John and Fanny Allan of Richmond, Virginia. Allan was a prosperous merchant who admired education and social refinement, benefits he bestowed upon his adopted son. In turn, young Edgar excelled in both letters and mathematics at well-regarded schools in Richmond and London. Although he later described his childhood as a lonely one, he seems to have had the usual number of boyhood playmates. No doubt his loneliness in part stemmed from the loss of his biological family, for he seems to have endured no unusual deprivations in the Allan household.

Poe and his adoptive parents spent five years in London, but when Allan's international business interests floundered, they returned to Richmond. Back home in America, the teenaged Edgar was known to his friends as a competitive young man who showed exceptional talent in poetry and languages. Poe entered the University of Virginia in 1826 as an enthusiastic scholar, but the university during these years was a chaotic, undisciplined place where, unfortunately, student life fostered excessive drinking and gambling. Even as Poe complained in letters sent home about the dissolute environment, he incurred gambling debts and lost his academic focus, behavior that quickly annoyed John Allan and eventually alienated him altogether from his son. Angry and dejected, Poe dropped out of the university and rather impetuously fled to Boston without any means of supporting himself.

Poverty, not patriotism, drove the 17-year-old college dropout in 1827 to falsify his name and age in order to enlist in the United States Army. Edgar "Perry" was a good soldier—conscientious and disciplined—but as an aspiring poet, he had no true interest in military life. He plotted an early discharge, but his plan failed; admitting that he had lied about his name and age was apparently not enough to win a release from his five-year commitment. Consequently, Poe decided to seek admission to the United States Military Academy at West Point, where he hoped to fulfill the terms of his enlistment in a more intellectually stimulating atmosphere. Poe entered West Point in 1830, but following yet another wave of bitter arguments with Allan, he deliberately provoked his own expulsion. Such rash behavior was an early, if not the first, sign of a predilection for self-defeat that Poe would display throughout his life and that probably lies behind his theory of "perversity," illustrated in several of his tales by characters compelled to hasten their own demise.

None of Poe's experiences at college, in the army, or at West Point ever tempered his passion for writing poetry, however. Indeed, throughout these years, and always encouraged by friends and classmates, he wrote and rewrote many of the works for which he is now famous. Before the end of 1829 when he was only 20, he had published two collections of poems, *Tamerlane and Other Poems* in 1827, and *Al Aaraaf, Tamerlane and Minor Poems* in 1829. Two years later in 1831, the world would see a third volume, *Poems by Edgar A. Poe.* Being a published poet had, so far, done nothing to ameliorate Poe's eternal financial woes, unfortunately. After leaving West Point, he lived a threadbare existence in New York City and in Baltimore, sometimes working at various low-level editorial jobs to earn a subsistence living while he continued to write.

Toward the end of 1833, Poe's fortunes began to improve slightly when he won a cash prize from the Baltimore *Saturday Visitor* for his sensational tale, "MS Found in a Bottle." His works had, moreover, begun to attract the attention of various magazine editors in Baltimore, including John Pendleton Kennedy. Recognizing Poe's incipient abilities, Kennedy exploited his own connections to help Poe find employment, and Poe returned to Richmond in 1835 to become an editor for the *Southern Literary Messenger.* There he began to develop in earnest the magazinist's skills and talents that apparently came to him so naturally.

In 1836, enjoying an improved financial situation, Poe married his 13-year-old tubercular cousin, Virginia Clemm. Although Poe's relationships with women had, so far, been disappointing, his reasons for marrying Virginia were more noble than deviant. The young girl and her mother, Maria, were desperately poor, a situation doubtless arousing sympathy in a sensitive man who himself had recently been hungry and coatless in winter. When he married Virginia, he brought both her and Maria to live with him.

During his years with the *Messenger,* Poe's career took definite shape. He was an exacting editor, a prolific writer, an astute if acerbic reviewer, and a meticulous critic attempting to set new standards for literary composition. He emphasized formal and aesthetic perfection of texts over moral content, political alignment, and authorial character. As a writer, Poe still favored poetry over prose, but he knew the latter, especially the novel, was more financially lucrative. With a new family to support, he set out deliberately to exploit the public taste while trying hard to maintain his own literary integrity. In 1838, he published *The Narrative of Arthur Gordon Pym,* a work evincing Poe's lifelong tendency in his prose tales to construct literary hoaxes with serious philosophical, even metatextual, dimensions.

Ambitious and hoping for still more prestigious employment in the north, Poe left the *Southern Literary Messenger* in 1837. In Philadelphia in 1839, he became assistant editor of *Burton's Gentleman's Magazine* and, when *Burton's* was sold and renamed *Graham's Lady's and Gentleman's Magazine* in 1841, Poe was the appointed editor. In 1840, he published *Tales of the Grotesque and Arabesque.* Launching a promising career in the burgeoning magazine trade of the nineteenth century, he dreamed of one day own- ing and editing his own periodical called *The Stylus.* Sadly, his dream was never realized owing to the ephemeral nature of magazines in a highly competitive market and to Poe's own financial limitations, not to mention his deteriorating health and his odd, self- destructive tendencies.

Though the facts concerning Poe's alleged alcoholism will never be known, his bizarre behavior, whatever the cause, spoiled his reputation and seriously diminished his business prospects. Friends and acquaintances remarked his apparent drunkenness on many occasions, but a few observed how Poe seemed to become disproportionately intoxicated after only one or two drinks. These reports, coupled with his debilitating headaches, nausea, and bouts of diarrhea, suggest that he might have suffered from a medical condition such as hypoglycemia or diabetes, serious maladies with symptoms that can resemble inebriation or even mental illness.

Endless financial problems, his own poor health, and the slow death of Virginia doubtless all contributed during the last decade of Poe's life to his rancorous, sometimes strangely obsessive relationships with others, including Rufus Griswold (whom Poe often lambasted in print), Henry Wadsworth Longfellow (whom Poe accused of plagiarism), and Thomas Dunn English (whom Poe sued for libel). Griswold, in particular, would emerge as Poe's nemesis, deliberately attempting to ruin his reputation both before and after Poe's death.

Even in the face of assaults on his moral character, the publication of "The Raven" in 1845 brought Poe more fame than he had ever before enjoyed. This haunting poem was reviewed enthusiastically all over the country, and it was reprinted 10 times within the month following its appearance in the New York *Mirror.* "The Raven" also inspired dozens of parodies, which Poe thoroughly enjoyed along with the public recognition that he had for so long ambivalently sought. He had always wanted to appeal to the popular taste without sacrificing his high literary standards, and he saw the mass appeal of "The Raven" as evidence of his success.

Also in 1845, Poe's professional star rose once again when he became an editor of the *Broadway Journal,* where he was also given a share in the magazine's profits. Charles Frederick Briggs, co-owner of the *Journal,* was a true friend to Poe, frequently defend- ing his reputation and contradicting the vicious lies spread by Griswold. During these years, Poe seemed to emerge once and for all from poverty and obscurity. He used his position to lobby against the "nativist" movement in American literature and to advocate an international copyright law. His high profile frequently tilted toward notoriety, how- ever, as he published numerous scathing reviews of contemporary drama and literature, escalated his private war with Longfellow, and made an embarrassing spectacle of him- self at a meeting of the Lyceum in Boston. Unfortunately, Poe's public disputes soon began to seem less edgy and entertaining than obsessive, paranoid, and cruel. Almost as quickly as he had gained them, he lost friends and popular approval.

Thus was the year of 1845 a dizzying time of glory and loss for Edgar Allan Poe. An even harder blow came during that same year when he briefly became sole propri- etor of his own magazine; the *Broadway Journal* fell into his hands, but it quickly per- ished in a maelstrom of inherited debt in early January of 1846. Almost exactly a year later his invalid wife died. During the months following her death, Poe apparently tried to mend his life through new and renewed connections with women. His financial, phys- ical, and emotional condition, however, probably made him more the object of female sympathy than an attractive prospect. When Sarah Helen Whitman broke their marriage engagement in 1848, Poe attempted suicide.

The suicide attempt failed, but only a few months later, the 40-year-old Poe's troubled existence came to a tragic end. On October 3, 1849, following a business trip to Philadelphia, Poe was found on a Baltimore street in a disoriented condition. Though he was taken immediately to a hospital, he died four days later from uncertain causes. According to the attending physician, whose credibility has been questioned repeatedly by Poe's biographers, he probably died of *delerium tremens* brought on by acute alcoholism. Some have speculated that he perished of encephalitis; another rather outlandish theory is that he had contracted rabies. The circumstances surrounding Poe's death, like so much about his personal, inner life, remain mysterious. When Maria Clemm named Rufus Griswold Poe's literary executor, the clouds of mystery engulfing aspects of Poe's biography thickened; Griswold continued to berate Poe after death, even forging passages from Poe's letters and other personal documents that Maria had turned over to him. Biographers still ponder Maria's reasons for delivering Poe's literary estate into the hands of an enemy.

Edgar Allan Poe was buried inconspicuously on October 8, 1849, in a small Presbyterian cemetery in Baltimore, where he lay until 1876. His remains were moved in that year to their present site in a commemorative monument. From among the literati, only Walt Whitman attended the 1876 ceremony, and indeed, for many years following Poe's death, he seemed forgotten by the literary world that had so consumed his energy. Like his younger contemporary, Herman Melville, Poe would not attain full recognition as an important American writer for decades after his passing.

MAJOR WORKS AND THEMES

Poe's early poems are indebted to the British Romantic poets, especially Byron, Coleridge, and Shelley. Most often, he explores the darker side of romanticism—death, loss, loneliness, fear inspired by the sublime. Today as well as during his lifetime, "To Helen" (1831), "The City in the Sea" (1831), "Sonnet—To Science" (1829), and "Israfel" (1831) are considered to be the best of his early poems. From among his latest poems, "The Raven" (1845) and "Annabel Lee" (1849) are doubtless the best known and most highly regarded.

Early in his career, Poe established the themes that run throughout his works. In *Tamerlane and Other Poems,* his main themes concern memory, idyllic youth, the conflict between body and spirit, the power of imagination, transcendence of the mundane world, the qualities of genius, ideal beauty, and the nature of reality. In the poems included in *Tamerlane,* as well as in "Al Aaraaf" in his second volume, Poe rejects cold, Cartesian science as the foe of beauty. "Sonnet—To Science" bitterly laments the chilling effect of Enlightenment thought on the poet's magical, mystical engagement with nature. Since Poe believes that the road to wisdom lies in the contemplation of ideal beauty, he fears the legacy of the Age of Reason for its barbarous implications.

According to Poe, the most perfect poetic subject is the death of a beautiful woman, a theme he develops in several poems such as "Annabel Lee" and in some of his tales, such as "Ligeia." This topic allows the poet to exploit a powerful mood—grief—and to induce in the reader the contemplation of ideal beauty—ideal because no longer embodied in a living being, but held in memory. As Poe explains in "The Philosophy of Composition" and "The Poetic Principle," his intention in all of his poems—indeed, the aim of poetry as he sees it—is to produce in the reader the inner state of the poet from which the poem springs. Poe also claims that in achieving such a purpose, the hypnotic, musical, emotional effects of language are far more significant than the meanings the words convey.

To explain how poetry accomplishes its ends, Poe points to the role of two human faculties—Ideality and Causality. The poet uses language and symbols (Causality) in ways that awaken the soul and stimulate the intuition, so that the reader perceives and thus shares the exalted state (Ideality) of the poet's imagination. Poe also argues that a poem must be brief, no more than 100 lines, because sustaining imaginative excitement for long periods is impossible. Poe's critical discourse on poetics reveals powerful intellectual tension between his romantic tendencies emphasizing such emotion, on the one hand, and his formalist proclivities emphasizing craft, on the other. Like Coleridge, whose "Shellingian" and "Kantian" phases are widely noted, Poe also struggled toward a compromise between expressive and objective poetic principles. In their mutual struggle, both Coleridge and Poe anticipate the work of twentieth-century formalists who sought to explain how poetic devices, rhetorical and stylistic features, and structural elements work together to produce a unified, aesthetic impression. In his analysis of the precise effects of specific poetic language in a single work, Poe also anticipates the New Critical claim that there can be no such thing as paraphrase.

Poe's deft management of deranged narrators—created in part to raise significant psychological and philosophical questions as well as to dupe the naive reader—is another feature of Poe's works that would not be fully appreciated until after the New Critical dictum forbidding the equation of authors and their narrators. The biographical fallacies that plagued Poe criticism during the early twentieth century were certainly augmented by Freudian readers, especially, who assumed that Poe must be channeling his own unmediated thoughts through the words of his narrators and poetic speakers.

Poe's innovative imagination does not end with his development of forward-looking critical views, or with his lessons in critical responses to unreliable narrators. Indeed, he also singlehandedly transformed the *Blackwood's* variety of gothic horror tale into a more serious genre, the likes of which appealed even to Henry James as a sophisticated vehicle for the exploration of such psychological and linguistic concerns as he entertains in *The Turn of the Screw*. Doubtless, James (and others) also perceived the comic dimensions of Poe's horror fiction, for *The Turn of the Screw*, to which James referred openly as a hoax, operates in many ways similar to Poe's best-known tales such as "The Fall of the House of Usher."

Poe's comic elements are widely recognized, and he is even known to have spoofed himself from time to time. In "Thou Art the Man" (1844), for instance, he makes fun of the ratiocinative tale that he, himself, invented and for which he is also well known. "The Murders in the Rue Morgue," "The Purloined Letter," "The Mystery of Marie Roget," and "The Gold-Bug" are among Poe's tales of ratiocination featuring the protagonist and paragon of rationality, Auguste Dupin, who inspired Arthur Conan Doyle's creation of Sherlock Holmes.

With his contemporaries Hawthorne and Melville, Poe shares a powerfully cynical vein of thought; consequently, like them he frequently crosses the threshold from romanticism to antiromanticism. In his most admired and anthologized gothic tales— "MS Found in a Bottle," "The Pit and the Pendulum," "Ligeia," "The Fall of the House of Usher," "William Wilson," "The Tell-Tale Heart," "The Cask of Amontillado," and "The Black Cat"—as well as in *The Narrative of Arthur Gordon Pym* and others, Poe employs formal devices designed to emphasize the terrifying side of poetic, transcendental aspiration beyond one's human limits. Live burial, descents into whirlpools and maelstroms, frightening encounters with doppelgangers—all are metaphors that Poe exploits to emphasize the potential for madness and self-destruction that accompanies efforts to escape ordinary existence. With Hawthorne and Melville, Poe will doubtless continue to be one of the most widely read and influential figures to have emerged during the American Renaissance.

CRITICAL RECEPTION

While he lived, as we have observed, Poe never achieved the type or amount of recognition he craved. Possibly, he might never have been satisfied, for his reactions to criticism were frequently capricious. For instance, when John Neal referred ambivalently to *Al Aaraaf, Tamerlane and Minor Poems* as "exquisite nonsense" that showed promise, young Poe took heart and declared Neal's words to be the first encouragement he had ever received (Silverman 54). Some years later, however, when he suspected Charles Dickens of writing a review that favorably compared his poems to Tennyson's, Poe took offense at what most other writers would have considered high praise from a literary lion. Apparently, Poe was easily insulted and frequently attacked those who might have otherwise been useful to him. His ill-considered remarks about the Transcendentalists, for instance, irritated Emerson, who in turn dismissed Poe's poetry out of hand. In any case, Poe's early poems have never been his most admired works; at first his critical reviews, and later, in the 1830s, his prose tales brought his name most prominently before the public. As we have already observed, 1845—the year of "The Raven" and the *Broadway Journal*—saw Poe in the brightest of limelights he would ever enjoy during his lifetime.

Poe's critical fortunes in the years since his death have been nearly as erratic as his lifelong financial situation. During the second half of the nineteenth century, the literary establishment in the United States dismissed him as a hack, while in Britain, the Pre-Raphaelites admired him. In fact, Dante Gabriel Rossetti is believed to have written "The Blessed Damozel" (1850) in response to "The Raven." Around the same time in France, Baudelaire proclaimed Poe's genius and openly acknowledged his own literary indebtedness to him. The younger French symbolists, including Mallarmé and Valéry, shared Baudelaire's enthusiasm. On the eve of the modernist era, this continental European view of Poe prompted an American change of heart toward his works and doubtless set the stage for the considerable Poe revival that developed after the middle of the twentieth century.

Poe's literary reputation was especially well served by formalist practices that prevailed in the United States from approximately the 1950s through the middle 1970s. New Critical close reading, tempered by the corrective influence of the Chicago School, was especially suited to analysis of Poe's carefully crafted tales such as "The Fall of the House of Usher," "William Wilson," "Ligeia," and others that exhibit Poe's own meticulous attention to formal structure and narrative management. Indeed, some of the most insightful criticism of Poe's works was produced during these years, which saw Darrel Abel's classic essay of 1949, "A Key to the House of Usher," Eric W. Carlson's collection of essays by such notables as Allen Tate and Georges Poulet in 1959, and Patrick Quinn's *The French Face of Edgar Allan Poe* in 1957, among others. The application of psychological theories to the interpretation of Poe's art during and after the 1960s was similarly enlightening and afforded a long-overdue substitute for simplistic Freudian readings of his texts that had, during the early twentieth century, naively equated Poe with his demented narrators.

Beginning in the 1970s in the United States, structuralism and its aftermath produced another wave of valuable insights into Poe's art. Studies by Jean Ricardou, John Carlos Rowe, and others throughout the 1970s reveal Poe not only as a consummate crafter of formally perfected tales, but also as a linguistically and philosophically astute writer of works, such as *The Narrative of Arthur Gordon Pym,* that metacritically dramatize the exigencies of verbal representation. *Pym* continues into the twenty-first century to interest a diverse group of critics examining topics ranging from political ideology to race and gender.

During the 1970s, critical preoccupation with Harold Bloom's theory of the "anxiety of influence" generated increased awareness of writers all over the world who, like the French symbolists, openly acknowledged their indebtedness to Poe. Apparently, even during those years in America when Poe was all but forgotten by scholars and critics, writers as diverse as Ellen Glasgow, Jules Verne, and H. G. Wells found him both inspiring and instructive. In the modern and postmodern periods, Henry James, William Faulkner, Paul Bowles, Vladimir Nabokov, Jorge Luis Borges, and many others acknowledge, in varying degrees, Poe's effects on their own creative imaginations. Critical assessment of Poe's influence on subsequent generations of writers has become an established thread in Poe scholarship today.

The 1970s were a turning point in literary studies, in general, when theoretical approaches to the interpretation of texts began to outnumber conventional, more historically grounded scholarship. The 1980s saw the development of an increasingly divisive critical community, and Poe studies were no exception. Traditionalists frequently complained that theorists ignored the solid scholarship of their predecessors and thus sometimes committed egregious errors; theorists, in turn, charged that the critical approaches of the past were staid and narrow. Both sides were often correct. Two booms in Poe studies that occurred in the early 1970s, and again in the middle 1980s, produced an array of Derridian, Lacanian, Kristevan, and other theoretically based arguments that strike out in new directions but vary dramatically in quality and validity. Such studies were invariably matched by a steady stream of critical works watering old ground. In the 1990s, culture studies that focus on Poe's overt and covert ideology, including racial and gender politics, tend to predominate; while some of these views of Poe's work shed light on previously undisclosed aspects of his thought and art, many others, though ingenious, remain unconvincing. During the 1990s, indeed, the mystique that Poe himself often deliberately cultivated seems intensified as he is alternately made out to stand on first this, and now that, side of the gender-racial-ideological divide. Ironically, Poe is once again subject to a variant of the moralistic, political criticism that he railed against in his own day, and that he countered in his critical works such as "The Philosophy of Composition" (1846) and "The Poetic Principle" (1850).

Fifteen decades of Poe scholarship have produced no universal view of his art, nor any full understanding of his psychological complexity. A definitive critical biography of Poe remains to be written and might never be, owing to the irresolvable mysteries enveloping his life and death. During the latter half of the twentieth century, however, many of the long-standing, erroneous myths about Poe have been dispelled. That he was eccentric, irascible, melancholy, self-destructive, and often down on his luck, we know; however, we also know that he was an astute journalist, a dedicated, even driven, intellect with keen insight into the literary world and his own deserved place within it. Twentieth-century criticism of Poe's art also corroborates his contemporaries' judgment that his tales of horror and ratiocination are, indeed, his best material. More definitively than any of his poems, they reveal Poe's sophistication, depth, and insight into the ontological and epistemological dilemmas of existence.

WORKS CITED

Silverman, Kenneth. *Edgar A. Poe: Mournful and Never-ending Remembrance.* New York: Harper Collins, 1991.

BIBLIOGRAPHY

Works by Edgar Allan Poe

Poems
Tamerlane and Other Poems. Boston: Calvin F. S. Thomas, 1827.
Al Aaraaf, Tamerlane and Minor Poems. Baltimore: Hatch and Dunning, 1829.
Poems by Edgar A. Poe. 2nd ed. New York, 1831.
The Raven and Other Poems. New York, 1845.
Eureka: A Prose Poem. New York: George P. Putnam, 1848.

Tales
The Narrative of Arthur Gordon Pym. New York, 1838.
The Journal of Julius Rodman, Burton's Gentleman's Magazine, Jan.–June 1840.
Tales of the Grotesque and Arabesque. 2 vols. Philadelphia: Lea and Blanchard, 1840.
The Murders in the Rue Morgue and The Man That Was Used Up. Philadelphia: William H. Graham, 1843.
Tales. New York: Wiley and Putnam, 1845.

Nonfiction
The Conchologist's First Book. Philadelphia, 1839.
Marginalia. 1844–49. Charlottesville: University Press of Virginia, 1981.

Studies of Edgar Allan Poe

Abel, Darrel. "A Key to the House of Usher," *University of Toronto Quarterly,* 18 (1949), 176–85.

Carlson, Eric W., ed. *The Recognition of Edgar Allan Poe.* Ann Arbor: U of Michigan P, 1959.

Caserio, Robert L. *Plot, Story and the Novel: From Dickens and Poe to the Modern Period.* Princeton: Princeton UP, 1979.

Davidson, Edward H. *Poe: A Critical Study.* Cambridge, MA: Harvard UP, 1957.

Jacobs, Robert D. *Poe: Journalist and Critic.* Baton Rouge: Louisiana State UP, 1969.

Kennedy, J. Gerald, and Liliane Weissberg, eds. *Romancing the Shadow: Poe and Race.* New York: Oxford, 2001.

Moldenhauer, Joseph J. "Murder As a Fine Art: Basic Connections Between Poe's Aesthetics, Psychology, and Moral Vision." *PMLA* 83 (1968), 284–97.

Poulet, Georges. "Poe." In Eric W. Carlson, ed. *The Recognition of Edgar Allan Poe.* Ann Arbor: U of Michigan P, 1959.

Quinn, Arthur Hobson. *Edgar Allan Poe: A Critical Biography.* New York: D. Appleton-Century, 1941.

Quinn, Patrick. *The French Face of Edgar Allan Poe.* Carbondale: Southern Illinois University Press, 1957.

Ricardou, Jean. " 'The Singular Character of the Water,' " transl. Frank Towne, *Poe Studies,* 9 (1976), 1–6.

———. "Gold in the Bug," transl. Frank Towne, *Poe Studies,* 9 (1976), 33–9.

Rowe, John Carlos. "Writing and Truth in Poe's *The Narrative of Arthur Gordon Pym,*" *Glyph* 2 (1977), 102–21.

Thomas, Dwight, and David K. Jackson. *The Poe Log: A Documentary Record of the Life of Edgar Allan Poe, 1809–1849.* Boston: G. K. Hall, 1987.

Thompson, G. R. *Poe's Fiction: Romantic Irony in the Gothic Tales.* Madison: U of Wisconsin P, 1973.

JAMES REDPATH (1833–1891)

John P. Koontz

BIOGRAPHY

James Redpath, the oldest child of Ninian and Maria Maine Redpath, was born on August 24, 1833, and christened in Berwick Upon Tweed, a border garrison town on the northeast coast of England. His mother was English and came from a seafaring family. His father was Scottish, and for a time he served as the master of schools in Berwick.

For reasons that have not been documented, the Redpath family emigrated to the United States in 1849 and settled on a farm in Allegan County near Kalamazoo, Michigan. Redpath, declaring "I won't be a farmer[.] I came to America to be a printer" (Horner 14), entered the trade in Kalamazoo, moving within a few months to Detroit. Soon he began writing impassioned antislavery copy under the pseudonym "Berwick." Horace Greeley (1811–72) discovered his work and quickly offered him a position as correspondent. Thereupon Redpath, who was barely 19, went to live in New York and to work for *The New-York Tribune.*

An early assignment at the *Tribune* involved compiling "Facts of Slavery," a regular series of articles gleaned from southern newspaper exchanges. Redpath resolved to examine the institution for himself. His first trip, in March 1854, convinced him that the slaves were willing and prepared to rebel. Upon returning to New York from his first visit, he produced a series of pseudonymous articles for William Lloyd Garrison (1805–79) to inform northern readers of the conditions he observed. During his second trip he sent articles, at some personal peril, to various northern newspapers while still traveling in the South. He later edited and expanded them for a book, *The Roving Editor, or, Talks with Slaves in the Southern United States* (1859), securing the financial assistance of Gerrit Smith to cover the costs of production.

In 1855 Redpath turned his attention to Kansas and began working for the *Missouri Democrat,* a Free Soil advocate, in June. For the next three years, he became active in Kansas affairs, writing dispatches, engaging in politics, securing support in New England for the Free Soil settlers, and writing poetry about Kansas. He also founded a Free Soil newspaper, *The Crusader of Freedom,* in Doniphan in December 1857, and defiantly announced "I enroll myself a Crusader of Freedom until slavery ceases to exist" (Horner 91).

During the Pike's Peak Gold Rush of 1859, Redpath and fellow journalist Richard J. Hinton prepared a guidebook for gold prospectors, *Hand-Book to Kansas Territory and the Rocky Mountains' Gold Region* (1859), in the hope that it would spur a greater number of Free Soil immigrants to settle in the Territory, the western part of which contained most of the gold fields. Redpath's activities there had taken a dramatic, perhaps histrionic, turn in May 1856 when he stumbled upon the camp of John Brown (1800–59) within days of the massacre at Pottawatomie Creek. He and Brown shared the same abolitionist views and he set about becoming Brown's most fervent publicist, fiercely denying Brown's role in the massacre and skillfully shaping the "Martyr for Freedom" image which prevailed in the public discourse for a generation after he published Brown's biography shortly after his execution in December 1859.

Redpath returned East from Kansas in July 1858, and soon became active in promoting Haiti, founding a Haitian Bureau of Emigration in Boston and New York and publishing a weekly newspaper, *Pine and Palm.* In 1860, he published *Guide to Hayti,* an anthology of articles and essays by various hands on a range of Haitian subjects.

After the outbreak of the Civil War, Redpath worked alternately as publisher and war correspondent. After Thayer and Eldridge, the Boston publishing firm with which he had become closely associated, failed, he set up a firm in his own name and began the series "Books for the Times," which included William Wells Brown's *The Black Man* (1863), John R. Beard's *Toussaint L'Ouverture* (1863), and Louisa May Alcott's *Hospital Sketches* (1863). In 1864 he published "Books for the Camp Fires," a series aimed at soldiers and civilians, and Brown's *Clotel; or the President's Daughter,* Alcott's *On Picket Duty, and Other Tales,* and reprints of works by Balzac and Hugo. In 1864, he abandoned publishing to serve as a war correspondent with the armies of Thomas and Sherman.

In 1868 Redpath started the Boston Lyceum Bureau, later known as the Redpath Bureau, to supply the renewed demand for speakers and performers for lyceums across the country. Representing figures such as Mark Twain, Julia Ward Howe, Charles Sumner, and Ralph Waldo Emerson, the Redpath Bureau became the most prominent and successful agency of its kind. In 1875, Redpath sold his interest in the bureau, and for the next few years, he lived alternately in Washington, D.C., and New York when not traveling. His health declined at the end of the decade, and he suffered a breakdown in 1879. In 1880, he was commissioned to cover Irish affairs, and for the next two years he reported on the famine and the land war in the west of Ireland.

Upon his return to the United States, he lectured on the lyceum circuit; wrote newspaper articles; published a collection of his lectures and articles, *Talks about Ireland;* and published *Redpath's Weekly,* devoted to the promotion of Irish causes.

In spite of failing health, Redpath remained productive. In 1886 he became an editor at the *North American Review.* In February 1891, he was run over by a vehicle while crossing Broadway in New York. He died of his injuries on February 10. At his request, his remains were carried to Fresh Pond, Long Island, and cremated.

MAJOR WORKS AND THEMES

As the summary of his life suggests, Redpath was an activist engaged in a lifelong attempt to shape public opinion. Throughout his career, he remained alert to the commercial potential of radical ideas and was remarkably resourceful in packaging them as consumable commodities. He insistently challenged popular opinion, and rarely consolidated it. Never a political or social insider, he observed and wrote with the keen but rarely jaundiced eye of estrangement.

His first important volume, *The Roving Editor, or, Talks with Slaves in the Southern United States* (1859), dedicated to John Brown, embodies these elements. The text, which is largely patched together from previously published newspaper articles, is Redpath's experiment in a new, if imperfect, democratic order. In the course of his inquiry, Redpath reveals the slave-holders not simply as liars but as dupes for believing their own ideology. The slaves as truth-tellers ironically come to enjoy a privileged moral standing. As slaves, their testimony is raised over the claims of slave-holders with often embarrassing and humorous results. This ascendence through humor helps make Redpath's larger point of moral ascendence, which in turn increases the sense of outrage at what is exposed as a manifestly unjust social order. Redpath is not motivated entirely by a sense of outrage, however. In contrast to the broad depiction of racial division in *Roving Editor*, he offers a detailed and ardent portrait of racial regeneration in *Guide to Hayti* (1861), in which he urges Americans of African descent to join Haiti in creating a new society and a new race, adding a Saxon discipline the Republic lacks. It is his most purely utopian work.

The Public Life of Capt. John Brown proved to be his most popular and influential work. Quickly exploiting his connections to Brown and his family and relying on his own accounts of Brown's experiences in Kansas, he gathered documents and testimony and produced a volume of 407 pages within a year of Brown's death. Insisting that Brown acted from principles of benevolence, he strenuously denied Brown's role in the Pottawatomie Creek massacre. Deftly addressing concerns about Brown's methods, he attempts to show that rather than causing social disorder, they promise to inaugurate a new, more permanent regime.

CRITICAL RECEPTION

Recorded opinion of any sort about James Redpath is sparse. Consideration of his work has largely been the province of historians. John R. McKivigan, who has edited a modern edition of *Roving Editor*, reports that there is no record of its sales. He quotes a friendly newspaper editor in Leavenworth, Kansas, who found it "eccentric and humorous" and effusively claimed it "for all Humanity" (*Roving Editor* xx). He says that Frederick Douglass promoted it, but that Bronson Alcott found its portraits "overdrawn, and tempered with prejudices unjust to all parties" (*Roving Editor* xx). McKivigan also notes that it is not widely used in slavery scholarship—and that when it is discussed, it is generally viewed with suspicion (*Roving Editor* xxiv). Redpath's *Life of Capt. John Brown* has received greater, but hardly more respectful, attention from historians because of its subject's protean importance. Most have rejected Redpath's characterization of Brown as hagiography. James C. Malin has dismissed Redpath as "a publicity agent for John Brown" (245). Recently, Merrill D. Peterson, acknowledging its importance, asserts that Redpath's analysis of Brown's failure at Harpers Ferry as tactical, not strategic, has influenced most subsequent analyses. As for his lyceum work, Redpath's biographer, Charles F. Horner, praised him extravagantly. Given his financial interest in the Redpath Bureau and his role in promoting lyceums throughout the Midwest and Texas, Horner's emphasis and interest is understandable, if not wholly disinterested.

WORKS CITED

Malin, James C. *John Brown and the Legend of Fifty-Six.* Memoirs of the American Philosophical Society 17. Philadelphia: APS, 1942.

McKivigan, John R., ed. Introduction. *The Roving Editor, or, Talks with Slaves in the Southern United States.* By James Redpath. 1859. University Park, PA: Pennsylvania State University Press, 1996.

BIBLIOGRAPHY

Works by James Redpath

The Roving Editor, or, Talks with Slaves in the Southern United States. 1859. Ed. John R. McKivigan. University Park, PA: Pennsylvania State University Press, 1996.

and Richard J. Hinton. *Hand-Book to Kansas Territory and the Rocky Mountains' Gold Region. accompanied by reliable maps and a preliminary treatise on the pre-emption laws of the United States.* New York: J. H. Colton, 1859.

The Public Life of Capt. John Brown, by James Redpath with an Auto-Biography of his Childhood and Youth. Boston: Thayer and Eldridge, 1860.

Echoes of Harper's Ferry. Boston: Thayer and Eldridge, 1860.

Guide to Hayti. Boston: Haytian Bureau of Emigration, 1861.

Shall we suffocate Ed. Green? Boston: J. Redpath, 1864.

Talks about Ireland. New York: P. J. Kenedy, 1881.

Studies of James Redpath

Boyd, Willis D. "James Redpath and American Negro Colonization in Haiti, 1860–1862." *Americas* 12.2 (1955): 169–82.

Dixon, Christopher. "Nineteenth-Century African American Emigrationism: The Failure of the Haitian Alternative." *Western Journal of Black Studies* 18.2 (1994): 77–88.

Hart, Jim A. "James Redpath, Missouri Correspondent." *Missouri Historical Review,* 57.1 (1962–63): 70–8.

Horner, Charles Francis. *The Life of James Redpath, and the development of the modern lyceum.* New York and Newark, NJ: Barse & Hopkins, 1926.

McKivigan, John R. "James Redpath, John Brown, and Abolitionist Advocacy of Slave Insurrection." *Civil War History* 37 (December 1991): 293–313.

———. "James Redpath and Black Reaction to the Haitian Emigration Bureau." *Mid-America* 69.3 (1987): 139–53.

Schackelford, Lynne P. "James Redpath." *Dictionary of Literary Biography 49: American Literary Publishing Houses, 1638–1899, Part 2: N–Z.* Ed. Peter Dzwonkoski. Detroit: Gale, 1986. 387–9.

JOHN ROLLIN RIDGE (1827–1867)

William Etter

BIOGRAPHY

On March 19, 1827, John Rollin Ridge (his Cherokee name was Cheesquatalawny or "Yellow Bird") was born to a wealthy, educated Cherokee family. His father, John, practiced law, and his grandfather fought with the United States against the Creek Indians and owned the planter's estate in Georgia on which his son and grandson lived. His mother, Sarah Northrup, was a white woman whom Ridge's father met while studying in New England. The Ridges elected to use their formidable political influence in the Cherokee nation to advance assimilation as the best means of resolving conflicts between Native American peoples and the United States. When the "Ridge faction" signed the Treaty of New Echoa in 1835, ceding Cherokee lands east of the Mississippi to the United States for five million dollars and territory in the West, it was opposed by the powerful "Ross faction," which rejected all proposals to remove the Cherokees from their ancestral lands. After accusing the Ridges of treason under an 1829 Cherokee statute which forbade unauthorized representatives from making treaties with the United States, the Ross faction organized the assassination of John Rollin Ridge's father, grandfather, and cousin on June 22, 1839. Young John was only 12 when he witnessed, as he later wrote, his father stabbed 29 times and his house surrounded by over 20 men. This event, during which the boy endured feelings of anger, terror, and powerlessness, is typically interpreted by scholars as the origin of his lifelong concern with revenge, frequently thematized in his writing.

An individual with a multi-ethnic identity, Ridge was also shaped by many regions. After his father's death, Ridge briefly studied at the Great Barrington Academy in Massachusetts, then returned to the South to live with his mother, now residing in Arkansas. For a time he studied law but was forced to relocate to Missouri after he killed David Kell, whom some historians believe had been ordered by the Ross faction to assassinate the adolescent Ridge. In 1850 Ridge moved to California to seek his fortune in the gold fields and lived in this state until his death. He soon discovered that searching for gold required labor more arduous than that performed, he wrote a friend, by "any slave I ever owned" (*The Life,* xviii). Mining proved no more attractive, and after two months Ridge turned to clerking for county officials and writing for newspapers.

From this period until the end of his life he published a steady stream of articles, primarily in San Francisco periodicals, and managed newspapers. In 1854, his only novel and the first by a Native American, *The Life and Adventures of Joaquín Murieta, The Celebrated California Bandit,* was published in San Francisco under the name "Yellow Bird." Ridge continued to work as a journalist during the Civil War. After the conflict ended, he traveled to Washington, D.C., with a Cherokee delegation to speak on behalf of Cherokees who had allied themselves with the Confederacy and now wished to be considered a people distinct from the "Ross-dominated Cherokee nation" (Weaver 80). Ridge died of a "brain fever" in California in 1867. A volume of his poetry, the first collection by a Native American, appeared posthumously the following year.

MAJOR WORKS AND THEMES

Ridge wrote in three major genres—the novel, journalism, and poetry—but his literary reputation is founded almost entirely on *Joaquín Murieta.* Based on the exploits of five real California outlaws, Ridge's novel is a story of revenge and "rough justice." The novel begins just after the Mexican War and tells the story of Joaquín Murieta, a Sonoran farmer who, in a vengeful rage, turns to a life of crime after he is forced off his land, his wife is raped, his half-brother is wrongly hanged, and Murieta himself is scourged by "lawless and desperate men, who bore the title of Americans but failed to support the honor and dignity of that title" (9). With a band of outlaws (among them the sadistic villain Three-Fingered Jack) and covert support from Mexican communities, Murieta robs and murders throughout the state until he is killed by Captain Harry Love, commissioned by the California state legislature to hunt down the outlaw. Despite some popularity when it was published in 1854, and the fact Ridge created the first California "folk hero," *Joaquín Murieta* remains relatively obscure. (In the nineteenth century pirated editions sold better than the original.) Printed, like many "frontier potboilers," as a cheap pamphlet, only one copy of the ninety-page first edition is known to survive.

Ridge's newspaper articles and editorials express conservative socio-political views. He promoted Native American assimilation to the Anglo-dominated culture, institutions, and economy of the United States. Other articles envisioned the Cherokee nation becoming "an integral part" of the American Union, with "Senators and Representatives in Congress." Ridge's most famous statements in support of Native-American rights and culture appeared in a series of three articles for *The Hesperian* magazine (1862), but his journalism did not voice unqualified praise for Native Americans. While he railed against the brutality California Indians suffered at the hands of whites, Ridge also told the readers of newspapers like the *Sacramento Bee* that California tribes were "uncivilized," "ignorant," and cowardly compared to "civilized" Eastern peoples like the Cherokees. The same racial stereotyping appears in *Joaquín Murieta.* During the Civil War the journalist expressed ideas his Unionist readers frequently found offensive: strong support for the Confederacy and slavery and virulent opposition to Lincoln's presidency.

Ridge's poems, most of which he composed before he was twenty, are generally sentimental in subject matter and tone and sometimes reflects his lifelong admiration for Romantic poetry.

CRITICAL RECEPTION

The majority of criticism on Ridge's work focuses on *Joaquín Murieta*. Though critics conventionally disparage the novel for its crude, even "abominable" style, they regard it as crucial to an understanding of cultural contact in the Far West. To this end, valuable scholarship has illuminated connections between the racial oppression depicted in the novel and nineteenth-century California history. (The Foreign Miners' Tax Law, passed in 1850 and aimed at driving Latin American miners away from the state, for instance, is an important subtext for understanding Murieta's struggle for justice.) In current scholarship, three dominant interpretations of *Joaquín Murieta* may be discerned. The first asserts that the novel speaks to interfactional conflict within the Cherokee nation using a Mexican-American hero as a "mask" for a Native-American one. The second understands the novel as Ridge's protest against the oppression of displaced Mexican people in the aftermath of the Mexican War and California statehood. The third contends *Joaquín Murieta* thematizes conflicts between individualist and communal values. When discussing this novel, virtually all critics identify two elements as significant: Murieta's daring escape on horseback with bullets whizzing about him and an original poem on Mount Shasta inserted into the narrative when Murieta rides north. Most refer to these elements as moments of Romantic "sublimity," and some call Murieta a "Byronic" hero.

Joaquín Murieta has been interpreted as a character who derives power from liminality, riding between the worlds of citizen and outlaw, the law and the spirit of justice, Sonoran and "American." Some critics choose to see him as a "trickster" figure while others interpret the novel and Ridge's own life from a postcolonial perspective. Populated with displaced Mexican, Native-American, and Chinese characters, *Joaquín Murieta* offers fertile ground for examining the relationship between identity and place, the meaning of homeland, the dynamics of a multicultural society, and the conflict between hegemonic and minority discourses. As Louis Owens observes, Ridge shared with his characters the unique experience of living as a mixed-blooded individual in the United States, which often demanded one construct one's public persona as a sort of "masquerade," a "mimic [of] the discourse of the privileged center" in order to be accessible to the dominant white culture (33). Many critics believe the cultural crises presented in the novel remain central concerns in Native-American literature.

WORKS CITED

Owens, Louis. *Other Destinies: Understanding the American Indian Novel.* Norman: University of Oklahoma Press, 1992.

Ridge, John Rollin. *The Life and Adventures of Joaquín Murieta.* Ed. Joseph Henry Jackson. Norman: University of Oklahoma Press, 1955.

Weaver, Jace. *That the People Might Live.* New York: Oxford UP, 1997.

BIBLIOGRAPHY

Works by John Rollin Ridge

The Life and Adventures of Joaquín Murieta, The Celebrated California Bandit. San Francisco: W. B. Cooke and Company, 1854.

Poems. San Francisco: Henry Payot & Co., 1868.

A Trumpet of Our Own: Yellow Bird's Essays on the North American Indian, Selections. Ed. David Farmer and Rennard Strickland. San Francisco: Book Club of America, 1981.

Studies of John Rollin Ridge

Lowe, John. " 'I Am Joaquin!': Space and Freedom in Yellow Bird's *The Life and Adventures of Joaquín Murieta, the Celebrated California Bandit.*" *Early Native American Writing.* Ed. Helen Jaskoski. New York: Cambridge UP, 1996.

Mondragon, Maria. " 'The (Safe) White Side of the Line': History and Disguise in John Rollin Ridge's *The Life and Adventures of Joaquín Murieta: The Celebrated California Bandit.*" *American Transcendental Quarterly* 8, no. 3 (September 1994): 173–87.

Parins, James W. *John Rollin Ridge: His Life and Works.* Lincoln: University of Nebraska Press, 1991.

Rowe, John Carlos. *Literary Culture and U.S. Imperialism.* New York: Oxford UP, 2000.

Ruoff, A. LaVonne Brown. *American Indian Literatures.* New York: MLA, 1990.

Walker, Cheryl. *Indian Nation: Native American Literature and Nineteenth century Nationalisms.* Durham: Duke UP, 1997.

CATHARINE MARIA SEDGWICK (1789–1867)

Maria Karafilis

BIOGRAPHY

Born on December 28, 1789, into a politically powerful family, Catharine Maria Sedgwick was the sixth of seven surviving children born to Theodore and Pamela Dwight Sedgwick. Her mother descended from a distinguished Connecticut River Valley family and her father was very active in state and federal government. Theodore Sedgwick fought in the Battle of White Plains, New York, during the Revolutionary War and was elected to a number of public offices in the early national period. He served in both houses of the Massachusetts legislature; the U.S. House of Representatives, where he was Speaker under George Washington; and the Senate, where he fought to gain ratification of the Constitution. He was an influential Federalist who maintained that only an elite leadership could sustain the nation and had a haughty suspicion of the lower orders. When the Federalists were defeated at the polls in 1800, Theodore resigned his congressional seat and was appointed to Massachusetts's highest court.

As a child growing up in Stockbridge, Massachusetts, Catharine Sedgwick subscribed to her father's Federalist beliefs and notes in her autobiography that "I remember well looking upon a Democrat as an enemy to his country, and at the party as sure, if it prevailed, to work its destruction" (*Power* 63). As she matured, while she retained some of her father's condescension and the notion of an elite based on culture and manners, if not on wealth, she aligned herself primarily with a Democratic social and political position. She would later write that the Federalists' greatest "misfortune . . . was a thorough distrust of the people" and in her fiction she often satirized an aristocracy of wealth (*Power* 64). In fact, what Catharine Sedgwick most loved about life in Stockbridge was its democratic nature. She considered living in the country "an essential advantage" because "one is brought into close social relations with all conditions of people. There are no barriers between you and your neighbors. The highest and lowest meet in their joys and sorrows, at weddings and funerals, in sicknesses and distresses of all sorts" (*Power* 77).

Sedgwick ultimately came to find her father's Federalist views detrimental to American democracy and also, on some level, found his unwavering commitment to his political duties detrimental to the well-being and smooth running of the family home. Her mother, Pamela, suffered from acute physical and mental debilitation, weakness that Catharine ascribed to two sources: the ignorance and "rough handling" of the medical profession and the weight of domestic cares that oppressed her as Theodore Sr. was in Boston, Philadelphia, or Washington, D.C., fulfilling his public duties (*Power* 60). After witnessing her mother's loneliness, depression, and physical ailments, along with the loveless and perhaps abusive marriage of her sister Frances, it is no wonder that Sedgwick expressed in several of her published works the sentiment that it was "a truth, which, if more generally received by her sex, might save a vast deal of misery, that marriage is not *essential* to the contentment, the dignity, or the happiness of woman" (*Hope Leslie* 350, original emphasis).

Sedgwick opted to remain single despite a number of suitors, a highly unusual choice in nineteenth-century America. Uncommonly close to all four of her brothers—Theodore Jr., Harry, Robert, and Charles—a great deal of her marital and maternal affections were transferred to them and their families. She was especially intimate with Harry and Robert and wintered with them in New York City. Her summers were spent either in Stockbridge with Theodore Jr. or in Lenox with Charles, where she maintained a suite of rooms. In her autobiography, Sedgwick writes, "All my brothers were beloved, and I can conceive of no truer image of the purity and happiness of the equal loves of Heaven than that which unites brothers and sisters. It has been my chiefest blessing in life and, but that I look to its continuance hereafter, I should indeed be wretched" (*Power* 89). Her close relationships with her siblings, her sisters-in-law, and her nieces and nephews no doubt contribute to one of the recurrent themes in her fiction: the home as an image of heaven. Not only in a didactic tale entitled *Home,* but in many of her other works, the virtuous, nurturing, and well-regulated home is a source of contentment, fulfillment, and even salvation. It is indeed "as perfect an image of heaven, as the infirmity of human nature, and the imperfections in the constitution of human affairs, would admit" (*Home* 99).

Her childhood home is also where Sedgwick received her most important schooling. Although she attended local district schools and respected private academies in New York City, Albany, and Boston, Sedgwick described her formal schooling as "fragmentary," "miscellaneous," "a waste," an experience in which "no one dictated my studies or overlooked my progress" (*Life and Letters* 43–4, *Power* 84). Sedgwick considered her most meaningful education to be that received at the family homestead. She writes that she "was reared in an atmosphere of high intelligence. My father had uncommon mental vigor. So had my brothers. Their daily habits, and pursuits, and pleasures were intellectual, and I naturally imbibed from them a kindred taste" (*Life and Letters* 46–7). Her brothers, especially Harry, charged her to channel her energies away from superficial "female" concerns such as personal appearance, dancing prowess, and etiquette and to cultivate her judgment and perception by a program of reading, observation, and reflection. Her father, when he was home from his public duties, kept the young Catharine beside him until late in the evening, reading aloud the works of David Hume, William Shakespeare, or Miguel de Cervantes. Before her adolescence, she was also studying histories by Rollins and Gibbons as well as reading the popular novels and miscellanies of the day. Although Sedgwick's upbringing compensated for some of the lapses in her schooling, she long felt the loss of a formal education; in the margins of a September 10,

1838, letter from Kenyon College informing her that she had been elected to the institution's literary society, she excitedly wrote "Diploma!!!" in large letters (Karafilis xxii).

The early love of reading and intellectual engagement that her father and brothers inspired served her well, as Sedgwick merged her loves of literature and history in her most successful works. Her brothers played a further role in her literary endeavors by being some of her earliest and most ardent supporters. Theodore Jr. and Robert echoed Harry's encouragement to turn a short religious tract into her first novel and they also acted as her agents, negotiating with publishers. Sedgwick dedicated her fourth novel, *Clarence* (1830), "to my brothers—my best friends," and the book stands as a testament to her enduring love for and appreciation of them.

While Catharine Maria Sedgwick's father and brothers pursued high-profile public careers as lawyers, politicians, and political activists, working to shape the future of the young nation, her education did not prepare her to follow such a path. She did, however, participate in the project of nation building through her writing, and her works reached a wide cross section of the young nation's citizenry. As her admirers informed her, her writing was read with the greatest interest by people from all walks of life—old and young, rich and poor. Her influence on American social and political life may not have been as explicit or "official" as that of her father and brothers, or as direct as that of some of her fictional heroines who, also denied an explicitly political arena in which to act, foist themselves into politics by freeing prisoners, serving as spies, or cornering heads of state in their own parlors to plead their cases. But Sedgwick's readers were very clear that in educating and morally instructing her readership, she provided a valuable benefit to her countrymen and women. Such praise must have been singularly gratifying to the author, who did not write just to entertain. Sedgwick died at the age of 78 in Roxbury, Massachusetts.

MAJOR WORKS AND THEMES

Over the course of her literary career, which spanned from 1822 to the advent of the Civil War, Sedgwick penned 10 novels and didactic works, over 100 tales and sketches, and a voluminous correspondence. In her novels and tales Sedgwick strove to instill traditional American republican values such as self-control, self-denial, and concern for the larger good, as well as demonstrate the benefits of Christian virtues and religious tolerance. Sedgwick's close relationship with her brothers and her idealization of the "equal love" evinced in the brother-sister bond perhaps also contributed to her imagining of an egalitarian American republic. The familial values translated into the political realm form the basis of the republican ideal—a political and cultural order rooted in the same values of intimate brotherhood, equality, and selflessness. She extolled such virtues in an attempt to shape a republican citizenry that, in her eyes, would be capable of fulfilling the American promise of democracy and building a nation in which merit and manners, instead of wealth, determined one's position. Her faith in merit and manners as the only basis for distinction—the belief that doing well and behaving well will equalize society—may seem facile to twenty-first-century readers, but it was a belief to which Sedgwick firmly held and which reveals the depth of her commitment to her nation's democratic experiment. For Sedgwick, then, writing can be viewed as the performance of a civic duty, a duty analogous to, if less publicly enacted than, those her father and brothers fulfilled in the congressional hall, the statehouse, and the courthouse. Such themes and sentiments run throughout virtually all of Sedgwick's writing, beginning with her first published novel, *A New England Tale* (1822).

After Sedgwick converted from Congregationalism to Unitarianism in 1821, she began *A New England Tale* as a religious tract criticizing orthodox Calvinism. At her brothers' encouragement, she turned it into a novel. Although it proved quite controversial in her native New England, and a number of her neighbors objected to her portrayal of hypocritical sectarians, the novel was praised for its depiction of village life, use of American materials and subject matter, and eloquence. The heroine of the novel is the orphan Jane Elton, who is sent to live with her hypocritical and dogmatic aunt, Mrs. Wilson. The conflicts between the two characters represent the ideological and theological contest between rigid Calvinist doctrine and a more liberal Christianity based on a merciful God. Part of Jane's maturation entails enduring the trials inflicted by her aunt and her dissolute cousins, David and Elvira, as well as coming to reject the affections of the charismatic and arrogant Erskine in favor of those of the generous and principled Quaker, Robert Lloyd.

Redwood (1824), published anonymously and initially incorrectly attributed to James Fenimore Cooper, received such praise that William Cullen Bryant declared it "absolutely unsafe and dangerous not to admire it" (Foster 56). It tells the story of an aristocratic Virginian and his spoiled and selfish daughter who, on a journey to the North, find peace and redemption on the Lenox farm, the homestead of a virtuous and hard-working New England family. In *Redwood,* Sedgwick also gained favorable reviews for her depiction of Deborah Lenox, the stalwart and down-to-earth New Englander whose characterization the famed British novelist Maria Edgeworth described as "first rate—in [Sir Walter] Scott's best manner, yet not an imitation of Scott" (*Life and Letters* 169).

Sedgwick's third novel, *Hope Leslie* (1827), was a more ambitious project than any she had yet attempted. A carefully researched historical romance set in seventeenth-century Massachusetts, *Hope Leslie* critiques colonial historiography, the role of women in American society, and Indian relations. The narrative tells the story of the Fletcher family: William, the kind and indulgent patriarch who comes to the New World but is soon disillusioned with the hypocrisy of the Puritan theocracy; his son, Everell; his adopted daughters, Hope and Faith; and his indigenous servants, the spoils of war, Magawisca and Oneco. The love relationship between Hope and Everell becomes a central plot element and is complicated by fighting between the Native Americans and the Puritans; the captivity of members of each group by the other; subsequent risky and intricate rescues engineered by the heroines, Hope and Magawisca; and potential romantic unions between the protagonists and other characters, both indigenous and Anglo.

Sedgwick's next novel, *Clarence* (1830), satirizes upper-class life in New York and contrasts an aristocracy of wealth with an aristocracy of talent and virtue. In the novel Sedgwick depicts an idyllic retreat from city life and the establishment of a cultured, rural society similar to Thomas Jefferson's vision of a virtuous, agricultural republic. Like her first three works, *Clarence* was an immediate success.

Sedgwick's last historical romance, the genre for which she is best known today, is *The Linwoods* (1835), written at the height of her fame as a writer during the Jacksonian era and set against the backdrop of the American Revolution. *The Linwoods* constructs the domestic romance as a political allegory in which national discord, rebellion, and reconciliation are figured in familial terms. The novel's primary narrative thread tells the story of two families: the Linwoods, who are loyalists, and the Lees, who are revolutionaries. Much of the novel narrates the transformation of the Linwood children, especially the heroine, Isabella, from Tory to Rebel. In the process, Isabella rebels not only against British control of the colonies, but also the institution of slavery, gender norms, and patriarchal authority. Her changing political affiliations are paralleled by her changing amorous alliances, as she rejects her childhood sweetheart, the studied and aristo-cratic Brit Jasper Meredith, for Eliot Lee, descendent of the Pilgrims and confidante of General Washington. Disguise, the intrigues of Rebel and Tory spies, and instances of cross-gender and cross-racial passing, as well as cases of mistaken identity, not only make for a compelling read, but foster an antiaristocratic skepticism of surface appear-ances and external markers of virtue and identity.

Sedgwick responded to the social, cultural, and political upheavals surrounding her by inculcating certain ideologies and virtues in her reading public. Her readership's receptivity to her literary instruction is demonstrated by the critical and public popular-ity of her works. Sedgwick's later writing, a series of didactic tales, continues to a great degree the cultural work of her early novels. These didactic tales, including *Home* (1835), *The Poor Rich Man and the Rich Poor Man* (1836), *Live and Let Live; or, Domestic Ser-vice Illustrated* (1837), and *Means and Ends, or Self-Training* (1839), encourage the common man to improve himself in the world by making use of his God-given talents. Critics have described these tales as conduct books of sorts, stories designed to teach "manners" to children as well as rough-hewn laborers and immigrants. Dedicated to such groups as "My Young Country Women" and "Farmers and Mechanics," they fall somewhere between a religious tract and a novel. The didactic works concern themselves with the dangers of market speculation and the commercialization of culture, detail the plights of recent immigrants, advocate marrying for love instead of for social position, portray fulfilled and productive spinsters, and depict the beauty and bounty of New England village life with all of Sedgwick's characteristic "purity of style," "bright imag-ination," "compassion," and "playful satire" (*Redwood, A Tale* 101, Hillard 73, Green-wood 411, Bryant 257). The didactic works were some of her most popular and, like many of her other works, emphasize the inherent goodness of people and suggest means of developing one's potential for personal and political virtue in a democratic society.

CRITICAL RECEPTION

In the early national period, Catharine Maria Sedgwick already had gained great fame as an author and was credited with helping to put American literature on the map. Ranked with James Fenimore Cooper, Washington Irving, and William Cullen Bryant, she was embraced by both literary critics and lay readers. Although Sedgwick slowly began to disappear from literary history in the late nineteenth century, readers have redis-covered her works in the past decade and she has enjoyed a resurgence of popularity.

While a handful of nineteenth-century critics faulted novels such as *Clarence* and her didactic pieces for improbable plot lines or characterizations and a lack of polish, Sedgwick's writing received largely favorable reviews in some of the most respected journals of the day, including the *North American Review* and the *U.S. Magazine and Literary Gazette,* and was praised by some of the most respected writers and thinkers, such as Edgar Allan Poe, Maria Edgeworth, and Harriet Martineau. Her works were pub-lished in both the United States and England and translated into French, Italian, and Swedish. Indeed, Sedgwick's critics could very well proclaim that "our most truthful novelist," as Nathaniel Hawthorne called her, was also our most famous novelist (quoted in Foster 20).

Part of the reason Sedgwick's works were so popular with her contemporary audi-ence was that her readers appreciated the aesthetics of her writing, an aesthetics that seems decidedly republican in its devotion to common sense, simplicity, and a lack of ostentation or ornament. Her critics also recognized the aid that her writings would provide in creating a national literature and discerned its usefulness in inculcating republican values in the young nation's readership. They saw in Sedgwick's writing a literature for the masses—a literature that would entertain the American people, engross them, and, most important, guide them through the relatively uncharted territory of democratic rights and responsibilities in the new republic. William Cullen Bryant perhaps most clearly states the cultural work Sedgwick's writings perform. In his review of *Redwood,* Bryant lauds Sedgwick's contributions to the consolidation of a unique domestic literature and her representations of the "national character" of the United States:

We are happy to see the author of this work connecting [the manners and character of our countrymen], as we find them connected in real life, with much that is ennobling and elevated, with traits of sagacity, benevolence, moral courage, and magnanimity. . . . When this is done, something is done to exalt our national reputation abroad, and to improve our national character at home. (272)

Many other critics also praised the democratic ethics of her works, finding in Sedgwick's writing, for example, "the marks of a true genius for commencing a literature for the mass of the American people, which shall bring up their moral tone to the spirit of their institutions. Her mind appreciates the peculiar dignity of republicanism, and her heart rejoices in its enacted poetry" (*American Monthly* 21).

Sedgwick believed that an intimate connection existed between literary production and didacticism, between her writing and the code of virtues that she wished to inculcate in her readership. This connection was clear to her critics as well, and her contemporary reviewers cite her blend of Christian and democratic ethics as a primary source of the power of her writing. Again from the widely read and influential journal the *North American Review,* nineteenth-century critic W. Hillard encapsulates the feelings of many readers when he comments that Sedgwick's writing

has that high and pure tone of moral and religious feeling, without which genius is a fatal curse. . . . She never makes vice interesting no[r] virtue repulsive, but paints each in its true colors, so that the mind obeying its natural instinct is enamored of the one and abhors the other. . . . She never makes merit ludicrous or contemptible, by connecting it with those low or ridiculous qualities which are offensive to taste, or vice attractive by a graceful garb. (76)

As critic F. W. P. Greenwood succinctly put it, Sedgwick's works were particularly satisfying because they "delight, instruct, and improve us." (413)

Most appealing to Sedgwick's nineteenth-century readership, then, were her clear and straightforward prose style; her contribution to a burgeoning national literature; her use of domestic history, settings, and mores; her moral guidance and instruction; and her "enlightened sympathies," a liberal Protestantism that often undergirded sensitive depictions of the marginalized—white women, African Americans, and immigrants, especially the Irish (*Literary World* 298).

More recent critics also have found much to praise in Sedgwick's writings. The majority of current criticism has focused on her third novel, *Hope Leslie,* which appeals to twenty-first century readers for many of the same reasons it appealed to her nineteenth-century audience: its depiction of a spirited and independent heroine and its engagement with its contemporary culture, especially in Sedgwick's treatment of "the Indian question" and her representations of the Pequod War and Native Americans. But with the republication of additional texts, such as *A New England Tale* in 1995, *The Linwoods* in 2002, and the anthologizing of a number of her tales, studies of Catharine Maria Sedgwick have expanded beyond *Hope Leslie* to include nuanced analyses of many of her other works as well.

WORKS CITED

Bryant, William Cullen. "*Redwood, A Tale.*" *The North American Review* (XX) 47, April 1825: 245–72.

Foster, Edward Halsey. *Catharine Maria Sedgwick.* New York: Twayne, 1974.

Greenwood, F. W. P. "*Hope Leslie; or, Early Times in the Massachusetts.*" *The North American Review* (XXVI) 59, April 1828: 403–20.

Hillard, W. "*Clarence; or, A Tale of Our Own Times.*" *The North American Review* (XXXII) 70, January 1831: 73–95.

Karafilis, Maria. Introduction. *The Linwoods or, "Sixty Years Since in America."* By Catharine Maria Sedgwick. Hanover: University Press of New England, 2002. xi–xxxv.

"Miss Sedgwick's Works." *The Literary World* October 6, 1849: 297–98.

"The Novels of Miss Sedgwick." *The American Monthly Magazine* January 1836: 15–25.

"*Redwood, A Tale.*" *The United States Literary Gazette* (1) 1, April 1, 1824: 101–02.

Sedgwick, Catharine Maria. *Home: Scenes and Characters Illustrating Christian Truth.* Boston: J. Munroe, 1835.

——. *Hope Leslie; or, Early Times in the Massachusetts.* 1827. New Brunswick: Rutgers University Press, 1987.

——. *Life and Letters of Catharine Maria Sedgwick.* Ed. Mary E. Dewey. New York: Harper and Brothers, 1872.

——. *The Power of Her Sympathy: The Autobiography and Journal of Catharine Maria Sedgwick.* Ed. by Mary Kelley. Boston: Massachusetts Historical Society and Northeastern University Press, 1993.

——. *Redwood, A Tale.* New York: E. Bliss and E. White, 1824.

BIBLIOGRAPHY

Major Works by Catharine Maria Sedgwick

Catharine Maria Sedgwick Papers I, II, III. Massachusetts Historical Society.

A New England Tale; or Sketches of New England Character and Manners. New York: E. Bliss and E. White, 1822.

Redwood, A Tale. New York: E. Bliss and E. White, 1824.

Hope Leslie; or, Early Times in the Massachusetts. New York: White, Gallaher, and White, 1827.

Clarence; or, A Tale of Our Own Times. Philadelphia: Carey and Lea, 1830.

Home: Scenes and Characters Illustrating Christian Truth. Boston: J. Munroe, 1835.

The Linwoods; or, "Sixty Years Since" in America. New York: Harper and Brothers, 1835.

Tales and Sketches. Philadelphia: Carey, Lea, and Blanchard, 1835.

The Poor Rich Man and the Rich Poor Man. New York: Harper and Brothers, 1836.

Live and Let Live; or, Domestic Service Illustrated. New York: Harper and Brothers, 1837.

Means and Ends, or Self-Training. Boston: Marsh, Capen, Lyon and Webb, 1839.

Letters From Abroad to Kindred at Home. New York: Harper and Brothers, 1841.

Tales and Sketches. Second Series. New York: Harper and Brothers, 1844.

Married or Single? New York: Harper and Brothers, 1857.

Life and Letters of Catharine Maria Sedgwick. Ed. Mary E. Dewey. New York: Harper and Brothers, 1872.

The Power of Her Sympathy: The Autobiography and Journal of Catharine Maria Sedgwick. Ed. by Mary Kelley. Boston: Massachusetts Historical Society and Northeastern University Press, 1993.

Studies of Catharine Maria Sedgwick

Baym, Nina. *American Women Writers and the Work of History, 1790–1860.* New Brunswick: Rutgers University Press, 1995.

———. *Woman's Fiction: A Guide to Novels By and About Women in America, 1820–1870.* Second ed. Urbana: University of Illinois Press, 1993.

Castiglia, Christopher. *Bound and Determined: Captivity, Culture Crossing, and White Womanhood from Mary Rowlandson to Patty Hearst.* Chicago: University of Chicago Press, 1996.

Fetterley, Judith, ed. *Provisions: A Reader from Nineteenth-Century American Women.* Bloomington: Indiana University Press, 1985.

Foster, Edward Halsey. *Catharine Maria Sedgwick.* New York: Twayne, 1974.

Gould, Philip. *Covenant and Republic: Historical Romances and the Politics of Puritanism.* New York: Cambridge University Press, 1996.

Karafilis, Maria. "Catharine Maria Sedgwick's *Hope Leslie:* The Crisis Between Ethical Political Action and US Literary Nationalism in the New Republic." *American Transcendental Quarterly* 12 (1998): 327–44.

Kelley, Mary. *Private Woman, Public Stage: Literary Domesticity in Nineteenth-Century America.* New York: Oxford University Press, 1984.

Nelson, Dana. "Sympathy as Strategy in Sedgwick's *Hope Leslie.*" In *The Culture of Sentiment: Race, Gender, and Sentimentality in Nineteenth-Century America.* Edited by Shirley Samuels. New York: Oxford University Press, 1992. 191–202.

Scheiber, Andrew J. "Mastery and Majesty: Subject, Object, and the Power of Authorship in Catharine Sedgwick's 'Cacoethes Scribendi.' " *American Transcendental Quarterly* 10 (1996): 41–58.

Stadler, Gustavus. "Magawisca's Body of Knowledge: Nation Building in *Hope Leslie.*" *Yale Journal of Criticism: Interpretation in the Humanities* 12.1 (1999): 41–56.

Steinberg, Stacy. " 'Unexpected and Inconvenient Notice': Domestic Entrapment and Servant Infidelity in *The Coopers* and *Live and Let Live.*" *Legacy: A Journal of American Women Writers* 15 (1998): 85–91.

Welsh, Sister Mary Michael. *Catharine Maria Sedgwick: Her Position in the Literature and Thought of Her Time Up to 1860.* Washington: Catholic University of America, 1937.

Zagarell, Sandra. "Expanding America: Lydia Sigourney's 'Sketch of Connecticut' and Catharine Sedgwick's *Hope Leslie.*" *Tulsa Studies in Women's Literature* 6 (1987): 225–45.

Nineteenth-Century Reviews

Bryant, William Cullen. "*Redwood, A Tale.*" *The North American Review* (XX) 47, April 1825: 245–72.

Greenwood, F. W. P. "*Hope Leslie; or, Early Times in the Massachusetts.*" *The North American Review* (XXVI) 59, April 1828: 403–20.

Hillard, W. "*Clarence; or, A Tale of Our Own Times.*" *The North American Review* (XXXII) 70, January 1831: 73–95.

"*The Linwoods; or, Sixty Years Since in America.*" *The North American Review* (XLII) 90 January 1836: 160–95.

Martineau, Harriet. "Miss Sedgwick's Works." *The London and Westminster Review* (VI) 1, October 1837–January 1838: 42–65.

"Miss Sedgwick." *The Southern Literary Messenger* (III) 4, April 1837: 331–4.

"Miss Sedgwick's Works." *The Literary World* October 6, 1849: 297–8.

"*A New England Tale; or, Sketches of New-England Character and Manners.*" *The Literary and Scientific Repository* (IV) 8, May 1822: 336–70.

"The Novels of Miss Sedgwick." *The American Monthly Magazine* January 1836: 15–25.

Poe, Edgar Allan. "Catharine M. Sedgwick." *Godey's Lady's Book* (XXXIII) 9, September 1846: 130–2.

———. "*The Linwoods.*" *The Southern Literary Messenger* (II) 8, December 1835: 57–9.

"*Redwood, A Tale.*" *The United States Literary Gazette* (1) 1, April 1, 1824: 101–2.

LYDIA HUNTLEY SIGOURNEY (1791–1865)

Grace Ann Hovet

BIOGRAPHY

Lydia Howard Huntley Sigourney, born on September 1, 1791, in Norwich, Connecticut, was the only child of Ezekiel Huntley and his second wife, Zerviah Wentworth Huntley. Her father, a gardener for the well-situated Mrs. Jerusha Lathrop, entrusted her to keep his accounts when she was only eight years old. By 12, she was sewing his shirts and stockings. Her mother was apparently freed from the contested second-wife role that plagued Sigourney. She named her only child after the deceased wife and, herself an avid reader, nurtured Lydia's early interest in language. She encouraged Lydia to write, provided her with reading materials, supplied her with journals, and supported her attempts to write a novel. With Mrs. Lathrop, Mrs. Huntley fostered Lydia's pursuit of intellectual knowledge and her less enthusiastic interest in the decorative arts young ladies were to master.

The Huntleys had lived as tenants of Mrs. Lathrop, and at her death in 1805, Lydia suffered a double separation: from her aged mentor and from her home. Her grief was so incapacitating that she had to take a two-week rest cure with Lathrop relatives in Hartford where she initiated her public career as an educator/writer. She spent the rest of her life trying to mesh the private with the public sphere, a task made urgent by her need to care for her parents and (eventually) appease her husband. She established schools, first in Norwich in 1811 and then in Hartford in 1814, for which Mrs. Lathrop's nephew, Daniel Wadsworth, recruited students from established families. After writing a great deal, she asked him about the appropriateness of using her own materials in class. Wadsworth's endorsement was so affirmative that he gathered 1,000 subscriptions at $1 a piece and arranged to have *Moral Pieces, in Prose and Verse* published in 1815. Lydia Huntley's emergence as a writer thus coincided with making the profit she needed to support herself, her parents, and, soon, her family.

In 1819 the "gardener's daughter" moved "up" by marrying Charles Sigourney, a well-educated, reputedly wealthy, prominent businessman 13 years her senior. Unlike her mother, Sigourney moved into a ready-made family. At any given time she cared for

15 to 18 individuals, among them her conservative husband, three trying stepchildren, and a resentful sister-in-law (DeJong 38). She bore five children (three dying in infancy) and housed her parents. Though she gave up formal teaching, she schooled the children and mastered domestic arrangements. She also wrote volume upon volume of poetry and prose about the blessings of home life. Because of need, she also became her own press agent, seeking publishers, contacting editors, bargaining for fees, and keeping meticulous records. Her omnipresent knitting needles became props whereby she maintained her image as a dutiful homemaker while, at the same time, advancing her career as writer.

She soon learned that her husband had overextended the family's finances. She knew she could contribute money by signing her articles, but he insisted on anonymity. Lydia initially acceded, even when her mass-market appeal, based on subject matter, style, and word-of-mouth intensified. In 1827 a vituperative Charles accused her of consorting with the enemy (literati). She unsuccessfully appealed for a separation and also religiously guarded against betraying the dichotomy between her private and public lives to her readers. By 1834, however, finances dominated family need and she decided to oppose her husband by publishing in her married name. The rest is history: her name sold, sales trebled, and popularity soared. At the end of her life, the "American Hemans," "the sweet singer of Hartford" annotated 55 volumes, to which must be added her posthumous *Letters of Life* (1866), some 2,000 articles, 1,500 letters of correspondence, and countless responses to requests for her work.

Her reputation as an upholder of the verities of the human hearth remained undiminished through the 1860s. While making her bibliographic annotations in *Letters of Life,* she states, "I am exceedingly tired of the list," but continues for another 38 pages (Letter XIII). She thus reinforced her almost compulsive will to instruct, comfort, and inspire readers—and to make a livelihood. She died on June 10, 1865. The church bells of Hartford rang for an hour.

MAJOR WORKS AND THEMES

Lydia Sigourney understood that being a woman's best-seller meant meeting the needs of an emerging middle-class readership. Decade by decade, she anticipated audience interests—the 40s sweep of gift annuals and the 50s interest in periodicals. Thematically, she focused on ideal womanhood, Christian piety, model lives, and acceptance of death. Almost 50 percent of her titles relate to children and mothers as, for example, children in *Sayings of the Little Ones, and Poems for their Mothers* (1855); young girls and boys in *The Girl's Reading-Book* (1838) and *The Boy's Reading-Book* (1839); young ladies in *Letters to My Pupils: with Narrative and Biographical Sketches* (1851); brides in *Whisper to a Bride* (1850); and mothers, especially those who had lost their loved ones, as in her encomium to her dead son in *The Faded Hope* (1853).

While her thematic unity belied her own bifurcated life, she nevertheless continued to champion images derived from current ideas (which she helped formulate) about "the angel in the house" and "true womanhood." Her view of the "woman's question" remained conservative; *mothers* influence the public sector by training their "children in patriotism and republican values" (Baym 70). Though an idealist, she had an astute business sense that led her to challenge homemakers to master finances. This she herself did, seldom hesitating to drive hard bargains for fees, arguing in one case for a 50 percent raise and in another securing stereotypes to republish work at will (Haight 129, 40). She routinely repackaged old works and lent her name for $500 as titular editor to Godey's

Lady's Book while, at the same time, submitting materials to its rival. She also, however, tithed 10 percent of her income, espousing favorite institutions and causes.

A hope she pursued throughout her lifetime was to be a model for her readers. This accounts in part for her persistent depiction (others say invention) of herself as leading an exemplary private life. It accounts, too, for her penchant for featuring the lives of pious or famous people—those who, like Nancy Maria Hyde and Margaret and Henrietta Flower, had recently died—and others who, like Marcus Aurelius and Job, had set historical precedent. In addition, she wrote for adopted causes such as the plight of the Native American Indians in *Traits of the Aborigines of America* (1822) and *Zinzendorff* (1835), temperance, and seamen, soldiers, and farmers. Her unstinting support of institutionalized children manifested itself at her funeral as participants included "officers of the Deaf and Dumb Asylum, the Retreat for the Insane, the Orphan Asylum, and the State Reform School" (*Letters of Life* 411). Women writers have frequently been the spokespeople for their own; Sigourney, with her humble background, limited education, intense aspiration, and passionate commitment to the ideals of hearth and home became the voice for white middle-class women facing the challenges of a new nation caught in her time between its recent Revolution and incipient Civil War.

CRITICAL RECEPTION

Sigourney's penchant for projecting her own causes and ideals—her exempla, brief lives, exhortations, "effusions," and even *Letters of Life*—colors her critical reception. Broadly stated, reactions to her work during her lifetime overbalance the merits of the person at the expense of literary value; those today undermine her merits as a person and attempt to clarify her position as a literary practitioner. As Karen Kilcup succinctly summarizes, during Sigourney's lifetime, with a few caveats, she was flatteringly termed Mrs. Hemans (a celebrated writer in England); by the turn of the century, her work was unmitigatedly disparaged, and in the past quarter century, her work is being reconstituted in terms of her life, practice, and historical position (263). Ann Douglas Wood heralds the current approach in a 1972 article analyzing Sigourney's "uncanny ability to adapt herself to the pattern laid out for women of her day" (181). Concern prevails over what Nina Baym poignantly summarizes as Sigourney's "reinventing" herself (66). A note close to outrage permeates reactions to her untoward practice of citing personal correspondence as public endorsement, name-dropping, double-dipping (republishing works and reissuing editions), fretting about fees, and appropriating material that was not hers (such as her dead son's journal). Though she did not work *for* money—and generously tithed—critics note a "once-deprived, always wanting" syndrome in her absorbing bookkeeping and accounting practices.

Studies of her relationship to the sentimental tradition clearly mark efforts to reconstruct Sigourney's reputation. Such studies position her *oeuvre* within an era where highly charged, romantic vocabulary, descriptions, and situations prevailed; her purple passages, euphemisms, and "greater glory" rhetoric anchor themselves to such currents. So, too, does her stance as moral legislator and arbiter of life and death. As bookends to her reception is Rev. E. B. Huntington, in 1868, contending that we cannot "doubt that their author (Sigourney) will continue to rank high even among the poets of her age" (97) and, in 1988, Annie Finch hoping "that before too long it will be possible to see the sentimental tradition (which Sigourney represents) as a literary movement in its own right, as a movement having . . . its own inheritors" (13). In between, as Dorothy Bowles explains, are Sigourney's multitudinous nineteenth-century readers who knew she "wrote for heart, not the intellect" and for whom "bad reviews had little effect because her readers were neither scholarly nor critical" (274). They were common folk looking for guidance and inspiration and unwittingly establishing what has come to be known as the mass market.

WORKS CITED

Baym, Nina. "Reinventing Lydia Sigourney." *Redefining the Political Novel: American Women Writers, 1797–1901*. Ed. Sharon Harris. Knoxville: U of Tennessee P, 1995.

Bowles, Dorothy A. "Lydia Sigourney." *Dictionary of Literary Biography* 73 (1988): 264–74.

DeJong, Mary G. "Lydia Howard Huntley Sigourney (1791–1865)." *Legacy: A Journal of Nineteenth Century American Women Writers.* 5: 1 (1988): 35–41.

Finch, Annie. "The Sentimental Poetess in the World: Metaphor and Subjectivity in Lydia Sigourney's Nature Poetry." *Legacy: A Journal of Nineteenth Century American Women Writers* 5: 2 (1988): 3–18.

Haight, Gordon. *Mrs. Sigourney: The Sweet Singer of Hartford.* New Haven: Yale UP, 1930.

Huntington, Rev. E. B., ed. "Lydia Sigourney." *Eminent Women of the Age: The Lives and Deeds of the Most Prominent Women of the Present Generation.* Hartford: Betts, 1868.

Kilcup, Karen. "Nineteenth-Century American Women Poets Revisited." Ed. Karen Kilcup. *Nineteenth-Century American Women Poets: a Critical Reader.* Malden, MA: Blackwell.

Sigourney, Lydia Huntley. *Letters of Life.* New York: Appleton, 1866.

Wood, Ann Douglas. "Mrs. Sigourney and the Sensibility of Inner Space." *The New England Quarterly: A Historical Review of New England Life and Letters* 45: 2 (1972): 163–181.

BIBLIOGRAPHY

Works by Lydia Huntley Sigourney

Poetry
Traits of the Aborigines of America, a Poem. By Anonymous. Cambridge, MA: Hillard & Metcalf, 1822.

Poems. Boston: Samuel G. Goodrich, 1827.

Poems. Philadelphia: Key & Biddle, 1834.

Poetry for Children. Hartford, CT: Robinson & Pratt, 1834.

Zinzendorff, and Other Poems. New York: Levitt, Lord, 1835.

Pocahontas, and Other Poems. New York: Harper, 1841.

The Poetical Works of Mrs. L. H. Sigourney. Edited by F. W. N. Bayley. London: Routledge, 1850.

Fiction, Nonfiction Prose, and Miscellaneous Writings
Moral Pieces, in Prose and Verse. Hartford, CT: Sheldon & Goodwin, 1815.

Sketch of Connecticut, Forty Years Since. By Anonymous. Hartford, CT: Oliver D. Cooke, 1824.

The Intemperate, and the Reformed. New York: Sleight & Van Norden, 1833.

Letters to Young Ladies. By Anonymous. Hartford, CT: P. Canfield, 1833.

Sketches. Philadelphia: Key & Biddle, 1834.

Tales and Essays for Children. Hartford, CT: F. J. Huntington, 1835.

Letters to Mothers. Hartford, CT: Hudson & Skinner, 1838.

Pleasant Memories of Pleasant Lands. Boston: James Munroe, 1842.

Myrtis, and Other Etchings and Sketches. New York: Harper, 1846.

Water-drops. New York: Robert Carter, 1848.

Past Meridian. New York: Appleton, 1854.

Lucy Howard's Journal. New York: Harper, 1858.

Letters of Life. New York: Appleton, 1866.

Studies of Lydia Huntley Sigourney

Baym, Nina. "Reinventing Lydia Sigourney." *Redefining the Political Novel: American Women Writers, 1797–1901.* Ed. Sharon Harris. Knoxville: U of Tennessee P, 1995.

Bowles, Dorothy A. "Lydia Sigourney." *Dictionary of Literary Biography* 73 (1988): 264–74.

DeJong, Mary G. "Lydia Howard Huntley Sigourney (1791–1865)." *Legacy: A Journal of Nineteenth Century American Women Writers* 5: 1 (1988): 35–41.

Finch, Annie. "The Sentimental Poetess in the World: Metaphor and Subjectivity in Lydia Sigourney's Nature Poetry." *Legacy: A Journal of Nineteenth-Century American Women Writers* 5: 2 (1988): 3–18.

Haight, Gordon. *Mrs. Sigourney: The Sweet Singer of Hartford.* New Haven: Yale UP, 1930.

Huntington, Rev. E. B. "Lydia Sigourney." *Eminent Women of the Age: The Lives and Deeds of the Most Prominent Women of the Present Generation.* Hartford: Betts, 1868.

Kot, Paula. "Lydia Huntley Sigourney." *Dictionary of Literary Biography* 239 (2001): 273–85.

Petrino, Elizabeth. "Nineteenth-century American Women's Poetry." *Cambridge Companion to Nineteenth-Century Women's Poetics.* Eds. Dale Bauer and Philip Gould. Cambridge: Cambridge UP, 2000.

Walker, Cheryl. "Nineteenth-Century American Women Poets Revisited." *Nineteenth-Century American Women Writers: A Critical Reader.* Ed. Karen Kilcup. Malden, MA: Blackwell: 1988.

Wood, Ann Douglas. "Mrs. Sigourney and the Sensibility of Inner Space." *The New England Quarterly: A Historical Review of New England Life and Letters* 45:2 (June 1972): 163–81.

Zagarell, Sandra A. "Expanding 'American': Lydia Sigourney's *Sketch of Connecticut,* Catharine Sedgwick's *Hope Leslie.*" *Redefining the Political Novel: American Women Writers, 1797–1901.* Ed. Sharon Harris. Knoxville: U of Tennessee P, 1995.

WILLIAM GILMORE SIMMS (1806–1870)

Ted Olson

BIOGRAPHY

Author William Gilmore Simms was born April 17, 1806, in Charleston, South Carolina. His father William Gilmore Simms Sr. was a merchant of Scots-Irish descent who emigrated to the South Carolina piedmont from Larne, Ireland, shortly after the Revolutionary War. In 1804, the elder Simms married Harriet Ann Augusta Singleton, who was from a pro-Revolution Virginia family that had relocated to Charleston before the War. William Gilmore Simms Jr. was the second, and only surviving, child of this union. William Gilmore Simms Sr., suffering the death of his wife in 1808 and the loss of his business soon afterward, departed for the frontier, where he eventually established a plantation near Columbia, Mississippi. William Gilmore Simms Jr. remained in Charleston with his maternal grandmother, Jane Miller Singleton Gates. In an 1816 court-imposed legal hearing, the future author chose to stay in Charleston with Gates rather than live in Mississippi with his father, who was suing for custody of the 10-year-old child.

Given his grandmother's marginal economic standing, William Gilmore Simms Jr. was formally educated in Charleston public schools. From an early age an avid reader of classical authors (especially Homer and Virgil), Simms also learned to appreciate frontier narrative traditions through listening to his grandmother's stories. Another formative influence was his extensive travel in the southern states, including a mid-1820s visit to Mississippi (at which time Simms again declined his father's invitation to leave Charleston for plantation life in the Old Southwest). In October 1826 Simms married Charlestonian Anna Malcolm Giles; the couple would produce one child—a daughter born in November 1827.

Initially considering a career in medicine, Simms, between 1825 and 1827, studied law and simultaneously pursued a literary career. The financial (if not aesthetic) success of his earliest books—five poetry volumes published between 1825 and 1830—led Simms, by the early 1830s, to cease practicing law and to instead write full-time. From 1830 to 1832 Simms suffered several personal setbacks, including the deaths of his wife, father, and grandmother; also, the controversial daily newspaper that he both owned and edited, the *Charleston City Gazette,* failed. Marrying Chevillette Eliza Roach in 1836, Simms moved onto his father-in-law Nash Roach's 7,000-acre plantation, "Woodlands," located beside the Edisto River near Orangeburg, South Carolina. This marriage, lasting until Chevillette Simms's death in 1863, would produce 14 children, only 5 of whom survived at the time of Simms's 1870 death.

Residing with his family at Woodlands for more than a quarter of a century, Simms divided his energies between writing, overseeing the plantation, and participating in local, state, regional, and national politics. Through these years, he became a vocal defender of the southern way of life. Ironically, in 1865, during the Civil War that resulted from the secession Simms had supported, soldiers from Union General William Tecumseh Sherman's army burned a section of the plantation house at Woodlands, including much of Simms' personal library and art gallery. Thereafter, Simms lived in Charleston, where he wrote and edited constantly in an effort to earn money for his now-destitute family. He died from colon cancer on June 11, 1870.

MAJOR WORKS AND THEMES

Scholar John Caldwell Guilds—acknowledging Simms's authorship of 82 books on diverse topics in several literary genres—asserted that "Simms the writer defies classification" (340). Simms's literary career began in 1825 when he published his first volume of lyric poetry and edited the short-lived periodical *The Album.* Over the next five years Simms produced four additional volumes of poetry, most of which were published in Charleston. In the early 1830s, Simms caught the attention of northern literary circles with two books from a prominent New York City press: the ambitious long narrative poem *Atalantis: A Story of the Sea* (1832) and his initial foray into fiction, the trial novel *Martin Faber; the Story of a Criminal* (1833). That novel was widely reviewed, mostly favorably, in northern as well as southern periodicals. Since his poetry volumes had received little notice, Simms subsequently concentrated on writing fiction, soon generating the novels upon which his literary reputation would be based.

Simms followed his well-received if formative 1834 novel *Guy Rivers: A Tale of Georgia* with his breakthrough novel *The Yemassee* and two less critically acclaimed novels, *The Partisan* (1835) and *Mellichampe* (1836). After the Panic of 1837, as economic recession spread across the United States, book sales plummeted nationally. Simms wrote four more novels in quick succession—none of which were as critically acclaimed or commercially successful as *The Yemassee.* Compelled to support his growing family and to sustain Woodlands primarily on money earned as a professional author, Simms from 1842 to 1850 chose to work primarily in more lucrative literary genres. While in personal letters he privately castigated southern society for its nonsupport of individual authors and of literary culture generally, Simms began to openly defend the antebellum southern way of life in his writings as well as in public roles, for two years serving as a member of the South Carolina legislature.

From 1849 to 1854, Simms edited a prestigious literary periodical, the *Southern Quarterly Review.* After 1850 he returned to fiction writing, producing four more historical romances set during the Revolutionary War. According to scholar Mary Ann Wimsatt, Simms's fiction of the 1850s incorporated new elements in his work: satire; backwoods humor; and an emphasis on exploring social manners. Despite their innovations, Simms's novels of the 1850s did not reclaim for the author a level of popularity comparable to what he had known in the 1830s. Damaging his national literary reputation during the 1850s was Simms's vocal support of the antebellum South and, more specifically, of such controversial issues as slavery (which he deemed defensible if practiced with compassion) and southern secession from the Union.

The majority of Simms's novels were historical romances set during one of four periods in American history. *The Lily and the Totem* (1850) chronicled some of the earliest explorations (i.e., before the 1607 settling of Jamestown) of what would become the southeastern United States. *The Yemassee* (1835) explored life in colonial South Carolina before the 1763 rise to power of King George III. Several other novels by Simms—including *The Sword and the Distaff* (1852; later retitled *Woodcraft* in 1854)—were set in Revolutionary War-era South Carolina. A few other novels—such as *Beauchampe* (1856)—constituted Simms's effort to represent pre–Civil War nineteenth-century southern society.

Simms confessed that his approach to writing fiction had been strongly influenced by the novels of two of his contemporaries, Sir Walter Scott and James Fenimore Cooper, both of whom were acknowledged masters of the historical romance. In his own historical romances, though, Simms exhibited distinctive stylistic and thematic elements. His finest novels were unique for their strikingly realistic portrayal—written in forceful prose that often evinced folk speech—of a complex frontier world. For instance, *The Yemassee* arguably offered a more insightful and epic portrayal of the American frontier—with a more realistic treatment of Native Americans—than had any of Cooper's Leatherstocking novels.

The author of nearly two dozen novels, Simms also wrote numerous short stories—many of them based on his experiences in the Southwestern frontier. One of the more acclaimed among Simms's books was the 1845 short story collection *The Wigwam and the Cabin.* In addition, Simms published books in two other literary genres: drama and nonfiction (including biographies, histories, and geography studies). Simms has never been considered a distinctive poet by critics, since his verses were heavily influenced by the poetry of William Cullen Bryant and such British poets as Lord Byron and John Keats. Yet, Simms's poetry—the bulk of it composed at the outset of his literary career—was integral to the development of his fictional voice. For example, Simms first defined himself as a chronicler of the frontier in numerous narrative verses that explored various historically significant incidents from the colonial and Revolutionary War period.

CRITICAL RECEPTION

During his lifetime, Simms developed a national reputation as the antebellum South's most significant author; his critical standing, though, has diminished over the years. Many mid-nineteenth century literary critics proclaimed Simms a major American writer. One such critic, J. Quitman Moore, asserted in 1860 that "The judgment of an impartial and enlightened criticism must assign him a proud and elevated niche in the Pantheon of American letters" (qtd. in Wimsatt 1). Some twentieth-century critics regarded Simms as having been of historical importance. In 1954, scholar Jay B. Hubbell called Simms "the central figure in the literature of the Old South" (572). Nevertheless, the consensus among twentieth-century literary critics is that Simms's achievements are inferior to the work of several of his northern contemporaries, including Cooper and Nathaniel Hawthorne. Wimsatt succinctly articulated this latter-day attitude: "[Simms's] books are verbose and in places overblown or awkward; they are sometimes melodramatic and sentimental; they are often poorly constructed; and their occasionally strident southern sectionalism grates harshly on twentieth-century ears" (7).

Simms's increasingly marginal role in American literature after the Civil War is no doubt traceable in part to the lack of a fair, comprehensive published biographical study of the author. Through much of the twentieth century, the most influential book on Simms and his work was William Peterfield Trent's biased 1892 biography, in which the biographer, a product of the New South, castigated Simms's work for its embodiment of the antebellum South's outmoded value system. According to Wimsatt, Trent's biography of Simms was "one of the least balanced and judicious treatments ever accorded an important author" (2). Unfortunately, Trent's negative assessment remained the dominant interpretation of Simms's literary career for a century. A far more objective treatment of the author and his work was offered in Guilds's 1992 study *Simms: A Literary Life.*

Scholars who have recently reexamined Simms's life and writings have affirmed that the author made distinctive contributions to American literature. While his poems, dramatic works, and nonfiction are generally viewed today as being either of relatively marginal quality or of interest solely as historical documents, Simms's fictional works have garnered increased attention from literary critics in recent years. Guilds, for instance, identified Simms's *Guy Rivers* as the first American novel to realistically portray "the ugliness, the lawlessness, the brutality of the early nineteenth-century American frontier" (58–9). Guilds also asserted that Simms's fiction depicted Indians more realistically than did Cooper's novels and that Simms represented women as progressively as had Hawthorne. Simms is also credited with playing a central role in the early development of a distinctively southern literary tradition.

WORKS CITED

Guilds, John Caldwell. *Simms: A Literary Life.* Fayetteville: University of Arkansas Press, 1992.

Hubbell, Jay B. *The South in American Literature, 1607–1900.* Durham, NC: Duke University Press, 1954.

Wimsatt, Mary Ann. *The Major Fiction of William Gilmore Simms: Cultural Traditions and Literary Form.* Baton Rouge: Louisiana State University Press, 1989.

BIBLIOGRAPHY

Works by William Gilmore Simms

Fiction

Martin Faber; The Story of a Criminal. New York: J. & J. Harper, 1833.

The Book of My Lady. A Melange. Philadelphia: Key & Biddle, 1833; Boston: Allen & Ticknor, 1833.

Guy Rivers: A Tale of Georgia. New York: Harper & Brothers, 1834.

The Yemassee. A Romance of Carolina. New York: Harper & Brothers, 1835.

The Partisan: A Tale of the Revolution. New York: Harper & Brothers, 1835.

Mellichampe. A Legend of the Santee. New York: Harper & Brothers, 1836.

Martin Faber, The Story of a Criminal; and Other Tales. New York: Harper & Brothers, 1837.

Pelayo: A Story of the Goth. New York: Harper & Brothers, 1838.

Carl Werner, An Imaginative Story; With Other Tales of Imagination. New York: George Adlard, 1838.

The Kinsmen; or The Black Riders of Congaree. A Tale. Philadelphia: Lea & Blanchard, 1841. (Revised as *The Scout.* New York: Redfield, 1854.)

Confession; or, The Blind Heart. A Domestic Story. Philadelphia: Lea & Blanchard, 1841.

Beauchampe; or The Kentucky Tragedy. A Tale of Passion. Philadelphia: Lea & Blanchard, 1842.

Castle Dismal: or, The Bachelor's Christmas. A Domestic Legend. New York: Burgess, Stringer & Co., 1844.

Helen Halsey: or, The Swamp State of Conelachita. A Tale of the Borders. New York: Burgess, Stringer & Co., 1845.

Count Julian; or, The Last Days of the Goth. An Historical Romance. Baltimore and New York: William Taylor, 1845.

The Wigwam and the Cabin. New York: Wiley & Putnam, 1845.

Katherine Walton: or, The Rebel of Dorchester. An Historical Romance of the Revolution. Philadelphia: A. Hart, 1851.

The Sword and the Distaff; or, "Fair, Fat and Forty," A Story of the South, at the Close of the Revolution. Charleston: Walker, Richards & Co., 1852. (Retitled *Woodcraft, or Hawks about the Dovecote. A Story of the South, at the Close of the Revolution.* New York: Redfield, 1854.)

Vasconselos. A Romance of the New World. New York: Redfield, 1853.

The Forayers, or the Raid of the Dog-Days. New York: Redfield, 1855.

Eutaw, A Sequel to The Forayers, or The Raid of the Dog-Days. A Tale of the Revolution. New York: Redfield, 1856.

Beauchampe, or The Kentucky Tragedy. A Sequel to Charlemont. New York: Redfield, 1856.

Joscelyn; A Tale of the Revolution. The Old Guard V (January–December 1867).

Poetry

Monody, on the Death of Gen. Charles Cotesworth Pinckney. Charleston: Gray & Ellis, 1825.

Lyrical and Other Poems. Charleston: Ellis & Neufville, 1827.

Early Lays. Charleston: A. E. Miller, 1827.

The Vision of Cortes, Cain, and Other Poems. Charleston: James S. Burges, 1829.

The Tri-Color; or, The Three Days of Blood, in Paris. London: Wigfall & Davis, 1830.

Atalantis: A Story of the Sea. New York: J. & J. Harper, 1832.

Southern Passages and Pictures. New York: George Adlard, 1839.

Donna Florida. Charleston, SC: Burges & James, 1843.

Grouped Thoughts and Scattered Fancies. A Collection of Sonnets. Richmond, VA: Wm. Macfarlane, 1845.

Areytos: or, Songs of the South. Charleston, SC: John Russell, 1846.

Lays of the Palmetto: A Tribute to the South Carolina Regiment, in the War with Mexico. Charleston, SC: John Russell, 1848.

Sabbath Lyrics; or, Songs from Scripture. A Christmas Gift of Love. Charleston, SC: Walker and James, 1849.

Poems Descriptive, Dramatic, Legendary and Contemplative. New York: Redfield, 1853. Charleston, SC: John Russell, 1853.

Drama

Norman Maurice; or, The Man of the People. An American Drama. Richmond, VA: J. R. Thompson, 1851.

Michael Bonham: or, The Fall of Bexar. A Tale of Texas. Richmond, VA: J. R. Thompson, 1852.

Nonfiction

The History of South Carolina. Charleston, SC: Babcock & Co., 1840.

The Geography of South Carolina: Being a Companion to the History of that State. Charleston, SC: Babcock & Co., 1843.

The Lily and the Totem, or, The Huguenots in Florida. A Series of Sketches, *Picturesque and Historical, of the Colonies of Coligni, in North America. 1562–1570.* New York: Baker and Scribner, 1850.

South Carolina in the Revolutionary War: Being a Reply to Certain Misrepresentations and Mistakes of Recent Writers, in Relation to the Course and Conduct of this State. Charleston, SC: Courtenay, 1853.

Sack and Destruction of the City of Columbia, S.C., to Which Is Added a List of Property Destroyed. Columbia, SC: Power Press of Daily Phoenix, 1865.

Biographies

The Life of Francis Marion. New York: Henry G. Langley, 1844.

The Life of Captain John Smith. The Founder of Virginia. New York: George F. Cooledge and Brother, 1846.

The Life of the Chevalier Bayard; "The Good Knight," Sans peur et sans reproche. New York: Harper & Brothers, 1847.

Scholarly Writing

Views and Reviews in American Literature, History and Fiction. New York: Wiley & Putnam, 1845.

Letters

The Letters of William Gilmore Simms. 5 volumes. Eds. Mary C. Simms Oliphant, Alfred Taylor Odell, and T. C. Duncan Eaves. Columbia: University of South Carolina Press, 1952–1956.

Studies of William Gilmore Simms

Guilds, John Caldwell. *Simms: A Literary Life.* Fayetteville: University of Arkansas Press, 1992.

Parks, Edd Winfield. *William Gilmore Simms as Literary Critic.* Athens: University of Georgia Press, 1961.

Ridgely, J. V. *William Gilmore Simms.* New York: Twayne Publishers, 1962.

Trent, William Peterfield. *William Gilmore Simms.* American Men of Letters Series. Boston: Houghton, Mifflin & Co., 1892. New York: Greenwood Press, 1969 [reprint].

Wakelyn, Jon L. *The Politics of a Literary Man: William Gilmore Simms.* Westport, CT: Greenwood Press, 1973.

Wimsatt, Mary Ann. *The Major Fiction of William Gilmore Simms: Cultural Traditions and Literary Form.* Baton Rouge: Louisiana State University Press, 1989.

ELIZABETH CADY STANTON (1815–1902)

Arthur K. Steinberg

BIOGRAPHY

Elizabeth Cady Stanton was born on November 12, 1815, in Johnstown, New York, to Margaret Livingston Cady and Daniel Cady. She was formally educated at the Johnston Academy, where she studied Latin, Greek, and mathematics, and at Emma Willard's Troy Female Seminary, which was renowned for its academic rigor. Her father, an eminent lawyer, state judge, and congressman, exposed Elizabeth, one of 11 children, to a large amount of legal training, which explains her penchant for the law and its use in the defense of women in a society that did not recognize their legal rights. In 1840, she married Henry B. Stanton, an avowed abolitionist orator. The couple honeymooned in London, where the World's Anti-Slavery Convention was being held. It was there that Stanton met women's rights activist Lucretia Mott. The two became fast friends and commiserated over the fact that women delegates from America were denied a seat at the convention because of their gender. After returning to Johnstown, Stanton assumed the duties of a housewife, and in time, she raised seven children, five boys and two girls.

In the fall of 1843, the Stantons moved to Boston, where Elizabeth was introduced to such luminaries as Bronson Alcott, Lydia Maria Child, Ralph Waldo Emerson, Nathaniel Hawthorne, Theodore Parker, and John Greenleaf Whittier. Her years in Boston were enjoyable, and she found the members of her social circle to be intellectually engaging. In 1847, however, her husband's poor health caused the family to move to the drier climate of Seneca Falls, New York.

In 1848, Stanton and Mott called for a Women's Rights Convention to be held in Seneca Falls. Stanton drafted a "Declaration of Sentiments," advocating various forms of reform for women and quickly emerged as a leader of the nineteenth-century women's movement. Spurred on by the gender-based denial of women's participation in the 1840 World Anti-Slavery Convention in London, Stanton also contributed in 1848 to New York State's passage of a bill granting married women property rights.

In 1851, Stanton met Susan B. Anthony, and the two formed a close collaborative partnership that would last for 50 years. While Anthony devoted her time to honing her oratorical skills, Stanton employed her hours at home to refining her writing abilities. Together they founded the short-lived *Revolution,* a weekly newspaper that promoted women's rights. In 1869, Stanton founded the National Woman Suffrage Association; her new position provided the platform from which she became an outspoken social and political activist. She launched campaigns debating issues relating to the place of women in modern society. Stanton eventually tired of being the torchbearer of numerous causes and turned her attention to producing the first three volumes of *History of Woman Suffrage* (1881–85), with the assistance of Anthony and Matilda Joslyn Gage. In 1887, following her husband's death, Stanton moved to New York City and became a syndicated columnist. In 1895, she published the *Woman's Bible,* a controversial argument that examined the relationship between organized religion and the subordination of women.

Stanton's autobiography, *Eighty Years and More,* published in 1898, was her last major work. In her final years, Stanton became a virtual recluse as a result of poor health. In October, 1902, at the age of 86, she died in New York City in the presence of two of her grown children. While she did not witness the passage of the nineteenth amendment, her historic role in the attainment of equality of women in American society has not been forgotten. A statue of her, Anthony, and Mott has been erected in the United States Capitol, to commemorate her efforts on behalf of women.

MAJOR WORKS AND THEMES

Eight years after attending the 1840 World Anti-Slavery Convention in London, Stanton drafted the "Declaration of Rights and Sentiments for Women," modeled upon the "Declaration of Independence." Lucretia Mott's husband James presided over the Women's Rights Convention in Seneca Falls, New York, where Stanton delivered the "Declaration." The convention was attended by some 300 people, including 40 men. Stanton began the "Declaration" with the proposition that "all men and women are created equal" and outlined 18 grievances endured by women, ranging from the denial of legal rights to their wages, to the lack of equal educational opportunities, to the automatic awarding of custody of children to the husband in cases of divorce. The "Declaration" also protested against the double standard of morality and women's exclusion from the ministry. Stanton followed the declaration with a series of 11 resolutions, including the demand for woman's suffrage. All of the resolutions were passed unanimously, with the exception of the ninth proclamation, which called for the right of women to vote. The suffrage resolution was passed by a slim margin, however, after Frederick Douglass made an impassioned plea for its adoption.

The *Revolution* magazine, a collaborative effort with Susan B. Anthony that was published between January 1868 and May 1870, was a vehicle for advancing women's rights. It was in the *Revolution* that Stanton proposed a sixteenth amendment to the constitution that would grant suffrage to all citizens. The paper also carried articles on the need for prison reform, the issue of prostitution, the plight of Native Americans, and the deplorable conditions in tenement houses. The magazine folded in 1870 as a result of financial problems.

The History of Woman Suffrage, published between 1881 and 1886, was a multivolume production. Stanton, Anthony, and others contributed the first three volumes of this expansive work. *The History of Woman Suffrage* is a detailed chronicle of the women's rights movement featuring articles, speeches, meeting minutes, clippings, and opinions about the feminist movement.

The Woman's Bible, first published in 1895 by Stanton and others, was the work of a committee of women intending to highlight the part played by women in biblical history. While the theological value may be questionable, the intent was to more accurately reflect the thoughts of women and the role they played in religion and the Bible. Stanton had little patience for the traditional interpretation of the Bible and viewed it as an obstacle to the intent of the Constitution. Of all her works, *The Woman's Bible* appears to have been the most disturbing for traditionalists, who embraced the gender-based subordination of women.

Stanton's autobiography, *Eighty Years And More* (1898), traces her journey along the road to feminist equality. The work describes her activities and illuminates her philosophy and the objectives of the numerous organizations of which she was a part. She was in the process of revising the work when she died in 1902.

CRITICAL RECEPTION

Despite the fact that Stanton received negative publicity as a result of the 1848 Seneca Falls Convention, she continued her crusade for women's rights. The *Revolution,* which she founded in 1868 with Susan B. Anthony, received mixed reviews. The *Troy* [New York] *Daily Times* praised the paper as being "readable, well-edited, and instructive" (qtd. in "Elizabeth Cady Stanton"), while the *New York Times* opined that the paper's motto, "Men, their rights and nothing more; Women their rights and nothing less," was "meaningless" (qtd. in "Elizabeth Cady Stanton").

While the *History of Woman Suffrage* is today regarded as an indispensable source of information about the nineteenth-century women's movement, contemporary reviewers were less kind. An anonymous reviewer in *The Nation* complained that "the three editors . . . have produced one of the most disorderly and ineffective works ever dignified with the name of history. It is, in its entirety, absolutely unreadable, and the last thing to be derived from it is a feeling of the steady progress of the cause which its authors have at heart" (*Nation* Sept. 1, 1881, 177).

The Woman's Bible, on the other hand, became an immediate best-seller and was translated into seven languages. Because of its radical message, however, the book was banned by several libraries and was censured by the National American Woman Suffrage Association.

Stanton's last substantial work, *Eighty Years and More,* received mixed notices. *The Nation* reported that the author "tells [her] story in a manner that is engaging, both because of the variety of her experience and because of her satisfaction and delight in the recital" (*The Nation,* May 5, 1898, 347). At the same time, however, the anonymous reviewer argues that the narrative is "overweighted with trivial minutia" (347) and cites various discrepancies in Stanton's account of her life. Nevertheless, many other critics viewed her memoirs "as lively and readable," noting that Stanton presented herself "as a heroic figure overcoming obstacles in her moral battle" ("Elizabeth Cady Stanton").

Today, there is a resurgence of interest in Stanton and her compatriot Susan B. Anthony, thanks in part to the documentary produced by filmmakers Ken Burns and Paul Barnes in 1999. *Not for Ourselves Alone: The Story of Elizabeth Cady Stanton & Susan B. Anthony,* which also appeared in book form, tells the story of their friendship over a half decade and chronicles their tireless efforts to improve the lives of American women.

WORKS CITED

"Elizabeth Cady Stanton." The Gale Group. 2000. November 16, 2002. <http://uncommonclasix.homestead.com/files/elizabethcady.html>

"A Review of *Eighty Years and More*." *The Nation*. Vol. LXVI, no. 1714 (May 5, 1898): 347–8.

"A Review of *History of Women's Suffrage*." *The Nation*. Vol. XXXIII, no. 844 (Sept. 1, 1881): 177–8.

BIBLIOGRAPHY

Works by Elizabeth Cady Stanton

Letter to the Woman's Rights Convention, Held at Worcester Oct. 1850 [and] *Letter to the Woman's Rights Convention, Held at Syracuse, Sept. 1852*. Syracuse, NY: Master's Print, 1852(?).

Address to the Legislature of New-York, Adopted by the State Woman's Rights Convention, Held at Albany, Tuesday and Wednesday, February 14 and 15, 1854. Albany, NY: Weed, Parsons & Co., 1854.

The Slave's Appeal. Albany, NY: Weed, Parsons and Co. 1860.

Free Speech: By Elizabeth Cady Stanton, at the Fourth Annual N.Y. State Anti-Slavery Convention at Association Hall, Albany, N.Y., February 4th and 5th, 1861. Albany, NY, 1861.

Address of Elizabeth Cady Stanton, on the Divorce Bill, before the Judiciary Committee of the New York Senate . . . Feb. 8, 1861. Albany, NY: Weed, Parsons and Co., 1861.

Address in Favor of Universal Suffrage, for the Election of Delegates to the Constitutional Convention Before the Judiciary Committee of the Legislature of New York, in the Assembly Chamber, January 23, 1867, in Behalf of the American Equal Rights Association. Albany, NY: Weed, Parsons and Co., 1867.

Address of Mrs. Elizabeth Cady Stanton, Delivered at Seneca Falls & Rochester, N.Y. July 19th & August 2d, 1848. New York: Robert J. Johnston, 1870.

Memorial of Elizabeth Cady Stanton, Isabella Beecher Hooker, Elizabeth L. Bladen, Olympia Brown, Susan B. Anthony, and Josephine L. Griffing, to the Congress of the United States, and the Arguments Thereon before the Judiciary Committee of the U.S. Senate, by Isabella Beecher Hooker, Elizabeth Cady Stanton, and Susan B. Anthony, Washington, January 12, 1872. Washington, DC: Chronicle Publishing Co., 1872.

History of Woman Suffrage, vols. 1–3. Eds. Elizabeth Cady Stanton, Susan B. Anthony, and Matilda Joslyn Gage. New York: Fowler & Wells, 1881–1886.

The Pleasures of Age: An Address Delivered by Elizabeth Cady Stanton on Her Seventieth Birthday. (N.p., 1885?).

Bible and Church Degrade Women (Chicago: H. L. Green, 1890?)—comprises *The Effects of Woman Suffrage on Questions of Morals and Religion, The Degraded Status of Woman in the Bible*, and *The Christian Church and Woman. Woman Suffrage: Hearing before the Judiciary Committee of the House of Representatives . . . February 11, 1890*. Washington, DC: U.S. Government Printing Office, 1890.

Suffrage a Natural Right. Chicago: Open Court Publishing Co., 1894.

The Woman's Bible, 2 vols. New York: European Publishing Co., 1895, 1898.

Eighty Years and More (1815–1897): Reminiscences of Elizabeth Cady Stanton. New York: European Publishing Co., 1898; London: Unwin, 1898.

Elizabeth Cady Stanton to Her Life-long Friend and Co-worker Susan B. Anthony on Her Eightieth Birthday, February 15, 1900. N.p., 1900.

Elizabeth Cady Stanton as Revealed in Her Letters, Diary and Reminiscences. Eds. Harriot Stanton Blatch and Theodore Stanton. New York and London: Harper, 1922.

Elizabeth Cady Stanton/Susan B. Anthony: Correspondence, Writings, Speeches. Ed. Ellen Dubois. New York: Schocken, 1981.

Studies of Elizabeth Cady Stanton

Banner, Lois W. *Elizabeth Cady Stanton, a Radical for Woman's Rights.* Boston: Little, Brown and Co, 1980.

Bohannon, Lisa Frederiksen. *Women's Rights and Nothing Less: The Story of Elizabeth Cady Stanton.* Greensboro, NC: Morgan Reynolds, 2002.

Clarke, Mary S. *Bloomers and Ballots; Elizabeth Cady Stanton and Women's Rights.* New York: Viking Press, 1972.

DuBois, Ellen Carol, ed. *The Elizabeth Cady Stanton—Susan B. Anthony Reader: Correspondence, Writings, Speeches.* Boston: Northeastern University Press, 1992.

Faber, Doris. *Oh Lizzie! The Life of Elizabeth Cady Stanton.* New York: Lothrop, Lee and Shepard, 1972.

Fowler, Lois J., and David H. Fowler, eds. *Revelations of Self; American Women in Autobiography.* Albany, NY: State University of New York Press, 1990.

Goodman, James E. "The Origins of the 'Civil War' in the Reform Community: Elizabeth Cady Stanton on Woman's Rights and Reconstruction." *Critical Matrix: The Princeton Journal of Women, Gender, and Culture* 1, no. 2 (1985): 1–29.

Griffith, Elisabeth. *In Her Own Right: The Life of Elizabeth Cady Stanton.* New York: Oxford University Press, 1984.

Huxman, Susan Schultz. "Perfecting the Rhetorical Vision of Woman's Rights: Elizabeth Cady Stanton, Anna Howard Shaw, and Carrie Chapman Catt." *Woman's Studies in Communication* 23, no. 2 (Fall 2000): 307–36.

Jelinek, Estelle C., ed. "The Paradox and Success Of Elizabeth Cady Stanton." *Women's Autobiography: Essays in Criticism.* Bloomington: Indiana University Press. 71–92.

Kern, Kathi. *Mrs. Stanton's Bible: Elizabeth Cady Stanton and the Woman's Bible.* Ithaca, NY: Cornell University Press, 2001.

Loeffelholz, Mary. "Posing the Woman Citizen: The Contradictions of Stanton's Feminism." *Genders* 7 (March 1990): 87–98.

Lutz, Alma. *Created Equal: A Biography of Elizabeth Cady Stanton 1815–1902.* New York: Day, 1940.

Miller, Diane H. "From One Voice A Chorus": Elizabeth Cady Stanton's 1860 Address to the New York State Legislature. *Women's Studies In Communications* 22.2 (Fall 1999): 152–189.

Oakley, Mary Ann. *Elizabeth Cady Stanton.* Old Westbury, NY: Feminist Press, 1972.

Pellauer, Mary. *Toward a Tradition of Feminist Theology: The Religious Social Thought of Elizabeth Cady Stanton, Susan B. Anthony, and Anna Howard Shaw.* Brooklyn, NY: Carlson Publishing, 1991.

Smith, Sidonie. "Resisting The Gaze of Embodiment: Women's Autobiography in the Nineteenth Century." *American Women's Autobiography: Feasts Of Memory.* Madison: University of Wisconsin Press, 1992. 75–110.

Stevenson-Moessner, Jeanne. "Elizabeth Cady Stanton, Reformer to Revolutionary: A Theological Trajectory." *Journal of the American Academy of Religion.* Vol. LXII, no. 3 (Fall 1994): 673–97.

Waggenspack, Beth M. *The Search for Self-Sovereignty: The Oratory of Elizabeth Cady Stanton.* New York: Greenwood Press, 1989.

Ward, Geoffrey C., and Ken Burns. *Not for Ourselves Alone: The Story of Elizabeth Cady Stanton and Susan B. Anthony: An Illustrated History.* New York: Knopf, 1999.

Wolff, Cynthia G. "Emily Dickinson, Elizabeth Cady Stanton, and the Task of Discovering a Usable Past." *Massachusetts Review* 30.4 (Winter 1989): 639–44.

Youman, Mary. "Elizabeth Cady Stanton and The Woman's Bible." *Kentucky Philological Association Bulletin* (1983): 73–86.

MARIA W. STEWART (1803–1879)

Mark G. Vásquez

BIOGRAPHY

Maria W. Stewart was the first American-born woman—let alone the first black woman—to deliver a political speech in front of an audience of both men and women. She is also, quite likely, the first American woman for whom we have texts of her public political lectures. Religiously fervent, Stewart decried through what one critic has called her "decidedly evangelical style" (Richardson xvii) the lack of freedom for both women and African Americans. Orphaned at five, widowed at 26, cheated out of her legal inheritance until her old age, Stewart anticipated the Grimké sisters, Sojourner Truth, Margaret Fuller, and others in her outspoken feminist rhetoric of social reform.

Maria Miller was born in 1803 in Hartford, Connecticut, to Negro parents about whom very little is known. Orphaned at the age of five (and with no known siblings), Maria was "bound out" to the family of a clergyman and trained for domestic duties. The family library served to provide the young Maria with a rudimentary educational background, while the clergyman's vocation illustrated the strength of religious morals (and of religious rhetoric) that would mark Maria's adulthood.

Leaving the clergyman's home in 1818, Maria Miller supported herself through domestic employment, concurrently attending a Sabbath school to augment her literary and religious education. In August 1826, Miller married James W. Stewart, a mulatto shipping agent about twice her age. Adding her husband's surname initial as her own middle initial, Maria W. Stewart entered Boston's small but growing African American middle-class society (the city's black population increased tenfold during the 1820s). Shortly after her marriage, Stewart met abolitionist writer David Walker through the Massachusetts General Colored Association. Walker became both a literary and political influence upon Maria, and he and James Stewart worked together to shelter runaway slaves. But this venture was short-lived; Stewart died of illness (likely heart disease) in December 1829.

In the two years following her husband's death, Maria Stewart became involved in litigation that resulted in the loss of property formerly owned by James Stewart. A penniless widow, Maria Stewart soon renewed her commitment to Christianity and, in the early 1830s, began writing her religious, economic, and political views. Although her publishing career in Boston lasted but three years (1831–34), Stewart published a political pamphlet (*Religion and the Pure Principles of Morality*), a series of religious meditations, and, in William Lloyd Garrison's *The Liberator,* her collected speeches. In September 1832, she delivered the first recorded speech by an American woman before a mixed-sex audience, lecturing against the expatriation of black Americans to West Africa; that same year she published *Meditations from the Pen of Mrs. Maria W. Stewart.*

Moving to New York in 1834, Stewart published a volume of her collected works (*Productions of Maria Stewart*) in 1835, joined the black "Female Literary Society," attended the Woman's Anti-Slavery Convention in 1837, lectured occasionally, and began a 40-year career in schoolteaching. Stewart taught in New York, Baltimore, and Washington, D.C.; after the Civil War she served as Matron of the Freedman's Hospital (now the Howard University Hospital). Income from this position allowed Stewart to establish a Sunday school. In 1878, thanks to new federal legislation, Stewart became eligible for a pension from James Stewart's war service. The following year, she published a new edition of her *Meditations,* augmented by a new preface, as well as biographic and testimonial material. Stewart died in December of that same year at Freedman's Hospital, and was buried on the fiftieth anniversary of her husband's death.

MAJOR WORKS AND THEMES

While Sarah Grimké is usually acknowledged as providing the foundation for American female political involvement, in fact it was Stewart who first charted that terrain early in the 1830s, boldly proclaiming her gospel of political reform; as Richardson has pointed out, Stewart's "original synthesis of religious, abolitionist, and political concerns places her squarely in the forefront of a black female activist and literary tradition" (xiv) and Stewart is thus "a seminal figure in nineteenth-century black intellectual history" (xvi). Adducing her argument with the support of scriptural, classical, and historical references, her emotionally charged rhetoric anticipated those of Grimké, Truth, Fuller, Frances Willard, and others; her unsparing examination of human and social conditions provided a tonic for various ills.

Stewart's writings and speeches persistently addressed three central themes: women's rights, abolition, and black separatism. For many of Stewart's readers and auditors (and certainly for Stewart herself), these themes were interwoven. For instance, Stewart—unlike some white female activists—differentiated between rights for white women and rights for black women, asserting that black women in many ways were moving toward liberation more quickly than white women due to their harsh cultural experience (Giddings 55). As a result, and in contrast to her white counterparts who framed feminism as analogous to the abolition movement, Stewart drew the line between sex and race more clearly: while she favored the empowerment of *all* women, and while she sometimes called for whites to engage in the abolition movement, she also never forgot that the oppression of women and men (especially women and men of color) was caused primarily by white society.

Nearly all Stewart's speeches and writings touched upon (if they did not always chiefly address) the subject of rights for women. Before Stewart, the lone woman to lecture publicly in the United States (to notorious notice) was Frances Wright in the late 1820s; but unlike Wright, who was born in Scotland, Stewart was the first native-born

American woman to deliver public addresses. While Stewart in great measure advocated the hegemonic, patriarchal views of domesticity, she also acknowledged that such domesticity could embolden female independence, organization, and power. Stewart called upon women—and black women in particular—to increase their intellectual capacity and achievement. In her April 1832 speech in Boston to the Afric-American Female Intelligence Society, Stewart called upon white females to educate themselves on the conditions of black women, and called upon black women (as she had in *Religion and the Pure Principles of Morality*) to tap into their latent physical, spiritual, and educational powers. Her concluding exhortation repositions the female as a powerful cultural force: "O woman, woman! Upon you I call; for upon your exertions almost entirely depends whether the rising generation shall be any thing more than we have been or not. O woman, woman! Your example is powerful, your influence great; it extends over your husbands and your children, and throughout the circle of your acquaintance" (Richardson 55). Although this appeal nods to the mainstream concept of True Womanhood, it also, in its apocalyptic call for a cross-racial sympathy, anticipates by 20 years the thematic and rhetorical approaches of Harriet Beecher Stowe. And in her final speech, in September 1833, Stewart illustrated principles later adopted by the Grimkés and Fuller as she parallels the women of biblical times and other eras to her contemporaries; she highlighted that speech with the admonition that just as "such women as are here described have once existed" then so too might contemporary women "strive, by their example[,] both in public and private" (Richardson 69).

As equally concerned with abolition as with feminism, Stewart in February 1833 spoke at the African Masonic Hall in Boston on "African rights and liberty . . . a subject that ought to fire the breast of every free man of color" (Richardson 56); for Stewart, such free blacks, as she had argued five months earlier in a speech at Franklin Hall, were little better than slaves. Outlining to her Masonic Hall audience the deplorable treatment of Africans, Stewart accuses ignorant, uneducated blacks of considering themselves as inferior to whites and "scarce superior to the brute," claims that Africans would never had been denied rights "[h]ad we as a people received one-half of the early advantages the whites have received" (61), exhorts blacks to petition Congress to abolish slavery, and again calls upon whites, through her fervent religious rhetoric, to assist in the effort: "Let me entreat my white brethren to awake and save our sons from dissipation and our daughters from ruin. Lend the hand of assistance to feeble merit; plead the cause of virtue among our sable race; so shall our curses upon you be turned into blessings" (Richardson 63). At once calling for a joint effort between races and placing responsibility for slavery on both blacks and whites, Stewart embraced a problematic abolitionist agenda that ultimately alienated all segments of her audience. In much the same way, Stewart as an assimilationist was opposed to colonization (the removal of free blacks to Africa), holding that a separatism of relocation reinforced the institution of slavery; instead, Stewart endorsed the ethos of self-reliance. First critiquing colonization in her September 1832 speech at Franklin Hall (before a mixed audience), Stewart more fully attacked the movement a few months later (before a predominantly black audience), calling the colonizationists "blind to heir own interests" and boldly imploring them instead, as "real friends to Africa," to fund American colleges for the "sons of Africa" (Richardson 71).

CRITICAL RECEPTION

Stewart's career as public speaker and author was short-lived because of economic necessity, to be sure, but also because of significant resistance to her ideas and language from both black and white audiences. Her own people resented her criticism of black attitudes and ignorance; white audiences bristled at the frankness of her rhetoric. And both communities no doubt recoiled as well at the severity of her reforms, especially coming from a woman. As Stewart admitted in her final speech in 1833, "I have made myself contemptible in the eyes of many, that I might win some" (Richardson 73). For nearly a half-century Stewart essentially disappeared from public view, until a chance meeting with Garrison led to the 1879 reprinting (with an autobiographical introduction) of *Meditations*.

Yet Stewart's influence gradually diminished in literary, religious, and political circles. By 1936, scholar Dorothy B. Porter would describe Stewart as "probably the earliest Negro woman lecturer and writer and one who has been neglected by historians and bibliographers" (569). For the following half-century, that assessment still held. In the 1980s, though, Judith Fetterley, Dorothy Sterling, and Paula Giddings brought forth Stewart as an important historical and literary figure, and Marilyn Richardson collected (for the first time since 1879) all of Stewart's political writings. In addition, Gail Hankins has identified Stewart as a forerunner of female and African American oratory, though she remarks that Stewart was unaware of her importance, and "unknowingly made a place for herself in rhetorical history" (20). More recently, Lora Romero has discussed "Stewart's remarkable but underanalyzed polemics against slavery and racism through which she expounded black nationalist objectives" (53).

WORKS CITED

Giddings, Paula. *When and Where I Enter: The Impact of Black Women on Race and Sex in America.* New York: William Morrow, 1989.

Hankins, Gail A. "In the Beginning . . . Maria W. Stewart: Forerunner of American Women Orators." *Women and Language* 15:2 (Fall 1992): 20–4.

Porter, Dorothy B. "The Organized Educational Activities of Negro Literary Societies, 1828–1846." *The Journal of Negro Education* 5:4 (October 1936): 560–75.

Richardson, Marilyn, ed. and intro. *Maria W. Stewart, America's First Black Woman Political Writer: Essays and Speeches.* Bloomington: Indiana Univ. Press, 1987.

Romero, Lora. *Home Fronts: Domesticity and Its Critics in the Antebellum United States.* Ithaca, NY: Cornell Univ. Press, 1997.

BIBLIOGRAPHY

Works by Maria W. Stewart

Religion and the Pure Principles of Morality, The Sure Foundation on Which We Must Build. Boston: Garrison and Knapp, 1831.

Meditations from the Pen of Mrs. Maria W. Stewart. Boston: Garrison and Knapp, 1832. Reprinted with a new introduction, 1879.

Productions of Maria Stewart Presented to the First African Baptist Church and Society. Boston: Friends of Freedom and Virtue, 1835.

Maria W. Stewart, America's First Black Woman Political Writer: Essays and Speeches. Ed. and intro. Marilyn Richardson. Bloomington: Indiana Univ. Press, 1987.

Studies of Maria W. Stewart

Fetterley, Judith. "Maria W. Stewart." In *Provisions: A Reader From 19th-Century American Women.* Ed. Judith Fetterley. Bloomington: Indiana Univ. Press, 1985. 60–5.

Moore, Opal. "The Productions of Maria W. Stewart: Rebellious Domesticity and Black Women's Liberation." *Early America Re-Explored: New Readings in Colonial, Early National, and Antebellum Culture.* Ed. and Intro. Klaus Schmidt and Fritz Fleischman. New York: Peter Lang, 2000. 441–65.

Sterling, Dorothy. *We Are Your Sisters: Black Women in the Nineteenth Century.* New York: Norton, 1984. 153–9.

HARRIET BEECHER STOWE (1811–1896)

Denise D. Knight

BIOGRAPHY

Harriet Elizabeth Beecher was born on June 14, 1811, in the quaint New England town of Litchfield, Connecticut, the seventh child of the stern and spirited Congregationalist minister, Lyman Beecher, and his wife, Roxana Foote Beecher. In 1816, when Harriet was just five, Roxana Beecher, a devoted helpmate and loving mother, died from tuberculosis. Shortly after Roxana's death, Lyman's half-sister, Esther Beecher, moved into the rambling parsonage to assume care of the household. Harriet's older sister, Catharine, who later gained fame as a writer and educator, became a surrogate mother to her younger siblings. Lyman Beecher remarried the year following Roxana's death, and although his new wife's relationship with his children was cordial, Catharine remained their primary caretaker. Characterized by her new stepmother as an "amiable, affectionate, and very bright" child (Cross 1, 273), young Harriet's precocity revealed itself in her appetite for reading and in the easy fluency with which she wrote. She excelled at the Litchfield Female Academy, where she studied geography, history, arithmetic, grammar, chemistry, logic, and moral philosophy. Under the tutelage of one of her instructors, Harriet, by the age of nine, began writing weekly essays; at age 12, her earliest extant composition, "Can the Immortality of the Soul be Proved by the Light of Nature?", was read before an assembly at the Academy's annual exhibition of student work. In 1824, at the age of 13, Harriet enrolled in sister Catharine's Hartford Female Seminary, an innovative experiment in the education of women. Harriet stayed at the Seminary until she was 21, first as a student and later as a teacher of rhetoric and composition. Her classmates included Sara Willis, who would later gain fame using the pseudonym Fanny Fern. When Catharine Beecher suffered a nervous breakdown in 1829, Harriet stepped in temporarily to assume the leadership of the school. In 1832, the Beechers moved en masse to Cincinnati, Ohio, after Lyman Beecher accepted the presidency of the Lane Theological Seminary. Homesick for the picturesque New England landscape she had left behind, Harriet eased the pain by immersing herself in writing. Her first publication, a textbook titled *Primary Geography for Children,* appeared in

1833. That same year she began contributing sketches, essays, and reviews to *Western Monthly Magazine.* She also became an active member of the Semi-Colon Club, a literary group that devoted itself to "the discussion of interesting questions belonging to society, literature, education, and religion" (qtd. in Hedrick 91). Among the members of the Club were Eliza Tyler Stowe, whom Harriet befriended, and her husband, Calvin Ellis Stowe, a theology professor at Lane. Shortly after Eliza's death from cholera in 1834, Calvin began courting Harriet; they married in January 1836. In September of that year, while Calvin was traveling in Europe, Harriet gave birth to twin girls; five more children eventually followed. Despite the time devoted to child care, Harriet Beecher Stowe continued to write, publishing in such forums as *Godey's Lady's Book* and the *New-York Evangelist.* Calvin supported Stowe's writing and urged her to develop her talents as "a *literary* woman" (qtd. in Hedrick 138), in part because her earnings were needed to supplement his own modest income. Stowe's first book of fiction, *The Mayflower; or, Sketches of Scenes and Characters Among the Descendents of the Puritans,* a collection of 15 domestic sketches, was published in 1843 by Harper and Brothers, but it did not meet with critical success. In 1846–47, Stowe spent 15 months at the Brattleboro Water Cure, in Vermont, where she was treated with good results for exhaustion and mental fatigue, brought on by the care of her children and the management of her household. The Stowes left Cincinnati in 1850 for Brunswick, Maine, where Lyman accepted an appointment to the faculty of Bowdoin College. It was there that Stowe wrote her epic antislavery novel, *Uncle Tom's Cabin,* shortly after the passage of The Fugitive Slave Act of 1850. The publication of the novel thrust Stowe into the public eye; within months of its appearance she was an international celebrity. In 1852, the Stowes moved to Andover, Massachusetts, where Calvin joined the faculty of the Andover Theological Institute. A second antislavery novel, *Dred: A Tale of the Great Dismal Swamp,* was published in 1856, followed by several more books, including *The Minister's Wooing* (1859), *The Pearl of Orr's Island* (1862), *Agnes of Sorrento* (1862), *Oldtown Folks* (1869), *Lady Byron Vindicated* (1870), *Pink and White Tyranny: A Society Novel* (1871) *Palmetto-Leaves* (1873), and *Poganuc People* (1878). None of Stowe's subsequent works rivaled the power of *Uncle Tom's Cabin;* consequently, none were accorded the same degree of critical acclaim. The Stowes moved again when Calvin retired in 1864, this time to Nook Farm in Hartford, Connecticut. Between 1868 and 1884, the couple spent their winters in Florida. In 1884, Calvin's rapidly declining health forced the Stowes to return to Hartford, where Calvin succumbed to Bright's disease in 1886. Although Stowe herself became increasingly ill and suffered from senility in her later years, she remained at Nook Farm until her death in 1896 at the age of 85. She is buried next to her husband in the Andover Chapel Cemetery at the Andover Theological Seminary.

MAJOR WORKS AND THEMES

If Harriet Beecher Stowe had never written another word after the publication of *Uncle Tom's Cabin* in 1852, her place in American literary history would still be secure. A powerful polemic against the institution of slavery, *Uncle Tom's Cabin* has been called "the most influential novel ever written" and today "remains the world's all-time best-seller" (Donovan 11).

During her 18 years in Cincinnati, Stowe witnessed race riots and heard graphic accounts of conditions suffered by former slaves, which she later used to authenticate her depictions in *Uncle Tom's Cabin.* Before the passage of The Fugitive Slave Act of 1850, however, Stowe was not publicly active in the antislavery cause, although she published a handful of anonymous pro-abolition columns in the *Cincinnati Journal* and engaged in passionate discussions on the evils of slavery with friends and family members. It was Stowe's sister-in-law, Isabella Beecher, who in 1850 finally encouraged her to take action: "Now Hattie," she wrote, "if I could use a pen as you can, I would write something that would make this whole nation feel what an accursed thing slavery is" (qtd. in Hedrick 207). Several months later, Stowe reported that while attending a service at the First Parish Church in Brunswick, Maine, she was visited by the vision of a slave being beaten to death; thus was born the climactic scene of *Uncle Tom's Cabin* in which Tom is murdered by his brutal master, Simon Legree. Throughout her life, Stowe insisted that God was the author of the book; she was simply the instrument through which he spoke.

The plot of *Uncle Tom's Cabin* is held together by the journeys of two slaves, Eliza and Tom, who, when the novel opens, are the property of Mr. Shelby, a Kentucky plantation owner. Forced by an economic crisis to generate some quick cash, Shelby arranges to sell Eliza's young son, Harry, and his long-time slave, Uncle Tom. When Eliza learns of the impending sale, she plans an escape to Canada with her child. The novel follows her dramatic flight toward freedom, during which she receives assistance from various members of the underground railroad. The second journey, which Stowe develops in considerably more detail, involves Tom, a devout Christian who submits to his fate and is sold down the river through a succession of owners, until he meets his death at the hands of the evil Legree.

While Stowe wrote *Uncle Tom's Cabin* in part to make the "whole nation feel what an accursed thing slavery is"—indeed, she relied on her background in rhetoric to construct and sustain a compelling argument—other important themes emerge. Throughout the novel, for example, Stowe repeatedly questions the moral fiber of a nation that allowed the institution of slavery to exist. In nearly every chapter, she reminds the reader that Christian ethics are incompatible with a social system that tolerates human bondage. The moral drama is examined and developed through the responses of various characters to the existence of evil, which Stowe addresses "on several levels: theological, moral, economic, political, and practical" (Donovan 33). Stowe also explores the power of Christian love—the antithesis of evil—most notably through little Eva St. Clare, an allegorical figure who exemplifies that love, and through her Christ figure, Uncle Tom.

Stowe's response to those who attacked *Uncle Tom's Cabin* as unsubstantiated propaganda was published in *A Key to Uncle Tom's Cabin* (1853), in which she passionately defended the novel, documented the facts behind it, and reaffirmed her commitment to the pro-abolitionist movement.

While *Uncle Tom's Cabin* is the major work in Stowe's oeuvre, others merit brief mention. *Dred: A Tale of the Great Dismal Swamp* (1856), is another antislavery novel set in North Carolina. Despite respectable sales in the months following its publication (it sold 150,000 copies in the United States during its first year in print), the novel is an inferior work in terms of both plot and structure. The title character, Dred, who does not appear until chapter 18, is an embittered and militant black man—the antithesis of Uncle Tom—who is driven by hatred in his quest for vengeance. A gloomy work with a contrived ending, *Dred* suffers from hasty writing and a slipshod plot.

The Pearl of Orr's Island (1862), set in New England, was a relatively minor work in Stowe's time but is now undergoing critical reappraisal. It is a powerful work in which Stowe explores the political and psychological dimensions of a young woman, Mara Lincoln, who hungers for adventure and opportunities in a world reserved solely for men. An insightful examination of the limitations imposed by socially prescribed roles, the novel is considered by some to be "as close as Stowe ever came to writing a fictionalized autobiography" (Hedrick 297). In *The Minister's Wooing* (1859), also set in New England, Stowe draws upon her family's theological roots in her depiction of Dr. Samuel Hopkins, a prominent divine who pursues a young woman with the intention of marrying her. While the novel was well known in the years following its publication, it suffers from a thin and utterly predictable plot.

CRITICAL RECEPTION

Despite the fact that she was a prolific author with nearly two dozen books to her credit, Stowe's literary reputation rests almost exclusively on the reception accorded *Uncle Tom's Cabin*. Legend has it that when she met President Abraham Lincoln at the White House in 1863, he greeted her as "the little lady who started this big war" (qtd. in Crozier 72). The controversy engendered by *Uncle Tom's Cabin* has been far-reaching: supporters hail it as an important work of cultural realism while detractors condemn it for promoting lies and distortions.

Initially appearing serially in the *National Era,* an antislavery newspaper, *Uncle Tom's Cabin* was published as a two-volume novel in 1852 and became an immediate best-seller. By the end of the first year, the novel had sold "300,000 copies in the United States and a million in England" (Donovan 11). By the mid 1970s, it had been translated into 58 languages.

Much of the early critical response to the novel was positive. British writer Charles Kingsley praised the book as "the greatest novel ever written" (qtd. in Donovan 16), a view that was shared by numerous critics on both sides of the Atlantic. Emerson applauded *Uncle Tom's Cabin* in his essay, "Success," for its ability to speak "to the universal heart" (*Complete Works* 7, 286), and Frederick Douglass hailed the novel as "the master book of the nineteenth-century" (quoted in Foner 227). Another former slave, Sella Martin, commented that in exposing details about slave auctions, Stowe had "thrown sufficient light upon that horrible and inhuman agency of slavery" (qtd. in Donovan 17). Similarly, William Wells Brown, an African American novelist, remarked that "*Uncle Tom's Cabin* has come down upon the dark abodes of slavery like a morning's sunlight . . . awakening sympathy in hearts that never before felt for the slave" (qtd. in Donovan 18). Throughout the remainder of the nineteenth century, the reception remained primarily positive, with some notable exceptions.

The southern response to the novel, and to *A Key to Uncle Tom's Cabin,* was, predictably, generally hostile. William J. Grayson, a South Carolina poet, excoriated Stowe as "a moral scavenger" who "sniffs up pollution with a pious air" (qtd. in Adams 39). In one of the most scathing reviews, William Gilmore Simms accused Stowe of possessing "a malignity so remarkable that the petticoat lifts of itself, and we see the hoof of the beast under the table" (qtd. in Gossett 190). In addition, a review by George F. Holmes in *The Southern Literary Messenger* attacked Stowe for "intermeddl[ing] with things which concern her not—to libel and vilify people from among whom have gone forth some of the noblest men that have adorned the race" and for using her pen to bring forth "allegations of cruelty towards the slaves" that are "absolutely and unqualifiedly false" (qtd. in Ammons 468, 475). Stowe was also censured for suggesting colonization as a solution to slavery.

Throughout the early twentieth century, *Uncle Tom's Cabin* was either dismissed for its sentimentalism, criticized for its unpolished style, or considered too marginal for serious critical inquiry. Some critics, most notably James Baldwin, angrily denounced the novel for its racial stereotypes and accused Stowe of divesting Tom of his manhood. In the second half of the century, however, and particularly in recent years, *Uncle Tom's Cabin* has become firmly reassimilated into the American literary canon. Edmund Wilson proclaimed it in 1962 to be "a much more impressive work than one has ever been allowed to suspect" (5) and Leslie Fiedler in *Love and Death in the American Novel* characterized it as "an astonishingly various and complex work" (261). Kenneth Lynn argued that the negative characterization of the novel as "good propaganda" was "one of the most unjust clichés in all of American criticism" (qtd. in Donovan 21). More recently, Paul Lauter observed that "The restoration of *Uncle Tom's Cabin*—even despite its racial stereotypes—to a degree of literary grace in the last decades testifies more to the impact of the civil rights movement than, as yet, to a shift in our literary aesthetic" (107). Indeed, both the civil rights and women's movements of the 1960s set the stage for a critical reassessment of the novel. Feminist critics have come to see the novel as a revolt against male patriarchy and to recognize the political dimensions inherent in the power struggles that are depicted. Jean Fagan Yellin suggests that the "problems of slavery in [the novel are] finally inseparable from the issue of women's political impotence" (91).

While the bulk of criticism addressing Stowe's works has focused on *Uncle Tom's Cabin,* some of her other works, most notably *Oldtown Folks* and *The Pearl of Orr's Island,* are also beginning to receive scholarly attention. John R. Adams characterizes *Oldtown Folks* as "the best book [Stowe] ever wrote" and "the most comprehensive of her New England novels" (63). Judith Fetterley suggests that "next to *Uncle Tom's Cabin,*" *The Pearl of Orr's Island* is "Stowe's most mythically charged and imaginatively compelling work" and that it "derives its deepest meaning from Stowe's vision of the value of the feminine principle in a masculine world" (379).

WORKS CITED

Adams, John R. *Harriet Beecher Stowe.* Boston: Twayne Publishers, 1989.

Ammons, Elizabeth, ed. *Uncle Tom's Cabin* (a Norton critical edition). New York: Norton, 1994.

Cross, Barbara M., ed. *The Autobiography of Lyman Beecher,* 2 vols. Cambridge: Harvard University Press, 1961.

Crozier, Alice C. *The Novels of Harriet Beecher Stowe.* New York: Oxford University Press, 1969.

Donovan, Josephine. *Uncle Tom's Cabin: Evil, Affliction, and Redemptive Love.* Boston: Twayne, 1977.

Emerson, Ralph Waldo. *The Complete Works of Ralph Waldo Emerson.* 12 vols. Cambridge: Riverside Press, 1903.

Fetterley, Judith. *Provisions: A Reader from 19th-Century American Women.* Bloomington: Indiana University Press, 1985.

Fiedler, Leslie. *Love and Death in the American Novel.* New York: Criterion Books, 1960.

Foner, Philip S., ed. *The Life and Writings of Frederick Douglass,* vol. 2. New York: International Publishers, 1950.

Gossett, Thomas F. *"Uncle Tom's Cabin" and American Culture.* Dallas: Southern Methodist University Press, 1985.

Hedrick, Joan D. *Harriet Beecher Stowe: A Life.* New York: Oxford University Press, 1994.

Lauter, Paul. *Canons and Contexts.* New York: Oxford University Press, 1991.

Wilson, Edmund. *Patriotic Gore.* New York: Oxford University Press, 1962.

Yellin, Jean Fagan. "Doing It Herself: *Uncle Tom's Cabin* and Women's Role in the Slavery Crisis," in *New Essays on "Uncle Tom's Cabin."* Eric J. Sundquist, ed. New York: Cambridge University Press, 1986. 85–105.

BIBLIOGRAPHY

Works by Harriet Beecher Stowe

Primary Geography for Children. Cincinnati: Corey & Fairbank, 1833.

The Mayflower; or, Sketches of Scenes and Characters Among the Descendents of the Puritans. New York: Harper and Brothers, 1843.

Uncle Tom's Cabin; or, Life Among the Lowly. 2 vols. Boston: John P. Jewett, 1852.

A Key to Uncle Tom's Cabin. Boston: John P. Jewett and Co., 1853.

Sunny Memories of Foreign Lands. 2 vols. Boston: Phillips, Sampson, 1854.

Dred: A Tale of the Great Dismal Swamp. 2 vols. Boston: Phillips, Sampson, 1856.

The Minister's Wooing. New York: Derby and Jackson, 1859.

Agnes of Sorrento. Boston: Ticknor and Fields, 1862.

The Pearl of Orr's Island: A Story of the Coast of Maine. Boston: Ticknor and Fields, 1862.

Little Foxes. Boston: Ticknor and Fields, 1866.

Religious Studies, Sketches, and Poems. Boston: Houghton, Mifflin, 1896.

Oldtown Folks. Boston: Fields, Osgood, 1869.

Lady Byron Vindicated: A History of the Byron Controversy, from Its Beginnings in 1816 to the Present Time. Boston: Fields, Osgood, 1870.

Pink and White Tyranny: A Society Novel. Boston: Roberts Brothers, 1871.

Palmetto-Leaves. Boston: J. R. Osgood, 1873.

Woman in Sacred History: A Series of Sketches Drawn from Scriptural, Historical, and Legendary Sources. New York: J. B. Ford, 1873.

Footsteps of the Master. New York: J. B. Ford, 1877.

Poganuc People: Their Loves and Lives. New York: Fords, Howard, and Hulbert, 1878.

Studies of Harriet Beecher Stowe

Adams, John R. *Harriet Beecher Stowe.* Boston: Twayne Publishers, 1989.

Ammons, Elizabeth, ed. *Approaches to Teaching Stowe's Uncle Tom's Cabin.* New York: Modern Language Association of America, 2000.

———. *Critical Essays on Harriet Beecher Stowe.* Boston: G. K. Hall, 1980.

———, ed. *Uncle Tom's Cabin* (a Norton critical edition). New York: Norton, 1994.

Ashton, Jean W. *Harriet Beecher Stowe: A Reference Guide.* Boston: G. K. Hall, 1977.

Baldwin, James. "Everybody's Protest Novel." In *Notes of a Native Son.* Boston: Beacon Press, 1955. 13–28.

Berlant, Lauren. "Poor Eliza." *American Literature: A Journal of Literary History, Criticism and Bibliography* 70, no. 3 (1998 Sept): 635–68.

Crozier, Alice C. *The Novels of Harriet Beecher Stowe.* New York: Oxford University Press, 1969.

Donovan, Josephine. "Harriet Beecher Stowe's Feminism. *American Transcendental Quarterly* 47–48 (Summer–Fall 1980): 141–57.

———. *Uncle Tom's Cabin: Evil, Affliction, and Redemptive Love.* Boston: Twayne, 1977.

Fields, Annie. *Life and Letters of Harriet Beecher Stowe.* Boston: Houghton, Mifflin, 1898.

Foster, Charles H. *The Rungless Ladder: Harriet Beecher Stowe and New England Puritanism.* Durham, NC: Duke University Press, 1954.

Furth, Isabella. "Manifest Destiny, Manifest Domesticity, and the Leaven of Whiteness in *Uncle Tom's Cabin.*" *Arizona Quarterly: A Journal of American Literature, Culture, and Theory* 55, no. 2 (1999 Summer): 31–55.

Gatta, John. "The Anglican Aspect of Harriet Beecher Stowe." *New England Quarterly: A Historical Review of New England Life and Letters* 73, no. 3 (2000 Sept.): 412–33.

Gilbertson, Catherine. *Harriet Beecher Stowe.* New York: D. Appleton-Century, 1937.

Goldner, Ellen J. "Arguing With Pictures: Race, Class, and the Formation of Popular Abolitionism through *Uncle Tom's Cabin.*" *Journal of American & Comparative Cultures* 24, no. 1–2 (2001 Spring–Summer): 71–84.

Gossett, Thomas F. *"Uncle Tom's Cabin" and American Culture.* Dallas: Southern Methodist University Press, 1985.

Graham, Thomas. "Harriet Beecher Stowe and the Question of Race." *New England Quarterly* 46, no. 4 (Dec. 1973): 614–22.

Grant, David. "Stowe's *Dred* and the Narrative Logic of Slavery's Extension." *Studies in American Fiction* 28, no. 2 (2000 Autumn): 151–78.

———. *"Uncle Tom's Cabin* and the Triumph of Republican Rhetoric." *New England Quarterly: A Historical Review of New England Life and Letters* 71, no. 3 (1998 Sept): 429–48.

Hamilton, Cynthia S. *"Dred:* Intemperate Slavery." *Journal of American Studies* 34, no. 2 (2000 Aug): 257–77.

Hedrick, Joan D. *Harriet Beecher Stowe: A Life.* New York: Oxford University Press, 1994.

———. " 'Peaceable Fruits': The Ministry of Harriet Beecher Stowe." *American Quarterly* 40, no. 3 (Sept. 1988): 307–32.

Hildreth, Margaret Holbrook. *Harriet Beecher Stowe: A Bibliography.* Hamden, CT: Archon Books, Shoe String Press, 1976.

Holmes, George F. "Rev. of *Uncle Tom's Cabin.*" *The Southern Literary Messenger* 18 (October 1852), n.p.

Karafilis, Maria. "Spaces of Democracy in Harriet Beecher Stowe's *Dred.*" *Arizona Quarterly: A Journal of American Literature, Culture, and Theory* 55, no. 3 (1999 Autumn): 23–49.

Kelley, Mary. "At War with Herself: Harriet Beecher Stowe as Woman in Conflict within the Home." *American Studies* 19 (Fall 1978): 23–40.

Kent, Kathryn R. " 'Single White Female': The Sexual Politics of Spinster in Harriet Beecher Stowe's *Oldtown Folks.*" *American Literature: A Journal of Literary History, Criticism, and Bibliography* 69, no. 1 (1997 March): 39–65.

Kirkham, E. Bruce. *The Building of "Uncle Tom's Cabin."* Knoxville: University of Tennessee Press, 1977.

Lynn, Kenneth S. *Introduction to Uncle Tom's Cabin: Or, Life among the Lowly.* Cambridge, MA: Harvard University Press, Belknap Press, 1962.

McCray, Florine Thayer. *The Life-Work of the Author of "Uncle Tom's Cabin."* New York: Funk and Wagnalls, 1889.

McCullough, David. "The Unexpected Mrs. Stowe." In *Brave Companions: Portraits in History.* New York: Prentice Hall, 1992.

Moers, Ellen. *Harriet Beecher Stowe and American Literature.* Hartford, CT: The Stowe-Day Foundation, 1978.

Noble, Marianne. "The Ecstacies of Sentimental Wounding in *Uncle Tom's Cabin.*" *Yale Journal of Criticism: Interpretation in the Humanities* 10, no. 2 (Fall 1997): 295–320.

O'Loughlin, Jim. "Articulating *Uncle Tom's Cabin.*" *New Literary History: A Journal of Theory and Interpretation* 31, no. 3 (2000 Summer): 573–97.

Sajé, Natasha. "Open Coffins and Sealed Books: The Death of the Coquette in Harriet Beecher Stowe's *Dred.*" *Legacy: A Journal of American Women Writers* 15, no. 2 (1998): 158–70.

Rowe, John Carlos. "Stowe's Rainbow Sign: Violence and Community in *Dred: A Tale of the Great Dismal Swamp* (1856)." *Arizona Quarterly: A Journal of American Literature, Culture, and Theory* 58, no. 1 (2002 Spring): 37–55.

Smith, Gail K. "Reading with the Other: Hermeneutics and the Politics of Difference in Stowe's *Dred.*" *American Literature: A Journal of Literary History, Criticism, and Bibliography* 69, no. 2 (1997 June): 289–313.

Smith, Rita J. "Those Who Go Before: Ancestors of Eva St. Clare." *New England Quarterly: A Historical Review of New England Life and Letters* 70, no. 2 (1997 June): 314–18.

Stoneley, Peter. "Sentimental Emasculations: *Uncle Tom's Cabin* and *Black Beauty.*" *Nineteenth-Century Literature* 54, no. 1 (1999 June): 53–72.

Stowe, Charles Edward. *Life of Harriet Beecher Stowe.* Compiled from Her Letters and Journals. Boston: Houghton, Mifflin, 1889.

Stowe, Charles Edward, and Lyman Beecher Stowe. *Harriet Beecher Stowe: The Story of Her Life.* Boston: Houghton, Mifflin, 1911.

Stowe, Lyman Beecher. *Saints, Sinners, and Beechers.* Indianapolis: Bobbs-Merrill, 1934.

Sundquist, Eric J., ed. *New Essays on Uncle Tom's Cabin.* New York: Cambridge University Press, 1986.

Tang, Edward. "Making Declaration of Her Own: Harriet Beecher Stowe as New England Historian." *New England Quarterly: A Historical Review of New England Life and Letters* 71, no. 1 (1998 March): 77–96.

Terrell, Mary Church. *Harriet Beecher Stowe: An Appreciation.* Washington, DC: Murray Brothers, 1911.

Tompkins, Jane P. "Sentimental Power: *Uncle Tom's Cabin* and the Politics of Literary History." In *The New Feminist Criticism: Essays on Women, Literature, and Theory,* edited by Elaine Showalter. New York: Pantheon, 1985. 81–104.

Wagenknecht, Edward. *Harriet Beecher Stowe: The Known and the Unknown.* New York: Oxford University Press, 1965.

Warner, Nicholas O. "Temperance, Morality, and Medicine in the Fiction of Harriet Beecher Stowe" In *The Serpent in the Cup: Temperance in American Literature,* edited by David S. Reynolds. Amherst: U of Massachusetts P, 1997. 136–152.

Wilson, Forrest. *Crusader in Crinoline: The Life of Harriet Beecher Stowe.* Philadelphia: J. B. Lippincott, 1941.

Wolff, Cynthia Griffin. " 'Masculinity' in *Uncle Tom's Cabin.*" In *Speaking the Other Self: American Women Writers,* edited by Jeanne Reesman. Athens: U of Georgia P, 1997. 3–26.

BAYARD TAYLOR (1825–1878)

Andrew Rennick

BIOGRAPHY

Bayard Taylor was born on January 11, 1825, in Kennett Square, Pennsylvania. He began writing poetry while attending local academies, publishing his first poem in the *Saturday Evening Post* at age 16. Unable to afford college, he became a printer's apprentice. In 1844 Taylor printed a volume of poems entitled *Ximena, or The Battle of the Sierra Morena.* The profits from *Ximena* enabled the young writer to buy out his apprenticeship and journey to Europe. Supporting himself by writing letters to American journals, he spent two years hiking through the Old World. Upon his return, Wiley and Putnam published his *Views A-foot; or, Europe Seen With Knapsack and Staff* (1846). Taylor's intrepid spirit won him immediate public acclaim; *Views* sold six editions in its first year (Smyth 50–51). Encouraged by this success, Taylor moved to New York. In 1849 he produced *Rhymes of Travel, Ballads and Poems* and covered the California Gold Rush for Horace Greeley's *Tribune,* resulting in the popular *Eldorado; or, Adventures in the Path of Empire* (1850). In 1850, however, his bright fortunes were marred when his wife Mary died after two months of marriage.

Over the next decades, Taylor solidified his reputation as America's best-known traveler. His letters from around the world appeared in the *Tribune* and were republished in celebrated volumes. Ambitious and indefatigable, he lectured extensively between journeys, helped his publishers promote and sell his books, and cultivated relationships with leading editors and poets (Greenspan 389). He continued to write poetry as well as novels, plays, and criticism, and contributed short stories to the *Atlantic Monthly.* In 1860 Taylor moved into a newly built estate near his boyhood home, intending to retire from travel writing. Yet after a stint with a diplomatic mission to Russia in 1862, he made several more journeys. In 1876, he delivered the Ode for the nation's centennial celebration in Philadelphia.

Taylor had a lifelong interest in German culture, encouraged by his German second wife, Marie. He translated Freilgrath and Goethe, completing Parts I and II of *Faust* in 1870 and 1871. His lectures on German literature at Cornell University were collected and published posthumously as *Studies in German Literature* (1879). In February 1878, Taylor was named Minister to Germany. He would not enjoy his post for long, succumbing to illness in Berlin on December 19, at age 53.

MAJOR WORKS AND THEMES

In his travel writing, Taylor plays adventurer and reporter, seeking out exotic experiences and recording life on the streets. The travelogues display Romantic sensibilities and staunch nationalism. Throughout his life, Taylor disdained his travel writing, considering himself a poet in the vein of Tennyson and Shelley. He is commonly associated with the "Genteel Tradition," a middle-class imitation of aristocratic "values, interests, and tastes" (Wermuth 23). Taylor's poetic theories find voice in his series of parodies and mock literary discussions, *The Echo Club and Other Literary Diversions* (1876). The poetry itself is marked by scrupulous attention to form, sonorous diction, and the idealization of beauty and virtue. *Poems of the Orient* (1854), featuring "Bedouin Song," marks Taylor's attempt to capture the exotic East.

Pastoralism pervades Taylor's work, especially later in his career. His novels, particularly *The Story of Kennett* (1866), celebrate idyllic rural America, nevertheless detailing the repressiveness of country life. *Hannah Thurston* (1862) satirizes various mid-century reform movements. Religion is one of Taylor's abiding interests, providing themes for the lyric dramas *The Prophet: A Tragedy* (1874) and *Prince Deukalion* (1878). Influenced by his Quaker mother and education, Taylor often draws on the sect for local color.

CRITICAL RECEPTION

To his frustration, Taylor was best known to the public as a travel writer. Praise for his poetry and fiction came most often from his many friends in literary circles, although "Bedouin Song" was set to music and performed by Glee clubs into the twentieth century (Beatty 177). While he was regularly able to find publishing venues, contemporaries often dismissed him as imitative, a charge echoed by later critics. However, Taylor's translation of *Faust,* rendered in Goethe's original meter, was widely acclaimed and has been used in editions as recently as 1969.

Twentieth-century critics agree that while Taylor's poems are technically competent, they lack imagination and rely too heavily on abstraction. His work is widely considered the epitome of mid-century American convention, a mix of Romantic sentimentalism and Victorian values that has found few recent supporters. In the most recent Taylor study, Paul Wermuth favors *The Echo Club,* which William Dean Howells called "the best set of parodies ever written" (qtd. in Wermuth 167). Of the novels, *The Story of Kennett* is lauded for its "freshness" and "picturesque simplicity" (Beatty 240); critics have also found it an interesting precursor to the realist movement (La Salle 20).

For years critical attention focused on Taylor's voluminous correspondence, providing insight into the New York publishing scene. However, recent interest has come from Queer Theorists, who note exquisite depictions of male beauty in poems such as "Hylas" and passionate male friendships in the travelogues and the novel *Joseph and His Friend* (1870). *Eldorado,* Taylor's most enduring work, is gaining a reputation as classic Americana.

WORKS CITED

Beatty, Richmond Croom. *Bayard Taylor: Laureate of the Gilded Age.* Norman, OK: University of Oklahoma Press, 1937.

Greenspan, Ezra. *George Palmer Putnam: Representative American Publisher.* University Park, PA: The Pennsylvania State UP, 2000.

La Salle, C.W. II. Introduction. *The Story of Kennett.* By Bayard Taylor. New Haven, CT: College & University Press, 1973. 7–21.

Smyth, Albert H. *Bayard Taylor.* Boston: Houghton, Mifflin, and Co., 1896.

Wermuth, Paul. *Bayard Taylor.* New York: Twayne Publishers, 1973.

BIBLIOGRAPHY

Works by Bayard Taylor

Travel Writings

Views A-foot; or, Europe Seen with Knapsack and Staff. New York: Wiley and Putnam, 1846. Reprint, Philadelphia: McKay, 1893.

Eldorado; or, Adventures in the Path of Empire: New York: Wiley and Putnam, 1850. Reprint, Introduction by James D. Houston. Afterword by Roger Kahn. Berkeley, CA: Heydey Books, 2000.

A Journey to Central Africa. New York: Wiley and Putnam, 1854.

The Lands of the Saracen. New York: Wiley and Putnam, 1854. Reprint, New York: Arno, 1977.

A Visit to India, China, and Japan in the Year 1853. New York: Putnam, 1855.

At Home and Abroad. New York: Putnam, 1859.

At Home and Abroad, Second Series. New York: Putnam, 1862.

Colorado: A Summer Trip. New York: Putnam, 1867. Reprint, Niwot, CO: UP of Colorado, 1989.

Novels

Hannah Thurston, A Story of American Life. New York: Putnam, 1862. Reprint, Upper Saddle River, NJ: Gregg, 1968.

John Godfrey's Fortunes: Related by Himself. A Story of American Life. New York: Putnam, 1864.

The Story of Kennett. New York: Putnam, 1866. Reprint, Edited by C. W. La Salle II. New Haven, CT: College & University Press, 1973.

Joseph and His Friend. New York: Putnam, 1870.

Beauty and the Beast, and Tales of Home. New York: Putnam, 1872. Reprint, New York: Garnet, 1969.

Poetry

Ximena, or the Battle of the Sierra Morena, and Other Poems. Philadelphia: Hooker, 1844.

Rhymes of Travel, Ballads and Poems. New York: Putnam, 1849.

A Book of Romances, Lyrics, and Songs. Boston: Ticknor, Reed, and Fields, 1851.

Poems of the Orient. Boston: Ticknor and Fields, 1854.

Poems of Home and Travel. Boston: Ticknor and Fields, 1855.

The Poet's Journal. Boston: Ticknor and Fields, 1862.

The Picture of St. John. Boston: Fields, Osgood, and Co., 1866.

Lars: A Pastoral of Norway. Boston, Osgood, 1873.

Home Pastorals, Ballads, and Lyrics. Boston: Osgood, 1875.

The National Ode. Boston: Gill, 1877.

Poetical Works of Bayard Taylor. Household edition. Boston: Houghton, Mifflin, and Co., 1880. Reprint, New York: AMS, 1970.

Dramatic Works of Bayard Taylor. Boston: Houghton, Mifflin, and Co., 1880. Reprint, New York: AMS, 1969.

Critical and Other Works

Faust. By Johann Wolfgang von Goethe. Part I. Boston: Fields, Osgood, and Co., 1870.

Faust. By Johann Wolfgang von Goethe. Part II. Boston: Fields, Osgood, and Co., 1871.

The Echo Club and Other Literary Diversions. Boston: Osgood., 1876.

Studies in German Literature. New York: G. P. Putnam's Sons, 1879. Reprint. Freeport, NY: Books For Libraries Press, 1972.

Critical Essays and Literary Notes. New York: G. P. Putnam's Sons, 1880.

Letters of Bayard Taylor. Edited by John Richie Schultz. San Marino, CA: Huntington Library, 1937.

Faust, Parts 1 & 2. By J. W. Goethe. Introduction and Afterword by J. M. Sneed. London: Sphere Books, 1969.

Selected Letters of Bayard Taylor. Edited by Paul Wermuth. Lewisburg, PA: Bucknell UP, 1997.

Studies of Bayard Taylor

Beatty, Richmond Croom. *Bayard Taylor: Laureate of the Gilded Age.* Norman, OK: University of Oklahoma Press, 1937.

Cary, Richard. *The Genteel Circle: Bayard Taylor and His New York Friends.* Ithaca, NY: Cornell UP, 1952.

Frentz, Horst. "Bayard Taylor and the Reception of Goethe in America." *Journal of English and Germanic Philology* 41 (1942): 121–39.

Krumpelmann, John T. *Bayard Taylor and German Letters.* Hamburg: Cram, de Gruyter and Co., 1959.

Martin, Robert K. *The Homosexual Tradition in American Poetry.* Iowa City: University of Iowa Press, 1998.

Smyth, Albert H. *Bayard Taylor.* Boston: Houghton, Mifflin, and Co., 1896.

Stedman, Edmund. *Poets of America.* Boston: Houghton, Mifflin, and Co., 1885.

Tumulty, Sharon. "From Persia to Peoria: Bayard Taylor as Travel Writer." Diss., U of Delaware, 1971.

Wermuth, Paul. *Bayard Taylor.* New York: Twayne Publishers, 1973.

HENRY DAVID THOREAU (1817–1862)

Stephen Hahn

BIOGRAPHY

Henry David Thoreau was born on a farm owned by his maternal grandmother in Concord, Massachusetts, on July 12, 1817, and christened by the eminent Dr. Ezra Ripley. His paternal grandfather, Jean Thoreau, descended from a French Huguenot family on the British Isle of Jersey, had been cast on New England shores in a shipwreck in 1773. Jean became a privateer in the Revolutionary War and amassed a substantial fortune as a merchant. Henry's father, John, lost most of the inheritance and alternately worked as a storekeeper, schoolteacher, and pencil-maker. His mother Cynthia Dunbar's family, descended from Scots, included Loyalists in the American Revolution and ministers in southern New Hampshire. Contrary to the popular image of Thoreau as a solitary, unattached, and even unsociable figure, family and personal relationships formed a central part of his life.

Henry was the third of four children, which included Helen (1812–49), John (1815–42), and Sophia (1819–76). None married or had children. Although Henry was the only family member to attend college, all were literate and contributing members of the community. As he was dying, Sophia assisted Thoreau in organizing his manuscripts and, with William Ellery Channing, played the part of guardian and executor of his literary remains. With his brother John, his companion on a two-week-long trip on the Concord and Merrimack rivers in 1839, Henry had an especially close relationship. They taught and ran schools together; courted the same young woman, who passed them over; and had such sympathetic relations that when John died rapidly and horribly in January 1842 of infectious tetanus ("lockjaw") from a razor cut, Henry suffered temporary psychosomatic paralysis. Henry took an active part in family affairs: the business of pencil-making (and later the supply of plumbago for electrotyping), inherited from his lucky but ne'er-do-well uncle Charles Dunbar; the building of houses in Concord as the family became established; and the support of his mother and sister Sophia after the death of his father in 1859 until his own early death in 1862.

In Thoreau's early childhood, the family moved from Concord to Chelmsford, Massachusetts, where his father briefly ran a grocery business that failed, and then to Boston in 1821, where his father even more briefly taught school, before returning to Concord in 1823 to take over the uncle's pencil-making operations. (Thoreau dated his earliest memory of Walden Pond from a visit at age four.) He accompanied his father on business trips to New York and elsewhere. None of John Thoreau's pencil-making innovations were patented, apparently because of the cost of doing so, and the family business was conducted secretively to protect their processes from imitation by competitors. In addition to these mechanical accomplishments, Thoreau became a surveyor and was noted for his horticultural prowess, winning local contests by growing large pumpkins and squashes.

As a youth, Henry attended a private "infant school" and the publicly supported Concord "Center School" before enrolling in the private Concord Academy with his brother John in 1828. During this time, the family was still in precarious financial circumstances and moved several times while taking in boarders to defray expenses. In 1829, at the age of 13, Thoreau began attending lectures on natural history at the Concord Lyceum, founded as part of a widespread movement for community education. In the late summer 1833, having barely passed its entrance exams—and supported by his brother, older sister, and aunts, in addition to his parents—Thoreau enrolled at Harvard College. Destined to become one of the most memorable graduates of any class at Harvard, he was distinguished more by the breadth of his study than by the points he earned in a system now arcane to higher education. Despite having achieved a middling record that placed him nineteenth in a class of 50 at his graduation in August 1837, he participated in an honors conference where he delivered a paper on "The Commercial Spirit of the Times" that took a decisive turn toward the transcendental. He was 21 years old.

While at Harvard, Thoreau studied broadly in literature and languages and wrote numerous essays. He took a six-week leave to teach school in Canton, Massachusetts, boarding with the Unitarian minister Orestes Brownson, with whom he studied German. He spent the months prior to commencement living with his friend and classmate Charles Stearns Wheeler in a hut on the shores of Flint's Pond in Lincoln, near Concord, and returned for the commencement exercises. We do not know if he stayed at the exercises long enough to hear Emerson's Phi Beta Kappa address, "The American Scholar," in August 1837. We do know, however, that he had already come within Emerson's ken. They met personally for the first time in April 1837 after Sophia showed Emerson's sister-in-law, Lucy Jackson Brown, who boarded with the Thoreaus, one of Thoreau's manuscripts. Emerson's intercession was instrumental in securing Thoreau a grant to defray the cost of completing his college studies. Fourteen years younger than Emerson, Thoreau soon became a member of discussion and editorial groups of a Transcendentalist persuasion while beginning his short-lived career as a school teacher and making the trip that would provide material for his first book, *A Week on the Concord and Merrimack Rivers,* composed largely during his stay at Walden Pond from July 4, 1845, to September 6, 1847. Critics assume that it was Emerson who provided the impetus for Thoreau's journal, and that it is Emerson who is remembered as the "friend" on its first page.

After graduating from Harvard, Thoreau taught school from 1837 to 1839, made pencils, tended to the affairs of the Emerson household from 1841 to 1843, and tutored the children of Emerson's brother William on Staten Island. His first published essay appeared in the locally produced Transcendentalist journal *The Dial,* followed by other essays and poems. Although he published only two books in his lifetime, liberal notions of fair use led to the dissemination of much of his writing in the press, notably in the New

York *Herald Tribune,* edited by Horace Greeley, who acted in part as an agent for his writing. He also gave numerous public lectures and became acquainted with a number of major writers in addition to Emerson, including Hawthorne, Whitman, Bronson Alcott (whose daughter Louisa May was one of Thoreau's students), William Ellery Channing, Margaret Fuller, and James Russell Lowell.

In the spring of 1845, Thoreau erected a small cabin on the shores of Walden Pond, on land owned by Emerson, with the help of Alcott, Channing, Emerson, and others from Concord. There he moved in July to begin the stay of two years, two months, and two days that provides the narrative frame (condensed to the cycle of a year) for *Walden* (1854). During this period, Thoreau led an active life away from as well as on the shores of Walden. He began writing *A Week,* gave lectures at the Concord Lyceum, was arrested for nonpayment of the poll tax, and made the first of his trips to the Maine woods.

After leaving Walden in September 1847, Thoreau tended to the affairs of the Emerson household, while Emerson spent the year in England. In the years following, Thoreau continued to give lectures and publish essays, to compose his journal, and to amass and edit material for what would become posthumous books. Despite his ironically self-deprecating comment that he had "traveled a good deal in Concord" (*Walden,* Rossi, 2), Thoreau traveled throughout the Northeast—to the Monadnock and White Mountain regions of New Hampshire frequently, to the Maine Woods, to Cape Cod, to Quebec, to Long Island in 1850 on a mission to recover the body of Margaret Fuller following a shipwreck, to Brattleboro, Vermont, and to Chappaqua and Brooklyn, New York. In his last years, he was one of the major surveyors in the town of Concord.

While Thoreau himself never participated in utopian communities, such as Brook Farm and the ephemeral Fruitlands, or social experiments other than his own, there is a current of social observation and critical commentary in all his writing. While he assisted in "conducting" on the Underground Railroad, there is understandably little documentation relating to such secretive resistance. He declined to join any anti-slavery or abolitionist society. Life events behind his political writings arose almost accidentally with his arrest in 1846 for nonpayment of a nominal poll tax, written up considerably in the 1849 essay "Resistance to Civil Government" (more familiarly known as "Civil Disobedience"). His activism continued with distanced but impassioned protest to the Fugitive Slave Law in the case of Anthony Burns in Boston in 1854, and culminated in his 1857 meeting with John Brown and his participation in public protest following Brown's raid on the arsenal at Harpers Ferry and the trial and execution of Brown for treason against the Commonwealth of Virginia in 1859.

Even after the onset in November 1860 of the last stage of the tuberculosis, Thoreau continued to write. As the cause and gravity of his illness became evident, he sought an environment that might allow the disease to go into remission. He traveled with Horace Mann Jr. to Minnesota in 1861 in search of such an environment, only to witness the vanishing of displaced Indians near the headwaters of the Mississippi at Lake Itasca, and to find no appreciable relief. He returned to Concord and began organizing his manuscripts for posthumous publication, and died on May 6, 1862, a few months before his forty-fifth birthday.

MAJOR WORKS AND THEMES

Thoreau published only two complete books in his lifetime, *A Week on the Concord and Merrimack Rivers* (1849) and *Walden; or Life in the Woods* (1854). Thematically and structurally the two books have certain similarities: both are organized loosely around cycles of the calendar; both deal with excursions or sojourns on or near water; and both exploit the possibility that the description of encounters with natural and historical objects and events can intimate or reveal other kinds or levels of experience—personal, linguistic, and spiritual or transcendental. Yet these books represent only a fraction of what Thoreau wrote in the approximately 25 years from the time he began his journal writing in 1837 until his death in 1862.

Thoreau's development as a writer can be said to begin, notwithstanding his protest about how little he learned at Harvard, in his undergraduate years under the discipline of writing periodic required themes. Topics ranged from issues in moral philosophy to more literary analysis. One can infer retrospectively the significance of this early practice by tracing a pattern of development in Thoreau's works from journal entries to lectures, essays, and published or nearly completed books. That pattern, along with evidence of Thoreau's process of revising the two books published in his lifetime, provides for textual scholarship a rich field of study. In the last decade of the twentieth century, new works by Thoreau—"The Dispersion of Seeds" and "Wild Fruits"—were being "rediscovered" and reconstructed from manuscripts; and in the last half of that century, textual scholars continued to discover and to reconstruct successive versions of *A Week* and *Walden.*

A Week can be described as an anthology of lyric, narrative, and reflective passages strung on the narrative frame of a week's journey (the actual journey lasted two weeks, August 31 to September 14, 1839)—the lyric portions including his own poems and prose descriptions and quotations from poems out of the English tradition, various scriptures, and epic and folk traditions, and the narrative including stories like that of the abduction of Hannah Dustin (who slew her Native American captors on an island on the Merrimack in March 1697) and other topics inspired by encounters on the trip, including a frequently extracted essay on friendship. The tone of the work is both elegiac—in memoriam to his brother John—and hopeful, a paradox central to Thoreau's work, alternating between the threat of despondency and the affirmation of hope.

The central achievement of Thoreau's career as a writer of extended prose narrative, *Walden,* may derive some of its spontaneous, colloquial tone from having been tried out in lecture pieces, delivered before an audience, that were integrated into the final work, but it is less obviously pieced together than *A Week.* It is organized around a seasonal cycle from summer to winter to spring (like *A Week,* collapsing a double cycle, here of two years, into one). While noting that the actual Walden encampment ended on the cusp of the transition of summer into fall, the book creates the impression of a falling and rising movement from opposition to and alienation from the contemporary scene ("I went to the woods" *Walden* 61), through "Solitude" (the title of a medial chapter), to a concluding reunion with society coupled with an ecstatic vision of the possibilities of life ("The sun is but a morning star" *Walden* 223) that is consonant with the opposition of metaphors of drought and desiccation to those of "freshets" and "flood" in the spring (*Walden* 222).

While many passages suggest the importance of the theme of the transcendence of temporality, division, and limitation advanced by Emersonian transcendentalism, *Walden* is only loosely allied with what might be called Transcendentalist doctrine, and its tropes—while pointing to the possibility of access to a higher world or understanding through experience of the natural world—remain figures of imagination and will. If philosophy focuses on what it is necessary to believe, *Walden* focuses thematically on questioning how we construct our ideas of what is necessary in life against other possibilities. The theme of "what man has made [and makes] of man," and implicitly what one makes of oneself, is in fact the subject of the opening chapter of *Walden*—"Economy"—and a central concern of the book as a whole. Moreover, Thoreau's version of Transcendentalism leans heavily toward a developing American pragmatism, as when he insists that "in view of the future or possible, we should live quite laxly and undefined in front" (*Walden* 216) and not be defined by what our fathers or their fathers believed or told us they believed. The sojourn at Walden is framed as a kind of experiment in living—"to front only the essential facts of life and see if I could not learn what it had to teach" (*Walden* 61)—and questions as much as it propounds.

Walden experienced a happier fate on publication than had *A Week*. Published in Boston by Ticknor and Fields, *Walden* sold nearly 1,750 copies in the first year. It was reviewed widely and well, according to the persuasions of its reviewers, who ranged domestically from Portland, Maine, to New Orleans, and included the British novelist George Eliot. Not only the prestigious imprint of his second publisher—a firm that counted Longfellow and Lowell among its authors—but the notoriety of essays such as "Slavery in Massachusetts," which appeared in *The Liberator* in July 1854, brought further attention to Thoreau. Large portions of *Walden,* including whole chapters, were excerpted in periodicals. Interest in Thoreau's writing grew, and Ticknor and Fields republished the remaining copies of *A Week* with a new title page in 1862, shortly after Thoreau's death. *Letters to Various Persons,* edited by Emerson, was published posthumously in 1865, followed by numerous editions of Thoreau's books, essays, and journals.

A Week and *Walden* were the products of sustained composition and successive revisions, resulting in the transformation of the quotidian into the symbolic. None of Thoreau's posthumously published book-length works were composed in the same way or to the same effect. Both *The Maine Woods* (1864) and *Cape Cod* (1865) grew out of long pieces prepared for periodicals. Thoreau began editing them and pieces collected in *Excursions* (1863) for book publication when it was clear he was dying, but the short interval of this awareness precluded sustained revision. They do not lack sublimity and poetry entirely (especially *The Maine Woods*), but they do reflect a more straightforward journalistic style. Greeley urged Thoreau toward periodical publication to gain a wider audience early on; his efforts took such a turn following the publication of *Walden.*

Separate note should be made of Thoreau's shorter compositions—the most well-known are the essay on Civil Disobedience ("Resistance to Civil Government," 1849), "Slavery in Massachusetts" (1854), and "The Succession of Forest Trees" (1860)—that are generally divided into categories of "natural history" and "social reform." Like his longer works, these reflect an attention to "principle," which could be described as an amalgamation of Transcendentalist and idealist impulses with observational or empiric impulses. Intellectually as well as morally, Thoreau endorsed an adherence to principle in the belief that persisting in the application of principle is informative.

CRITICAL RECEPTION

Evidence of the critical reception of Thoreau's work in his lifetime comes primarily from reviews of *Walden,* but these vary according to the reviewer's persuasion and temperament. Because these reviews focus on one work received in the periodical press, they are not enough to establish a critical tradition, although the dominance of *Walden* as a focus of attention is significant. A sustained tradition of critical reception begins only after Thoreau's death, with Emerson's eulogy in the August 1862 *Atlantic Monthly* and with an extended critical essay by James Russell Lowell in the *North American Review* in October 1865. These two retrospective views had an influence far beyond their time, being quoted, excerpted, and anthologized as the reports of eminent writers who had known Thoreau. Emerson's "Thoreau" is more balanced, though it tends to be remembered as an expression of Emerson's disappointment that despite "his rare powers of action, . . . [Thoreau] had no ambition" rather than of his concern that "the country knows not yet . . . how great a son it has lost" (Glick 33). Lowell's "Thoreau" expresses disdain for what Lowell regards as Thoreau's hubris, humorlessness, and priggishness. (The two had a falling out when Lowell as editor of the *Atlantic Monthly* removed without consultation a "pantheistic" sentence from Thoreau's series on the Maine Woods.) Like Emerson's essay, Lowell's emerges from blame to praise—"his whole life was a rebuke of the waste and aimlessness of our American luxury" (Glick 46)—but for Lowell this is a compromised virtue. Awarding Thoreau a high place as a stylist, Lowell finds that morally he is a contradiction and a nullity, for "Thoreau's experiment [at Walden] actually presupposed all that complicated civilization which it theoretically abjured" (Glick 45). Much of the critical commentary that follows Lowell's essay can be read as attempts to support, argue against, set aside, or deconstruct this one proposition. Subthemes emerge, such as whether Thoreau was ever in any significant sense a "naturalist" (Lowell claims that Thoreau did not know, until he went to Walden, that hickory trees grew in Concord [Glick 39]), but the main concern is whether Thoreau "discovered nothing" (Glick 39) or actually revealed some things worth knowing. What tends to be retained of these appraisals is the image of one who turns his back in conceit of himself against the rest of society or the worthiness of social action. (See, a century later, Richard Poirier, *A World Elsewhere,* 1966.)

Reception of Thoreau's writing can be divided into aspects that are appreciative and those that are critical, corresponding to a distinction Lowell makes: "His appreciation is of the highest quality; his critical power, from want of continuity of mind, very limited and inadequate" (Glick 39). Appreciation appears in many forms in the reception of Thoreau's writing—from memoirs, such as Edward Waldo Emerson's *Henry Thoreau as Remembered by a Young Friend,* to homage paid by writers and artists such as Henry Beston, Aldo Leopold, Edwin Way Teale, and N. C. Wyeth; to influence or response evident in such unlikely writers as Yeats (the bean row in "The Lake Isle of Innisfree"), Virginia Woolf, and Marcel Proust. Among other significant appreciative acts is the production of the fine "Walden Edition" of Thoreau's *Collected Writings* by Houghton Mifflin in 1906, illustrated with photographs by Herbert W. Gleason, who also published and photographically illustrated a collection of gleanings from Thoreau's journals, *Through the Year with Thoreau,* in 1917.

In 1890 the English writer and social activist Henry S. Salt published *Life of Henry David Thoreau,* a remarkably balanced and informed work that provides a readable and useful introduction to Thoreau's work. It is especially significant because, unlike other early biographies—those by W. E. Channing and F. B. Sanborn, for instance—it was written by someone who was not personally familiar with Thoreau. Salt argues against two possible extreme views of Thoreau, claiming that he gave himself neither to misanthropic pursuit of metaphysical abstractions nor to fruitless documentation of natural phenomena; rather, Thoreau "was a firm believer in the gradual progress and ultimate renovation of mankind," insisting on "the independence of the individual mind" and the adoption of "simple, practical modes of living which alone can keep a man independent" to achieve greater human freedom (Salt 112).

The achievement of even a temporarily "balanced" view in the critical tradition is significant because it helps to establish Thoreau's writing as a permanent object of critical attention and because it provides parameters for critical discussion. Nearly every major critic or historian of American literature and every major socioliterary critic between the two world wars had something to say about Thoreau. Notable figures include Mark Van Doren, Lewis Mumford, and Vernon Louis Parrington. Critical discussion focuses on Thoreau's role in defining what it means to be an American and the direction that progress in the United States might take as it affects what Salt called "the independence of the individual mind" (Salt 112).

In the 1940s, criticism began to focus on assessing and exploring the more specifically literary qualities of Thoreau's writing, beginning with F. O. Matthiessen's *American Renaissance.* Matthiessen emphasizes the coordination of architectonic structure and constitutive symbol in an organic whole (citing the romantic esthetic theories of Horatio Greenough), though still with reference to the social and humanistic concerns of prior criticism. In the major works that followed World War II, critics such as Reginald L. Cook, in *Passage to Walden* (1949), and Sherman Paul, in *The Shores of America* (1958), extended these explorations of esthetic, symbolic, and mythographic qualities in *Walden* and other writings. Others such as Leo Stoller continued the discussion of the social and political implications of Thoreau's writing. Stoller's *After Walden* is one of the earliest post-war studies of the implications of Thoreau's having other lives to live and what he did with them. With the exception of naturalist readers who tended to migrate toward appreciative comment on the journals (see Zwinger and Teale, in *A Conscious Stillness,* for instance), critics working under the emergent paradigm of concern with the organic unity and symbolic resonance of individual works focused more or less exclusively on *Walden.* The opportunity for comment on other works was not lost, as these continued to be reprinted, with introductions and opportunities for editing, but from a literary standpoint all roads led to and circulated around one book and one geographical location.

By the centennial of Thoreau's death in 1962, *Walden* had become a revered text in the canon of the American literary tradition, to be interpreted and explored, but only seldom to be questioned as a significant contribution to American letters. The primary critical questions to be answered, according to the editor of a volume based on a commemorative edition of the *Massachusetts Review,* John Hicks, had to do with "Thoreau's relevance in the climate of post-existentialist thought" and "Thoreau's significance for persons caught up in important or typical contemporary events" (1). The tone of nearly all the contributors to the book based on this representative volume is celebratory, with the interesting exception of Theodore Baird, who continues the Lowellian complaint in the essay "Corn Grows in the Night." Although Baird published very little in his career, he exerted an enormous influence in literary studies through his control of curriculum at Amherst College during World War II, and indirectly at Harvard in the 1950s. For Baird, Thoreau appeals chiefly "to the individual's profound dissatisfaction with the part he must play in earning a living, in just being a member of the human race" (68). Thoreau's influence is divisive and pernicious, owing to the "incoherence in . . . [his] systems of thought" (74). The early vision of *Walden* and its use of language in elaborating that vision "proved not to be durable" (75). According to Baird, it is a profound disappointment that Thoreau as a writer ended, as he characterizes him in the notebooks, periodicals, and posthumous books, "counting and measuring and labeling according to Gray's *Botany*" (77).

If the reception of *Walden* needed a new focus to be delivered from its own obsessions, such a refocusing was provided from outside literary studies by the philosopher Stanley Cavell in *The Senses of Walden* (1972), which also provides an antidote to Baird's invective. For Cavell, Thoreau's attentiveness to such acts as counting and measuring and labeling always involves questions of what it means to count, et cetera, in an environment where we "have already philosophized our lives almost beyond comprehension" (91). That is, Thoreau's rigor in writing from experience, including the experience of his reading, is that he "praises nothing that he has not experienced and calls nothing impossible that he has not tried" (4) on the basis of theory or precept handed down to him. These acts are among those by which we orient ourselves, and reflection upon them as acts helps to ensure the authenticity of our orientation. Cavell also considers, as does Paul Lauter in an earlier essay ("Thoreau's Prophetic Legacy"), Thoreau's relation to a biblical, prophetic tradition.

Critical bibliography since the 1970s is enormous and permits only a summary consideration. Thoreau criticism at the turn of the millennium ranges throughout the Thoreau canon with a confidence that Thoreau is a permanently significant writer and that the exploration of works heretofore subjected to summary judgments—for instance, the journals (in Sharon Cameron's *Writing Nature* [1985]) or the writings on John Brown (in Samuel McGuire Worley's *Emerson, Thoreau, and the Role of the Cultural Critic* [2001])—is a worthy pursuit. Major biographical and psychological reassessments include Richardson's *Henry Thoreau: A Life of the Mind* (1986) and Milder's *Reimagining Thoreau* (1995). The most profound advance in Thoreau's critical reception in the last quarter of the century was concurrent with the rise of environmental studies and eco-criticism. It includes Lawrence Buell's compendious work *The Environmental Imagination* and the work of literary and cultural critics of whom nearly 20 contributed to *Thoreau's Sense of Place* (Schneider 2000). In works such as *Thoreau's Country,* by David R. Foster and more popularly in John Hanson Mitchell's *Walking towards Walden: A Pilgrimage in Search of Place* (1995), Thoreau's writing continues to provide a focal point for cultural understanding and reorientation.

WORKS CITED

Baird, Theodore. "Corn Grows in the Night." *Thoreau in Our Season.* Ed. John H. Hicks. Amherst: University of Massachusetts Press, 1966: 68–78.

Cavell, Stanley. *The Senses of Walden.* New York: Viking, 1972.

Glick, Wendell. *The Recognition of Henry David Thoreau: Selected Criticism Since 1848.* Ann Arbor: The University of Michigan Press, 1969.

Hicks, John H., ed. "Introduction." *Thoreau in Our Season.* Amherst: University of Massachusetts Press, 1966: 1–12.

Salt, Henry S. *Life of Henry David Thoreau* [1890]. Ed. Hendrick, Hendrick, and Oehlschlager. Chicago: University of Illinois Press, 1993.

Thoreau, Henry David. *Walden and Resistance to Civil Government.* 2nd ed. Ed. William Rossi. New York: Norton, 1992.

BIBLIOGRAPHY

Works by Henry David Thoreau

A Week on the Concord and Merrimack Rivers. Boston: James Munroe and Company, 1849.

Walden; or Life in the Woods. Boston: Ticknor and Fields, 1854.

Excursions. Boston: Ticknor and Fields, 1863.

The Maine Woods. Boston: Ticknor and Fields, 1864.

Cape Cod. Boston: Ticknor and Fields, 1865.

Letters to Various Persons. Ed. Ralph Waldo Emerson. Boston: Ticknor and Fields, 1865.

A Yankee in Canada with Anti-Slavery and Reform Papers. Boston: Ticknor and Fields, 1866.

Collected Writings. Walden Edition. Ed. Torrey and Allen. Boston: Houghton Mifflin, 1906.

Collected Poems of Henry David Thoreau. Ed. Carl Bode. Chicago: Packard Publishers, 1943.

Correspondence. Ed. Harding and Bode. New York: New York University Press, 1958.

The Annotated Walden. Ed. Philip Van Doren Stern. New York: Potter, 1970.

The Writings of Henry David Thoreau. Vols. 1–. Ed. Harding et al. Princeton: Princeton University Press, 1971–.

Henry David Thoreau: A Week . . . [Etc.]. Ed. Robert F. Sayre. New York: Library of America, 1985.

Faith in a Seed: "The Dispersion of Seeds" and Other Late Natural History Writings. Ed. Bradley P. Dean. Washington, DC: Island Press, 1993.

Walden: An Annotated Edition. Ed. Walter Harding. Boston: Houghton Mifflin, 1995.

"Wild Fruits": Thoreau's Rediscovered Last Manuscript. Ed. Bradley P. Dean. New York: W. W. Norton, 2000.

Henry David Thoreau: Collected Essays and Poems. Ed. Elizabeth Witherell. New York: Library of America, 2001.

Studies of Henry David Thoreau

Adams, Stephen, and Donald Ross Jr. *Revising Mythologies: The Composition of Thoreau's Major Works*. Charlottesville: University Press of Virginia, 1988.

Anonymous Review [of *Walden*]. *Worcester* (MA) *Palladium*. August 16, 1854. Quoted in Borst, *The Thoreau Log*. New York: G. K. Hall, 1992: 305–6.

Bennett, Jane. *Thoreau's Nature: Ethics, Politics, and the Wild*. Lanham, MD: Rowman and Littlefield Publishers, 2000.

Bickman, Martin. Walden: *Volatile Truths*. New York: Twayne Publishers, 1992.

Borst, Raymond R. *A Thoreau Log: A Documentary Life of Henry David Thoreau 1817–1862*. New York: G. K. Hall, 1992.

Bridgman, Richard. *Dark Thoreau*. Lincoln: University of Nebraska Press, 1982.

Buell, Lawrence. *The Environmental Imagination: Thoreau, Nature Writing, and the Formation of American Culture*. Cambridge: Harvard University Press, 1995.

Cain, William E., ed. *A Historical Guide to Henry David Thoreau*. New York: Oxford University Press, 2000.

Cameron, Sharon. *Writing Nature: Henry Thoreau's Journal*. Chicago: University of Chicago Press, 1985.

Christie, John Aldrich. *Thoreau as World Traveler*. New York: Columbia University Press, 1955.

Cook, Reginald L. *Passage to Walden*. Boston: Houghton Mifflin Company, 1949.

Emerson, Edward Waldo. *Henry Thoreau as Remembered by a Young Friend*. Boston: Houghton Mifflin Company, 1917.

Emerson, Ralph Waldo. "Thoreau." *Atlantic Monthly* (August 1862): 239–49. Rpt. in Glick, *The Recognition of Henry David Thoreau*, 18–34.

Foster, David R. *Thoreau's Country: Journey through a Transformed Landscape*. Cambridge: Harvard University Press, 1999.

Garber, Frederick. *Thoreau's Fable of Inscribing*. Princeton: Princeton University Press, 1991.

———. *Thoreau's Redemptive Imagination*. New York: New York University Press, 1977.

Gleason, Herbert W. *Thoreau Country: Photographs and Texts Selections from the Work of H. D. Thoreau by Herbert W. Gleason*. Ed. Mark Silber. San Francisco: Sierra Club Books, 1975.

———. *Through the Year With Thoreau*. Boston: Houghton Mifflin Company, 1917.

Hahn, Stephen. *On Thoreau*. Belmont, CA: Wadsworth, 2000.

Harding. Walter. *The Days of Henry Thoreau: A Biography* [1965]. Revised Edition. New York: Dover Publications, 1982.

Howarth, William L. *The Book of Concord: Thoreau's Life as a Writer*. New York: Viking, 1982.

Johnson, Linck C. *Thoreau's Complex Weave: The Writing of* A Week on the Concord and Merrimack Rivers. Charlottesville: The University Press of Virginia, 1986.

Lauter, Paul. "Thoreau's Prophetic Legacy." In John H. Hicks, ed. *Thoreau in Our Season.* 80–90.

LeBeaux, Richard. *Young Man Thoreau.* Amherst: University of Massachusetts Press, 1977.

Lowell, James Russell. "Thoreau." *North American Review* (October 1865): 597–608. Rpt. in Glick, *Recognition,* 38–46.

Matthiessen, F. O. *American Renaissance.* New York: Oxford University Press, 1941.

Meyer, Michael. *Several More Lives to Live: Thoreau's Political Reputation in America.* Westport, CT: Greenwood, 1977.

———. "Thoreau, Abolitionists, and Reformers." In *Thoreau Among Others: Essays in Honor of Walter Harding.* Ed. Rita K. Gollin and James B. Scholes. Geneseo, NY: State University of New York, College at Geneseo, 1983.

———. "Thoreau and Black Emigration." *American Literature* 53 (1981): 380–96. Ed. Joel Myerson. *The Cambridge Companion to Henry David Thoreau.* New York: Cambridge University Press, 1995.

Milder, Robert. *Reimagining Thoreau.* New York: Cambridge University Press, 1995.

Mitchell, John Hanson. *Walking towards Walden: A Pilgrimage in Search of Place.* Reading, MA: Addison-Wesley Publishing Company, 1995.

Paul, Sherman. *The Shores of America: Thoreau's Inward Exploration.* Urbana: University of Illinois Press, 1958.

Peck, H. Daniel. *Thoreau's Morning Work: Memory and Perception in "A Week . . . [Etc.]".* New Haven: Yale University Press, 1990.

Poirier, Richard. *A World Elsewhere: The Place of Style in American Literature.* New York: Oxford University Press, 1966.

Richardson, Robert D., Jr., *Henry Thoreau: A Life of the Mind.* Berkeley: University of California Press, 1986.

Sattelmeyer, Robert. *Thoreau's Reading: A Study in Intellectual History.* Princeton: Princeton University Press, 1988.

Sayre, Robert F., ed. *New Essays on* Walden. New York: Cambridge University Press, 1992.

———. *Thoreau and the American Indians.* Princeton: Princeton University Press, 1977.

Schneider, Richard, ed. *Thoreau's Sense of Place: Essays in American Environmental Writing.* Iowa City: University of Iowa Press, 2000.

Seybold, Ethel. *Thoreau: The Quest and the Classics.* New Haven: Yale University Press, 1951.

Shanley, J. Lyndon. *The Making of* Walden. Chicago: University of Chicago Press, 1957.

Smith, Harmon. *My Friend, My Friend: The Story of Thoreau's Relationship with Emerson.* Amherst: University of Massachusetts Press, 1999.

Stoller, Leo. *After* Walden: *Thoreau's Changing Views on Economic Man.* Stanford, CA: Stanford University Press, 1957.

Torrey, Bradford. "Thoreau." *Atlantic Monthly* (December 1896): 822–32. Rpt. in Glick, *Recognition,* 138–49.

Walls, Laura Dassow. *Seeing New Worlds: Henry David Thoreau and Nineteenth Century Natural Science.* Madison: University of Wisconsin Press, 1995.

Whicher, George F. Walden *Revisited: A Centennial Tribute.* Chicago: Packard and Company, 1945.

Worley, Samuel McGuire. *Emerson, Thoreau, and the Role of the Cultural Critic.* Albany: State University of New York Press, 2001.

Zwinger, Ann, and Edwin Way Teale. *A Conscious Stillness: Two Naturalists on Thoreau's Rivers.* Cambridge, MA: Harper and Row, 1982.

THOMAS BANGS THORPE (1815–1878)

John J. Han

BIOGRAPHY

A humorist and realist of the Old Southwest, Thomas Bangs Thorpe was born on March 1, 1815, in Westfield, Massachusetts. He was the first son of the Reverend Thomas and Rebecca Farnham Thorp (the "e" in Thorpe was a later addition). Thomas Thorp died when the boy was four years old. Several months later, Rebecca Thorp and her three children moved to Albany, New York, to live with her parents; the boy attended the public schools in the city.

In 1827, when Thomas Bangs was 12, the family moved to New York City, where he completed his elementary education. In 1830, deciding to become a historical painter, he began studying with figure painter John Quidor, an illustrator of Washington Irving (*Reminiscences* 3). In fall 1834 Thorpe enrolled at Wesleyan University in Middletown, Connecticut. Because of his deteriorating health, however, he withdrew from the university in summer 1836. Next year, he went to the South in search of a milder climate and settled in Baton Rouge, Louisiana; he was to reside in Louisiana for the next 17 years.

In 1838 Thorpe married Anne Maria Hinckley, who bore him three children. The following year Thorpe published his first character sketch, "Tom Owen, the Bee-Hunter," in William T. Porter's magazine *Spirit of the Times*. In 1840 he published a sketch, "Wild Turkey Shooting," and an essay, "Primitive Forests of the Mississippi," in the *Spirit of the Times,* and an essay, "The Mississippi," in the *Knickerbocker Magazine*. The following year the *Spirit of the Times* published "The Big Bear of Arkansas," Thorpe's most widely anthologized story. With the publication of this work, Thorpe's popularity soared, and he continued to write many humorous tales and character sketches set in the Old Southwest for magazines. He also painted portraits, frontier scenes, and animals. From 1843 to 1847, he edited several Whig newspapers, including the *Concordia Intelligencer* and *The Louisiana Conservative*.

In 1845 *The Big Bear of Arkansas, and Other Sketches, Illustrative of Characters and Incidents in the South and Southwest,* Thorpe's first collection of humorous stories, was published; the following year another volume, *The Mysteries of the Backwoods; or Sketches of the Southwest: Including Character, Scenery, and Rural Sports,* saw the light of day. During the Mexican War, Thorpe accompanied General Zachary Taylor's army and subsequently published three volumes detailing his war-time experiences: *Our Army on the Rio Grande* (1846); *Our Army at Monterey* (1847); and *The Taylor Anecdote Book: Anecdotes and Letters of Zachary Taylor* (1848).

In 1853 Thorpe moved to New York. The following year he published an expansion of his *Mysteries* volume as *The Hive of "The Bee-Hunter": A Repository of Sketches, Including Peculiar American Character, Scenery, and Rural Sports* and his only novel, *The Master's House; A Tale of Southern Life.* Thorpe's wife died in 1855, and he married Jane Fosdick two years later. He worked on the staff of *Frank Leslie's Illustrated Newspaper* and became part owner of the *Spirit of the Times.* During the Civil War he enlisted in the volunteer army, serving as a staff officer in the military government of New Orleans and then as a member of the Louisiana Constitutional Convention. In 1864 he returned to the North, worked at the New York City Customhouse, and contributed articles to several magazines, including *Harper's, Appleton's Journal,* and *Baldwin's Monthly.* His final book was *Reminiscences of Charles L. Elliott, Artist,* published in 1868. Thorpe died of Bright's disease in New York City on September 20, 1878.

MAJOR WORKS AND THEMES

Thorpe's literary fame rests on several tall tales and humorous sketches included in *The Mysteries of the Backwoods* and *The Hive of "The Bee-Hunter."* They portray the sights and sounds of the Old Southwest: backwoods scenery, rural characters and their customs, frontier occupations, and local sports. The author has a keen eye for the sham of backwoodsmen, although, unlike the vitriolic humorist Mark Twain, his main purpose in these stories is to amuse the reader, not to change society. "Tom Owen, the Bee Hunter" sketches an eccentric frontier hero who is compared to Nimrod, the mighty hunter of the biblical times, and to Davy Crockett, the legendary American hunter. When he sees a bee going into a tree, Tom Owen chops down the tree, and then collects the sweets. He claims that he can see a bee over a mile away, which is a hyperbole typical of frontier tall tales. The urbane narrator of "The Big Bear of Arkansas" records the adventures of a mighty hunter, Jim Doggett, whom he met during the steamboat trip up the Mississippi from New Orleans. A braggart, Doggett tells his curious audience about a huge, ferocious bear that he once encountered in the wilderness. After failed attempts at killing the bear, Doggett spotted the animal by accident and killed it easily. The "unhuntable" animal died, Doggett believes, simply because his time came. The story "A Piano in Arkansas" depicts a comic episode related to the piano. The inhabitants of the little village of Hardscrabble hear the news that a real piano has arrived at their town. The prevailing opinion among the curious villagers is that a piano is an animal because it has four legs. The all-knowing Moses Mercer—son of "Old Mercer," a congressman in the State Senate—proudly informs the villagers that the piano is a musical instrument. The problem is that Mercer himself has not seen a piano and, at a party, mistakenly points at a washing machine as a piano.

Among his less-known works are the novel *The Master's House* and the three non-fiction books that resulted from his involvement in the Mexican War. *The Master's House* was a counter to *Uncle Tom's Cabin,* Harriet Beecher Stowe's abolitionist novel, which many viewed as propaganda. It was written, to borrow Milton Rickels's words, "within the framework of the romantic and sentimental novel of reform" (180). The protagonist,

Graham Mildway, is a Southerner who goes to a New England college and falls in love with a girl, a Northerner. The two characters marry and settle in the South, where they operate a plantation. Throughout the novel, Thorpe launches a moral argument against slavery by using such characters as Major Dixon, a slave trader, and a young female slave who is forced to part with her child.

In *Our Army on the Rio Grande,* Thorpe provides first-hand accounts of the American Army's conquest of the city of Matamoros, Mexico. Patriotic in tone, this work lacks artistic merits; however, it contains historical information on major battles and military documents. *Our Army at Monterey,* Thorpe's second book on the Mexican War, concerns the brilliant leadership of General Zachary Taylor and the valor of the American troops. Finally, *The Taylor Anecdote Book* consists of over 300 anecdotes exemplifying the heroism of the American soldiers and the brutality of the Mexicans.

CRITICAL RECEPTION

Critics generally see Thomas Bangs Thorpe as a minor writer. He is remembered mainly as an author of humorous tales and sketches set in the Old Southwest. In his *Thomas Bangs Thorpe: Humorist of the Old Southwest* (1962), the only biography—for that matter the only book-length work—on Thorpe, Milton Rickels calls Thorpe a "versatile . . . minor figure" (vii). The author considers Thorpe the greatest of all the humorists and realists of the Old Southwest in the 1840s and 1850s. Thorpe was "the keenest observer of his times, the most productive writer, perhaps the most complex and interesting figure" (3). Meanwhile, Norris W. Yates comments that Porter served as a kind of literary agent for "two of the most popular southern writers, Thomas Bangs Thorpe and Johnson Jones Hooper" (44).

Thorpe's well-known stories have been received favorably. Franklin Meine, for example, notes that the story "The Big Bear of Arkansas" is "characteristically Western and vastly amusing"; it is "a match for Münchhausen" (xxv). According to Milton Rickels, the story "represents the most notable achievement of the time in reproducing the character of the American frontiersmen." No other tall tales of Thorpe's time surpasses "The Big Bear of Arkansas" in its "complexity of structure and richness of content" (50–1). Norris W. Yates comments that the "epic breadth and dramatic conflict" in the "The Big Bear of Arkansas" come from "the vital personality of the narrator and his somewhat awed feeling 'that bar was an unhuntable bar, and died when his time come' " (175–6). To J. A. Leo Lemay, Thorpe's piece is clearly "the classic story . . . of the humor of the Old Southwest"; the power of the story comes from Thorpe's "use of traditional symbols and mythic archetypes operating within an intellectually complex fictive world" (322, 341). John Caldwell Guilds considers "The Big Bear of Arkansas" as "the story that of all Arkansas literature best captures the spirit, the symbolism, the mythology of the state"; it is "a masterpiece of its kind" (139). Regarding *The Hive of "The Bee-Hunter,"* Milton Rickels notes that in content and writing style the volume is better than any other books written by the author (178). Alexander Nicolas DeMenil identifies Thorpe's Tom Owen, the bee-hunter, as "a famous character in the *antebellum* fiction of the country" (138).

Criticism on Thorpe's novel and three volumes of nonfiction have been rare and mostly unfavorable. Milton Rickels comments that the progression of the plot in *The Master's House* is awkward and loose (181). Several critics have discussed Thorpe's attitude toward the institution of slavery in the novel. In Shields McIlwaine's opinion, the author was "essentially the early anti-slavery man of the Old South" although he opposed radical social changes (23). Rickels concurs with McIlwaine's view, pointing out that Jennette Tandy in her article "Pro-Slavery Propaganda in American Fiction of the Fifties" and Francis Pendleton Gaines in his book *The Southern Plantation* both erroneously identify the novel as a pro-slavery one; he notes that Thorpe "did not accept the institution of slavery as morally defensible or as good for either the master or the slave" (183). Rickels notes that Thorpe's ideas in *Our Army on the Rio Grande* consist mostly of "intellectual clichés or emotional commonplaces"; that the careless form of *Our Army at Monterey* diminishes the value of its content; and that in *The Taylor Anecdote Book* Thorpe's evaluations of General Taylor are "campaign propaganda before they are biography" (124, 149, 155).

WORKS CITED

DeMenil, Alexander Nicolas. *The Literature of the Louisiana Territory.* St. Louis, MO: St. Louis News Company, 1904.

Gaines, Francis Pendleton. *The Southern Plantation: A Study in the Development and the Accuracy of a Tradition.* New York: Columbia University Press, 1924.

Guilds, John Caldwell. *Arkansas, Arkansas: Writers and Writings from the Delta to the Ozarks 1541–1969.* Fayetteville: University of Arkansas Press, 1999. Vol. 1.

Lemay, J. A. Leo. "The Text, Tradition, and Themes of 'The Big Bear of Arkansas.' " *American Literature* 47 (1975): 321–42.

McIlwaine, Shields. *The Southern Poor-White: From Lubberland to Tobacco Road.* Norman: University of Oklahoma Press, 1939.

Meine, Franklin. Introduction. *Tall Tales of the Southwest: An Anthology of Southern and Southwestern Humor 1830–1860.* Ed. Franklin Meine. New York: Alfred A. Knopf, 1930. xv–xxxii.

Rickels, Milton. *Thomas Bangs Thorpe: Humorist of the Old Southwest.* Baton Rouge: Louisiana State University Press, 1962.

Yates, Norris W. *William T. Porter and the Spirit of the Times: A Study of the Big Bear School of Humor.* Baton Rouge: Louisiana State University Press, 1957.

BIBLIOGRAPHY

Works by Thomas Bangs Thorpe

Tales and Sketches
The Big Bear of Arkansas, and Other Sketches, Illustrative of Characters and Incidents in the South and Southwest. Philadelphia: Carey & Hart, 1845.

The Mysteries of the Backwoods; or Sketches of the Southwest: Including Character, Scenery, and Rural Sports. Philadelphia: Carey & Hart, 1846.

The Hive of "The Bee-Hunter": A Repository of Sketches, Including Peculiar American Character, Scenery, and Rural Sports. New York: D. Appleton, 1854.

Novel
The Master's House; A Tale of Southern Life. New York: T. L. McElrath, 1854.

Nonfiction
Our Army on the Rio Grande. Philadelphia: Carey & Hart, 1846.
Our Army at Monterey. Philadelphia: Carey & Hart, 1847.
The Taylor Anecdote Book. Anecdotes and Letters of Zachary Taylor. New York: D. Appleton, 1848.
Reminiscences of Charles L. Elliott, Artist. New York: Evening Post, 1868.

Studies of Thomas Bangs Thorpe

DeMenil, Alexander Nicolas. *The Literature of the Louisiana Territory.* St. Louis, MO: St. Louis News Company, 1904.

Gaines, Francis Pendleton. *The Southern Plantation: A Study in the Development and the Accuracy of a Tradition.* New York: Columbia University Press, 1924.

Guilds, John Caldwell. *Arkansas, Arkansas: Writers and Writings from the Delta to the Ozarks 1541–1969.* Fayetteville: University of Arkansas Press, 1999. Vol. 1.

Lemay, J. A. Leo. "The Text, Tradition, and Themes of 'The Big Bear of Arkansas.' " *American Literature* 47 (1975): 321–42.

McIlwaine, Shields. *The Southern Poor-White: From Lubberland to Tobacco Road.* Norman: University of Oklahoma Press, 1939.

Meine, Franklin. Introduction. *Tall Tales of the Southwest: An Anthology of Southern and Southwestern Humor 1830–1860.* Ed. Franklin Meine. New York: Alfred A. Knopf, 1930. xv–xxxii.

Rickels, Milton. *Thomas Bangs Thorpe: Humorist of the Old Southwest.* Baton Rouge: Louisiana State University Press, 1962.

Tandy, Jennette. "Pro-Slavery Propaganda in American Fiction of the Fifties." *South Atlantic Quarterly* 3 (1922): 48–69.

Yates, Norris W. *William T. Porter and the Spirit of the Times: A Study of the Big Bear School of Humor.* Baton Rouge: Louisiana State University Press, 1957.

HENRY TIMROD (1828–1867)

Geoff Bender

BIOGRAPHY

Henry Timrod was born in Charleston, South Carolina, on December 8, 1828, to William Henry Timrod and Thyrza (Prince) Timrod. He was the third of four children. William was a bookbinder whose shop became an informal gathering spot for Charleston's intellectuals. A minor poet in his own right, William is best known for his ode, "Sons of the Union," written in response to the Nullification controversy of 1832–33.

By 1836, Henry was enrolled at a small school run by the German Friendly Society. By 1840, he had transferred to Christopher Coates' prestigious Classical School, where he met Paul Hamilton Hayne. Hayne, a well-known southern poet of his day, became Timrod's lifelong friend and a champion of his work after Timrod's untimely death. In January 1845, Timrod entered the University of Georgia in Athens at the beginning of the second term. He was evidently better prepared than many of his peers, for he entered as a sophomore. Due to poor health and financial struggle, Timrod was forced to withdraw from the university sometime before August 1846.

A young man with little means, Henry Timrod returned to Charleston to become an apprentice to the well-known attorney, James Louis Petigru. In 1850, however, Timrod left Petigru, feeling unsuited to the law, and began work as a private tutor in low-country plantations. He continued this work, with intermittent stints as a teacher and clerk, for over a decade. Meanwhile, Timrod began to make a name for himself as a poet. In January 1849, he started to contribute poetry to the *Southern Literary Messenger* under the pseudonym "Aglaus." By the early 1850s, Timrod was frequenting the back room of John Russell's bookshop, a place popular among Charleston's literati. Out of this back room was born *Russell's Magazine,* designed as a superior rival to William Gilmore Simms's *Southern Quarterly Review.* The first issue emerged in April 1857, carrying Timrod's narrative poem, "The Arctic Voyager." Timrod contributed to *Russell's* regularly thereafter. By 1859, he had collected enough work to publish his first volume of poetry. The book, whose thematic material was inspired largely by English Romanticism, received little national attention, and the copies from the first printing did not sell out during Timrod's lifetime. In 1861, however, the South's shifting political landscape gave Timrod the material to shape a more authentic expression.

On February 8, 1861, a provisional Confederate Congress met in Montgomery, Alabama. On February 23, Charleston's *Daily Courier* carried a poem by Timrod, "Ode on Occasion of the Meeting of the Southern Congress," which he later titled "Ethnogenesis," his first significant war poem. Another ode, "Cotton Boll," followed in the summer of that year. Together, they optimistically praised southern nationalism and imagined a glorious future for the newborn Confederacy. By July, Timrod had enlisted in a military company whose aim was to defend the Beaufort coastline, and in early 1862, he joined the Thirtieth South Carolina Regiment.

In April 1862, on a three-month leave of absence, Timrod set out for the western front as a war correspondent for the Charleston *Mercury*. This was to be a decisive experience in Timrod's evolving view of the war. Once there he participated in the Confederate retreat from Shiloh. Close observation of the bloody battlefield, of war's sheer destructive capacity, muted Timrod's strident nationalism and complicated his understanding of war's consequences. In "Charleston," written later that year and under the threat of Union naval assault on his home city, Timrod imagines a less certain military outcome while maintaining the city's unquestionable nobility in the face of mounting adversity. And in "Christmas," published in December 1862, Timrod concludes with a fervent wish not for victory but for simple peace. In that same month, he was discharged from the Confederate Army due to ill health.

After a feeble attempt to re-enlist in the summer of 1863—he lasted a single day in military service before a tubercular hemorrhage necessitated his withdrawal—Henry Timrod joined the Charleston *Mercury* as assistant editor. He moved to Columbia in early 1864 to become an associate editor and partner in the Daily South Carolinian. In Columbia, he delivered a lecture before the Methodist Female College that was to become his most famous essay, "A Theory of Poetry." Soon after, on February 16, 1864, Timrod married Katie Goodwin. They had one child, Willie, who was born on Christmas Eve, 1864; he lived less than a year.

On February 17, 1865, Union troops sacked Columbia and Timrod hid, briefly, fearing northern retaliation for his outspoken southern nationalism. He returned to a city destroyed, and his personal prospects followed suit. In 1866, after finding no lucrative position at the *Daily South Carolinian*, Timrod briefly worked as a private secretary to Governor James L. Orr. At this time Timrod wrote what many critics consider his finest poem, simply titled "Ode," designed to be sung at the Magnolia Cemetery in Charleston on June 16, 1866, in praise of the fallen Confederate dead. In spite of his local literary success, Timrod failed to interest New York publishers in his work. His health failing, he retired to Copse Hill, near Augusta, Georgia, to convalesce in the company of his old friend, Paul Hamilton Hayne. His health was not long restored, however. In 1867, amidst a flurry of plans for further newspaper work and perhaps another book, Henry Timrod lost his life to a consumption that he had fought for over a decade. He died on October 7 and was buried at the Trinity Church cemetery, in Columbia, beside the body of his son.

MAJOR WORKS AND THEMES

Although Henry Timrod could be described, at best, as a "lukewarm secessionist," it is the South's act of secession from the Union that created the circumstances out of which Timrod's best poetry emerged (Parks 91; Rubin 219). Nevertheless, the moniker by which he is often known, "the Laureate of the Confederacy" (Parks 115), belies the scope of his war poetry. As described briefly above, Timrod's attitude toward southern independence and the nature of war as a means to secure that independence evolved significantly over the course of his wartime experience. The brief review that follows will endeavor to trace the broad contours in his evolving views through the lenses of a few key poems.

As mentioned, Timrod's initial odes, "Ethnogenesis" and "Cotton Boll," ring with an almost unremitting optimism for a Confederate future and stake the South's moral claim to victory. However, it is important to note that Timrod's expression of a utopian vision of nationhood, seeking to "give labor to the poor" (*Collected* 95) through the mechanism of a cotton-based economy, remains wholly unreflective of the moral implications of the institution of slavery, which enabled such an economy to thrive. Chattel slavery, though a primary cause of the war, is a topic that Timrod never openly addressed. His defense of the war is rather rooted in a regional loyalty that approaches religious zeal in its intensity, best illustrated in "Carolina" with the very first line: "The despot treads thy sacred sands" (*Collected* 109).

As the carnage of war mounted, however, and Timrod witnessed first-hand the physical toll it could take, the tone of his work becomes notably more mournful. In "Spring," for example, first published in April 1863, the poet located, amidst a pastoral scene of vernal awakening, the startling presence of the war dead brought in by the western wind. The eerie juxtaposition is heightened by the shocking image, placed near the end of the poem, of a field of "bloody daisies" lifting from a blood-soaked, battle-weary earth (*Collected* 124). In "The Unknown Dead," published later that year, on July 4—the day Grant gained Vicksburg and Lee began to retreat to Virginia after losing at Gettysburg—the speaker laments the lives lost to history: soldiers of common families, buried in unmarked graves, whose names will soon be forgotten to all but a few loved ones and the cold statistics of war casualties. While Timrod's meditations on the fallen dead do not entirely obfuscate his nationalistic sentiments—for these soldiers were, to him, "true martyrs of the fight" (*Collected* 126)—they do complicate his understanding of "martyrdom" beyond the wooden rhetoric of his earlier patriotism.

The problem of reconciling the tragedy of war death with the wounded pride of a defeated army is most poignantly captured in his last important war poem, "Ode." Critic John Budd considers this poem to be the "epitome of the desperation of Timrod and of the Southern people" (444). In an attempt to rebound from desperation and find, instead, a unified response to an irreconcilably fragmenting experience, Timrod resorted to a much quieter religious patriotism when he argued, at the poem's conclusion, that the holiest ground is found "where defeated valor lies" (*Collected* 130).

CRITICAL RECEPTION

In spite of Timrod's frantic publishing efforts at the end of his life, his war poetry remained uncollected until 1873, when his close friend Paul Hamilton Hayne assembled it, together with some of Timrod's other lyrics, in a volume that he prefaced with a long memoir. The book sold well, for the second edition appeared a few months after the first. Although the work elicited some praise from the North, notably from Richard Henry Stoddard and John Greenleaf Whittier, national attention soon moved on.

The year 1899, however, saw the commencement of a Timrod revival. The Timrod Memorial Association brought out a Memorial Edition of his work that year, which included 82 poems, 73 from Hayne's 1873 text. Four thousand copies of this volume sold and, again, it garnered some national critical attention. Nevertheless, concerted scholarly interest in Henry Timrod did not begin in earnest until the 1940s, with the publication of *The Last Years of Henry Timrod* (1941), a study by Jay B. Hubbell; *The Uncollected Poems of Henry Timrod* (1942), edited by Guy A. Cardwell Jr.; and *The Essays of Henry Timrod* (1942), edited by Edd Winfield Parks. To this day, interest in the work of Henry Timrod seems largely confined to scholars of southern writers.

WORKS CITED

Budd, John. "Henry Timrod: Poetic Voice of Southern Nationalism." *Southern Studies: An Interdisciplinary Journal of the South* 20, no. 4 (1981): 437–46.

Parks, Edd Winfield. *Henry Timrod.* New York: Twayne, 1964.

Rubin, Louis D., Jr. *The Edge of the Swamp: A Study in the Literature and Society of the Old South.* Baton Rouge: Louisiana State UP, 1989.

Timrod, Henry. *The Collected Poems of Henry Timrod.* Eds. Edd Winfield Parks and Aileen Wells Parks. Athens: U of Georgia P, 1965.

BIBLIOGRAPHY

Works by Henry Timrod

Poems. Boston: Ticknor, 1859.

The Poems of Henry Timrod. Ed. Paul H. Hayne. New York: Hale, 1873.

Poems of Henry Timrod. Memorial Edition. 1899. Richmond: Johnson, 1901.

The Essays of Henry Timrod. Ed. Edd Winfield Parks. Athens: U of Georgia P, 1942.

The Uncollected Poems of Henry Timrod. Ed. Guy A. Cardwell Jr. Athens: U of Georgia P, 1942.

The Collected Poems of Henry Timrod. Eds. Edd Winfield Parks and Aileen Wells Parks. Athens: U of Georgia P, 1965.

Studies of Henry Timrod

Budd, John. "Henry Timrod: Poetic Voice of Southern Nationalism." *Southern Studies: An Interdisciplinary Journal of the South* 20, no. 4 (1981): 437–46.

De Bellis, Jack. *Sidney Lanier, Henry Timrod, and Paul Hamilton Hayne: A Reference Guide.* Boston: Hall, 1978.

Green, Claud B. "Henry Timrod and the South." *The South Carolina Review* 2, no. 2 (1970): 27–33.

Hubbell, Jay B., ed. *The Last Years of Henry Timrod.* 1941. New York: AMS P, 1966.

Murphy, Christina. "The Artistic Design of Societal Commitment: Shakespeare and the Poetry of Henry Timrod." *Shakespeare and Southern Writers: A Study of Influence.* Ed. Philip C. Kolin. Jackson: UP of Mississippi, 1985.

Parks, Edd Winfield. *Ante-Bellum Southern Literary Critics.* Athens: U of Georgia P, 1962.

———. *Henry Timrod.* New York: Twayne, 1964.

Rubin, Louis D., Jr. *The Edge of the Swamp: A Study in the Literature and Society of the Old South.* Baton Rouge: Louisiana State UP, 1989.

SOJOURNER TRUTH (c. 1797?–1883)

Lori N. Howard

BIOGRAPHY

Sojourner Truth was born circa 1797, second youngest of the 10 or 12 children of James "Bomefree" and Betsey "Mau-mau Bett," slaves owned by Colonel Johannes Hardenbergh and then by his son Charles Hardenbergh in Rosendale, Ulster County, New York. She remembered most of her brothers and sisters only faintly because the Hardenberghs had sold them either before her birth or while she was a baby. Truth, whose birth name was Isabella, lived with her parents and her younger brother Peter until she too was sold at approximately the age of nine after Charles Hardenbergh's death (Painter 11). The Hardenbergh family freed James and Betsey after their owner's death, but Sojourner and Peter were sold to new masters. John Nealy (or Neely) bought the young girl, who suffered her worst treatment in his household. Misunderstandings arose between Truth and Nealy's wife because Truth did not understand English. Her first language was Dutch, the language of Ulster County's settlers; she learned English only after being sold to Nealy (Fitch 11).

Betsey instilled a belief in God in her children, but Truth had no formal religious or biblical education. In the *Narrative of Sojourner Truth,* she explains that she prayed her father would come to her at Nealy's and find her a new master; she got her wish. James did visit, and then Martin Scriver bought Truth; she worked for him for about a year and a half (Truth and Gilbert 28). John J. Dumont bought Truth from Scriver and took her to New Paltz, New York, where she lived and worked on the Dumont farm from 1810 to 1826. While owned by Dumont, Truth lived with his slave Thomas, who probably fathered her five children. She referred to having a second husband, possibly a slave named Robert who lived near the Dumonts. Four of Truth's children are confirmed by census data: Diana, Elizabeth, Sophia, and Peter; a fifth child may have died in infancy (Fitch 12).

In 1817, the state of New York passed a law freeing all slaves born before 1799 when they reached specified ages. Truth's emancipation from Dumont should have occurred on July 4, 1827. A broken promise from Dumont about an earlier release prompted Truth to walk away from her owner's home one night in the fall of 1826 to freedom. Isaac S. and Maria Van Wagenen took her in after her flight from slavery; the Van Wagenens had to buy out the remaining term of her enslavement so that she would not have to return to Dumont. Her gratitude toward and respect for the family is evident in Truth's adoption at that time of the family's surname.

Truth's path to preaching started in her childhood when Mau-mau Bett taught Isabella and Peter about a heavenly father who would protect them even if they were separated from their parents and each other. After emancipation, Truth moved to New York City to pursue religious studies, where she spent time in the corrupt mystic Robert "Matthias" Matthews's religious community. Upon recognizing Matthias's immoral and materialistic nature, she followed God's direction and left the city to start a lifetime of itinerant preaching as "Sojourner Truth," because she was to travel the land sharing God's truth (Stewart xxxviii). She preached at various meetings in New England and then joined the Northampton Association of Education and Industry, a Transcendentalist commune in Northampton, Massachusetts, and settled in the area for a few years after the community disbanded. There Truth met Olive Gilbert, to whom she would dictate the *Narrative*. Her involvement with the antislavery cause also began during this period.

Truth's *Narrative* was first published in 1850, and she began speaking for the antislavery cause at about this time, lecturing and promoting her autobiography. She settled down in Battle Creek, Michigan, in the late 1850s, but continued to travel the United States, preaching and singing, until the early 1880s. Her last documented lecture was given on October 31, 1882, in Michigan. Truth died on November 26, 1883, and is buried in Battle Creek (Finch 12, 226).

MAJOR WORKS AND THEMES

Truth was illiterate, so she dictated her story to her friend Olive Gilbert, whose own opinions color the memoir. Frances Titus edited the "Book of Life" section that was added later. The first third of the *Narrative* graphically details Truth's life as a slave and the beginning of her religious journey. The bulk of the memoir focuses on her life after emancipation, including her successful lawsuit to emancipate her son Peter who was illegally taken to Alabama; her spiritualism; her experiences with various religious groups; and the beginning of her speaking career. The *Narrative* provides the basis for her public appearances, during which she preached and sang in support of a range of causes including the end of slavery, women's rights, woman's suffrage, and temperance.

Truth's faith and religious fervor run through both the *Narrative* and her recorded speeches. She was known for her persuasive rhetorical style, for an unflagging dignity, and for using humor and a sharp wit to expose people who hid behind religion to support slavery or deny equal rights. Many of Truth's speeches were published, including her most famous given at the May 1851 Women's Rights Convention in Akron, Ohio. Several conflicting texts of the "Ain't I a Woman?" speech exist, some giving Truth a southern slave's dialect. The month after Truth spoke in Akron, the speech was published in the *Anti-Slavery Bugle* and reported in part in the *New York Tribune* and the *Liberator.* Twelve years later, the convention's head officer, Frances D. Gage, published a version in the *National Anti-Slavery Standard* that first reported the repeated line, "Ar'n't I a woman?". Regardless of the exact wording of the text, it is a landmark in Truth's career because it joins her two most important causes: abolishing slavery and women's rights.

CRITICAL RECEPTION

The *Narrative* received little critical attention at the time of its publication, but many reactions to Truth's speeches survive. For example, a reporter for the *Detroit Post* described the speaker as "Keen and quick-witted, with a memory that never dropped a single thread, she was always ready with an answer that went straight to the mark, and often withered her opponent into silence" ("Sojourner Truth" 4). Truth was known for her strong rhetorical ability to grab and keep a crowd's attention, her ease in disabling hecklers, and the riveting hymns, or sorrow songs, that she would sing at the beginning or close of her speeches.

Harriet Beecher Stowe secured Truth's renown with her April 1863 article in the *Atlantic Monthly,* "Sojourner Truth, the Libyan Sibyl." Stowe described Truth as "perfectly self-possessed and at her ease; in fact, there was almost an unconscious superiority, not unmixed with a solemn twinkle of humor, in the odd, composed manner in which she looked down on me" (Stowe 152). Stowe's presentation of Truth combated the distorted image created by Olive Gilbert's rendering of her in the *Narrative.* Jeffrey C. Stewart suggests that, "Like many another amanuensis for former slaves, Gilbert was trapped in her paternalistic view of slaves and was unable to respect Sojourner's superior moral and spiritual sensibilities" (xl).

Very little critical work was produced on the *Narrative of Sojourner Truth* until it was reprinted in the 1990s. Henry Louis Gates Jr. included the *Narrative* in the Schomburg Library of Nineteenth-Century Black Women Writers; Oxford University Press published the Schomburg edition in 1991. The resulting critical work has examined many facets of Sojourner Truth's legacy including her autobiography, spiritual life, career as an orator, and rhetorical strategies. Most critics of the twentieth and twenty-first century are skeptical of the filtered presentation of Truth's *Narrative* and of the transcriptions of her speeches. Jean Humez notes that although the *Narrative* "contains only the skeletal structure of the full spiritual autobiography that we might have had if Truth had had direct access to the pen, there is still plenty of rich material, particularly in the core stories, that illuminates Truth's midlife understanding of her religious experience" (36). Even with the interference of the writers that put Truth's words into print, the value of her life story as a northern slave narrative, spiritual autobiography, and protest manifesto is evident.

WORKS CITED

Fitch, Suzanne Pullon, and Roseann M. Mandziuk. *Sojourner Truth as Orator: Wit, Story, and Song.* Westport, CT: Greenwood P, 1997.

Humez, Jean. "Reading the Narrative of Sojourner Truth as a Collaborative Text." *Frontiers: A Journal of Women Studies* 16.1 (1996): 29–52.

Painter, Nell Irvin. *Sojourner Truth: A Life, A Symbol.* New York: Norton, 1996.

"Sojourner Truth." *Detroit Post.* 26 June 1871: 4.

Stewart, Jeffrey C. "Introduction." *Narrative of Sojourner Truth.* New York: Oxford UP, 1991.

Stowe, Harriet Beecher. "Sojourner Truth, the Libyan Sibyl." 1863. Rpt. *Narrative of Sojourner Truth.* New York: Oxford UP, 1991.

Truth, Sojourner, and Olive Gilbert. *Narrative of Sojourner Truth: A Bondswoman of Olden Time.* Battle Creek, MI: 1881.

BIBLIOGRAPHY

Works by Sojourner Truth

(With Olive Gilbert). *Narrative of Sojourner Truth: A Bondswoman of Olden Time, Emancipated by the New York Legislature in the Early Part of the Present Century; with a History of Her Labors and Correspondence Drawn from Her "Book of Life."* Battle Creek, MI: 1878. Rpt. New York: Oxford UP, 1991.

Studies of Sojourner Truth

Alliaume, Karen Trimble. "The Risks of Repeating Ourselves: Reading Feminist/Womanist Figures of Jesus." *Cross Currents: The Journal of the Association for Religion and Intellectual Life* 48.2 (1998): 198–217.

Asher, Sandra. *A Woman Called Truth: A Play in Two Acts Celebrating the Life of Sojourner Truth.* Woodstock, IL: Dramatic P, 1993.

Fitch, Suzanne Pullon, and Roseann M. Mandziuk. *Sojourner Truth as Orator: Wit, Story, and Song.* Westport, CT: Greenwood P, 1997.

Humez, Jean. "Reading the Narrative of Sojourner Truth as a Collaborative Text." *Frontiers: A Journal of Women Studies* 16.1 (1996): 29–52.

Joseph, Gloria I. "Sojourner Truth: Archetypal Black Feminist." *Wild Women in the Whirlwind.* Ed. Joanne Braxton and Andrée McLaughlin. New Brunswick, NJ: Rutgers UP, 1990. 35–47.

Krieg, Joann P. "Whitman and Sojourner Truth." *Walt Whitman Quarterly Review* 16.1 (1998): 32–6.

Lipscomb, Drema R. "Sojourner Truth: A Practical Public Discourse." *Reclaiming Rhetorica: Women in the Rhetorical Tradition.* Ed. Andrea A. Lunsford. Pittsburgh, PA: U of Pittsburgh P, 1995. 227–45.

Mabee, Carleton, and Susan Mabee Newhouse. *Sojourner Truth: Slave, Prophet, Legend.* New York: New York UP, 1993.

Mandziuk, Roseann M., and Suzanne Pullon Fitch. "The Rhetorical Construction of Sojourner Truth." *Southern Communication Journal* 66.2 (2001): 120–38.

Massa, Suzanne Hotte. "Sojourner Truth (1797, 1800?–1883)." *African American Authors, 1745–1945: A Bio-Bibliographical Critical Sourcebook.* Ed. and preface Emmanuel S. Nelson. Westport, CT: Greenwood, 2000. 418–23.

McKissack, Patricia C., and Frederick McKissack. *Sojourner Truth: Ain't I a Woman?* New York: Scholastic, 1992.

Painter, Nell Irvin. *Sojourner Truth: A Life, A Symbol.* New York: Norton, 1996.

———. "Sojourner Truth's Religion in Her Moment of Pentecostalism and Witchcraft." *Spellbound: Women and Witchcraft in America.* Ed. Elizabeth Reis. Wilmington, DE: Scholarly Resources, 1998. 145–55.

Sachez-Eppler, Karen. "Ain't I a Symbol?" *American Quarterly* 50.1 (1998): 149–57.

Stowe, Harriet Beecher. "Sojourner Truth, the Libyan Sibyl." *Atlantic Monthly* April 1863: 473–80.

Yellin, Jean Fagan. *Women & Sisters: Antislavery Feminists in American Culture.* New Haven: Yale UP, 1989.

JONES VERY (1813–1880)

Aleta Cane

BIOGRAPHY

Born in Salem, Massachusetts, August 18, 1813, Jones Very was the first of four sons and two daughters of a sea captain, Jones Very, and his first cousin, Lydia. While Captain Very was at sea, Mrs. Jones passionately tended her gardens by day and wrote poetry and read late into the evenings. The young Jones Very was a contemporary and neighbor of Nathaniel Hawthorne. The trajectories of their lives were similar: in the early losses of their seafaring fathers; their tendency toward solitude; their abiding interests in literature; and their literary friends and mentors.

At age nine the younger Very served as his father's cabin boy on a voyage that allowed them to visit Elsinor Castle, a visit that would hold significance for the poet in later life. During a second voyage together, to New Orleans, they met Captain Cook, about whom Very would later write a sonnet. Their return to Salem coincided with the town's celebration of the visit of Lafayette. Shortly thereafter, and in quick succession, the family suffered the deaths of Captain Very and Lydia's father, Charles. A rift developed between Charles's widow and Lydia over the contents of his will. Taken to court by her father's second wife, Lydia won a case against the complaint that she had concealed monies named in the will.

The shy and solitary Very was awarded a prize for his academic work in 1826 but in 1827 he was forced to leave school to help support the family. He was an errand boy at an auction house in Salem. There, he discovered and bought a rare Shakespeare volume, which he subsequently sold to purchase needed texts to prepare himself for entry into Harvard College. He obtained a teaching post at a private school presided over by Henry Oliver, who tutored Very so well that he was able to enter Harvard as a sophomore.

Very was encouraged in his writing of poetry by his tutors and published poems in the *Salem Observer* beginning in August 1833. His second poem, in heroic couplets, excoriated the evils of slavery. That poem demonstrates the influence on Very of Goldsmith and Crabbe.

When Very entered Harvard in 1834, he broke the family's link to the sea just as Salem itself began to turn to nonmaritime pursuits. Very's age and his self-reliance made him a receptive scholar. He continued to contribute verses to the *Observer*. His third published poem, in blank verse, shows a Wordsworthian influence in its theme—the presence of God in nature. The poem is also notable for what Lawrence Buell has identified as a hallmark of Transcendental verse, its reliance on aphorism.

A brief hiatus from college found him at home writing poetry. He published "The Death of Lafayette" in the *Observer* which, by 1834, had published five of Very's submissions. In his poem about his sick brother, Franklin, the child catches a bee in the garden, which is emblematic of vice, and the boy's experience symbolizes all human experience. Very did not publish again until he returned to Harvard in January 1835, where he submitted eight poems for the student magazine, *Harvardiana*. He graduated third in his class and delivered the English oration, entitled "Individuality," at commencement. It was a preview of several of his mature themes of intellectual independence and religious fervor.

Very met Elizabeth Peabody in Salem. She was a friend of Emerson's, a passionate abolitionist, and a Unitarian. She was familiar with William Ellery Channing, Bronson Alcott, and Margaret Fuller and introduced them to Very. Emerson was much taken by Very's purity of soul and clarity of expression and mentored him in his writing.

At college, Very had been a fine Greek scholar and was appointed a Greek tutor at Harvard in 1836. By then he had decided to prepare for the ministry. His tutor's job paid his Divinity School fees. He was a self-assured young man who took great personal interest in his students, often visiting them in their rooms and walking and talking with them. Thoreau was one of his favorite students.

Over time, Very became more religious. He perceived God to be an ever-present spirit, flowing into all receptive nature and individuals. He worked to become more receptive and worthy of God's presence in his life. His poem, "The Voice of God," affirms his resolve. His fervor became monomania and led him to assert that God had revealed Himself to him, giving him a message for New England youth. Many of Very's students saw in him an ascetic figure who deserved the designation of "saint." However, the faculty and administration at Harvard were distressed by his utterances.

Jones Very articulated the belief that he was the Second Coming incarnate and was committed to McLean's Hospital for a monthlong treatment. There he met the Reverend J. F. Clarke who edited the *Western Messenger* magazine. Very submitted several poems to the magazine, and the March 1839 issue contained nine Very poems. In time, the *Messenger* would publish 40 of his religious verses. Emerson encouraged Very to publish a book of his poetry but Very demurred, saying that the words were God's and to sign his name to them would be irreverent. Nonetheless, Emerson prevailed and edited the poems and essays himself. At the completion of the editing, Emerson wrote to Elizabeth Peabody saying that he expected the book to be "a little gem of a volume" (Bartlett 67).

The book, *Three Essays and Verses,* contained 65 poems and three literary essays and was published by Little Brown in Boston in September 1839. He tried to convert his friends and acquaintances to his vision of Christ, yet remained without disciples and alienated many of his friends and patrons. Emerson was to call him his "brave saint" (qtd. in Bartlett 78) but personally withdrew from him. Very spent the rest of his life as an itinerant preacher and in writing religious poetry at the family home in Salem where he died in 1880.

MAJOR WORKS AND THEMES

In both his poetry and published prose Very focuses on one overriding theme: the apprehension and celebration of Christ in nature and in all human endeavor. For example, in his essay, "Hamlet," he argues that Hamlet never found happiness because his mind "could never reach the assurance of external existence which Christ alone can give" (Bartlett 78). Life failed to satisfy Hamlet because it was ephemeral. Very argued that Hamlet's "To be or not to be" soliloquy explained the poet's own longing for the transcendent experience (Bartlett 78).

The poems are divisible into three thematic groups: poems of nature, poems of religion, and autobiographical poems (of which there are but a few). Very's nature poems, such as "The Hummingbird," underscore the poet's sympathy with the natural world. Like Bryant's poetry, Very's celebrates American flowers and birds. Very sees them as emblematic of God's work in America. Bartlett views this as "Very's unique contribution to American literature" (84). The poem, "Columbine," demonstrates how Very placed himself in the natural world as he gazes at the flower. In "The Song" he praises nature without preaching while remarking on an idealized youth. A poem as lovely as this, remarks Bartlett, made him seem less "repelantly . . . Puritan" (87), whereas the poem "Life" shows Very's deep longing to be with his God: "To grow fixed with deeper roots in Thee," he prays. As he became more involved in his spiritual quest his poetry became more mystical so that in "The Prisoner," he perceives God in his own room.

CRITICAL RECEPTION

Margaret Fuller published the first review of Very's book in *The Boston Quarterly Review* for January 1840. "In these little poems . . . you will find an elasticity of spirit, a genuine flow of thought and unsought nobleness and purity almost unknown amid the factitious sentiment and weak movement of our overaught over ambitious literature, if indeed we can say we have one" (Bartlett 103). Emerson wrote for the June 16, 1841, edition of the *Dial* that Very "casts himself into the state of the high and transcendental obedience to the inward spirit" and that "the verses rather flow through him than from him" (Bartlett 105). Richard Henry Dana commended the poems to Bryant, calling them "quite apart in poetic merit" containing within "extraordinary grace and originality" (Bartlett 107).

William P. Andrews reviewed a new edition of Very's verse that appeared from Houghton Mifflin in 1883. Writing in *The Literary World* for June 1883, he notes that Very compared favorably with Blake, Herbert, and Swedenborg. Taking some of the poems to task for repetitious thematic material, he concludes, however, that "evidence of original power, genuine feeling and unconscious art" suffuse the volume. An unsigned review of the same volume which first appeared in the *New York Tribune* and was reprinted in *The Boston Evening Transcript* for August 28, 1883, opines that Very's poetry is a blend of "Buddhist ecstasy and a sweet sedate Puritanism" (Bartlett 107).

Louis Untermeyer, writing in the preface to his *American Poetry from the Beginning to Whitman* (1931), compares Very and T. H. Chivers as "two independents, who scorned in their time, are now recognized as geniuses" (Bartlett 38). Contemporary reappraisal of Very's oeuvre can be summed up by Lawrence Buell's observation that Very's poems administer their best "electric jolt" when they display his "prophetic rage" (103).

WORKS CITED

Bartlett, William. *Jones Very, Emerson's "Brave Saint."* New York: Greenwood, 1968.
Buell, Lawrence. "The American Transcendentalist Poets." *The Columbia History of American Poetry.* Ed. Jay Parini. New York: Columbia University Press, 1993. 97–120.

BIBLIOGRAPHY

Works by Jones Very

Jones Very: The Complete Poems. Ed. Helen Deese. Athens: Georgia University Press, 1993.
Poems of Jones Very. Ed. James Freeman Clarke. Boston: Houghton Miflin, 1886.
Very, Jones. *Three Essays and Verses.* Boston: Little Brown, 1839.

Studies of Jones Very

Cameron, Kenneth Walter. *Lowell, Whittier, Very and the Alcotts Among Their Contemporaries: A Harvest of Estimates, Insights and Anecdotes from the Victorian Literary World and Index.* Hartford: Transcendental Books, 1978.
Clayton, Sarah Turner. *The Angelic Sins of Jones Very.* New York: Peter Lang, 1999.
Cole, Phyllis. "Jones Very's 'Epistle to the Unborn.' " *Studies in the American Renaissance* (1982): 160–83.
Deese, Helen. "A Calendar of the Poems of Jones Very." *Studies in the American Renaissance* (1986): 305–72.
———. "The Peabody Family and the Jones Very 'Insanity': Two Letters of Mary Peabody." *Harvard Library Bulletin* 35.2 (1987): 218–29.
———. "Selected Sermons of Jones Very." *Studies in the American Renaissance* (1984): 1–78.
———. "Unpublished and Uncollected Poems of Jones Very." *ESQ* 30.3 (1984): 154–62.
Gittleman, Edwin. *Jones Very: The Effective Years, 1833–1840.* New York: Columbia University Press, 1967.
Robinson, David. "Jones Very." *The Transcendentalists: A Review of Research and Criticism.* Ed. Joel Myerson. New York: MLA, 1984.
Seed, David. "Alone with God and Nature: The Poetry of Jones Very and Frederick Goddard Tuckerman." *Nineteenth Century American Poetry.* Totowa, NJ: Barnes and Noble, 1985.

SUSAN WARNER (1819–1885)

Jana L. Argersinger

BIOGRAPHY

Susan Bogert Warner was born in New York on July 11, 1819, to Henry and Anna Bartlett Warner. Her paternal family traced its ancestry to the *Mayflower;* after the Revolution, her grandparents settled in Canaan, New York, where they raised a large family and sustained themselves mostly by farming. Henry, with older brother Thomas, left the plough to make his way through college, and after studying law launched a practice in New York City. Anna Bartlett's family boasted similarly longstanding American roots, but their affluence joined with Anna's gender apparently precluded the opportunity and burden of self-creation that presented itself to the Warner boys. In 1817 Anna married Henry and, shortly after, Susan arrived. The loss of three small children concentrated the couple's love on this daughter, until the birth of another in the mid-1820s—a devotion that likely made fertile ground for the lofty will that took hold in Susan; younger sister Anna (named for the mother) observes in her biography that Susan had a lifelong, self-confessed "relish for the right of way that might have served a boy" (*Susan Warner* 34).

When the mother died early, Henry's sister Frances came to take her place, and as Henry prospered, the family enjoyed the ease and culture that money afforded, moving in 1835 to an elegant home on St. Mark's Place. On the walls hung fine artwork, and Henry developed an extensive library, which the girls explored in the geography and history games he assigned. He also taught them Greek and grammar; read to them from the Bible, Shakespeare, Edgeworth, and Scott; and engaged tutors in mathematics and foreign languages. More conventional female accomplishments—drawing, music, sewing—found their place, as did social skills. One friend recalled that the tall, high-strung Susan conducted herself awkwardly in public, and Susan sometimes made similar self-judgments, but according to her sister's memory, she "grew to be intensely fond of society . . . coming into a coolness of self possession [Anna had] not often seen equalled" (*Susan Warner* 117). Disdainful of physical effort and something of a voluptuary, the bright young Susan inclined to an indoor world of imagination and especially of books, a passion her father closely oversaw. Her love of tales expressed itself in an early gift for "talking stories," played out with Anna and several cousins during summers at Canaan—in group narrations of which she was the undisputed leader.

During Susan's late teens, the Panic of 1837 initiated a great change. The Warners' fortunes plunged, and they had to leave the city for an isolated farmhouse on Constitution Island, across the Hudson River from West Point. This property was intended for development as a resort, but ambition gave way to subsistence; Henry became less and less able to support the family, and his speculations and legal entanglements drew them into such straits that in 1849 all but essentials went to pay off debt. Displaced from genteel society and deprived of likely marriage prospects, the young women turned to evangelical Christianity and their own resources for the means of surviving in spirit and body. In 1841, they experienced conversion and together joined the Mercer Street Presbyterian Church, where their father was a member, striving to re-anchor themselves in submission to God's providence. Thereafter, although the contrary pulse of Susan's desires continued, the sisters' days moved largely to the rhythm of church activity, which helped fill the need for both meaningful purpose and society. Religious and social impulses—blended with the strong family patriotism—made for enduring ties with the academy across the river, where they had visited during their Uncle Thomas's term as chaplain, and where they now often attended chapel as well as secular functions.

Though spiritual life grew rich, material needs still pressed. Correcting school examinations, practicing household economies, and creating and selling a natural history game helped finances, but not enough. One evening in 1848, Aunt Fanny planted a potent idea: "Sue, I believe if you would try, you could write [and, implicitly, sell] 'a story' " (*Susan Warner* 263). Thus prompted, Susan began *The Wide, Wide World,* weaving the story of a young girl's tribulations from the bitterly familiar threads of legal trouble, parental abandonment, and privation, made comprehensible as a narrative of Christian soul-forging. In early 1850, Henry offered the bulky manuscript to New York's publishing houses, meeting here with disinterest and there with a derisive "Fudge!," but at last George Putnam, swayed against his own doubts by his mother's enthusiasm, agreed to publish. Caught up in the sheer pleasure of writing, Susan immediately began a new book, *Queechy,* and Anna did likewise; from the beginning, authorship was a collaborative affair, regularly taking the form of a three-woman writing group (Aunt Fanny making the nonauthorial third) and at times issuing in coauthored texts. Indeed, from the time of their move to Constitution Island, the sisters became so closely bound together by shared isolation, faith, and literary vocation that Susan's history can hardly be spun out separately.

The Wide, Wide World appeared under the pseudonym Elizabeth Wetherell in December 1850, and it made an extraordinary hit, ultimately becoming (next to *Uncle Tom's Cabin*) the century's best-seller—a category whose beginnings some historians trace to Warner's debut. Notices were good, and in 1852 Putnam ordered an unprecedented run of 5,000 copies for *Queechy,* which sold well if not as brilliantly. Income began to flow, enough to keep the Warners from the edge of poverty for limited stretches of time, but despite publishing steadily for most of their adult years, the sisters would not regain their lost security. The gold- and silver-lined drawer suggestively hidden in the escritoire that Susan imagines in her original conclusion to *The Wide, Wide World* never came to be. Inadequate copyright law was partly to blame: then, books could be reprinted outside their country of origin without return to the author, so that, although Susan's novels were popular in Europe, little profit found its way to her. And when later sales settled to unexceptional levels—a decline often attributed to Susan's deepening didacticism—both sisters sold their books outright, forfeiting potential royalties for the sake of ready cash. Most of Susan's subsequent publications traded on the fame of the "the author of *The Wide, Wide World.*"

In the 1850s, following that heady success, Susan published a Bible textbook with Carter's—the religious house that would later become her principal publisher; in 1860, she and Anna together brought out *Say and Seal;* and in 1862 they launched the *Little American,* a juvenile miscellany whose range of topics recalled the plenitude of their girlhood education. The economic effects of the Civil War contributed to this project's failure, depressed the literary industry in general, and intensified the sisters' reliance on the over-taxed strength of their own hands for rural essentials. From 1851 on, however, publication income and contacts did provide modest opportunities for travel and society; at winter lodgings in New York they received guests during Saturday evening "at homes," and at gatherings hosted by literary friends they met such writers as Thackeray and Sedgwick. Through the 1860s, 1870s, and early 1880s, Susan and Anna constantly gestated projects aimed explicitly at doing God's work and keeping the household solvent—these urgent motives always enlivened with delight in the work of writing. A coauthored series of Biblical interpretations appeared in1865–78, and several more novels by Susan, including a trilogy for juveniles (an audience for which both often wrote), followed *Say and Seal* in the 1860s.

In 1875, the undramatic current of island life shifted with Henry's death, which grieved the women but had little effect on domestic economy, since Susan had become the main breadwinner. Henry's absence opened the way for spending winters in a town outside West Point rather than undertaking more distant and arduous removals, and the academy played an ever more important role: the sisters began to conduct Bible studies, over tea and gingerbread, for groups of cadets, many of whom remained devoted to them after graduation. In every year except one from the time of her father's death to her own, apparently from a stroke, on March 17, 1885, Susan produced a novel. She was buried in the West Point Cemetery, to be joined 30 years later by Anna—whose identification with the older sister remained so powerful that she inscribed both names in new books long after the two had been separated by death.

MAJOR WORKS AND THEMES

Warner worked in the mid-nineteenth-century genre called "sentimental" (often a dismissive label), "domestic," "woman's," or "exploratory" fiction, which American female authors penned abundantly and to immense popular acclaim, especially in the 1850s and 1860s. *The Wide, Wide World* unfolds a tale of women's experience that Warner and such novelists as Maria Cummins would tell repeatedly—a form of bildungsroman that overtly celebrates what we now consider the cult of domesticity and true womanhood. It typically follows a young woman who, bereft of parental support, must make her way through the troubles of the wide world to a mature selfhood that, paradoxically for modern readers, depends on subjecting the self to male authority, divine and human. Once she has become what she ought to be, the protagonist wins home and marriage: a domestic heaven governed by a benevolent husband but illumined by her self-effacing piety, a place where sexuality conspicuously does not figure.

Warner's first child-heroine, Ellen Montgomery, has a passionately self-willed nature that must, as a succession of painful losses and tutelary figures insists, be subdued to God's loving discipline; once this training is complete, John Humphreys (spiritual mentor, father, brother, and lover all in one) will make her a wealthy wife. While sharing sentimental preoccupations with the life of feeling, human relation, and home, Ellen's narrative reflects its creator's particularities: Perhaps most central is Warner's sharply personal concern with the gendered and class-inflected dynamics of power, which embodies itself in the flawed father figure, among other males, and refers more generally to the psychological crux of her life: the conflict between a vital, autocratic sense of self and the requirement that she empty out that self to make way for God. Other marks of individuality include the nuanced translation of autobiography into fiction; the vivid rendering of rural surroundings (though sometimes with a sniff of snobbish distaste); and the interplay between an attraction to New World gentility, European aristocracy, and material ease, on one hand, and an allegiance to the ideals of American democracy, Christian unworldliness, and selfless industry, on the other. All these elements appear, in modulated form, throughout her writings.

Queechy plots a similar path but with an important reversal: its heroine, Fleda Ringgan, is a model of Christian virtue and practical ability from the start, and her example wins a rich Englishman to Christ, thus fitting him as her husband and (ironically) guide in all things spiritual and worldly. The novel's middle stretches showcase the adolescent Fleda's resources: facing adversity as part of God's providence, she manages both home and farm at Queechy (a setting patterned after the Canaan homestead) and helps sustain her family by publishing poetry and selling produce. During interludes in New York's high society, Fleda joins in debates on the varied theme of power, and she ably holds up the side of American democratic ideals—all the while remaining untainted by "masculine" commerce and urban corruption. Warner counterposes this portrait of an American woman's potential autonomy, however, with the concluding idyll of married bliss on an English estate, where Fleda's aristocrat, after lifting her free of toil, enfolds her in tender dominion.

While attending in some detail to these better-studied first novels risks reinforcing the imbalance that exists in Warner scholarship, a brief overview of lesser-known works may at least pique readerly interest. Two noteworthy works are theological: *The Law and the Testimony* (1853), a collection of biblical passages arranged by theme; and *The Word* (1865–78), a series of scriptural interpretations, which a reader just back from Israel praised as valuable guides (though Susan herself had no first-hand experience of the Holy Land). *The Hills of the Shatemuc* (1856) characteristically chronicles a young woman's lessons in selfless piety, but in this case the story is as much about the male protagonist—an apotheosized version of Henry Warner as self-fashioned American man, one too perfect to fall into ineffectuality like the original and his other doubles elsewhere in Warner's fiction.

Say and Seal (1860), the first of three novels coauthored with Anna, sets Christian romance in a New England village; it is regarded as a richly realized work of local color that yet supports a pastoral fantasy or Pauline allegory of Christ's marriage to the church—the paradoxical mix of realism and idealized dreamscape that runs through much of Susan's work. One scene, unusually, does more than intimate the lovers' erotic passion for each other. In novels written from the 1860s forward, Warner seems to tend away from the luxurious, if straitened, private identity imaged in the endings of her first two and to engage more closely with communal issues, reflecting her move from Presbyterianism to a strain of Methodism that called for social action. The spiritual welfare of the unfortunate, however, usually supersedes their corporeal needs, as the three-part story of another wealthy, virtuous heroine in *Melbourne House, Daisy,* and *Daisy in the Field* (1864–69) attests. Abolition is a pressing issue here, but because publication postdated the Civil War, the effect is less one of reformist fervor directed at concrete change than one of moral reflection. In the coauthored *Wych Hazel* and its sequel, *The Gold of*

Chickaree (1876), social critique takes the form of an ambitious idea for bettering the lives of mill workers, made practicable when a rich young heroine gives up the autonomy and freedom from moral responsibility she loves and joins resources with the man who wants to marry her. Warner's antidemocratic drift embodies itself in this elite pair, without whose guidance the laboring masses would not be relieved.

During her last years, Warner concentrated on a series of eight didactic novels advertised as "true" stories. In the 1980s, one of these, *Diana,* attracted the attention of novelist Joyce Carol Oates, who gauged the historical and psychological distance between Warner's time and ours by way of her own divided response to the Warneresque heroine—an engagingly passionate, independent woman whose progress to maturity extinguishes just those qualities. The protagonists of the other factual novels are likewise exemplary, but the persuasive representation of vigorous individuality in some characters—coupled with dialogue passages that wrestle over the difficulty of relinquishing one's will—suggest that the pivotal conflict of Warner's life occupied her until its end. Completion of the last "true" book, *Daisy Plains,* fell to Anna, in a poignant close to their lives together.

CRITICAL RECEPTION

In Warner's day, critical and popular attention concentrated on *The Wide, Wide World* and *Queechy,* and while judgment often turned on their moral center, it did not overlook their more literary merits. Most critics joined the general public in praise of what the novels preach: the *Newark Daily Advertiser* and the *New York Times,* for example, hailed the unmatched pious power of Ellen's narrative in the same tone as letters from individuals; one admirer in Philadelphia, expressing the common sentiment, wrote to say both books had not only given him " 'exquisite pleasure' " but also taught him to be " 'a better man—more strengthened to duty, more reconciled to suffering' " (*Susan Warner* 354). The aesthetic appeal implied in "exquisite pleasure" also won notice from critics and writers (among them Barrett Browning, James, and Kirkland), who compared Warner to Stowe, Flaubert, and Dickens and complimented her polished style and skillful evocation of New England customs and landscapes. Kirkland, in particular, made much of the quintessential "American" character of Warner's work and its contribution to a new national literature.

Not all of Warner's first-generation audience was impressed, however. Hawthorne and Melville, notably among "belletristic" writers, took issue in private with female "scribblers" like Warner for flooding the marketplace with what they saw as bromidic rehearsals of conventional values. As the nineteenth century progressed and the twentieth began, such reactions prevailed. None of the many publications that followed Warner's first two enjoyed the same success, though they attracted a modest readership and occasionally good reviews (especially from religious commentators). Scholars have suggested that Warner's popularity waned, at first, because her impulse to preach overtook the impulse to tell a gripping story with fully realized characters and places, and later because her work as a whole fell out of step with the postbellum turn toward secular materialism and realism. When mentioned at all from 1900 to 1977, Warner typically suffered contempt for her sentimental piety and perceived lack of artistry: a turn-of-the-century writer for the *Critic* compiled, for satiric effect, a one-sentence paragraph out of Warner's many descriptors for Ellen Montgomery's tears; in 1903 Charles Kingsley retitled her best-seller *The Narrow, Narrow World;* and in the mid-twentieth century (as formalism took hold), the few scholars who troubled themselves to consider Warner made much the same dismissive gestures.

In the 1970s and 1980s, when Americanists interested in cultural history began to recover the record of forgotten women's experience, Warner reemerged from near-invisibility. Such path-breakers as Nina Baym and Jane Tompkins discovered in her early novels, especially the first, a story of female identity-making worth the notice of academics, primarily as a socioreligious artifact showing what women could make of themselves within nineteenth-century constraints rather than as a work of imaginative literature or feminist exploration. The 1987 Feminist Press edition of *The Wide, Wide World,* with an afterword by Tompkins, made the novel readily available for inclusion in university courses, where it is no longer rare. Following up these early efforts, scholars have uncovered disregarded riches, though again almost exclusively in Warner's first two novels: as the selective bibliography below suggests, recent studies consider them worthy of a broad array of approaches, including those concerned with gender and sexuality (finding in various degrees complicity with or—now more often—resistance to limiting ideologies), race, psychology, reader response, Bakhtinian analysis, and literary history. The last puts Warner in conversation with Emerson and also recognizes her, along with other female local colorists, as a precursor of realism, whose contributions to a national literature have been slighted in the modern era. One of the newer strains of argument returns to the vexed question of aesthetic quality, maintaining that contemporary treatments, especially those that look fixedly at the cultural functions of sentimental texts, have underplayed signs of original artistry, which may be appreciated by refining traditional criteria for separating "good" from "bad" to do justice to the distinctive aims and linguistic practices of the genre.

The critical move toward particularized considerations is not far advanced, leaving room for a yet more textured understanding of Warner. The biographical record, for instance, would bear further attention—especially to the near-symbiotic but perhaps subtly combative bond of sisterhood and mutual authorship between Susan and Anna. And finally, while Warner's declining sales and the critical focus on her first two novels suggest that her later works are less compelling, this exclusion may rest partly on assumptions akin to those that kept her entire corpus in the dark for decades.

WORK CITED

Warner, Anna. *Susan Warner.* New York: Putnam's Sons, 1909.

BIBLIOGRAPHY

Works by Susan Warner

Essay
"How May an American Woman Best Show Her Patriotism?" *Ladies' Wreath* 5 (1851): 313–27.

Fiction (Adult and Juvenile)
The Wide, Wide World. New York: Putnam, 1850.
Queechy. New York: Putnam, 1852.
Carl Krinken: His Christmas Stocking. New York: Putnam, 1853.
The Hills of the Shatemuc. New York: Appleton, 1856.
The Old Helmet. New York: Carter, 1863.
Melbourne House. New York: Carter, 1864.
Daisy. Philadelphia: Lippincott, 1868.
Daisy in the Field. New York: Carter, 1869.

A Story of Small Beginnings
What She Could. New York: Carter, 1870.
Opportunities. New York: Carter, 1870.
The House in Town. New York: Carter, 1870.
Trading. New York: Carter, 1872.

Stories on the Lord's Prayer
The Little Camp on Eagle Hill. New York: Carter, 1873.
Sceptres and Crowns. New York: Carter, 1874.
Willow Brook. New York: Carter, 1874.
Bread and Oranges. New York: Carter, 1875.
The Flag of Truce. New York: Carter, 1875.
The Rapids of Niagara. New York: Carter, 1876.
Pine Needles. New York: Carter, 1877.
Diana. New York: Putnam's Sons, 1877.
My Desire. New York: Carter, 1879.
The End of a Coil. New York: Carter, 1880.
The Letter of Credit. New York: Carter, 1881.
Nobody. New York: Carter, 1882.
Stephen, M. D. New York: Carter, 1883.
A Red Wallflower. New York: Carter, 1884.
Daisy Plains. New York: Carter, 1885.

Theological Works (Adult and Juvenile)
The Law and the Testimony. New York: Carter, 1853.
Lessons on the Standard Bearers of the Old Testament. New York: Randolph, 1872.

The Word
Walks from Eden. New York: Carter, 1865.
The House of Israel. New York: Carter, 1866.
The Broken Walls of Jerusalem and the Rebuilding of Them. New York: Carter, 1870.
The Kingdom of Judah. New York: Carter, 1878.

Works Coauthored with Anna Warner
Say and Seal. Philadelphia: Lippincott, 1860.
The Golden Ladder. New York: Randolph, 1862.
The Little American: A Series of Stories and Sketches for Young Folks. October 1862–December 1864.
Wych Hazel. New York: Putnam's Sons, 1876.
The Gold of Chickaree. New York: Putnam's Sons, 1876.

Studies of Susan Warner

Argersinger, Jana. "Family Embraces: The Unholy Kiss and Authorial Relations in *The Wide, Wide World.*" *American Literature* 74 (2002): 251–85.

Ashworth, Suzanne. "Susan Warner's *The Wide, Wide World,* Conduct Literature, and Protocols of Female Reading in Mid-Nineteenth-Century America." *Legacy* 17 (2000): 141–64.

Baker, Mabel. *Light in the Morning: Memories of Susan and Anna Warner.* West Point: Constitution Island Association Press, 1978.

Barnes, Elizabeth. *States of Sympathy: Seduction and Democracy in the American Novel.* New York: Columbia Univ. Press, 1997.

Baym, Nina. *Woman's Fiction: A Guide to Novels by and about Women in America, 1820–1870.* 2nd ed. 1978; Ithaca: Cornell Univ. Press, 1978.

Brodhead, Richard. *Cultures of Letters: Scenes of Reading and Writing in Nineteenth-Century America.* Chicago: Univ. of Chicago Press, 1993.

Dobson, Joanne. "The Hidden Hand: Subversion of Cultural Ideology in Three Mid-Nineteenth-Century American Women's Novels." *American Quarterly* 38 (1986): 223–42.

Foster, Edward. *Susan and Anna Warner.* Boston: Twayne, 1978.

Goshgarian, G. M. *To Kiss the Chastening Rod: Domestic Fiction and Sexual Ideology in the American Renaissance.* Ithaca: Cornell Univ. Press, 1992.

Harris, Susan. *Nineteenth-Century American Women's Novels: Interpretive Strategies.* Cambridge: Cambridge Univ. Press, 1990.

Hovet, Grace, and Theodore Hovet. "Tableaux Vivants: Masculine Vision and Feminine Reflections in Novels by Warner, Alcott, Stowe, and Wharton." *ATQ,* n.s., 7 (1993): 335–56.

Noble, Marianne. *The Masochistic Pleasures of Sentimental Literature.* Princeton: Princeton Univ. Press, 2000.

Oates, Joyce Carol. "Pleasure, Duty, Redemption Then and Now: Susan Warner's *Diana.*" *American Literature* 59 (1987): 422–27.

Roberson, Susan. "Ellen Montgomery's Other Friend: Race Relations in an Expunged Episode of Warner's *Wide, Wide World.*" *ESQ* 45 (1999): 1–31.

Sanderson, Dorothy. *They Wrote for a Living: A Bibliography of the Works of Susan Bogert Warner and Anna Bartlett Warner.* [West Point]: Constitution Island Association, 1976.

Schnog, Nancy. "Inside the Sentimental: The Psychological Work of *The Wide Wide World.*" *Genders* 4 (spring 1989): 11–25.

Stewart, Veronica. "Mothering a Female Saint: Susan Warner's Dialogic Role in *The Wide, Wide World.*" *Essays in Literature* 22 (1995): 59–74.

Stokes, Olivia. *Letters and Memories of Susan and Anna Bartlett Warner.* New York: Putnam's Sons, 1925.

Tompkins, Jane. *Afterword to* The Wide, Wide World. New York: Feminist Press, 1987.

———. *Sensational Designs: The Cultural Work of American Fiction, 1790–1860.* New York: Oxford Univ. Press, 1985.

Weiss, Jane. "Susan Warner." In *Nineteenth-Century American Women Writers: A Bio-Bibliographical Critical Sourcebook.* Ed. Denise D. Knight. Westport, CT: Greenwood, 1997.

Williams, Cynthia. "Susan Warner's *Queechy* and the *Bildungsroman* Tradition." *Legacy* 7, no. 2 (1990): 3–16.

Williams, Susan. "Widening the World: Susan Warner, Her Readers, and the Assumption of Authorship." *American Quarterly* 42 (1990): 565–86.

FRANCES MIRIAM BERRY WHITCHER (1812?–1852)

Anne Razey Gowdy

BIOGRAPHY

Frances Miriam Berry, thirteenth (some say eleventh) of 15 children of Lewis and Elizabeth Wells Berry, was born in Whitesboro (also called Whitestown), New York, on November 1. Linda A. Morris, a recent Whitcher biographer, concludes that 1812 is "most probable" as her birth year (227, n. 38). Despite the inscription on her tombstone that says she was 39 when she died in January 1852, other researchers contend that she may have been born in 1811, 1813, or even 1814.

A posthumous biographical essay by her younger sister suggests that Miriam's creative talent surfaced early as caricature in prose, poetry, and pictorial sketches. Kate Berry quotes from a letter in which Miriam acknowledges having a "remarkably strong sense of the ridiculous," a perspective that shaped her later writing (Berry 50, 53).

After Miriam entertained a local literary society with adventures of the Widow Spriggins, the comic story was published in 1839 by a friend who edited the Rome, New York, *Gazette.* Using the pen name of Frank (a family nickname), Miriam earned her first pay for an 1846 series of comic monologues, "The Widow Bedott's Table Talk," published in Joseph Neal's *Saturday Gazette and Lady's Literary Museum.*

In 1832, Miriam joined her family's church, Whitesboro Presbyterian; however, the 1844 arrival in Oneida County of a young Episcopalian missionary created far-reaching consequences in Miriam's life. In 1846, she affiliated herself with the new St. John's Episcopal Church and became engaged to its pastor, the Rev. William Whitcher. Soon after their marriage in January 1847, William became pastor of Trinity Episcopal Church in Elmira, New York. Miriam continued to write Bedott stories and other pieces she sold to the prestigious *Godey's Lady's Book,* although her sister asserts defensively that "no ill-managed household, badly-cooked dinners, or disarranged attire could have been pointed at as indications that she was a 'literary woman' " (Berry 110).

The bride adjusted with difficulty to life as a minister's wife in a town she apparently judged provincial and petty. The Whitchers suffered the loss of a stillborn child in April 1848. By the time a second daughter, Alice Miriam, was born late in 1850, the couple had returned to Whitesboro. William's resignation from the Elmira church was prompted, at least in part, by the revelation that his wife was the author of increasingly popular local color sketches in *Godey's*. William's career thereafter included a series of temporary positions that separated him intermittently from his family.

Even as Miriam's already precarious health declined, she continued to write. When she died from consumption on January 4, 1852, she left her husband of five years, an infant daughter, and an unfinished novel. She was buried in Whitesboro.

MAJOR WORKS AND THEMES

Frances Miriam Berry Whitcher created three distinct humorous literary heroines who speak in American vernacular voices, using them to critique pretensions to gentility that she observed in a rising American middle class. In Whitcher's earliest published writing, the Widow "Permilly" Ruggles Spriggins recounts how her late husband Jabez had won her only by courting her in the exaggerated style of her favorite novel, Maria Roche's *The Children of the Abbey* (1796). Whitcher creates broad farce from the widow's untutored local dialect, her frequent malapropisms, and her equating real life with current conventions of the literary romance.

Whitcher's most enduring character is the socially ambitious Widow Priscilla Bedott of Wiggletown, whose affectionate nickname "Silly" reveals much. The Bedott monologues record the widow's pursuit of a new husband, culminating in her "conversion" and subsequent remarriage to the widowed Baptist preacher O. Shadrack Sniffles, who mistakenly believes she is wealthy. Her frequent poems and the interspersed verses attributed to the local poet "Hugelina" parody sentimental poetry then in vogue.

Finally, in the "Aunt Maguire Letters," Priscilla Bedott's common-sense sister, "Aunt Maguire" of Scrabble Hill, emerges as a central character whose comments provide an implied corrective for social blunders of other characters. "Aunt Maguire's Description of the Donation Party," probably Whitcher's most famous and controversial piece, details a custom that required the minister's family to entertain church members, who in turn bring gifts to compensate for his poor salary. When the story appeared anonymously in *Godey's Lady's Book* in March 1848, depicting stingy guests who wreak havoc at the parsonage, Trinity parishioners felt maligned. Likewise, when "The Contemplated Sewing Circle" was published by *Godey's*, its overbearing matron, Mrs. Samson Savage of Scrabble Hill, caused serious offense to an influential church officer, who claimed Mrs. Savage was intended as an uncomplimentary portrait of his own wife. This incident sparked the church's confrontation with the Reverend Whitcher and his subsequent resignation. Interestingly, nearby communities also took offense at the portrayal of Mrs. Savage, recognizing her as their own.

In a letter from Elmira, Whitcher proclaims, "I am heartily sick of Bedotting and Maguiring, and only wish I could be as well paid for more sensible matter" (M. L. Ward Whitcher 32). In the months of her final illness, she was able to write only a few chapters of a sentimental novel, *Mary Elmer,* intended as serious fiction that her daughter might someday read.

CRITICAL RECEPTION

Whitcher's publications were immediately successful. Kate Berry records Joseph Neal's observation in September 1846: "The world is full of Bedott. Our readers talk of nothing else, and despise 'Neal' if the Widow be not there" (110). The first collection of Widow Bedott stories appeared posthumously in 1855, edited by Alice Neal. The book sold more than 100,000 copies by the time a successful 1879 stage adaptation by David Ross Locke ("Petroleum V. Nasby") created the demand for a new edition in 1883.

Capitalizing on the favorable market for Widow Bedott stories, Benjamin Whitcher's second wife in 1867 collected Miriam's Widow Spriggins episodes. Mrs. M[artha]. L. Ward Whitcher included in that volume a biographical sketch of the author, a newly completed version of Miriam's unfinished novel *Mary Elmer*, and miscellaneous sketches including several framed narratives grouped as "Letters from Timberville."

In her own time, Whitcher's stories were appreciated for their successful dialect humor and recognizable parodies of small-town characters and customs. Despite Whitcher's obviously successful creation of on-target and well-received comedy, male critics persisted in the assertion that female authors possessed no real wit. In response, Kate Sanborn's 1886 anthology *The Wit of Women* introduced examples from numerous women writers as convincing evidence to the contrary, but Sanborn included only a discussion of Whitcher with no selections because "every one who enjoys that style of humor knows them by heart" (68). As late as 1901, Oscar Fay Adams's *Dictionary of American Authors* labeled Whitcher "a still popular humorist."

Dialect fiction was less favored during most of the twentieth century, but a reassessment of nineteenth-century women writers returned Whitcher's books to print and prompted renewed academic interest in her work (see Langworthy, O'Donnell, and Curry). Contemporary scholars appreciate Whitcher's themes and characters as strongly felt social commentary. Linda Morris and Nancy Walker point out in her work a scathing critique of the genteel mode that emerged in Whitcher's time. Among her lively characters, readers can recognize cautionary models for behavior in the escapades of Permilly Spriggins and "Silly" Bedott, contrasted with the commonsense views of Aunt Maguire, the observing voice of the author.

WORKS CITED

Adams, Oscar Fay. *A Dictionary of American Authors*. 4th ed. Boston: Houghton Mifflin, 1901.

[Berry, Kate.] "Passages in the Life of the Author of Aunt Maguire's Letters, Bedott Papers, Etc. in two parts. By her sister." *Godey's Lady's Book,* 47 (July 1853): 49–55; (August 1853): 109–115.

Curry, Jane. "Yes, Virginia, There Were Female Humorists: Frances Whitcher and Her Widow Bedott." *University of Michigan Papers in Women's Studies* 1 (1974): 74–90.

Langworthy, Margaret Wyman. "Frances Miriam Whitcher." *Notable American Women, 1607–1950.* Cambridge: Harvard University Press, 1971. Vol. 3, 580–81.

Morris, Linda A. *Women's Humor in the Age of Gentility: The Life and Works of Frances Miriam Berry Whitcher.* Syracuse, NY: Syracuse University Press, 1992.

O'Donnell, Thomas F. "The Return of the Widow Bedott: Mrs. F. M. Whitcher of Whitesboro and Elmira." *New York History* 55 (1974): 4–34.

Sanborn, Kate. *The Wit of Women.* New York: Funk and Wagnalls, 1886.

Walker, Nancy. "Sut and His Sisters: Vernacular Humor and Genteel Culture." *Sut Lovingood's Nat'ral Born Yarnspinner: Essays on George Washington Harris.* Ed. James E. Caron and M. Thomas Inge. Tuscaloosa: University of Alabama Press, 1996. 261–71.

Whitcher, Mrs. M. L. Ward. "Biographical Introduction." In *The Widow Spriggins, Mary Elmer, and Other Sketches* by Frances Miriam Berry Whitcher. New York: George W. Carleton, 1867. 11–35.

BIBLIOGRAPHY

Works by Frances Miriam Berry Whitcher

Whitcher, Frances Miriam Berry. *The Widow Bedott Papers.* With an introduction by Alice B. Neal. New York: J. C. Derby, 1856.
———. *Widow Spriggins, Mary Elmer, and Other Sketches.* Edited with a memoir by M. L. Ward Whitcher. New York: George W. Carleton, 1867.
(Miriam Whitcher's unpublished letters are in the Manuscript Collection of the New York Historical Society, New York City.)

Studies of Frances Miriam Berry Whitcher

Kiskis, Michael J. "Frances Miriam Berry Whitcher (1814–1852)." *Nineteenth-Century American Women Writers.* Ed. Denise D. Knight. Westport, CT: Greenwood, 1997. 463–7.
Preston, Robyn M. "Frances Miriam Whitcher." *Dictionary of Literary Biography. Vol. 202, Nineteenth-Century American Fiction Writers.* Ed. Kent P. Ljungquist. Detroit: Gale, 1999. 296–301.
Wade, Clyde W. "Frances Miriam Whitcher." *Dictionary of Literary Biography. Vol. 11: American Humorists, 1800–1950.* Ed. Stanley Trachtenberg. Detroit: Gale, 1982. 560–67.
Walker, Nancy. *Women Vernacular Humorists in Nineteenth-Century America: Ann Stephens, Frances Whitcher, and Marietta Holley.* New York: Garland, 1988.

JAMES MONROE WHITFIELD (1822–1871)

Edward Whitley

BIOGRAPHY

Born in Exeter, New Hampshire, on April 10, 1822, to free African American parents, James Monroe Whitfield lived briefly in Boston before settling in Buffalo, New York, where he showed an early interest in politics and literature. At age 16 he spoke at a convention urging black separatists to settle in California, and by the late 1840s he was publishing both political and conventionally romantic poetry in *The Liberator, The North Star,* and *Frederick Douglass' Paper* while working full time as a barber. Whitfield continued to write poems over the next few years, culminating with the 1853 publication of *America and Other Poems.* He hoped that publishing a book of poetry would herald the beginning of his career as a professional writer. Whitfield writes in the introduction to *America and Other Poems,* "This volume is presented . . . in the hope that it may find a favorable reception with our people, and 'put money in the purse' of the writer, that he may be able to cultivate, improve, and fully develop the talent which God hath given him" (viii). While the collection of poems was well received, it did not provide Whitfield with the financial windfall he had hoped for.

Instead of dedicating himself to poetry, however, Whitfield became increasingly involved in politics, particularly the separatist movement led by Martin R. Delany (the person to whom *America and Other Poems* is dedicated) which encouraged African Americans to establish black settlements outside of the United States. Along with participating in the 1854 National Emigration Convention in Cleveland, Whitfield defended the emigration movement against detractors such as Frederick Douglass, with whom he had a heated exchange in the black press. Whitfield was slated to edit the pro-emigration journal *African-American Repository* in 1858, but no record of the publication has ever been found. He is also believed to have traveled to Central America between 1859 and 1861 to look for potential emigration sites, but no historical documents have confirmed the voyage. With the outbreak of the Civil War, Whitfield put aside plans for emigration and publicly supported the Union. He returned to poetry following the Civil War in his new home of California, writing poems commemorating the fourth anniversary of the Emancipation Proclamation and the ratification of the Fifteenth Amendment. While in California he was the Grand Master of the Prince Hall Masons and worked again as a barber. He died on April 23, 1871, in San Francisco and was buried in the Masonic Cemetery.

MAJOR WORKS AND THEMES

America and Other Poems displays the characteristic invective abolitionists raised against the failure of American democracy and Christianity to end slavery. The title poem of the volume, "America," opens as a parody of the patriotic song of the same name by changing lines such as "Sweet land of Liberty" to "Thou boasted land of liberty," and proceeds to question how the Revolutionary War, a war fought in the name of universal human rights, ended up securing the right to hold slaves. The poem ends by comparing the United States to both biblical Egypt and Babylon, and not the New Jerusalem its Puritan forebears considered it. "How Long," a 200-line poem concerned not only with national but also global injustice, provides a detailed catalogue of the crimes attendant with European despotism and the African slave trade. Similar to "America," "How Long" asks how the United States, which claims to be an international standard of liberty, can continue the practice of slavery. The poem ultimately ends on a hopeful note in that it sees the potential for a world freed from bondage. "The Misanthropist," the other major poem in *America and Other Poems,* takes the Byronic theme of the alienated romantic artist and applies it to the plight of the black poet. There are also shorter abolition poems in the volume, such as "To Cinque," which is a panegyric to the leader of the 1839 revolution on the slave ship *Amistad,* and "Lines on the Death of J. Quincy Adams," which praises this "champion of the free" for his support of antislavery causes. While abolitionist poetry dominates *America,* there are also a number of conventional poems on the topics of love, music, and self-reliance, along with occasional poems written to celebrate Christmas, New Year's, and the dedication of several churches. Whitfield's 1867 poem commemorating the fourth anniversary of the Emancipation Proclamation returns to the similar themes of "America" and "How Long" in that it takes American history and politics as its subject to say that even though slavery has ended, the nation still has much to do if it is to live up to its promise to be the "country of the free." His last poem, the 1870 "Poem by J. M. Whitfield," still bears the marks of the poet's earlier abolitionist verses but is remarkably conciliatory toward the United States, going so far as to praise the nation for being a world leader in culture, economics, and human rights.

CRITICAL RECEPTION

Whitfield's poetry was praised by some of the most prominent African American political leaders of his time, including Frederick Douglass, William Wells Brown, and Martin R. Delany, who, in *Blake; or, The Huts of America,* has the novel's black revolutionaries recite Whitfield's poetry. Critical commentary since the nineteenth century has consistently praised Whitfield not only for the abolitionist message he championed but also for his technical skill as a poet, specifically, his control of meter and rhyme, his prolific use of classical imagery, and his keen sense of history. But this praise is always qualified: a persistent critical leitmotif has been to lament what Whitfield's achievements could have been had he been given the opportunity to develop himself as a poet. His contemporaries saw in him a potential equal to Edgar Allan Poe and John Greenleaf

Whittier, while twentieth-century critics saw him as approaching but falling shy of the achievements of the Harlem Renaissance poets. Another critical tendency is to position Whitfield's poetry as part of a developing tradition and to see Whitfield as one of the first in a long line of African American poets and writers to question their relationship with the United States. In this sense, Whitfield is revered more as a placeholder in the African American literary tradition rather than as a poet in his own right, as reflected in the overabundance of anthologies and historical surveys that feature Whitfield and the dearth of actual criticism devoted exclusively to his life and work.

BIBLIOGRAPHY

Works by James Monroe Whitfield

Poetry
America and Other Poems. Buffalo: James S. Leavitt, 1853.
"A Poem Written for the Celebration of the Fourth Anniversary of President Lincoln's Emanci-
    pation Proclamation." In Ezra Rothschild Johnson, *Emancipation Oration by Dr. Ezra R.
    Johnson, and Poem, by James M. Whitfield.* San Francisco: Elevator Office, 1867.
"Poem by J. M. Whitfield." *San Francisco Elevator.* 22 April 1870: 3.

Prose
[Letters to *The North Star.*] *Arguments, Pro and Con, on the Call for a National Convention, to
    be Held in Cleveland, Ohio, August 24, 1854.* Ed. M. T. Newsom. Detroit: George E. Pomery
    & Co., 1854.

Studies of James Monroe Whitfield

Brawley, Benjamin. *Early Negro American Writers: Selections with Biographical and Critical
    Introductions.* Chapel Hill: University of North Carolina Press, 1935.
———. *Negro Genius.* New York: Dodd, Mead, 1937.
Brown, Sterling. *Negro Poetry and Drama.* Washington, D. C.: Associates in Negro Folk Edu-
    cation, 1937.
Brown, William Wells. *The Black Man, His Antecedents, His Genius, and His Achievements.* New
    York: Thomas Hamilton, 1863.
Delany, Martin. *Blake; or, The Huts of America.* 1970 Ed. Floyd Miller. Boston: Beacon, 1989.
———. *The Condition, Elevation, Emigration, and Destiny of the Colored People of the United
    States.* Philadelphia, 1852.
Douglass, Frederick. *Anti-Slavery Bugle.* 24 August 1850: 1.
Jackson, Blyden. *A History of Afro-American Literature.* Vol. 1. Baton Rouge: Louisiana State
    University Press, 1989.
Laryea, Doris Lucas. "James Monroe Whitfield." *Dictionary of Literary Biography.* Vol. 50. Ed.
    Trudier Harris. Detroit: Gale Research, 1986. 260–63.
Levine, Robert. "'I, Too, Sing America': James M. Whitfield's *America and Other Poems* (1853)."
    http://www.iath.virginia.edu/fdw/volume1/levine/. 2001.
Loggins, Vernon. *The Negro Author: His Development in America to 1900.* New York: Columbia
    University Press, 1931.
Miller, Floyd J. *The Search for a Black Nationality: Black Emigration and Colonization,
    1787–1863.* Urbana: University of Illinois Press, 1975.
Redmond, Eugene. *Drumvoices: The Mission of Afro-American Poetry.* Garden City, NY: Anchor,
    1976.
Robinson, William H. *Early Black American Poets: Selections with Biographical and Critical
    Introductions.* Dubuque, IA: W. C. Brown Co., 1969.

Sherman, Joan R. *Invisible Poets: Afro-Americans of the Nineteenth Century.* Urbana: University of Illinois Press, 1989.

Wagner, Jean. *Black Poets of the United States: From Paul Laurence Dunbar to Langston Hughes.* Urbana: University of Illinois Press, 1973.

Whitlow, Roger. *Black American Literature: A Critical History.* Chicago: Nelson Hall, 1973.

SARAH HELEN WHITMAN (1803–1878)

Noelle A. Baker

BIOGRAPHY

Sarah Helen Power Whitman was born to Nicholas and Anna Marsh Power on January 19, 1803, in Providence, Rhode Island. In this state, founded on religious freedom, Anna Power and her daughters struggled with double standards commonly experienced by other nineteenth-century women. Nicholas Power abandoned his family in 1813, forcing them into an imperiled financial and social position. Although the male members of the Power family matriculated from Brown, Sarah Helen Power enjoyed only limited educational opportunities. Nonetheless, as an adult, Sarah Helen Whitman held court among Providence's literary elite: she learned German at home and established her own intellectual circle.

Sarah Helen Power's childless marriage to John Winslow Whitman in 1828 was unhappy and ended in his death in 1833. However, Whitman, an amateur editor of two literary journals, introduced his fiancée to literary life. During their engagement, Sarah Helen Power published her early poetry as "Helen" in the *Boston Spectator and Ladies' Album,* a journal that Whitman helped edit. Through him, she met another contributor to the *Spectator,* Sarah Josepha Hale. In the 1830s, Hale published Whitman's poetry in *The Ladies' Magazine, Godey's Lady's Book,* and *The Ladies' Wreath.* In the 1830s and 1840s, Whitman also published her poetry in the *Providence Journal, The Literary Journal & Weekly Register of Science and the Arts,* and *The Democratic Review,* as well as giftbooks like *The Rhode Island Book* (1841) and *The Token* (1842).

After her husband's death, Whitman returned to Providence. She remained single and in her mother's home for many reasons: chief among them were financial considerations; both women's marital history; and the mental instability of a younger sister, Susan Anna, who required care until her death. Within these domestic constraints, however, Whitman lived an active intellectual life, participating in the Coliseum Club; Anne Lynch's Providence "Coterie"; and the Phalanstery, a club based on Fourier's principles. Such social and literary circles foregrounded her essays on Shelley (1834), genius (1835), Goethe (1840), and Emerson (1845) in the *Providence Journal, The Literary*

Journal and Weekly Register, the *Boston Quarterly Review,* and *The United States Magazine and Democratic Review.*

In February 1848 Whitman addressed a valentine to Edgar Allan Poe for one of Anne Lynch's Valentine parties. The valentine intrigued Poe and initiated a literary romance ending in scandal by December 1848, when Poe was erroneously reported to have been evicted from Whitman's home for drunkenness and disorderly conduct. Despite the dishonor of being jilted and then maligned alongside her former fiancé in Rufus Griswold's "Ludwig" obituary, Whitman enjoyed a certain status as Poe's beloved. Her verse appeared thereafter in Caroline May's *The American Female Poets* (1848), Rufus Griswold's *The Female Poets of America* (1849), and Sarah Josepha Hale's *Woman's Record* (1853). She published a volume of poetry in 1853, *Hours of Life and Other Poems.*

In the 1850s and 1860s, Whitman became a Spiritualist, publishing testimonial letters in the *New York Tribune* and E. W. Capron's *Modern Spiritualism* (1855). In her journalism, she also advocated women's liberation, the establishment of public parks, and abolition. For her work, Whitman was elected vice president of the Rhode Island Suffrage Association in 1868; in 1870 and 1871, New York suffragists also honored her.

During her last 18 years, Whitman defended Poe's reputation in *Edgar Poe and His Critics* (1860) and in journalistic pieces, primarily in the *Providence Journal.* In the 1870s she became a primary source of information for Poe's biographers. Whitman died in 1878 while collecting her works for publication.

MAJOR WORKS AND THEMES

Whitman represents both the antebellum "poetess" and the rising class of female journalists emerging at mid-century. While much of her work treats nature, love, friendship, reformist causes, and philosophy, Poe appears prominently throughout.

Both *Hours of Life* and the posthumous *Poems* demonstrate the variety that Rufus Griswold recognized in Whitman's verse. Representative poems like "In Memoriam" and "She Blooms No More" elaborate the beautiful death; "A Day of the Indian Summer" and "A November Landscape" celebrate nature. Whitman's French and German translations, as well as the autobiographical poem *Hours of Life,* consider philosophical subjects.

Whitman's essays of the late 30s and 40s—particularly on Goethe and Emerson—explicate idealism from Plato to Emerson. In the journalism that followed, Whitman experimented with travel writing, art criticism, and reformist essays.

Whitman's prose and poetry about Poe constitute a significant feature of her literary production from the mid-1840s to her death. Six sonnets for Poe and verse like the "Arcturus" poems, "The Raven," and "Resurgemus" promote Spiritualism and the couple's relationship. *Edgar Poe and His Critics* emphasizes Poe's connectedness with his period; both prose and verse defend Poe when his critics considered him a demonic figure.

CRITICAL RECEPTION

Whitman's early reputation to the 1840s was regional, primarily because she published pseudonymously. In a letter of May 21, 1828, to Winslow Whitman, for example, Sarah Josepha Hale asked him to influence the writer of "charming poetry over the signature of 'Helen' " to contribute to the *Ladies' Magazine* (qtd. in Varner 74). Similarly,

George W. Curtis wrote Whitman privately about Emerson's and Thoreau's admiration of her essay on Emerson (qtd. in Ticknor 25). By the 1850s, however, Whitman was publishing under her own name. In his anthology of American women poets, Rufus Griswold singles out Whitman's "high and sustained . . . range of poetic art" (8), while Caroline May compliments Whitman's vigorous and perceptive prose (235).

Response to *Hours of Life* varied. Reviewers likened the sonnets to Poe's and Whitman's exploration of traditional subject matter. They were less impressed with the title poem, finding it too scholarly. The Spiritualist journal *Shekinah,* however, designated *Hours of Life* a "song of the soul" (Green 291).

Typically, reviewers regarded *Edgar Poe and His Critics* in light of Whitman's history. Even her friend Curtis wrote in *Harper's* that it was "impossible" to read the book without remembering "the brave woman's arm thrust through the slide to serve as a bolt against the enemy" (qtd. in W. F. C. 9). By century's end, Poe's reputation overshadowed Whitman's writing.

Poe scholars kept the lamp burning in the twentieth century, publishing Whitman's correspondence. Varner's unpublished dissertation, a biography of Whitman, is especially important in this context. Such attention, however, tended to focus on Poe, rather than Whitman. But the 1990s signaled a turn in her reception as feminists began recovering antebellum women's verse. More recent critical studies continue to theorize the Poe-Whitman relationship and to demonstrate her significance within the contexts of Spiritualism, women's writing, and the canon.

WORKS CITED

Green, Fanny. "Mrs. Whitman's Poems." Review of *Hours of Life and Other Poems,* by Whitman. *The Shekinah* 3 (October 1853): 290–6.

Griswold, Rufus Wilmot. *The Female Poets of America.* Philadelphia: Carey and Hart, 1849.

Hale, Sarah Josepha. *Woman's Record: or Sketches of all Distinguished Women from "The Beginning" till A.D. 1850.* New York: Harper and Brothers, 1853.

May, Caroline. *The American Female Poets: With Biographical and Critical Notices by Caroline May.* Philadelphia: Lindsay & Blakiston, 1848.

Ticknor, Caroline. *Poe's Helen.* New York: Charles Scribner's Sons, 1916. 25.

Varner, John Grier. "Sarah Helen Whitman: Seeress of Providence." Ph.D. diss., University of Virginia, 1940.

W. F. C. [William Francis Channing]. "Preface to the Second Edition." *Edgar Poe and His Critics.* By Whitman. Providence, RI: Tibbitts and Preston, 1885. 9–11.

BIBLIOGRAPHY

Works by Sarah Helen Whitman

Poetry
Hours of Life and Other Poems. Providence: George H. Whitney, 1853.
Poems. Boston: Houghton, Osgood and Company, 1879.

Nonfiction
"Character and Writings of Shelley." *The Literary Journal, and Weekly Register of Science and the Arts* 1 (1834): 352–353.
"On the Nature and Attributes of Genius." *The Boston Pearl* 5 (1835): 108.

Review of *Conversations with Goethe, in the Last Years of His Life*. Translated by S. M. Fuller. *Boston Quarterly Review* 3 (1840): 20–57.

"Emerson's Essays." *The United States Magazine, and Democratic Review* 16 (1845): 589–602.

Edgar Poe and His Critics New York: Rudd & Carleton, 1860.

"The Woman Question." *Providence Daily Journal,* 11 February 1868, 2.

"Woman's Suffrage." *Providence Daily Journal,* 10 December 1868, 2.

"Byronism." *Providence Daily Journal,* 18 October 1869, 2.

"Progressive Women and 'Average Young Men.'" *Providence Daily Journal,* 15 May 1869, 2.

"Immortality as Viewed by Scholars and Scientists." *Providence Daily Journal,* 20 March 1876, 2.

"Mr. Geo. W. Curtis on the 'True Mischief of Spiritualism.'" *Providence Daily Journal,* 29 September 1876, 1.

Letters

Miller, John Carl, ed. *Poe's Helen Remembers*. Charlottesville: University of Virginia Press, 1979.

Studies of Sarah Helen Whitman

Baker, Noelle A. "'This Slender Foundation . . . Made Me Immortal': Sarah Helen Whitman vs. Poe's Helen." *Poe Studies/Dark Romanticism* 32 (1999): 8–26.

Conrad, Susan P. *Perish the Thought: Intellectual Women in Romantic America 1830–1860.* New York: Oxford University Press, 1976.

Reilly, John E. "Sarah Helen Whitman as a Critic of Poe." *University of Mississippi Studies in English,* n.s., 3 (1982): 120–127.

Richards, Eliza. "Lyric Telegraphy: Women Poets, Spiritualist Poetics, and the 'Phantom Voice' of Poe." *Yale Journal of Criticism* 12 (1999): 269–294.

———. "'The Poetess' and Poe's Performance of the Feminine." *Arizona Quarterly* 55 (1999): 1–29.

St. Armand, Barton Levy. "Veiled Ladies: Dickinson, Bettine, and Transcendental Mediumship." *Studies in the American Renaissance.* Ed. Joel Myerson. Charlottesville: University of Virginia Press, 1987. 1–51.

Ticknor, Caroline. *Poe's Helen.* New York: Scribner's, 1916.

Walker, Cheryl, ed. *American Women Poets of the Nineteenth Century: An Anthology.* New Brunswick: Rutgers University Press, 1992.

WALT WHITMAN (1819–1892)

Steven Olsen-Smith

BIOGRAPHY

The family of Walter and Louisa Van Velsor Whitman, working-class parents of the man who would come to be known as America's representative poet, embodied the unique potential and internal contradictions of the young nation upon which their son would project his own exuberant sense of self-worth. An outspoken supporter of democratic ideals and the rights of common Americans, and an opponent of religious orthodoxy after the example of Thomas Paine, the senior Walter Whitman failed repeatedly as a businessman, is thought to have been emotionally volatile with his wife and children, and was probably an alcoholic. Louisa, who from youth absorbed the best qualities of the Quaker faith and bearing, suffused warm maternal affection and maintained cohesiveness within the family before and after the death of her husband in 1855. Born Walter Whitman Jr. in West Hills, Long Island, on May 31, 1819, "Walt" was their second child, following elder brother Jesse and followed by younger sisters Mary Elizabeth and Hannah Louisa Whitman, and by the patriotic namesakes Andrew Jackson, George Washington, and Thomas Jefferson Whitman. A fifth brother had died in infancy, and the Whitmans' ninth and last child, Edward, was mentally retarded and physically disabled but beloved by Walt Whitman throughout life and the main beneficiary of the poet's will in 1892.

When Whitman was four years old his father moved the family from West Hills to Brooklyn, where he hoped to succeed as a house-builder. There Walt attended public school until he was 11, when he went to work first at an attorney's and then at a doctor's office. At 12 or 13 he became a printer's apprentice for a local newspaper, which led at age 16 to his position with a printing office in Manhattan, where Whitman had already begun publishing his writing in the popular New York *Mirror.* But by this point his father abandoned efforts to make a living in construction and moved the family back to the country, where Walt eventually joined them and taught school in various Long Island villages, worked as a printer, and briefly established his own newspaper, the *Long-Islander.* Rarely successful at holding down a job, Whitman disliked systematic labor and tended to roam, as indicated in his late prose work, *Specimen Days,* where he recalled wandering Long Island in "all seasons . . . absorbing fields, shores, marine incidents, characters, the bay-men, farmers" (*Prose Works* 12). The profound regional influence and affiliation would emerge in his poems "Starting from Paumanok" (*Paumanok* being an early Algonquian name for the island) and "Out of the Cradle, Endlessly Rocking."

More than the average person, Whitman seems to have needed stimulation and bustle to bring out his resourcefulness and dedication to employment, and these he eventually found by reporting on New York social and political life after returning to Manhattan in 1841, first working for the fashionable New York *World* and editing (in 1842) the New York *Aurora.* For these and other papers Whitman wrote conventional literature (including poetry and temperance fiction) bearing little meaningful resemblance to his later writings. Much more relevant to Whitman's work of distinction is the journalism he produced throughout the 1840s. As a frequent part of his work routine he strolled Broadway, the Battery, and other lively Manhattan locales—a dandified man-about-town, decked out with hat, cane, and boutonnière—thoughtfully observing and recording the plenitudes of mid-century urban American life and mingling with "people of all classes and stages of rank," as he stated in the *Aurora* ("Our City" 17). Whitman's journalistic forays among a young American populace that ranged from opera-goers to stage drivers to street gangs created the basis for his exaltations of social diversity in the work of his fame, *Leaves of Grass.*

In 1848 Whitman was dismissed after nearly two years as editor of the Brooklyn *Daily Eagle* because of his unyielding support of the Wilmot Proviso of 1846, which sought to outlaw slavery in new territories. He immediately took a position in New Orleans with the *Crescent* but after three months returned to Brooklyn (where his family had resettled) to establish a Free Soil newspaper, the *Brooklyn Freeman,* in turn resigning that position before the end of 1849. Though he spent only three months in Louisiana, the journey there and back by mid-Atlantic rail, stagecoach, and the Mississippi River furnished Whitman with the raw materials for American regional depictions in *Leaves of Grass.* All but unprecedented in form and content when it appeared in 1855, yet archetypal to subsequent literary traditions, *Leaves of Grass* embodies principles of innovation inspired by the eminent New England essayist Ralph Waldo Emerson. In particular, Emerson's essay on "The Poet" (1844) contains passages that welded Whitman's fervid nationalism with his rising literary aspirations, and provided confirmation of his own intellectual potential and of the opportunity for realizing it on a national level. Emerson received a presentation copy of *Leaves of Grass* and replied to Whitman with a letter greeting him "at the beginning of a great career," which Whitman promptly published in the New York *Tribune* and included in the second (1856) edition of *Leaves,* cloth versions of which displayed Emerson's "greeting" at the base of the spine (Myerson 25). Critics condemned the self-promotion, and Whitman annoyed reviewers still further by including in the 1856 edition his open reply to Emerson—a prose manifesto echoing and extending the older writer's views, and foretelling a national literature that would promote not only the political and cultural destiny of Americans, but also the sexuality of humanity and nature.

The 1855 and 1856 *Leaves* represent an exuberant triumph in Whitman's aspiring self-image as poet of his era, but the achievement was attended by personal crises. His father died in 1855, and near the end of the decade he recorded into a notebook his sequence of 12 poems entitled "Live Oak, with Moss," which seems to document Whitman's involvement in a failed homosexual attachment. After editing the Brooklyn *Daily*

Times from 1857 to 1859, he published the greatly expanded third edition of *Leaves* (1860). The Civil War broke out the next year, and when New York newspapers listed Whitman's brother George among the soldiers wounded at Fredericksburg in December 1862, he traveled to Virginia in search of him. Although the wound turned out to be superficial, Whitman was overcome by the carnage he beheld and settled in Washington, D. C., where for the duration of the war he ministered without pay to sick and wounded soldiers in the capital's hospitals. Supported by a succession of government jobs, he continued as family patriarch from afar, sending portions of his salary to his mother in Brooklyn. Throughout the war he wrote the poems that would appear as *Drum-Taps,* many of which bear the powerful stamp of his hospital ministrations. After the assassination of President Lincoln in April 1865, Whitman delayed publication until October in order to add a sequel containing his elegy for the fallen leader, "When Lilacs Last in the Dooryard Bloom'd."

Not long after Lincoln's death Whitman lost his job as a clerk in the Bureau of Indian Affairs after the newly appointed Secretary of the Interior James Harland objected to sexual imagery in *Leaves of Grass.* He quickly secured employment in the U. S. Attorney General's Office through the agency of friends such as William Douglas O'Connor, who in 1866 lauded Whitman's character and writings in a pamphlet entitled *The Good Gray Poet.* This was followed in 1867 by John Burroughs' *Notes on Walt Whitman as Poet and Person,* partly authored by Whitman himself to promote the appearance of a fourth edition of *Leaves* that same year. Whitman's residence in Washington came to an end in 1873, when after suffering his first paralytic stroke he relocated permanently to Camden, New Jersey, where George had settled, and where their mother had died earlier that year. His first few years in Camden were lonely and included a second stroke in 1875; but he continued to publish prose and poetry in newspapers and magazines and in 1876 brought out a centennial "Author's Edition" (not an actual resetting) of his work. Throughout the last half of the decade he received visits from a widening circle of people who admired his writings, himself traveling in 1879 as far west as Colorado and, in 1880, to Canada.

In the last full decade of his life Whitman's literary fortunes rose as his health declined. In 1881 a Boston firm printed a new authorized edition of his writings, but in 1882 the publisher suppressed the book after the Massachusetts District Attorney threatened to prosecute on the basis of obscenity laws. Publication was quickly resumed by a Philadelphia firm, and sales multiplied as a result of the publicity. In 1884 he purchased his own home, at 328 Mickle Street, where he continued to receive visits and financial support from disciples and benefactors. Last in a succession of young male friends who looked after his physical needs as a paralytic was Horace Traubel, whose 11-volume *With Walt Whitman in Camden* is based on daily conversations with the poet. Worn down by repeated fits of paralysis and a prolonged struggle with tuberculosis, Whitman died of pneumonia at 6:43 pm on Saturday, March 26, 1892. His wake and funeral were attended by thousands, many of whom knew Whitman not by his writings but by his familiar presence on Camden's streets, wharves, and ferries, where, true to its origins, his career ended among the lives and occupations of common people.

MAJOR WORKS AND THEMES

Whitman's major theme was the self, proclaimed throughout the successive publications of his major work *Leaves of Grass.* In America, the work appeared as six different editions in 1855, 1856, 1860, 1867, 1871, and 1881–82; separately published reprintings appeared in 1876 and 1892; and the *Complete Poems and Prose* appeared in 1888. Whitman's emphasis on individual experience aligns him with nineteenth-century American Romanticism, particularly as manifested in Ralph Waldo Emerson's emphasis on the preeminence and integrity of the human soul as the true source of moral wisdom—knowledge obtained through the mind's powers of intuition, or insight, rather than through its rational comprehension of external reality. Yet Whitman's belief in individual worth was likewise a natural outgrowth of the democratic principles he espoused throughout his journalistic and literary careers. In his newspaper editorials of the 1840s he had championed America's working class as the true embodiment of the ideals set forth in the *Declaration of Independence* and the United States *Constitution.* As he announced in his preface to the 1855 edition of *Leaves,* "the genius of the United States is not best or most in its executives or legislators, nor in its ambassadors or authors or colleges or churches or parlors, nor even in its newspapers or inventors . . . but always most in the common people" (*Leaves* 1855 iii)

Egalitarian vision punctuates Whitman's best-known poem "Song of Myself." The familiar frontispiece of the first edition pictures Whitman in working-class garb with an attitude of self-possession (insolence, some reviewers felt)—an image likewise projected by his literary persona, whose tanned face, virility, and overall physical health reflect Whitman's conception of an ideal American populace. Similarly, by inaugurating free-verse forms in defiance of established metrical standards, and by employing slang expressions, colloquialisms, and grammatically incorrect syntax, Whitman incorporated a common vernacular familiar enough on America's streets and docks but rarely exhibited in serious poetry. In addition to such exploits in poetic diction, Whitman eschewed rhyme and meter for verse-forms he hoped could be readily grasped by an audience that included common readers. Prose-like in its straightforward syntax and declarative voice, and characterized by supple, unobtrusive poetic devices like anaphora, alliteration, and parallelism, "Song of Myself" contrasts pointedly with the elaborate verse structures and ornamental diction of then-conventional poetic modes. Whitman's signature use of the catalogue device (long lists depicting figures, actions, and vocations in American urban and rural life) aptly reflects his admiration for the boundless North American landscape and the diversity of its peoples.

No less integral to Whitman's individualism than his politics is his belief in the cleanliness of both body and soul. Though he disavowed religious affiliations and creeds, Whitman took the existence of the human soul seriously and considered it nothing less than a manifestation or projection of universal divinity. If any definable category of religious belief approximates his views in this area, it would be the doctrine of pantheism, which locates divinity within the material universe and all of its phenomena. Whitman at times makes reference in his writings to the nominative "God" of Christian tradition; yet he far more frequently addresses manifestations of godhood in stars, earth, rocks, plants, animals, and—most important for his theme of selfhood—human flesh. In *Leaves of Grass* sensual states and enjoyments are deemed just as important a part of spiritual fulfillment as intuitive processes. Indeed the most provocative aspect of Whitman's commitment to selfhood is his unabashed celebration of anatomical parts and sexual behavior. In keeping with his pantheistic tendencies, Whitman felt that his frankness about sexual matters received validation from the workings of the natural world, which displays openly its "procreant urge" and constant "breed of life" (*Variorum* I.3). Whitman's sense of the natural world as a simultaneously spiritual and sexual entity enabled him to address the greatest universal threat to selfhood, declaring early in "Song of Myself" that the "smallest sprout shows there is really no death,

/ And if ever there was it led forward life" (I.8). The theme of death recurs throughout much of Whitman's verse not as the great spoiler of human life but as a deep and beautiful mystery illuminated, if not solved, by nature's exhaustless pattern of birth and renewal. It is not clear from his verse that Whitman believed a person's conscious identity survives the event of physical death, but with few exceptions he remained steadfastly true to his announcement in "Song of Myself" that "to die is different from what any one supposed, and luckier" (I.8).

Critics often invoke Whitman's period of "crisis" in the late 1850s to account for developments in his poetic content and style after the 1855 and 1856 *Leaves of Grass.* In "Out of the Cradle, Endlessly Rocking" (first published as "A Child's Reminiscence" in 1859) Whitman identifies "unsatisfied love" as the central motive for poetry, never to be alleviated except by "death" (*Variorum* II.350) In "As I Ebb'd with the Ocean of Life" (published as "Bardic Symbols" in 1860) he pursues similar themes of detachment and isolation, considering "drift and debris" along the seashore as potentially fitting images of human identity and desire (II.321). Unfulfilled love and the pain of isolation figure prominently in "Live Oak, with Moss," which Whitman recorded into a private notebook from now-lost drafts early in 1859. Much in keeping with technical advancements displayed by the two "sea-shore" poems, the 12 "Live Oak" poems present a frank, formally balanced, unified account of a failed love affair and its aftermath. Never published intact, the sequence was dismantled by Whitman and the individual poems dispersed among 33 others in the "Calamus" cluster of the 1860 edition of *Leaves of Grass*—their original narrative of love and abandonment muted. "Calamus" celebrates the phrenological concept of *adhesiveness* (denoting friendship among men) as distinct from the concept of *amativeness* (love of men for women), to which Whitman devoted a cluster of poems entitled "Enfans d'Adam," later retitled "Children of Adam." "Calamus" alternates back and forth between expressions of personal desire and declarations about the social power of robust "manly attachment" (II.356). Whitman later described the cluster as political in nature—a poetic program for social cohesiveness at a time of cresting civil tensions between the American North and South.

Whitman redoubled his poetic loyalty to the nation with *Drum-Taps* (1865), commemorating America's Civil War and its fallen president, Abraham Lincoln. Addressing the enormity of the conflict and calling the North to arms, Whitman's opening pieces have been disparaged as overly rhetorical and jingoistic—critical evaluations that fail to appreciate Whitman's realistic sense of the war's epochal magnitude (as in "Beat! Beat! Drums!") and his heartfelt commitment to the preservation of the union. Objective, detailed depictions of wartime images in such poems as "Cavalry Crossing a Ford" and "An Army Corps on the March" added yet another facet to his poetic craftsmanship and made him a forerunner of literary realism. But the best poems of the *Drum-Taps* collection apply familiar themes and techniques to the new subject of national strife. In such works as "Vigil Strange I Kept on the Field One Night" and "As Toilsome I Wander'd Virginia's Woods," Whitman countered the horrors and hatred of war by illustrating emotional attachment and manly sympathy among soldiers. Also in keeping with earlier motifs, both poems depict a natural world that endorses and sanctifies isolated acts of humanity and love in the midst of fratricidal carnage. These themes culminate in Whitman's elegy for Lincoln, "When Lilacs Last in the Dooryard Bloom'd," where the unification of love and death once again figures as the provocation and preoccupation of poetic utterance.

After *Drum-Taps,* Whitman's literary work diminished in quantity and quality, although he continued to augment *Leaves of Grass* until 1881. His most extensive late undertakings were in prose, such as *Democratic Vistas* (1871), which excoriates politi-cal and cultural corruption in the Gilded Age while still envisioning a glorious future for the United States. *Specimen Days* (1882) collects autobiographical notes and mem-oranda from the 1860s onward, and contains important biographical information about Whitman's Long Island childhood. *Two Rivulets,* an experimental arrangement of old and new verse, appeared as a companion volume to the 1876 impression of *Leaves of Grass;* and a collection of new poems, *November Boughs,* appeared in 1888 along with a prefatory essay entitled "A Backward Glance O'er Travel'd Roads." These last two titles were separately annexed to the 1891–92 "deathbed" version of *Leaves of Grass,* which contains the final authorized collection of Whitman's poetry.

CRITICAL RECEPTION

Although it was an immediate drawing room sensation when it appeared in May 1855, the first edition of *Leaves of Grass* received few reviews from newspapers and magazines, and the second (1856) edition was hardly noticed at all in print. The few reviewers who approved of Whitman's overall purpose acknowledged the originality of *Leaves of Grass* as a bold advancement in the quest for a national literature. *Life Illus-trated* advised "all who are fond of new and peculiar things to procure" *Leaves of Grass,* and the New York *Daily News* declared, "We enjoy enterprise in speech and writing as thoroughly as in steam vessels, revolving rifles or new-found Nicaraguas" (Price 8; Olsen-Smith 210). Such reviewers welcomed deft innovations in form and content as manifestations of the national spirit, and Whitman himself chimed in with an anony-mous notice (in the *United States Review*) that opened, "An American bard at last!" (Price 8). Ironically, however, the majority of favorable criticism sprang directly from tradi-tional aesthetic standards. Friendly reviewers praised Whitman's profound powers of description and the effectiveness of his diction and phraseology. Even more, they applauded Whitman's authentic appreciation of nature and his profound ability to absorb and express in words the beauty and sublimity of natural phenomena.

Along with publicizing a letter of endorsement by Ralph Waldo Emerson, Whitman wrote anonymous reviews of his own book, and these were instrumental in goading a number of hostile critics into noticing *Leaves of Grass.* Rufus W. Griswold in the *Crite-rion* apologized to readers for reviewing the book and called it "a mass of stupid filth" (Price 26) A reviewer in *Frank Leslie's Illustrated Newspaper* promised to burn his own copy of *Leaves* and excoriated Emerson for dragging Whitman's "slimy work into the sanctum of New England firesides" (Olsen-Smith 214). The overt sensuality of Whit-man's language and subject matter tasked the ingenuity of his defenders as much as it emboldened his detractors. Some favorable reviewers in the 1850s felt obliged to cen-sure it as the one regrettable flaw in an otherwise new and exciting literary work. A very few mounted counterattacks by pointing to the erotic elements of mainstream literary tradition. For example, Fanny Fern in the New York *Ledger* dared a hostile critic of Whit-man to "look carefully between the gilded covers of books, backed by high-sounding names, and endorsed by parson and priest, lying unrebuked upon his own family table, where the asp of sensuality lies coiled amid rhetorical flowers" (Price 47). But such rea-soning carried little weight with a critical establishment no less contemptuous of Whit-man's method of versification than of his sexual imagery. Differences between erotic qualities of great literature and "indecencies" in *Leaves of Grass,* insisted the New York *Christian Examiner,* were as clear as "the difference between the nudity of a statue and the gestures of a satyr" (Price 60).

Contemporaneous reception clashed along similar lines in England, and critics on both sides of the Atlantic remained deeply divided over *Leaves of Grass* throughout Whitman's career. Only when Whitman himself ceased using sensual subject matter did the subject cease to be a defining factor in critical appraisals of his work. Reviewers of *Drum-Taps,* for instance, focused primarily on the structure and artistry of his writing and argued about whether or not Whitman was truly a poet. William Dean Howells and Henry James, the two best-known commentators, concluded that he was not. But an expurgated *Poems by Walt Whitman,* coordinated by the English editor and critic William Michael Rossetti, appeared in England in 1868 and greatly increased Whitman's British readership over the following decade. In 1876 Whitman's unsigned essay, "Walt Whitman's Actual American Position," ignited a transatlantic newspaper debate among supporters and critics concerning America's neglect of the poet.

Benefactors and disciples accumulated throughout the last three decades of Whitman's life, beginning with William Douglas O'Connor, John Burroughs, and Richard Maurice Bucke, all of whom published hagiographic monographs on Whitman. The most influential advocate to appear outside Whitman's own circle was Edmund Clarence Stedman, a respected critic whose support was the most important boost to Whitman's popular reputation since Emerson greeted him "at the beginning of a great career." Whitman's followers cultivated his posthumous reputation with unflagging resolve into the first decade of the twentieth century, when biographies of Whitman were published by Henry Bryan Binns in 1905 and Bliss Perry in 1906. But the real turning point came in 1911 at the hands of the Harvard professor and philosopher George Santayana, who was instrumental in transforming the American poetic canon then dominated by trinomial worthies such as Henry Wadsworth Longfellow, John Greenleaf Whittier, and William Cullen Bryant. Walt Whitman, Santayana argued in "The Genteel Tradition in American Philosophy," had proven the one nineteenth-century poet strong enough to go deeper into the American psyche than the dominant tradition, and in so doing had harnessed "the spirit and inarticulate principles" of his nation, creating the groundwork in America for "a noble moral imagination, a worthy filling for the human mind" (52, 53). Four years after Santayana's essay, his student Van Wyck Brooks asserted in *America's Coming of Age* that Whitman had "precipitated the American character" (109).

On the basis of such endorsements, academic studies of Whitman proliferated in the 1920s and 30s, when Whitman was increasingly admired as a forerunner of modernism. In declaring Whitman a predecessor of prevailing critical and literary culture, the academic world began to devote focused attention to the structure and style of Whitman's texts and to the ways biographical, political, and historical forces shaped his work. Whitman was never favored by proponents of the New Criticism, whose fondness for densely rhetorical, tightly constructed literary works was ill-suited for Whitman's free-flowing artistic method. Nonetheless, close formalist readings of Whitman's writings proliferated within the New Critical reign of the late 1940s, 50s, and 60s. The resilience of Whitman criticism and scholarship in this period can be accounted for in large part by the fact that Whitman himself was quickly turning into an academic institution. The English departments of major universities were gradually yielding more space in their curriculums to American literature and American studies—producing undergraduate and graduate courses in which Whitman figured prominently along with Emerson, Thoreau, Hawthorne, Poe, Melville, and Dickinson.

In 1955 (the hundredth anniversary of the publication of *Leaves of Grass*) New York University Press issued the first number of the *Walt Whitman Newsletter*—devoted to criticism and scholarship on Whitman—which thrives today as a refereed academic journal, the *Walt Whitman Quarterly Review,* published by the University of Iowa Press. That same year Gay Wilson Allen, who had been writing informed, scholarly articles on Whitman since the early 30s, published *The Solitary Singer*—a biography of surpassing archival research that remained standard until the end of the century. Formalist critical approaches were spear-headed by Richard Chase's *Walt Whitman Reconsidered* (1955) and James E. Miller Jr.'s *A Critical Guide to Leaves of Grass* (1957). The surge of scholarly and critical activity required complete, reliable texts of Whitman's writings, and in the centennial year New York University Press announced the commencement of *The Collected Writings of Walt Whitman,* a project currently consisting of 22 published volumes, and still in progress at Peter Lang Press.

Throughout the second half of the twentieth century, studies of Whitman diverged widely in orientation and intent owing to theoretical permutations introduced by psychoanalytic criticism, deconstruction, post-structuralism, and post-colonialism. The change in scholarly perspective since Brooks described Whitman as an instigator of the modern American character is exemplified by recent studies such as David S. Reynolds's new historicist *Walt Whitman's America: A Cultural Biography* (1995), which depicts Whitman primarily as an embodiment of his political and social culture rather than as a poet endeavoring to think ahead of his time. Yet traditional scholarship continues amidst the proliferation of theoretical viewpoints, as demonstrated by Jerome Loving's *Walt Whitman: The Song of Himself* (1999), the new standard biography. One important aspect of Loving's biography is that he leaves open the subject of Whitman's homosexuality— a subject largely shunned by scholars and at times vehemently denied throughout most of the past century (and by Whitman himself in old age). The significance of Whitman's sexual orientation was first addressed in depth by Robert K. Martin in *The Homosexual Tradition in American Poetry* (1979), where the author argues not only that Whitman was gay, but that he strove to communicate his homosexuality through his writings. The claim has prompted both support and opposition among American literary scholars, and the role of Whitman's sexuality in his works will likely prove the prevalent topic in Whitman studies for the foreseeable future.

WORKS CITED

Brooks, Van Wyck. *America's Coming of Age.* New York: B. W. Huebsch, 1915.

Myerson, Joel. *Walt Whitman: A Descriptive Bibliography.* Pittsburgh, PA: University of Pittsburgh Press, 1993.

Olsen-Smith, Steven. "Two Views of Whitman in 1856: Uncollected Reviews of *Leaves of Grass* from the New York *Daily News* and *Frank Leslie's Illustrated Newspaper.*" *Walt Whitman Quarterly Review* 12 (Spring 1996): 210–6.

Price, Kenneth M., ed. *Walt Whitman: The Contemporary Reviews.* New York: Cambridge University Press, 1996.

Santayana, George. *The Genteel Tradition: Nine Essays by George Santayana.* Ed. Douglas L. Wilson. Cambridge: Harvard University Press, 1967.

Stedman, Edmund Clarence. "Walt Whitman." *Scribner's Magazine* 21 (November 1880): 47–64.

Whitman, Walt. *Leaves of Grass.* 1855 facsimile reprint. New York: Collectors Reprints, Inc., 1992.

———. *Leaves of Grass: A Textual Variorum of the Printed Poems.* 3 vols. Edited by Sculley Bradley, Harold W. Blodgett, Arthur Golden, and William White. New York: New York University Press, 1980.

———. "Our City." In *Walt Whitman and the New York Aurora.* Edited by Joseph Jay Rubin and Charles H. Brown. Westport, CT: Greenwood Press, 1972. 17–9.

————. *Prose Works 1892.* 2 vols. Edited by Floyd Stovall. New York: New York University Press, 1963, 1964.

BIBLIOGRAPHY

Works by Walt Whitman

Franklin Evans, or The Inebriate. New York: J. Winchester, 1842.

Leaves of Grass. Brooklyn, NY: 1855; second edition, Brooklyn, NY, 1856; third edition, Boston: Thayer & Eldridge, 1860; fourth edition, New York, 1867; fifth edition, Washington, DC, 1871; sixth edition, Boston: James R. Osgood and Company, 1881, and Philadelphia: Rees Welsh & Co. and David McKay, 1882.

Drum-Taps. New York, 1865.

Poems by Walt Whitman. Ed. William Michael Rossetti. London: John Camden Hotten, 1868.

Passage to India. Washington, DC, 1871.

Democratic Vistas. Washington, DC, 1871.

As a Strong Bird on Pinions Free, and Other Poems. Washington, DC, 1872.

Memoranda During the War. Camden, NJ, 1876.

Two Rivulets. Camden, NJ, 1876.

November Boughs. Philadelphia: David McKay, 1888.

Complete Poems and Prose. Philadelphia: Ferguson Brothers, 1888.

Good-Bye My Fancy. Philadelphia: David McKay, 1891.

Specimen Days & Collect. Philadelphia: Rees Welsh & Co., 1882.

Complete Prose Works. Philadelphia: David McKay, 1891.

The Complete Writings of Walt Whitman. 10 vols. Edited by Richard Maurice Bucke, Thomas B. Harned, and Horace Traubel. New York: Putnam, 1902.

An American Primer. Edited by Horace Traubel. Boston: Small, Maynard & Company, 1904.

The Gathering of the Forces: Editorials, Essays, Literary and Dramatic Reviews and Other Material Written by Walt Whitman as Editor of the Brooklyn Daily Eagle in 1846 and 1847. 2 vols. Edited by Cleveland Rodgers and John Black. New York: Putnam, 1921.

I Sit and Look Out: Editorials from the Brooklyn Daily Times. Edited by Emory Holloway and Vernolian Schwarz. New York: Columbia University Press, 1932.

The Collected Writings of Walt Whitman. 23 vols. to date. Edited by Gay Wilson Allen et al. New York: New York University Press, 1961–1984; New York: Peter Lang, 1998–.

The Early Poems and the Fiction. Edited by Thomas L. Brasher. New York: New York University Press, 1963.

Prose Works 1892. 2 vols. Edited by Floyd Stovall. New York: New York University Press, 1963, 1964.

Leaves of Grass: Comprehensive Reader's Edition. Edited by Harold W. Blodgett and Sculley Bradley. New York: New York University Press, 1965.

The Correspondence. 6 vols. Edited by Edwin Haviland Miller. New York: New York University Press, 1961–77.

Daybooks and Notebooks. 3 vols. Edited by William White. New York: New York University Press, 1878.

Leaves of Grass: A Textual Variorum of the Printed Poems. 3 vols. Edited by Sculley Bradley, Harold W. Blodgett, Arthur Golden, and William White. New York: New York University Press, 1980.

Notebooks and Unpublished Prose Manuscripts. 6 vols. Edited by Edward F. Grier. New York: New York University Press, 1984.

The Journalism. 1 vol. to date. Edited by Herbert Bergmann. New York: Peter Lang, 1998.

Studies of Walt Whitman

Allen, Gay Wilson. *The New Walt Whitman Handbook.* New York: New York University Press, 1975.

————. *The Solitary Singer: A Critical Biography of Walt Whitman.* New York: Macmillan, 1955. Revised, Chicago: University of Chicago Press, 1985.

Allen, Gay Wilson, and Ed Folsom, eds. *Walt Whitman and the World.* Iowa City: University of Iowa Press, 1995.

Arvin, Newton. *Whitman.* New York: Macmillan, 1938.

Asselineau, Roger. *The Evolution of Walt Whitman: The Creation of a Book.* Cambridge: Harvard University Press, 1962.

Bauerline, Mark. *Whitman and the American Idiom.* Baton Rouge: Louisiana State University Press, 1991.

Beaver, Joseph. *Walt Whitman: Poet of Science.* New York: King's Crown Press, 1951.

Binns, Henry Bryan. *A Life of Walt Whitman.* London: Methuen, 1905.

Black, Stephen A. *Walt Whitman's Journey into Chaos.* New Brunswick, NJ: Rutgers University Press, 1975.

Bowers, Fredson, ed. *Whitman's Manuscripts: Leaves of Grass (1860).* Chicago: University of Chicago Press, 1955.

Bucke, Richard Maurice. *Cosmic Consciousness.* New York: Dutton, 1923.

————. *Walt Whitman.* Philadelphia: David McKay, 1883.

Burroughs, John. *Notes on Walt Whitman as Poet and Person.* New York: American News Company, 1867.

————. *Whitman: A Study.* Boston: Houghton Mifflin, 1896.

Canby, Henry Seidel. *Walt Whitman: An American.* Boston: Houghton Mifflin, 1943.

Chase, Richard. *Walt Whitman Reconsidered.* New York: William Sloane, 1955.

Erkkila, Betsy. *Whitman: The Political Poet.* New York: Oxford University Press, 1989.

Erkkila, Betsy, and Jay Grossman, eds. *Breaking Grounds: Whitman and American Cultural Studies.* New York: Oxford University Press, 1996.

Folsom, Ed. *Walt Whitman's Native Representations.* New York: Cambridge University Press, 1994.

————. *Walt Whitman: The Centennial Essays.* Iowa City: University of Iowa Press, 1994.

Golden, Arthur, ed. *Walt Whitman's Blue Book: The 1860–61 Leaves of Grass, Containing His Manuscript Additions and Revisions.* 2 vols. New York: New York Public Library, 1968.

Greenspan, Ezra. *Walt Whitman and His English Admirers.* Leeds: Leeds University Press, 1962.

Holloway, Emory. *Whitman: An Interpretation in Narrative.* New York: Knopf, 1926.

Hutchinson, George B. *The Ecstatic Whitman: Literary Shamanism and the Crisis of the Union.* Columbus: Ohio State University Press, 1986.

Kaplan, Justin. *Walt Whitman: A Life.* New York: Simon & Schuster, 1980.

Killingsworth, M. Jimmie. *Whitman's Poetry of the Body: Sexuality, Politics, and the Text.* Chapel Hill: University of North Carolina Press, 1989.

Klammer, Martin. *Whitman, Slavery, and the Emergence of Leaves of Grass.* University Park: Pennsylvania State University Press, 1995.

Kuebrich, David. *Minor Prophecy: Walt Whitman's New American Religion.* Bloomington: Indiana University Press, 1990.

LeMaster, J. R., and Donald D. Kummings, eds. *Walt Whitman: An Encyclopedia.* New York: Garland, 1998.

Loving, Jerome. *Emerson, Whitman, and the American Muse.* Chapel Hill: University of North Carolina Press, 1982.

————. *Walt Whitman: The Song of Himself.* Berkeley: University of California Press, 1999.

Martin, Robert K., ed. *The Continuing Presence of Walt Whitman: The Life after the Life.* Iowa City: University of Iowa Press, 1992.

————. *The Homosexual Tradition in American Poetry.* Austin: University of Texas Press, 1979.

Miller, Edwin Haviland. *Walt Whitman's Poetry: A Psychological Journey.* Boston: Houghton Mifflin, 1968.

————. *Walt Whitman's "Song of Myself": A Mosaic of Interpretations.* Iowa City: University of Iowa Press, 1989.

Miller, James E., Jr. *A Critical Guide to Leaves of Grass.* Chicago: University of Chicago Press, 1957.

Moon, Michael. *Disseminating Whitman: Revision and Corporeality in Leaves of Grass.* Cambridge: Harvard University Press, 1991.

O'Connor, William Douglas. *The Good Gray Poet.* New York: Bunce & Huntington, 1866.

Perry, Bliss. *Walt Whitman.* Boston: Houghton, Mifflin, 1906.

Price, Kenneth M., ed. *Walt Whitman: The Contemporary Reviews.* New York: Cambridge University Press, 1996.

Reynolds, David S. *Walt Whitman's America: A Cultural Biography.* New York: Knopf, 1995.

Schively, Charles, ed. *Calamus Lovers: Walt Whitman's Working Class Camerados.* San Francisco: Gay Sunshine Press, 1987.

Schmidgall, Gary. *Walt Whitman: A Gay Life.* New York: Dutton, 1997.

Symonds, John Addington. *Walt Whitman: A Study.* London: George Routledge, 1893.

Thomas, M. Wynn. *The Lunar Light of Whitman's Poetry.* Cambridge: Harvard University Press, 1987.

Traubel, Horace. *With Walt Whitman in Camden.* Vol. 1, Boston: Small, Maynard & Company, 1906; Vol. 2, New York: Appleton, 1908; Vol. 3, New York: Mitchell Kennerley, 1914; Vol. 4, edited by Sculley Bradley, Philadelphia: University of Pennsylvania Press, 1953; Vol. 5, edited by Gertrude Traubel, Carbondale: Southern Illinois University Press, 1964; Vol. 6, edited by Gertrude Traubel and William White, Carbondale: Southern Illinois University Press, 1982; Vol. 7, edited by Jeanne Chapman and Robert MacIsaac, Carbondale: Southern Illinois University Press, 1992; Vols. 8 and 9, edited by Jeanne Chapman and Robert MacIsaac, Oregon House, CA: W. L. Bentley, 1996.

Warren, James Perrin. *Walt Whitman's Language Experiment.* University Park: Pennsylvania State University Press, 1990.

Woodress, James., ed. *Critical Essays on Walt Whitman.* Boston: G. K. Hall, 1983.

Zweig, Paul. *Walt Whitman: The Making of the Poet.* New York: Basic Books, 1984.

Bibliographies, Reference Guides, and Other Scholarly Resources

Folsom, Ed, and Ken Price, eds. *The Walt Whitman Archive.* <http://jefferson.village.virginia.edu/whitman/>.

Giantvalley, Scott. *Walt Whitman, 1838–1939: A Reference Guide.* Boston: G. K. Hall, 1981.

Golden, Arthur, ed. *Walt Whitman's Blue Book: The 1860–61 Leaves of Grass, Containing His Manuscript Additions and Revisions.* 2 vols. New York: New York Public Library, 1968.

Kummings, Donald D. *Walt Whitman, 1940–1975: A Reference Guide.* Boston: G. K. Hall, 1982.

Myerson, Joel, ed. *The Walt Whitman Archive: A Facsimile of the Poet's Manuscripts.* 6 vols. New York: Garland, 1993.

———. *Walt Whitman: A Descriptive Bibliography.* Pittsburgh, PA: University of Pittsburgh Press, 1993.

———, ed. *Walt Whitman: A Documentary Volume.* Detroit: Gale Group, 2000.

JOHN GREENLEAF WHITTIER (1807–1892)

Patrick M. Erben

BIOGRAPHY

John Greenleaf Whittier was born on December 17, 1807, on a farm near Haverhill, Massachusetts, the second child of the poor Quakers John and Abigail Whittier. His Quaker roots, family bonds, and interests in New England folklore became lifelong influences on Whittier's literary and political careers. While his family's poverty and the Quaker emphasis on a guarded education limited Whittier's formal schooling, he early on displayed a strong penchant for writing poetry. Before enrolling for only two self-supported terms at Haverhill Academy in 1827, Whittier had already published over 80 poems in local newspapers, including the *Newbury Free Press,* a liberal paper edited by William Lloyd Garrison. Standing at the beginning of a career as a renowned abolitionist, the young Garrison admired Whittier's literary abilities and secured him a position as editor of a liberal Boston paper, the *American Manufacturer,* in 1829.

Whittier's editorial work and involvement in politics, however, did not deter him from his poetic endeavors, which bore fruit in his first collection of tales and poems, published in February 1831 as *Legends of New-England.* His literary talent and political enthusiasm—particularly for humanitarian issues—further attracted the attention of Garrison, who enlisted Whittier in the burgeoning abolitionist movement. In 1833, Whittier published the antislavery manifesto *Justice and Expediency,* which not only opposed slavery in general but also rejected the widely popular belief, sponsored by the "Colonization Society," that racial tensions in America could be resolved by the settlement of free and enslaved blacks in Africa. In December of that year, Whittier became a founding member of the American Anti-Slavery Society.

Throughout the 1830s and early 40s, Whittier vehemently supported the cause of eradicating slavery. Collections of poetry such as *Poems Written During the Progress of the Abolition Question* and *Voices of Freedom* harnessed his literary talent for humanitarian and political purposes. In close succession, Whittier edited several newspapers with an openly abolitionist agenda, including *The Pennsylvania Freeman* (1838–40), *The American and Foreign Anti-Slavery Reporter* (1841), and *The Emancipator*

(1841–44), while contributing to Garrison's famous *Liberator*. In 1835, Whittier joined the Massachusetts state legislature, and he used his term to lobby his home district for the antislavery cause. With resentment against abolitionism remaining strong in New England, however, Whittier's activism narrowed his access to fashionable literary circles and even jeopardized his safety. In 1835, during a rally in Concord, New Hampshire, he barely escaped an angry mob throwing stones and rotten eggs. When his office at the *Pennsylvania Freeman* was burned and sacked in 1838, he saved some of his papers by joining, in disguise, the crowd of looters.

In 1839, Whittier and Garrison parted ways in their methods and style of pursuing the abolitionist cause. Whittier disliked Garrison's radical advocacy of overturning the Constitution to topple slavery and hoped to effect change through the established political system. He was instrumental in founding the Liberty Party, which sought abolition while aiming to preserve the Union. Whittier gradually withdrew from an active political career during the late 1840s and 50s. He had sold the family farm in 1636 and moved with his mother and sisters to Amesbury, Massachusetts. Living more frequently at Amesbury after 1840, Whittier also returned to the publication of poetry dedicated to the folklore of New England. In quick succession, he published several volumes of poetry, including *Lays of My Home, Songs of Labor,* and *The Chapel of the Hermits,* as well as his only novel, *Leaves from Margaret Smith's Journal.* Two other landmarks, however, contributed to Whittier's elevation to literary fame. In 1857, the founding of the *Atlantic Monthly* provided a regular outlet for Whittier's poetry alongside the work of other prominent New England writers, including Ralph Waldo Emerson, Henry Wadsworth Longfellow, and Harriet Beecher Stowe. With the publication of his most famous poetical work, *Snow-Bound,* in 1866, Whittier gained both literary fame and financial success, earning $10,000 from the sale of the first edition.

The end of the Civil War also brought Whittier's political and humanitarian struggles to a conclusion, yet his personal life appeared less gratifying. In spite of romances with Mary Emerson Smith and Evelina Bray during his school years, as well as a more mature relationship with the Abolitionist Elizabeth Lloyd during the 1850s, Whittier never married. Biographers consider his strict Quaker upbringing, strong commitment to political activism, and late financial security as possible reasons. The death of his younger sister Elizabeth in 1864 affected Whittier profoundly and contributed to his renewed interest in the ideals of family and friendship, as well as the tales of his childhood. Whittier increasingly retired to his house in Amesbury and, after 1876, to his new estate in Danvers, named Oak Knoll. The elderly Whittier relished the company of his extended family, particularly his niece Elizabeth. He also cultivated friendships and correspondences with several women writers of the period, including Lydia Maria Child, Lucy Larcom, and Sarah Orne Jewett. Whittier reciprocated their admiration with literary advice and patronage. Larcom and Whittier, for instance, collaborated on three anthologies of verse and prose.

Whittier spent the last decades of his life in relative seclusion, while continuing to publish several volumes of poetry, including *The Pennsylvania Pilgrim, The Vision of Echard,* and *At Sundown.* Revered mainly for his work capturing the idyllic New England life of the early nineteenth century, Whittier had gained the status of a national poet whose birthdays were celebrated like public holidays. He died on September 7, 1892.

MAJOR WORKS AND THEMES

Although Whittier's oeuvre spans five decades and comprises numerous volumes of poetry, numerous prose tales, and countless newspaper editorials, literary historians have drawn a surprisingly clear distinction between works dedicated to social causes and writings that celebrate the rural folk life and legends of New England. The apparent oppositions between public and personal, political and sentimental, national and regional concerns in his poetry, however, are subsumed in Whittier's enduring ardor for the ideals of universal brotherhood and freedom, as well as a hopefulness guided by his belief in a benevolent God. The persecution of Quakers in colonial New England, along with their insistence on a personalized faith, instilled in Whittier a general hatred of the social and racial inequities of slavery and the religious intolerance of Puritanism. For Whittier, the nurturing environment he experienced within his family as well as the simplicity of communal life in rural New England exemplified larger principles of social harmony. His poetic celebrations of the folk tales and everyday scenes of early nineteenth-century New England life, therefore, do not simply reflect nostalgia for a simpler past but represent an optimistic alternative to the stupefying political and social conflicts characterizing pre– and post–Civil War America.

Whittier's earliest writings in prose and poetry, collected in *Legends of New-England* (1831), display his interests in the folklore of his rural Massachusetts home, presented in a romantic style. Though he had read little outside of Quaker devotional works, his youthful poetry was influenced by the poet Robert Burns, whose celebrations of the beauty found in the commonplace occurrences of the Scottish countryside and the simplicity of its dialect voices strongly appealed to Whittier's sensibility. Whittier soon rejected the gothic tendencies of his earliest work and even repressed the sale of *Legends,* yet he returned to the subjects and imagery of this volume throughout his career.

During his editorship at various newspapers, his friendship with William Lloyd Garrison, and his active involvement in the antislavery movement, however, Whittier channeled much of his poetic powers into poetry championing abolitionism. *Poems Written During the Progress of the Abolition Question* contains polemical but emotionally genuine attacks on the institution of slavery. Mirroring his abolitionist manifesto *Justice and Expediency,* Whittier demanded the immediate abolition of slavery, guided by a true adherence to Christ's command of brotherly love. After Senator Daniel Webster had stunned abolitionists by supporting the Fugitive Slave Law of 1850, Whittier expressed his anger in the poem "Ichabod!" The title of the poem, which was printed in *Songs of Labor,* is a scriptural reference to 1 Samuel 4.21, meaning "The glory is departed from Israel." Whittier's abolitionist poems—including the caustic "Hunters of Men"—also noted the paradox between the American claim for freedom and the country's continuing support of the slave system. When the passage of the 13th Amendment finally emancipated all slaves, Whittier responded with the joyous poem "Laus Deo!"

With the end of the Civil War, Whittier more permanently returned to rural themes, particularly in his winter idyll *Snow-Bound.* The isolation and physical transformation caused by a New England snowstorm highlights the family circle, the warmth of the hearth, and the exchange of memories and tales. The poem's main appeal lies in its intriguing details of early nineteenth-century New England life and its celebration of the enduring affection of the family in times of physical trial or change. Besides its autobiographic tendencies, critics such as James Rocks have recently stressed the poem's reconciliatory tone at a moment when the nation emerged from the chaos of war.

In his mature poetry, Whittier further blended humanitarianism and a deep-seated Christianity, advocating the liberalization of American religion. In his earlier works, including the fictional account of a seventeenth-century Quaker woman, *Leaves from Margaret Smith's Journal,* and his prose sketches *The Supernaturalism of New England,* Whittier had critically revisited Puritanism. In later poems such as "The Eternal Goodness" and "Our Master," Whittier stressed Christ as the incarnation of God's love and the idea of universal salvation, thus contradicting the Puritans' grim Calvinist doctrines of predestination and the depravity of man. Many of Whittier's religious lyrics were set to music and became popular hymns. Combining his message of a benevolent God with his moral assertions lodged in familiar images of the landscape and people of nineteenth-century New England, Whittier provided poetic assurances for a troubled and disunited national audience.

CRITICAL RECEPTION

Whittier's critical and popular reception has undergone a steady decline from being esteemed as one of the nation's most celebrated poets at the time of his death to the status of a minor poet today. Gathered with Longfellow, Bryant, Holmes, and Lowell under the belittling terms "Schoolroom Poets" or "Fireside Poets," Whittier and his work are frequently chided for a blatant moralizing, overt didacticism, empty sentimentalism, and a modest, if not inferior, artistic accomplishment. Rather than reflecting new research and critical insights into his life and work, changing scholarly attitudes toward Whittier trace a fundamental transformation of the literary tastes, aesthetic sensibilities, and basic world-views of American society from the mid-nineteenth century to the present day.

From the first appearance of Whittier's poetry in the 1830s to the rise of his literary fame shortly after the Civil War, critical reception remained mixed. Literature, it was widely believed, should provide moral and spiritual elevation to the public. The didacticism and clear moral lessons of Whittier's poetry fulfilled such expectations, though his stringent social reform program also shocked those who believed that political activism was beyond the pale of the artist. For audiences favoring the cause of abolitionism, Whittier's vehement poetic attacks on slavery compensated for defects of his work. Some of his literary contemporaries, such as Edgar Allan Poe and Nathaniel Hawthorne, however, commented that Whittier was not a first-rate poet. In 1841, Poe characterized Whittier as a "fine versifier, so far as strength is regarded independently of modulation. . . . But in taste, and especially in imagination . . . he is ever remarkably deficient" (286).

Certainly, such earlier criticism could not take into account some of the more mature and accomplished poetry Whittier wrote after the Civil War, particularly the poems collected in *Snow-Bound* and *The Tent on the Beach.* From the time of his rising literary fame in the 1860s until the early twentieth century, Whittier was mythologized as one of the greatest poets of the American nation. His popularity at the end of his life far outranked today's critical favorites Henry James and Walt Whitman. Amounting to hero worship, the widespread approval of this time focused on the public impact of Whittier's New England reminiscences, his ardent reformism, and optimistic faith in God. For critics and biographers such as his nephew Samuel T. Pickard, the author's social eminence compensated for any artistic shortcomings.

With the onset of literary modernism in the 1910s and 20s, critics suddenly dismissed the very qualities in Whittier's work that their predecessors had lauded, especially his unshakable trust in an absolute truth. In a time of alienation and disillusionment, critics, according to Jayne Kribbs, attacked "what they saw as Whittier's outworn sentimentalism, his showy (empty, some said) display of the good, noble, and lofty, and his participation in a long since faded romantic tradition" (xxxii). Literature, these critics believed, had to represent a voice apart from society. Whittier's reflection of the popular sentiments of nineteenth-century America proved his lack of imaginative depth and artistic vision.

Since the 1950s, a more balanced view of Whittier's literary work has prevailed. Following a more rigorously historicist approach to literature, critics now judge Whittier less by an ostensibly unchanging standard of artistic greatness, but consider more carefully the place of his work within his personal and historical context, particularly the constraints and demands of his abolitionist activism. Accordingly, Whittier's poetry had to balance the conflicting demands of literary subtlety and propagandist directness. Critics also admit, however, that many of Whittier's over 300 poems were hastily conceived and written, and they elevate other works that combine emotion, moral instruction, and reformist ardor with a diligent poetic framework. Recent critics such as James Rocks and Shirley Marchalonis investigate the relationships between Whittier's poetry and sociocultural issues such as the development of the antislavery movement and the relationship between male and female literary figures, as well as the Victorian ideal of domesticity.

WORKS CITED

Kribbs, Jayne K. "Introduction." *Critical Essays on John Greenleaf Whittier.* Boston: G. K. Hall, 1980. xiii–xl.
Poe, Edgar Allan. "A Chapter on Autography." *Graham's Magazine.* December 1841. 286.

BIBLIOGRAPHY

Works by John Greenleaf Whittier

Selected Poetry
Legends of New-England. Hartford, CT: Hanmer & Phelps, 1831.
Poems Written During the Progress of the Abolition Question in the United States, Between the Years 1830 and 1838. Boston: Isaac Knapp, 1837.
Lays of My Home, and Other Poems. Boston: Ticknor, 1843.
Voices of Freedom. Philadelphia: Thomas Cavender, 1846.
Songs of Labor and Other Poems. Boston: Ticknor, Reed & Fields, 1850.
The Chapel of the Hermits and Other Poems. Boston: Ticknor, Reed & Fields, 1853.
The Panorama and Other Poems. Boston: Ticknor & Fields, 1856.
Home Ballads and Poems. Boston: Ticknor & Fields, 1860.
In War Time and Other Poems. Boston: Ticknor & Fields, 1864.
Snow-Bound. A Winter Idyl. Boston: Ticknor & Fields, 1866.
The Tent on the Beach and Other Poems. Boston: Ticknor & Fields, 1867.
Among the Hills and Other Poems. Boston: Fields, Osgood, 1869.
The Vision of Echard and Other Poems. Boston: Houghton, Osgood, 1878.
At Sundown. Cambridge: Privately printed at the Riverside Press, 1890; Boston: Houghton, Mifflin, 1892.

Selected Prose
Justice and Expediency; or, Slavery Considered with a View to Its Rightful and Effectual Remedy, Abolition. Haverhill, MA: C. P. Thayer, 1833.
The Stranger in Lowell. Boston: Waite, Peirce, 1845.
The Supernaturalism of New England. New York & London: Wiley & Putnam, 1847.

Leaves from Margaret Smith's Journal in the Province of Massachusetts Bay, 1678–9. Boston: Ticknor, Reed & Fields, 1849.

Old Portraits and Modern Sketches. Boston: Ticknor, Reed & Fields, 1850.

Literary Recreations and Miscellanies. Boston: Ticknor & Fields, 1854.

Whittier on Writers and Writing: The Uncollected Critical Writings of John Greenleaf Whittier. Eds. Edwin Harrison Cady and Harry Hayden Clark. Syracuse, NY: Syracuse University Press, 1950.

Editions, Introductions, and Letters

The Journal of John Woolman. Edited, with an introduction by Whittier. Boston: Osgood, 1871.

Child Life: A Collection of Poems. Edited by Whittier, with the assistance of Lucy Larcom. Boston: Osgood, 1872.

Child Life in Prose. Edited by Whittier, with the assistance of Lucy Larcom. Boston: Osgood, 1874.

Songs of Three Centuries. Edited by Whittier, with the assistance of Larcom. Boston: Osgood, 1876.

Letters of Lydia Maria Child. Introduction by Whittier. Boston & New York: Houghton, Mifflin, 1883.

"Whittier Letters to Sarah Orne Jewett." Edited by Richard Cary. *Emerson Society Quarterly* 50 (1968): 11–22.

"More Whittier Letters to Jewett." Edited by Richard Cary. *Emerson Society Quarterly* 58 (1970): 132–9.

The Letters of John Greenleaf Whittier. Edited by John B. Pickard. 3 vols. Cambridge: Harvard University Press, 1975.

Studies of John Greenleaf Whittier

Burdick, E. Miller. "The Immortalizing Power of Imagination: A Reading of Whittier's Snow-Bound." *ESQ: A Journal of the American Renaissance* 31.2 (1985): 89–99.

Currier, Thomas Franklin. *A Bibliography of John Greenleaf Whittier.* Cambridge: Harvard University Press, 1937.

Frank, Albert J. von. "John Greenleaf Whittier." *Dictionary of Literary Biography 243.*

———. *Whittier: A Comprehensive Annotated Bibliography.* New York: Garland, 1976.

Grant, David. " 'The Unequal Sovereigns of a Slaveholding Land': The North as Subject in Whittier's 'The Panorama.' " *Criticism—A Quarterly for Literature & the Arts* 38 (1996): 521–49.

Hubbard, George U. "Ina Coolbrith's Friendship with John Greenleaf Whittier." *The New England Quarterly* 45.1 (1972): 109–18.

Kribbs, Jayne K., ed. *Critical Essays on John Greenleaf Whittier.* Boston: Hall, 1980.

Leary, Lewis. *John Greenleaf Whittier.* New York: Twayne, 1961.

Marchalonis, Shirley. "A Model for Mentors? Lucy Larcom and John Greenleaf Whittier." *Patrons and Protegees: Gender, Friendship, and Writing in Nineteenth-Century America.* Ed. Shirley Marchalonis. New Brunswick, NJ: Rutgers UP, 1994. 94–121.

Miller, Perry. "John Greenleaf Whittier: The Conscience in Poetry." *Esq-A Journal of the American Renaissance* 50 (1968): 128–42.

Peterson, Beverly. "Stowe and Whittier Respond in Poetry to the Fugitive Slave Law." *Resources for American Literary Study* 26 (2000): 184–99.

Pickard, John B. *John Greenleaf Whittier: An Introduction and Interpretation.* New York: Holt, Rinehart, and Winston, 1966.

———. "Whittier's Abolitionist Poetry." *Emerson Society Quarterly* 50 (1968): 105–13.

Rocks, James E. "Whittier's *Snow-Bound:* 'The Circle of Our Hearth' and the Discourse on Domesticity." *Studies in the American Renaissance 1993.* Charlottesville: University of Virginia Press, 1993. 339–53.

Vella, Michael. "Fire in the Ashes of Puritanism: The Conflict of Discourse between John Green-leaf Whittier and Reverend George Ellis." *American Transcendental Quarterly* 5.4 (1991): 301–15.

Wagenknecht, Edward. *John Greenleaf Whittier: A Portrait in Paradox.* New York: Oxford University Press, 1967.

Warren, Robert Penn. *John Greenleaf Whittier's Poetry.* Minneapolis: University of Minnesota Press, 1971.

Woodwell, Roland H. *John Greenleaf Whittier: A Biography.* Haverhill, MA: Trustees of the Whittier Homestead, 1985.

NATHANIEL PARKER WILLIS (1806–1867)

Mark G. Vásquez

BIOGRAPHY

Nathaniel Parker Willis was born in Portland, Maine, in 1806; his family moved to Boston when he was six years old. Nathaniel's father, a clergyman with literary aspirations of his own, founded a religious newspaper, *The Boston Recorder.* This newspaper, in fact, became the first publishing arena for Nathaniel's own writing: he printed several poems in the *Recorder* during his days as a Yale student. Upon his graduation in 1827, Willis published a collection of poems and, at 22, assumed the editorships of the *Legendary,* the *Token,* and the *American Monthly Magazine.* Despite such a busy schedule, Willis found time to publish another collection of poems (*Fugitive Poetry*) in 1829. In 1831 Willis left Boston to join the editorial staff at the *New York Mirror.* This position allowed him to travel extensively; in the next few years he would visit France, Italy, the Near East, and points around the Mediterranean, arriving finally in England, where he resumed writing for periodicals. In late 1835, he published *Pencillings by the Way,* an account of his travels, and married Mary Stace.

Willis returned to America in 1836, at the age of 30, and continued to write for periodicals, publish poetry collections, pen a style guide (*Lectures on Fashion*) and two plays, and establish and edit periodicals. After Mary died in childbirth in 1845, Willis again traveled to Europe; the next year he married Cornelia Grinnell. Maintaining his prolific output, Willis continued to write both prose and poetry, publishing five books in the next five years. In 1852 he sailed to Bermuda and the West Indies to help alleviate some health problems (finally diagnosed as epilepsy). Yet his literary production did not slow much; he produced one of his most popular collections (*Rag-Bag*) in 1855 and his only full-length novel (*Paul Fane*) in 1856. Now 50 years old, Willis had been one of the most influential and highly paid editors and publishers of the mid-nineteenth century, as well as one of its most widely read (if not widely admired) writers. During the Civil War, Willis wrote a series of war reports for the *Home Journal* (a journal that later became *Town and Country*). He died in 1867 on January 20, his 61st birthday.

MAJOR WORKS AND THEMES

Willis suffered from a troubled reputation—a reputation that to some degree he helped to construct. Regarded in his own time as a prolific editor and writer, later as a genteel, aloof author of "social writing" and "polite literature," and regarded generations later primarily as the brother of Fanny Fern (Sarah Parton Willis), "Natty" Willis has remained difficult to categorize both because of his dabblings in so many literary genres and because he himself continually resisted such labelling, reinventing himself several times over. During his lifetime, Willis published more than two dozen books of prose, several collections of poetry, a novel, and two plays, in addition to writing for and/or editing numerous periodicals. Such a prolific and various body of work complicates the task of identifying "major works and themes." Willis was a versatile writer whose reputation, founded upon his essays, short stories, and editorial work, is also augmented by his large body of verse and his pair of plays.

As a travel writer, Willis focused not on cataloguing his travels—on providing his readers with a confusing itinerary—but on describing, in vivid detail, scenes into which readers might place themselves. A travel book without this descriptive quality, Willis remarked, was to a sense of place what a skeleton is to a sense of the human figure. In his popular *Pencillings by the Way*—the compilation of Willis's travel letters for the *New York Mirror*—the conversational, impressionistic style of Willis's "pencillings" was peppered, notably, with social criticism. For example, Willis expressed clear disdain of the artifice of Parisian society, and equally clear sympathy for Polish exiles. Sometimes Willis was criticized for authorial indiscretion—including incendiary comments about the wealth and social habits of the Catholic clergy in Italy—but Willis here and throughout his career (and in his personal life) concerned himself with "turning the so-called private experience to public account" (Baker 8).

As a sketcher, Willis successfully modeled his early efforts upon the work of Washington Irving. First published in the *Legendary* and the *Token,* Willis's short stories, such as those featured in "Leaves from a Colleger's Album," centered on commonplace personalities and their humorous (mis)adventures, often climaxing with surprise endings. By the time he worked for the *American Monthly Magazine,* Willis had developed tales and sketches in three areas: travel sketches, such as "Notes Upon a Ramble" or "A Winter Scene in New England," again focused on impressionistic yet often richly detailed descriptions of places and incidents; sentimental and romantic tales; and humorous stories of manners. These final two categories moved Willis away from his previous interests, and Willis struggled somewhat with the new genres. His early sentimental and romantic tales—for instance, "The Death of the Gentle Usher"—have been criticized for being too cloying and melodramatic, while his better works—for example, "Incidents in the Life of a Quiet Man"—employ Gothic elements reminiscent of the work of Edgar Allan Poe (whom Willis, notably, hired in 1844 to work at the *Evening Mirror*). Yet Willis seemed more successful creating the light humorous tale of manners. Stories such as "The Elopement" and "The Fancy Ball" comment extensively upon miscellaneous details of high society. These attempts at these various genres perhaps signal a market savvy that was to serve Willis throughout this career.

Willis's one completed novel, *Paul Fane* (1856), repeats many of the characterizations from earlier sketches, especially the autobiographical details. Paul Fane, a young man attending college in preparation for the ministry, secretly wishes to become an artist instead. An agreeable socialite, Paul is treated indifferently by Mildred Ashly; this spurs him to prove himself as an artist and to travel to Florence. Paul's entrance into Florentine society highlights his sensitivity to criticism, a sensitivity that increases when he encounters Mildred Ashly's brother and sister, both of whom he eventually helps marry off. Rededicating himself to his art, Paul vows to return to America. *Paul Fane* was very popular, printed in American and English editions, and in his focus on intricate details of social classes and their important consequences, Willis anticipates, in some respects, George Eliot and Henry James. As a poet, Willis preferred blank verse and adhered to conventional subjects for romantic poetry. Influenced by Byron, Wordsworth, and Coleridge, Willis also turned out the sentimental lyrics or humorous poems, again aware of what periodical readers might prefer.

As a dramatist, Willis employed his blank verse in constructing two oft-staged plays, *Bianca Visconti* and *Tortesa the Userer,* both of which focus on Willis's favored themes of social standing, "false position," the role of the artist, and troubled love. *Bianca Visconti* centers on the class-conscious father of the title character, who has apprehensions about Bianca's marriage to Francesco Sforza, whom he considers of low birth. It is revealed both that Bianca is a child born out of wedlock and that her brother (thought dead) is still alive. This brother, Giulio, has been present in disguise the whole time; he facilitates the marriage between Bianca and Sforza, although Sforza (like Willis himself?) fears he is not courtly enough for acceptance. Despite these fears, and despite an attempt on Sforza's life by the court poet Pasquali, the marriage indeed takes place. After Giulio is mistakenly killed and Bianca goes mad, Sforza is crowned; yet his ascent is, to say the least, bittersweet. In *Tortesa the Userer,* Tortesa is engaged to Isabella, daughter of Count Falcone. Again, the father opposes the marriage; but the Count, noting Tortesa's desire for achieving a higher social position, agrees to give his blessing, hoping that Tortesa may help the Count to regain his lost lands. Tortesa's conflict with the envious Zippa leads to multiple disguises, betrayals, and misunderstandings, with the result that Isabella falls in love, and then out, with the painter Angelo. Distraught, and not wanting to marry Tortesa, she attempts suicide by poison. She revives, but the Count thinks her a ghost, and shuts her out. Tortesa enters Angelo's studio, where he believes the painter has hidden Isabella's body, and is stunned by the painting of Isabella he finds there. In fact, however, it is Isabella herself, standing still; Tortesa and Angelo soon duel; Angelo wins Isabella, and Tortesa takes Zippa for his bride. Building on some of the same themes present in *Bianca Visconti,* Willis in *Tortesa the Userer* fashioned what Poe called the best American play yet written.

CRITICAL RECEPTION

Among his contemporaries (and Poe would be a notable exception), Willis was generally seen as someone who, despite his prodigious editorial and authorial production, was widely (and justifiably) condemned. As Sandra Tomc remarks, "no writer, with the possible exception of James Fenimore Cooper, attracted more criticism and ill-will," though "biographers remain puzzled by the vituperation he attracted" (792). Even when they praised him, contemporary reviewers tempered their praise with admonishment; they admitted that Willis was a fine writer, but they condemned his "personality," his affectations, his languid tone. This "extended campaign of slander" (Tomc 793) continued for the rest of Willis's life.

In 1885, Henry Beers wrote the first biography of Willis, and the reputation of Willis as an central literary figure remained strong into the 1920s, when Fred Lewis Pattee called him "the most important figure in the American mid-century school of fiction" (78). But Willis drifted into obscurity until the late 1960s, when Cortland Auser's book-length treatment of Willis revived some limited interest. It was Auser, in fact, who noted that "literary historians have discredited Willis with cursory references to his dandyism in dress and what they considered his affectations in writing. They have perpetuated earlier partisan judgments" (10). In the 1970s and 80s, with the recovery by feminist critics of less-examined works by nineteenth-century women, Willis again surfaced, first (in Ann Douglas's assessment) as a "male sentimentalist," (235) and second, as brother (and foil) to his sister, Fanny Fern.

Finally, however, Willis is being assessed on his own (admittedly problematic) terms; Thomas Baker's *Sentiment of Celebrity* (1999) centers on the "cultural politics of self-dramatization in the life of Willis," who "lived a life that cast him as a perennial player in the grand theater of public life" (5). Most vexing for critics of Willis, both his contemporaries and modern-day scholars, is the seeming paradox of what Sandra Tomc has referred to as "an idle industry"—"Willis promoted the notion that one could go places by lacking direction or acquire commodities and money through relaxation" so that "the dominant theme of his career was not that he went places in spite of his idleness, but that he never got anywhere because of it: he never managed to attain the life of ease he seemed already to be leading" (791–792).

WORKS CITED

Auser, Cortland P. *Nathaniel Parker Willis*. New York: Twayne, 1969.
Baker, Thomas N. *Sentiment of Celebrity: Nathaniel Parker Willis and the Trials of Literary Fame*. New York: Oxford University Press, 1999.
Douglas, Ann. *The Feminization of American Culture*. New York: Knopf, 1977.
Pattee, Fred Lewis. *The Development of the American Short Story: An Historical Survey*. New York, 1923.
Tomc, Sandra. "An Idle Industry: Nathaniel Parker Willis and the Workings of Literary Leisure." *American Quarterly* 49:4 (December 1997): 780–805.

BIBLIOGRAPHY

Works by Nathaniel Parker Willis

Sketches. Boston: S. G. Goodrich, 1827.
The Legendary: Consisting of Original Pieces, Principally Illustrative of American History, Scenery, and Manners. Ed. N. P. Willis. 2 vols. Boston: S. G. Goodrich, 1828.
Fugitive Poetry. Boston: Pierce and Williams, 1829.
The Token: A Christmas and New Year's Present. Ed. N. P. Willis. 2 vols. Boston: S. G. Goodrich, 1829.
Pencillings by the Way. 3 vols. London: John Macrone, 1835.
Bianca Visconti; or, the Heart Overtasked. New York: Samuel Colman, 1839.
Tortesa the Userer. New York: Samuel Colman, 1839.
The Poems, Sacred, Passionate, and Humorous. New York: Clark and Austin, 1844.
Hurry-Graphs; or, Sketches of Scenery, Celebrities, and Society, Taken from Life. New York: Charles Scribner, 1851.
The Rag-Bag: A Collection of Ephemera. New York: Charles Scribner, 1855.
Paul Fane; or, Parts of a Life Else Untold. New York: Charles Scribner, 1856.

Studies of Nathaniel Parker Willis

Auser, Cortland P. *Nathaniel Parker Willis*. New York: Twayne, 1969.
Baker, Thomas N. *Sentiment of Celebrity: Nathaniel Parker Willis and the Trials of Literary Fame*. New York: Oxford University Press, 1999.

Beers, Henry A. *Nathaniel Parker Willis.* Boston: Houghton Mifflin, 1885.

Lang, Hans-Joachim. "*Paul Fane* and *Ruth Hall:* Or, Two Geniuses in One Family." *Transatlantic Encounters: Studies in American-European Relations.* 157–75.

Tomc, Sandra. "An Idle Industry: Nathaniel Parker Willis and the Workings of Literary Leisure." *American Quarterly* 49:4 (December 1997): 780–805.

HARRIET E. WILSON (1827?–1863?)

Tammy Cole

BIOGRAPHY

By examining census records, marriage certificates, and city directories, Henry Louis Gates Jr. has pieced together a rough outline of Harriet (Adams) Wilson's biography, which he includes in the introduction of his 1983 republication of Wilson's 1859 *Our Nig*. Gates's investigation establishes that the Wilson who penned the controversially titled work was Harriet Adams Wilson, a free African American woman who resided in Boston from 1856 until 1863. Contradictions in census data, however, prevent a definitive outline of Wilson's biography. Although the death certificate of the author's son settles the initial uncertainty of Wilson's race, other inconsistencies remain: one census, for example, suggests that Wilson might have been born as early as 1808; another that she was born in Fredericksburg, Virginia. Acknowledging that record keeping was both sporadic and unreliable at that time, most scholars agree that Wilson was born around 1827 or 1828 and most likely died in 1863 (Gates 268, White 43).

While few definite details exist about Harriet E. Wilson's life, many can be garnered by examining the autobiographical elements of *Our Nig* and searching public records for comparable information. Gates proposes that Wilson may have been an indentured servant for the Samuel Boyles family in Milford, New Hampshire, and that the Bellmont family in *Our Nig* was modeled after the Boyleses. In 1993, however, Barbara A. White published the most thorough study to date of Wilson's life in which she introduces the Nehemiah Hayward family of Milford, New Hampshire, as the inspiration for the novel's fictional Bellmont family. Careful to present an accurate interpretation of the historical data she collected, for the families' demographics do not match up exactly, White points out that the number of Hayward children and their ages differ slightly from those of the Bellmont family. The similarities between the two families far outweigh the differences, however. White discovered that an 1840 Milford census lists an African American girl residing with the Hayward family (22). Establishing the Hayward family as the model for the Bellmonts casts a shadow on a well-known family with strong abolitionist ties (Davis 485; White 297). Mrs. Rebecca Hayward, a descendant of Anne Hutchinson, was related to the Hutchinson Family Singers who traveled in support of abolitionism and other social issues. The Hayward-abolitionist connection may partly explain why Wilson published her work as a novel instead of as a pure autobiography and why she expressed such contempt for abolitionists in general.

Nothing is known about Wilson as a youngster. We can surmise that Wilson, like her protagonist Alfrado, probably had a white mother and a black father and was abandoned and thus indentured at a young age to a cruel and hypocritical family. The physical and emotional abuse that she suffered led to her chronic illness as an adult. Wilson's experience as a so-called free African American more closely mirrored that of her enslaved southern counterparts.

Marriage records indicate that in 1851 Harriet Adams married Thomas Wilson and bore a son, George Mason Wilson, about nine months later. Like Frado's husband Samuel, Thomas Wilson was a fake fugitive slave involved in the abolitionist lecture circuit. Deserted by her husband and in debilitating health, Wilson turned to writing as a means of economic sustenance in the hopes of retrieving her sickly child, who resided on poor farms or in foster care several times throughout his short life (White 25). A death certificate shows that George died on February 15, 1860, shortly after *Our Nig* was published in Boston. No historical data exists for Harriet E. Wilson after 1863.

MAJOR WORKS AND THEMES

Our Nig, which appears to be Wilson's sole text, combines two modes of writing popular in the 1850s: the slave narrative and the sentimental novel (Gates 268). The result is a unique narrative type that combines elements of biography and fiction, creating a new hybrid: fictionalized autobiography (Ellis 73). The narrative voice shifts throughout *Our Nig* from the use of the first-person pronoun to a third-person omniscient narrator. The injustice of slavery and the consequences of racism for all African Americans, free and enslaved, is the primary theme of *Our Nig,* as evidenced in the extended title—*Our Nig; or, Sketches from the Life of a Free Black, in a Two-Story White House, North. Showing that Slavery's Shadows Fall Even There. By "Our Nig."* northern abolitionists receive the same indictment as their southern slave-owning counterparts. Adhering to characteristics of the slave narrative, *Our Nig* contains letters of authenticity to remove reader doubt about the credibility of the author. Whether these letters are fictional creations of Wilson or true testimonials remains unsettled (Breau 458; Ellis 68). Wilson's tale also has the formulaic slave narrative epiphany. One cannot read *Our Nig* without thinking of Frederick Douglass's challenging of Mr. Covey's power over him (Ellis 67). Frado has a similar moment in *Our Nig.* After years of physical abuse, Frado determines she will stand up for herself against Mrs. Bellmont and tells her if she is beaten again, she will quit working for good. After threatening Mrs. Bellmont, Frado "feels the stirrings of free and independent thought" (Wilson 344). At this turning point in Frado's life, she recognizes her commodial worth in the marketplace of slavery.

To expound upon the work's slavery theme, Wilson uses a dog motif whereby Frado, the protagonist of the work, and her dog Fido serve as character foils. Fido is bought and sold in the novel according to the whims of various members of the Bellmont family. When Frado's own indentured servitude expires as she reaches the age of 18, she laments that she must leave Fido behind. Although originally bought for Frado by Jack Bellmont, Fido does not belong to her. He is part of the Bellmont estate and must remain figuratively fettered, left behind when she frees herself. Wilson uses this motif to align the novel with the slave narrative.

Although Wilson clearly employs elements of the sentimental novel in her writing of *Our Nig,* she modifies the characteristics of sentimental fiction. Instead of Frado finding solace in the home, doing good works, or in her trust of God, she ultimately dismisses domesticity and the conversion experience as means for salvation. No model of good-Christian-family stability exists in *Our Nig.* Frado's mother Mag is outcast when she becomes pregnant out of wedlock. Although the baby dies, Mag is never welcomed back into the fold, and rather than face the "sneering world" (Wilson 290) of Singleton, Mag marries Jim, a black man, the only man who cares for her. As a result, Mag is thrust further "down the ladder of infamy" (Wilson 293). While the members of the Bellmont family profess to be Christians, their actions (overt abuse and covert denial and/or impotence) speak louder than their words. When Frado seeks religious solace, she finds instead hypocrisy. Any benefit of her occasional attendance at revival meetings with Aunt Abby or her prayer vigils with the dying James is overshadowed by Mrs. Bellmont's violent and unchristian treatment. Religion proves to offer false hope to Frado, for she never reaches sanctification as she is never able to reconcile the ill treatment she receives from so-called Christians with the prospect of an eternal life in heaven.

CRITICAL RECEPTION

Wilson appears to have paid to publish *Our Nig* herself. The novel, printed by George C. Rand and Avery, was virtually ignored by Wilson's contemporaries. By studying many of the extant copies of *Our Nig,* Eric Gardner has been able to establish that about 50 percent of the owners he has traced were children and that none of the owners he has traced were African American. Further, most of the original owners of the copies he has studied resided within three counties of New Hampshire, which suggests that Wilson peddled the copies of *Our Nig* herself (238–40).

While never completely lost or forgotten, the novel was not widely circulated until Gates's 1983 republication, when it then enjoyed a large critical reception as the first novel written by an African American woman in English. Wilson's status as the first African American female novelist was challenged in 2001, however, when Gates purchased a manuscript penned by Hannah Crafts called *The Bondswoman's Narrative.* Crafts is now considered the first African American female novelist as her work possibly dates back as far as 1843.

WORKS CITED

Breau, Elizabeth. "Identifying Satire: *Our Nig.*" *Callaloo* 16.2 (1993): 460–6.

Davis, Cynthia J. "Harriet E. Wilson (1827?–1863?)." *Nineteenth-Century American Women Writers: A Bio-Bibliographical Sourcebook.* Ed. Denise D. Knight. Westport, CT: Greenwood P, 1997. 484–9.

Ellis, R. J. "Traps Slyly Laid: Professing Autobiography in Harriet Wilson's *Our Nig.*" *Representing Lives: Women and Auto/Biography.* Ed. Alison Donnell and Pauline Polkey. New York: St. Martin's P, 2000. 65–76.

Gardner, Eric. " 'This Attempt of Their Sister': Harriet Wilson's *Our Nig* From Printer to Readers." *New England Quarterly* 66.2 (1993): 226–46.

Gates, Henry Louis, Jr. "Harriet E. Adams Wilson." *Afro American Writers Before the Harlem Renaissance.* Detroit, MI: Gale Research Co., 1986. 268–71.

White, Barbara A. "*Our Nig* and the She-Devil: New Information about Harriet Wilson and the 'Belmont' Family." *American Literature* 65.1 (1993): 19–52.

Wilson, Harriet E. *Our Nig; or Sketches from the Life of a Free Black. Three Classic African-American Novels.* Ed. William L. Andrews. New York: Vintage, 1983. 286–367.

BIBLIOGRAPHY

Works by Harriet E. Wilson

Wilson, Harriet E. *Our Nig; or Sketches from the Life of a Free Black. Three Classic African-American Novels.* Ed. William L. Andrews. New York: Vintage, 1983. 286–367.

Studies of Harriet E. Wilson

Bassard, Katherine Clay. " 'Beyond Mortal Vision': Harriet E. Wilson's *Our Nig* and the American Racial Dream-Text." *Female Subjects in Black and White: Race, Psychoanalysis, Feminism.* Ed. Elizabeth Abel. Berkeley: U of California P, 1997. 187–200.

Breau, Elizabeth. "Identifying Satire: *Our Nig.*" *Callaloo* 16.2 (1993): 460–6.

Cole, Phyllis. "Stowe, Jacobs, Wilson: White Plots and Black Counterplots." *New Perspectives on Gender, Race, and Classes in Society.* Ed. Audrey T. McCluskey. Bloomington: Indiana UP, 1990. 23–45.

Davis, Cynthia J. "Harriet E. Wilson (1827?–1863?)." *Nineteenth-Century American Women Writers: A Bio-Bibliographical Sourcebook.* Ed. Denise D. Knight. Westport, CT: Greenwood P, 1997. 484–9.

———. "Speaking the Body's Pain: Harriet Wilson's *Our Nig.*" *African American Review* 27 (1993): 391–404.

Doriani, Beth M. "Black Womanhood in Nineteenth Century America: Subversion and Self Construction in Two Women's Autobiographies." *American Quarterly* 43.2 (1991): 199–222.

Douglas Wood, Ann. " 'The Fashionable Diseases': Women's Complaints and Their Treatment in Nineteenth-Century America." *Journal of Interdisciplinary History* 4 (1973): 25–52.

Ellis, R. J. "Body Politics and the Body Politic in William Wells Brown's *Clotel* and Harriet Wilson's *Our Nig.*" *Soft Canons: American Women Writers and Masculine Tradition.* Ed. Karen L. Kilcup. Iowa City: U of Iowa P, 1999. 99–122.

———. "Traps Slyly Laid: Professing Autobiography in Harriet Wilson's *Our Nig.*" *Representing Lives: Women and Auto/Biography.* Ed. Alison Donnell and Pauline Polkey. New York: St. Martin's P, 2000. 65–76.

Ernest, John. "Economies of Identity: Harriet E. Wilson's *Our Nig.*" *PMLA* 109.3 (1994): 424–38.

Foreman, P. Gabrielle. "The Spoken and the Silenced in *Incidents in the Life of a Slave Girl* and *Our Nig.*" *Callaloo* 13.2 (1990): 313–24.

Gardner, Eric. " 'This Attempt of Their Sister': Harriet Wilson's *Our Nig* From Printer to Readers." *New England Quarterly* 66.2 (1993): 226–46.

Gates, Henry Louis, Jr. "Harriet E. Adams Wilson." *Afro American Writers Before the Harlem Renaissance.* Detroit, MI: Gale Research Co., 1986. 268–71.

Herndl, Diane Price. *Invalid Women: Figuring Feminine Illness in American Fiction and Culture 1840–1910.* Chapel Hill: U of North Carolina P, 1993.

———. "The Invisible (Invalid) Woman: African American Women, Illness, and Nineteenth-Century Narrative." *Women's Studies* 24 (1995): 553–72.

Johnson, Ronna. "Said But Not Spoken: Ellison and the Representation of Rape, Race, and Gender in Harriet E. Wilson's *Our Nig.*" *Speaking the Other Self: American Women Writers.* Ed. Jeanne Campbell Reesman. Athens: U of Georgia P, 1997. 96–116.

Jones, Jill C. "The Disappearing 'I' in *Our Nig.*" *Legacy* 13.1 (1996): 38–53.

Leveen, Lois. "Dwelling in the House of Oppression: The Spatial, Racial, and Textual Dynamics of Harriet Wilson's *Our Nig.*" *African American Review* 35 (2001): 561–80.

Lindgren, Margaret. "Harriet Jacobs, Harriet Wilson and the Redoubled Voice in Black Autobi-ography." *Obsidian II: Black Literature in Review* 8 (1993):18–38.

Lovell, Thomas B. "By Dint of Labor and Economy: Harriet Jacobs, Harriet Wilson, and the Salu-tary View of Wage Labor." *Arizona Quarterly* 52.3 (1996): 1–32.

Marfo, Florence. "Marks of the Slave Lash: Black Women's Writing of the 19th Century Anti-Slavery Novel." *Diaspora: Journal of the Annual Afro-Hispanic Literature and Culture Con-ference* 11 (2001): 80–6.

Mitchell, Angelyn. "Her Side of the Story: A Feminist Analysis of Two Nineteenth-Century Ante-bellum Novels–William Wells Brown's *Clotel* and Harriet E. Wilson's *Our Nig*." *American Literary Realism* 24. 3 (1992): 7–21.

Mullen, Harryette. "Runaway Tongue: Resistant Orality in *Uncle Tom's Cabin, Our Nig, Incidents in the Life of Slave Girl,* and *Beloved*." *The Culture of Sentiment: Race, Gender, and Senti-mentality in Nineteenth Century America*. Ed. Shirley Samuels. New York: Oxford UP, 1992. 244–64.

Nelson, Emmanuel S. "Harriet E. Wilson (1827–1863?)." *African American Authors, 1745–1945: A Bio-Bibliographical Critical Sourcebook*. Westport, CT: Greenwood P, 2000. 483–7.

Savitt, Todd L. "Black Health on the Plantation: Masters, Slaves and Physicians." *Science and Medicine in the Old South*. Eds. Ronald L. Numbers and Todd L. Savitt. Baton Rouge: Lou-isiana State UP, 1989. 327–55.

Short, Gretchen. "Harriet Wilson's *Our Nig* and the Labor of Citizenship." *Arizona Quarterly: A Journal of American Literature, Culture, and Theory* 57 (2001): 1–27.

Stern, Julia. "Excavating Genre in *Our Nig*." *American Literature* 67 (1995): 439–66.

Tate, Claudia. "Allegories of Black Female Desire: Or, Rereading Nineteenth Century Sentimen-tal Narratives of Black Female Authority." *Changing Our Own Words: Essays on Criticism, Theory, and Writing by Black Women*. Ed. Cheryl A. Wall. New Brunswick, NJ: Rutgers UP, 1989. 98–126.

West, Elizabeth J. "Reworking the Conversion Narrative: Race and Christianity in *Our Nig*." *MELUS: The Journal of the Society for the Study of the Multi-Ethnic Literature of the United States* 24 (1999): 3–27.

White, Barbara A. "*Our Nig* and the She-Devil: New Information about Harriet Wilson and the 'Belmont' Family." *American Literature* 65.1 (1993): 19–52.

SELECT BIBLIOGRAPHY

Abel, Darrel. *Ruined Eden of the Present: Hawthorne, Melville, and Poe: Critical Essays in Honor of Darrel Abel.* Eds. G. R. Thompson and Virgil L. Lokke. West Lafayette: Purdue UP, 1981.

Abrams, M. H. *The Mirror and the Lamp: Romantic Theory and the Critical Tradition.* New York: Oxford UP, 1981.

American Women Writers: A Critical Reference Guide from Colonial Times to the Present. 4 vols. Eds. Lina Mainiero and Langdon Lynne Faust. New York: Frederick Ungar Publishing Co., 1979–82.

Andrews, William L. *Literary Romanticism in America.* Baton Rouge: Louisiana State UP, 1981.

Avallone, Charlene. "What American Renaissance? The Gendered Genealogy of a Critical Discourse." *PMLA* 112, 5 (Oct. 1997): 1102–20.

Baym, Nina. *American Women Writers and the Work of History, 1790–1860.* New Brunswick, NJ: Rutgers UP, 1995.

———. *Woman's Fiction: A Guide to Novels by and About Women in America 1820-1870.* Ithaca, NY: Cornell UP, 1978.

Bloom, Harold. *The Western Canon.* New York: Harcourt Brace & Co., 1994.

Branch, Edward Douglas. *The Sentimental Years, 1836–1860.* New York: D. Appleton-Century Co., 1934.

Brooks, Van Wyck. *The Flowering of New England, 1815–1865.* New York: E. P. Dutton and Co., 1936.

Brown, Gillian. *Domestic Individualism: Imagining Self in Nineteenth-Century America.* Berkeley: U of California P, 1990.

Brown, Herbert Ross. *The Sentimental Novel in America, 1789–1860.* Durham, NC: Duke UP, 1940.

Browne, Anita, ed. *The 100 Best Books by American Women, 1833–1933.* Chicago: Associated Authors Service, 1933.

Budick, Emily M. *Fiction and Historical Consciousness: The American Romance Tradition.* New Haven, CT: Yale UP, 1989.

Buell, Lawrence. *Literary Transcendentalism: Style and Vision in the American Renaissance.* Ithaca, NY: Cornell UP, 1973.

———. *New England Literary Culture from Revolution through Renaissance.* Cambridge: Cambridge UP, 1986

Chai, Leon. *The Romantic Foundations of the American Renaissance.* Ithaca, NY: Cornell UP, 1987.

Conrad, Susan P. *Perish the Thought: Intellectual Women in Romantic America, 1830–1860.* New York: Oxford UP, 1976.

Cott, Nancy F. *The Bonds of Womanhood: "Woman's Sphere" in New England 1780–1835.* New Haven, CT: Yale UP, 1977.

Davidson, Cathy N. *Revolution and the Word: The Rise of the American Novel.* New York: Oxford UP, 1986.

Deegan, Dorothy Yost. *The Stereotype of the Single Woman in American Novels.* New York: Columbia UP, 1951.

Dobson, Joanne. "The American Renaissance Reenvisioned." In *The (Other) American Traditions: Nineteenth-Century Women Writers.* Ed. Joyce W. Warren. New Brunswick, NJ: Rutgers UP, 1993. 164–82.

Donovan, Josephine. "Toward the Local Colorists: Early American Women's Tradition." In *New England Local Color Literature: A Woman's Tradition.* New York: Frederick Ungar Publishing Co., 1983. 25–37.

Doriani, Beth M. "Black Womanhood in Nineteenth-Century America: Subversion and Self-Construction in Two Women's Autobiographies." *American Quarterly* 43.2 (June 1991): 199–223.

Douglas, Ann. *The Feminization of American Culture.* New York: Alfred A. Knopf, 1977.

Elbert, Monika M. *Separate Spheres No More: Gender Convergence in American Literature 1830–1930.* Tuscaloosa: U of Alabama P, 2000.

Fetterley, Judith. "Commentary: Nineteenth-Century American Women Writers and the Politics of Recovery." *American Literary History* 6 (1994): 600–11.

———, ed. *Provisions: A Reader from 19th-Century American Women.* Bloomington: Indiana UP, 1985.

Fiedler, Leslie. *Love and Death in the American Novel.* New York: Criterion Books, 1960.

Foster, Edward Halsey. *The Civilized Wilderness: Backgrounds to American Literature, 1817–1860.* New York: Free Press, 1975.

Foster, Frances Smith. *Witnessing Slavery: The Development of Ante-Bellum Slave Narratives.* Westport, CT: Greenwood, 1979. Rpt. 1994.

———. *Written by Herself: Literary Production by African American Women, 1746–1892.* Bloomington: Indiana UP, 1993.

Frederick, John T. "Hawthorne's 'Scribbling Women.'" *New England Quarterly* 48 (June 1975): 231–40.

Freibert, Lucy M., and Barbara A. White, eds. *Hidden Hands: An Anthology of American Women Writers, 1790–1870.* New Brunswick, NJ: Rutgers UP, 1988.

Gates, Henry Louis, Jr. *The Schomburg Library of Nineteenth-Century Black Women Writers.* New York: Oxford UP, 1988.

Geary, Susan. "The Domestic Novel as a Commercial Commodity: Making a Best Seller in the 1850s." *Papers of the Bibliographical Society of America* 70 (July–September 1976): 365–95.

Gilbert, Sandra, and Susan Guber. *The Madwoman in the Attic: The Woman Writer and the Nineteenth-Century Literary Imagination.* New Haven, CT: Yale UP, 1979.

Grey, Robin. *The Complicity of Imagination: The American Renaissance, Contests of Authority, and the 17ʰ-Century English Culture.* New York: Cambridge UP, 1997.

Habegger, Alfred. *Gender, Fantasy, and Realism in American Literature.* New York: Columbia UP, 1982.

Hale, Sarah Josepha. *Women's Record; or, Sketches of All Distinguished Women, from the Creation to A.D. 1854.* New York: Harper and Brothers, 1855.

Harris, Susan K. "But is it any good?: Evaluating Nineteenth-Century American Women's Fiction." *American Literature* 63, 1 (Mar. 1991): 43–61. Rpt. in *The (Other) American Traditions: Nineteenth-Century Women Writers.* Ed. Joyce W. Warren. New Brunswick, NJ: Rutgers UP, 1993. 263–79.

———. *19th-Century American Women's Novels: Interpretive Strategies.* Cambridge: Cambridge UP, 1990.

Hart, James D. "Home Influence." In *The Popular Book: A History of America's Literary Taste.* New York: Oxford UP, 1950. 85–105.

Hart, John Seely. *The Female Prose Writers of America With Portraits, Biographical Notices, and Specimens of Their Writings.* Philadelphia: E. H. Butler and Co., 1852.

Higginson, Thomas Wentworth. "Woman in Literature." In *Woman: Her Position, Influence, and Achievement Throughout the Civilized World.* Ed. William C. King. Springfield, MA: King-Richardson Co., 1901. 493–505.

Hofstader, Beatrice. "Popular Culture and the Romantic Heroine." *American Scholar* 30 (Winter 1960–61): 98–116.

Howe, Daniel Walker. "American Victorianism as a Culture." *American Quarterly* 27 (December 1975): 507–32.

Hubbell, Jay B. *The South in American Literature, 1607–1900.* Durham, NC: Duke UP, 1954.

Hull, Raymona E. " 'Scribbling' Females and Serious Males: Hawthorne's Comments from Abroad on Some American Authors." In *The Nathaniel Hawthorne Journal 1975.* Ed. C. E. Frazer Clark Jr. Englewood, CO: Microcard Editions Books, 1975. 35–58.

Johannsen, Albert. *The House of Beadle and Adams and Its Dime and Nickel Novels.* 2 vols. Norman: U of Oklahoma P, 1950.

Kelley, Mary. "The Literary Domestics: Private Woman on a Public Stage." In *Ideas in America's Cultures.* Ed. Hamilton Cravens. Ames: Iowa State UP, 1982. 83–102.

———. *Private Woman, Public Stage: Literary Domesticity in Nineteenth-Century America.* New York: Oxford UP, 1984.

Lauter, Paul. *Canons and Contexts.* New York: Oxford UP, 1991.

———. *Reconstructing American Literature.* Old Westbury, NY: Feminist Press, 1983.

Leverenz, David. *Manhood and the American Renaissance.* Ithaca, NY: Cornell UP, 1989.

Lewis, R. B. *The American Adam: Innocence, Tradition, and Tragedy in the Nineteenth Century.* Chicago: U of Chicago P, 1955.

Loewenberg, Bert James, and Ruth Bogin, eds. *Black Women in Nineteenth-Century American Life: Their Words, Their Thoughts, Their Feelings:* University Park: Pennsylvania State UP, 1976.

Loshe, Lillie Deming. *The Early American Novel.* New York: Columbia UP, 1907.

Matthiessen, F. O. *American Renaissance: Art and Expression in the Age of Emerson and Whitman.* London: Oxford UP, 1941.

McNall, Sally Allen. *Who Is in the House: A Psychological Study of Two Centuries of Women's Fiction in America, 1795 to the Present.* New York: Elsevier North-Holland, 1981.

Michaels, Walter Benn, and Donald E. Pease, eds. *The American Renaissance Reconsidered.* Baltimore: Johns Hopkins UP, 1985.

Miller, Perry. *The Raven and the Whale: The War of Words and Wits in the Era of Poe and Melville.* New York: Harcourt, 1956.

Moylan, Michele, and Lane Stiles, eds. *Reading Books: Essays on the Material Text and Literature in America.* Amherst: U Mass P, 1997.

Nye, Russel B. *Society and Culture in America, 1830–1860.* New York: Harper and Row, 1974.

Parker, Gail. "Introduction." In *The Oven Birds: American Women on Womanhood, 1820–1920.* Ed. Gail Parker. Garden City, NY: Doubleday and Co., 1972.

Pattee, Fred Lewis. *The Feminine Fifties.* New York: D. Appleton-Century Co., 1940.

———. *First Century of American Literature.* New York: D. Appleton-Century Co., 1935.

Pease, Donald E. "Historicizing the American Renaissance." *Modern Philology* 89.1 (Aug. 1991): 36–51.

———. *Visionary Compacts: American Renaissance Writings in Cultural Context.* Madison: U of Wisconsin P, 1987.

Petter, Henri. *The Early American Novel.* Columbus: Ohio State UP, 1971.

Porte, Joel. *In Respect to Egotism: Studies in American Romantic Writing.* Cambridge: Cambridge UP, 1991.

Reynolds, David S. *Beneath the American Renaissance: The Subversive Imagination in the Age of Emerson and Melville.* Cambridge: Harvard UP, 1988.

Rosenfelt, Deborah S. "The Politics of Bibliography: Women's Studies and the Literary Canon." In *Women in Print I.* Ed. Joan E. Hartman and Ellen Messer-Davidow. New York: Modern Language Association, 1982. 11–35.

Ruoff, John C. "Frivolity to Consumption: or, Southern Womanhood in Antebellum Literature." *Civil War History* 18 (September 1972): 213–29.

Sale, Maggie. "Critiques From Within: Antebellum Projects of Resistance." *American Literature* 64.4 (Dec. 1992): 695–719.

Samuels, Shirley, ed. *The Culture of Sentiment: Race, Gender, and Sentimentality in Nineteenth-Century America.* New York: Oxford U P, 1992.

Shapiro, Ann R. *Unlikely Heroines: Nineteenth-Century American Women Writers and the Woman Question.* New York: Greenwood, 1987.

Smith, Henry Nash. "The Scribbling Women and the Cosmic Success Story." *Critical Inquiry* 1 (September 1974): 47–70.

Smith, Leslie. "Through Rose-Colored Glasses: Some American Victorian Sentimental Novels." In *New Dimensions in Popular Culture.* Ed. Russel B. Nye. Bowling Green, OH: Bowling Green U Popular Press, 1972. 90–106.

Stafford, John. *The Literary Criticism of "Young America": A Study of the Relationship of Politics and Literature, 1837–1850.* New York: Russell & Russell, 1967.

Stanford, Ann. "Images of Women in Early American Literature." In *What Manner of Woman: Essays on English and American Life and Literature.* Ed. Marlene Springer. New York: New York UP, 1977. 184–210.

Sterling, Dorothy. *We Are Your Sisters: Black Women in the Nineteenth Century.* New York: Norton, 1984.

Stern, Madeleine B., ed. *Publishers for Mass Entertainment in Nineteenth Century America.* Boston: G. K. Hall and Co., 1980.

Stern, Milton R., and Seymour L. Gross, eds. *American Literature Survey: The American Romantics 1800–1860.* New York: Viking P, 1962.

Sundquist, Eric J. "Slavery, Revolution and the American Renaissance." In *The American Renaissance Reconsidered.* Eds. Walter Benn Michaels and Donald E. Pease. Baltimore: Johns Hopkins UP, 1985. 1–33.

Tandy, Jeannette Reid. "Pro-Slavery Propaganda in American Fiction of the Fifties." *South Atlantic Quarterly* 21 (Jan. 1922): 41–50; (April 1922): 170–8.

Tompkins, Jane P. *Sensational Designs: The Cultural Work of American Fiction, 1790–1860.* New York: Oxford UP, 1985.

Van Doren, Carl. *The American Novel, 1789–1939.* New York: Macmillan Co., 1947.

Voloshin, Beverly R. "The Limits of Domesticity: The Female *Bildungsroman* in America, 1820–1870." *Women's Studies* 10, no. 3 (1984): 283–302.

Walker, Cheryl, ed. *American Women Poets of the Nineteenth Century: An Anthology.* New Brunswick, NJ: Rutgers UP, 1992.

Warren, Joyce W. *The (Other) American Traditions: Nineteenth Century Women Writers.* New Brunswick, NJ: Rutgers UP, 1993.

Watts, Emily Stipes. *The Poetry of American Women from 1632 to 1945.* Austin: U of Texas P, 1977.

Welter, Barbara. "The Cult of True Womanhood, 1820–1860." *American Quarterly* 18 (Summer 1966): 151–74.

———. *Dimity Convictions: The American Woman in the Nineteenth Century.* Athens: Ohio UP, 1976.

Williams, Kenny. *They Also Spoke: An Essay on Negro Literature in America, 1787–1930.* Nashville, TN: Townsend Press, 1970.

Wolf, Bryan J. *Romantic Re-Vision: Culture and Consciousness in Nineteenth-Century American Painting and Literature.* Chicago: U of Chicago P, 1982.

Wood, Ann Douglas. "The 'Scribbling Women' and Fanny Fern: Why Women Wrote." *American Quarterly* 23 (Spring 1971): 3–24.

Wright, Lyle J. "A Statistical Survey of American Fiction, 1774–1850." *Huntington Library Quarterly* 2 (April 1939): 309–18.

INDEX

Abbott, A. W., 225

Adams, John R., 349

Addams, Jane, 11

Addison, Daniel Dulany, 48

Albertine, Susan, 95

Alcott, Amos Bronson, 1–6; early years, 1; death, 2; educational theories, 2–3; Fruitlands, 2, 4; literary friendships, 2, 3; literary reputation, 4; marriage, 1; Orchard House, 2; public lectures, 2; teaching career, 1–2. Works: *Concord Days*, 3, 4; "Consociate Family Life," 3; *The Doctrine and Discipline of Human Culture*, 5; "The Forester," 3; *The Journals of Bronson Alcott*, 3; *New Connecticut*, 3; *Observations on the Principles and Methods of Infant Instruction*, 3; "Orphic Sayings," 2, 3, 4; "Personal Theism," 3; "Philosophemes," 3; *Ralph Waldo Emerson*, 3; *Record of Conversations on the Gospels*, 2; *Sonnets and Canzonets*, 3, 4; *Table-Talk*, 3; *Tablets*, 2, 4; "Transcendentalist Club," 3

Alcott, Louisa May, 7–14; admiration of Thoreau, 7; contemplation of suicide, 8; death, 9; favorite authors, 7; Fruitlands, 7; literary friendships 7; literary reputation, 11–12; literary themes, 10; siblings, 7, 8, 9; use of a pseudonym (A. M. Barnard), 10, 12; volunteerism

during Civil War, 8; youth, 7–8. Works: "Behind a Mask, or A Woman's Power," 11; *Eight Cousins*, 9, 10, 11; *Flower Fables*, 8; *Good Wives*, 9; *Hospital Sketches*, 11; *The Inheritance*, 8, 12; *Jo's Boys*, 9, 10; *Journals*, 9; *Little Men*, 9, 10; *Little Women*, 2, 8, 9, 10, 11; *Lulu's Library*, 9; *Merry's Museum*, 8; *A Modern Mephistopheles*, 11, 12; *Moods*, 8; *An Old-Fashioned Girl*, 9; *The Olive Leaf*, 8; "Pauline's Passion and Punishment," 8; *The Pickwick Portfolio*, 8; "Rival Painters," 8; *Rose in Bloom*, 9, 10; "To the First Robin," 7; "Transcendental Wild Oats," 2; "A Whisper in the Dark," 11; *Work: A Story of Experience*, 9, 12

Allen, Gay Wilson, 34

American Anti-Slavery Society, 138, 139, 151

Ames, Mary Clemmer, 40, 44

Andrews, William L., 106

Andrews, William P., 382

Apess, William, 15–18; death, 15; literary reputation, 16; marriage, 15; military service, 15; views on Christianity, 16; views on racism, 16; youth, 15. Works: *Eulogy on King Philip*, 16; *The Experience of Five Christian Indians of the Pequot Tribe*, 16; *The Increase of the Kingdom of Christ*, 16; *Indian Nullifi-*

ABOUT THE CONTRIBUTORS

JANA L. ARGERSINGER is coeditor of two scholarly journals published at Washington State University: *ESQ: A Journal of the American Renaissance* and *Poe Studies/Dark Romanticism.* She also serves as an officer of the Council of Editors of Learned Journals. She has published on Susan Warner's best-selling first novel, *The Wide, Wide, World,* and is currently working on Elizabeth Stoddard and Northwest regionalist Carol Ryrie Brink.

ANNE BAKER is an assistant professor of English at North Carolina State University. She has published articles on Margaret Fuller and Herman Melville and is currently working on a book about geography and antebellum American literature and culture.

NOELLE A. BAKER is an assistant professor of English at the University of Wisconsin Oshkosh. Her publications include essays on Jane Campion, Sarah Helen Whitman, and William Ware.

ANN BEEBE is an assistant professor of English at the University of Texas at Tyler. She is revising articles on Pocahontas and the 1907 Jamestown Exposition as well as a longer study of Elizabeth Stuart Phelps and the Civil War.

SAMUEL I. BELLMAN is professor of English, emeritus, at California State Polytechnic University, Pomona. Bellman's published works include two volumes for Twayne Publishers, numerous articles and reviews and poems, and academic fiction. His most recent academic tale is "This Man's Art and That Woman's Scope."

GEOFF BENDER is an adjunct instructor for Syracuse University's English department and Writing Program. His interests include nineteenth-century American and British writers. He lives in Syracuse, New York, with his wife, daughter, and poetic aspirations.

JANA A. BOUMA received her Ph.D. in English from the University of Nebraska–Lincoln and is an independent scholar residing in St. Peter, Minnesota.

AMY L. BURTNER is a lecturer in the English Department at SUNY Cortland. A transplant from the midwest, she lives in Binghamton, New York, and earned her Ph.D. from Binghamton University in 2002.

ALETA CANE, senior lecturer in English at Northeastern University, University College, is the co-editor, with Susan Alves, of *The Only Efficient Instrument: 19th-Century American Women Writers and the Periodical* (2001). She is also the author of articles on Charlotte Perkins Gilman, Anzia Yezierska, Gerard Manley Hopkins, and Fay Weldon. She is currently at work on a new book, *Radigals: Progressive Era Women Editors.*

TAMMY COLE is a Ph.D. candidate in American literature at Georgia State University.

MARY G. DE JONG, associate professor of English and Women's Studies at Penn State Altoona, has published several articles on antebellum poetry. She is working on a book about the writing and performance of hymns.

CECILE ANNE DE ROCHER teaches at Georgia State University. She reads literature of the American Renaissance and wrote her dissertation on Elizabeth Manning Hawthorne.

LYNN DOMINA is the author of a collection of poetry, *Corporal Works,* and a reference book, *Understanding A Raisin in the Sun.* She has published scholarly articles on several nineteenth- and twentieth-century writers, including Elizabeth Keckley, Zora Neale Hurston, Mary McCarthy, and N. Scott Momaday. She currently teaches at the State University of New York, Delhi, in the Catskill region of New York.

GREGORY EISELEIN is associate professor and Director of Graduate Studies in the Department of English at Kansas State University. He is the author of *Literature and Humanitarianism in the Civil War Era* (1996) and editor of *Emma Lazarus: Selected Writings* (2002) and *Adah Isaacs Menken: Infelicia and Other Writings* (2002). With Anne K. Phillips, he has co-edited *The Louisa May Alcott Encyclopedia* (2001) and the forthcoming Norton Critical Edition of *Little Women.*

MONIKA ELBERT is professor of English at Montclair State University and also serves as associate editor of *The Nathaniel Hawthorne Review.* She has written extensively on Hawthorne and on nineteenth-century American literature and is currently co-editing a collection on the Peabody sisters.

PATRICK M. ERBEN is a Ph.D. candidate at Emory University in Atlanta. He is broadly interested in early American literature, with a specific focus on multilingual and multicultural encounters. His dissertation examines connections between German and English discourses of community in colonial Pennsylvania. He also teaches and studies the impact of American cultural formations, including literature, on the natural environment.

PAUL J. ERICKSON is a doctoral candidate in the Department of American Studies at the University of Texas at Austin. He has published essays on antebellum popular urban fiction and on the history of the book.

WILLIAM ETTER is a Ph.D. candidate in American literature at the University of California at Irvine.

THERESA J. FLOWERS is a continuing lecturer in the Department of English at the University of North Texas.

LUCY M. FREIBERT, professor emerita of English at the University of Louisville, is the author of articles on Herman Melville, Hilda Doolittle, Margaret Atwood, and utopian fiction. With Barbara A. White, she edited *Hidden Hands: An Anthology of American Women Writers, 1790–1870* (1985). She is currently preparing an annotated bibliography of American wit and humor to 1876.

THERESA STROUTH GAUL is an assistant professor of English at Texas Christian University. She has published several articles on contacts between whites and Native Americans as depicted in the literature of the early nineteenth century.

FREDRICA BEARG GLUCKSMAN is a student in the D. Litt program at Drew University, Madison, New Jersey. She has written book reviews for *Women Artists News* and curriculum guides for the Center for Learning in Rocky River, Ohio. She has also taught literature and writing at Kean University and Livingston High School.

CATHERINE J. GOLDEN is professor of English at Skidmore College. She most recently edited *Book Illustrated: Text, Image, and Culture 1770–1930* and *The Mixed Legacy of Charlotte Perkins Gilman,* with Joanna Zangrando (2000). She is currently writing a book on depictions of the woman reader in Victorian and American illustrated literature.

ANNE RAZEY GOWDY, formerly associate professor of English at Tennessee Wesleyan College, is now instructor in English at the University of Mississippi. She edited *A Sherwood Bonner Sampler, 1869–1884,* published in 2000 by the University of Tennessee Press. Her academic interests include nineteenth-century women, particularly regional and local color writers.

SHARON L. GRAVETT, professor of English at Valdosta State University, has published work on American Civil War literature as well as on writers such as Henry David Thoreau, Toni Morrison, and Thomas Carlyle and on films such as *Blade Runner, Citizen Kane, Double Indemnity,* and *Body Heat.*

STEPHEN HAHN is associate provost and professor of English at The William Paterson University of New Jersey. He has published books on Thoreau and Derrida and numerous essays on British and American literature and rhetoric and composition. He has co-edited two books on teaching the work of William Faulkner.

JOAN WYLIE HALL, instructor of English at the University of Mississippi, is the author of *Shirley Jackson: A Study of the Short Fiction.* She has published articles on Ruth McEnery Stuart, Eudora Welty, Lee Smith, Ann Patchett, Josephine Humphreys, and other southern writers.

JOHN J. HAN is associate professor of English at Missouri Baptist University, where he teaches American literature, world literature, and minority literature. He has also taught at Kansas State University, the University of Nebraska-Lincoln, and Nebraska Wesleyan University. Han has scholarly publications on Flannery O'Connor and about Asian American writing and serves as editor of *Intégrité: A Faith and Learning Journal.*

HILDEGARD HOELLER is assistant professor of English at the College of Staten Island—CUNY. She is the author of "Edith Wharton's Dialogue with Realism and Sentimental Fiction" (2000) and has published articles on nineteenth- and twentieth-century American writers as well as African literature.

GRACE ANN HOVET is a professor emerita at the University of Northern Iowa (UNI), Cedar Falls, where she taught in the Department of English Language and Literature. She was instrumental in founding both the Women's Studies and Leadership Studies programs at UNI. She has published articles on nineteenth- and twentieth-century women writers. Hovet currently resides in Fearrington Village, North Carolina, and is a visiting scholar at the University of North Carolina–Chapel Hill.

THEODORE R. HOVET is professor emeritus at the University of Northern Iowa, Cedar Falls, where he taught in the Department of English Language and Literature. He was instrumental in establishing an American Program at UNI. He has written and taught extensively on novelists such as Susan Warner, Harriet Beecher Stowe, and Harper Lee. He currently resides in Fearrington Village, North Carolina, and is a visiting scholar at the University of North Carolina–Chapel Hill.

LORI N. HOWARD is a doctoral candidate at Georgia State University and the managing editor of the *South Atlantic Review.* Her dissertation examines shifting gender roles in nineteenth-century American novels.

PHILLIP HOWERTON received his B. S. in history from Drury College in 1997 and his M.Ed from Drury in 1999. He is currently a Ph.D. candidate in nineteenth-century American literature at the University of Missouri, Columbia.

MARIA KARAFILIS is an assistant professor at the California State University, Los Angeles. Her essays on antebellum U.S. literature have appeared in *American Transcendental Quarterly* and *Arizona Quarterly,* and she is editor of a reprint of Catharine Maria Sedgwick's *The Linwoods or, "Sixty Years Since in America."*

DENISE D. KNIGHT is professor of English and director of Graduate Studies at the State University of New York, Cortland. She is the author of *Charlotte Perkins Gilman: A Study of the Short Fiction* (1997) and a recognized authority on Gilman. Knight received SUNY Chancellor's Awards for Excellence in Teaching and Excellence in Scholarship in 2002.

JOHN P. KOONTZ is a graduate student at Drew University, pursuing a doctorate in English Literature.

ANNETTE JAEL LEHMANN is an assistant professor of Comparative Literature and Media Studies at the Freie Universität in Berlin, Germany. Her publications include *Im Zeichen der Shoah: Aspekte der Dichtungs-und Sprachkrise bei Rose Ausländer und Nelly Sachs,* 1999; *Un/Sichtbarkeiten der Differenz. Beiträge zur Gender-Debatte in den*

Künsten, 2001; (with Jutta Eming und Irmgard Maassen) *Mediale Performanzen. His-torische Konzepte und Perspektiven* 2002; and (with Philip Ursprung) *Interactions–Between Arts and Architecture,* 2003.

VALERIE D. LEVY is a recent Ph.D. graduate at the University of Georgia, Athens. Her publications and conference presentations include a book chapter on Zora Neale Hurston and essays on Alice Walker, Judith Ortiz Cofer, and Pat Mora, as well as abo-litionists Maria Weston Chapman, Frances Ellen Watkins Harper, and John Greenleaf Whittier.

VERONICA MARGRAVE graduated Summa Cum Laude from SUNY Cortland with a degree in English. She has been published in *She Said She Said, Parnassus,* and the *Ithaca Journal* and has won numerous awards in the study of English. She plans to attend law school and get a dual degree in both law and English.

TERRY NOVAK is an associate professor of English at Johnson and Wales University in Providence, Rhode Island. Much of her teaching and research focuses on the writings of American women and African Americans.

STEVEN OLSEN-SMITH is an assistant professor of English at Boise State Univer-sity. He has published articles on Herman Melville and Walt Whitman, and he is coor-dinating (with Peter Norberg) a new edition of Melville's marginalia.

TED OLSON teaches at East Tennessee State University, where he also serves as interim director of the Center for Appalachian Studies and Services. His books include *Blue Ridge Folklife* (1998).

MARYBETH SHORT PAGE graduated from SUNY Cortland summa cum laude with a Secondary English Education degree. She is a middle school English teacher and resides in upstate New York.

WILLIAM PANNAPACKER, assistant professor of English at Hope College in Hol-land, Michigan, has published articles on Emerson, Poe, and Whitman. He is currently revising his dissertation on self-refashioning in American autobiographical writing.

TIM PRCHAL is a visiting assistant professor at Oklahoma State University, specializ-ing in nineteenth-century and early twentieth-century American literature. His most recent work focuses on immigrant fiction, race, and national identity. His work has appeared in the journal *Studies in American Fiction* and has been anthologized in *F. Scott Fitzgerald in the Twenty-First Century* and *Theory and Practice of Classic Detective Fic-tion.*

CATHERINE RAINWATER is professor of English at St. Edward's University in Austin, Texas. Among her publications are several essays on Poe. Most recently she is the author of *Dreams of Fiery Stars: The Transformation of Native American Fiction* (1999).

ANDREW RENNICK is a Ph.D. candidate in American literature at the University of Maryland, College Park. He has authored articles on Thomas Carlyle and William Dean Howells.

TODD RICHARDSON, a visiting assistant professor at the University of South Carolina, is currently writing a book on the construction of Emerson's reputation in the Boston periodical press. He has published articles on Emerson, Whitman, Melville, and Poe.

JOSEPH ROSENBLUM teaches English in Greensboro, North Carolina, where he lives with two cats and a rabbit. He has contributed to various journals and reference works. Occasionally, these contributions have been accepted.

DOROTHY J. RUMENIK, a former high school English teacher, is an elementary school guidance counselor in Tallahassee, Florida. Caroline Howard Gilman is her great, great, great, great, great grandmother.

ROBERT A. RUSS is an adjunct assistant professor of English at Elon University in North Carolina. He is co-editor, with Victor Kramer, of *The Harlem Renaissance* (1997), and he performs a one-man-show based on portions of Homer's *Iliad*.

REBECCA R. SAULSBURY is an assistant professor of English at Florida Southern College. She teaches early and nineteenth-century American literature, African American literature, American women writers, and literature of the American West. She has published essays and presented papers on Maria Cummins, Catharine Sedgwick, Willa Cather, and Elinore Pruitt Stewart, and she is currently revising her dissertation on Maria Susanna Cummins into a book manuscript.

WILLIAM J. SCHEICK is the J. R. Millikan Centennial Professor at the University of Texas at Austin. His books include *The Slender Human Word: Emerson's Artistry in Prose* (1978); *The Half-Blood: A Cultural Symbol in Nineteenth-Century American Fiction* (1979); and *The Ethos of Romance at the Turn of the Century* (1994).

ARTHUR K. STEINBERG, Ph.D. and J.D., teaches American history at Central Piedmont Community College. He practiced law for 18 years and publishes on topics on legal history.

MARK G. VÁSQUEZ is a senior lecturer in English at Western New England College and also teaches American literature at Anna Maria College. He has recently published articles on nineteenth-century American preachers, the presentations of Native Americans in early U. S. novels, and antebellum tract literature. He is the author of *Authority and Reform: Religious and Educational Discourse on Nineteenth-Century New England Literature* (2003).

EDWARD WHITLEY is a Ph.D. candidate in English at the University of Maryland, College Park.